THE PAPERS OF
BENJAMIN FRANKLIN

SPONSORED BY

The American Philosophical Society

and Yale University

Benjamin Franklin

THE PAPERS OF

Benjamin Franklin

VOLUME 37   *March 16 through August 15, 1782*

ELLEN R. COHN, *Editor*

JONATHAN R. DULL, *Senior Associate Editor*

KAREN DUVAL, *Associate Editor*

JUDITH M. ADKINS, KATE M. OHNO, AND

MICHAEL A. SLETCHER, *Assistant Editors*

CLAUDE A. LOPEZ, *Consulting Editor*

NATALIE S. LESUEUR, *Editorial Assistant*

New Haven and London   YALE UNIVERSITY PRESS, 2003

As indicated in the first volume, this edition was made possible through the vision and generosity of Yale University and the American Philosophical Society and by a substantial donation from Henry R. Luce in the name of Life Magazine. *Additional funds were provided by a grant from the Ford Foundation to the National Archives Trust Fund Board. Subsequent support has come from the Andrew W. Mellon Foundation. Major underwriting of the present volume has been provided by the Barkley Fund, the Florence Gould Foundation, the Norman and Lyn Lear Foundation, the National Trust for the Humanities, and the Pew Charitable Trusts through Founding Fathers Papers, Inc. We gratefully acknowledge the bequest of Raymond N. Kjellberg, which will continue to sustain our enterprise. We are grateful for the generous support of Curran W. Harvey, Jr., Candace and Stuart Karu, Richard N. Rosenfeld, Phyllis Z. and Fenmore R. Seton, and Malcolm N. Smith, and we offer special appreciation to Ralph Gregory Elliot. Gifts from many other individuals as well as donations from the American Philosophical Society, the New York Times Foundation, the Friends of the Franklin Papers, and the* Saturday Evening Post Society *help to sustain the enterprise.* The Papers of Benjamin Franklin *is a beneficiary of the generous and long-standing support of the National Historical Publications and Records Commission under the chairmanship of the Archivist of the United States. The National Endowment for the Humanities, an independent federal agency, has provided significant support for this volume. For the assistance of all these organizations and individuals, as well as for the indispensable aid of archivists, librarians, scholars, and collectors of Franklin manuscripts, the editors are most grateful.*

Publication of this volume was assisted by a grant from the Pew Charitable Trusts.

Library of Congress catalog card number: 59–12697
International standard book number: 0–300–10077–9

⊗ The paper in this book meets the guidelines for permanence and durability of the Committee on Production Guidelines for Book Longevity of the Council on Library Resources.

Printed in the U.S.A.

Contents

Foreign-language surnames and titles of nobility often run to great length. Our practice with an untitled person is to provide all the Christian names at the first appearance, and then drop them; a chevalier or noble is given the title used at the time, and the full name is provided in the index.

*Denotes a document referred to in annotation.

CONTENTS

List of Illustrations

xxviii

Contributors to Volume 37

The ownership of each manuscript, or the location of the particular copy used by the editors of each rare contemporary pamphlet or similar printed work, is indicated where the document appears in the text. The sponsors and editors are deeply grateful to the following institutions and individuals for permission to print or otherwise use in the present volume manuscripts and other materials which they own.

INSTITUTIONS

Académie royale des sciences, Paris
American Philosophical Society
Archives du Ministère des affaires
étrangères, Paris
Archives Nationales, Paris
British Library
John Carter Brown Library
William L. Clements Library
Columbia University Library
Connecticut Historical Society
First Federal Savings & Loan
Association of Boston
Fitzwilliam Museum, Cambridge,
England
Historical Society of Pennsylvania

Library of Congress
Massachusetts Historical Society
Musée de Blérancourt
National Archives
New-York Historical Society
Public Record Office, London
Royal Archives, Windsor Castle
Sheffield Central Library
South Carolina Historical Society
University of Pennsylvania Library
University of South Carolina
Library
Western Reserve Historical Society,
Cleveland, Ohio
Yale University Library

INDIVIDUALS

Mrs. Archibald M. Crossley,
Princeton, New Jersey
Kaller's Historical Documents, Inc.,
New Jersey
Elisha K. Kane, Kane, Pennsylvania
Joseph Kleiner, Trenton, New
Jersey
Mrs. Frederick G. Richards,
Annapolis, Maryland

Statement of Methodology

Arrangement of Materials

The documents are printed in chronological sequence according to their dates when these are given, or according to the date of publication in cases of contemporary printed materials. Records such as diaries, journals, and account books that cover substantial periods of time appear according to the dates of their earliest entries. When no date appears on the document itself, one is editorially supplied and an explanation provided. When no day within a month is given, the document is placed at the end of all specifically dated documents of that month; those dated only by year are placed at the end of that year. If no date is given, we use internal and external evidence to assign one whenever possible, providing our explanation in annotation. Documents which cannot be assigned a date more definite than the entire length of Franklin's stay in France (1777–85) will be published at the end of this period. Those for which we are unable to provide even a tentative date will be published at the conclusion of the series.

When two or more documents have the same date, they are arranged in the following order:

1. Those by a group of which Franklin was a member (*e.g.*, the American Commissioners in Paris)
2. Those by Franklin individually
3. Those to a group of which Franklin was a member
4. Those to Franklin individually
5. "Third-party" and unaddressed miscellaneous writings by others than Franklin.

In the first two categories letters are arranged alphabetically by the name of the addressee; in the last three, by the name of the signatory. An exception to this practice occurs when a letter to Franklin and his answer were written on the same day: in such cases the first letter precedes the reply. The same rules apply to documents lacking precise dates printed together at the end of any month or year.

Form of Presentation

The document and its accompanying editorial apparatus are presented in the following order:

1. *Title.* Essays and formal papers are headed by their titles, except in the case of pamphlets with very long titles, when a short form is substituted. Where previous editors supplied a title to a piece that had none, and this title has become familiar, we use it; otherwise we devise a suitable one.

Letters written by Franklin individually are entitled "To" the person or body addressed, as: To John Adams; To John Adams and Arthur Lee; To the Royal Society.

Letters to Franklin individually are entitled "From" the person or body who wrote them, as: From John Adams; From John Adams and Arthur Lee; From the Committee of Secret Correspondence.

Letters of which Franklin was a joint author or joint recipient are titled with the names of all concerned, as: Franklin and Silas Deane to Arthur Lee; Arthur Lee to Franklin and Silas Deane. "Third-party" letters or those by or to a body of which Franklin was a member are titled with the names of both writers and addressees, as: Arthur Lee to John Adams; The American Commissioners to John Paul Jones.

Documents not fitting into any of these categories are given brief descriptive headings, as: Extract from Franklin's Journal.

If the name in the title has been supplied from external evidence it appears in brackets, with a question mark when we are uncertain. If a letter is unsigned, or signed with initials or an alias, but is from a correspondent whose handwriting we know, the name appears without brackets.

2. *Source Identification.* This gives the nature of the printed or manuscript version of the document, and, in the case of a manuscript or a rare printed work, the ownership and location of the original.

Printed sources of three different classes are distinguished. First, a contemporary pamphlet, which is given its full title, place and date of publication, and the location of the copy the editors have used. Second, an essay or letter appearing originally in a *contemporary* publication, which is introduced by the words "Printed in," followed by the title, date, and inclusive page numbers, if necessary, of the publication. Third, a document, the manuscript or contemporary printed version of which is now lost, but which was printed at a later date, is identified by the words "Reprinted from," followed by the name of the work from which the editors have reproduced it. The following examples illustrate the distinction:

Printed in *The Pennsylvania Gazette,* October 2, 1729.

Reprinted from William Temple Franklin, ed., *Memoirs of the Life and Writings of Benjamin Franklin* . . . (3 vols., 4to, London, 1817–18), II, 244.

The Source Identification of a manuscript consists of a term or symbol (all of which are listed in the Short Title List) indicating the character of the manuscript version, followed by the name of the holder of the manuscript, as: ALS: American Philosophical Society. Because press copies replicate the manuscripts from which they were made, we indicate the character of the original manuscript, as: press copy of L. Since manuscripts belonging to individuals have a tendency to migrate, we indicate the year in which each private owner gave permission to publish, as: Morris Duane, Philadelphia, 1957. When two or more manuscript versions survive, the one listed first in the Source Identification is the one from which we print.

3. An editorial *Headnote* precedes some documents in this edition; it appears between the Source Identification and the actual text. Such a headnote is designed to supply the background of the composition of the document, its relation to events or other writings, and any other information which may be useful to the reader and is not obtainable from the document itself.

4. The *Text* of the document follows the Source Identification, or Headnote, if any. When multiple copies of a document are extant, the editors observe the following order of priority in determining which of the available versions to use in printing a text: ALS or ADS, LS or DS, AL or AD, L or D, and copy. An AL (draft) normally takes precedence over a contemporary copy based on the recipient's copy. If we deviate from the order set forth here,

we explain our decision in the annotation. In those instances where multiple texts are available, the texts are collated, and significant variations reported in the annotation. In selecting the publication text from among several copies of official French correspondence (*e.g.*, from Vergennes or Sartine) we use the version which is written in the best French, on the presumption that the French ministers used standard eighteenth-century spelling, grammar, and punctuation.

The form of presentation of the texts of letters is as follows:

The place and date of composition are set at the top, regardless of their location in the original manuscript.

The signature, set in capitals and small capitals, is placed at the right of the last line of the text if there is room; if not, then on the line below.

Addresses, endorsements, and notations are so labelled and printed at the end of the letter. An endorsement is, to the best of our belief, by the recipient, and a notation by someone else. When the writer of the notation has misread the date or the signature of the correspondent, we let the error stand without comment. Line breaks in addresses are marked by slashes. Different notations are separated by slashes; when they are by different individuals, we so indicate.

5. *Footnotes* to the Heading, Source Identification, Headnote, and Text appear on the pages to which they pertain. References to documents not printed or to be printed in later volumes are by date and repository, as: Jan. 17, 1785, APS.

Method of Textual Reproduction

1. *Spelling* of all words, including proper names, is retained. If it is abnormal enough to obscure the meaning we follow the word immediately with the current spelling in brackets.

2. *Capitalization and Punctuation* are retained. There is such variety in the size of initial letters, often in the same manuscript, that it is sometimes unclear whether the writer intended an upper or lower case letter. In such cases we make a decision on the basis of the correspondent's customary usage. We supply a capital letter when an immediately preceding period, colon, question mark, exclamation point, or dash indicates that a new sentence is intended. If a capital letter clearly indi-

cates the beginning of a new thought, but no mark of punctuation precedes it, we insert a period. If neither punctuation nor capital letter indicates a sentence break, we do not supply them unless their absence renders comprehension of the document nearly impossible. In that case we provide them and so indicate in a footnote.

Dashes were used for a variety of purposes in eighteenth-century personal and public letters. A dash within a sentence, used to indicate a break in thought, is represented as an em dash. A dash that follows a period or serves as a closing mark of punctuation for a sentence is represented as an em dash followed by a space. Occasionally correspondents used long dashes that continue to the end of a line and indicate a significant break in thought. We do not reproduce the dash, but treat it as indicating the start of a new paragraph.

When there is an initial quotation mark or parenthesis, but no closing one, we silently complete the pair.

3. *Contractions and abbreviations* are retained. Abbreviations such as "wd", "honble", "servt", "exclly", are used so frequently in Franklin's correspondence that they are readily comprehensible to the users of these volumes. Abbreviations, particularly of French words, that may be unclear are followed by an expanded version in brackets, as: nre [navire]. Superscript letters are brought down to the line. Where a period or colon is a part of the abbreviation, or indicates that letters were written above the line, we print it at the end of the word, as: 4th. for 4.th. In those few cases where superscript letters brought down to the line result in a confusing abbreviation ("Made" for "Mad^e"), we follow the abbreviation by an expanded version in brackets, as: Made [Madame].

The ampersand by itself and the "&c." are retained. Letters represented by the "y" are printed, as: "the" and "that". The tailed "p" is spelled out, as: "per", "pre", or "pro". Symbols of weights, measures, and money are converted to modern forms, as: *l.t.* instead of ₶ for *livres tournois*.

4. *Omissions, mutilations, and illegible words* are treated as follows:

If we are certain of the reading of letters missing in a word because of a torn or taped manuscript or tightly bound copy-book, we supply the letters silently.

If we cannot be sure of the word, or of how the author spelled it, but we can make a reasonable guess, we supply the missing letters in brackets.

When the writer has omitted a word absolutely required for clarity, we insert it in italics within brackets.

5. *Interlineations* by the author are silently incorporated into the text. If they are significant enough to require comment a footnote is provided.

Textual Conventions

/	denotes line break in addresses and different hands in notations.
⟨roman⟩	denotes a résumé of a letter or document.
[*italic*]	editorial insertion explaining something about the manuscript, as: [*one line illegible*]; or supplying a word to make the meaning clear, as: [*to*].
[roman]	editorial insertion clarifying the immediately pre-ceding word or abbreviation; supplies letters missing because of a mutilated manuscript.
(?)	indicates a questionable reading.

Abbreviations and Short Titles

AAE	Archives du Ministère des affaires étrangères.
AD	Autograph document.
Adams Correspondence	Lyman H. Butterfield, Richard A. Ryerson, *et al.*, eds., *Adams Family Correspondence* (6 vols. to date, Cambridge, Mass., 1963–).
Adams Papers	Robert J. Taylor, Gregg L. Lint, *et al.*, eds., *Papers of John Adams* (11 vols. to date, Cambridge, Mass., 1977–).
ADB	*Allgemeine Deutsche Biographie* (56 vols., Berlin, 1967–71).
Adm.	Admiral.
ADS	Autograph document signed.
AL	Autograph letter.
Allen, *Mass. Privateers*	Gardner Weld Allen, ed., *Massachusetts Privateers of the Revolution* ([Cambridge, Mass.], 1927) (Massachusetts Historical Society *Collections*, LXXVII).
Almanach des marchands	*Almanach général des marchands, négocians, armateurs, et fabricans de France et de l'Europe et autres parties du monde* . . . (Paris, 1779).
Almanach royal	*Almanach royal* (91 vols., Paris, 1700–92). Cited by year.
Almanach de Versailles	*Almanach de Versailles* (Versailles, various years). Cited by year.
Alphabetical List of Escaped Prisoners	Alphabetical List of the Americans who having escap'd from the Prisons of England, were furnish'd with Money by the Commissrs. of the U.S. at the Court of France, to return to America.

	A manuscript in the APS, dated 1784, and covering the period January, 1777, to November, 1784.
ALS	Autograph letter signed.
ANB	John A. Garraty and Mark C. Carnes, eds., *American National Biography* (24 vols., New York and Oxford, 1999).
APS	American Philosophical Society.
Archaeol.	Archaeological.
Assn.	Association.
Auphan, "Communications"	P. Auphan, "Les communications entre la France et ses colonies d'Amérique pendant la guerre de l'indépendance Américaine," *Revue Maritime*, new series, no. LXIII and LXIV (1925), 331–48, 497–517.
Autobiog.	Leonard W. Labaree, Ralph L. Ketcham, Helen C. Boatfield, and Helene H. Fineman, eds., *The Autobiography of Benjamin Franklin* (New Haven, 1964).
Bachaumont, *Mémoires secrets*	[Louis Petit de Bachaumont *et al.*], *Mémoires secrets pour servir à l'histoire de la république des lettres en France, depuis MDCCLXII jusqu'à nos jours; ou, Journal d'un observateur . . .* (36 vols. in 12, London, 1784–89). Bachaumont died in 1771. The first six vols. (1762–71) are his; Mathieu-François Pidansat de Mairobert edited them and wrote the next nine (1771–79); the remainder (1779–87) are by Barthélemy-François Mouffle d'Angerville.
Balch, *French in America*	Thomas Balch, *The French in America during the War of Independence of the United States, 1777–1783* (trans. by

	Thomas Willing Balch *et al.*; 2 vols., Philadelphia, 1891–95).
BF	Benjamin Franklin.
BF's accounts as commissioner	Those described above, XXIII, 20.
BF's journal of the peace negotiations	Printed below, pp. 291–346. Unless otherwise noted, this refers to the copy in Josiah Flagg's hand with corrections by BF, at the Library of Congress.
BFB	Benjamin Franklin Bache.
Bigelow, *Works*	John Bigelow, ed., *The Works of Benjamin Franklin* (12 vols., New York and London, 1887–88).
Biographie universelle	*Biographie universelle, ancienne et moderne, ou histoire, par ordre alphabétique, de la vie publique et privée de tous les hommes qui se sont fait remarquer . . .* (85 vols., Paris, 1811–62).
Bodinier	From information kindly furnished us by Cdt. Gilbert Bodinier, Section études, Service historique de l'Armée de Terre, Vincennes.
Bodinier, *Dictionnaire*	Gilbert Bodinier, *Dictionnaire des officiers de l'armée royale qui ont combattu aux Etats-Unis pendant la guerre d'Indépendance* (Château de Vincennes, 1982).
Bowler, *Logistics*	R. Arthur Bowler, *Logistics and the Failure of the British Army in America, 1775–1783* (Princeton, 1975).
Bradford, *Jones Papers*	James C. Bradford, ed., *The Microfilm Edition of the Papers of John Paul Jones, 1747–1792* (10 reels of microfilm, Alexandria, Va., 1986).
Burke's Peerage	Sir Bernard Burke, *Burke's Genealogical and Heraldic History of the Peerage*

Baronetage and Knightage with War Gazette and Corrigenda (98th ed., London, 1940). References in exceptional cases to other editions are so indicated.

Burnett, *Letters*   Edmund C. Burnett, ed., *Letters of Members of the Continental Congress* (8 vols., Washington, 1921–36).

Butterfield, *John Adams Diary*   Lyman H. Butterfield *et al.*, eds., *Diary and Autobiography of John Adams* (4 vols., Cambridge, Mass., 1961).

Cash Book   BF's accounts described above, xxvi, 3.

Chron.   *Chronicle.*

Claghorn, *Naval Officers*   Charles E. Claghorn, *Naval Officers of the American Revolution: a Concise Biographical Dictionary* (Metuchen, N.J., and London, 1988).

Clark, *Ben Franklin's Privateers*   William Bell Clark, *Ben Franklin's Privateers: a Naval Epic of the American Revolution* (Baton Rouge, 1956).

Clark, *Wickes*   William Bell Clark, *Lambert Wickes, Sea Raider and Diplomat: the Story of a Naval Captain of the Revolution* (New Haven and London, 1932).

Clowes, *Royal Navy*   William Laird Clowes, *The Royal Navy: a History from the Earliest Times to the Present* (7 vols., Boston and London, 1897–1903).

Cobbett, *Parliamentary History*   William Cobbett and Thomas C. Hanssard, eds., *The Parliamentary History of England from the Earliest Period to 1803* (36 vols., London, 1806–20).

Col.   Column.

Coll.   *Collections.*

comp.   compiler.

Croÿ, *Journal*   Emmanuel, prince de Mœurs et de Solre

	et duc de Croÿ, *Journal inédit du duc de Croÿ, 1718–1784* (4 vols., Paris, 1906–07).
d.	*deniers.*
D	Document unsigned.
DAB	*Dictionary of American Biography.*
DBF	*Dictionnaire de biographie française* (19 vols. to date, Paris, 1933–).
Dictionary of Scientific Biography	Charles C. Gillispie, ed., *Dictionary of Scientific Biography* (18 vols., New York, 1970–90).
Deane Papers	*The Deane Papers, 1774–90* (5 vols.; New-York Historical Society *Collections,* XIX–XXIII, New York, 1887–91).
DF	Deborah Franklin.
Dictionnaire de la noblesse	François-Alexandre Aubert de La Chesnaye-Dubois and M. Badier, *Dictionnaire de la noblesse contenant les généalogies, l'histoire & la chronologie des familles nobles de la France* . . . (3rd ed.; 19 vols., Paris, 1863–76).
Dictionnaire historique	*Dictionnaire historique, critique et bibliographique, contenant les vies des hommes illustres, célèbres ou fameux de tous les pays et de tous les siècles* . . . (30 vols., Paris, 1821–23).
Dictionnaire historique de la Suisse	*Dictionnaire historique & biographique de la Suisse* (7 vols. and supplement, Neuchâtel, 1921–34).
DNB	*Dictionary of National Biography.*
Doniol, *Histoire*	Henri Doniol, *Histoire de la participation de la France à l'établissement des Etats-Unis d'Amérique. Correspondance diplomatique et documents* (5 vols., Paris, 1886–99).
DS	Document signed.

Duane, *Works* William Duane, ed., *The Works of Dr. Benjamin Franklin* . . . (6 vols., Philadelphia, 1808–18). Title varies in the several volumes.

Dubourg, *Œuvres* Jacques Barbeu-Dubourg, ed., *Œuvres de M. Franklin* . . . (2 vols., Paris, 1773).

Dull, *French Navy* Jonathan R. Dull, *The French Navy and American Independence: a Study of Arms and Diplomacy, 1774–1787* (Princeton, 1975).

Ed. Edition or editor.

Edler, *Dutch Republic* Friedrich Edler, *The Dutch Republic and the American Revolution* (*Johns Hopkins University Studies in Historical and Political Science*, ser. XXIX, no. 2; Baltimore, 1911).

Elias and Finch, *Letters of Digges* Robert H. Elias and Eugene D. Finch, eds., *Letters of Thomas Attwood Digges (1742–1821)* (Columbia, S.C., 1982).

Etat militaire *Etat militaire de France, pour l'année* . . . (36 vols., Paris, 1758–93). Cited by year.

Exper. and Obser. *Experiments and Observations on Electricity, made at Philadelphia in America, by Mr. Benjamin Franklin* . . . (London, 1751). Revised and enlarged editions were published in 1754, 1760, 1769, and 1774 with slightly varying titles. In each case the edition cited will be indicated, *e.g.*, *Exper. and Obser.* (1751).

f. florins.

Fauchille, *Diplomatie française* Paul Fauchille, *La Diplomatie française et la ligue des neutres de 1780 (1776–1783)* (Paris, 1893).

xli

Ferguson, *Power of the Purse* — E. James Ferguson, *The Power of the Purse: a History of American Public Finance . . .* (Chapel Hill, N.C., 1961).

Fitzmaurice, *Life of Shelburne* — Edmond George Petty-Fitzmaurice, *Life of William, Earl of Shelburne, Afterwards First Marquess of Lansdowne, with Extracts from His Papers and Correspondence* (3 vols., London, 1875–76).

Fitzpatrick, *Writings of Washington* — John C. Fitzpatrick, ed., *The Writings of George Washington . . .* (39 vols., Washington, D.C., 1931–44).

Ford, *Letters of William Lee* — Worthington Chauncey Ford, ed., *Letters of William Lee, 1766–1783* (3 vols., Brooklyn, N.Y., 1891).

Fortescue, *Correspondence of George Third* — Sir John William Fortescue, ed., *The Correspondence of King George the Third from 1760 to December 1783 . . .* (6 vols., London, 1927–28).

France ecclésiastique — *La France ecclésiastique pour l'année . . .* (15 vols., Paris, 1774–90). Cited by year.

Freeman, *Washington* — Douglas S. Freeman (completed by John A. Carroll and Mary W. Ashworth), *George Washington: a Biography* (7 vols., New York, 1948–57).

Gaz. — *Gazette.*

Gaz. de Leyde — *Nouvelles extraordinaires de divers endroits,* commonly known as *Gazette de Leyde.* Each issue is in two parts; we indicate the second as "sup."

Gen. — General.

Geneal. — *Genealogical.*

Gent. Mag. — *The Gentleman's Magazine, and Historical Chronicle.*

Giunta, *Emerging Nation* — Mary A. Giunta, *et al.,* eds., *The Emerg-*

ing Nation: a Documentary History of the Foreign Relations of the United States under the Articles of the Confederation, 1780–1789 (3 vols., Washington, D.C., 1996).

Harlow, *Second British Empire* — Vincent T. Harlow, *The Founding of the Second British Empire, 1763–1793* (2 vols., London and New York, 1952–64).

Hays, *Calendar* — I. Minis Hays, *Calendar of the Papers of Benjamin Franklin in the Library of the American Philosophical Society* (5 vols., Philadelphia, 1908).

Heitman, *Register of Officers* — Francis B. Heitman, *Historical Register of Officers in the War of the Revolution* . . . (Washington, D.C., 1893).

Hillairet, *Rues de Paris* — Jacques Hillairet, pseud. of Auguste A. Coussillan, *Dictionnaire historique des rues de Paris* (2nd ed.; 2 vols., [Paris, 1964]).

Hist. — Historic or Historical.

Hoffman and Albert, eds., *Peace and the Peacemakers* — Ronald Hoffman and Peter J. Albert, eds., *Peace and the Peacemakers: the Treaty of 1783* (Charlottesville, Va., 1986).

Idzerda, *Lafayette Papers* — Stanley J. Idzerda *et al.*, eds., *Lafayette in the Age of the American Revolution: Selected Letters and Papers, 1776–1790* (5 vols. to date, Ithaca, N.Y., and London, 1977–).

JA — John Adams.

JCC — Worthington Chauncey Ford *et al.*, eds., Journals of the Continental Congress, 1744–1789 (34 vols., Washington, 1904–37).

Jefferson Papers — Julian P. Boyd, Charles T. Cullen, John Catanzariti, Barbara B. Oberg, *et al.*,

	eds., *The Papers of Thomas Jefferson* (30 vols. to date, Princeton, 1950–).
Jour.	Journal.
JW	Jonathan Williams, Jr.
Kaminkow, *Mariners*	Marion and Jack Kaminkow, *Mariners of the American Revolution* (Baltimore, 1967).
Klingelhofer, "Matthew Ridley's Diary"	Herbert F. Klingelhofer, ed., "Matthew Ridley's Diary during the Peace Negotiations of 1782," *William and Mary Quarterly*, 3rd series, XX (1963), 95–133.
L	Letter unsigned.
Landais, *Memorial*	Pierre Landais, *Memorial, to Justify Peter Landai's Conduct during the Late War* (Boston, 1784).
Larousse	Pierre Larousse, *Grand dictionnaire universel du XIXe siècle* . . . (17 vols., Paris, [n.d.]).
Lasseray, *Les Français*	André Lasseray, *Les Français sous les treize étoiles, 1775–1783* (2 vols., Paris, 1935).
Laurens Papers	Philip M. Hamer, George C. Rogers, Jr., David R. Chestnutt, *et al.*, eds., *The Papers of Henry Laurens* (16 vols. to date, Columbia, S.C., 1968–).
Le Bihan, *Francs-maçons parisiens*	Alain Le Bihan, *Francs-maçons parisiens du Grand Orient de France* . . . (Commission d'histoire économique et sociale de la révolution française, *Mémoires et documents*, XIX, Paris, 1966).
Lee Family Papers	Paul P. Hoffman, ed., *The Lee Family Papers, 1742–1795* (University of Virginia *Microfilm Publication* No. 1; 8 reels, Charlottesville, Va., 1966).

Lewis, *Walpole Correspondence*	Wilmarth S. Lewis *et al.*, eds., *The Yale Edition of Horace Walpole's Correspondence* (48 vols., New Haven, 1939–83).
Lopez, *Lafayette*	Claude A. Lopez, "Benjamin Franklin, Lafayette, and the *Lafayette*," *Proceedings* of the American Philosophical Society CVIII (1964), 181–223.
Lopez, *Mon Cher Papa*	Claude-Anne Lopez, *Mon Cher Papa: Franklin and the Ladies of Paris* (rev. ed., New Haven and London, 1990).
Lopez and Herbert, *The Private Franklin*	Claude-Anne Lopez and Eugenia W. Herbert, *The Private Franklin: the Man and His Family* (New York, 1975).
LS	Letter or letters signed.
l.t.	*livres tournois.*
Lüthy, *Banque protestante*	Herbert Lüthy, *La Banque protestante en France de la Révocation de l'Edit de Nantes à la Révolution* (2 vols., Paris, 1959–61).
Mackesy, *War for America*	Piers Mackesy, *The War for America, 1775–1783* (Cambridge, Mass., 1965).
Madariaga, *Harris's Mission*	Isabel de Madariaga, *Britain, Russia, and the Armed Neutrality of 1780: Sir James Harris's Mission to St. Petersburg during the American Revolution* (New Haven, 1962).
Mag.	*Magazine.*
Mass. Arch.	Massachusetts Archives, State House, Boston.
Mazas, *Ordre de Saint-Louis*	Alexandre Mazas and Théodore Anne, *Histoire de l'ordre royal et militaire de Saint-Louis depuis son institution en 1693 jusqu'en 1830* (2nd ed.; 3 vols., Paris, 1860–61).

Medlin, *Morellet*	Dorothy Medlin, Jean-Claude David, Paul LeClerc, eds., *Lettres de Morellet* (3 vols., Oxford, 1991–96).
Métra, *Correspondance secrète*	[François Métra *et al.*], *Correspondance secrète, politique & littéraire, ou Mémoires pour servir à l'histoire des cours, des sociétés & de la littérature en France, depuis la mort de Louis XV* (18 vols., London, 1787–90).
Meyer, *Armement nantais*	Jean Meyer, *L'Armement nantais dans la deuxième moitié du XVIIIe siècle* (Paris, 1969).
Meyer, *Noblesse bretonne*	Jean Meyer, *La Noblesse bretonne au XVIIIe siècle* (2 vols., Paris, 1966).
"Mission of Col. Laurens"	"The Mission of Col. John Laurens to Europe in 1781," *The South Carolina Historical and Genealogical Magazine,* I (1900), 13–41, 136–51, 213–22, 311–22; II (1901), 27–43, 108–25.
Morison, *Jones*	Samuel E. Morison, *John Paul Jones: a Sailor's Biography* (Boston and Toronto, 1959).
Morris, *Jay: Peace*	Richard B. Morris *et al.*, eds., *John Jay, the Winning of the Peace: Unpublished Papers, 1780–1784* (New York, Cambridge, London, 1980).
Morris, *Jay: Revolutionary*	Richard B. Morris *et al.*, eds., *John Jay, the Making of a Revolutionary: Unpublished Papers, 1743–1780* (New York, Evanston, San Francisco, 1975).
Morris Papers	E. James Ferguson, John Catanzariti, Mary A. Gallagher, Elizabeth M. Nuxoll, *et al.*, eds., *The Papers of Robert Morris, 1781–1784* (9 vols., Pittsburgh, Pa., 1973–99).

Morton, *Beaumarchais Correspondance*	Brian N. Morton and Donald C. Spinelli, eds., *Beaumarchais Correspondance* (4 vols. to date, Paris, 1969–).
MS, MSS	Manuscript, manuscripts.
Namier and Brooke, *House of Commons*	Sir Lewis Namier and John Brooke, *The History of Parliament. The House of Commons, 1754–1790* (3 vols., London and New York, 1964).
Neeser, *Conyngham*	Robert Walden Neeser, ed., *Letters and Papers Relating to the Cruises of Gustavus Conyngham, Captain of the Continental Navy, 1777–1779* (New York, 1915).
NNBW	*Nieuw Nederlandsch Biografisch Woordenboek* (10 vols. and index, Amsterdam, 1974).
Nouvelle biographie	*Nouvelle biographie générale depuis les temps les plus reculés jusqu'à nos jours . . .* (46 vols., Paris, 1855–66).
p.	pence
Pa. Arch.	Samuel Hazard *et al.*, eds., *Pennsylvania Archives* (9 series, Philadelphia and Harrisburg, 1852–1935).
Palmer, *Loyalists*	Gregory Palmer, ed., *Biographical Sketches of Loyalists of the American Revolution* (Westport, Conn., 1984).
Phil. Trans.	The Royal Society, *Philosophical Transactions.*
PMHB	*Pennsylvania Magazine of History and Biography.*
Price, *France and the Chesapeake*	Jacob M. Price, *France and the Chesapeake: a History of the French Tobacco Monopoly, 1674–1791, and of Its Relationship to the British and American Tobacco Trade* (2 vols., Ann Arbor, Mich., 1973).

Proc.   *Proceedings.*

Pub.   *Publications.*

Quérard, *France littéraire*   Joseph Marie Quérard, *La France lit-*
                                                téraire ou Dictionnaire bibliographique
                                                des savants, historiens, et gens de lettres
                                                de la France, ainsi que des littérateurs
                                                étrangers qui ont écrit en français, plus
                                                particulièrement pendant les XVIIIe et
                                                XIXe siècles . . . (10 vols., Paris,
                                                1827–64).

Rakove, *Beginnings of*   Jack N. Rakove, *The Beginnings of Na-*
    National Politics   *tional Politics: an Interpretive History of*
                                                the Continental Congress (New York,
                                                1979).

RB   Richard Bache.

Repertorium der diplo-   Ludwig Bittner *et al.*, eds., *Repertorium*
    matischen Vertreter   *der diplomatischen Vertreter aller Länder*
                                                seit dem Westfälischen Frieden (1648)
                                                (3 vols., Oldenburg, etc., 1936–65).

Rev.   *Review.*

Rice and Brown, eds.,   Howard C. Rice, Jr., and Anne S.K.
    Rochambeau's Army   Brown, eds., *The American Campaigns*
                                                of Rochambeau's Army, 1780, 1781,
                                                1782, 1783 (2 vols., Princeton and
                                                Providence, 1972).

s.   *sou.*

s.   shilling.

Sabine, *Loyalists*   Lorenzo Sabine, *Biographical Sketches of*
                                                Loyalists of the American Revolution
                                                . . . (2 vols., Boston, 1864).

SB   Sarah Bache.

Schelle, *Œuvres de Turgot*   Gustave Schelle, ed., *Œuvres de Turgot*
                                                et documents le concernant (5 vols.,
                                                Paris, 1913–23).

Schulte Nordholt, *Dutch*   J. W. Schulte Nordholt, *The Dutch Re-*
    Republic   *public and American Independence*

xlviii

(trans. Herbert M. Rowen; Chapel Hill, N.C., 1982).

Sellers, *Franklin in Portraiture*
Charles C. Sellers, *Benjamin Franklin in Portraiture* (New Haven and London, 1962).

Sibley's Harvard Graduates
John L. Sibley, *Biographical Sketches of Graduates of Harvard University* (17 vols. to date, Cambridge, Mass., 1873–). Continued from Volume IV by Clifford K. Shipton.

Six, *Dictionnaire biographique*
Georges Six, *Dictionnaire biographique des généraux et amiraux français de la Révolution et de l'Empire (1792–1814)* (2 vols., Paris, 1934).

Smith, *Letters*
Paul H. Smith *et al.*, eds., *Letters of Delegates to Congress* (26 vols., Washington, D.C., 1976–2000).

Smyth, *Writings*
Albert H. Smyth, ed., *The Writings of Benjamin Franklin . . .* (10 vols., New York, 1905–7).

Soc.
Society.

Sparks, *Works*
Jared Sparks, ed., *The Works of Benjamin Franklin . . .* (10 vols., Boston, 1836–40).

Stevens, *Facsimiles*
Benjamin F. Stevens, ed., *Facsimiles of Manuscripts in European Archives Relating to America, 1773–1783* (25 vols., London, 1889–98).

Taylor, *J. Q. Adams Diary*
Robert J. Taylor *et al.*, eds., *Diary of John Quincy Adams* (2 vols. to date, Cambridge, Mass., and London, 1981–).

Tourneux, *Correspondance littéraire*
Tourneux, Maurice, *Correspondance littéraire, philosophique et critique par Grimm, Diderot, Raynal, Meister, etc. revue sur les textes originaux comprenant outre ce qui a été publié à diverses*

	époques les fragments supprimés en 1813 par la censure les parties inédites conservées à la Bibliothèque Ducale de Gotha et l'Arsenal à Paris (16 vols., Paris, 1877–82).
Trans.	Translator or translated.
Trans.	*Transactions.*
Van Doren, *Franklin*	Carl Van Doren, *Benjamin Franklin* (New York, 1938).
Van Doren, *Franklin-Mecom*	Carl Van Doren, ed., *The Letters of Benjamin Franklin & Jane Mecom* (American Philosophical Society *Memoirs,* XXVII, Princeton, 1950).
Villiers, *Commerce colonial*	Patrick Villiers, *Le Commerce colonial atlantique et la guerre d'indépendance des Etats-Unis d'Amérique, 1778–1783* (New York, 1977).
W&MQ	*William and Mary Quarterly,* first or third series as indicated.
Ward, *War of the Revolution*	Christopher Ward, *The War of the Revolution* (John R. Alden, ed.; 2 vols., New York, 1952).
Waste Book	BF's accounts described above, XXIII, 19.
WF	William Franklin.
Wharton, *Diplomatic Correspondence*	Francis Wharton, ed., *The Revolutionary Diplomatic Correspondence of the United States* (6 vols., Washington, D.C., 1889).
Willcox, *Portrait of a General*	William B. Willcox, *Portrait of a General: Sir Henry Clinton in the War of Independence* (New York, 1964).
WTF	William Temple Franklin.
WTF, *Memoirs*	William Temple Franklin, ed., *Memoirs of the Life and Writings of Benjamin Franklin, L.L.D., F.R.S., &c . . .* (3 vols., 4to, London, 1817–18).

l

WTF's accounts   Those described above, XXIII, 19.

Yela Utrilla, *España*   Juan F. Yela Utrilla, *España ante la Independencia de los Estados Unidos* (2nd ed.; 2 vols., Lérida, 1925).

Note by the Editors and the Administrative Board

As we noted in volume 23 (pp. xlvi–xlviii), the period of Franklin's mission to France brings with it roughly two and a half times as many documents as those for the other seventy years of his life. In the present volume once again we summarize a portion of his incoming correspondence in collective descriptions; they appear in the index under the following headings: favor seekers; offerers of goods and schemes; commission seekers.

As we noted in volume 30 (p. lx), Franklin's French secretary Jean L'Air de Lamotte was responsible for keeping the official letterbook. Many of the copies produced by L'Air de Lamotte are severely flawed. They contain errors of spelling, punctuation, and syntax that could not have been present in Franklin's originals. Regrettably, however, these copies are the only extant versions of much of Franklin's official correspondence dating from this period, and we publish them as they stand, pointing out and correcting errors only when they threaten to obscure Franklin's meaning.

A revised statement of textual methodology appeared in volume 28 and is repeated here. The original statement of method is found in the Introduction to the first volume, pp. xxiv–xlvii. The various developments in policy are explained in xv, xxiv; xxi, xxxiv; xxiii, xlvi–xlviii.

While this volume was in production, the Franklin Papers lost two good friends. Edward C. Carter II, Librarian of the American Philosophical Society, was a loyal supporter and a long-standing member of our Administrative Board. I. Bernard Cohen served on our Advisory Committee since the inception of this project. We and our predecessors benefited tremendously from their expertise and friendship. We shall miss them both.

Natalie LeSueur left the project in 2002. Jennifer Macellaro provided editorial assistance for the final stages of this volume. Our thanks to both of them.

Introduction

In the spring and summer of 1782 Franklin established the framework for a peace agreement with Great Britain. This proved to be one of his most difficult diplomatic challenges, and represented one of his greatest triumphs. His success was based on the same strengths he had exhibited four-and-a-half years earlier when seeking an alliance with the French government: he had absolute confidence in the American cause, a shrewd understanding of the political climate, patience, and an aptitude for one of the diplomat's most subtle arts—the ability to create contrasting impressions for different audiences. Dependent on France for continuing financial support, he reassured French Foreign Minister Vergennes that America would not make a separate peace with Britain; to encourage British concessions, however, he allowed the British to believe that he would sign a peace treaty without French consent. Franklin chronicled his activities, beginning with the events of late March, in a journal he wrote from May 9 to July 1.

The peace negotiations began soon after the resignation of British Prime Minister North on March 20. One of the two secretaries of state in the new government announced by the Marquess of Rockingham was the Earl of Shelburne, an old acquaintance from Franklin's days in London and himself a master of subtlety and diplomatic skill. Shelburne's mandate was British internal affairs; foreign affairs fell to his rival, Charles James Fox. Each man sought control over the negotiations with America.[1] It was Franklin, however, who through a serendipitous circumstance initiated contact with Shelburne and gave the new secretary of state for the home department his opening.

Franklin's opportunity presented itself in the person of the Earl of Cholmondeley, an acquaintance of Madame Brillon, who arrived in Paris on March 21 en route to London.[2] When Cholmondeley offered to carry messages to England, Franklin

1. See the headnote to Shelburne to BF, April 6.
2. XXXVI, 456–8, 504–6.

(who had not yet learned of the fall of the North administration) gave him a note for Shelburne congratulating him on the House of Commons' recent initiatives to end offensive operations in America and explore ways to end the war.[3] "Great Affairs," as Franklin reflected in his journal, "sometimes take their Rise from small Circumstances."

Shelburne, who received Franklin's letter on April 5, wasted little time. He immediately secured the King's permission to send Richard Oswald as an official representative to sound out Franklin. Oswald—an unpretentious man of Franklin's generation, and an old friend of Henry Laurens—proved the perfect choice to win the American minister's confidence. He was accompanied by Caleb Whitefoord, an old friend of Franklin's, who made the introduction.[4]

On the last day of these initial discussions, however, Franklin made what he came to realize was a serious mistake. On the morning of Oswald's departure, April 19, Franklin met him in Paris for a final confidential conversation. Franklin suggested that if Britain were truly interested in reconciliation, it ought to cede Canada to the United States; this concession would permit the Americans in turn to make provisions for dispossessed Loyalists. When proposing these ideas Franklin referred to a set of handwritten notes, which Oswald persuaded him to surrender so that he might accurately represent Franklin's ideas to Shelburne.

Surrendering the paper was Franklin's mistake, as it provided written evidence that he was acting outside the boundaries of his instructions. Congress had never authorized him to offer concessions regarding the Loyalists. Moreover, his notes indicated his willingness to negotiate without notifying the French. Had Shelburne leaked this information, he could have

3. BF to Shelburne, March 22, and BF's journal of the peace negotiations.
4. For Oswald's arrival see BF to Vergennes, April 15, and BF's journal of the peace negotiations. BF evidently met Oswald in 1766 during a meeting of Nova Scotia land investors, but Oswald left the group after that evening and we have no evidence that BF remembered him: George C. Rogers, Jr., "The East Florida Society of London, 1766–1767," *Florida Historical Quarterly*, LIV (1975–76), 488.

undermined both Congress' and Vergennes' trust in Franklin. Franklin quickly recognized his error and vowed never to commit future offers to paper.[5] Fortunately, Shelburne kept Franklin's notes confidential, but his expectations about the Loyalists would make later phases of the negotiations more difficult for the American commissioners.

Not long after Oswald's visit, Fox sent his own representative, Thomas Grenville, to begin discussions with Vergennes. Fox also instructed Grenville to make contact with Franklin. Franklin told him what he had told Oswald, that the United States would never negotiate apart from France.[6] Grenville, however, reported to Fox that he had gotten the impression that Franklin might in fact do just that. Grenville then tried to induce Franklin to negotiate with him rather than Oswald by promising to secure the immediate acknowledgment of American independence, which Fox (but not Shelburne) was prepared to make. Franklin was suspicious of this offer—correctly, since the cabinet ultimately sided with Shelburne—and did not accept it. When pressed, however, he did allow that America's refusal to make a separate peace might not stand, should the other powers make extravagant demands on England in subsequent stages of the negotiations.[7]

A month later Rockingham died, Shelburne succeeded him as Prime Minister, and Fox resigned. Shelburne appointed two trusted subordinates, Thomas Townshend and Baron Grantham, as his secretaries of state but retained personal direction of all the peace negotiations. On July 10 Shelburne hinted to the House of Lords that Britain might have to acknowledge American independence, but only in case of necessity. That same day, in France, Franklin met with Oswald and delivered what amounted to an ultimatum. He outlined a series of four articles he considered "necessary to be granted." These included Amer-

5. Notes for a Conversation with Oswald, [on or before April 19]; BF's journal of the peace negotiations.

6. BF's conversation with Oswald occurred on April 15; that with Grenville on May 14: see our headnote to BF's April 15 letter to Vergennes, and BF's journal of the peace negotiations.

7. BF and Grenville's conversation was June 1: BF's journal of the peace negotiations. See also Shelburne to BF, April 6.

ican independence, settling boundaries of the British colonies, the curtailment of Canada to its old borders, and free access to the Newfoundland fisheries. Among the articles he deemed "advisable" were that Britain make reparations to American citizens, issue a public acknowledgement of wrongdoing, allow American ships to trade with Britain and Ireland, and surrender all of Canada.[8]

Two days later, Franklin suspended diplomatic discussions with Oswald. Grenville, Franklin said, had assured him that an acknowledgement of independence would precede peace negotiations. Franklin had reason to doubt Britain's sincerity, and declared that until such an acknowledgment arrived, any further discussions seemed "untimely." That same day he wrote a gracious note to Shelburne congratulating him on his appointment as Prime Minister, and characterizing the position as "an Extension of your Power to do Good." Oswald forwarded it with an alarmed letter of his own, seeking further instructions.

Franklin now had merely to wait, just as he had waited four-and-a-half years earlier for Vergennes to approach him about an alliance. For the moment, he had an advantage he had lacked on the earlier occasion. Then he had been burdened with two meddlesome colleagues, Arthur Lee and Silas Deane.[9] In July, 1782, Franklin was acting alone. Peace Commissioners Henry Laurens and John Adams had declined the invitation to join him in Paris, and John Jay, who had come at the end of June, was ill with influenza.

It did not take long for Shelburne to capitulate. On July 27, the Prime Minister informed Oswald that he would soon receive a commission empowering him to negotiate a treaty based on Franklin's necessary articles. Not only was Shelburne prepared to concede American independence as part of a preliminary peace agreement, he also accepted Franklin's demands concerning the Canadian border and American access to the fisheries.[1]

An unsigned preliminary copy of Oswald's commission arrived in early August. Franklin immediately forwarded it to Ver-

8. See our headnote to BF to Lafayette, July 9.
9. See, for example, XXV, 207.
1. See the headnote to Shelburne to BF, July 27.

gennes, whose own negotiations with Great Britain were stalled until its arrival. Vergennes recommended that the Americans begin negotiations; Franklin agreed. Peace might have been within easy reach had it not been for the objections of John Jay, who by this time had recovered from his illness. Jay observed that Oswald's commission referred to the American Peace Commissioners as representatives of the thirteen colonies, rather than the United States. New to the negotiations, humiliated by the two difficult years he had spent begging assistance from the Spanish, and deeply suspicious of Great Britain, Jay demanded that Parliament explicitly recognize American independence before the negotiations began.[2] The discussions between Jay, Franklin, and Vergennes on this point would continue into September, and negotiations would remain paralyzed until Shelburne amended Oswald's commission. The outline of the treaty, however, remained firmly in place, and became the foundation for the detailed discussions that would culminate in the preliminary peace agreement of November 30.

Overshadowed in our documents by Oswald's arrival in April and the commencement of negotiations was the news that George III had finally approved a prisoner exchange on April 7. Franklin, who throughout the war had received reports of the American prisoners' mistreatment, had fought passionately to effect this exchange. His inability to achieve it had been one of his greatest frustrations. In spite of the prisoner release, and the fact that an end to hostilities seemed possible, Franklin continued to dwell on the horrors of British cruelty. This rage fueled one of his most elaborate hoaxes, a pair of political pieces designed to influence British public opinion.

The hoax was based on the same idea Franklin had emphasized to Oswald during the emissary's April visit, that Britain should acknowledge its war atrocities and offer reparations to the Americans. Franklin composed a pair of letters, ostensibly published in America, that he hoped would be reprinted in the British press. The first was a grisly account of torture and scalpings performed on innocent American townspeople, written from the point of view of an American Indian in the British

2. For Jay's intervention see BF to Vergennes, Aug. 8.

service. The second, in the form of a letter from John Paul Jones, portrayed the captain defending himself against the British charge of piracy and accusing George III of being a ruthless murderer. Franklin printed these pieces on a broadside that mimicked exactly the format of a single-sheet supplement to an American newspaper, complete with advertisements. He sent this "Supplement to the Boston Independent Chronicle" to various correspondents in England and the Netherlands. One of the pieces was reprinted in *The Public Advertiser;* the other appeared in *The Remembrancer.*[3]

During the summer Franklin also wrote two important essays on the law of nations which he sent to England in July: an argument against privateering, and "A Thought Concerning the Sugar Islands." These essays were immediately circulated in manuscript, and appeared in print shortly before Franklin's death.[4]

Franklin's press was unusually active during the spring and summer of 1782. In addition to the "Supplement" mentioned above, he printed new promissory note forms, a bond form, a passport for ships, and a new personal passport form inaugurating the 52-point script type that Fournier le jeune had cut for him in 1780. For the last, he employed a two-pull printing system that allowed him to simulate handwriting.[5] Franklin also printed a forty-six-page treatise on perpetual peace written by the former galley slave Pierre-André Gargaz. This "shabbily dressed" individual had walked from the south of France to Paris carrying his manuscript. He and Franklin not only discussed world politics, theories of war and peace, and social reform, but they also discovered a mutual enthusiasm for phonetic spelling systems.[6]

During periods of diplomatic calm, Franklin turned to science. In early April he visited one of Chaumont's quarries, where four live toads had been discovered fifteen feet under-

3. See "Supplement to the Boston Independent Chronicle," [before April 22].
4. These two essays are published below, [after July 10].
5. Passport for Rawle and Walker, May 8, 1782.
6. See Gargaz's letter of *c.* July 10.

ground in small, discreet cells in the limestone. He wrote up his findings and submitted them to the Académie des sciences.[7] In April or May he may have succeeded in viewing the much-advertised but as yet nonfunctional flying machine invented by Jean-Pierre Blanchard, who begged him to postpone his visit by a week.[8] In June he finally finished for Jan Ingenhousz an analysis of an Italian pamphlet describing the effects of a lightning strike on the Cremona church weathervane. He sent it with a long-postponed letter he had been writing in installments.[9]

Throughout the spring, Franklin also made time (occasionally with the prodding of the frantic author) to review page proofs of Michel-René Hilliard d'Auberteuil's second volume of *Essais historiques et politiques sur les Anglo-Américains,* a history of the colonies, their conflicts with Great Britain, and the Revolution up to 1778.[1] In July he received St. John de Crèvecœur's newly published *Letters from an American Farmer.*[2] The young Joseph Wright, in Paris during the summer of 1782, painted four oil portraits of Franklin, two of which were for Richard Oswald and Caleb Whitefoord.[3] Franklin himself, it seems, tried his hand at drawing. We publish in this volume a sketch identified as a scene in Chaumont's gardens attributed to Franklin and dated March 27.

Marring the excitement and promise of these months was a prolonged dispute between Franklin and Chaumont over their accounts. The dispute infuriated Franklin, and the accounts themselves have long been a source of frustration to historians, as the various versions were separated from one another over time and are now scattered in several different repositories. We have finally sorted them out, and publish in this volume the fully documented story of the dispute and its settlement. The ac-

7. His report is dated April 6.
8. See Blanchard to BF, *c.* April.
9. BF's analysis is published under the date of June 21. The serial letter in which it was enclosed is in XXXV, 544–51.
1. BF's side of the correspondence is lost, but his comments are reflected in Hilliard's letters.
2. See Target to BF, July 13.
3. See Patience Wright to BF, July 30.

counts reveal, among other things, the agreement over Franklin's rent.[4]

Chaumont's unscrupulous behavior during this period, induced by his financial decline, might have permanently severed the two men's friendship had Franklin not called a moratorium on the arbitration. He used Chaumont's example as a moral lesson for Jonathan Williams, Jr., cautioning him to recognize "a Man naturally honest thus driven into Knavery by the Effect of imprudent Speculations."[5] Franklin's views on mankind in general did not improve with the approach of a peace treaty. Elated as he was to see the end of hostilities, his rage against the atrocities commited on innocent victims was if anything more focused as he began negotiations. The more he mused on the human race, he wrote, the more disgusted he was. Men "are generally more easily provok'd than reconcil'd, more dispos'd to do Mischief to each other than to make Reparation, much more easily deceiv'd than undeceiv'd, and having more Pride & even Pleasure in killing than in begetting one another."[6]

4. See the headnote to the exchange about accounts between Chaumont and Franklin, [before April 26]. For the rent agreement, see Ferdinand Grand's Report on Chaumont's Account with Franklin, [May 7].
5. To JW, June 13.
6. To Joseph Priestley, June 7.

Chronology

May 4: Oswald arrives again in Paris.

May 7: Thomas Grenville joins Oswald.

May 9: Franklin and Grenville meet with Vergennes; Franklin begins his journal of the peace negotiations.

May 10: Grenville meets with Vergennes and Aranda.

May 10–September 24: Laurens travels to Netherlands and France.

May 14–21: Oswald returns to London for further instructions.

May 21–June 23: John and Sarah Jay travel from Madrid to Paris.

May 26: Grenville presents Vergennes his powers to negotiate.

c. May 28: Laurens meets with Adams at The Hague.

May 31: Oswald is back in Paris.

June 1: Grenville unsuccessfully offers Franklin British recognition of American independence.

June 7: Franklin receives loan of 2,352,899 *l.t.* 15 *s.* 4 *d.* from French government.

June 9: Franklin releases Cornwallis from his parole.

June 15: Grenville presents new powers to Vergennes.

June 19: George III gives his assent to Enabling Act.

July 1: Death of Rockingham.

July 4: Shelburne becomes first lord of the treasury; Fox resigns.

July 10: Franklin presents Oswald with a list of American demands; Thomas Townshend becomes secretary of state for the home department.

July 11: British army evacuates Savannah.

July 16: Franklin and Vergennes sign contract for repayment of French loans.

July 17: Baron Grantham becomes secretary of state for foreign affairs.

July 27: Shelburne authorizes Oswald to negotiate on basis of Franklin's "necessary articles."

July 31: New instructions for Oswald authorize sweeping concessions.

August 3: Jay begins discussions with Aranda.

August 6: Oswald receives commission enabling him to negotiate.

August 7: Jay objects to Oswald's commission.

THE PAPERS OF
BENJAMIN FRANKLIN

VOLUME 37

March 16 through August 15, 1782

Editorial Note on Franklin's Accounts

During the period of this volume, Franklin attempted to settle his accounts with his landlord, le Ray de Chaumont. We publish the successive versions of these accounts, and we provide an overview of the dispute in a headnote to the first of them, [before April 26].

The following previously identified accounts still apply: VI and VII (XXIII, 21); XII (XXV, 3); XVII (XXVI, 3); XIX and XXII (XXVIII, 3–4); XXV, XXVII, and XXVIII (XXXII, 3–4). We offer here a summary of items which have not found a place elsewhere in our annotation, but which provide insights into Franklin's private and public life.

Account XVII (Franklin's Private Accounts with Ferdinand Grand, XXVI, 3) gives insight into Franklin's personal and household affairs. On April 5, Franklin withdrew 7,000 *l.t.* in cash, and on July 29 he purchased seven shares in the Caisse d'escompte. Mlle de Chaumont was paid in March, June, July, and August.[1] Campo-de-Arbe, the maître d'hôtel, received 3,011 *l.t.* 10 *s.* 6 *d.* for household expenses on June 17,[2] and a final salary payment on June 21. He was replaced by Duchemin, who was paid monthly thereafter.[3] The cook, Coimet, received one payment in June; Frémont, who supplied linen,[4] collected his annual payment in August. On April 3, Franklin resubscribed to the *Gazette de Leyde,* and on July 2 a case of books was delivered.[5] On

---

1. A separate memorandum in WTF's hand, marked "Paid Miss Cht", itemizes the vegetable bill for July. Listed are sums for peas, carrots, beans, turnips, currants, and water cress (APS).

2. Campo-de-Arbe's signed receipt for that amount is at the APS. Other receipts at the APS that may have been paid by the maître d'hôtel include two for bread from Pharon l'aîné, the Passy *boulanger,* one covering April and the other June 1–15. Each lists standard loaves of four and five *livres,* as well as "Pain de table" and "Pain a caffé." On June 21, the frères de Manounry signed a receipt for 122 bottles of "Champaigne non mousseux."

JW provided porter for the household; he notified WTF on July 5 that he had debited BF's account for a cask and a case containing 80 bottles (APS).

3. He had been offered the position 18 months earlier: XXXIV, 266.

4. XXXV, 6.

5. Among BF's papers at the APS is a circular dated June 12 from Robert-André Hardouin announcing various books for sale. In the margin, crosses were made next to the second installment of Charles Bonnet's *Œuvres d'histoire naturelle et de philosophie* (8 vols., Neuchâtel, 1779–83), and the Société Typographique de Genève's *Œuvres posthumes de J.-J. Rousseau* . . . . BF's complete set of Bonnet's *Œuvres* is now at the APS.

March 28, Franklin paid the abbé Rochon 510 *l.t.* This entry may represent the purchase of Rochon's micrometer.[6]

Franklin himself drew a quarter's salary on April 4 and July 4, and on July 13 deposited thirty-two coupons from the Caisse d'Escompte. The account received its quarterly review on July 17, when it was signed by both Grand and Franklin.[7]

Account XXV (Account of Postage and Errands, XXXII, 3) was at this time being kept by L'Air de Lamotte, based in part on monthly bills from Berthelot, the postman, and Julien, the *commissionaire*. The gardener, Jean-Nicolas Bonnefoÿ (Bonefoi), was also paid for errands. On March 31, Moses Young was sent by carriage to Paris with dispatches. On April 25, taxes were paid at Customs for three cases sent to Rochefort.[8] The deliveryman who brought a case of limes received a gratuity on July 2. July 6 saw the highest volume of mail for a single day: packages and letters amounted to 112 *l.t.* 16 *s.*

Account XXVII (Accounts of the Public Agents in Europe, XXXII, 4) lists the payment of L'Air de Lamotte's salary. Pissot's bill for books was settled on September 10, when the bookbinder Gauthier was also paid.

Editorial Note on Promissory Notes

By the time Franklin issued the first of the promissory notes in March described below, he was using a new triplicate form, set in *gros romain* italic, with slight variations in wording. This form lasted him through the end of the French mission.[9]

---

6. BF had described the instrument ("a kind of telescope") in 1780, after having seen it once. We know he purchased one before returning to America in 1785; he showed it to Rittenhouse in 1786, and it was listed on the inventory of his estate: XXXII, 120–1n.

7. A three-page variant of part of this account exists, covering only July 17, 1782, through Jan. 20, 1783 (APS). The only differences are variations in phraseology.

8. These cases may have contained the books requested by the secretary of foreign affairs, Robert R. Livingston. BF told Morris that he intended to send them to America with Lafayette, who was expected to sail in April: XXXVI, 401–2, 651, 672; BF to Livingston, March 30; BF to Morris, March 30, both below.

9. In the new form the payee is "Superintendent of Finances" instead of "President"; the amount is now given in *l.t.* rather than *louis d'or;* and there

On March 25 Joseph Gould of Massachusetts, a mariner on the *Raven* from Boston, and Moses How of Rhode Island, taken on the *Polly*, each received signed notes for 72 *l.t.* Benjamin Slocum of Rhode Island, who carried Franklin a letter of introduction from Francis Coffyn, signed a note for the same amount on April 27.[1] Francis Ming and Capt. John Norcom,[2] commander of the privateer *Friends*, each received 168 *l.t.* on May 9. Six days later William Allcock, who served under Norcom, signed for 336 *l.t.* This sum was shared by Allcock and the five men who accompanied him to Passy; see his letter to Franklin of May 6. On May 22, two men identified as George Cabit and William Stephenson (both of whom signed with an X) each received 48 *l.t.*[3] On August 3, "S. Simondes", whose first name was probably Samuel, signed a promissory note for 96 *l.t.*[4]

To John Jay

ALS: First Federal Savings & Loan Association of Boston; copies: Columbia University Library, Henry E. Huntington Library, Library of Congress, National Archives

Dear Sir,   Passy, March 16. 1782

I have received your several Favours of Jan. 30. Feb. 11. and March 1.[5] and propose to write fully to you per next Post. In the mean time this Line may serve to acquaint you that I have paid duly all your former Bills drawn in favour of Mr Cabarrus;[6] and

---

are two additional lines to be filled in by the recipient indicating his home state and the name, owner, and home port of the ship on which he had been taken. For the previous forms see XXXI, 497; XXXV, 6. All the promissory notes discussed below are at the APS, and all the men who signed them (except Benjamin Slocum) are on the Alphabetical List of Escaped Prisoners.

1. Coffyn's letter is below, April 21.

2. Claghorn, *Naval Officers*, p. 223, where his name is spelled Norcombe.

3. Francis Coffyn, who aided both men, calls them "Cabot" and "Stevenson": Coffyn to BF, May 16.

4. Account XXVII records a disbursement of this amount to a "Samuel Simmons" on Nov. 26. A Samuel Simon, Simmonds, or Symons is also listed in British records: Kaminkow, *Mariners*, pp. 172, 185.

5. XXXVI, 496–7, 558–60, 634–5.

6. Between Feb. 6 and 11, BF's banker Ferdinand Grand honored 19 bills which Jay had drawn on the French-born Spanish banker François Cabarrus.

that having obtain'd a Promise of Six Millions for this Year, to be paid me Quarterly,[7] I now see that I shall be able to pay your Drafts for discharging the Sums you may be oblig'd to borrow for paying those upon you, in which however I wish you to give me as much time as you can, dividing them so as that they may not all come upon me at once. Interest should be allow'd your Friends who advance for you. Please to send me a compleat List of all the Bills you have accepted, their Numbers & Dates, marking what are paid, and what are still to pay. I congratulate you on the Change of Sentiment in the British Nation.[8] It has been intimated to me from thence, that they are willing to make a separate Peace with us exclusive of France, Spain and Holland, which, so far as relates to France, is impossible; and I believe they will be content that we leave them the other two.[9] But Holland is stepping towards us; and I am not without Hopes of a second Loan there.[1] And since Spain does not think our Friendship worth cultivating, I wish you would inform me of the whole Sum we owe to her, that we may think of some Means of paying it off speedily. With sincerest Regard, I am, Dear Sir, Your most obedient and most humble Servant   B FRANKLIN

The Marquis de la Fayette has your Letter. I shall soon write to Mr Carmichael.

His Excelly. J. Jay Esq

Endorsed: Recd 26 March 1782[2]

The total amount of these bills was 76,681 *l.t.* 13 *s.* 6 *d.*: Account XXVII (XXXII, 4).

7. Two weeks earlier French Foreign Minister Vergennes had informed BF of the new loan from the French government: XXXVI, 650.

8. The change of sentiment was marked particularly by a vote of the House of Commons during its session of Feb. 27–28 condemning the further prosecution of offensive warfare in North America: XXXVI, 621–2.

9. BF recently had rebuked David Hartley for such suggestions: XXXVI, 435–8, 583–4.

1. A few months before this, the French government had raised a loan of 5,000,000 *f.* in the Netherlands on behalf of the United States: XXXVI, 16n, 200, 211, 452n.

2. Someone has added, "By Hon: J. Jay".

From Francis Coffyn

ALS: American Philosophical Society

Monsieur   Dunkerque ce 16 mars 1782.

J'ai l'honneur de vous ecrire la presente qui vous sera remise par les nommés Joseph Gole & Moses howes[3] tous deux matelots americains qui ont été pris sur Differents navires & conduits en Angletterre, d'ou ils se sont sauvés des prisons, et sont arrivés ici manquant de tout, comme ils cherchent a retourner en Amerique Je leurs ai fourni Pour le compte de votre Excellence une somme de L. 96 pour payer les frais de leur route, suivant leur recepicé.[4]

J'ai l'honneur d'etre avec un tres profond respect Monsieur Votre tres humble & tres obeissant Serviteur   F. Coffyn

Addressed: A Son / Excellence M. B. Franklin / Ministre pleni-potentiaire des etats unis / de l'amerique Septentrionale a la cour / de france / a Passi pres Paris

Notation: Coffyn 16. Mars 1782.

From John Jay

AL (draft):[5] Columbia University Library

Dr Sir   Madrid 18 March 1782

All our Trouble and anxiety abt the Bills payable here this Month has been in vain they are protested. The following are the Reasons which I have desired the Notary to recite exactly in the Protest vizt (here insert Reasons verb. [verbatim])[6] It is proper

3. Joseph Gould and Moses How reached Passy by March 25. See our headnote on Promissory Notes, above.

4. 96 *l.t.*, for which sum Grand, on BF's order, reimbursed him: Account XXVII (XXXII, 4).

5. Printed, with many of Jay's cancellations indicated, in Morris, *Jay: Peace*, pp. 143–4.

6. When the bills were protested, Jay explained that he did not have time to have recourse to Congress for paying his outstanding debts, which were no more than £25,000 sterling. He did not blame BF for his inability to help (XXXVI, 451–2): Morris, *Jay: Peace*, p. 144n. Jay's efforts to avoid defaulting on the loans are detailed in Morris, *Jay: Peace*, pp. 130–4. Jay might have been spared the embarrassment had BF not waited until March 16 (above) to tell him that Vergennes had promised a new loan of 6,000,000 *l.t.*, news he

you shd be informed that Mr. Garbarrus [Cabarrus], some Months ago voluntary offered (thro Mr. Carmichael) to furnish me even with 100,000 Dollr. per Month provided the Minister wd agree to put it on the same footing on which he had contracted to furnish certain Supplies to Govt.— I need not observe that this did not take place.[7] You know that Mr Cabarrus had advanced about 30,000 Dollars towards our Bills.[8] The Minister lately gave him an order for 26,000 Dollars being somewhat more than the Ballance due on the 150000 Dollars of which my former Letters have often made mention so that my Debt to Mr Cabarrus has been considerably diminished.[9] This Gentleman has also often authorised Mr Carmichael to assure me of his Readiness to advance what might be necessary to pay the Residue of our Bills if the Minister or the Embassador of France wd. become responsible for the Reimbursmt. with Interest in a convenient Time. The twelve Day of the Month he renewed this offer to me in very express Terms telling me he would wait ten or twelve Months for the Money.

On the 15th. Inst. the Minister consented that Mr Cabarrus shd. supply me to the Amount of 40 or 50 thousd. Current Dollars on these Terms. But Mr Cabarrus then insisteed that the Rents of the post office shd be charged with the Repaymt of this Sum at the Rate of 200,000 Reals of Vollon pr. Month. With this *new* Condition the Minister refused to comply—and the protest of the Bills became inevitable.

This is a Subject on which I could make some interesting Remarks & add some Singular Circumstance but they must be deferred to another opportunity.

Wd it be posible to take up & pay these Bills at Paris?

---

communicated to Robert Morris on March 4 (XXXVI, 650). Neither, apparently, did he suggest to Vergennes that he pass the news to Jay through French Ambassador Montmorin, as Vergennes only informed the ambassador about it on March 14 (AAE).

7. Spanish Chief Minister Floridablanca refused to cooperate with Cabarrus, claiming the Spanish government needed whatever money the banker could command: Morris, *Jay: Peace*, p. 131.

8. Jay had reported this to BF on Jan. 11: XXXVI, 424.

9. See Jay's March 1 letter to BF: XXXVI, 635.

I am Dr Sir with sincere Esteem and Regarrd your obliged &
obt Servt   J J.

His Exy Dr Franklin

To Dr. Franklin 18 March 1782.

From Henry Wyld[1]   ALS: American Philosophical Society

Most Excellent sir   Hatherlowe March 18th. 1782

I Arrived at my own house on the 15th. of January past and
laid the answer you thought proper to return, before the Gentlemen to whom the Same was addressed, all of whom return
you their most humble and harty Thanks, for the kindness
shewed to me, and are sensible of the respect shewed to them in
a merchantile Capacity by the Credid you gave my draft on my
Friend Mr. Edmund Clegg, which has rec'd due honour.[2]

We, notwithstand the negative you gave to the second Article
of our propositions in the way the same was proposed, do perce-
vere in our plan of Emigration, and therefore desire you will,
immediately on the receipt of this transmit us the certificate
promised, to operate as a Protection, provide we should fall into
the hands of the Crusers of either you or your Allies, And also
we desire you will recommend us, either to the general Congress
or the Congress for Pensylvania, for the Expence, provide we
shall have occasion for the same to inable us to establish such
Businesses as proposed, and by so doing will discover your desires, to establish, a few Virtuous tho' not rich persons, in America, who have it in their power, to render essential service, to any
State where such manufacturies are wanted.

We also desire you to forward our solicitation respecting the

1. One of a group of textile manufacturers based in Manchester and Stockport who had formed an association called the Emigrant Club for the purpose of establishing textile manufactories in America. Wyld delivered the
group's petition to BF on Jan. 2: XXXVI, 105–7, 354, 367.

2. BF's answer was to Henry Royle *et al.*, Jan. 4. He loaned Wyld 10 guineas
in exchange for a draft drawn on Clegg, which he forwarded to William
Hodgson: XXXVI, 374–5, 389.

Expence and other requests to the Congress of Pensilvania, that on our arrival we may not be suspected, as enemies to the liberties of the Citizens of the United States, for this you may be assured of that though I appied to you witht. any Commendation from the Friends of liberty in this Country of whom you had any knowledge, yet the persons concerned are as great for supporting the liberties of America, according to their Capacities, as any person whatsoever either in England or America, and we are since my return joined by some of the greatest Geniusses of Our Country, who ardently wish to be gone, and only wait for your Excellencies protection from your Crusers, hoping to be at Philadelphia about the 30th. of June if yours arrives timely enough.

There seems something going forward in the House of Commons towards establishing peace, may God of his providence avert the designs of his Majesty and his Accursed ministry from frustrating the desirable prospect. I send this because I with every one else who I represented are impatient for an Answer, having wrote to you on the same subject five weeks since[3] and expected an answer the last week, but none coming causes this, If any thing is wrote which you think imprudent, attribute the same to an over warmness in the Cause I with others have so long and still are the warmest advocates for I am for myself and Co. Your Excellencies Most humble servant   HENRY WYLD

Addressed: To his Excellency Benjn. Franklin LLD at Passey near / Paris / Haste

Notation: H. Wyld— Hatherlow— 18. Mars 1782

From Jonathan Williams, Jr.

ALS: American Philosophical Society; copy: Yale University Library

Dear & hond sir.   Nantes March 19. 1782

I inclose you an Accot of what I have paid to the Custom House for Duty, on Public Goods amounting to £5271..

---

3. On Feb. 12: XXXVI, 567–8.

13.10.[*l.t.*] I send a Voucher for the principal sum, the two small ones are included in other payments for different Concerns; if it is neccessary I will have other Receipts taken & sent to you.— I have had a deal of Trouble in this Business and on the whole think I have got off tolerably well for if all the duties had been paid it would have amounted to six times the Sum.[4]

I have received Billys Favour covering Capt Robesons Commn &ca for which I thank you.[5] I knew the Terms I offered to freight my Brig on were high & had little Expectation of your accepting them, the Reason is she is so small & yet so fine a Vessell that I can more than fill her with private Freight at a higher price. Mr Moylan & myself have had thoughts of buying a fine large Ship which will carry 300 Tons & sails well, but we will not buy her without first being certain of having the public Freight. If you will insure her without a premium as the King does, we will let her go on the same Terms or if you will take the whole ship by the Measurement of her 250 Tons as the neutral men offer, you shall have her, but you know the difference of freighting per measurement of the Ship or of the Goods. Please to favour me with an Answer, & say decisively on what Terms you will take the Ship which will determine us to buy her or not, & with this view I have suspended my determination with the proprietor for 8 days.[6]

I have at length got the seeds & they will go by the next messagerie.[7] I am sorry the Wine has been so long on the Way but

---

4. On March 9, jw had reported that he and the farmers general had settled the amount of duty he owed on the goods shipped aboard the captured *Marquis de Lafayette*: xxxvi, 677. The account he enclosed was later forwarded to Barclay (see wtf's notation) and is now missing, but a copy is in jw's letterbook (Yale University Library): the "principal sum" was just over 4,595 *l.t.*, and the two smaller sums, one for eleven bales and the other for "sundry," along with his 2½ percent commission, brought the total to the figure he quotes here.

5. wtf wrote on March 13, according to the notation on jw's March 9 letter: xxxvi, 678. The commission was for the brig *Spry*, commanded by William Robeson.

6. Since late January bf had been trying to arrange for the shipping of supplies that would replace those lost on the *Marquis de Lafayette*: xxxvi, 546, 556, 558, 677–8.

7. On Feb. 24, 1781, wtf had asked rb to purchase three cases of Ameri-

that is always the Case with Goods that go up the River. I cannot send you the Cramberrys[8] whole as I intended because they are too ripe to bear the jolting of the Carriage but Mrs Williams is busy in preserving some for you which will be sent in little Pots.

I will take Care of Mr Johonnott & Mr Warrens Bills.[9]

I am as ever most affectionately & Dutifully Yours

JONA WILLIAMS J

my best affection to Billy.

Please to spare me a few quire of Paper for the press and a pacquet or two of Ink Powder, I expect some but it is not yet come to hand.

Notations: Williams M. Jona. Nantes, March 19 1782.— / [*In William Temple Franklin's hand:*] The Acct. inclosed was given to Mr. Barclay this 16 June 1785— W. T. F.

From John Bondfield   ALS: American Philosophical Society

Sir   Bordeaux 20 March 1782

Within this month past have arrived from Ireland upwards of Thirty Captains Officers and Seamen who by bribing the Centeries or out the Hospitals have escaped by Neutral Vessels and come safe off. The reports they make of the misery they endured and that of their fellow Companions is incredible they have re-

---

can seeds for the comte de Barbançon and ship them on three different vessels (Library of Congress). Bartram prepared the three cases in the fall and added a smaller box of seeds as a gift for BF. BF's box was sent on the *Betsey,* the first of the three ships to sail; see XXXVI, 186, 677. The *Betsey's* cargo was what JW had just received, and he forwarded the gift box and Barbançon's first case to Passy, via Versailles, on March 22. See JW's letter of April 18.

8. Which he had received from Boston earlier in the month: XXXVI, 677.

9. JW was arranging to have BF reimbursed in Boston for money he had lent Winslow Warren and Gabriel Johonnot: XXXV, 10n, 491; XXXVI, 470, 578; JW to Warren, Feb. 19 (Yale University Library). On April 18, he forwarded their bills to his father, instructing him to disburse the money according to BF's orders (Yale University Library).

quested me to represent their sufferings to you tho. I have assured them of your repeated application to obtain redress they persist in requiring that I write you on the Subject and streniously request your outmost exertion to obtain an exchange or a mitigation of treatment during their imprisonment some that are here have been eighteen months confined in various prisons & prison Ships naked without a change of Linnen to preserve them from the inclementcy of the Weather or from filth a power [poor?] worthy Captain Lewis had only a thin pair of Linnen Breeches wrent & slit from top to bottom—[1] I have also had complaints of late from Seamen taken by force in the West Indies being in the service of American Vessels put on board french Merchantmen and sent to Europe this is a greivance of a momentary nature tho attended with Injury to the individuel publick service may be supposed renderd nessessary and may not be again repeated.

Our Neutral Consuls give a latitude to the late resolves in parlement[2] that their Flag is intitled to transport Goods to the United States under the privalidges and restrictions observed in Europe and at present in the West Indies please to give me your construction by which I may be governd not only for my private intruction but to serve to the Trade here who will apply to me for information. I dined yesterday with the prussien Consul[3] who is ready to embark deeply in conections with us so soon as licence is Granted we have upwards of one hundred sail of Neutral Vessels now in this Port. I have the Honor to be with due respect Sir Your most Obedient Humble Servant

JOHN BONDFIELD

Addressed: Son Excellence / Son Excellence Benj Franklin Esqr. / Ministre pleinipenta des Etats Unies / de l'Amerique / a / Paris

1. Elijah Lewis, Job Whipple, and two other escaped prisoners, all traveling together, were aided by Bondfield on March 18: Account XXVII (XXXII, 4). By March 24 they were in Nantes, where they described prison conditions in Kinsale to JW. See their letter to BF, March 24, and JW's letter of March 26.

2. On April 7, 1781, Congress approved new instructions for privateers which permitted the free navigation of neutral vessels: XXXVI, 638n.

3. Jean-Georges Streckeisen, of the firm Texier & Streckeisen: XXXIII, 279n; *Almanach royal* for 1782, p. 268.

From Anne-Louise Boivin d'Hardancourt Brillon de Jouy

L:[4] American Philosophical Society

[March 20, 1782]

PLAIDOYER POUR MADAME
Brillon de Jouy
francaise native de Paris, demeurant
ordinairement à Passy de present à Nice
Contre Monsieur
Benjamin Franklin
americain né à Boston ci devant
académicien, phisicien, Logicien & & &ca
aujourdhui Ambassadeur en france des
Provinces unies de L'amerique resident
à Passy.

C'est avec regret que Le Sanctuaire de la Justice S'ouvre, et que cette deesse ecoute des plaintes portées contre un homme Celebre, que ses ennemis mêmes ont respecté comme le plus sage, et Le plus juste des philosophes de son Siecle; Sa Partie adverse même Longtems abusée sur son merite, n'osoit reclamer une dette qu'elle croyait d'autant plus sacrée, qu'elle regardait comme inutile La signature de Monseigneur Benjamin franklin, et que sa parole lui paraissait plus Sure que tous Les contrats; aujourdhuy Lesée dans tous ses droits, opprimée sous le poids de L'injustice, elle craindrait peut-être encore de ternir la reputation de L'homme qui L'a trompé de la maniere La plus outrageante, si la Societé n'était interessée à devoiler un crime d'autant plus atroce, et dangereux à son repos, qu'il est commis par un homme en place dont L'etat et la reputation semble Lui assurer L'impunité.

O Justice, ô deesse image du dieu, qui regit L'univers, qui devoile les actions Les plus cachées pour recompenser la vertu ignorée, et punir Le vice orgueilleux qui leve sa tête altiere se croyant a L'abri de la foudre, Justice je t'implore en faveur de La Dame Brillon, pese dans tes balances redoutables les conventions reciproques de L'ambassadeur, et de la femme qu'il abusa d'une maniere cruelle, ne te Laisses seduire ni par L'eloquence Sublime

---

4. This mock legal plea to the goddess of Justice is written in the same secretarial hand as that of Mme Brillon's *placet* of Dec. 24, 1781: XXXVI, 292–3.

de L'ameriquain coupable, ni par sa Science dangereuse, ni par sa reputation que la renommée s'est enorgueillie d'etendre d'un pôle à L'autre, plus Le coupable est grand, plus il cause L'admiration des deux hemispheres, plus ta gloire s'accroitra, deesse, en proportionant La punition à L'offense en Laissant tomber ton tonnere sur celui qu'on assure avoir enchainé La foudre, comme il entraina tous Les Cœurs.

FAITS

En 1776 Messire BENJAMIN FRANKLIN fit une societé d'amitié conjointement avec La dame BRILLON,[5] par La quelle ils se promirent reciproquement de se voir souvent Lorsqu'ils seroient à portée de Le faire sans prejudicier à Leurs affaires reciproques

2°. de s'ecrire Lorsqu'ils seroient separés

3°. de repondre exactement à toutes Les Lettres ecrittes par L'un où par L'autre

4°. de n'alleguer aucunes raisons pour se dispenser des conventions cy dessus enoncées.

En 1781 Madame BRILLON obligée de faire un long Voyage pour cause de santé, prit congé de Monsieur BENJAMIN FRANKLIN avec une veritable douleur, il parut touché de son depart Lui rappella Leurs conventions, Lui ecrivit à sa premiere Station en lui faisant de nouveaux Serments; Madame BRILLON croyant d'après cette premiere demarche que sa dette etait assurée, ecrivit souvent à L'ambassadeur, il repondit d'abord, ensuitte Les reponses s'eloignerent, ensuitte il ne fit plus aucunes reponses aux Lettres de Madame BRILLON, et n'en fit même Qu'une très courte au placet Le plus touchant que cette dame et sa famille Lui adresserent dans Leur detresse,[6] La Dame BRILLON apprit dans ce tems par Monsieur LE VEILLARD dont Le temoignage peut faire foi, que ce n'etoit pas fautte de tems de la part dudit BENJAMIN puisqu'il avoit le Loisir de courtiser au moins deux Jolies femmes par jour dans ses moments de disette; elle pria Monsieur LE VEILLARD de lui rappeller ce qu'il lui devoit et de L'engager à Suspendre ses galanteries un quart d'heure tous Les quinze

5. The "peace treaty" alluded to here was concluded most likely during the summer of 1778: XXVII, 332–3.
6. BF's reply to the *placet* was hardly brief: XXXVI, 380–2.

jours, et payer petit à petit Les arerages du fonds qu'il doit à Madame BRILLON, Le dit BENJAMIN s'avoua Coupable, mais ne paya rien; La Dame BRILLON poussée à bout par La recidive des torts de son adversaire s'est determinée à se pourvoir devant vous A CES CAUSES requiert La Suppliante que Le dit Messire BENJAMIN FRANKLIN soit condamné envers elle à tous depens, dommages, et interets qu'il vous plaira fixer relativement aux faits exposés

Nous oui Me. [Maître] D'orengo, pour la dame Brillon, et Maitre Tondu nommé d'office pour Messire franklin; Lequel nous a demandé du tems pour avoir des instructions de sa partie, leur avons donné acte de leurs dires et requisitions, ce faisant avons accordé un mois de delay à La partie de Me. Tondu, et cependant attendu que les plaintes faittes par la partie d'orengo nous paraissent infiniment justes et Equitables, Condamnons provisoirement Le dit franklin à ecrire dans Les vingt-quatre heures de la signification du present arrêt une premiere Lettre Longue, où il demandera de L'indulgence pour ses fautes passées, et Six Lettres plus courtes (Les sujets à son choix) et pour les quelles Lui accordons six mois depens reservés. A Nice Le 20 Mars 1782. Signés Le Comte de Marié premier president, Le comte trinquiery de St Antonin 2e. president, Langosco, dé Oresti, Reynardy, ayberti, roubiony, Bataglini, maccarani, Leotardy, Caravadosy, Senateurs. Collationé Conforme à L'original.   CRESPEAUX DE PISCATORY
                                                            Greffier

From Samuel Hubbart   Two ALS:[7] American Philosophical Society

Honored sir   Mill Prison March 20th. 1782

I Wrote you the thirteenth of Feby. last[8] by Capt. J. Foster Williams, wherein I informed you of my situation being taken by his Majestys Ship Recovery & Carried into Ireland, & from thence Conveyed within these Walls & being destitute of both Money & Cloths do therefore take the Liberty to write you for

---

7. Which differ slightly in wording and punctuation.
8. Hubbart's letter is actually dated Feb. 12: XXXVI, 567.

some, & am in hopes of your granting my Request. My Fathers family was well when I left home together with my Uncle Greenes & Mrs Mecom,[9] if you will comply with my Request You will most greatly oblige your most Hble Servt.[1]

SAML HUBBART

Addressed: To / The / Honble / Benja: Franklin Esqr / Embassador at the Court / of France. Paris.

Notation: Hubbart M. Samuel March 20 1782.

From George James Cholmondeley, Earl of Cholmondeley[2]

Copy:[3] Library of Congress; transcripts: Massachusetts Historical Society, National Archives

Thursday Evn: [March 21, 1782][4] Hotel de Chartres.
Lord Cholmondeley's compliments to Dr. Franklin, he sets out

---

9. His father, Thomas Hubbart, was the stepson of BF's brother John. His mother, who had died in 1775, was the sister of Catharine Ray Greene, wife of R.I. governor William Greene. The Greenes and the Hubbarts were great friends of BF's sister Jane Mecom: V, 502n; XXXVI, 567n.

1. Hubbart wrote a final plea on May 12. Still confined in "this horrid Place," he begged BF for assistance. Hist. Soc. of Pa.

2. George James Cholmondeley, the 4th Earl of Cholmondeley, had met Mme Brillon at Nice in January. When he began his journey northward, Mme Brillon warmly recommended him to BF but was not certain her letter would arrive in time: XXXVI, 457, 504–6.

3. This letter is the first of some 40 documents that BF marked for insertion in his journal of the peace negotiations, printed below under the date of May 9. As we explain in our annotation there, BF's draft of the journal is missing. So, too, are many of the autograph letters he marked for insertion. The present document is one of eight for which no original or contemporary copy survives. We therefore publish the text from the copy of BF's journal made by Josiah Flagg, the best of the three surviving versions. (The two transcripts listed here are from the other two versions.) As with all the inserted letters, this one is briefly summarized in its chronological place in the journal itself.

4. Dated by BF's journal of the peace negotiations. Cholmondeley called on BF the following morning.

for London tomorrow Evening, and Shou'd be glad to see him for Five Minutes before he went, Ld. C will call upon him at any time in the morning that he shall please to appoint.

From David Hartley

Reprinted from William Temple Franklin, ed., *Memoirs of the Life and Writings of Benjamin Franklin* . . . (3 vols., 4to, London, 1817–18), II, 289–90.

My Dear Friend,   London, March 21, 1782.

You will have heard before this can reach you, that Lord North declared yesterday in the House of Commons that his Majesty intended to change his ministers.[5] The House is adjourned for a few days to give time for the formation of a new ministry. Upon this occasion therefore I must apply to you to know whether you would wish me to transfer the late negociation to the successors of the late ministry; in these terms; (vide yours to me of January 15, 1782) viz. "that you are empowered by a special commission to treat of peace whenever a negociation for that purpose shall be opened. That it must always be understood that it is to be in conjunction with your allies conformable to the solemn treaties made with them. That the formal acknowledgment of the Independence of America is not made necessary."[6] And may I add that upon these terms you are disposed to enter a negociation. It is not known who will succeed the late ministry, but from the circumstances which preceded its dissolution we are to hope that they will be disposed to enter into a negociation of peace upon fair and honourable terms. I have no doubt that there were some persons in the late ministry of that disposition.

I told you in my last letters to you of the 11th and 12th instant,[7] that I had received information, whilst I was in the course of cor-

5. With the King's reluctant approval, North resigned as prime minister in order to forestall the humiliation of having the House of Commons vote to remove him: Ian R. Christie, *The End of North's Ministry, 1780–1782* (London and New York, 1958), pp. 363–9; Alan Valentine, *Lord North* (2 vols., Norman, Okla., 1967), II, 309–16.

6. Hartley silently dropped half a dozen sentences that came before the final sentence of this quotation: XXXVI, 436–7.

7. XXXVI, 684–5, 688–9.

respondence with the ministry myself on the subject of peace, that some part of the ministry were transmitting some communications or enquiries upon that subject with Mr. Adams, unknown to me. I had informed the ministry from you the names of the four persons empowered to treat. I saw the minister upon the occasion (I should now call him the late minister). I took the liberty of giving him my opinion upon the matter itself. So far as it related personally to me, I expressed myself fully to him that there was no occasion that such a step should have been taken unknown to me, for that I was very free to confess that if they thought my partiality towards peace was so strong that they could drive a better bargain through another channel, I could not have any right of exclusion upon them. I relate this to you because I would wish to have you make a corresponding application to your own case. If you should think *that my strong desire for peace*, although *most laudable and virtuous in itself, should mislead me*,[8] and that my being so as you may suppose misled, may be of any prejudice to the cause committed to your trust, I desire by no means to embarrass your free conduct, by any considerations of private or personal regard to myself. Having said thus much, I will now add that I am not unambitious of the office of a peace maker, that I flatter myself the very page which I now am writing will bear full testimony from both sides of the impartiality of my conduct. And I will add once more what I have often said and repeated to each side, viz. that no fallacy or deception, knowing or suspecting it to be such, shall ever pass through my hands.

Believe me I sympathize most cordially and sincerely with you in every anxiety of yours for peace. I hope things are tending (although not without rubs) yet in the main to that end. Soon! as soon as the course of human life may be expected to operate on the great scale and course of national events, or rather in the creation and establishment of a new world. I am sometimes tempted to think myself in patient expectation the elder sage of the two. I say the elder, not the better. Yours, &c. D. H.

8. On Jan. 15, BF had written, "I am persuaded that your strong Desire for Peace has misled you"; later in the same letter he called that desire "laudable & virtuous": XXXVI, 435, 437.

From William Jackson[9]   ALS: University of Pennsylvania Library

Sir,   Calais 21st. March 82.

Although I cannot boast the happiness of being personally known to you, yet I flatter myself that my name as formerly conductor of the Public Ledger, and the literary efforts I made in favor of America, must be familiarized to your mind.[1]

I was at Paris in the month of May 1777, and, a fortunate concurrence of circumstances enabled me to communicate to Mr. Carmichael, some very important intelligence relative to the secret correspondonce carried on, between Maurepas and Lord Mansfield.[2] I afterwards accompanied Mr. Carmichael to Dunkirk, where I dictated a series of such facts as he deemed worthy of record, and, for which, I recieved from him letters expressive of gratitude on my return to England.[3]

---

9. Born in Dublin, Jackson (1737?–1795) moved to London at an early age, took holy orders, served briefly as a cleric, and then became a journalist. He was known for his smooth demeanor and abusive pen. From 1766 to 1777, he edited the *Public Ledger*, an anti-ministerial daily newspaper that consistently opposed the war. Between 1778 and 1783, he lived under the protection of two wealthy patrons, Elizabeth Chudleigh, mentioned below, and Samuel Clay Harvey. He published the first British edition of *The Constitutions of the Several Independent States of America . . .* in 1783, and from 1784 to 1786 was the editor of *The Morning Post*. Convicted of high treason in 1795, he committed suicide just before he was to receive his sentence: *DNB;* Lucyle Werkmeister, "Notes for a Revised Life of William Jackson," *Notes and Queries,* CCVI (1961), 43–7, 266–7; Lucyle Werkmeister, *The London Daily Press, 1772–1792* (Lincoln, Nebr., 1963), pp. 80, 411; Solomon Lutnick, *The American Revolution and the British Press, 1775–1783* (Columbia, Mo., 1967), pp. 77–8, 84, 135, [225].

1. In 1774, the *Public Ledger* published BF's anonymous essay, "The Question Discussed: or, Reasons Why America Should Suspend All Trade with Great Britain," (XXI, 351–9). Jackson was the author of a series of letters signed "Curtius", many of which were pro-American, and of an attack on Samuel Johnson's "Taxation No Tyranny": *DNB;* Fred Junkin Hinkhouse, *The Preliminaries of the American Revolution as Seen in the English Press, 1763–1775* (New York, 1926), pp. 124–5.

2. British intelligence in France reported Jackson's arrival in early May and speculated on his communications with Deane: Stevens, *Facsimiles,* II, nos. 154, 168.

3. Carmichael sent reports to the Commissioners on his mission to Dunkirk. Shortly after his arrival there at the end of June, he transmitted to

20

I am now, Sir, at Calais, on a visit to the Duchess of Kingston. It is possible I may accompany her to Petersburgh,[4] and, if there be a service which could be rendered America at the Court of Russia, I should be singularly happy to be employed and empowered on the occasion. The Connection of the Duchess with the Empress, might surely be improved to advantage; and the sphere in which she moves, must afford opportunity for elevated observation.

To a Man of your experience and penetration it would be impertinent to say more. I will only beg leave to add, that I have suffered inconveniencies even to the being deprived of an income by my attachment to the cause of America; but, I think myself amply honoured by the privilege I now assume, of professing my sincere veneration for the character, conduct, and abilities, of Doctor Franklin.

I have the honor to be, Sir, Your Most Devoted, And obedient Hble Servt. Wm. Jackson.

A Letter will come safe addressed to Me at The Duchesses House.

His Excellency Doctor Franklin.

Notation:[5] Jackson 21. March 1782

---

them a copy of a letter said to have been written by Maurepas to Nathaniel Parker Forth, who, according to an anonymous note, was a conduit to Lord Mansfield: XXIII, 49; XXIV, 243–5, 294–6.

4. Elizabeth Chudleigh (1720–1788), while maid of honor to Augusta, Princess of Wales, contracted a secret marriage, which was unhappy and was soon dissolved without benefit of a formal divorce. Her second marriage, to the Duke of Kingston (1711–1773), was challenged as bigamous by the duke's heirs in 1776, and she fled to Calais before she could be restrained from leaving the country. The following year she made the first of four visits to Russia, where she acquired several properties including a townhouse and a country estate, and courted the favor of Catherine II. She resided in Calais between her second and third visits, from the summer of 1781 until the summer of 1782: *DNB;* Anthony Cross, "The Duchess of Kingston in Russia," *History Today,* XXVII (1977), 390–5.

5. On the same sheet as the notation is a pencil sketch of an object or apparatus we cannot identify.

From Larwood, Van Hasselt & Van Suchtelen[6]

ALS: American Philosophical Society

Honnourable Sir!   Amsterdam the 21st March 1782

We are honnoured with your Excellency's much respected favour of 11th Instt.[7] and well observe the Contents, for which please to accept our Thanks; the honnourable John Adams Esqr. hath accepted the 51 bills in question to gether f. 40958:—Bank[8] & in consequence thereof these bills have been duely paid to us.

We beg leave to make Your Excellency an offer of our best Services here & we have the honnour to remain most sincerely Honnourable Sir! Your Excellencys Most Obedt & most humble Servants   LARWOOD VAN HASSELT VAN SUCHTELEN

Addressed: The Honnourable Benjn: / Franklin Esqr. / Commissioner for the United States / of North America / at / Passy / near Paris

To Joseph-Mathias Gérard de Rayneval

ALS: Archives du Ministère des affaires étrangères; copy: Library of Congress

Sir,   Passy, March 22. 1782

With this I have the honour of sending you *all the Letters* I have received from or written to England on the Subject of Peace.[9] M. de Vergennes should have seen them sooner if I had imagined them of any Importance: for I have never had the least

---

6. This is the last extant letter from this Amsterdam merchant firm (XXXVI, 575n).

7. XXXVI, 681.

8. 40,958 florins banco, which were worth slightly more than florins: XXXIII, 360n, 361n, 492n.

9. These included nine letters he had received since December and his four replies; see XXXVI, 253n. In addition to four letters from David Hartley and his three replies, there was one letter each from Edmund Burke, Winchcombe Hartley, and Robert Strange. BF also sent the three letters exchanged with William Alexander about the latter's trip to England. All 13 letters are published in vol. 36. French translations are at the AAE.

Desire of keeping such Correspondence secret.[1] I was, as you will see, accidentally drawn into this; and conceiving it of no Use, I have been backward in continuing it.

I send you also some Papers which show the attentive Care of Congress respecting the Laws of Nations, and which were intended to accompany my Letter relating to Denmark,[2] but then omitted.

Herewith you will also receive the Vote of Congress impowering the Commissioners to borrow Money.[3]

With great Esteem I have the honour to be Sir, Your most obedient and most humble Servant   B Franklin

De Raynevall

1. Since 1778, BF had made a practice of providing the French foreign ministry with copies of correspondence; see XXV, 701–2, and subsequent volumes.

2. BF's Dec. 22, 1779, letter to Danish Foreign Minister Bernstorff (XXXI, 261–5), a copy of which is at the AAE. The papers may have been the Congressional resolutions of May 10 and 11, 1778 (*JCC*, XI, 486, 487–9), copies of which were sent to the Spanish government in November, 1778: XXVIII, 19–20.

3. Such empowerment derived from the resolution of Dec. 23, 1776, authorizing them to borrow up to £2,000,000 (about 47,000,000 *l.t.*): XXIII, 56–7; *JCC*, VI, 1036–7.

To the Earl of Shelburne[4]

ALS: Public Record Office; AL (draft) and two copies:[5] Library of Congress; transcripts: Massachusetts Historical Society, National Archives

Passy, March 22. 1782.

Lord Cholmondeley having kindly offer'd to take a Letter from me to your Lordship,[6] I embrace the Opportunity of assuring the Continuance of my ancient Respect for your Talents and Virtues, and of congratulating you on the returning good Disposition of your Country in favour of America, which appears in the late Resolutions of the Commons. I am persuaded it will have good Effects. I hope it will tend to produce a general Peace, which I am persuaded your Lordship, with all good Men, desires, which I wish to see before I die, & to which I shall with infinite Pleasure contribute every thing in my Power.— Your Friends the Abbé Morellet & Madam Helvetius are well.[7] You have made

---

4. William Fitzmaurice Petty, 2nd Earl of Shelburne, was a prominent member of the opposition in Parliament and supporter of America. Apparently BF first became acquainted with him in 1763: X, 348–9. On March 26, 1782, George III accepted a new government with Charles Watson-Wentworth, 2nd Marquess of Rockingham (XII, 362n), as prime minister, Shelburne as home secretary (handling negotiations with the Americans), and Charles James Fox as foreign secretary. (The three former secretaryships, those for the northern department, southern department, and American colonies, were abolished.) The King also agreed not to exercise a royal veto over American independence. On the following day the Rockingham government took office: John Norris, *Shelburne and Reform* (London and New York, 1963), pp. 149–50; Fitzmaurice, *Life of Shelburne*, II, 87–91; Sir F. Maurice Powicke and E. B. Fryde, comps., *Handbook of British Chronology* (London, 1961), pp. 108, 115–16. For Shelburne's role in the peace negotiations see Harlow, *Second British Empire*, I, 223–407; C. R. Ritcheson, "The Earl of Shelburne and Peace with America, 1782–1783," *International History Review*, V (1983), 322–45; Jonathan R. Dull, "Vergennes, Rayneval, and the Diplomacy of Trust," in Hoffman and Albert, eds., *Peace and the Peacemakers*, pp. 101–31.

5. One of the copies and both transcripts are in BF's journal of the peace negotiations (below, under the date of May 9).

6. See BF's journal of the peace negotiations.

7. Morellet met Shelburne in Paris in 1771 and not only became his lifelong friend but also played a major part in Shelburne's conversion from mercantilism to free trade. The following year, when Morellet visited him in England, Shelburne introduced Morellet to BF: XIX, 177n; Ritcheson, "Earl

the latter very happy by your kind Present of Gooseberry Bushes, which arriv'd in five Days, and in excellent Order.—[8] With great and sincere Esteem, I have the honour to be, My Lord, Your Lordship's most obedient and most humble Servant

B FRANKLIN

Lord Shelburne

Endorsed: 22d. March 1782 Dr. Franklin

Notation: Rd. by Earl Cholmondeley. Entd.

From Thomas Digges[9]

Reprinted from William Temple Franklin, ed., *Memoirs of the Life and Writings of Benjamin Franklin . . .* (3 vols., 4to, London, 1817–18), II, 290–3.

Sir,   Amsterdam, March 22[–26], 1782.

I left England a few days back, and until my conversation and some consultations with Mr. Adams on a matter which will be mentioned to you by him,[1] and more particularly explained in this letter, my determination was to have seen you, as well on that business as on a matter of much consequence to my private reputation.[2] I feel the disadvantages under which I labour when

---

of Shelburne," pp. 328–30. Shelburne had known Mme Helvétius since his 1771 visit to France, when he attended her salon: Fitzmaurice, *Life of Shelburne,* I, 425–6.

8. William Alexander had brought the gooseberry bushes on his return from a recent visit to England (XXXVI, 639–40). Shelburne, who knew of Mme Helvétius' passion for gardening, had sent sets of rose bushes before the war and had offered to send some trees for her "jardin anglais" in 1780. Mme Helvétius had refused; the small space was already filled, and, besides, they should wait until the war was over and communication between their two countries was easier: Medlin, *Morellet,* I, 242, 244n, 422, 425, 458.

9. Digges's first letter to BF since Dec. 29, 1780. Three months after that BF was informed that Digges had misappropriated funds intended for the relief of American sailors imprisoned in England: XXXIV, 221–3, 475–6.

1. JA wrote BF on March 26, below.

2. Digges wanted to clear himself of the charge of misappropriating funds. When those accusations and BF's response (XXXIV, 507) were made

writing to you on a matter which cannot be explained or cleared up but by personal conversation. I do not give up my intended purpose of personally speaking to you, but it being found better and more convenient to my purpose to return immediately hence to England, and from thence to Paris, in preference of going first to Paris, it must be unavoidably delayed for some days.

It would take up more than the length of a letter to explain the whole opening and progression of a matter I am here upon, which was and is meant to be jointly communicated to you with Mr. Adams; I will therefore take the liberty to give you an abbreviation of it in as few words as I can.

About a fortnight ago a direct requisition from ministry, through Lord Beauchamp,[3] was made to Mr. R. Penn[4] to know if he could ascertain *that any person or persons in Europe were commissioned by Congress to treat for peace, whether they were NOW willing to avail themselves of such commission, and of the present sincere disposition in ministry to treat, and whether they would receive an appointed commissioner to speak for a truce, and mention a place for the meeting, &c.*

Mr. Penn's referring Lord Beauchamp to me, as knowing the nature of Mr. Adams's former commission, was the sole cause of my being privy to or a party in the matter. I had various meetings with Lord Beauchamp in company with Mr. Penn on the subject; the particular memorandums of which, and Lord B.'s statement of what the ministry wanted to obtain, together with every other circumstance relative to the matter, I regularly consulted Mr. Laurens and Mr. D. Hartley upon; and the result was my taking the journey hither, and to Paris in order to put the questions (as they are before stated from Lord B. to Mr. Penn)

---

public, he claimed he actually had paid the prisoners, "but not by the common agents employed for that purpose": Elias and Finch, *Letters of Digges*, pp. 24n, 357, 361n.

3. Francis Seymour Conway, Viscount Beauchamp, was a supporter of Lord North's and, as a member of Parliament, held the post of cofferer of the household: *DNB* under Seymour; Namier and Brooke, *House of Commons*, III, 424.

4. Richard Penn, Jr., the former lieutenant governor of Pennsylvania (XXVII, 579n), was an acquaintance of Digges's: XXIX, 581; XXXIII, 427; Elias and Finch, *Letters of Digges*, pp. 37, 40n, 300.

and to bring an answer thereto. I am well convinced by Lord Beauchamp's pledge of his personal honour, as well as from Mr. Hartley's telling me he knew the matter to come directly from Lord North (for he visited him more than once to ascertain the fact) that it is a serious and sincere requisition from ministry, and that they will immediately take some steps to open a treaty provided I go back with assurances that there is a power vested in Americans in Europe to treat and conclude, and that they are willing to avail themselves of such power when properly applied to.[5]

I have stated the whole transaction to Mr. Adams, read every memorandum I had made, informed him of every circumstance I knew, and when I put the questions (as they are before stated from Lord B. to Mr. Penn) he replied, "that there were certainly commissioners in Europe, of which body he was one, who had powers to treat and conclude upon peace; that he believed them willing to enter into such a treaty, provided a proper offer was made; but that no questions now or to be made in future could be answered by him without previously consulting his colleagues, and afterwards acquainting the ministers of the belligerent powers thereof." Mr. Adams recommended that any future questions might be made directly to you, for that the present, as well as any subsequent propositions would be immediately communicated to you and Mons. de Vergennes.

His answers to my questions were nearly what I foretold and expected, and is substantially what Lord Beauchamp seemed so anxious to procure. When I relate this answer to his Lordship my business will be finished in that quarter. I will here explain to you my only motive for being a messenger from him whom I had never known or been in company with before. It will enable me to say, I have done one favour for you, and I claim of you another, viz. to obtain a restoration of my papers from Lord Hillsborough's office, which were in a most illegal and unjustifiable manner seized from me near a twelvemonth ago, and are yet

---

5. Hartley provided Digges with a cautious letter of recommendation to BF, one of two letters from Hartley enclosed with the present letter: XXXVI, 684–5, 688–9. Digges's mission seems to have been the work of the North government, which still hoped for a compromise settlement with the Americans.

withheld notwithstanding the personal applications for them from Lord Coventry, Lord Nugent, and Mr. Jackson, each of whom have explained the injury and very extraordinary mischief the want of my papers for so long a time has and is now doing me.[6]

On my first conversation with Mr. Adams I had concluded to go to you, partly by his advice to do so; but as the expence of two journies where one may serve is of some import to me, and from supposing your answer would be substantially the same as that from Mr. Adams, I have thought it better to go back immediately to London, and then set out for Paris with the probability of being able to bear my papers.[7]

I will take the liberty to trouble you with another letter if any thing occurs on my arrival in London. I am to leave this with Mr. Adams for forwardance; and for the present I have only to beg a line acknowledging the receipt of it. If your letter is put under *a cover to Mr. Stockdale, Bookseller, Piccadilly, London,* it will the more readily get to hand. I am, with great respect, Sir, your very obedient servant,   T. DIGGES.

Ostend, 26th March.

On my last visit to Mr. Adams, Friday evening,[8] to explain to him the substance of the foregoing letter, and ask his forwar-

6. The Earl of Hillsborough was North's final secretary of state for the southern department. The three men who interceded for Digges had disparate backgrounds and political opinions. George William Coventry, the 8th Earl of Coventry, was an opponent of the North government: G. E. Cokayne *et al.*, eds., *The Complete Peerage of England, Scotland, Ireland, Great Britain and the United Kingdom* . . . (13 vols., rev. ed., London, 1910–40), III, 473–4. Robert Nugent, a vice-treasurer of Ireland, was a North supporter: *DNB;* Namier and Brooke, *House of Commons*, III, 218–22. George Jackson, the second secretary of the Admiralty, was a member of administration, who soon would be forced from office by a new first lord of the Admiralty. When Digges returned to England he was permitted to search for his papers and he took "documents & Letters" from Jackson's office: N. A. M. Rodger, *The Insatiable Earl: a Life of John Montagu, Fourth Earl of Sandwich, 1718–1792* (New York and London, 1993), p. 306; Elias and Finch, *Letters of Digges*, pp. liv, lviii.

7. Digges did not go to Paris, and the present letter is the last extant one between him and BF.

8. March 22.

dance of it to you, we had some farther conversation on the matter, the ultimate conclusion of which was, that it was thought better I did not send the annexed letter to you, or mention my business with him until my going in person from England. Mr. Adams's reasons were these. That if I made the communication *then* he should be necessitated to state the matter in a long letter to you and others of his colleagues; that the matter as it then stood was not of such importance but he could save himself the trouble of the explanation; and that as he recommended any future questions or applications to be made directly to you, your situation making it more convenient sooner to inform the French court thereof, he thought my letter had better be postponed, and the substance of it given in person as soon as I could possibly get from London to Paris. I acquiesced, though reluctantly, and having thought much on the matter on my journey hither, I have at length determined to forward the foregoing letter with this postscript, and at the same time to inform Mr. Adams of my exact feelings on the matter,[9] viz. that my wishes and intentions when I left England were to see, and make known the matter to you; that through Mr. Hartley or some other channel you must hear that I had been at Amsterdam, and my seemingly turning my back upon you might be thought oddly of; and finally that I could not answer for carrying the inclosure from Mr. Hartley back to England, not knowing the consequence it might be of. I hope and think I have done right in this matter. The purpose for my moving in the business I went to Mr. A. upon, has, I own, been with a double view of serving myself in a matter of much consequence to me, for after delivering the explanations I carry, I can with some degree of right and a very great probability of success, claim as a gratuity for the trouble and expence I have been at, the restoration of my papers; the situation of which I have already explained to Lord Beauchamp, in order to get him to be a mover for them, and I have very little doubt that a few days will restore them to me, and give me an opportunity to speedily speak to you on a matter which gives me much uneasiness, vexation, and pain. Excuse the hurry in which I write, for I am very near

9. He wrote JA on the same day: Elias and Finch, *Letters of Digges*, pp. 362–4.

the period of embarkation. Paul Wentworth embarked this day for England, I trod on his heels chief of the way from the Hague which he left suddenly.[1] General Faucit is on his road hence to Hanover.[2]

From René-Georges Gastellier

ALS: American Philosophical Society

Monsieur et très illustre docteur

à montargis ce 22 mars 1782

Je viens de recevoir une lettre de Mademoiselle de fay par la quelle J'apprends avec un plaisir vraiment indicible que vous aviés bien voulú jetter un Coup d'oeil favorable sur les deux ouvrages qu'elle vous a presentés en mon nom.[3] Ma satisfaction seroit Complette si j'etois persuadé que vous les avés trouvés dignes sinon de votre suffrage aumoins de votre indulgence: tels qu'ils sont daignés les agréer Comme un bien foible hommage des sentimens de respect et de veneration dont votre celebrité m'a penetré pour toujours.

L'acte d'association dont vous faites esperer m'honorer un jour fera une des époques les plus agreables de ma vie, j'en apprendrai la réalité avec autant de joye que de réconnoissance.

Je suis avec le plus profond respect Monsieur et très illustre docteur votre trés humble trés obeissant serviteur

GASTELLIER

Notation: Gastelier, Montargis 22 Mars 1782.

1. Wentworth left after an unsuccessful attempt to procure a separate peace with the Netherlands: XXXVI, 537n; James H. Hutson, *John Adams and the Diplomacy of the American Revolution* (Lexington, Ky., 1980), p. 107.
2. Maj. Gen. William Fawcett or Faucitt made various recruiting missions abroad and was promoted to lieutenant general later in the year: *DNB*.
3. On Feb. 6, Mlle Defay sent BF Gastellier's works and his request to be named a corresponding member of the APS: XXXVI, 547–8.

From William Hodgson   ALS: American Philosophical Society

Dear sir   [March 22, 1782?]

I recd yesterday from Mr Grand your Remittance for £300 for the use of the Prisoners, this together with the former Remittance in Jany makes in all £460..10 s. recd this Year,[4] from the Number of Prisoners which I have before informed you were about 1000 Men,[5] you will easily judge that I was all the amount of this last remise in advance prior to my receiving it, as the weekly payments come to £50 a fraction more or less, at one Shilling per week to each man pursuant to your former orders, I shall go on advancing as I have hitherto done, not in the least doubting but you will cause me to be reimbursed, a little temporary disburse, makes no material Inconvenience to me.

I have wrote several Letters to which I have not yet rec'd your Reply,[6] I am rather apprehensive that some accident may have happened which has prevented my hearing from you, in full Confidence however that you will give me Credit for the goodness of my Intention, I shall now communicate to you the great Revolution that has happened in the Administration of this Country, there is a total Change, the whole of the Old Ministry, so hostile & so inimical to America are to Retire & the Goverment is to be lodged in the hands of those who have ever repro-

---

4. These remittances are listed in Hodgson's account described in XXXVI, 605–6n; the £300 is also listed under the date of March 2 in Account XXVII (XXXII, 4). Hodgson's account lists a further payment of £200 from Grand in May (remitted on April 18: Account XXVII) and various expenditures by Hodgson on behalf of prisoners: Miles Saurey, Hodgson's agent at Mill Prison, Plymouth, was sent £190 in March and £70 in April; Thomas Wren, the agent at Forton Prison, Portsmouth, was sent £70 in March and £62 12 s. in April; and £48 was sent to Plymouth in March for clothing. Another account, submitted by Hodgson on Oct. 24, 1783 (APS) includes several other expenditures between March and October, 1782: £21 "to Mr Benjn Cook Commissary to Genl Greens Army . . . for his passage Home", £3 3 s. "to Capt Dunlop in gt distress", and 16 s. for "Pepper Mint Drops". The peppermint drops were for Gérard de Rayneval: BF to Gérard de Rayneval, Sept. 4, 1782 (AAE).

5. In January, he had estimated the number of prisoners at nearly 900: XXXVI, 440.

6. Since BF's latest extant letter, that of Jan. 7, Hodgson had written BF at least three times (XXXVI, 389, 439–41, 605–6, 633–4).

bated the American War & the Principles upon which it was carried on;[7] I congratulate you upon this Event because I hope & trust it will lead to that great Epoch which must be the wish of your Heart, Peace, upon such a footing as will ensure to America all that she has so nobly & so gloriously contended for— *I Know* the rising Ministers will cooperate in any Measures that may tend to Peace, My late Letters mentioned to you that in Case the Event took place which now has actually happened I shou'd wish to have your Instructions—[8] I am upon tender ground; allow me to say only that in aspiring to the Honor, of being an Introductor to a Negotiation, I aspire to what I shou'd consider as the greatest honor of my Life— I make no pretensions to your Confidence from my Abilities I pretend only to plain common Sense & goodness of Intention, if they will entitle me to what I aspire after, yo[u may] depend upon it I will never *Knowingly* deceive you, or *Knowingly* be the Instrument of Deception in others; Mr Burke has introduced into Parliament a Bill for the exchange of American Prisoners to this I alluded in a former Letter,[9] the Bill has passed the Commons & will soon I have no doubt pass the Lords likewise—[1] In consequence I flatter myself that there will soon be a resolution taken to exchange under the Terms & Conditions you formerly mentioned & pursuant to which I presented a Memorial on the 4th day of last Decemr—[2] I submit it to you whether it may not be judged proper that you shou'd expressly authorise in a particular Letter or Power the exchange under the Terms & Conditions agreed upon— Messrs

7. The composition of the impending Rockingham government was a subject of speculation in the London press, although its predictions did not always prove accurate. The March 22 issue of the *London Courant, Morning Gazette, and Daily Advertiser,* for example, erroneously predicted the Duke of Grafton as first lord of the Admiralty, Lord Camden as chancellor, Lord Thurlow as lord president of the council, Fox as chancellor of the exchequer, and the Duke of Richmond as a secretary of state.

8. XXXVI, 278.

9. XXXVI, 633–4.

1. Burke's bill to facilitate the exchange of prisoners received the King's assent on March 25: Thomas W. Copeland *et al.,* eds., *The Correspondence of Edmund Burke* (10 vols., Cambridge and Chicago, 1958–78), IV, 428n. For BF's description of it see BF to Jay, April 24.

2. For Hodgson's memorial see XXXVI, 278.

Curson & Gouverneur have been released from their Confinement upon Bail, in the same manner as Mr Laurens, themselves £1000 each & two Sureties £500. each[3] I made no hesitation to be one of their Sureties—I shall be waiting with anxiety for your Reply, I beg you will believe me to be on all occasions with the greatest Respect Dr sr Your's Sincerely   WILLIAM HODGSON

Addressed: To / Benj. Franklin Esqr

Endorsed: Suppos'd 22 March 1782

From Robert Morris

LS and copy:[4] American Philosophical Society; copy: Library of Congress

Sir   Office of Finance Philada March the 22d. 1782
The Bearer of this Letter Monsieur le Baron d'Arndt[5] will shew you a Certificate for Two Thousand Nine hundred & Ninety Seven Dollrs. & 37/90ths signed by Joseph Nourse Esquire Register of the Treasury of the United States and issued by Virtue of a Warrant this Day from me.[6] This Money is on In-

3. For Hodgson's earlier efforts on behalf of Samuel Curson and Isaac Gouverneur, Jr., see XXXV, 344, 439; XXXVI, 62, 270, 277, 640.

4. We cannot be sure when Morris sent this LS. The fair copy was lost in transit; see Morris to BF, June 10. In this LS, the secretary left blanks for specific amounts and for the date from which interest was to accrue. Morris filled these in and also added the complimentary close and postscript, which all subsequent copies include. (Morris' insertions are specified in *Morris Papers*, IV, 436–7.) The copy at the APS is a duplicate enclosed with Morris' cover letter of June 10, below.

5. Henry Leonard Philip, baron d'Arendt, was appointed commander of the German battalion in America in 1777 and went on leave in 1778: XXVIII, 298n; *JCC*, VII, 185. In 1780, he asked BF to help him justify his stay in Europe beyond his one-year furlough: XXXII, 391–3, 407.

6. The printed certificate, dated March 23 (APS), authorized payment of d'Arendt's back pay and depreciation up to Jan. 1, 1781. Congress ordered the settlement in July, 1781, concluding that d'Arendt should be compensated for time spent abroad in unsuccessful trade negotiations: *Morris Papers*, III, 168n; *JCC*, XX, 740–2. On the verso of the certificate is a receipt for the full amount dated Oct. 13, 1782, in WTF's hand and signed by d'Arendt.

terest at six per Cent from the Eighteenth Inst. and is the Ballance still due after a partial Payment, Should it be perfectly convenient to you it will be a great Favor to him and agreable to me that this Balance be paid to Monsieur le Baron d'Arndt taking his Receipt in full of all Demands against the United States on the Back of the Certificate with three Copies thereof signed by him and sending them by different Opportunities. I mention the Balance as it stands in the Certificate without noticing the Interest because in Case of Payment by you the Transaction will be substantially as if I had given him here a Bill of Exchange.

I have the honor to be sir Your most Obedient & most hble Servant ROBT MORRIS

PS On the final adjustment of the Baron's Acct I find the balance larger than was expected, therefore it is probable that a partial Payment from You may answer his purpose, the Receipts to be indorsed on the Certificate & Copies transmitted as already mentioned. R M

His Excellency Benjamin Franklin.

From Georg Wilhelm von Pachelbel and Other Favor Seekers
ALS: American Philosophical Society

During the period of this volume Franklin is frequently asked to forward mail or to help in obtaining information about relatives in America. The letter from Georg Wilhelm von Pachelbel, printed below, is the earliest and briefest of these requests. He is minister plenipotentiary to the court of France for the duc de Deux-Ponts and chargé d'affaires for the Landgrave of Hesse-Darmstadt.[7]

On April 23, M. Faucon writes from Riom, in the Auvergne, to ask Franklin's assistance in obtaining news of his twenty-six-year-old

---

7. The diplomatic career of Pachelbel (1717–1784) is described in Hans Ammerich, *Landesherr und Landesverwaltung: Beiträge zur Regierung von Pfalz-Zweibrücken am ende des Alten Reiches* (Saarbrücken, 1981), p. 214, and in *Repertorium der diplomatischen Vertreter*, II, 184–5, 280; III, 193, 198, 306. Unless otherwise noted the letters discussed in this headnote are in French and are at the APS.

son, Julien, reportedly living in Boston. Julien made several crossings as an apprentice pilot on ships belonging to the Bordeaux firm of Reculès de Basmarein & Raimbaux. When that firm went bankrupt, he took passage in 1780 on the "Boxquine" or *Buckskin*, a frigate out of Baltimore. Julien's last letter to his father, dated July 21, 1780, was written as the ship headed out to sea from Bordeaux.[8] His uncharacteristic silence since then greatly worries the father. Julien's younger brother, living at Paris and employed as an assistant to M. de Celse, director of the tollhouse Saint-Jacques, can provide more details.

Franklin receives two letters concerning the effects of Mrs. Battier, recently deceased at Ghent.[9] Mlle Murray, who nursed Mrs. Battier through her final illness, writes from Ghent on April 25. In her last days Mrs. Battier suggested that Franklin, who had shown her great kindness, might be willing to forward to her father, Thomas Ivers of Boston, a small box containing a gold chain and a miniature portrait surrounded by small diamonds. Mlle Murray is settling her friend's estate, as none of the London relatives bothered to come. Fortunately, she has inherited all the lady's effects and silver, and can sell a watch to cover the funeral expenses. Franklin may reply to Mlle Murray "chez Milady Findlater a son hôtel a Bruxelles."[1] On May 14, B. C. Cutler[2] writes in English from Paris. He understands that Miss Murray asked Franklin to forward the portrait to him to send to Boston. Since he is on the point of leaving Paris he asks Franklin to forward it directly to Mr. Ivers.

Franklin receives another pair of requests to forward letters to General von Steuben. On June 8, the general's father, writing in German from Cüstrin, congratulates Franklin on America's successful

---

8. The *Buckskin* had arrived in Bordeaux by April 1780: XXXII, 230n. The bankruptcy of Basmarein & Raimbaux is discussed in XXVI, 677n, and XXVIII, 550n.

9. Le Roy had mentioned Mme Battier to BF the year before: XXXIV, 401–2.

1. Christina Theresa Josepha Murray (*c.* 1755–1813) married James Ogilvy, 7th earl of Findlater, at Brussels in 1779: Lewis, *Walpole Correspondence*, XXXII, 55n; Sir James Balfour Paul, ed., *The Scots Peerage* (9 vols., Edinburgh, 1904–14), IV, 40; IX, 90. Her father, Joseph Jacob, Graf Murray de Melgum (1718–1802), had five daughters and we assume that Lady Findlater and Mlle Murray were sisters or half-sisters: Constant von Wurzbach, *Biographisches Lexikon des Kaiserthums Oesterreich* (60 vols., Vienna, 1856–91), XIX, 467–70; G. E. Cokayne, *Complete Baronetage* (6 vols., Exeter, 1900–09), IV, 421.

2. Presumably a relative of Thomas Ivers' second wife, Mary Cutler, whom he married in September, 1776: *Boston Town Records [1634]–1822* (39 vols., Boston, 1876–1909), XXX, 437.

prospects.[3] He encloses yet another letter to his son from whom he has had no word for a year. Three days later Major General de Bouvinghausen writes from Stuttgart, enclosing a letter for the general in answer to one from him dealing with family affairs.[4]

Captain Vernié of the Royal Regiment of Hesse-Darmstadt writes on June 27 from Hennebont, in Brittany, to inquire about the fate of his brother, Major Pierre-Joseph-François Vernié. Could Franklin tell him what he knows or direct him to someone who can inform him?[5]

In a letter dated only "Juillet 1782," the sieur d'Averton[6] writes from the château de Bonnevaux near Milly, in the Gâtinais, to inquire after his son, the chevalier Charles-François d'Averton,[7] an officer who left his regiment in 1778 to serve in the "états unis de La nouvelle Angleterre". His family has not heard from him since. The sieur humbly beseeches Franklin to forward whatever information he can to him at his château.

Seven months to the day after his first request, Andreas Bermbach writes Franklin in German on August 8, from Niederselters. He asks him to forward a second letter to Theodor Mieger, care of the magistrate at Philadelphia.[8]

A smaller number of correspondents seek Franklin's assistance on a variety of projects, most of them commercial. Dutch recognition of the United States prompts Etienne Caÿrol & Cie.[9] to establish an entrepôt at Amsterdam for textiles from its royal manufactory of Gobelins. On May

3. Wilhelm Augustine von Steuben (xxx, 617n) had inquired of his son's well-being six months earlier: xxxvi, 308–9. We are grateful to Liselotte Davis of Yale University for reading the 18th-century German script and providing us with a résumé of this letter.

4. Bouvinghausen twice before had asked BF to forward letters to the baron: xxxv, 12; xxxvi, 309.

5. Capt. Vernié (Vernier) is listed in the *Etat militaire* for 1781, p. 337. His brother had been killed in 1780: xxxvi, 311, 416–17.

6. Louis-Marc-Antoine (1718–1804) was a retired cavalry major and chevalier de Saint-Louis: *DBF*. His letter is at the Yale University Library.

7. Also known as Antoine-Charles-Marie, the chevalier (b. 1759) had been a first lieutenant in the infantry, Picardy Regiment (later renamed the Colonel-général Regiment). In America he participated in the siege of Gloucester during the Yorktown campaign: Bodinier, *Dictionnaire*, pp. 20–1; Rice and Brown, eds., *Rochambeau's Army*, i, 56n; *Etat militaire* for 1779, p. 147, and for 1781, p. 174.

8. For Bermbach and his earlier letter see xxxvi, 309; Eugen Caspary *et al.*, eds., *Geschichte von Niederselters* (Selters, 1994), p. 75. Filed with the present letter from Bermbach is a summary in French.

9. For Caÿrol see xxiii, 441n; xxiv, 275n.

4, and again four days later, the firm requests a letter of introduction to John Adams for its agent at Amsterdam, Paul Charlé, in the expectation that Adams will promote its textiles among American speculators.[1]

The firm of B. Gannan & Zoon (Son) writes from Ostend on June 25[2] in excellent English to inform Franklin that it is fitting out one of the fastest-sailing cutters ever built in England, the *Maarstrand*, to sail to Philadelphia under Imperial colors. The vessel has just crossed from there in seventeen days, fully loaded with tobacco shipped by Samuel Inglis & Co.[3] The captain, "born English & naturaliz'd Imperial", desires the protection of the American Ministers. Franklin is offered the opportunity to send dispatches or goods. The Gannans, residents of Dunkirk,[4] are well known in the bureau of the marine at Versailles as well as among many Americans. Franklin endorsed the letter, "Answer refus'd."

Franklin's support is also sought for two projects less obviously commercial. The Italian Anton-Benedetto Bassi, who wrote Franklin twice in 1780,[5] writes again on May 6. Just as Franklin's election to the Padua Academy has brought honor to the Academy,[6] so too Franklin's subscription to Bassi's *Recueil complet des plus beaux morceaux de poésies italiennes* will bring luster to that work. He enclosed an eight-page prospectus and a subscription form.[7] On August 8, when this attempt has gone unanswered, Bassi writes that he is unable to complete his work because of illness. He recalls Franklin's help with his earlier publication[8] and implores his aid anew. The bearer will await Franklin's answer.[9]

1. The firm writes again on July 30. Cäyrol is mortified to have had no answer to the two letters of May and assures BF that their firm at Amsterdam will not injure the business of Dutch textile manufacturers. He encloses an unspecified letter from their firm in Amsterdam and asks BF to supply the address (as only he can), and have a servant post it.

2. This letter is at the University of Pa. Library.

3. Inglis (1745–1783) was a Philadelphia merchant long associated with Robert Morris: *Morris Papers*, III, 121–2n, 518.

4. B. Gannan's son may be the Dunkirk merchant James Gannan: Edward Church to BF, Nov. 19, 1784 (APS).

5. XXXIII, 35.

6. For BF's election see Daniele Delfino's letter of April 6.

7. The prospectus is missing; the blank subscription form remains with the letter. Bassi eventually published an Italian version of this work: *Scelta di poesie italiane dé piu celebri autori d'ogni secolo* (2 vols., Paris, 1783–84).

8. The brochure *Observations sur les poètes italiens . . .* (1780): XXXIII, 35n.

9. Both these letters are printed in Antonio Pace, *Benjamin Franklin and Italy* (Philadelphia, 1958), pp. 48, 49.

On May 7, M. Le Roux[1] solicits Franklin's support for a work by his father-in-law. He promises that the prospectus (not found) is full of useful discoveries which Franklin is bound to appreciate. Le Roux's praise of his father-in-law, who has saved the life of Le Roux's wife and whose work has benefitted humanity, suggests that he has something to do with medicine.[2]

As always, people seek Franklin's assistance with financial matters, in particular with payment of money owed to them. On May 10, Denis Baucher, a sergeant of the French marines, recounts his service as a volunteer on the *Bonhomme Richard* in 1779.[3] Having lost a foot and several fingers on his right hand in the fighting against the *Serapis*, he was discharged and remains unable to work, confined to his bed, and entirely dependent on the charity of others for his livelihood. He has heard that the crew of the privateer *Grandville* has been awarded its part of the prizes.[4] He hopes that the claims will be settled so that he might receive the three shares of the prizes promised him when he signed on at Lorient.[5] He hopes also that Franklin will provide for him in his present circumstances.

A Monsieur de Beauquesne writes on July 17 from Paris. He was a commanding captain of a volunteer corps stationed in Senegal when he obtained permission to return to France for health reasons.[6] Cap-

1. Le Roux was *secrétaire de la chambre* of the comte d'Artois: *Almanach de Versailles* for 1781, p. 203.

2. Le Roux's letter is at the University of Pa. Library.

3. Born *c.* 1739 at Couvains, in Normandy, Baucher (Bauché, Beauchez, Bouchinet) had made sergeant in the Berwick Regiment: Bodinier, *Dictionnaire*, p. 488. See also the roster of the *Bonhomme Richard* in Augustus C. Buell, *Paul Jones, Founder of the American Navy* ... (2 vols., New York, 1906), II, 405–6, 410.

4. For the *Grandville*'s claims see XXXII, 209–10, 265–6; XXXIV, 460–1; and XXXVI, 482.

5. For the settlement of prize claims see XXXVI, 529–30. Baucher's name ("Bauché ou Buchinet") appears on a copy of the distribution of the prize money certified by John Paul Jones on Sept. 5, 1785 (National Archives). His three shares amounted to 649 *l.t.* 5 *s.* 9 *d.*

6. The British colony was captured in January, 1779, by French troops under the duc de Lauzun. When Lauzun prepared to return to France six weeks later, the climate and lack of provisions had taken such a toll on the troops that he had two hundred Africans trained in artillery and incorporated into the French garrison he left behind. He also authorized bringing from the island of Gorée the "Volontaires d'Afrique": XXIX, 172n, 180n; Comte Roger de Gontaut Biron, *Un Célèbre Méconnu: le duc de Lauzun (1747–1793)* (Paris, 1937), pp. 91, 93, 106.

tured on his return voyage, he was robbed of almost everything and detained at Kinsale. Later, the neutral ship bringing him to France sank within sight of Havre de Grace and again he lost everything. Now lodged in a commercial hotel with his 15-year-old daughter whom he feels he cannot leave, he sends Franklin an unnamed project. On August 11, he sends an expanded copy of the project, saying that the marquis de Castries will also receive a copy presented by the chevalier de Beauteville,[7] lieutenant general in the French army, former ambassador to Switzerland, and *ami intime* of the marquis. He himself should have gone to Versailles long ago to seek reparations for his losses, but his financial straits have inhibited him. If Franklin will lend *un petit secours*, he will soon be in a position to repay him.[8]

Franklin receives applications from a steady number of people wishing to emigrate. The earliest of these is a merchant named Trouillot, writing on April 26 from Lyon. The fifth living son of a former notary, he knows something of agriculture, has a small inheritance as well as some merchandise, and has a brother in commerce at Bordeaux with whom he could work. Several of his friends are prepared to accompany him to America. He left his studies three years ago to throw himself into commerce, without success. He is 23 years old, has no physical defects, and stands five feet, eight inches. These details, he explains, will help the minister to advise him whether to go or to stay.

M. Imbault, an employee at the *bureau général des fermes* in Orleans, has until now been discouraged from emigrating by the cost of the voyage. But prospects abroad have brightened, especially for French immigrants, he feels, so on May 4 he asks whether Franklin would favor his passage from Europe. Perhaps it would help if he told the minister that for seven years he has been "vegetating" in an office where fortune has served him poorly, and that his promotion depends on the passing into eternity of one or two of his colleagues, something they have no intention of doing and which he cannot decently suggest they do. Nonetheless, he wishes to enlarge his sphere of activity, and in America he can live free and try out various professions forbidden him in France by his parents' prejudices.[9]

A 38-year-old widower and father of eight healthy children (the eldest son is 16), Alard du Perier writes from Grenoble on June 12. He

---

7. Pierre de Buisson, *dit* chevalier de Beauteville (1703–1792): *DBF; Repertorium der diplomatischen Vertreter*, III, 109, 117, 137, 138; *Dictionnaire de la noblesse*, IV, 487.

8. The first of Beauquesne's letters is at the University of Pa. Library.

9. This letter is at the University of Pa. Library.

has money, and experience both in manufacturing and in agriculture, and he is willing to go over with his family in exchange for citizenship and a plot of uncleared land. He can supply a certificate of good citizenship and good morals.[1]

Franklin's goodness of heart and charity toward all have determined one stranger, the abbé de Klinglin, to write on June 29, from his sickbed at Paris. He requests a letter of recommendation for one La Coste, who goes to Philadelphia to establish a business. Franklin evidently told Mme de La Coste, who delivered the abbé's letter, to apply for the recommendation on July 4. On that day, Mme de la Coste, writing from Paris, follows his orders by sending for the promised recommendation, on which she places all her hopes.[2]

Three people apply to Franklin for the post of consul or agent. C. Barthélemy Martin fils aîné, writing from Cette (Sète) on April 14, reiterates a request he made in February.[3] Addressing Franklin this time as "Milord", Martin is eager to smooth the way for American merchants in the lucrative market of Languedoc and to extend a helping hand in case of need. He prays for the Supreme Being to bestow His most holy blessings on Franklin's worthy person.

James Price, an American merchant in partnership with John Bondfield at Bordeaux,[4] writes in English from that city on April 20 to recommend as agent for the relief of American prisoners Anthony Lynch, a partner in the house of V. & P. French & Nephew.[5]

Laurence Joseph Wagner, the Dutch consul general at Trieste, Fiume, and other Austrian ports on the Adriatic, begs Franklin to forward to Congress his offer to represent the commercial interests of the United States as well. He offers the double advantage of being a native of Trieste and a master of English, as his July 26 letter in English demonstrates.

1. His letter is at the University of Pa. Library.
2. Both these letters are at the University of Pa. Library.
3. XXXVI, 304.
4. Price had arrived in France the year before: XXXV, 338, 488.
5. Lynch was probably the nephew in the firm's title. On April 25, JW acknowledged an April 23 letter from the firm requesting his "Interference with Dr. Franklin in respect of yr. Nephew." JW assured them that BF knew Mr. Lynch's merits, but said that he had made it a rule not to ask favors of the minister. However, JW would speak to Thomas Barclay on Lynch's behalf. Yale University Library.

Monsieur, Paris ce 22 Mars 1782

La lettre ci-jointe[6] m'a été envoïée de Ratisbonne, avec la Requisition de vous prier de vouloir bien la faire passer à son adresse. Pardonnez, Monsieur, si j'ose en conséquence vous importuner à ce sujet, n'aïant pû me refuser à cette demande qui m'a été faite de si loin.

J'ai l'honneur d'être avec un attachement respectueux, Monsieur, Votre très humble et très obéissant serviteur

DE PACHELBEL

Notation: Pachelbel Paris 2 Mars 1782

To Jonathan Williams, Jr.

Copy: Library of Congress

Dear Jonathan, Passy, March 23, 1782.

I have received yours of the 19th. Inst. with the Account of the Duties you have paid. I do not comprehend the Policy of burthening their own Manufactures; but the Laws of the Country we trade with must be observed.

I have determin'd to rely on the Government entirely for the Transport of the Goods. I am instructed not to send them but under Convoy directly to Philadelphia and I cannot trust myself in making Bargains for Ships, being too ignorant in such Matters. Particularly I will enter into no such Bargain with my Cousin. If it should prove a hard one for you, it would hurt my Feelings of Friendship; and if a profitable one, I shall be reflected on as having given you a lucrative Jobb at the expence of the Publick. I believe the Government would still take more Ships if offer'd soon, so that you may there find Employ for the Ship you propose to buy if you like the Terms. Our Occasions are not so pressing as to Justify my giving extravagant Freights. By Advices from America it appears that our Army was provided with Clothing for this Year; that the Cargo of the Marquis de la Fayette was arrived at Philada. from St. Thomas's and lay upon the Hands of the Importers; the arms taken with Cornwallis and

6. Not found.

41

large Quantity arriv'd at Boston, put us at our Ease on that Article;[7] and we have therefore more than a Year before us to get our Goods over. Mr. Morris writes me that he is sorry the Purchase has been made, and wishes the Value had still remain'd in Money at our Disposal.[8] So I can only thank you for your offer, and decline it.

I hope the seeds will arrive soon, or the Season of Planting will be lost, and they become useless. Billy will send you the Paper & Ink powder. My Love to the good Wife, & believe me ever

Your affectione Uncle.

P.S. The St. Domingo Fleet if it arrives will furnish a good many Ships.

Mr. Williams.

From Thomas Barclay

ALS: American Philosophical Society

Sir, Ghent 23d. March 1782

I left Amsterdam the 10th. and have been here ten days; I Came on the incouragement given me by a Merchant of this City, that he wou'd exchange the products of the Netherlands, for such British Manufactures as wou'd suit him, chosen from those in my hands belonging to the United States, and which I Cou'd not ship to America unless I did it in Contradiction to a Resolution of Congress in the View of all the Trading people of Amsterdam who are interested in the Commerce of that Country,[9] The amount of those goods is about a Hundred thousand Guilders, I did every thing in my power to dispose of them or exchange them at Amsterdam but to No purpose, the determination in America against receiving such goods has operated

7. Robert Morris corrected this overly optimistic assessment; see BF to Morris, March 30, and Morris' reply of July 1.

8. XXXVI, 403–6.

9. The goods in Barclay's care consisted mostly of cloth for uniforms: XXXVI, 382, 620–1. Some of these goods came from Britain, with which Congress had forbidden all commercial intercourse: *JCC*, XIX, 315–16.

against them to such a degree in that place, as put it out of my power, and it being equaly necessary that both parties shou'd see the goods they were to receive, the person from hence is to meet me at Amsterdam this day two weeks, when I doubt not but we shall settle the Matter finaly— I have taken some Samples of the goods which he is to furnish me with, amongst them are white & Check'd linen shirts for Soldiers and Seamen— The former at 31 stivers Dutch Money, about 2/7 d [2 s., 7 p.] sterling, greatly supperior to those worn by the Imperial troops, and the later at 27½ stivers equal to 2/3 sterling— Of those I expect to get part ready to send by the ship General Sulivan, which was not got to Amsterdam when I heard from thence last post—[1] I have taken the opportunity of being here to Examin Mr. Deanes Accounts agreeable to a Resolution of Congress,[2] they are Very long as You will Naturaly immagine, and are Comprised under four heads— His personal Expences of every kind for about four Years— A Salary of about Twelve thousand livres per annum for some time— Twenty thousand livres paid the French Officers going to America, and a Commission of 5 per Cent on all the Goods purchased by Mr. Beaumarchais, Mr. Montieu, and Mr. Chamont, the amount of the supplies sent by Mr. Beaumarchais is about five Million of livres, on which He had charged a Commission of 10 per Cent, so that the whole Commission on that account amounts to Upwards of 15 per Cent.[3]

I shall transmit to Congress the particulars of Mr. Deanes Accounts, recommend to them to appoint a Committee to make a report upon them, to state their objections and allow Me to set-

1. Barclay, who had purchased a share in the *General Sullivan*, expected the privateer at Amsterdam by March 10: XXXVI, 612, 621.

2. Barclay himself had never received this resolution, which reversed what he expressly had been told before leaving America. He saw it for the first time when he met Deane in Ostend. Deane described their stalemate in a letter to BF of Feb. 1 (XXXVI, 507). Deane eventually persuaded Barclay to proceed with the examination despite his lack of direct orders, and on Feb. 26 Barclay volunteered to spend a day or two with Deane in Ghent: *Deane Papers*, V, 61–2, 64–6, 68–9.

3. Deane had sent a copy of his accounts to Ferdinand Grand the preceding October: *Deane Papers*, IV, 480–8. In 1776, he had signed contracts with Beaumarchais and Montieu for sending uniforms and military supplies to the United States: *ibid.*, III, 33–6.

tle them in Europe by an Arbitration of four or five Men of Charracter—[4] If the Matter is ever to be ended I see no better manner, for it is of so Complicated a Nature that I can do nothing farther untill I have particular orders from Congress— I have the honour to be with the greatest respect, Sir Your Excellencys Most Obedient Huml Servant   THOS BARCLAY

His Excellency Benjn. Franklin Esqre.[5]

Endorsed: March 23

From Robert Morris

LS: Historical Society of Pennsylvania; copy: Library of Congress

Sir,   Office of Finance, Philada. March 23d. 1782.

Applications being frequently made by the several Loan Officers for Orders to Renew Setts of Exchange in consequence of proof made to them by the Proprietors of Interest bills,[6] that the first Second, third and fourth bills have been lost and destroyed, or by Accident prevented from reaching the Persons to whom they were Remitted, and as it is but just in such Instances to Renew the Same, I have Caused a Number of Bills to be Struck of the same denomination and in the same Stile, Manner and Tenor except that they are fifth, sixth seventh and eighth Bills and when made use of will be filled up in the same Manner as the first four were and Issued from the Same office.

I give you this Notice that you may direct the Banker to pay due honor to any one of these bills in all instances where no One of the Sett Consisting of Eight, has before been paid and of

4. Deane agreed to the arrangement, anticipating that the arbitrators would meet in Paris: Wharton, *Diplomatic Correspondence*, V, 245; *Deane Papers*, V, 78. See also Deane's letter to BF of March 30.

5. On March 27, BF showed this letter to Matthew Ridley, who paraphrased it in his journal (XXXVI, 165n).

6. Congress used bills of exchange on France to pay interest on loan office certificates issued before March 1, 1778. Holders could sell the bills for close to their face value in specie. For a detailed explanation see *Morris Papers*, III, 51–2n.

course he will before such payment always Satisfy himself that none of the others have been honored. This general Advice will I think answer the purpose and render unnecessary particular advice with each Renewed Sett of Exchange.

I have the Honor to be Sir Your Excellency's Most Obedient and Humble Servant   ROBT MORRIS

His Excellency Benjm. Franklin Esqr.

From Joseph Nourse[7]   ALS: American Philosophical Society

Hona. Sir,   Philadelphia the 23d March 1782

Altho I never had the honor of a personal Acquaintance with your Excellency, yet as my Patron, the Hon' R Morris, hath in some measure, by his Letter of the 22d. Instant respecting the Baron D'Arndt, presented me to your knowledge as an Officer under Congress, and presuming in that humanity which hath been shown to our poor Bretheren, confined in the Jails in England, I cannot help, acquainting your Excellency that my Brother Mr. William Nourse was taken a Prisoner on Board the Ship of War Confederacy, and that he was sent, and by Letter from him of the 23d November last remained a Prisoner in the Jail of Forton.[8] Cou'd your Excelleny be of any Service in effecting his Exchange, it wou'd confer the greatest Obligation on his Anxious Parents, in Virginia.[9]

Permit me to inform your Excellency that he is in Service of

7. Register of the Treasury: XXXVI, 196n. On this date Nourse signed a certificate for money due to the baron d'Arendt; see Morris' letter of March 22.

8. The *Confederacy* was captured in April, 1781, and Nourse was committed to Forton on Aug. 9. Just three days before the present letter was written, he was pardoned to serve in the Royal Navy: XXXV, 434n; Kaminkow, *Mariners*, p. 142.

9. James Nourse (1731–1784) and his wife, Sarah Fouace (d. 1784), owned a plantation near Charlestown in what is now West Virginia. Nourse had been a court justice for Berkeley County and in 1778 represented Berkeley in the Va. House of Delegates: *Morris Papers*, I, 158n; Maria C. N. Lyle, "James Nourse of Virginia," *The Va. Mag. of History and Biography*, VIII (1900), 199–202.

the United States, as an Acting Midshipman, that he is young, and a long Confinement, may prevent his views in Life which are in the Marine, & to subscribe myself, with the greatest Respect, Your Excellencys most obedient & most humble Servant

JOSEPH NOURSE.

From John Bondfield

ALS: American Philosophical Society

Sir   Bordeaux 24 March 1782

Mr. William Vernon Junr of Boston son to the president of the Navy Board of the Eastern department having been with me these three Years past[1] intending to return shortly to America is desireous to pass a few Days at Paris. Permit me to introduce him to your Civilities his Prudent conduct in the midst of sceenes of disipations has procured him very respectable conections at this City which I flatter myself will correspond with the Wishes and Views of his Father.

I have given him a draft on you for two Thousand four hundred livres which I request the favor of you to pay him and pass the Amount to the debit of my account.[2]

I have the Honor to be with due respect Sir Your most Obedient Humble Servant   JOHN BONDFIELD

I have receivd a large Caise which by the Acquit a Caution contains hats addrest to me by Mr Des Arneaux by order of Mr Regnier by your directions. I have not any instructions pr Letter from Mr Regnier. I have lodged the Case in Store until further orders— If you see Mr Regnier please to inform him not having the Honor to know him or his address.

Addressed: His Excellency / Benj Franklin / Esq / Passi

1. Vernon had written to BF in May, 1779, when searching for a position: XXIX, 482–3.

2. BF did so, and Bondfield's account was debited on July 6: Account XXVII (XXXII, 4).

From Jean-Baptiste-Jacques Elie de Beaumont[3]

ALS: American Philosophical Society

Monsieur   Paris 24 mars 1782.

Il y a bien longtems que je n'ai pu avoir l'honneur de vous voir. Vos occupations pour une portion du monde, et les miennes pour quelques individus souffrans nous tiennent respective-ment Éloignés. Je vous rends dans mon Cœur l'hommage que je ne puis gueres vous offrir par mes visites. Voici cependant une occasion que je m'empresse de saisir en presentant a Votre Ex-cellence un memoire dont le sujet a quelque droit de vous inte-resser: je desire qu'il puisse obtenir quelques uns de vos mo-ments.[4]

J'ai aussi l'honneur de vous adresser une lettre qui est deja d'une ancienne date et qu'on m'a prié de vous faire parvenir.[5] Je

3. An old friend of BF's and a fellow member of the Neuf Sœurs, Elie de Beaumont was a prominent jurist who had collaborated with Voltaire on more than one case. His legal briefs were distinguished for their elegance as well as their concern for social justice: XVI, 205; XVII, 123; XXVIII, 616–17; XXXI, 371–2; David A. Bell, *Lawyers and Citizens: the Making of a Political Elite in Old Regime France* (New York and Oxford, 1994), pp. 131–2, 136, 175.

4. That brief must have just been presented; the publication was an-nounced three days later in the *Mémoires secrets* (XX, 143–4). Entitled *Mé-moire pour le sieur Benjamin Beresford, prêtre de l'église anglicane, chapelain du duc de Bedford, recteur des deux paroisses de la ville de Bedford*, it concerned the case of an English parson who eloped with 15-year-old Sidney Hamilton in November, 1780. The girl's mother abducted her and fled to Lille, where the daughter gave birth to a baby girl in August, 1781. There the mother ob-tained an arrest decree against Beresford and had the case moved to Paris. Beresford protested a French court's competence to judge the validity of his marriage. Elie was acting as *avocat consultant* for Beresford's advocate, Guy-Jean-Baptiste Target. On March 25, the Parlement delivered its decision in favor of Beresford.

In addition to recounting the facts of the case, Elie undertook a compar-ison of French and English law, derived, as he saw it, from the different char-acters of the two nations. The brief was widely praised and was discussed, along with the case, in both Paris and London: Bachaumont, *Mémoires se-crets*, XX, 143–4, 146–8, 150–1; *Jour. de Paris*, May 24, 1782; *A Narrative of circumstances attending Mr. Beresford's marriage with Miss Hamilton* (Lon-don, 1782).

5. Possibly the June 15, 1781, letter from the physician David reminding

me le proposois de jour a autre mais l'incertitude de vous trouver et mes occupations m'en ont jusqu'ici empêché. Je desirerois sçavoir s'il y a un jour fixe dans la semaine ou l'on soit sur de vous trouver a passy. J'aurois grand plaisir a vous y renouveller de vive voix le respect et l'attachement avec lesquels j'ai l'honneur d'être Monsieur Votre tres humble et tres obeissant serviteur

ELIE DE BEAUMONT.

Madame de Beaumont[6] a l'honneur de vous faire bien des Complimens. Je vous prie de faire agreer les miens a Monsieur votre petit fils.

Notation: Beaumont, Elie de Paris 24 Mars 1782.

From Isaac Hazlehurst

ALS: American Philosophical Society

Sir   Nantes 24th. March 1782

The very polite attention that you did me the honor to shew me during my stay in Paris,[7] claims my warmest acknowledgements & a due sense thereof will always be held in gratefull remembrance.

I promis'd to inform Your Excellency in what vessel I propos'd to embark for America, it is the Brigantine Betsey Capt. Gallagher,[8] I expect she will sail by the first of next month, If I

BF of a promise to help him obtain a chair of anatomy at Philadelphia: XXIV, 274n. On July 27, 1782, Elie asked WTF to remind BF of "la promesse qu'il a bien voulu me faire d'une lettre de recommendation pour Monsieur David medecin, auquel je prends un très grand interêt, ce qui me fait la desirer vivement." APS.

6. Anne-Louise Morin Du Mesnil Elie de Beaumont (1729–1783), novelist and *salonnière: DBF*, XII, 1197; Bell, *Lawyers and Citizens*, p. 132.

7. Hazlehurst had arrived in Paris a year earlier but made a journey to the Netherlands in the interim. In February, BF had provided him and James Grubb with letters of recommendation to John Holker: XXXIV, 455; XXXV, 112–13; XXXVI, 553n, 617. On March 9, as he prepared to leave Paris for Nantes, he thanked WTF for his civilities and attention (APS). This is his only extant letter to BF.

8. The *Betsey* had arrived from Philadelphia in January: XXXVI, 456n, 556. JW called her a "remarkable fine Brig" and put goods aboard for her return

can take charge of any papers you may be sure of the utmost care or if in any other mode I can be serviceable, I hope you will command me. I am with great respect Your Excellcys. Most obt. humle. serv   ISAAC HAZLEHURST

Addressed: His Excellency / Benj: Franklin Esqr. / Passy

Notation: Haslehurt Nantes 24 March 1782.

From Job Whipple and Elijah Lewis[9]

ALS:[1] American Philosophical Society

Hond. Sir   Nantes 24 March 1782.

We beg leave to inform you that we are two of those fortunate Persons who lately made their escape from Kingsale Prison in Ireland. Before we effected it the Prisoners of War confined there requested us to lay before your honor a state of their wretched disagreeable situation, praying you to redress their grievances as soon as in your power lieth.— The most nay every one of them is destitute of cloathing not sufficient to keep them warm from the inclemency of the Weather in a cold Prison without fire— Beg your honor will take it into consideration and appoint such ways and means as in your Wisdom shall seem meet to supply them with Cloathing and other necessaries.

We need not say any more on the subject resting assured you'll do what is possible in the Premises— We are with the utmost respect possible your Hble Servts[2]   JOB WHIPPLE
ELIJAH LEWIS

The Honble. Benja. Franklin Esqr.

---

voyage: JW to Bache & Shee, March 22; to Jacob Morris & John Woodward, March 22; and to Desegray & Co., March 23 (Yale University Library).

9. Lewis served as captain of the 1st Rhode Island Regiment from January, 1777, until his resignation in January, 1781. Shortly thereafter he was named master of the schooner *Betty*. Whipple, who had served in the American army since May, 1775, was captain of the 5th Massachusetts Regiment: Heitman, *Register of Officers*, pp. 263, 430; Claghorn, *Naval Officers*, p. 185.

1. In Whipple's hand.

2. Whipple and Lewis must have also enclosed the letter of introduction

Addressed: The Honble / Benja. Franklin Esqr. / Paris

Notation: Lewis, Elija, Nantes 24 March 1782.

From ———— Champion and ———— Lescuyer, and Other Offerers of Goods and Schemes

ALS: American Philosophical Society

During the months covered by this volume Franklin received but a few offers to supply goods or to promote commercial relations. The first letter, printed below, comes from a supplier to the French army at the Invalides and a merchant-manufacturer in Beauvais, an important textile center. On this letter Franklin drafted a note for a negative reply. We have found no traces of any replies to the following unsolicited offers.[3]

On March 27, Montesquieu l'aîné has heard that Franklin is proposing to purchase cloth in the southern region of Languedoc and writes the "député Du Congrès" to offer his assistance from Toulouse. At the beginning of the war he furnished several Bordeaux outfitters, including 10,000 uniforms for Mr. Delap.[4] Examples were forwarded to Franklin at Paris, but arrangements were suspended following new orders from Congress. His prices are far lower than those Congress has received before.

On April 20, the bishop of Le Puy-en-Velay writes from that city to offer woolen blankets manufactured there in workshops set up to assist the poor.[5] The main industry of his diocese is a form of silk lacework which the English used to buy in great quantity for export to America. He would like to reestablish that commerce without any in-

---

they were carrying from Richard Hare, Jr.: XXXVI, 606–7. Our annotation to that letter describes local efforts on behalf of the Kinsale inmates.

3. Unless otherwise noted, the letters discussed in this headnote are in French and are at the APS.

4. Samuel and J. H. Delap had long been involved in the American trade: XXII, 445n. For Congress' earliest order for military supplies, including uniforms, see XXIV, 122–6.

5. Marie-Joseph de Galard de Terraube (1736–1804) began his ecclesiastical career as prior at the Sorbonne and then canon at Notre-Dame de Paris. He was consecrated bishop of Le Puy-en-Velay in 1774: *DBF* under Galard; *Dictionnaire de la noblesse,* VIII, 797.

termediaries. He closes by recalling the time he and Franklin conversed at some length in 1778 at M. Bertin's country estate.[6]

On April 23, M. Tezenad writes from Passy on behalf of M. Carrier, M. de Montieu's uncle,[7] to offer Franklin the opportunity to view a rifle at Mr. Molley's, near the Grand Chatelet. The firearm is four feet, eight inches long and so finely worked in gold and ivory that it would make a proper offering to His Excellency General "Wasinghton".

A merchant from Abbeville, M. Meurice,[8] sends Franklin on May 30 a small sample of his "curative powder" which has proved successful on all kinds of wounds, however ancient. He encloses instructions for its application. The powder is inexpensive and easily distributed to soldiers in small blotting paper packets as a form of first aid. If Franklin needs confirmation of its efficacy and has no occasion to test it for himself, Meurice has treated a local worker with a badly wounded leg who would be willing to travel to the capital to report on his case in person. Franklin would only have to pay the two *louis* for the worker's journey.

Perhaps anticipating new trade opportunities presaged by the peace negotiations, J. U. Pauly writes from Hamburg on May 20[9] proposing a commercial treaty between that city and the United States. The arrangement, using Philadelphia as the initial American port, would give preference to the merchandise of Russia and the Austrian Empire. Eventually other cities in America and the Hanseatic League could be included in this commercial exchange. He outlines the terms

6. Bertin had entertained BF at least once that year at Chatou: XXVI, 506. JA, who accompanied BF and WTF on that occasion, described that visit and others to Chatou that year: Butterfield, *John Adams Diary*, II, 314–15, 318; IV, 117–18, 161. Bertin retired as secretary of state in May, 1780: Michel Antoine, *Le Gouvernement et l'administration sous Louis XV: Dictionnaire biographique* (Paris, 1978), p. 34.

7. Jean-Joseph Carié (Carrier) de Montieu, the former *entrepreneur de la manufacture royale des fusils* accused of furnishing defective firearms to the royal arsenal and later to the Americans: XXII, 464n.

8. He is listed among the principal merchants of the town in the *Almanach des marchands*, p. 7. Meurice signs his letter with an abbreviated first name, "Aen.", probably for Adrien. This letter is at the University of Pa. Library.

9. The original letter in German is not extant. We have a French translation (Hist. Soc. of Pa.) prepared at BF's request by a M. Tillier, who appended a brief note and signed himself an officer of the *Gardes*. He is listed among the second lieutenants of the Swiss Guards in the *Etat militaire* for 1781, p. 156. In a postscript Tillier added: "Je Vous prie dassurer de mes respects a Vos Dames." The letter is undated as to year.

of the treaty, and refers Franklin to the ambassadors of Vienna and Russia[1] for further details.

a Paris Le 25e mars 1782./.

Les soussignés ont L'honneur d'offrir Leurs Services Pour Les fournitures de L'habillements des trouppes Ameriquaines Conformement aux models qui Leurs sera donné, ou a Ceux qu'ils ont Envoies a nantes a Monsieur Villiammes neveux de Monsieur francklin ministre et deputé En La Cour de france[2]

Scavoir

1er Uniforme en Brun Veste et Culotte Blanche
2e Uniforme en Rouge de Garence veste et Culotte Blanche
3e Uniforme en Jeaune Veste et Culotte Blanche
4e Uniforme en Bleu Veste Et Culotte Blanche
avec Les Boutons Uniformes Conformes aux Models qui Leurs Seront Presentés, Les dits Entrepreneurs offrent de faire les Models Cy dessus designés Pour que L'entreprise qui Leurs Seroit donné Fut de même dans Son Execution

CHAMPION
fournisseur des troupes du Roy
LESCUYER
negt. et fabriquand a Beauvais

1. The comte de Mercy-Argenteau (XXIII, 590n) and Prince Bariatinskoy (XXIV, 49n), respectively. Also among BF's papers at the Hist. Soc. of Pa. is a title page of a pamphlet printed at Hamburg in May, 1782, addressed to Catherine II and the Economic Society of St. Petersburg, and proposing the establishment of commercial ties between Russian and Hanseatic merchants. A note on this title page, in an unknown hand, identifies Pauly as the author: "Prospectus addressé à la Chambre Economique de Petersbourg pour l'Etablissement dun commerce en General entre les deux Nations Russes & ameriquaines, fait par lautheur de la lettre & terminé *par des passages du vieux Testament*".

2. Champion had introduced himself to BF two years before: XXXIII, 107–8. Lescuyer, listed as Lescuyer Vuatrin on p. 81 of the *Almanach des marchands,* supplied JW with textiles from the summer of 1777 (XXIV, 456, 474) until his death in the spring of 1782: JW's accounts and his letters to Mme Lescuyer of May 25 and June 22, 1782 (Yale University Library).

Memoire

Endorsed: Que je garderai le Proposition mais qu'actuellement
je n'ai point d'achats a faire

From Cuming & Macarty[3] ALS:[4] American Philosophical Society

Sir   L'Orient 25th. March 1782

We take the Liberty of Inclosing your Excellency a Copy of
a Letter we have received from a certain Mr. Bright[5] (Son to a respectable Citizen of Philada) who has lately made his Escape
from Fortune Prisson in England where he has been detaind
since January 1781. This Young Man was taken at the same time
with our WM to whom he was particularly recommended—[6]
We have Constantly supplyd him with Money wich has Facili-
tated his getting away.

We have wrote to the Commandant at Brest, requesting His
and a Mr. Woods. discharge (he is also of Philadelphia) but least
we shoud not Succed, we beg leave to request, Your asistance, in
returning those two Young Men to their Families, by procuring
leave for their coming here to Embark in the Helena for Philadelphia.

We have the Honour to be with great respect Your Exellencys— Most Obedt. Humble Servt.   CUMING & MACARTY

Notation: Cuming & MacCarty L'orient 25 March 1782.

3. James Cuming and William Macarty, American merchants in Lorient,
announced their partnership on July 15, 1781: JW to Cuming & Macarty, July
24, 1781 (Yale University Library).

4. It appears to be in William Macarty's hand.

5. Michael Bright and others, including Champion Wood (mentioned below), appealed to BF on Feb. 21 and 26. Bright's letter to Cuming, enclosed
with this letter and now at the APS, was also dated Feb. 26: XXXVI, 598–9,
659n.

6. William Macarty had been captured en route to France and arrived in
Passy within days of Bright's incarceration at Forton: XXXIV, 429; Kaminkow, *Mariners,* p. 23.

From Jonathan Williams, Jr.

ALS: American Philosophical Society

Dear & hond sir.   Nantes March. 25. 1782

I embrace the Opportunity the departure of Mr Meyers[7] gives me to send you two Bottles of Cramberrys: I will send you more by the first messagerie.

I beg leave at the same time to introduce Mr Meyers to your kind Notice and Friendship.

I am as ever your dutifull & affect Kinsman

JONA WILLIAMS J

Addressed: His Excellency / Doctor Franklin &c &c.

Notation: J. Williams, Nantes March 25. 1782.

To ———[8]

AL (draft): American Philosophical Society

ce 26 Mars 82

J'ai reçu, avec ma petite Dialogue, votre charmante Epitre & Puisque je trouve que Madame la Goutte est de votre Connoissance, ma tres chere Amie je vous prie de grace que quand elle me fait une autre Visite, vous voudriez bien l'accompagner. Votre Présence me dedommagera de la sienne. Avec une telle Garde, la Peine deviendra Plaisir.[9]

---

7. Samuel Myers, a New York merchant in partnership with his brother Moses: XXXIV, 238n; *Morris Papers*, VI, 215n. Myers was on his way to Amsterdam, where the firm had established its base of operations. BF gave him a pass to that city on April 14: XXXVI, 379.

8. We can identify neither the intended recipient nor the letter she evidently sent. Mme Brillon, who had introduced the character of "Madame La Goutte" and to whom BF had replied with his dialogue on the gout more than a year earlier (XXXIII, 529–31; XXXIV, 11–21), had not yet returned from Nice.

9. On the verso the owner of a tin plate manufactory identified himself: "M. falatieu proprietaire de la manufr. Rle. [Royale] de Bain a Epinal en loraine." His name is listed as "Falacieu" in the *Almanach des marchands,* p. 202, where the Bains manufactory, outside of Epinal, is called the finest in the kingdom. Above this note BF has written "300 feuilles pesant 160 livres / 90 livres—12 Inches long by 9 1/2" and underneath, "Fer blanc". He also made a series of related calculations and drew a right isosceles triangle.

From John Adams

ALS: Robert Castle Norton Autograph Letters of U.S. Presidents, Western Reserve Historical Society; copy: Massachusetts Historical Society; copy, two press copies of copies, and transcript: National Archives

Sir   The Hague March 26. 1782

One day, last Week, I recd at Amsterdam a Card from Diggs, inclosing two Letters to me from Mr David Hartley. The Card desired to see me upon Business of Importance: and the Letters from Mr Hartley contained an Assurance that to his Knowledge the Bearer came from the highest Authority.—[1] I answered the Card, that in the present Situation of Affairs here and elsewhere, it was impossible for me to See any one from England without Witness, but if he was willing to see me in Presence of Mr Thaxter my Secretary and that I should communicate whatever he should Say to me to Dr Franklin and the Comte de Vergennes, I would wait for him at home at ten O Clock, but that I had rather he should go to Paris without Seeing me and communicate what he had to say to Dr Franklin, whose situation enabled him to consult the Court without loss of time. At ten, however he came, and told me a long story about Consultations with Mr Pen, Mr Hartley Lord Beauchamp and at last Lord North, by whom he was finally sent, to enquire of me, if I, or any other, had Authority, to treat with Great Britain of a Truce.—[2] I answered, that I came to Europe last with full Powers to make Peace,[3] that those Powers had been announced to the public upon my Arrival, and continued in force untill last Summer, when Congress Sent a new Commission, containing the Same Powers to five Per-

1. Digges's letter, written on the evening of March 20, asked for half an hour's conversation about both a public matter and a private affair which he expected would lead him to see BF in a few days. The first of Hartley's letters, dated Feb. 19, asked about JA's and Laurens' commissions, while the second, dated March 11, was a letter of introduction for Digges: Elias and Finch, *Letters of Digges*, pp. 352–4.

2. Digges described their meeting in his letter to BF of March 22[–26], above, and in a memorandum to Shelburne that BF sent JA on April 20, below.

3. XXX, 226–7; Butterfield, *John Adams Diary*, IV, 178–9, 181–3; *Adams Papers*, VIII, 203, 220–1. Congress did set conditions on the exercise of his powers: *JCC*, XIV, 956–60.

sons, whom I named.—[4] That if the King of England were my father, and I the Heir apparent to his Throne, I would not advise him to think of a Truce, because it would be but a real War under a simulated appearance of Tranquility, and would end in another open and bloody War, without doing any real good to any of the Parties.

He Said, that the Ministry would send, Some Person of Consequence over, perhaps General Conway,[5] but they were apprehensive, that he would be ill treated or exposed.— I Said that if they resolved upon such a measure, I had rather they would send immediately to Dr Franklin, because of his Situation near the French Court.— But there was no doubt, if they sent any respectable Personage properly authorised, who should come to treat honourably, he would be treated with great Respect.— But that if he came to me, I could give him no opinion upon any thing without consulting my Colleagues, and should reserve a Right of communicating every Thing to my Colleagues, and to our Allies.

He then Said, that his Mission was finished. That the Fact to be ascertained was Simply, that there was a Commission in Europe to treat and conclude, but that there was not one Person in G. Britain who could affirm or prove that there was such a Commission, altho it had been anounced in the Gazettes.[6]

I desired him and he promised me not to mention Mr Laurens, to the Ministry without his Consent, and without informing him that it was impossible he should Say any thing in the Business, because he knows nothing of our Instructions, because altho it was possible that his being in such a Commission might

4. JA, BF, Jay, Laurens, and Jefferson were appointed to the joint peace commission, although Jefferson declined to serve: XXXV, 161–7, 436n.

5. Henry Seymour Conway was a leader of the movement in the House of Commons that toppled the North government: XXXVI, 674n, 684n. Nonetheless, Digges, upon returning to London, wrote JA that Conway "was privy to & at the bottom of my message to You." Digges's veracity is open to question. When JA saw the account Digges gave Shelburne of their interview, sent to him by BF on April 20, he denied the bulk of its claims: Elias and Finch, *Letters of Digges*, pp. 365–7.

6. JA had not officially notified the British government of his mission in 1780 because of Vergennes' objections: XXXII, 18–19; XXXIII, 52n.

induce them to release him, yet it was also possible, it might render them more difficult concerning his Exchange.

The Picture he gives of the situation of Things in England, is gloomy enough for them. The Distresses of the People and the Distractions in Administration and Parliament, are such as may produce any Effect, almost that can be imagined.

The only Use of all this I think is, to Strike decisive strokes at New York and Charlestown. There is no Position so advantageous for Negotiation, as when We have all an Ennemies Armies Prisoners. I must beg the favour of you, Sir, to Send me, by one of the C de Vergennes's Couriers to the Duc de la Vauguion, a Copy in Letters of our Peace Instructions. I have not been able to decypher one Quarter Part of mine. Some Mistake has certainly been made.

Ten or Eleven Cities of Holland, have declared themselves in favour of American Independence, and it is expected that to day or tomorrow, this Province will take the decisive Resolution of Admitting me to an Audience.[7] Perhaps Some of the other Provinces, may delay it for, three or four Weeks. But the Prince[8] has declared that he has no hopes of resisting the Torrent and therefore that he shall not attempt it. The Duc de la Vauguion has acted a very friendly and honourable Part in this Business, without, however doing any ministerial Act, in it.

With great Respect, I have the Honour to be, Sir, your most obedient and most humble servant   J. ADAMS

His Excellency B. Franklin Esqr.

7. Two days later the States of the Province of Holland made such a recommendation to the States General of the Netherlands: Wharton, *Diplomatic Correspondence*, v, 316.

8. Prince William V of Orange, the Stadholder of the Netherlands, a longstanding opponent of American recognition.

From the Abbé Labat de Mourlens

ALS: American Philosophical Society

Monseigneur   Toulouse ce 26 mars 1782

Pour remplir la tâche dont j'ai ete chargé par ma Compagnie, j'ai du Celebrer la gloire et les vertus du roi mon maitre. J'ai du aussi y rendre un juste homage à la nation genereuse que vous representés à la Cour de france. La reunion de Ces deux Circonstances m'engage à prendre la liberté de vous presenter ci-joint un éxemplaire de mon ouvrage.[9]

Je suis avec respect Monseigneur de votre éxellence Le tres humble et tres obeissant serviteur   L'ABBÉ DE MOURLENS

Pour Monseigneur francklin ministre plenipotentiaire des états unis de L'Amerique Septentrionale à passy près paris.

Notation: Mourlens M. L'abbé de 26 Mars 1782.

From Jonathan Williams, Jr.

ALS: American Philosophical Society; copies: American Philosophical Society, Yale University Library

Dear & hond sir.   Nantes March 26. 1782.

I beg leave to trouble you with the present, which has for its subject the distresses of our Countrymen who escape hither from Prison. I am an Enemy to extravagant supplies, because extravagant People would take the advantage of the public Generisity &

---

9. The published version of a speech the abbé had delivered as *Maître des jeux floraux: Semonce Ou Discours Pour l'ouverture de séances publiques de l'Académie des Jeux Floraux, prononcé le 31 Janvier 1782, dans la Salle des Illustres de l'Hôtel-de-Ville de Toulouse* (Paris, 1782). The speech contains a tribute to the Americans, with references to BF, JA, Washington, Nathanael Greene, and John Hancock: Durand Echeverria and Everett C. Wilkie, Jr., comps., *The French Image of America* (2 vols., Metuchen, N.J., and London, 1994), I, 497–8. During the academy's annual "floral games," instituted in 1323, the poets of Languedoc competed for the prize of the golden amaranth and other gold or silver flowers: *Encyclopædia Britannica*, 11th ed., under "Toulouse."

indulge themselves in dependant Idleness; but the necessary assistance of meat & Cloathing I think no state should refuse to its subjects under Misfortune. Five Americans, of which two are Captains in our Army, have come hither from Bordeaux where they were set on shore after escaping from the Prison at Kingsale in Ireland, They applied to me supposing me a public Agent, & tho' I have no Authority from the public I could not avoid paying thirty Livres per man for their Carriage hither and engaging for their Board 'till I could know further. Capt Lewis & Capt Whipple are the two in the service, tho' the latter had resigned his Commission (after serving 6 Years) on accot of his Health; to establish which appears to have been his motive for coming to sea. These Gentlemen have Representations to make to you about the situation of 400 American Prisoners in Kingsale, I advised them to send you these Representations in writing rather than go to Paris themselves & accordingly you will hear from them.[1]

I beg Sir you will consider the situation of these unhappy Men & put in my power to distribute such supplies in future as they and others who may Come may stand in absolute need off. I repeat that nothing further than necessity ought to be allowed by a state, but so far as the Laws of humanity dictate they surely ought to provide, & no Individual can be expected to furnish what a state refuses.

I am Dear & hond sir as evr most respectfully & affecty Yours

J WILLIAMS J

Notation: Williams Mr. Jona. Nantes March 26 1782.—

1. They wrote on March 24, above. The other three escaped prisoners were naval captain Joseph Hardy, Mr. Bacon (possibly the Edward Bacon aided by Coffyn on Feb. 3: Account XXVII, xxxii, 4), and Mr. French: JW's account of expenses, Aug. 12, 1782 (Yale University Library).

To the Marquis de Lafayette Copy:[2] Library of Congress

Dear Sir, Passy, March 28. 1782.

I have considered the Proposal of getting the American Prisoners out of Forton Goal & bringing them over in Companies to France in smuggling Vessels; but as to effect this there must be some Place found on the Coast where the Prisoners may assemble to wait for the Vessel may lye to wait for the Prisoners, as the Case may happen, without Danger of being discovered and seized, (it being hardly possible to regulate & time the different Operations by Land & Water so as to meet exactly at the same time) and there being I imagine, no such Place on that Part of the Coast, I apprehend the Project to be impracticable.[3] Mr. Young[4] may however, makes the Enquiry he proposes at Dunkirk of Mr. Coffyn, in his way to Ostend, and writes to us the Opinion of that Gentleman. With great & sincere Esteem & Affection, I am, dear Sir, Your most obedient & most humble Servt.

Mr. De la Fayette.

From the Veuve de Précorbin and Other Commission Seekers ALS: American Philosophical Society

Even as the peace negotiations were getting under way, Franklin continued to receive letters soliciting commissions in the American army.[5] The earliest of these, printed below, is from a widowed mother of four who seizes on Franklin's reputation for generosity toward the unfortunate to plead the case of her irresponsible eldest son. Franklin's endorsement indicates a negative reply.

2. A letterbook copy by L'Air de Lamotte, who may have been confused by a heavily edited draft. Whatever the case, his mangling of the first sentence does not altogether obscure BF's point.

3. We know nothing further about this proposal.

4. Moses Young, Laurens' former secretary, who once had been a prisoner at Forton and now was employed by BF: XXXIII, 363n; XXXV, 187n; XXXVI, 163–4, 198–9. Young's employment with BF ended on April 14: Young to BF, July 10, below.

5. Unless otherwise noted, the letters discussed in this headnote are in French, are at the APS, and carry no indication that BF replied.

Franklin's Sketch of the Garden at Passy

On April 5, two young officers write from Donaveschingen (in the small German principality of Fürstenberg), where one, Ferdinand de Rembau, is a lieutenant in the Hohenzollern Cavalry Regiment in the service of the circle of Swabia, and the other, Dupont d'Aisÿ, from Normandy, is in the 6th Regiment of Light Cavalry. Their greatest desire is for glory and thus they seek to serve the American cause. They expect to receive a rank higher than their present one, though to prove their sincerity, they will accept short term appointments as gentlemen cadets. Since neither of them has come into an inheritance yet, they will also require pay suitable to their station. Extracts of their baptismal records and certificates of nobility and conduct will be forwarded on request. They await Franklin's orders impatiently and would prefer to embark at Ostend.[6]

The chevalier O'Gorman recommends Dr. O'Connor on April 11 for service in the American army or its hospitals. Both he and Dr. MacMahon have a high opinion of the doctor: he studied medicine at the University of Paris,[7] has practiced in military hospitals in France and the West Indies for nine years, and his doctor's certificates are in order. O'Connor himself will deliver this letter.

On June 4, the sieur de La Bassée, captain of dragoons and chevalier de Saint-Louis, presents his respects and the service of one of his sons, who for the past four months has pestered him to be allowed to serve America.[8] While he could call on any number of influential people to press his case, he has allowed himself to write only his relative M. de Saint-Paul, a high official in the *bureau de la guerre*.[9] The young man, eighteen years old, is strong, handsome, and very brave, and he has served as an officer on different privateers out of Dunkerque and

6. A note filed with their letter states that on April 8 it was sent to Capt. Frey, who had left some time before. Capt. Frey, originally from Konstanz, 40 miles from where the two officers were stationed, was then at Paris: XXIV, 156n, XXXVI, 690n.

7. Where MacMahon was on the medical faculty: XXV, 4n.

8. Charles-Marie-Hubert de La Bassée writes from Boulogne. His son Mathieu (1764–1830) served in the French army during the Revolution and the Empire, passing through the ranks to become brigadier general in 1803. He was made a baron in 1809: Jean-François-Eugène Robinet *et al.*, *Dictionnaire historique et biographique de la Révolution et de l'Empire, 1789–1815* ... (2 vols., Paris, 1898); *DBF* under "Delabassée"; Six, *Dictionnaire biographique*.

9. Saint-Paul's duties included nominations, commissions, and brevets for officers: *Almanach royal* for 1782, p. 247.

Boulogne. The father received favorable reports on his son's conduct from each commanding officer.[1]

On June 16, the prince de Sulkowski[2] writes from Paris to "l'Ami de l'Humanité" to introduce a Polish gentleman for whom he is confident Franklin will find a place in the American service. The attached memoir describes M. de Kurowski as a young infantry officer who advanced through the ranks to become captain and aide-de-camp to Lieutenant General comte de Stipkowski. Seeing that further advancement would be very slow, Kurowski obtained the Polish King's permission to resign and seek his fortune abroad.

From Simmern near Mannheim on July 20 the baron de Strasser relates in what he admits is "unfirm" English a tale of romance and disappointed expectations. As an ensign in the Hessian service when war with America was declared, he was one of the 12,000 auxiliaries to enter British pay for service in the colonies. In Charleston, S.C., he managed to win the heart of Miss Nancy Elliott, descended of Bernard Elliott, whom Franklin must have known.[3] The "handsome and lovely Nancy" promised to help him obtain a commission in the continental service and gave him several letters to carry to Generals Moultrie, Lincoln, and Scott, held on parole at Haddrel's Point.[4] The generals assured this German auxiliary that he would be appointed major of a

1. WTF's notation "Repe." indicates that an answer was sent.

2. August Casimir Sulkowsky (1729–1786), Duke of Bielitz and Palatine of Posen, had been a contender for the crown of Poland: Lewis, *Walpole Correspondence*, XXXIII, 279–80.

3. While living in Charleston under British occupation, Ann (Nancy) Elliott (1752–1848) was called "the beautiful rebel" for the bonnet she wore with 13 small plumes as a sign of her attachment to republican principles. She subsequently married Lewis Morris (1752–1824), aide-de-camp to Gen. Greene: Walter Whipple Spooner, *Historic Families of America* (2 vols., New York, [1907]), II, 219–20.
There are several Bernard Elliotts in this family; see Henry A. M. Smith, "The Baronies of South Carolina," *S.C. Hist. and Geneal. Mag.*, XV (1914), 70–1, 162–3; Edward McCrady, LL.D., *The History of South Carolina in the Revolution 1775–1780* (London, 1901), p. 179.

4. Haddrel's Point, in Charleston Harbor, was occupied by the British on April 25, 1780. When Lincoln surrendered the American army on May 12, the officers were confined there. The events recounted here must have occurred soon after the capitulation, for Lincoln was in Philadelphia in July: Mark Mayo Boatner III, *Encyclopedia of the American Revolution* (New York, 1966), pp. 474, 636, 750, 995; Alexander R. Stoesen, "The British Occupation of Charleston, 1780–1782," *S.C. Hist. and Geneal. Mag.*, LXIII (1962), 76.

brigade. He obtained his discharge, but was imprisoned, sent to England, and returned to his native country, where he has no employment and is "deprived of the Sweet hopes to accept the advantageous match with miss Nancy Elliott". He begs Franklin to support his petition to rejoin his regiment at his former rank. The baron de Siking, ambassador of the Elector Palatine, well acquainted with his uncle, baron de Ritter, minister at Vienna, will inform Franklin of his family background.[5]

A low-ranking officer of a distinguished Languedoc family writes on July 23 from Paris where he is staying with relatives on the chaussée d'Antin. This Dupuy, in service to the German infantry regiment of Laczj, has done his utmost to distinguish himself, but only a very small number of individuals are able to advance in times of peace. He wishes a position at his current rank in one of the French or German units serving in America and hopes that Franklin will write letters on his behalf to Washington. He has all the necessary supporting documentation as well as 18 years' tactical experience in the best troops of Germany. His desire for honor and to serve honorably will compensate for his lack of fortune. Wishing no longer to impose on his relatives, he urges Franklin to grant him an interview as soon as possible.

Next come two letters from the south of France. On July 28, Henry O'Neill, writing in English from Tournay, is furious with Franklin for obstructing his military career. He is on his way back to Ireland from Madrid where he failed to obtain even a lieutenant's commission, and accuses Franklin of thinking it in the interest of America that the Irish be ill-treated in Europe so that more of them will emigrate to America. He holds the French ministry and the conde de Aranda responsible as well. His own family, now ruined by service to the French and Spaniards, had deposited a sum of money in the Irish community in Paris sufficient for two of the name and family to be educated on the interest.[6] If O'Neill carries the story of his mistreatment back to Ire-

5. Karl Heinrich Josef, Graf von Sickingen zu Sickingen (XXVII, 391), a count since 1773, was the joint Bavarian and Palatine envoy to France until his death in 1791: *Repertorium der diplomatischen Vertreter*, III, 21, 304; *Almanach royal* for 1782, p. 148.

Heinrich Josef, Freiherr von Ritter, was named Bavarian minister plenipotentiary to Vienna in 1777 and remained so until his death in July, 1783: *Repertorium der diplomatischen Vertreter*, III, 18.

6. Among BF's papers is an undated note from a Mr. ONeill, who invites BF to the defense of his thesis, hoping that the Doctor will "condesend if possible to honour him forever with a moment of his presence." Hist. Soc. of Pa.

land, his countrymen may be moved "to joyn Sincearly with England and supply thire Armies and navy with numbers of brave men." Under this threat Franklin is directed to let O'Neill know if something can be done for him.

The vicomte de Lomagne writes from Berenx on August 12 hoping to enlist Franklin's assistance in obtaining a rank in the French army equal to the one he held in the American army. The long memoir he encloses recounts his five years of service in the United States, beginning with Lafayette's recommendation for a commission in February, 1778, and a promotion two months later to major in Colonel Armand's legion.[7] In May, 1781, von Steuben sent him to Philadelphia where he contracted smallpox. Congress granted him permission to recuperate in France and he arrived finally with the marquis de Chabert.[8] He is mortified now to find that other French officers with much less experience and rank in the American service might be given positions of higher rank than he.[9] He also wishes Franklin to help him receive payment for a loan office certificate left with Jonathan Williams, Jr.[1]

Monseigneur⠀⠀⠀⠀⠀⠀a Caen rüe St Etienne ce 28 mars 1782.

La veuve d'un gentilhomme, qui avoit servy sa patrie avec honneur, chargée de quatre Enfants prend La Liberté de s'adresser à vous, sans en Etre Connüe; parcequ'elle sait quelle est La sensibilité de vôtre Coeur, et vôtre inclination à secourir les malheureux. Mon fils ainè, nommè alexandre, felix, moisson, apres avoir été Elevé à L'Ecole Royal militaire, Etoit entré dans Le Rgmt. de Neustrie;[2] des discussions avec ses Camarades L'ont

7. Jean de Lomagne-Tarride, known as Maj. Lomagne, had benefited from BF's assistance once before: XXIV, 499n. The present letter is at the University of Pa. Library.
8. Joseph-Bernard, marquis de Chabert (1724–1805), commander of the *Saint-Esprit*, 80, was promoted *chef d'escadre* in 1782: Larousse; Ministère des Archives étrangères, *Les Combattants français de la guerre américaine 1778–1783* (Paris, 1903), p. 152; *Almanach royal* for 1783, pp. 169–70.
9. Lomagne was unable to obtain a commission in the French army until the Revolution: Gilbert Bodinier, *Les Officiers de l'armée royale combattants de la guerre d'Indépendance des Etats-Unis: De Yorktown à l'an II* (Vincennes, 1983), pp. 265, 406; Bodinier, *Dictionnaire*, p. 495.
1. Lomagne had been reimbursed for back pay and given a gratuity in bills of exchange and loan office certificates: *JCC*, XXI, 998; *Morris Papers*, II, 360–1n.
2. Précorbin was a *sous-lieutenant* of this infantry regiment: *Etat militaire* for 1781, p. 186.

engagé à en quitter; et il se trouve aujourdhuy sans Etat. Son pere Etoit chevalier de st. Loüis pensionnaire de sa majesté, et Lieutenant de Nos SS. Les Marechaux de france à Caen, sa fortune Etoit au desous de La Mèdiocrité;[3] ses pensions sont Eteintes avec Luy, et il ne reste à ses Enfants, que le souvenir cruel d'estre sorty de luy sans pouvoir L'imiter. La derniere avanture de Lainé le prive de toute resource, sy vôtre, exelence, ne daigne Luy subvenir, en ayant La bonté de luy procurer D'occasion de servir la juste Cause des Etats unis de L'amerique; et de luy menager un pasage dans vôtre patrie et luy procurer un grade qui le mette en Etat de supsister.

Daignés Monseigneur, ne pas refuser une veuve Desolée, et l'honorer d'une reponce favorable.

Je suis avec un profond respect, Monseigneur, Vôtre tres humble et tres obeissante servante   VE. DE PRÈCORBIN

Notation: Precorbin Mde. De 28. Mars 1782.

Endorsed: The Armies of America full Not possible

From Jonathan Williams, Jr.

ALS: American Philosophical Society; copy: Yale University Library

Dear & hond sir.   Nantes Mar. 28. 1782

I have received your Favour 23 Inst and perfectly agree in Opinion with you. I thank you very much for your kind Expressions of Friendship which I will always study to deserve. The Seeds you will before this have received, I hope in good Order.

I beg leave to introduce to your Notice my Friend Mr William Vernon of Boston.[4] You will find him worthy of your Friendship & I request you will show him every mark of Civility, which will highly oblige Dear & hond sir Your dutifull & affectionate Kinsman   JONA WILLIAMS J

---

3. M. Moisson de Précorbin was a *lieutenant des maréchaux de France: Etat militaire* for 1781, p. 47; Mazas, *Ordre de Saint-Louis*, I, 440.

4. Vernon was preparing to return to America: Bondfield to BF, March 24, above.

His Excellency Doctor Franklin.

Addressed: A Monsieur / Monsieur Franklin / en son Hotel / a Passy / prés Paris

Notation: J. Williams, Nantes March 28 1782.

From Charles-Guillaume-Frédéric Dumas

ALS: American Philosophical Society

Monsieur   La haie 29e. Mars 1782

Il ne me reste qu'un instant, pour vous communiquer ma joie de ce que vous lirez dans ma Lettre au Congrès,[5] dans le paquet ci-joint, qu'il importe de faire passer le plutôt possible, & de la maniere la plus sûre en Amérique. Dans environ un mois tout sera fait avec cette Rep. à notre satisfaction, c'est-à-dire l'admission de Mr. Adams. Nous demeurerons ici & vivrons heureux ensemble dans la Maison que je lui ai achetée.[6] La semaine prochaine j'aurai l'honneur de vous écrire plus amplement, & de justifier mon silence depuis quelque temps, qui étoit nécessaire: car je suis toujours de coeur & d'ame avec l'attachement le plus respectueux, Monsieur Votre très-humble & très obéissant serviteur   DUMAS

Nous venons de remporter la plus noble victoire ici sur l'Anglomanie, grace sur-tout à mon excellent Ami Mr. Gyzelaer[7] digne pensionaire de Dort.

Vous voudrez bien, Monsieur, avoir la bonté de bien cacheter le paquet.

a Son Exc. Mr. B. Franklin

5. Dumas' March 29 letter to Robert R. Livingston announcing that the provinces of Friesland and Holland had recommended that the States General of the Netherlands permit JA to present his diplomatic credentials: Wharton, *Diplomatic Correspondence*, V, 276.

6. In the middle of May JA moved into this house in The Hague, the first building acquired by the United States as a foreign legation: Butterfield, *John Adams Diary*, III, 4–5n; *Adams Correspondence*, IV, 323.

7. Cornelis de Gijselaar (Gyselaar) (1751–1815), the pensionary of Dordrecht (Dort): *NNBW*, X, 309–10.

From John Jay

AL (draft): Columbia University Library; copies:[8] Columbia University Library, Henry E. Huntington Library, National Archives

Dear Sir   Madrid 29th. March 1782

On the 18 Inst I informed you of my having been reduced, by Mr Cabarrus's want of good Faith to the mortifying Necessity of protestg a Number of Bills which were then payable.

Your favor of the 16th. Inst. reached me three day ago it made me very happy, and enabled me to retrieve the Credit we had lost here by those Protests. I consider your Letter as giving me sufficient Authority to take the necessary Arrangements with the Marqs. D Yranda for paying the Residue of my Debts here as well as such of the protested Bills as may be returned for that Purpose.[9] The Account you request of all the Bills I have accepted is making out, & when finished shall be transmitted by the first good opportunity that may offer. You may rely on my best Endeavours to render my Drafts as little inconvenient to you as possible.

The british Parliament it seems begin to entertain less erroneous Ideas of us, and their Resolutions afford an useful Hint to the other Powers of Europe. If the Dutch are wise they will proffit by it. As to this Court their System (if their Conduct deserves that Appellation) with Respect to us, has been so opposite to the obvious Dictates of sound Policy that it is hard to devine whether any thing but Experience can undeceive them. For my Part I really think that a Treaty with them daily becomes less important to us.

That Britain should be desirous of a separate Peace with us is very natural; but as such a Proposal implies an Impeachment of our Integrity I think it ought to be rejected in such a Manner as

---

8. All of which are misdated March 19. Jay did not receive BF's letter of March 16 (acknowledged here) until March 26 (Wharton, *Diplomatic Correspondence*, V, 369), so we assume that the date on the draft is correct. Where Jay made significant changes to his draft, we indicate the original wording in annotation. For other revisions see Morris, *Jay: Peace*, pp. 144–6.

9. Jay rebuffed Cabarrus' attempts at reconciliation, choosing henceforth to use Yranda and others as his bankers: Wharton, *Diplomatic Correspondence*, V, 370–2; Morris, *Jay: Peace*, p. 133.

to shew that[1] we are not ignorant of the Respect due to our Feelings on that Head. As long as France continues faithful to us I am clear that we ought to continue Hand in Hand to prosecute the War until all their as well as all our reasonable Objects can be attained by a peace—for I would rather see America ruined than dishonored. As to Spain and Holland we have as yet no Engagements with them and therefore are not obliged to consult either their Interest or their Inclinations further than may be convenient to ourselves, or than the Respect due to our good Allies may render proper. France in granting you six Million has acted with Dignity as well as Generosity— Such Gifts, so given, command both Gratitude and Esteem, and I think our Country possesses sufficient Magnanity to receive & to remember such Marks of Friendship with a proper Degree of Sensibility.[2]

I am pleased with your Idea of paying whatever we owe to Spain. Their pride perhaps might forbid them to receive the Money—but our Pride has been so hurt by the Littleness of their Conduct that I would in that Case, be for leaving it at the Gate of the Palace and quit the Country. At Present such a Step would not be expedient, tho the Time will come when Prudence instead of restraining will urge us to hold no other Language or Conduct to this Court than that of a just, a free, and a brave People, who have Nothing to fear from, nor to request of them.

With perfect Regard & Esteem I am Dr Sr your obligd & affe Servt

To Dr Franklin 29 March 1782

1. The remainder of this sentence initially was drafted as "our Feelings are hurt by such invidious Suspicions of our Honor."

2. Jay here drafted but deleted "very different has been the Conduct of this Court—pompous in Assurances, niggardly in their Grants daily making promises & daily breaking them. All high & mighty in Words, all mean and little in".

From Jean Rousseaux

ALS: University of Pennsylvania Library

Monsieur.   Brest Le 29. Mars 1782

Je me Suis fait Lhonneur de vous Ecrire deux Lettre[3] par Les quelle je vous priay de vouloir massiste dans Le besoin ou jette et vous demandant une Chose que jay Bien garnie [gagnée] a La Sueur de mon Cord. Je crois Monsieur que Je ne vous demande pas une chose qui met pas deu [qui ne m'est pas due] informe vous a Monsieur Cornic a qui jay mene une prize a Morlaix et je vous avez Envoye meme de Dunkerque La Lettre de mr. Cornic qui vous prouvoit le juste et vous Mave fait reponse a Dunkerque.[4] Jespere Monsieur que vous vouderee Mesurer dun mot de lettre mon adresse est Chez Mr. Latapie Dantiste du roy rue de riche a Brest.

Jay Lhonneur Dettre avec respect Monsieur Votre tres heumble et tres obs. Serviteur   JN. ROUSSEAUX

Ne Moublie pas je vous prie Monsieur.

Addressed: A Monsieur / Monsieur Le Doctheur / frankelin Embassadeur / Du Congray a Passy / Par Paris

To Robert R. Livingston

LS,[5] copy, and transcript: National Archives; copy: Library of Congress

Sir,   Passy, March 30th. 1782.

In mine of the 9th Inst. I acknowledg'd the receipt of yours of Jany. 7.[6] & I have not since received any of later Date.

The Newspapers which I send you by this Conveyance will acquaint you with what has since my last passed in Parliament. You will there see a Copy of the Bill brought in by the Attorney Genl: for impowering the King to make Peace with the Col-

---

3. Feb. 16 and March 6: XXXVI, 586–7.

4. Rousseaux's letter of Feb. 28, 1779, enclosed a now-missing certificate from Veuve Mathurin Cornic & fils concerning the prize *Jason*. BF responded two weeks later: XXVIII, 636–7.

5. In WTF's hand.

6. XXXVI, 390–402, 671–2.

onies.[7] They still seem to flatter themselves with the Idea of dividing us; and rather than name the Congress, they impower him generally to treat with *any Body or Bodies of Men, or any Person or Persons &ca.* They are here likewise endeavouring to get us to treat separately from France, at the same time they are tempting France to treat separately from us, equally without the least Chance of Success. I have been drawn into a Correspondence on this Subject which you shall have with my next. I send you a Letter of Mr Adams's just received which shews also that they are weary of the War, and would get out of it if they knew how.[8] They had not then received the certain News of the loss of St Christophers; which will probably render them still more disposed to Peace.—[9] I see that a Bill is also passing thro the House of Commons for the Exchange of American Prisoners, the Purport of which I do not yet know.[1]

In my last[2] I promised to be more particular with respect to the Points you mentioned as proper to be insisted on in the Treaty of Peace. My Ideas on those Points are I assure you full as strong as yours. I did intend to have given you my Reasons for some Addition, and if the Treaty were to be held on your side the Water, I would do it; otherwise it seems on second Thought, to be unnecessary, and if my Letter should be intercepted may be inconvenient. Be assured I shall not willingly give up any im-

7. The so-called Enabling Act (for which see XXXVI, 688n). It did not clear Parliament until June 17 and received the royal assent two days later: *Journals of the House of Commons* (51 vols., reprint, London, 1803), XXXVIII, 1060, 1064. It is puzzling that BF does not also discuss Lord North's resignation, which was reported in the London press on March 21.

8. An accurate appraisal of the North government's attempts, using Thomas Digges to contact the Americans, Nathaniel Parker Forth the French, and Paul Wentworth the Dutch. BF had just learned of the first from JA's letter of March 26, above; for the second see XXXVI, 684n; for the third see Digges's letter of March 22[–26].

9. De Grasse landed 6,000 troops on the island of St. Christopher (commonly called St. Kitts) on Jan. 11, forcing the British to retreat to a fort on Brimstone Hill, which surrendered after a month's siege: *Courier de l'Europe,* XI (1782), 235–6; *London Courant, Morning Gazette, and Daily Advertiser,* March 27, 1782; Mackesy, *War for America,* pp. 455–6.

1. Burke's bill, for which see Hodgson to BF, March 22.

2. XXXVI, 671–2.

portant Right or Interest of our Country, and unless this Campaign should afford our Enemies some considerable Advantage, I hope more may be obtained than is yet expected.

I have purchased for you all the Books you desired,[3] except four which we have sent for to England. I shall request our excellent Friend the Marquis de la Fayette, to take them under his Care, and I hope they will get safe to hand.— The others shall follow by the first Opportunity after I receive them.

Our Affairs go on generally well in Europe. Holland has been slow, Spain slower, but Time will I hope smooth away all Difficulties. Let us keep up not only our Courage but our Vigilance, and not be laid asleep by the pretended Half Peace the English make with us without asking our Consent. We cannot be safe while they keep Armies in our Country.

With great Esteem, I have the honour to be, Sir, Your most obedient & most humble Servant   B Franklin

His Exy. Robt. R. Livingston Esqre.

To Robert Morris   Copy:[4] Library of Congress

Sir,   Passy, March 30. 1782.

With this if it comes to Hand you will receive Copies of several preceeding Letters to you which went by the Alliance, Capt. Barry, who sail'd the 15. without taking any of our Supplies, conceiving his Vessel not fit for such Service, and I am still uncertain whether any Part can go by the Convoy.[5] If the St. Domingo

3. For which see xxxvi, 401–2.

4. By L'Air de Lamotte. We have not corrected his occasional lapses into French spelling and we gloss one word that he may have misread.

5. The *Alliance* sailed for America on March 16: xxxvi, 692n. The convoy was a French one for Virginia which had been scheduled to depart in mid-March: xxxvi, 546n, 557–8. Beaumarchais met with BF on March 22 and offered to ship 1,000 tons of the supplies to America, but the plan fell through: Beaumarchais to Francy, March 22, 1782, in Jules Marsan, ed., *Beaumarchais et les affaires d'Amérique: Lettres inédites* (Paris, 1919), pp. 28–9. The supplies were replacements for those aboard the ships *Marquis de Lafayette* and *Rusé. Intendant général des armées* Palteau de Veimerange

Fleet, which has long been expected, were arrived, Transports would not be so scarce.[6] Capt. Barry tells me there is Aboundance of Arms & ammunition at Boston, and the Capture of Cornwallis having furnished more, I hope those Articles will not be much wanted; I have also been informed, that the Cargo of Clothing sent by the Ship Marquis de la Fayette, is arrived with you from neutral Ports, & offered at a low Price. If this be true, the unavoidable Delay of the Goods we have here on hand will not on the whole be so prejudicial to our Affairs.— We do not however rely on these Informations, but press continually for the Aid of Government to get them transported safely. Mr. Barclay is still in Holland, endeavouring to ship the unfortunate Purchase left there by Gillon; and if his Ships go safe, you will be furnished from thence with something considerable.

Since my last I have paid in Holland a Number of Bills of Exchange drawn in favour of Mr. Ross amounting to 40,958 banck Florins, and by that Means prevented their Protest. No Demand has been made on me by Mr. Wm. Lee. I do not know where he is; and I think he did so little for the 3000 Guineas he receiv'd, that he may wait without much Inconvenience for the Addition. I have paid Capt. Frey and taken the Receipts you required. In the other Dispositions you have ordered, I shall do the best I can.[7]

Before I was sufficiently assured myself, or could assure Mr. Jay of having herewithal—to assist him in discharging his Acceptations, I heard he had began to suffer some of them to be protested. As soon as I found it was possible for me to help him,

---

finished assembling the replacements by early spring and loaded them on three ships that sailed from Brest at the end of May but were forced into Rochefort: Palteau de Veimerange to BF, Sept. 6, 1782 (APS).

6. A convoy of 150 ships had sailed from Saint Domingue in January under the escort of five French ships of the line. It arrived safely at La Coruña and Ferrol in late March: *Chef d'escadre* chevalier d'Albert Saint-Hypolite to Castries, March 22, 1782, Archives de la Marine B⁴ CXCIII: 192–195; Dull, *French Navy,* pp. 268, 374; Auphan, "Communications," p. 510.

7. For Morris' requests to pay Lee, Ross, and Frey see XXXVI, 155, 194–5, 196–7, 652, 673. On March 10, Ferdinand Grand paid 2,500 *l.t.* to Frey on BF's behalf (XXXVI, 690) and five days later he remitted 91,889 *l.t.* 1 *s.* 6 *d.* to Fizeaux, Grand, & Cie. to discharge bills drawn in favor of Ross: Account XXVII (XXXII, 4).

I wrote to him to draw upon me for the Sum he wanted,[8] being near Thirty Thousand Pounds Sterling, which will put a Stop to those Protestations, and enable him to pay all honourably.

By the News-Papers I send to Mr. Secy. Livingston you will see the Change of Sentiment respecting us in the English Nation. I do not know whether this will diminish your Expence for the coming Campaign, because while they have an Army in our Country, I do not think their proposed Inactivity is to be trusted, tho' it is said that after such Resolutions of Parliament, no Minister will dare to order offensive Operations. Their Papers say that Orders are given both in England and Ireland to stop the Embarkation of the Troops intended for North America; but what I rely on more, is some Information I have just received from Germany,[9] that the March of Recruits there to the Seaside is also countermanded. If from what *it is their Interest to do,* one could conclude *what they will do,* I should imagine that alarmed with the Loss of St. Christopher, they would withdraw their Troops from the Continent in order to defend their remaining Islands.[1] But this Ministry have hitherto so constantly acted contrary to the true Interest of their Nation & so inconsistantly with common Raison & Judgment, that one cannot fairly draw such a Conclusion.

The Goods for replacing the Cargo of the Marquis de La Fayette had been purchased long before we knew that you could have wished it otherwise.[2] I hope the Invoice you sent me of Goods to be bought by Mr. Barclay & Ridley,[3] will be partly rendered unnecessary by the Purchase, because I see no Possibility of paying the Sum, required for the Invoice viz, near Two millions, having received the most explicit & positive Assurances,

---

8. BF's letter is above, March 16, but he had learned of the grant on March 1: XXXVI, 650.

9. Not found.

1. On this very day the new ministry decided to order New York, Charleston, and Savannah evacuated. The troops would be sent to Halifax and the West Indies: Fortescue, *Correspondence of George Third,* V, 435–6; Mackesy, *War for America,* p. 474.

2. See XXXVI, 153–4, 405.

3. These were for the Board of War: XXXVI, 154–5; *Morris Papers,* III, 289–90n.

that more Money than I have mentioned cannot this Year be obtained.

Permit me to hope also and for the same Raison that the Bills you will find yourself obliged to draw on me may not amount to a very large Sum. Hitherto I have accepted & paid all Drafts upon myself, and enabled my Colleagues to discharge those upon them, with Punctuality & Honour, the few abovementioned on Mr. Jay only excepted. I wish to finish this Part of my Emploiment with the Credit I have hitherto supported both for myself and for my Constituants. I must in June next pay M. Beaumarchais near 2,500,000 Livres.[4] I have often been in great Distress & suffered much Anxiety; I still dread at times the same Situation: But your Promise that after this Month no more Bills shall be drawn on me, keeps up my Spirits, and affords me the greatest Situation [Satisfaction?].[5]

I am extreamly pleased with the various prudent Measures you have with so much Industry put in Practice to draw forth our internal Strength, I hope they will be attended with the Success they merit; and I thank you for the Communication.

Our former Friend Mr. Deane has lost himself entirely. He and his Letters are universally condemned. He cannot well return hither, and I think hardly to America. I see no Place for him but England. He continues however to sit croaking at Ghent, chagrin'd, discontented, & dispirited. You will see by the enclosed what Mr. Barclay says of his Accounts.[6] Methinks it would be well to have them examined, and to give Orders for the Payment of what is found justly due to him. Whether the Commission he charges on the Purchases made by Mr. Beaumarchais, comes under that Description I cannot say; the Congress will judge.

I will endeavour to send the Books with the Marquis, who does not go yet for 3 or 4. Weeks.[7] I shall write farther by that

4. Bills of exchange worth 2,400,000 *l.t.* were payable on June 15: XXIX, 707n; XXXVI, 147, 155, 650. Beaumarchais had provided military supplies to the United States on credit: XXII, 454.

5. XXXVI, 140, 146, 155, 561, 673.

6. Barclay to BF, March 23, above.

7. The books presumably are those Morris had requested the previous September: XXXV, 484–5. While awaiting his departure for America, La-

Opportunity. At present I can only add, that I am ever, with the sincerest Esteem, & Respect, Dear Sir, Your &c—

Robt. Morris Esq. Supt. of Finances.

From Michel-Guillaume St. John de Crèvecœur

ALS: American Philosophical Society

Sir   Paris 30th. March 1782.

You'll not think it Improper, I flatter myself, if I beg you'd direct me how to send some letters, either to Philadelphia or to Boston, those Last are for the Honoble. John Hancock;[8] so many have hitherto miscaried for want of care in those in whose hands I had Placed them, that I find myself forced to ask you, what means I shall make use of & whether you'd not permit me to send them to your office, whence in due Time & more safely, they might be conveyed to America; my frequent disappointments on that head are the Cause of my Taking this freedom, which I beg you'd Excuse.

You had great reasons for doubting the other day the Taking of St. Christopher. It was then primature, but now, happily confirmed: Permit me to felicitate you on this Conquest.

I am with unfeigned Respect sir Your very Humble Servant

ST. JEAN DE CREVECŒUR

Hôtel Turgot Isle St. Louis Paris[9]

---

fayette was helping the French government prepare campaign plans. With the advent of serious peace discussions his departure was postponed: Idzerda, *Lafayette Papers*, v, 30–2, 48.

8. Crèvecœur was asking the governor to assist him in sending money to the two children he had left behind in Orange County, N.Y. On April 7, Crèvecœur explained this request in a letter to Caleb Davies of Boston, of whom he asked the same favor. BF, he said, had encouraged him to write Hancock and had himself written to the governor. He enclosed bills of exchange for Davies to use on behalf of his children (Mass. Hist. Soc.). The children, América-Francès (1770–1823) and Philippe-Louis (1774–1850), were living with a family in Boston: Robert de Crèvecœur, *Saint John de Crèvecoeur, sa vie et ses ouvrages (1735–1813)* (Paris, 1883), pp. 56, 85–8, 288; Julia Post Mitchell, *St. Jean de Crèvecoeur* (New York, 1916), pp. 62–4, 121–35, 314–15.

9. The Paris residence of the marquis Turgot, where Crèvecœur stayed

His Excellency Benjamin Franklin

Addressed: A / Son Excellence Benjamin Franklin Ecuyer / Passy

Notation: Crevecœur M. St. Jean de Paris 30 March 1782.

From Silas Deane

ALS: American Philosophical Society

Sir   Ghent March. 30th: 1782

Mr. Barclay who set out on his return to Holland last Monday passed Several Days here in examining my Accompts,[1] & had his powers from Congress authorized him, an end might have been made of my embarrassments, & Complaints on that subject. I gave him duplicates of them, & every explanation which he desired; he promised to remit them to Congress, and to request particular Orders on the subject, it was his Opinion that the Accompts might be easily, and readily closed; if Congress would authorize him, or some other to do it, and that for the satisfaction of all Parties, that in Case any question, or difference should arise on any of the Charges on either side, that the same should be submitted to persons of known Character for their knowledge, and impartiality; I perfectly agreed with him on the subject; and wrote myself at the same Time to Congress praying of them to adopt that, or any other measure equally just, for the decision of this Affair;[2] but as I am apprehensive that Congress may delay from various Causes the coming to any resolution on the subject, and as You are interested in having all the Accts. of Our joint, or separate Transactions closed as speedily as may be, I have taken the Liberty of requesting of You to write to Congress on the subject, and doubt not but Your Letters will have sufficient weight with them to bring this affair to a close in a just

---

on his arrival from Normandy: XXXV, 527; Robert de Crèvecœur, *Crèvecoeur,* pp. 67–8; Mitchell, *Crèvecoeur* (New York, 1916), p. 67.

1. The preceding Monday was March 25. For Barclay's examination see his letter to BF of March 23.

2. Deane's letter was dated March 17: Wharton, *Diplomatic Correspondence,* V, 245.

and equitable way. I am sensible of the multiplicity of important Business on Your hands, and therefore do not expect an Answer, to the long Letter I sent You by Mr. Wilkinson,[3] but hope You will honor Me with a Line, acknowledging the Rect. of this and that if You judge any other method for adjusting those Accts. preferable to that which I have proposed, You will be so kind as to point it out. The Changes which have taken place, within a few Weeks past, at London give Me grounds to hope, that a Peace, is not so distant an Object, as what I lately feared it to be, and makes me more than ever anxious to close those Affairs by which I have suffered so greatly as soon as it is possible, that on so happy an Event, I may not be left still to suffer by the embarrassments, of past Transactions unsettled; but free to repair if possible my losses, which is the only advantage I expect, or wish for personally from Peace. I have the honor to be with the utmost respect sir Your most Obedt & Very huml. servt.   S Deane

his Excelleny B Franklin Esqr.

Notation: Deane, Ghent March 30. 1782

To John Adams   ALS: Massachusetts Historical Society

Sir,   Passy, March 31. 1782.

I received yours of the 10th Instant,[4] and am of Opinion with you, that the English will evacuate New York & Charlestown, as the Troops there, after the late Resolutions of Parliament, must be useless, and are necessary to defend their Remaining Islands where they have not at present more than 3000 Men.[5] The Prudence of this Operation is so obvious, that I think they can hardly miss it: otherwise I own that, considering their Conduct for several Years past, it is not reasoning consequentially, to con-

---

3. William Wilkinson carried Deane's Feb. 1 letter (XXXVI, 507–25) to Edward Bancroft, along with Deane's covering letter giving Bancroft the choice of whether to forward it to BF: XXXVI, 411n; *Deane Papers*, V, 63–4.

4. XXXVI, 679.

5. An underestimate, as the British had 8,756 effectives in the West Indies or en route there in March, 1782: Mackesy, *War for America*, p. 525.

clude they will do a thing because the doing it is required by Common Sense.

Yours of the 26th. is just come to hand. I thank you for the Communication of Digges's Message. He has also sent me a long Letter, with two from Mr Hartley.[6] I shall see Mr. de Vergennes tomorrow, and will acquaint you with everything material that passes on the Subject. But the Ministry by whom Digges pretends to be sent being changed, we shall, by waiting a little, see what Tone will be taken by their Successors. You shall have a Copy of the Instructions by the next Courier: I congratulate you cordially on the Progress you have made among those slow People. Slow, however, as they are, Mr Jay finds his much slower. By an American who goes in about Ten Days to Holland,[7] I shall send you a Packet of Correspondence with Mr Hartley, tho' it amounts to little.

With great Esteem I have the honour to be Your Excellency's most obedient & most humble Servant   B Franklin

To David Hartley

ALS: Historical Society of Pennsylvania; LS:[8] Keya Gallery, New York (1997); copy: William L. Clements Library

Dear Sir,   Passy, March 31. 1782

I have just received your Favours of March 11 & 12. forwarded to me by Mr. Digges, and another of the 21st. per Post.[9] I congratulate you on the returning good Disposition of your Nation towards America, which appears in the Resolutions of Parliamt. that you have sent me: and I hope the Change of your Ministry will be attended with salutary Effects. I continue in the same Sentiments express'd in my former Letters;[1] but as I am but one of five in the Commission, and have no Knowledge of the

6. Digges's letter is above, March 22[–26].

7. Possibly Matthew Ridley, who, according to his journal (Mass. Hist. Soc.), left Paris on May 9 and attempted to call on JA on May 20. Ridley was ill for much of April.

8. In the hand of Moses Young.

9. For the first two see XXXVI, 684–5, 688–9; the latest is above.

1. In his latest statement on the subject, written six weeks earlier (XXXVI, 585), BF had encouraged the British government to make peace proposals.

Sentiments of the others, what has pass'd between us is to be considered merely as private Conversation. The five Persons are Messrs. Adams, Jay, Laurens, Jefferson and myself, and in case of the Death or Absence of any the Remainder have Power to act and conclude.[2] I have not written to Mr Laurens, having constantly expected him here: but shall write to him by next Post; when I shall also write more fully to you, having now only time to add, that I am ever, with great Esteem and Affection, Dear Sir, Your most obedient & most humbl. Servt   B FRANKLIN

D. Hartley Esqr.

Addressed: To / David Hartley Esqr / Golden Square / London

Endorsed: D F Mar 31 1782 / D F Mar 31 1782

To William Hodgson   Copy: William L. Clements Library

Passy, March 31, 1782.

It is long since I have been able to afford myself the pleasure of writing to you;[3] but I have had that of receiving several Letters from you, and I sent you in consequence a credit for 300 £ which I hope you received.[4] I am sorry that you had been obliged to advance: The trouble you so kindly take is sufficient. I just hear from Ireland, that there are 200 of our People, prisoners there, who are destitute of every Necessary, and die daily in numbers.[5] You are about to have a new Ministry, I hear. If a sincere reconciliation is desired, Kindness to the Captives on both sides may promote it greatly. I have no Correspondent in Ireland. Can you put me in a way of sending those poor Men some Relief? And if you think the new Ministry better dispos'd than the last, I wish you would lay before them the slighted proposition I formerly

2. XXXV, 161–5.

3. His last extant letter to Hodgson was written in early January: XXXVI, 389.

4. Hodgson acknowledged it in his letter of March 22, above. His three previous letters explained the difficulties of providing relief to American prisoners of war: XXXVI, 439–41, 605–6, 633–4.

5. See XXXVI, 606–7, as well as Whipple and Lewis' letter of March 24.

sent you, for the Exchange of Prisoners.[6] I see in your News-papers that an Act is passing thro' the House of Commons rela-tive to that Subject. I beg you would send me a Copy of the Bill. Of the Dispositions on your side towards peace or Continuance of War, you must know more than me: I can only assure you of mine to finish this devilish Contest as soon as possible; and I have not lost sight of your request.[7]   B. FRANKLIN.

To Mr. Wm. Hodgson, Merchts., Coleman-Street./

Notation: Passy, March 31, 1782. Copy of a Letter from Doctr. Franklin to Mr. Wm. Hodgson. Recd. 8th. April 1782.

From the Abbé de St. Farre   LS: American Philosophical Society

Monsieur   ce 31 Mars 1782.

M. le chevalier d'uvet de contour officier dans la marine agé de dix-huit a vingt ans est venû me trouver hier, et m'exposer ses malheurs pour m'engager a venir a son secours.[8] Quelqu'in-téressant que soit ce récit et la grande douceur dont il l'accom-pagne, je n'ai pas crû devoir me prêter facilement a ses vües dans la crainte de fournir a sa grande jeunesse des moïens de se per-dre: je ne lui ai point laissé ignorer mes inquiétudes, et il a pensé qu'il les dissiperoit en se réclamant de vous; il ne pouvoit pas en effet me citer d'authorité plus respectable pour moi: vous l'avez envoïé, dit-il, a M. de beaumarchais pour recevoir la gratification que l'on accorde a tous ceux qui sont prisonniers de guerre, et l'absence de M. de beaumarchais pour plusieurs jours le laisse sans ressources. Votre réponse, Monsieur, déterminera ma sen-sibilité, et je me trouverai tres heureux de pouvoir etre de quelqu'utilité a un jeune infortuné avoüé par vous. Si au con-

6. Conveyed by Hodgson nearly four months earlier, his proposal had not received a formal response: XXXVI, 62–3, 278, 440–1; Hodgson to BF, March 22, above.

7. The request was that BF give him advance notice of the probability of peace (which would be useful in speculations on the stock market); BF had agreed to do so: XXXIV, 476–7, 508, 539, 573; XXXV, 46.

8. Two years earlier, BF had received an inquiry about M. de Contour, who claimed to be in the service of the American Navy: XXXII, 49.

traire il se trouve que son histoire est un petit roman, je gemirai pour l'humanité de voir que le vice se trouve avec les années les plus tendres et tous les déhors de la candeur. Je ne gouterai que la satisfaction d'avoir pû vous assurer des sentiments respectueux avec les quels j'ai l'honneur d'etre Monsieur votre tres humble et tres obéïssant serviteur   L'ABBÉ DE ST. FARRE
Prieur de St. Martin[9]

M. franklin.

Notation: L'abbé de St. Favre. 31. mars 1782.

To St. Farre

Copy: Library of Congress

Sir,   Passy, March 31. 1782.

I do not recollect that I have ever known or seen the Person you mention; and it is certain that I never knew or heard that Mr. De Beaumarchais was charged with the Payment of Gratifications to those who had been Prisoners of War or that any such Gratifications were allowed, so that I could not have sent any Person to that Gentleman for such Purpose. I honour the Goodness of your Heart, and I ought not to permit by my Silence your being imposed on by these Deceivers. Success might encourage this young Impostor to rely on such Artifices for a Subsistence; he might by Practice become more expert, and become a Pest to Society. Such Frauds are vastly more pernicious than Simple Theft, for they wrong not only the Person deceived of the Sum obtained, but they create a Diffidence which prevents the relief of Persons whose Misfortunes & Distress are real.[1] I have the honour to be, Sir, &c—

Mr. L'Abbé de St. Favre, Prieur de St. Martin.

La Lettre cy dessus à été envoyée en François

9. Saint-Martin-des-Champs, part of which now houses the Conservatoire des Arts et Métiers at 292 rue Saint-Martin, was a Benedictine priory affiliated with the Abbey of Cluny: Hillairet, *Rues de Paris*, II, 468–70. A contemporary description and brief history of the priory is in Pierre-Thomas-Nicolas Hurtaut, *Dictionnaire historique de la ville de Paris et de ses environs* (4 vols., Paris, 1779), III, 500–3; IV, 155–6.

1. BF had recalled a number of such "frauds" in a recent list: XXXVI, 375–6.

To Henry Wyld

Copy: William L. Clements Library

March 31. 1782.

I have received yours of the 18th. Instant. I omitted answering your former, being informed that your Bill had not been honoured, whence I conceived that you had imposed on me.[2] I am glad to hear that it is otherwise. Since you were here, I have received notice that no more such Passports are to be granted, the Traders having abused them: So that I must renew my first Advice to you and your Friends, not to attempt the Voyage till a peace, which, by the good Disposition that has lately appeared in your Parliament, I hope is not far off. You would in my Opinion hazard too much, and act imprudently by going sooner. When you do go, you may depend on my doing you every Service in my power; being really a Friend and Well-wisher to all honest industrious people, and desirous of promoting their happiness. *From Dr. Francklin. Not signed.*

Mr. Henry Wild, Schoolmaster, at Hatherlow near Manchester.

Notation: March 31. 1782. Copy of a Letter from Docr. Franklin to Mr. Henry Wild. Recd. 8th. April 1782.

From William Royal[3]

ALS: American Philosophical Society

Honour'd Sir   March 31st. 1782

I humble hope your Goodness will excuse the freedom of one who is intirely a Stranger to you, of troubling you with a few lines, tho I have great reasons to believe by my Parents letter to me was inclos'd under Cover of a letter thay sent to your Excellency,[4] that you was no stranger to them I have made bold to write to your Excellency by their desciption of your generous

---

2. XXXVI, 605.

3. Though he spells his name differently, William was the son of the late Joseph Royle (d. 1766) and Rosanna Hunter Royle, and the stepson of John Dixon. Royle and Dixon were successive editors of the *Virginia Gazette* and both known to BF. Dixon had written on the youth's behalf in 1780; see XXXI, 394, and the references cited there.

4. The only extant letter from either of his parents during this period is the one cited above.

Disposition to assist any one that was a Native of america. I have made bold to send you a letter inclose'd to my Parents hoping you will be so generous as to forward the same to them I am the Son of one Mr. Royal Deceas'd, Whose widow married Mr. John Dixon who is now living in Williamsburgh and who i dont [*doubt*] by a letter that I receiv'd a little time ago you was personlly acquainted with. [*Torn:* I m]ake no doubt but you are well acquainted with the Reason of my being in England, which if my Parents have not acquainted you with, I came to St. Thomas, Hospital to be Cut for the stone and as I was in England my Mother Consented I should be sent to my Father in laws own Mother[5] which a bout two Years ago I had the misfortune to lose, which as she was the only friend I had in these parts, I am now in great distress and knows not how to get home, tho my Parents has desir'd me to make Applycation to you but was Intirely ignorant which way I should proseed to get a letter convayd to you untel a friend told me he was sure I might send a letter safe by the Way of Ostend which accordingly I have done, and the letter I have sent to my Parents in Answer to theirs I have left unseald for your Perrusal in case you should dispute the truth of what I have inserted and I hope you will be so kind as to forward the same to my Dear Parents whome I long to be with and dont in the least doubt but I should before now had I had as thay desired but I had not Whearewithal to have Cum to you when I receiv'd thair letter as thay said you would upon their Account let me have what was necessary for the Voyag I have nothing more to add only to this obligation if you should be so very Good as to add one more to one whose Parents I am sencible has the highest veneration and Respects for you so I Conclude Hond. Sir Your most humble Servant[6]   WM ROYAL

Addressed: To / The Right Honourable / Doctor Frankling Minister / Plenipotentiary for the United / American States / at / Paris

Notation: Royal Mr Wm. March 31. 1782.

5. By father-in-law he means stepfather. Dixon's parents lived in Hull: XXXI, 394.

6. The letter he enclosed, no longer with BF's papers, may have been forwarded to Virginia.

From Jean-Jacques Caffiéri ALS: American Philosophical Society

Monsieur   De Paris ce premier Avril 1782
   Unne Maladie et Le mauvais temps m'ont empeches D'avoir
Lhonneur D'aller vous assurer de mes tres humbles Civivilités
et de vous prier de vouloir bien vous resouvenir de moi dans Les
occasions ou vous series charge de La part de La republique
ameriquaine de quelque morçeau de Sculpture soit tombeaux ou
Statue en marbre ou en Bronze, vous aves eû La Bonté de me
promettr de ne pas oublier quand L'occasion s'en presenteroit.[7]
Il n'est pas douteux que La republique voudra Constater par des
Monuments Ses heureux Succés et Les hérauts [héros] qui se sa-
crifies pour La patrie, mes talens vous sont Connus. J'ose esperer
que vous voudres bien me preferer aux propositions que pouroit
vous faire D'autre Sculpteurs.
   Jay Lhonneur D'etre avec respect Monsieur Votre tres humble et tres obeissant Serviteur   Caffieri

Permette je vous presente La Discription de La Sculpture que je
vien de finir pour La vant Scene de La Nouvelle Sale de La
Comedie françoise.[8]

Notation: Caffiery, Paris 1er. avl. 1782.

7. Though he had proposed a monument to Pulaski two years earlier, the
sculptor had not received any commissions from the Americans since completing the marble monument to Gen. Montgomery and the terra-cotta bust
of BF in 1777: XXIV, 160n, 161n; XXV, 266–7; XXXII, 474.
   8. Caffiéri enclosed a description of the group just completed: four cary-
atids in the form of sirens and tritons supporting a cornice where Apollo's
lyre is held up by Melpomene and Thalia. The Théâtre François (now the
Ódéon), built for the *comédiens français* at the King's direction near the Luxembourg, opened its doors the following week, on April 9: *Jour. de Paris,* issues of April 7, 8, 9, and 10.

From Thomas Mumford[9]

ALS: American Philosophical Society

Sir   Norwich 1st. April 1782

The Conduct of our Late intimate freind Silas Deane Esqr. respecting these States & our worthy allies, Convinces me he must have Left France some time since, this Leaves my agreeable nephew Mr. Gurdon S. Mumford destitute of the advice & assistance his father[1] (my only Brother) & friends depended on to fix & Continue him in business during his Minority, I am among the number of mr. Deans Old freinds to whom he has wrote Largely on Politicks, his Last to me was 24th. Septemr. 1781[2] in which he informs me he had some months before sent his Son to the netherlands, & shou'd *then* go to him in a few days, he further informs me he advised my kinsman's remaining with you untill he had inteligence from his father & me (the reason why I am Consulted respecting my nephew who has a father is I am fond of him & have pleasure in giving him aid,) as youth always needs advice, *at Least* I shall Consider my Self under particular Obligation to you while you Continue to extend yours to him, who will need it more now *Mr. Deane* his former patern has withdrawn himself than before, he shall have remittance as often as are necessary, have wrote my nephew if he inclines to spend a Year or Two at Amsterdam in a good Compting House to perfect him in the method of doing Large business I will introduce him to my friends Messrs. John De Neufville & Son,[3] your advice & assistance to my nephew as before requested (to whom please deliver the inclos'd) will Lay the greatest Obliga-

9. The Conn. merchant and shipowner who was supervising his nephew's education: XXII, 277n; XXXIV, 449–50.

1. David Mumford (1731–1807): XXXIV, 449, 452–3; James G. Mumford, *Mumford Memoirs . . .* (Boston, 1900), pp. 129, 178.

2. Livingston had forwarded BF a copy of this letter in January: XXXVI, 468n.

3. In fact, Neufville & fils had already informed Deane that they would take Gurdon, but the youth preferred a position with JW. He left BF's household in January or February: XXXVI, 331n; WTF to JW, Dec. 19, 1781 (Library of Congress).

tion on him who is with perfect esteem Sir Your Excellency's most Obedt. & very Huml servt. THOS. MUMFORD

His Excellency Benjamin Franklin Esqr

Addressed: His Excellency Benjamin Franklin Esquire / at / Passa / near / Paris

Notation: Tho: Mumford 1st. April 1782.

From James Searle[4]

AL: American Philosophical Society

Hotel de suede Rue de l'Universite F.S.G.[5]

Monday Evening 1st. of april 1782

Mr. Searle's respectfull compliments to Doctor Franklin & begs leave to inform him that he means to Leave Paris for Nantes on Thursday. He requests Therefore That Doctor Franklin woud be pleased to order the necessary passports to be made out for Mr. Searle & one Domestique for Nantes which place Mr. S will first go to.[6]

Mr. Searle will have the honour of waiting on Dor. Franklin before his departure.

Addressed: A Monsieur / Monsieur Franklin / A Passy

Notation: Searle 1st. april 1782.

---

4. This is the last extant letter from Searle, who was returning to America after an unsuccessful mission to obtain a loan for Pennsylvania (XXXIII, 63n). He arrived in June: William B. Reed, *Life and Correspondence of Joseph Reed* . . . (2 vols., Philadelphia, 1847), II, 464.

5. Faubourg Saint-Germain.

6. On April 3, BF granted Searle a passport for Nantes and Bordeaux: XXXVI, 379.

To the Marquis de Castries

LS:[7] William L. Clements Library; copy: Library of Congress

Sir, Passy, April 2d. 1782

I received the Letter your Excellency did me the honour of writing to me the 31st of March, relating to Messrs. *Agnew Father & Son*, and *Capt Parker*,[8] Englishmen taken Prisoners in America & brought to France. I know nothing of those Persons or of the Circumstances that might induce the Delegates of Virginia to desire their Detention, no Account of them from that State being come to my Hands; nor have I received any Orders from the Congress concerning them. I therefore cannot properly make any Oposition to their being permitted to reside at Caen on their Parole of Honour, or to ther being exchanged in pursuance of the Cartel, as his Majesty in his Wisdom shall think proper to direct.

I am with Respect, Sir, Your Excellency's most obedient & most humble Servant, B Franklin

His Exy, the Marqs. de Castries.

To George Washington

LS[9] and two copies: Library of Congress

Sir, Passy, April 2. 1782.

I received duly the Honour of your Letter accompanying the Capitulation of Gen. Cornwallis.[1] All the World agree that no Expedition was ever better plann'd or better executed. It has made a great Addition to the military Reputation you had already acquired, and brightens the Glory that surrounds your Name and that must accompany it to our latest Posterity. No

---

7. In WTF's hand.

8. Castries' letter is missing. Loyalists John Agnew, a chaplain, Capt. Stair Agnew, an engineer, and Capt. James Parker were captured aboard H.M.S. *Romulus* in February, 1781 (see XXXIV, 554n), and at this time were imprisoned in Saint Malo: Evan Nepean to BF(?), Nov. 23, 1782 (APS); Sabine, *Loyalists*, I, 154–5; II, 148.

9. In L'Air de Lamotte's hand, except for the last eight words of the complimentary close, which are in BF's hand.

1. XXXV, 637–8.

News could possibly make me more happy. The Infant Hercules has now strangled the two Serpents that attack'd him in his Cradle,[2] and I trust his future History will be answerable. This will be presented to you by the Count de Segur. He is Son of the Marquis de Segur Minister of War, and our very good Friend. But I need not claim your Regards to the young Gentleman on that Score; his amiable personal Qualities, his very sensible Conversation and his Zeal for the Cause of Liberty will obtain & secure your Esteem, and be a better Recommendation than any I can give him.[3]

The English seem not to know either how to continue the War, or to make Peace with us. Instead of entring into a regular Treaty, for putting an End to a Contest they are tired of, they have voted in Parliament that the Recovery of America by Force is impracticable, that an offensive War against us ought not to be continued, and that whoever advises it shall be deemed an Enemy to his Country.

Thus the Garrisons of New York and Charlestown, if continued there, must sit still, being only allowed to defend themselves. The Ministry not understanding or approving this making of Peaces by halves, have quitted their Places, but we have no certain Account here who is to succeed them, so that the Measures likely to be taken are yet uncertain: probably we shall know something of them before the Marquis de la Fayette takes his Departure. There are Grounds for good Hopes however, but I think we should not therefore relax in our Preparations for a vigorous

2. The two serpents were the armies of Burgoyne and Cornwallis. BF had used the comparison before: XXXVI, 115, 454, 644.

3. Louis-Philippe, comte de Ségur (1753–1830), enjoyed a distinguished career as soldier, diplomat, writer, and, under Napoleon, senator and Grand Master of Ceremonies: Bodinier, *Dictionnaire;* Harold Nicolson, *The Age of Reason: the Eighteenth Century* (Garden City, N.Y., 1960), pp. 36–9. Having recently become *colonel en second* of the Soissonnais Regiment, which was with Rochambeau's army, he finally received his father's permission to go to America. He traveled to Brest in early April, embarked on the frigate *Gloire,* and reached Philadelphia in September: Rice and Brown, eds., *Rochambeau's Army,* I, 79–80, 327; Louis-Philippe, comte de Ségur, *Mémoires ou souvenirs et anecdotes* (3 vols., Paris, 1827), I, 286–336. Washington greeted him warmly, praising Louis XVI, Rochambeau and his army, and Ségur's father: Ségur, *Mémoires,* I, 376–7.

Campaign, as that Nation is subject to sudden Fluctuations; and tho' somewhat humiliated at present, a little Success in the West Indies may dissipate their present Fears, recal their natural Insolence, and occasion the Interruption of Negociation & a Continuance of the War. We have great Stores purchased here for the use of your Army, which will be sent as soon as Transports can be procured for them to go under good Convoy.

My best Wishes always have and always will attend you, being with the greatest and most sincere Esteem & Respect, Sir, Your Excellency's most obedient and most humble Servant

B FRANKLIN

His Exy. Genl. Washington

Endorsed: Passy April 2d. 1782 from Doctr Franklin Comte de Segur Ansd. 18th Octo.

Officers of the Admiralty of Guadeloupe to the American Peace Commissioners

LS: American Philosophical Society

Messieurs,   à la Basseterre Guadeloupe Le 3. Avril 1782.

En conformité des ordres du Roi, les Officiers de l'Amirauté de la Guadeloupe ont l'honneur d'adresser à Vos Excellences, deux copies de procedures instruites au sujet des prises amenées à la Guadeloupe par des corsaires Americains.[4]

Nous Sommes avec respect, Messieurs, de Vos Excellences, Les très-humbles & très-obéissans Serviteurs

SALMON
BATRIAT
[?] DUPUCH Gfr.

MM. les Députés des Etats unis de l'Amerique septentrionalle à Paris.

Notation: Salimon 3. avl. 1782

4. The enclosures have not been found, but they may have related to Benjamin Putnam's claims to prizes brought into Guadeloupe. See our annotation to Putnam to BF, June 13.

From Christian Schneider[5]

ALS: American Philosophical Society, Historical Society of Pennsylvania

Sir, Germantown April 3th. 1782

Your Excellency having been pleased, to advise the Widow Anne Catharine Hacklin at Ebingen in the Dukedom of Würtenberg, that I should pay a certain Sum of money, due from me as Administrator to said Widow, into the hands of Your Excellency's Son-in-law Mr. Richard Bache at Philadelphia, I have done according to Your Excellency's Advise, have paid 200 pounds in specie to Mr. Richard Bache, and have received four Receipts of same Tenor and Date, of which, I take the Liberty to inclose No: 2. in this Letter.[6] And having no Oportunity to acquaint said Anne Catharine Hacklin of my procedings, I humbly beseech Your Excellency, to forward the inclosed Letter to said Widow Hacklin at Ebingen in the Dukedom of Würtenberg. I am Your Excellency's most humble and most obedient Servant

CHRISTIAN SCHNEIDER.

Notation: Schneider Christian 3 apl. 1782.

5. The brother-in-law of a woman whose case was first presented by M. Auer in 1779: XXX, 189–90. In that letter, written in German, Auer spelled her name "Höklin." In a subsequent letter (summarized in XXX, 190n) he spelled it "Höklerin." Between those German letters, the translations of them made for BF, and contemporary misreadings of those documents, her name has appeared in a variety of ways: *ibid.* and XXXV, 274–5, 280. "Höklin" is the variation most similar to her brother-in-law's anglicized spelling in the present letter ("Hacklin").

6. Höklin's son Frederick, who died in 1776, had saved this sum while working as a tanner for Schneider. BF had suggested that if Schneider remitted the sum to RB, BF would arrange for payment to the mother in Ebingen; see the letters cited above. RB's signed receipt, marked by Schneider "No: 2.", attests that on April 2 he received £200, equivalent to 1,200 guilders, for the widow. (A copy of that receipt, in an unknown hand, is also at the APS.)

From Edmund Clegg

ALS: American Philosophical Society

No 2 Wilks Street Spitalfields London Apr. 4: 1782

Highly respected Sir,

In the beginning of last Jany. Mr Henry Wyld from the Neighbourhood of Manchester waited upon you, respecting the emigration of himself, and a Number of his friends to the State of Pensilvania; at the same time he presented a Note from me, design'd to aid his introduction to You.[7]

We are all getting ready as fast as Possible, and purpose to go for Liverpool about the 20th of next Month in order to proceed according to your directions—and they write me, to request the Promised Protections may be sent to my care with all convenient speed for the Persons Named in their Proposals. Also for Myself and two sons—John 21 Years & Richard 19 Years of Age.— Another for John Billington and Ann His Wife with a child of 2 Years old— If it be in due order about 10 more not fill'd up for Persons, who are as yet uncertain, as to taking this Opportunity of going with us.

We are amply provided with all kinds of Models for the perfecting of our Purpose when we arrive at the much Longed for Country— Which if it please God to grant, in his good Providence— We have not the least doubt of Joining all the Manufactories of Spitalfields & Manchester together, in the most Perfect manner, as far as circumstances will admitt.

It will be our highest Worldly Glory to contribute all we are able to the internal riches of a rising Empire, that expected Prosperity animates our minds more than Private advantage.

I am greatly at a loss for the knowledge of the dift. kinds of Silks Produced in N. America & the Prices they are respectively worth in that Country I beg that information from you with samples—for I can get no acct here but what is very contradictory.

I should have wrote, on Mr Wylds return, but delay'd in hopes of being able to wait upon you myself— For I own I am affraid of Speaking my mind by Letter— But as the undertaking is of such extent I am very anxious that nothing be omitted.

If you have a trusty friend here, to whom I might fully open

---

7. XXXVI, 299.

my mind, I beg to have us brot together for there are very many things, which I'm affraid to mention by Letter, which I wish you to be well acquainted with.

It is my wish, if you Judge it right to take some Chains of Silk Handkercheifs that is Webbs unwoven and Shute, or Weft for them ready Prepared so as to be able at our Arrival to go to Work without loss of time, but in this I wait to be govern'd by your direction.

I have my fears respecting that part of our Utencils called Reeds being to be got in that Country, that may be fine enough for the Silk business, If that was known to be the Case we would try to get some ready made ones over with us—but the Laws make it very dangerous to attempt such a thing— The Company have wrote me by all means to see Mr Laurens, I have applied at Mr Mannings but have not seen him as he was at that time gone out of Town.

You may be assured Sir that a Person of Your eminence & Political principals stands very high in our esteem and if the time should ever arrive that we may have your Visits to see our Works in the much desired Country we shall much rejoice— In the mean time hope, thro' Your recommendations to meet with that Countenance which We shall endeavour to merit— Therefore entreat Your Letters for that Purpose— Mr Wyld has not in the course of his correspondance, told me wether you knew the Precise time fix'd for our setting out. But the Change of Men & We hope of Measures in this Government make us wish to be gone sooner than the 20th of May if it can be done. Please therefore to expedite all your directions to me as soon as Possible. As Mr Hodson very kindly takes the sending of this under his care I am more easy about its coming safe— I should hope he will not take it amiss if you return Your ansr by the same Channel of conveyance— Mr Wyld told me you would send a Special Messenger over when all things were ready— My Country frds have sold the Cattle & are making a full end of their affairs, and it is our earnest wish that we may not have to wait long for the Ship— I am With the highest esteem Your Excellencys most obedient & very Humble servant   EDMUND CLEGG

P.S. If we arrive Safe on the Continent a great Number more of usefull hands intend to follow us—and we have hitherto none but Religious, Sober Moral Persons

His Excellency B Franklin LLD &c &c

Addressed: A / Monsuer á / Monsr Franklin / Passi

Notation: Edmund Clegg

From Jonathan Williams, Jr.

ALS: American Philosophical Society; copy: Yale University Library

Dear & hond sir.   Nantes April. 4 1782

The object of the Present is to inform you that the ship The Count de Grasse belonging to Newbury has arrived here from Guadaloupe with 300 hhds of Sugar, & a prise taken on the Coast bound from Dartmouth in England to Newfoundland; The Ship & Prise I understand are to my Address but as the Captain is not yet up I am not able to give Particulars. I have however placed in Prison 12 Prisoners at the Expence of the United States, & beg you in Course to give Orders for their subsistence. There are a number (I suppose about a dozen) of other Prisoners who have been laying near 12 Months in Prison here, as this is a continual Charge on the States it may be well to exchange them.

By the Commercial Regulations of France Foreign ships are subject to a *freight Duty* on their Tonnage when bringing Goods from one part of the french Dominions to another. The spirit of this Law is the same with the English Navigation Act, to preserve the Carrying Trade to themselves. But in Consequence of our alliance & the real incapacity of France to furnish ships enough to bring home all the produce of their Islands (which are much increased since the War) I obtained an exemption, when the Aurora arrived at L'Orient to my Address from St Domingo,[8] I shall apply for a like Exemption for the Count de Grasse & beg leave

---

8. BF supported JW's application for this exemption in early 1781: XXXIV, 348, 526.

to claim your support to my sollicitation; The Court I am sure will see the National Interest too clearly to refuse it.

I am as ever with the highest Respect Your most dutifull & Affectionate   J WILLIAMS J

Please to read the inclosed Note.

[*On a separate sheet:*] I hear Mr. Jay has been obliged for want of Cash to suffer the Bills he had accepted to be protested for non Payment—is it true?

Addressed: Doctor Franklin.

Notations: J. Williams— April 4. 1782. / [*in William Temple Franklin's hand:*] Ansd

To David Hartley   Copy: Library of Congress[9]

My dear Friend,   Passy, April 5. 1782.

I wrote a few Lines to you the 31st. past, and promised to write more fully. On pursuing again your Letters of the 11th. 12th. & 21st. I do not find any Notice taken of one from me dated Feby. 16. I therefore now send you a Copy made from it in the Press.[1] The uncertainty of safe Transmission discourages a free Communication of Sentiments on these important Affairs; but the Inutility of Discussion between Persons, one of whom is not authoris'd but in Conjunction with others, and the other not authoris'd at all, as well as the obvious Inconveniences that may attend such previous handling of Points that are to be considered when we come to treat regularly; are with me a still more effectual Discouragement, and determine me to waive that Part of Correspondence. As to Digges I have no Confidence in him, nor

---

9. A substantial extract, made by Hartley, is among the Shelburne papers at the William L. Clements Library. Marked "From Dr Franklin to D H", it begins "You justly observe, in yours of the 12th." and stops one sentence short of the end.

1. The press copy is missing. In this letter (XXXVI, 583–5), BF discouraged Hartley from hoping the United States would treat for peace separately from France.

in any thing he says or may say of his being sent by Ministers. Nor will I have any Communication with him, except in receiving & considering the Justification of himself which he pretends he shall be able to make and intends for his excessive Drafts on me on Account of the Relief I ordered to the Prisoners, and his Embezzlement of the Money. You justly observe, in yours of the 12th. that "the first object is to procure a Meeting of qualified and authorized Persons" and that you "understand the Ministry will be ready to proceed towards opening a Negociation as soon as the Bill shall pass, and therefore it is necessary to consult of Time and Place, and Manner and Persons on each Side."[2] If the new have the same Intentions, & desire a general Peace, they may easily discharge Mr. Laurens from those Engagements that make his acting in the Commission improper; and except Mr. Jefferson, who remains in America, and is not expected here, we the Commissioners of Congress can be easily got together; ready to meet yours at such Place as shall be agreed to by all Powers at War, in Order to form the Treaty. God grant that there may be Wisdom enough assembled, to make if possible a Peace that shall be perpetual, and that the Idea of any Nations being natural Enemies to each other may be abolished, for the honour of Human Nature.

With regard to those who may be commissioned from your Government, whatever personal Preferences I may conceive in my own Mind, it cannot become me to express them. I only wish for wise and honest Men. With such a Peace may be speedily concluded. With contentious Wranglers the Negociation may be drawn into length & finally frustrated.

I am pleased to see in the Votes & parliamentary Speeches, and in your public Papers that in mentioning America, the Word *Reconciliation* is often used.[3] It certainly means more than a mere Peace. It is a sweet Expression. Resolve in your Mind, my dear Friend, the means of bringing about this *Reconciliation*. When you consider the Injustice of your War with us, and the barbarous manner in which it has been carried on, the many suffer-

2. XXXVI, 689. Hartley's extract here contains a phrase missing from the copy: "This you wrote while the old ministry existed;".
3. See, for example, XXXVI, 622n.

ing Families among us from your Burnings of Towns Scalpings by Savages &c. &c. will it not appear to you, that tho' a Cessation of the War may be a Peace, it may not be a Reconciliation? Will not some voluntary Acts of Justice and even of Kindness on your Part, have excellent Effects towards producing such a Reconciliation? Can you not find means of reparing in some Degree those Injuries? You have in England and Ireland twelve Hundred of our People Prisoners, who have for Years bravely suffered all the Hardships of that Confinement rather than enter into your Service to fight against their Country. Methinks you ought to glory in Descendants of such Virtue. What if you were to begin your Measures of Reconciliation by setting them at Liberty? I know it would procure for you the Liberty of an equal Number of your People, even without a previous Stipulation; and the Confidence in our Equity with the apparent Good Will in the Action would give very good Impressions of your Change of Disposition towards us. Perhaps you have no Knowledge of the Opinions lately conceived of your King and Country in America, the enclos'd Copy of a Letter[4] may make you a little acquainted with them, & convince you how impossible must be every Project of Bringing us again under the Domination of such a Sovereign. With great Esteem, I am, Dear Sir, Your most obedient & most humble Servant.

Mr. Hartley.

To the Chevalier de Chastellux[5]

LS:[6] private collection (1985); copy: Library of Congress

Dear Sir,   Passy, April 6. 1782.

It gave me great Pleasure to hear by the Officers returned last Winter from your Army, that you continued in good Health.

---

4. Not found. It is possible that BF enclosed a manuscript version of the fictitious letter from John Paul Jones which he later printed in his "Supplement to the Boston Independent Chronicle": below, [before April 22].

5. BF had given Chastellux letters of recommendation when the chevalier left France to serve with Rochambeau: XXXII, 135, 136.

6. In the hand of L'Air de Lamotte.

You will see by the Public Papers, that the English begin to be weary of the War, and they have reason; having suffered many Losses, having four Nations of Enemies upon their Hands, few Men to spare, little Money left, and very bad Heads. The latter they have lately changed. As yet we know not what Measures their new Ministry will take. People generally think they will be employ'd by the King to extricate him from his present Difficulties by obtaining a Peace, and that then he will kick them out again, they being all Men that he abominates, and who have been forced upon him by the Parliament.

The Commons have already made a Sort of half Peace with us Americans, by forbidding the Troops on the Continent to act offensively; and by a new Law they have impower'd the King to compleat it. As yet I hear nothing of the Terms they mean to propose; indeed they have hardly had time to form them. I know they wish to detach us from France; but that is impossible.

I congratulate you on the Success of your last glorious Campaign. Establishing the Liberties of America will not only make the People happy, but will have some Effect in diminishing the Misery of those who in the other parts of the World groan under Despotism, by rendering it more circumspect, and inducing it to govern with a lighter hand. A Philosopher endow'd with those strong Sentiments of Humanity that are manifested in your excellent Writings, must enjoy great Satisfaction in having contributed so extensively by his Sword as well as by his Pen to the *Felicité Publique.*[7]

M. Le Comte de Segur has desired of me a Line of Recommendation to you. I consider his Request rather as a Compliment to me, than as asking what may be of use to him; Since I find that all who know him here esteem & love him, and he is certainly not unknown to you.[8]

7. An allusion to Chastellux's *De la félicité publique,* the most important of his philosophical writings and the work which earned him membership in the Académie française: XXI, 505n; XXXIV, 333n; Chastellux, *Travels in North America in the Years 1780, 1781 and 1782,* ed. and trans. Howard C. Rice, Jr. (2 vols., Chapel Hill, N.C., 1963), I, 8–14.

8. Chastellux was a close relative of the comte's and an intimate friend of his father's: Louis-Philippe, comte de Ségur, *Mémoires ou souvenirs et anecdotes* (3 vols., Paris, 1827), I, 368–72.

Dare I confess to you that I am your Rival with Madame G.?[9] I need not tell you that I am not a dangerous one. I perceive that She loves you very much; and so does, Dear Sir, Your most obedient and most humble Servant   B FRANKLIN

Mr. Chevalier de Chatellux

Franklin: Account of Living Toads Found Enclosed in Limestone[1]

AD: Académie royale des sciences; copy: Library of Congress

In submitting the following report to the Académie des sciences, Franklin joined a long tradition of people who had marveled over the improbable discovery of toads living in niches in solid rock or in the middle of tree trunks. The *Annual Register* for 1761 published a survey of some of this literature, including translations of two accounts published by the Académie des sciences in 1719 and 1731 of live toads discovered in the trunks of mid-sized trees.[2] The author of the survey also alluded to several accounts of toads living in stone formations that had been reported by the ancient Greeks. Some of these reports he discounted as specious; others he was hard-pressed to explain, except by speculating that eggs must have been deposited in the crevices of saplings and somehow managed to derive sustenance from the moisture in the niches they created.[3] Dr. Charles Leigh in *The Natural History of Lancashire* . . . (Oxford, 1700), and other early British naturalists, also reported having seen living toads emerge from cells in seemingly solid rock.[4] In Hebron, Connecticut, a similar incident was described in 1770 by S. A. Peters. After detonating a large

9. The comtesse de Golowkin, whose correspondence with BF reflects concern for her *ami intime* as well as affection for her *cher papa*. See, for example, her earliest letters: XXXIV, 234–7, 331–2, 343–5.
1. La Rochefoucauld read this account to the Academy of Sciences at its meeting of April 20: *procés verbaux* for 1782.
2. We have not been able to find these reports in the Academy's memoirs.
3. *The Annual Register, or a View of the History, Politicks, and Literature, of the Year 1761* (London, 1762), pp. 82–3, second pagination.
4. Their findings are quoted in *The Lying Stones of Dr. Johann Bartholomew Adam Beringer* . . . , trans. and annotated by Melvin E. Jahn and Daniel J. Woolf (Berkeley and Los Angeles, 1963), pp. 180, 200.

rock on his property, he discovered a frog living in a small cavity laid open by the explosion. The cavity appeared to have been accessible only by a small crevice as wide as a knitting needle. Peters' letter was later forwarded to Thomas Jefferson, who submitted it to the American Philosophical Society.[5]

[April 6, 1782]

At Passy near Paris, April 6, 1782. being with Mr de Chaumont, viewing his Quarry, he mention'd to me that the Workmen had found a living Toad shut up in the Stone. On questioning one of them he told us they had found four in different Cells which had no Communication: That they were very lively and active when set at Liberty: That there was in each Cell some loose soft yellowish Earth, which appeared to be very moist. We ask'd if he could show us the Parts of the Stone that form'd the Cells; he said no, for they were thrown among the rest of what was dug out, and he knew not where to find them. We asked if there appear'd any Opening by which the Animal might enter? He said no, not the least. We ask'd if in the Course of his Business as a Labourer in Quarries he had often met with the Like? He said never before. We ask'd if he could show us the Toads? He said he had thrown two of them up on a higher Part of the Quarry, but knew not what became of the others. He then came up to the place where he had thrown the Two, and finding them, he took them by the foot and threw them up to us, upon the Ground where we Stood. One of them was quite dead; and appeared very lean: the other was plump and still living. The Part of the Rock in which they were found is at least 15 feet below the Surface, and is a kind of Limestone. A Part of it is fill'd with ancient Sea Shells, and other marine Substances. If these Animals have remained in that Confinement since the Formation of the Rock, they are probably some thousands of Years old. We have put them in Spirits of Wine to preserve their Bodies a little longer. The Workmen have promis'd to call us if they meet with any more that we may examine their Situation. Before a suitable Bottle could be found to receive them, that which was living when

5. The letter is quoted in Murphy D. Smith, *A Museum: the History of the Cabinet of Curiosities of the American Philosophical Society* (Philadelphia, 1996), pp. 203–4.

we first had them, appear'd to be quite dead and motionless; but being in the Bottle, and the Spirits pour'd over them, he flounc'd about in it very vigorously for Two or Three Minutes, and then expired.[6]

It is observed that Animals who perspire but little can live long without Food; such as Tortises whose Flesh is cover'd with a thick Shell, and Snakes who are cover'd with Scales which are of so close a Substance as scarcely to admit the Passage of perspirable Vapour thro' them. Animals that have open Pores all over the Surface of their Bodies, and live in Air which takes off continually the perspirable Part of their Substance, naturally require a continual Supply of Food to maintain their Bulk. Toads shut up in solid Stone which prevents their losing anything of their Substance, may perhaps for that reason need no Supply, and being guarded against all Accidents, and all the Inclemencies of the Air and Changes of the Seasons, are it seems Subject to no Diseases and become as it were immortal.[7]

6. BF related this incident to William Thornton in 1784, when the young medical student visited Passy. As Thornton heard the story, WTF and Bancroft were also present at the quarry, and Bancroft quipped that the newly revived toad "was in high spirits." BF evidently saved the preserved toads, which he showed to Thornton: Thornton Papers, folio 3060, Library of Congress. Thornton also described a session of the Society of Natural Historians at the University of Edinburgh, at which a number of similar incidents were related: a living toad found in a slab of marble and in the cornerstone of a 300-year-old building. *Ibid.*, folio 3061.

7. According to WTF, BF annexed to his retained copy of this report a copy of a letter from Sir John Pringle to Alexander Small dated April 25, 1780. It reported that certain large moths known as mosquito hawks survived 71 days after Pringle had removed their heads with a scissors: WTF, *Memoirs*, III, 450–1.

From Daniele Andrea Delfino[8]

AL: American Philosophical Society

Paris. ce 6me. avril 1782./.

L'Accademie des Sciences et arts de Padoüe D'esiroit ajouter Le nom de Monsieur franklin aux noms qui honorent déja La Liste des membres dont elle est composée.[9] Le chevalier Delfino Ambassadeur de Venise Seroit bien flatté de pouvoir donner cette satisfaction à un corps n'aissant, qui est specialment protegé par Le Gouvernement.[1] Il Joint pour cela ses instances á celles des accademiciens, et il á L'honneur de assurer Monsr. franklin de la plus sincére Consideration./.

Notation: Mr. Delfino Paris 6. Avril 1782.

To Delfino

Copy: Library of Congress

[between April 6 and 26, 1782][2]
Mr. Franklin is extreamly sensible of the honour done him by the Academy of Siences and Arts at Padua in electing him one of

---

8. Delfino, or Dolfin (1748–1798), served as Venetian ambassador to the French court from December, 1780, through the end of 1785. He had previously introduced the Pennsylvania fireplace to Venice, and his diplomatic dispatches reflect his continued admiration for BF: *Repertorium der diplomatischen Vertreter,* III, 463; Alberto M. Ghisalberti *et al.,* eds., *Dizionario biografico degli Italiani* (53 vols. to date, Rome, 1960–); Antonio Pace, *Benjamin Franklin and Italy* (Philadelphia, 1958), pp. 77, 87, 113–14, 122.

9. The certificate announcing BF's election to the Academy was signed by its principal officers on Dec. 20, 1781: XXXVI, 273. Also elected at Paris were d'Alembert, Lalande, the abbés Mably and Arnaud, Condorcet, Marmontel, Duhamel du Monceau, Macquer, and Antoine Louis: *Courier de l'Europe,* XI (1782), 297–8.

1. The Academy, founded in 1778 or 1779, was about to publish its first volume of proceedings: *Dizionario biografico,* XVI, 554; XXIV, 224; *Courier de l'Europe,* XI (1782), 298. Melchior Cesarotti, the Academy's secretary, published an account of the public sessions for the years 1780–98: *Relazioni accademiche* (2 vols., Pisa, 1803). See also Pace, *Franklin and Italy,* p. 331.

2. The dates on which Delfino notified BF of his election (above) and BF wrote to the president of the Academy, Caldani (below).

their Numbers, and of the very obliging Manner in which Mr. l'Ambassador de Venise has been pleased to communicate to him the notice of that election. Mr. Franklin will himself make his Acknowledgements to the Academy in a Letter, and begs M. L'Ambassador to be assured of his great & sincere Respect.

La lettre cy dessus a été envoyé en François.

Chevalier Delfino.

From the Earl of Shelburne

Copy:[3] Library of Congress; ALS (draft): Public Record Office; transcripts: Massachusetts Historical Society, National Archives

Under the previous division of responsibilities among three secretaries of state, the British government had assigned American affairs to the secretary of state for the American colonies. With the abolition of that post,[4] a struggle for control of negotiations with the American peace commissioners ensued between the Earl of Shelburne, the newly named secretary of state for the home department, and Charles James Fox, the newly named secretary of state for foreign affairs.[5] Not only were the two men bitter personal rivals, but also they held vastly different goals for negotiations with the Americans. Shelburne wished to maintain some formal connection between Great Britain and America. Fox, like Prime Minister Rockingham, was prepared to concede American independence in order to obtain a separate peace with them. This would force France, Spain, and the Netherlands to make peace on British terms. It would also eliminate Shelburne's claims as home secretary to deal with the Americans and consolidate all the various

---

3. The copy and both transcripts are in BF's journal of the peace negotiations. BF gave the recipient's copy of the letter to Vergennes, who prepared a French translation: Doniol, *Histoire*, V, 81. We note below major changes from the draft.

4. Explained in our annotation of BF to Shelburne, March 22, to which this is the reply.

5. George III, ultimately responsible for foreign policy, recognized Shelburne's authority over the American negotiations, but did not cut off the subsequent struggle. See Fortescue, *Correspondence of George Third*, V, 445.

peace negotiations in Fox's hands.[6] Franklin's letter of March 22 encouraged Shelburne's hopes and gave him an excuse to send to Passy a representative, the wealthy merchant and landowner Richard Oswald, whom he here introduces.[7] Fox named his own representative to negotiate with the French, his friend Thomas Grenville, and gave him a letter of introduction to Franklin as well (below, May 1). Grenville did not reach Paris, however, until May 7, more than three weeks after Oswald's arrival.[8] In spite of Oswald's head start, the competition between Shelburne and Fox over the American negotiations was far from resolved.

Dear Sir   London 6th. April 1782

I have been favour'd with your Letter, and am much oblig'd by your remembrance. I find myself return'd nearly to the same Situation, which you remember me to have occupied nineteen years ago, and should be very glad to talk to you as I did then, and afterwards in 1767,[9] upon the means of promoting the Happiness of Mankind, a Subject much more agreeable to my Nature, than the best concerted Plans for spreading Misery and Devastation. I have had a high Opinion of the Compass of your Mind and of your Foresight. I have often been beholden to both and shall be glad to be so again, as far as is Compatible with your Situation. Your Letter discovering the same disposition has made

6. H. M. Scott, *British Foreign Policy in the Age of the American Revolution* (Oxford, 1990), p. 320; Andrew Stockley, *Britain and France at the Birth of America: the European Powers and the Peace Negotiations of 1782–1783* (Exeter, 2001), p. 41; Esmond Wright, "The British Objectives, 1780–1783: 'If Not Dominion Then Trade,'" in Hoffman and Albert, eds., *Peace and the Peacemakers,* pp. 12–13; Harlow, *Second British Empire,* I, 227–9, 237.

7. Richard Oswald (1705–1784) had helped Henry Laurens raise bail: XXXVI, 373n; *DNB;* Price, *France and the Chesapeake,* II, 1048–9; Fitzmaurice, *Life of Shelburne,* II, 119n.

8. Harlow, *Second British Empire,* I, 247–52. Grenville (1755–1846) at present was a member of Parliament, representing Buckinghamshire: Namier and Brooke, *House of Commons,* II, 548. His lengthy future career included a brief tenure as first lord of the Admiralty: *DNB.*

9. Shelburne had been a leading peace advocate at the end of the last war and on Dec. 9, 1762, had introduced the motion approving the preliminaries of peace. He entered the cabinet in 1763 as president of the Board of Trade: X, 348n; *DNB,* under Petty. In 1767, BF had conferred on American affairs with Shelburne, by then secretary of state for the southern department: XIV, 242–3, 324–5, 331–2.

me send to you Mr. Oswald.[1] I have had a longer acquaintance with him, than even I have had the pleasure to have with you. I believe him an Honest Man, and after consulting some of our common Friends, I have thought him the fittest for the purpose. He is a Practical Man, and conversant in those negotiations, which are most Interesting to Mankind. This has made me prefer him to any of our Speculative Friends, or to any Person of higher Rank. He is fully appriz'd of my mind, and You may give full credit to every thing he assures you of. At the same time if any other Channell occurs to you, I am ready to embrace it. I wish to retain the same Simplicity and Good Faith, which subsisted between us in Transactions of less Importance.[2]

I[3] have the Honour to be with great and Sincere Esteem Dr. Sr. Your faithful and most Obedt. Servt.   SHELBURNE

From John Thornton[4]   ALS: American Philosophical Society

Sir   Clapham 6th April 1782
     My Friend Joseph Walker Esq having acquainted me with his intention of visiting paris;[5] I thought I might avail of myself of

1. Shelburne, hoping to forestall Rockingham and Fox, lost no time. On April 5, the day he received BF's March 22 letter, he met with Cholmondeley and Oswald: Fortescue, *Correspondence of George Third*, v, 442–3. Rockingham suggested two candidates of his own to Shelburne, William Hodgson (BF's agent for prisoner relief) and Henry Seymour, a former member of Parliament living in France (for whom see Namier and Brooke, *House of Commons*, III, 423): C. R. Ritcheson, "The Earl of Shelburne and Peace with America, 1782–1783: Vision and Reality," *International History Review*, v (1983), 331n.
     2. The draft had the additional phrase "when we were not at so great a difference."
     3. Shelburne's draft shows the deleted phrase "I beg my compts. to Madame Helvetius and the Abbé Morellet, and".
     4. Thornton (1720–1790), the heir to a large fortune, was a prominent merchant and "munificent" philanthropist, who generously supported Evangelical causes: *DNB* under Henry Thornton (John's son); Donald M. Lewis, ed., *The Blackwell Dictionary of Evangelical Biography 1730–1860* (2 vols., Oxford and Cambridge, Mass., 1995), II, 1103–4.
     5. According to Matthew Ridley, Walker was the son of a Yorkshire iron

that opportunity of getting some Letters to America thro your benevolence.

If I am deemed impertinent, I hope you'l attribute it, to the true Cause; the opinion I have of Dr Franklins Candour, & the desire I have not to be intirely blotted out of the Mind of those at a great distance I much esteem. I have left them open as I thought they would pass best so & they contain nothing that can I hope, offend any one.

I remember once paying my respects to you many years since, I shall be happy to see the day when I can do it again & apologise in person for this intrusion from sir Your very hum servt

JOHN THORNTON

P.S. Permit me to request your acceptance of some poems of a friend of mine who has been many years excluded from the World, as not being in his right Mind & considers himself as a Non Entity & reads nothing beyond a News paper, & yet he wrote the most of these poems last Year.[6]

Dr Franklin

Notation: Thorton, 6. april 1782.

To Samuel Cooper
Copy: Library of Congress

My dear Friend,   Passy, April 7. 1782.

This will be delivered to you by Mr. le Comte de Segur, (Son of the Marquis de Segur Ministre de la Guerre) a Young Nobleman whose amiable Qualities and sensible Conversation will I am sure give you Pleasure. I therefore make no Apology for the Liberty I take of introducing him to you, recommending him to your Civilities and Friendship, and requesting you would do the same by him to your Friends, the principal Gentlemen of your

---

master who came to France "for the purpose of learning what is said about peace": Matthew Ridley's Journal, entry for May 6, 1782 (Mass. Hist. Soc.).

6. *Poems by William Cowper, of the Inner Temple, Esq.* (London, 1782). For Cowper (1731–1800), to whom Thornton provided financial assistance, see the *DNB*.

State, civil & military. He goes over to fight for a Cause he loves,[7] and on many other Accounts will merit the Attentions that may be shown him. Your Grandson[8] is well and I am ever with sincerest Esteem & Respect. Dear Sir, &c.

Dr. Cooper.

To Cuming & Macarty

AL (draft): American Philosophical Society; copy: Library of Congress

Gentlemen,   Passy, April 7. 1782

I have just received the Letter you did me the honour of writing to me the 3d Instant[9] relating to some accepted Bills, amounting to 1671 Dollars that have been protested for Nonpayment at Madrid. I am sorry for the Uneasiness this Accident has occasioned to you, and shall immediately give Orders to have them taken up and the Money paid by my Banker, to Messrs Pache, Freres & Co.[1]

I have the honour to be Gentlemen.

Master Macarty[2] is well.—

Messrs Cuming and Macarty

---

7. Many years later, Ségur wrote of the general enthusiasm in Europe for the American cause, "On appelait alors les Américains *insurgés,* et *Bostoniens;* leur courageuse audace électrisa tous les esprits, excita une admiration générale, surtout parmi la jeunesse, amie des nouveautés et avide de combats." Louis-Philippe, comte de Ségur, *Mémoires ou souvenirs et anecdotes* (3 vols., Paris, 1827), I, 77.

8. Samuel Cooper Johonnot, BFB's schoolmate in Geneva.

9. Not found.

1. BF's letter to Grand is immediately below. For Pache frères & Cie. see XXV, 70.

2. George William René Macarty, son of William Macarty.

To Rodolphe-Ferdinand Grand

AL (draft): American Philosophical Society; copy: Library of Congress

Sir,   Passy, April 7. 1782

This is to request you would immediately discharge and take up sundry Bills of Exchange, amounting to One Thousand Six hundred and seventy one Dollars, which were accepted by Mr Jay at Madrid, & afterwards protested for Nonpayment, and are now in the hands of Messrs. Pache, freres & Co at Paris.[3] I am, Sir Your most obedt Servant

[*In the margin:*] Dollars 1671

Mr Grand,

Mr Grand Banker at Paris

To Catharine Greene   Copy: Library of Congress

My dear old Friend,   Passy, April 7. 1782.

If the Comte de Segur, Son of the Minister of War should happen to be in your Neighbourhood, I recommend him warmly to your Civilities & Friendship, and to those of the good Governor.[4] You will find him as amiable and deserving as any of the French Officers whose good Conduct you so much applauded last Year.[5] I continue as hearty and well as when you first knew me, which I think is near 30. Years, tho' perhaps you will not care to own so much.[6] Make my respectful Compliments acceptable to Mr. Greene, give my Love to my Friend Ray,[7] and believe me ever my dear Friend, Your most affectionately. &c—

Madam Green.—

---

3. Grand paid the bills on April 23: Account XXVII (XXXII, 4).
4. Her husband William was governor of Rhode Island.
5. XXXIV, 218, 243; XXXV, 188–9.
6. They met in the late fall of 1754: V, 502n.
7. William and Catharine's son: V, 502n.

From Henry Laurens

Copy:[8] Library of Congress; transcripts: Massachusetts Historical Society, National Archives

Dear Sir,   London 7th April 1782.

Richard Oswald Esq. who will do me the honour of delivering this, is a Gentleman of the strictest candour and integrity, I dare give such assurance from an experience little short of thirty Years[9] and to add, You will be perfectly safe in conversing freely with him on the business which he will introduce; a Business which Mr. Oswald has disinterestedly engaged in from motives of benevolence,[1] and from the choice of the Man a persuasion follows that the Electors mean to be in earnest. Some people in this Country, who have too long indulg'd themselves in abusing every thing American, have been pleas'd to circulate an opinion that Doctor Franklin is a very Cunning Man, in answer to which I have remark'd to Mr: Oswald, "Doctor Franklin knows very well how to manage a Cunning Man, but when the Doctor converses or treats with a Man of Candour there's no Man more Candid than himself, I dont know whether you will ultimately agree in political Sketches but I am sure as Gentlemen, you will part very well pleas'd with each other."

Should you Sir, think it proper to communicate to me your sentiments and advice on our Affairs, the more amply, the more acceptable and probably the more serviceable, Mr. Oswald will take charge of your dispatches and afford a secure means of conveyance. To this Gentleman I refer you for general Information of a Journey which I am immediately to make partly in his Company, at Ostend to file off for the Hague;[2] I feel a willingness, in-

8. The copy and transcripts are in BF's journal of the peace negotiations.

9. Laurens' first correspondence with Oswald dates from 1756. Laurens eventually acted as his agent, receiving a commission on the slaves Oswald acquired: Esmond Wright, "The British Objectives, 1780–1783: 'If Not Dominion Then Trade,'" and Charles R. Ritcheson, "Britain's Peacemakers, 1782–1783: 'To an Astonishing Degree Unfit for the Task'?" in Hoffman and Albert, eds., *Peace and the Peacemakers*, pp. 14, 75n; *Laurens Papers*, II, 169.

1. Oswald, however, had served the North government as an adviser on American affairs, showing himself as a mercantilist and an opponent of American independence: Ritcheson, "Britain's Peacemakers," pp. 79–80.

2. Laurens left that day to meet JA; he and Oswald traveled together be-

firm as I am, to attempt doing as much good as can be expected from, such, a Prisoner upon Parole. As General Burgoyne is certainly Exchanged, a circumstance by the bye which possibly might have embarrassed us had your late proposition been accepted,[3] may I presume at my return to offer another Lieutenant General now in England a Prisoner upon Parol,[4] in Exchange, or what shall I offer in Exchange for myself, a thing in my own estimation of no great Value?

I have the honor to be with great Respect and permit me to add, great Reverence sir Your faithful fellow Labourer and Obedient servant   HENRY LAURENS

His Excellency Benjamin Franklin Esquire Passy

To Richard Bache: Three Letters

(I), (II), and (III) Copy: Library of Congress

I.

Dear Sir,   Passy, April 8. 1782.

This will be delivered to you by M. le Prince de Broglie, who goes to America to join the Army of General Rochambeau.[5] He

---

tween Margate and Ostend. Shelburne, who had met with Digges, asked Laurens to ascertain whether JA really had said "the American Ministers can treat for Peace with Great Britain Independent of France": *Laurens Papers*, XV, 400–2, 478; Richard Oswald's Journal, in Giunta, *Emerging Nation*, I, 344.

3. The proposition to exchange Laurens for Burgoyne: XXXV, 221–2, 362–5, 566, 594; XXXVI, 13, 279n, 300–2, 326–7, 371, 621n. On Feb. 9, Burgoyne was exchanged for 1,047 American officers and soldiers: F. J. Hudleston, *Gentleman Johnny Burgoyne: Misadventures of an English General in the Revolution* (Indianapolis, 1927), p. 302. He was named commander-in-chief in Ireland on June 7: *DNB*.

4. Cornwallis. Laurens was asking approval for something he had already done; he had met with Shelburne on April 6 and, refusing unconditional release, had suggested that Congress would release Cornwallis in exchange: *Laurens Papers*, XV, 476–8.

5. Charles-Louis-Victor, prince de Broglie (1756–1794), the eldest surviving son of Victor-François, maréchal-duc de Broglie. He accompanied the comte de Ségur on the *Gloire: DBF*; Bodinier, *Dictionnaire*; Rice and

is a zealous Friend of our Cause and Country, and much esteem'd by all that know him. I recommend him earnestly to your Civilities, and request you would render him all the Services in your Power. I am ever. Your Affectionate Father. &c.

My Love to Sally & the Children. Ben is well

Mr. Bache.

II.

Dear Sir,   Passy, April 8. 1782.

You will have the honour of receiving this by the Hands of the Count de Segur, Son of the Minister of War, a most amiable and intelligent young Nobleman, who goes over to join the Army of M. le Comte de Rochambeau, and fight for America & the Cause he loves of Liberty. I request you would introduce him to General Lincoln,[6] to the Governor,[7] to Mr. Morris and to such others of your principal People as you judge proper, and that you would render him all the Services in your Power which will very much oblige, Your Affectionate Father.

Mr. Bache.

III.

Dear Son,   Passy, April 8. 1782.

Mr. Moulan who will present this to you, goes over to join the Army of M. le Comte de Rochambeau, having an Appointment into some Employ in the Artillery.[8] He bears a good Character among respectable People here, and I recommend him to your Civilities. I am ever, Your affectionate Father.

Mr. Bache

Brown, eds., *Rochambeau's Army*, I, 79–80, 166–7n, 289–90; E. W. Balch, trans., "Narrative of the Prince de Broglie, 1782," *Mag. of American History*, I (1877), 181–4. On April 7, the prince had requested letters of recommendation; see his letter of April 9.

6. Benjamin Lincoln was now the secretary of war: *DAB*.

7. William Moore (c. 1735–1793): *DAB; Morris Papers*, III, 187n.

8. See Moulan and Rose's notes of this date. BF also wrote a similar letter of introduction on April 8 to Jonathan Williams, Sr. (Library of Congress).

To Samuel Cooper

Dear Sir,   Passy, April 8. 1782.

The Prince de Broglie, Son of the Marechal Duc de Broglie has desired of me a few Letters of Introduction. With regard to Boston I cannot do better than to present him to you, who have a Pleasure in showing Civilities to Strangers of Merit, & who can introduce him to the principal Persons civil & military of your State.[9] You already love with reason the French Nation; you will find more Reason for loving them, the more Opportunities you have of conversing with their Nobless who have had a good Education, and know the World. This Gentleman has a most amiable Character, loves America & the Cause of Liberty, & is happy in the Thought of going to fight in defence of it. I have no Doubt that his Reception in New-England will be such as to increase rather than diminish the Esteem & affection he bears towards us. With great and sincere Respect. I am ever, Dear Sir, Your most obedient & most humble Servant.

Your fine Boy is well & goes on well at Geneva.

Dr. Cooper.

To William Greene

Sir,   Passy, April 8. 1782.

If M. le Prince de Broglie in passing thro' your State should happen to be near you, I request you would show him all the Civilities that are due to Strangers of Merit & Character. His good Will to our Country and Zeal for its Cause, join'd to his amiable personal Qualities, will make it a Pleasure to you to render him any Services he may stand in need of.— You will therefore excuse my taking this Liberty. With great & sincere Esteem and Respect, I have the honour to be, Sir, Your Excellency's &c. &c.

---

9. De Broglie recorded his impressions of his American visit, including a character sketch of Cooper, in E. W. Balch, trans., "Narrative of the Prince de Broglie," *Mag. of American History*, 1 (1877), 181–6, 231–5, 306–9, 374–80.

To His Exy. Govr. Greene & the same to Governor Trumbull.—

To Robert R. Livingston: Two Letters

(I) LS,[1] press copy of LS, and transcript: National Archives; copy: Library of Congress; (II) LS: New-York Historical Society; copy: Library of Congress

I.

Sir,   Passy, April 8. 1782.

Since my last[2] an extraordinary Revolution has taken place in the Court of England. All the old Ministers are out and the Chiefs of the Opposition are in their Places. The News Papers that I send will give you the Names as correctly as we yet know them. Our last Advices mention their kissing Hands;[3] but they had yet done nothing in their respective Offices, by which one might judge of their projected Measures; as whether they will ask a Peace of which they have great need, the Nation having of late suffered many Losses, Men grown extreamly scarce, and Lord North's new Taxes proposed as Funds for the Loan meeting with great Opposition;[4] or whether they will strive to find new Resources and obtain Allies to enable them to please the King and Nation by some vigorous Exertions against France, Spain & Holland. With regard to America, having while in Opposition carried the Vote for making no longer an offensive War

1. The LS of both (I) and (II) are in L'Air de Lamotte's hand, with the last seven words of the complimentary close by BF.

2. Of March 30, above.

3. Rockingham and his cabinet performed this ritual act of submission to the monarch when they assumed office on March 27: Alan Valentine, *Lord North* (2 vols., Norman, Okla., 1967), II, 319.

4. At the end of February North, wishing to raise almost £800,000, proposed new or expanded taxes on property, bills of exchange, promissory notes, public entertainment, tea, beer, tobacco, salt, soap, and common carriers. Meanwhile, a consortium of bankers had proposed loaning the government £13,500,000: Fortescue, *Correspondence of George Third*, V, 371–2; Valentine, *Lord North*, II, 303.

with us, they seem to have tied their own Hands from acting against us. Their Predecessors had been tampering with this Court, for a separate Peace.[5] The King's Answer gave me great Pleasure. It will be sent to M. de la Luzerne and by him communicated to Congress.[6] None of their Attempts to divide us met with the least Encouragement and I imagine the present Set will try other Measures.

My Letters from Holland give pleasing Accts. of the rapid Progress our Affairs are making in that Country. The Pacquet from Mr. Dumas which I forward with this will give you the Particulars.—[7]

M. Le Prince de Broglie will do me the favour of delivering this to you. He goes over to join the French Army, with the more Pleasure as it is employ'd in the Cause of Liberty, a Cause he loves, and in establishing the Interests of America a Country for which he has much regard and Affection. I recommend him earnestly to the Civilities & Services it may be in your Power to render him, and I request you would introduce him to the President of Congress and to the principal Members civil and Military.

Our excellent Friend the Marquis de la Fayette will sail in about three Weeks. By that time we may have more interesting Intelligence from England, and I shall write you fully.

With great Esteem, I have the honour to be Sir, Your most obedient and most humble Servant   B Franklin

Honble. Robt. R. Livingston

No 6.

II.

Sir,   Passy, April 8. 1782.

M. le Comte de Segur, who will put this into your hands, is an amiable young Nobleman, of excellent Character, who goes

5. By sending Nathaniel Parker Forth to negotiate with the French government.

6. Louis XVI refused to begin negotiations without the participation of his allies, as Vergennes informed La Luzerne on March 23: Giunta, *Emerging Nation*, I, 320–1.

7. Dumas had sent a packet with his letter of March 29, above.

over to fight for the American Cause under General Rocham-beau. He is the Son of the Minister of War, our good and kind Friend. You will I am sure have a Pleasure in rendring him every Service and Civility in your Power; and I request you would in-troduce him to the President of Congress and the other princi-pal Persons who may contribute by their Civilities to make his Residence in our Country agreable.[8]

I have the honour to be, with great Esteem, Sir, Your most obedient and most humble Servant   B FRANKLIN

M. Robt. R. Livingston Esqe.

Endorsed: 8th. Apl. 1782 Docr Franklin private Letter

To Robert Morris

Copy: Library of Congress; copy and transcript: National Archives

Sir,   Passy April 8. 1782.
The Bills accepted by Mr. Jay, and afterwards protested for Nonpayment, are come & coming back to France & Holland, and I have ordered them to be taken up and discharged by our Banker, I hope none will be return'd to America.

There is a Convoy just going, and another, it is said, will fol-low in about 3 Weeks.[9] By these two I hope the best Part, if not all our Goods, will be got out. Since my last of the 30th. past we hear that the old ministry are all out to a man, and that the new ministry have kiss'd Hands, and were about to enter on their re-spective Functions. As yet we know nothing of their Projects. They are all of them Men who have in Parliament declar'd

8. La Luzerne introduced Ségur to Livingston, Morris, and Lincoln: Louis-Philippe, comte de Ségur, *Mémoires ou souvenirs et anecdotes* (3 vols., Paris, 1827), I, 353–4.

9. The French navy was preparing convoys at Brest to transport rein-forcements to India, the West Indies, and North America. The first to sail de-parted for India on April 19, but a large British squadron intercepted it two days later, capturing two ships of the line, a dozen transports, and more than 1,000 troops. The convoys for North America and the West Indies likewise were unsuccessful: Dull, *French Navy*, pp. 278–80, 284.

strongly against the American War as unjust. Their Predecessors made various separate & private Essays to dispose us to quit France, and France to forsake us; but met with no Encouragement. Before our Friend the Marquis[1] Sails, we shall probably receive some interesting Information, which I will take care to forward to you.

Our Public Affairs go on swimmingly in Holland; and a Treaty will probably soon be entered into between the two Republicks. I wish I could give you as good News of our private Business. Mr. Barclay is still detained by it, and I am depriv'd of his Assistance here.—

This will be delivered to you by M. le Prince de Broglie, who goes over to join the Army of M. de Rochambeau. He bears an excellent Character here, is fond of America and its glorious Cause, and will have great satisfaction in fighting for the Establishment of Liberty. I recommend him earnestly to those Civilities, which I know you have a Pleasure in showing to Strangers of Merit & Distinction.

Your two fine Boys continue well. They dine with me every Sunday being at School in my Neighbourhood.[2]

With great Esteem & Regard, I have the honour &c. &c

Honble. Robt. Morris Esqe.

To George Washington

ᴌꜱ[3] and copy: Library of Congress

Sir, Passy, April 8. 1782.

I did myself the honour of writing to you a few Days since by the Comte de Segur.[4] This Line is chiefly to present the Prince de Broglie to your Excellency, who goes over to join the Army

1. Lafayette.
2. For the Morris boys and their education see xxxv, 592–3; xxxvi, 80–1n. They were expected to dine with ʙꜰ on Sundays whenever their guardian Matthew Ridley was absent: Matthew Ridley's Journal, entry of Dec. 10, 1781 (Mass. Hist. Soc.).
3. In the hand of L'Air de Lamotte, with ʙꜰ adding the final six words of the complimentary close.
4. Above, April 2.

of M. de Rochambeau. He bears an excellent Character here, is a hearty Friend to our Cause, and I am persuaded you will have a Pleasure in his Conversation. I take leave therefore to recommend him to those Civilities which you are always happy in showing to Strangers of Merit and Distinction.

I have heretofore congratulated your Excellency on your Victories over our Enemy's *Generals,* I can now do the same on your having overthrown their *Politicians.* Your late Successes have so strengthened the hands of Opposition in Parliament, that they are become the Majority, and have compelled the King to dismiss all his old Ministers and their Adherents. The unclean Spirits he was possessed with, are now cast out of him: but it is imagined that as soon as he has obtained a Peace, they will return with others worse than themselves, and *the last State of that Man,* as the Scripture says, *shall be worse than the first.*[5]

As soon as we can learn anything certain of the Projects of the new Ministry, I shall take the first Opportunity of communicating it.— With the greatest Esteem & Respect, I am Sir, Your Excellency's most obedient and most humble Servant

B FRANKLIN

His Exy. Gen. Washington

Notation: [Passy April 8th. 1782.] from Doctr Franklin prince de Broglie Ansd. 18th. Octo.

From Daniel Edwards *et al.*[6]

ALS: American Philosophical Society

Sir   L'Orient April 8th: 1782.

Haveing had the good fortune to make our Escape from Forton Prison in England on the 13th March last[7] and to take a small

5. Matthew 12:43–5.
6. All the signatories are listed in Kaminkow, *Mariners.* Isaac Allen was BF's grandnephew; see our annotation to Alice Freeborn's May 4 letter.
7. Descriptions of 13 of the escapees were circulated by prison authorities on March 13. Edwards, Allen, and Fulton appear on that list: 26, 30, and 40 years old, respectively, they all had dark complexions, dark hair, and ranged

Sloop from Portsmouth in the Night in which 32 of us landed safe at Cape Bellflour from whence we marched to Le Hague where we met with a French Gentlemen a Commissary who gave us a Pass a pair of Shoes & 10 Livres each to go as far as St. Maloes. When we arrived there 19 of us being not able to travell any farther they went on board a Privateer for a Months Cruize 5 got Passes and have gone to Nantes in order to make the best of their way to America & 8 of us came here for the like purpose wanting to get home as soon as Possible haveing been a long time prisoners some of us sent to England from the West Indies & some from New York. We arrived here the 25th: Ultio. & the American Agent not being here nor no Continental Ships we were Obliged to take Lodgeings for 11 Days before we could get a Vessell to go on Board off & the Capt. has it not in his power to give us any thing but our Victuals for our Work he haveing his Complement of hands already Shipped however he has promissed us a passage home but cannot give us any Money untill he Arrives in Philadelphia. And as there is no other Vessell in the Harbour Bound to America that will Sail this 3 or 4 Months and this Ship being almost Ready to sail we have thought it best to come on Board of her upon them Conditions.

And as we are destitute of both Money and Clothes we have made bold to apply to your Excellency requesting (If you please) some Assistance that will enable us at least to satisfy the Gentleman who was so kind as to take us in and Board us for the above mentioned time. (his Name is John Dager)

Two of us belong to Continental Ships Joshua Goss Midshipman belonging to the Boston Frigate was taken in one of her Prizes on the 8th: of July 1778 by the Porcupine Ship of War of 24 Guns and Carried to England where he has been a Prisoner ever since untill this present Escape.— The Other Eliphalet Rogers belonging to the Alliance Frigate was taken in one of her Prizes the 18th: Septr. 1779 and has likewise been a Prisoner in Forton Prison untill this present time. Therefore they would be extremely Obliged to your Excellency (if in your Power) to ad-

---

in height from five feet, five inches to five feet, eight inches. Sheldon S. Cohen, *Yankee Sailors in British Gaols: Prisoners of War at Forton and Mill, 1777–1783* (Newark, Del., and London, 1995), p. 184.

vance them a trifle of their Wages as their Necessities at present are very Pressing— Your Excellencie's granting this our Humble Petition would be gratefully Acknowledged by your Excellencies Most Obdt. Humble Servts. DANIEL EDWARDS
JOSHUA GOSS
GEORGE CLARK
JAMES FULLER
ELIPALET ROGERS
ROBERT FULTON
ISAAC ALLEN
WILLIAM JAMES His Mark

P.S. There is two more prisoners arived here that wrote to your Excellency from Havre de Grace and two of their Companions that Escaped in the Cartell with the french are detained in the [Kian] at Brest who would be glad of your assistance in setting them at Liberty. their Names are Levi Younger & Bartholemew Cashwood[8]

His Excellency Doctr. Franklin Esqr.

Addressed: His Excellency / Doctr. Franklin Esqr. / At / Paris.

Notation: [*torn:* Edwar]ds Daniel, [*torn:* Goss]]oshua, &c. L'orient [*torn*] 1782.

From Ferdinand Grand, with a Draft of Franklin's Reply

LS:[9] American Philosophical Society

sir   ce lundi [April 8, 1782][1]
    I just hear from Amsterdam that Bills accepted by Mr. J. Jay at Madrid are come back unpaid & protested to the Amount of 20000 Ducats. If you are desirous they should be paid you will be so Kind as to send me your Orders for that purpose & I shall

---

8. Yonger, Cashman, and their two companions wrote on Feb. 21: XXXVI, 598–9.
    9. In the hand of his son Henry.
    1. April 8, when BF drafted his response, was a Monday.

pursuant thereto write by tomorrow's Mail to the above friends to give notice to the holders of the Bills that they may send them back again to Madrid & that they will be surely paid.

I am most respectfully sir Your most ob hbl se   GRAND

[*Postscript in Ferdinand Grand's hand:*] Jay fait prevenir messr Pache d'envoyer recevoir chez moy les acceptations de Mr Jay, dont ils Sont porteurs, Suivant vos ordres. 20/mls Ducats font environ deux Cent mille Livres de france

Addressed: A Monsieur / Monsieur le Docteur Franklin / Passy.

[*In Franklin's hand:*]

Sir   Passy April 8. 1782
I approve of your Writing as you propose to Holland, that the Bills being sent back to Madrid will be paid;² or if the Holders chuse to take the Money here you will pay them at Paris, or in Amsterdam. I am with great Esteem, Sir, Your humble Servant
                                                                    B F.

From Robert Morris   LS:³ University of Pennsylvania Library

Sir,   Office of Finance, April 8th., 1782.
Since my Letter of the twenty sixth ultimo,⁴ I have compleated the sale of the Bills on Mr. grand to the extent of the livres five hundred thousand proposed as you will perceive by the letters and lists sent under your cover for that gentleman.⁵ I

2. Grand continued to pay Jay's bills. For example, he paid 115,410 *l.t.* (plus 2,058 *l.t.* 2 *s.* in protest charges) on May 8: Account XXVII (XXXII, 4).

3. The body of this letter is written in a numerical substitution cipher, possibly Office of Finance Cipher No. 3: xxxv, 266n; *Morris Papers,* IV, 541n. We publish the decipher interlined on the LS by L'Air de Lamotte and WTF.

4. He may have meant March 23 (above). No letter of March 26 has been found.

5. Morris' March 28 letter to Grand enclosed a list of 35 bills; his April 8 letter included a list of numbers 36 through 42. Morris had informed BF of his plan to draw the bills in a now-missing March 9 letter, described in Morris' letters of the same date to President of Congress Hanson and to Grand: *Morris Papers,* IV, 377–8, 378, 469–70, 541–2.

was in hopes that this sum would have carried me thro' untill payments from some of the States on account of their first quarterly quota of the requisition of Congress for the service of the present year,[6] should come to my relief, but unfortunately the delays which are almost unavoidable in the tedious forms of Business conducted by public Bodies of men in commonwealths have thrown back the collection of taxes so that I am left at the moment of preparation for a vigorous campaign without any other Resources than those which my own Credit and address is able to supply; and altho' I sold the Bills above mentioned at a high price[7] yet you must be sensible that the sum produced is very smal compared to my wants. I have just perfected a contract for supplying our moveing Army with rations thro' out the present campaign at ten pence per ration which I think vastly cheap it is made with men who combine an interest and influence equal to the undertakeing and you may depend that it will be performed, as I wish you to be fully informed of everything that can be usefull for you to know or that tends to give satisfaction to the court. I will enclose herewith a copy of the contract and a copy of a circular letter written to the Several States on the ninth February last, The first will sheew that I am attentive to our expenditures and the latter, that I mean to excite such exertions as will relieve our alies from future demands altho' the immediate inference is to induce a compliance on their parts of those aids that have already been requested for the service of the present year.[8] At any rate I expect that necessity will soon compell me to draw for another half million of livres, and perhaps the like sum after that, but sir, you may assure yourself and the Ministers of his most Christian majesty that I shall not exceed the aggregate of

6. The states had been ordered to pay by April 1 a quarter of the $8,000,000 requisitioned: *JCC*, XXI, 1087–8.

7. About £34,758 in Pa. currency: *Morris Papers*, IV, 545.

8. BF endorsed the first enclosure "Contract for Supplying the Army with Provisions" (Hist. Soc. of Pa.). Negotiated by April 6, the contract was in effect from May 1 to Dec. 31, 1782. The second enclosure, deciphered by L'Air de Lamotte, was Morris' appeal to the governors (Library of Congress). It stressed the improbability of additional foreign aid and the need for continuing resolve. The enclosures are published in *Morris Papers*, IV, 191–7, 525–33.

these sums without proper encouragement from you, as I expect that the Money which I shall raise upon the sale of those Bills will carry me forward untill the taxes from several of the states come to my aid. I will venture also to assure you that if reimbursement of the sums which I shall draw should be demanded toward the close of the Year I will repay them on your Drafts, let what will be the consequence my word is sacred, and the united States are at this moment supported by the belief that it is so, for you may depend that we are not less than fourhundd. thousd. Dollars advanced on the Credit of the Taxes for this Year; at which however I do not feel any uneasiness as our preparations for the Campaign are fast advanceing & the spirit of exertion in the Several Governments Is gaining ground so, that I see plainly I shall be tollerably well supported by a vigorous Collection of the Taxes which in the end will enable me to perform what I promise; at the same Time I cannot help observing that the sum asked of the Court for the Service of the current Year,[9] Is not large, especially if it enables us to give permanancy to arrangements calculated to relieve France entirely from our importunities: I do not however promise that we shall entirely cease to ask aids, but I promise to do everything in my Power to prevent the necessity of such solicitations and again I repeat, that nothing will make me so happy as to see America in condition not only to defend herself but able to render essential service to her allies. This letter will prepare you for farther drafts, my next will advise of them unless some favourable supply of Money should turn up to prevent the necessity of that measure which I wish to avoid if possble.—

I am, Sir, your obedient humble Servant   ROBT MORRIS

Addressed: His Excellency Mr. Franklin, / Minister Plenipo: &c, / Court of Versailles / Passy / near / Paris

Endorsed: Mr Morris April 8. 1782 Money Affairs

9. 12,000,000 *l.t.:* XXXVI, 155, 570.

From ———— Moulan and the Abbé Rose: Two Notes[1]

AL: Historical Society of Pennsylvania

[*c.* April 8, 1782][2]

Moulan conducteur surnumeraire des convois d'artillerie pour l'armée françoise en amerique.

————

Monsieur de franclin voudra bien avoir la bonté d'adresser a monsieur L'abbé Rose chez l'archeveque de Cambraŷ rüe du regard faub. st. germain;[3] Les lettres de recommandation pour monsieur moulan.

Endorsed:[4] This Mr Moulan was recommended to me by L'Abbé Rose & by Mr Gebelin BF.

1. These notes—the first written by a man who wanted letters of introduction, the second by the friend who intended to take charge of those letters—were penned on a small sheet of paper. Moulan, a civilian employee of the army ministry equivalent to a subordinate officer, was of too low a status to have left any trace in the army's records: Bodinier. Rose may have been the abbé L. Nicolas Roze or Rose (1745–1819), a composer. He and Court de Gébelin (mentioned in the endorsement) became members of the same masonic lodge: Stanley Sadie, ed., *The New Grove Dictionary of Music and Musicians* (29 vols., 2nd. ed., London and New York, 2000); Le Bihan, *Francsmaçons parisiens*, pp. 140, 431.

2. The date of BF's letters on Moulan's behalf; the one to RB is above.

3. The archbishop of Cambrai was Ferdinand-Maximilien-Mériadec de Rohan-Guéménée (1738–1813), who rented a residence at 3, rue du Regard: Larousse; *Dictionnaire de la noblesse*, XVII, 512–13; Hillairet, *Rues de Paris*, II, 327.

4. BF also wrote on this sheet two lists of names representing letters he wrote on April 8. The first was of people to whom he recommended Moulan: RB and Jonathan Williams, Sr. The second was a longer list of people to whom he recommended the prince de Broglie: "Dr. Cooper, Gen. Washington, Mr. Morris, Mr Bache, Govs. Greene and Trumbull, Secry. Livingston". Under Livingston he added, "K's answer noble", evidently a note to himself to include a reference to Louis XVI's refusal to engage in separate negotiations.

From the Prince de Broglie

AL: American Philosophical Society

Paris the 9th. of april 1782.
Prince of Broglie's best respects and compliments to his Excellency Mr. Franklin, begs leave to Send to him for the Packets he mentioned, the Day before yesterday, finds himself very much honoured With the trust being confident that he Will not fail to be very Well received in a Country Wherein Every body pays So great and So Well deserved a regard to one of the greatest men in the World.[5]

Notation: Le Prince de Broglie 9th. avril 1782.

From Catherine de Wesselow Cramer

ALS: American Philosophical Society

Genève ce 9 avril 1782.
Les Représentans & les Natifs ont pris les Armes hier au soir, Monsieur, dans un moment où l'on avait si peu sujet de le Soubçonner, qu'il ne m'a pas été possible de mettre votre Enfant, & les miens en sûreté: cependant je crois pouvoir vous répondre qu'il ne lui arrivera rien. Il se porte à merveilles, & dès qu'on laissera sortir quelqu'un de la ville je me flatte de lui en obtenir la permission. La crise violente qui se prépare n'est point à craindre pour les Etrangers; mais si elle ne boulverse pas de fond en comble notre malheureuse patrie; elle nous ramènera nécessairement la paix.[6]

5. BF wrote a series of recommendations for de Broglie on April 8. The prince left Paris for Brest on April 12: E. W. Balch, trans., "Narrative of the Prince de Broglie, 1782," *Mag. of American History,* 1 (1877), 181. This is the only extant letter from him to BF.

6. The political tensions at Geneva, described in XXXIV, 486n, erupted on the night of April 8 when the *Natifs* took control of the arsenal and the city gates to demand recognition of the edict admitting them to burgher status. Shots were fired, several people were killed or wounded, and some 18 *Négatifs* were taken hostage. In protest, the French envoy left the city. The following month France, Bern, and Sardinia prepared to restore the former government by force. On July 2, the city surrendered to their besieging armies and the hostages were freed: *Gaz. de Leyde,* issues of April 23, 1782,

Agréez, Monsieur, l'estime distinguée & tous les sentimens avec lesquels j'ai l'honneur d'être. V. T. H. &. T. O. S.

DE WESSELOW CRAMER

Notation: Cramer 9. Avril 1782.

From William Hodgson: Two Letters

(I) and (II) ALS: American Philosophical Society

I.

Dear sir   London 9 April 1782

Since my last on the 22 Ultimo I have rec'd your favor of the 31 March, inclosed I send you a Copy of the Memorial I had delivered to the Lords of the Admiralty prior to the reception of your Letter[7] & also of the note I have rec'd from Ld shelburne relative to this Business—[8] you may conclude it done, as soon as the official Forms can be got thro', to the tediousness & delatoriness of which, you are no Stranger— I coud wish to Know, as some Objections have been made, to the whole expence of Transports & Provisions being born by this Country whether you will give way, to any accommodation in that matter I mean

---

and following; Alexandre Jullien, ed., *Histoire de Genève des origines à 1798* (Geneva, 1951), pp. 469–74.

7. Hodgson's enclosure, a letter to the Admiralty Board dated April 6, renewed the proposals he had made the previous December (for which see our annotation of BF's March 31 letter). He offered them a choice of how to conduct a prisoner exchange. If they sent to France Americans from English and Irish jails, BF would acknowledge receiving them and engage to deliver an equal number of prisoners (soldiers, sailors, or a combination) in America. Alternately they could send their prisoners directly to America for exchange, using English ships to transport them. APS.

8. The note, written by Shelburne's undersecretary Evan Nepean (*DNB*), was dated April 7 at 9:30 P.M. The King was "graciously pleased to consent to an exchange of the American Prisoners, confined in Forton and Mill Prisons," and Hodgson should inform BF. Hodgson was also summoned to Shelburne's office the following day to discuss the matter. APS. Shelburne had told Henry Laurens about the King's decision a few days earlier: *Laurens Papers*, XV, 399.

as to America bearing any share of the expence, for I cou'd wish so fully to possess your Sentiments, as Not to make the least mistake in the arrangement— I presume you will make no Objection to Administration asking for any particular Class, or Corps of Men, I have allready said that I had no conception any Difficulty cou'd arise on that head, you will please to consider whether it will not be necessary to send regular passes for the Vessells that shall be employed in the Transport of the Prisoners & whether it may not be necessary to give some directions respecting the Victualling the Ships in America for the homeward Voyage shou'd Administration determine on having the Men delivered in Exchange, returned to Europe for by the Conversation, I have had with them tis not yet settled whether they will have them home or have them left at New York— I desire you will turn the whole of this Subject in your Mind & give me every necessary instruction & Information so that I may settle the matter to your Satisfaction— Respecting the Prisoners in Ireland, I have allready spoke to the Marquiss of Rockingham & Ld Shelburne about them & they took a Minute to give the Duke of Portland [*in the margin:* who is going Ld Lt of Ireland][9] directions to pay attention to the Situation of those Men & to grant them Relief— In regard to any allowance you may judge proper to make them I can with great ease & equal Pleasure settle that matter by means of Funds in Kinsale at which place the Men you mention are, their No about 150 as I have been informed from the Sick & Hurt office— I beg you will answer me as soon as you conveniently can, for the Prisoners will begin to be very Impatient, as they are allready apprised of the Intentions of Goverment & I heartily wish to see them once fairly shipped off I am with great Respect Dr sr yr most obedt sert

WILLIAM HODGSON

P.S. Ld Shelburne particularly desired I wou'd inform you that the first official Act he did in his Department was to give directions that the Prisoners shou'd be exchanged & he further gave me his word that the Prisoners shou'd be sent away with marks of attention to their wants so as to make their Voyage Comfort-

9. William Henry Cavendish-Bentinck, Duke of Portland (1738–1809), a future prime minister: *DNB* under Bentinck.

able— inclosed you have a Letter from Clegg & also another from a Prisoner to his friends in Philadelphia which he begs you wou'd forward.[1]

Addressed: To / His Excellency Benj: Franklin Esqr. / Passy—

II.

Dear sir   London 9th April 1782

I have this evening wrote you a general Letter to which I beg to be referred— my last of the 22 March (which I presume you had not rec'd when you wrote yours of the 31st of the same month) gave you an Acc't of the Change in our Administration, I gave you therein to understand that I *knew* the new Ministers, wou'd cooperate, in any measures, that might tend to peace, when I said this, I did not say it lightly or conjecturally, I spoke from Authority, given me from themselves, with whom, you will clearly see, I have of late had much conference, indeed my Connexion, & manner of thinking, had lead me, to some degree of Intimacy with them, before any Change was expected, insomuch, that they had thoughts, of charging me with a Commission to you, to see if any plan cou'd be hit upon to bring about, that object, that seems so much, to be the wish of all Parties, *Peace*—

I must own, that my Vanity, wou'd have been much gratified, to have been charged with such a Commission, but I was told Yesterday, that on Acc't of the publicity of my Connections & Principles, it had been judged adviseable, to drop that Idea—[2] The reason, tho' perhaps a good one, I cou'd easily see, was not the true one, the true one, as I conjecture, is much more substantial & tho' I do not certainly know it, yet I have no doubt you do, or will do, before this reaches you, by seeing a person of the first rank & great consideration, upon the same Errand, I am by no means, dissatisfied at this, on the contrary, I think, they have made a much better choice, & it convinces me, that they really mean to do, that which they profess; all this while, I am not sup-

1. The former must be Clegg's letter of April 4, above, but we know nothing further about the latter.
2. Rockingham had proposed him to Shelburne but Richard Oswald was chosen instead; see our annotation of Shelburne to BF, April 6.

posed to know, any thing of this, nor in fact do I, but from Combination of Circumstances, the other Letter therefore I meant for Communication, this not, shoud the Person I allude to, I mean Mr Laurens, appear— The person who will deliver you this pacquet, is not personally known to me, but he is to a very confidential Friend of mine, [*in the margin:* he may be trusted][3] he will make a short stay of a few days at Paris & will come direct to London, I therefore beg the favor of you to take that opportunity of answering my general Letter, in as full a manner as you shall think proper, he will have instruction to wait a day or two for that purpose shou'd you be pressed in point of Time & I coud wish that in that Letter which regards the exchange of Prisoners & all that relates thereto, you woud make it such a Letter as I can with propriety produce, as my Instructions in the Business which is to be settled.

You will, I am sure excuse me, in wishing to be informed of the probable success, of the measure I have alluded to, & the more so because I see in your very last Letter that you remind me of your attention to a similar request made some Time agoe— I beg the favor of you therefore, at the same Time you write me the public & official Letter that you wou'd oblige me so far as to write a few Lines private & Confidential, just to inform me if the Weather is likely to be fair or foul or in any other way you may judge most proper & circumstanced as I am at present with our Ministers, any Communications you may wish to have made I can do with the greatest Ease & procure you the speediest & most direct Answers— The Bearer of this will be desired to leave his address & to call upon you to know when you shall have any commands for London I am with great Esteem Dr sir your most obedt Hbl sert   WILLIAM HODGSON

Addressed: To / His Excellency Benj: Franklin, Esqr / PRIVATE

---

3. The friend probably was the merchant John Thornton who wrote BF on April 6 (above), in which case the messenger is Joseph Walker, whom Thornton introduced.

From the Comtesse d'Houdetot

LS: American Philosophical Society

paris Le 9. Avril 1782.

Monsieur Le Duc D'harcourt[4] Vient De me faire dire Mon Cher Docteur que Monsieur De Castries Luy Mande qu'il n'attend que Votre Consentement pour donner la Liberté sur parole aux prisonniers Detenus au Chateau De St. Malo Dont Mr. De St. Jean[5] Et moy avons Eû L'honneur De Vous parler; ayez donc la Bonté Mon Cher Docteur De Vouloir bien ou M'Envoyer le Consentement par Ecrit pour que je L'Envoye a Monsieur Le Duc D'harcourt ou de le faire passer Sur le Champs Vous Même a Monsieur De Castries affin de perdre le moins De tems possible pour soulager Des Malheureux Malades Blessés Et detenus deja depuis Long-tems, a la liberté Desquels Vous Mavés assuré n'avoir aucune Raison De Vous oposer. Recevés Mon Cher Docteur mes Excuses Et mes plus tendres Sentimens

LA CTESSE DHOUDETOT

Les noms Des trois prisonniers Sont Mrs. Reverend agnew, Capitaine Stair agnew Son fils, Mr. Parker Marchand, tous trois De Virginie.[6]

Notation: D'Houdetot 9. avril 1782.

From Jean-Charles-Pierre Lenoir[7]

LS: American Philosophical Society

a Paris ce 9. avril 1782.

Je remets à M Fox,[8] Monsieur, la permission, que vous m'avez demandée, pour que la malle Contenant ses livres lui Soit remise à la douane, Sans passer à la Chambre Syndicale.

---

4. François-Henri, duc d'Harcourt, governor general of Normandy: *DBF.*
5. St. John de Crèvecœur.
6. For these three loyalists see BF to Castries, April 2.
7. For whom see XXXIV, 330n.
8. We do not know who this is. George Fox had left France for Brussels

J'ai L'honneur d'être avec un respectueux attachement, Monsieur, votre très humble et trés obéissant serviteur.   LENOIR

M. Francklin.

Notation: Le Noir Paris 9. avril 1782.

From Alexander McNutt[9]

ALS: Historical Society of Pennsylvania

Sir   Salem April. 9th. 1782
    Haveing lately done my self the honor of writing to you, and forwarding Sundry Copies of the Constitution of New Ireland, with Several Numbers Adressed to the Peace Makers &c—[1] at present I have very little more Interesting to Acquaint you of, but Expect Shortly to have it in my power to write you more fully.

---

the previous winter and remained abroad until the summer of 1782: XXXV, 649n; Fox to WTF, Aug. 17, 1782 (APS).
    9. The ambitious land promoter who, in the mid-1760s, had interested BF in a share of a large tract in Nova Scotia (XI, 470n; XII, 20n, 345–50). McNutt persuaded families from both New England and Ireland to join him in settling this property. The British soon disallowed emigration from Ireland, and McNutt's reputation for making exaggerated claims made dealings difficult with the authorities in Canada. In 1778 he moved to Massachusetts and, representing himself as the leader of a parallel independence movement, urged Congress to involve Nova Scotia in the war. *DAB;* Arthur W. H. Eaton, "Alexander McNutt, the Colonizer," *Americana,* VIII (1913), 1065–87.
    1. This 1780 publication was listed in a Jan. 8, 1782, inventory of BF's library: XXXVI, 343. The pamphlet's full title was *The Constitution and Frame of Government of the Free and Independent State of New Ireland.* Ostensibly a plan of government for an independent Nova Scotia, it was also an advertisement for emigrants to the new (but as yet unrecognized) nation. Bound with it were McNutt's three addresses "To the Peace Makers," those "European Powers, That may be engaged in Settling Terms of Peace, among the Nations at War," that appeared under the collective title *Considerations on the sovereignty, independence, trade and fisheries of New Ireland (formerly known by the name of Nova Scotia).* BF's copies of these, as well as McNutt's broadside addressed "To the Inhabitants of the State of New Ireland and All Others on Both Sides of the Atlantic, Who Are Interested in the Great and Important Contest Between the Rising Empire of North America and the Island of Great Britain," are now at the Hist. Soc. of Pa.

The Occasion of the trouble I give you at present, is to Solicit your Interest in favour of a friend in Mill Prison near Plymouth, his name is Benjamin Brown[2] of Salem, State of Massachusetts, Your Order for his release in the next Exchange of Prisoners and any Other Good Offices you Can render him will be most Gratefully Acknowledged and honorably rewarded. I have the Honor to be, with due respect Sir your most Obedient & most humble sevt.   A. M. N

The Honorable Benjamin Franklin Esqr Minister Plenipotentiary of the United States of America at the Court of Versaillis

Notation: S. M. N. April 9. 1782.

From Henry Wyld   ALS: American Philosophical Society

Most excellent Sir   Hatherlow 9th April 1782

The Company I represented to your Excellency together with my self, desire to represent ourselves to you, in terms of the highest respect for the reception of me, and the kindness shewed by giving credit to the negotiating the Bill, which recd. due honour; But at the same time beg leave to express our surprize, that you have not made any reply to our former, as the papers to satisfy your Crusers, together with those of your Allies, are the only thing that stop us, having now sent a person into Ireland, to engage a Vessel, and our afairs we have adjusted, so that a failure in that would be a matter of very serious Consequences to many of us; which causes us, thus freely to express ouselves to your Excellency, being satisfied, that you, on mature consideration by imagining yourself in our situation, will easily forgive any thing that is disgusting assuring you, that nothing of that kind is designed, And altho' we may appear not worthy your Excellencies notice, or that of a Free state, yet you may be satisfied that we flatter ourselves, and we hope without Vanity, that in any Country where manufactures are wanted, we should meet with

2. A mariner who was committed to Mill Prison in early July, 1781: Kaminkow, *Mariners,* p. 25.

more indugeances than we wished to ask for, from the states you so honorably represent.

Therefore we desire you to transmit such a passport as may satify your Crusers to be here on or before the Fourteenth of May next, and direct the same to Mr. Henry Wyld schoolmr. of Mellor, to the Care of M. Henry Merril Currier of Chapel in la firth Derbyshire, or to Mr. Edmd. Clegg and Co. at No. 2 Wilks Street Spittlefields London, either of which ways the same will come safe.

Further we desire you, to commend us to the Congress of Pensilvania, that they may if they think proper advance a small sum, if our afairs may require the same, the repayment of which we not only secure, from the Profits of the Business, but from our own property, which we shall take, and we desire you to apprize the Inhabitants or some of them, whom you may think proper of our comming that the ship may not be detained in the Harbour upon any pretence, but return with the sea-Men to Caracfargus, and if consistent to be allowed to load with the produce of the Country, Contraband Goods always excepted but these things I submit to your pleasure.

Further, on my return from Paris, I met with two Gentlemen in Derby who were acquainted with my Business and who on the first of this Inst. signified their determined Resolution, to go over to Virginia, and there fix Engins to cast silk by upon the same Model of those at Derby, were they satisfied the should be well recd. If you mention your opinion thereof the same will be esteemed an Additional favour, as they desired me to mention the same, They are M[en of] extensive fortunes, and their Religious and Civil Principles such, that a free Government will not despise.

Our numbers are increased by some of the ablest Artisans in the Country, who rejoice much at the turn Politics have taken with us, and impatiently wish to be gone, pray delay not, I am for my self and Company Your Excellencies much obliged and most humble servt.   HENRY WYLD

Addressed: To his Excellency Benjm. Franklin / Minister plenipotentiary from the / united states of Amerca at Passey / near / Paris

Notation: H. Wyld— Watherlow 9 April 1782.

From Samuel Courtauld II[3]

ALS: American Philosophical Society

Sir   Paris 10 April 1782
    I have the honor to acquaint you my departure is put off 'till Sunday next, being under the necessity of returning to Versailles tomorrow for an Order to go with the Convoy.[4]
    I have the honor to be with Respect sir Your most Obt. humble servt.   SAML. COURTAULD

Notation: Saml. Courtauld Paris 10. april 1782.

From Michel-René Hilliard d'Auberteuil[5]

ALS: American Philosophical Society

Monsieur   A Paris le 10e. Avril 1782
    Je prends la liberté d'Envoyer à votre éxcellence la premiere

3. Identified in XXXVI, 406n. In anticipation of his emigration to America he signed an oath of allegiance to the United States: XXXVI, 545n.
4. In a letter dated only "Friday morng." (April 12), Courtauld informed BF that his departure was fixed for Sunday evening, on which day he would wait on BF to receive his commands (APS). BF gave him a passport on April 14: XXXVI, 379. The convoy never made it out of French waters (see our annotation of BF to Morris, April 8), and Courtauld was still in Paris in September: XXXVI, 406n.
5. Hilliard d'Auberteuil, historian and economist, was best known at this time as the author of *Considérations sur l'état présent de la colonie française de Saint-Domingue . . .* (2 vols., Paris, 1776–77). This work, based on Hilliard's experience as a barrister in the colony, was sharply critical of the colonial administration and after publication was suppressed by order of the *Conseil d'Etat.* Hilliard escaped prosecution by traveling to North America, but was back by July, 1779, when he published a prospectus for a history of the American revolution through 1778 (the subject of the present letter), a work said to have been subsidized by Sartine. After one arrest in 1784 and a near-arrest in 1786, Hilliard returned to Saint Domingue and is rumored to have been assassinated: *DBF;* Tourneux, *Correspondance littéraire,* XIII, 155–6; *Jour. de Paris,* issue of July 29, 1779; Durand Echeverria and Everett C. Wilkie, Jr., comps., *The French Image of America* (2 vols., Metuchen, N. J. and London,

épreuve de la 3e. partie de mes Essais[6] d'après la permission que vous m'en avez donnée et la promesse que vous avez bien voulu me faire de m'avertir des erreurs involontaires dans les quelles je pourrais tomber.

J'ai lu avec autant de plaisir que d'attention et de respect, la collection de vos memoires politiques.[7] Heureux les Americains d'avoir trouvé tant de lumieres, de zêle et de vertus dans un seul de leurs concitoyens!

Recevez je vous prie les temoignages de ma reconnaissance pour toutes les bontés que vous m'accordez.

Je suis avec une profonde veneration de votre Excellence Le très humble & trés Obéissant serviteur

D'AUBERTEUIL
Rue st. Louis au Marais

P.S. Je prie V. E. de renvoyer l'Epreuve le plus tot possible

Notation: D'auberteuil paris 10. avril 1782.

1994), I, 451, 496; Max Bissainthe, *Dictionnaire de bibliographie haïtienne* (Washington, D.C., 1951), pp. 529–30.

Though this is the first extant letter from Hilliard to BF, the two may have met years earlier through the Neuf Sœurs. Hilliard was a member of the lodge from 1777 through 1779: Louis Amiable, *Une Loge maçonnique d'avant 1789* . . . (Paris, 1897), pp. 280, 391–2; Le Bihan, *Francs-maçons parisiens.*

6. *Essais historiques et politiques sur les Anglo-Américains* (2 vols., Brussels and Paris, 1781–82), comprised four parts published in two volumes. The first volume, which concluded with the declaration of independence, was reviewed at length in the *Jour. de Paris* on May 11, when the second volume was announced as imminent. That estimate was optimistic, as Hilliard's correspondence with BF indicates. Volume II, beginning with June, 1776, traced both the military action in America and the diplomatic efforts in France up through the treaties of alliance and commerce. Hilliard summarized the constitutions of many of the states and provided, in one of the appendices, a list of French officers who had served in America. The volume was published around Aug. 15, the day a lengthy review appeared in the *Jour. de Paris,* praising Hilliard as the best-qualified historian to have treated the topic.

7. For BF's *Political, Miscellaneous, and Philosophical Pieces* (London, 1779), see XXXI, 210–18.

From Thomas Barclay

ALS: American Philosophical Society

Sir   Amsterdam, 11th. April 1782

I had the honour of writing to your Excellency the 23d. of last Month from Ghent, since which Nothing has arisen of Consequence enough to give You the trouble of a letter. I shall be detain'd here longer than I wish, owing to the ship which I Expect to take in the goods not being Yet arrived. As she Comes a Neutral vessell I am obliged to keep a Neutral Captain on board, he is lying at Ostend waiting for a Southerly wind, and all I Can say is that if an American had the Command of her, she wou'd have been here long ago— Captain Du Shone who I mention'd to You as the person I intended for her, return'd from Ostend and sail'd in another Vessell to America contrary to his Engagement with Me—[8] However this is no kind of disapointment as it happens, for I wrote to Nantes to Engage Captain Smedley, who is every way qualified for the business, and who I am inform'd is on his way hither,[9] shou'd any accident prevent his arrival I have a Very good Man here. A few hours of a favourable wind will bring the ship round, and I expect her every day. Mr. Peter Buyck of Ghent is here on the business of the Exchange of the Goods, but as we have not Yet finish'd, I need say nothing further—[1]

I received a letter from Mr Grand desiring Me to send him a Bill on You for the amount of the disbursements on the Alliance, which I have Accordingly done at 20 days sight for 15216 livs. tourns.— After the return of the Alliance from her Cruise, another small account of Disbursements arose, I have not Yet re-

---

8. Daniel Deshon, Jr. (XXXVI, 621n), had departed Amsterdam on the *Enterprize*, which arrived in Boston on May 14: Louis F. Middlebrook, *History of Maritime Connecticut during the American Revolution, 1775–1783* (2 vols., Salem, Mass., 1925), I, 145.

9. Samuel Smedley of Fairfield, Conn., was given command of the *Heer Adams* (ex-*General Sullivan*), which Barclay had chartered. She arrived in Philadelphia on Sept. 10: XXXVI, 612, 621; Barclay to BF, April 29, below; Middlebrook, *History of Maritime Connecticut*, II, 123; Claghorn, *Naval Officers*, p. 283; *Morris Papers*, VI, 351, 372–3.

1. Pieter Buyck had written BF in February, 1781: XXXIV, 365–6.

ceiv'd it, but when I do I shall Value on You for the amount—[2] Part of the Cloathing which was ship'd in the Marquis de la Fayette now lyes at Ostend, and I was offerd about 1000 suits at 20 sterg each, but I wou'd not take them. I believe I shall purchase about 3400 suits of the same Cloathing in much lower terms, in which Case I shall draw on You for about £2400 Sterling, unless You absolutely forbid me— I think such an Opportunity of a supply ought not to be miss'd. I suppose I need scarce inform Your Excellency that Friesland, Holland, Zealand and Overyssell have agreed Upon Mr. Adams being received as Minister from America, and that the States General have recommended it to the three other Provinces to Conform to the Resolutions of these.[3]

I have the honour to be with the greatest respect and sincerity Sir Your Excellencys Most Obed. & most hum Servant

THOS. BARCLAY

His Excellency Benjamin Franklin Esqre. at Passy

Mr. Gillon was at the Havanna in January with five Valuable prizes— All of them Jamaica ships bound to England— A M. Le Roy who was on board the South Carolina frigate, writes that he saw an English Fleet that had the Garrison of South Carolina on Board but Gillon do's not Mention any such Circumstance.[4] Since writing this letter there is an account from Utrecht that the Province, Yesterday, agreed to the reception of Mr. Adams.

Endorsed: April 11.

2. Grand honored Barclay's bill on April 6, and, on May 31, another one for 12,836 *l.t.* 9 *s.* 9 *d.* Gourlade & Moylan had disbursed about 40,000 *l.t.* for the *Alliance:* XXXV, 76n; Account XXVII (XXXII, 4).

3. On April 19, JA sent Livingston English translations of the resolutions of the various Dutch provinces (including Utrecht, mentioned in Barclay's postscript): Wharton, *Diplomatic Correspondence,* V, 315–19.

4. Commodore Gillon, finding that Charleston was still in British hands, sailed to Havana, capturing in the Bahama Channel five ships, which he sold on arrival: James A. Lewis, *Neptune's Militia: the Frigate* South Carolina *during the American Revolution* (Kent, Ohio, and London, 1999), pp. 51–2,

To Henry Laurens

LS:[5] South Carolina Historical Society; copies: William L. Clements Library, Library of Congress

Sir, Passy, Apl. 12. 1782.

I should sooner have paid my Respects to you by Letter if I had not till lately expected you here, as I understood it to be your Intention. Your Enlargement gave me great Pleasure; and I hope that the Terms exacted by the late Ministry will now be relax'd;[6] especially when they are informed that you are one of the Commissioners appointed to treat of Peace. Herewith I send you a Copy of the Commission;[7] the Purport of which you can Communicate to the Ministers if you find it proper. If they are disposed to make Peace with us and our Ally at the same time, I will on Notice from you, send to Mr Jay to prepare for Meeting at such Time and Place as shall be agreed on. As to our treating separately, and quitting our present Alliance, which the late Ministry seem'd to desire, it is impossible. Our Treaties,[8] and our Instructions,[9] as well as the honour and Interest of our Country forbid it. I will communicate those Instructions to you as soon as I have the Pleasure of seeing you. If you have occasion for Money, please to acquaint me with the Sum you desire, and I will endeavour to supply you.

61–2. The intelligence provided by Herman Le Roy (xxxv, 590n) about the British garrison in Charleston was inaccurate. The Rockingham government planned to evacuate it but had not yet begun to assemble the shipping to do so: Mackesy, *War for America*, p. 475.

5. In WTF's hand. It was carried by Moses Young: BF to Laurens, April 20, below.

6. The terms had been relaxed, allowing Laurens to be released from a pending legal hearing: xxxvi, 372n.

7. xxxv, 161–5.

8. The American-French treaties of alliance and of amity and commerce: xxv, 583–95, 595–626. See particularly Article Eight of the former treaty: xxv, 589.

9. xxxv, 166–7.

With very great Esteem & Respect, I have the Honour to be, Sir, Your most obedient & most humble Servant.

B Franklin

Honble. Hy: Lawrens Esqre

Endorsed: Recd 28th. Answd. 30th.

Notation: Benjamin Franklin— Passy 12th April 1782.

To Robert R. Livingston

Press copy of LS,[1] and transcript: National Archives; copy: Library of Congress

Sir,   Passy Apl. 12. 1782.

Being at Court on Tuesday, I learnt from the Dutch Minister,[2] that the new English Ministry have offer'd thro' the Ministers of Russia, a Cessation of Arms to Holland, and a renewal of the Treaty of 1674.[3] M. de Berkenrood seem'd to be of Opinion, that

1. In WTF's hand. Also at the National Archives is an incomplete press copy of a copy by L'Air de Lamotte.

2. Mattheus Lestevenon von Berkenrode (XXVIII, 324n).

3. On March 29, Foreign Secretary Fox made the offer to Russian Minister Ivan Matveevich Simolin (the Dutch having agreed to Russian mediation): Francis Piggott and G. W. T. Omond, eds., *Documentary History of the Armed Neutralities 1780 and 1800* (London, 1919), pp. 323–4; Fortescue, *Correspondence of George Third*, V, 427; Madariaga, *Harris's Mission*, pp. 387–8. For Simolin (1720–1799) see Nina N. Bashkina *et al.*, *The United States and Russia: the Beginning of Relations, 1765–1815* (Washington, D.C., [1980]), p. 1138; *Repertorium der diplomatischen Vertreter*, III, 355. The Anglo-Dutch commercial treaty of 1674 conceded extensive rights to Dutch shipping in case the Netherlands was neutral during a British war. Although these terms were favorable to the Netherlands, she could not risk a separate peace because her French ally occupied many of the Dutch colonies. Not only did the States General refuse but it also insulted Britain by admitting JA as American diplomatic representative: H. M. Scott, *British Foreign Policy in the Age of the American Revolution* (Oxford, 1990), pp. 284–5, 318; Andrew Stockley, *Britain and France at the Birth of America: the European Powers and the Peace Negotiations of 1782–1783* (Exeter, 2001), p. 43.

the Offer was intended to gain Time, to obstruct the Concert of Operations with France for the ensuing Campaign, and to prevent the Conclusion of a Treaty with America: It is apprehended that it may have some Effect in strengthening the Hand of the English Party in that Country, and retard Affairs a little, but it is hoped that the Proposal will not be finally agreed to. It would indeed render the Dutch ridiculous. A. having a Cane in his Hand meets his Neighbour B, who happens to have none, takes the Advantage, & gives him a sound Drubbing: B. having found a Stick, and coming to return the Blows he received; A says, My old Friend, why should we quarrel? We are Neighbours, let us be good ones, and live peaceably by each other as we used to do. If B. is so easily satisfied, and lays aside his Stick, the rest of the Neighbours as well as A. will laugh at him.— This is the light in which I stated it. Enclosed I send you a Copy of the Proposition.

I see by the News-papers, that the Spaniards having taken a little Port called St Joseph, pretend to have made a Conquest of the Ilinois Country.[4] In what light does this Proceeding appear to Congress? While they decline our offer'd Friendship, are they to be suffer'd to encroach on our Bounds, & shut us up within the Apalachian Mountains? I begin to fear they have some such Project.

Having seen in the English Prints an Article from Lisbon, that two American Ships under French Colours being arrived in that Port, were seized by the Government, I asked the Portuguese Ambassador[5] if it was true. He said he had no Advice of it, as he certainly should have had if such a Thing had happen'd; he therefore did not give the least Credit to it; and said we might make ourselves perfectly easy, no such Treatment would in his Opinion be offer'd us in their Ports: and he further observed on the Falsehood of English News Papers, their having lately as-

---

4. The troops were from the Spanish post at St. Louis. They reached St. Joseph (now in Michigan) on Feb. 12, 1781, and claimed the region in the name of Charles III: Eric Beerman, *España y la Independencia de Estados Unidos* (Malaga, Spain, 1992), pp. 62–5.

5. The conde de Sousa Coutinho.

serted that the Congress had issued Letters of Marque for Cruizing against the Portuguese.

With great Esteem, I have the honour to be, Sir, Your most obedt & most humble Servant. B FRANKLIN

[*Postscript in Franklin's hand:*] My No 6. was dated the 8th Inst.—

Honble. Robt. R. Livingston Esqre.

No. 7.

From Madame Cramer

ALS: American Philosophical Society

Genève ce 12 avril [1782]

Votre petit fils est en sureté, Monsieur, il est en suisse avec Mr Marignac.[6] Je l'aurais mené avec moi si j'avais pû sortir, mais on m'en a refusé la permission pour mes Enfans & pour moi. Agréez, Monsieur, l'assurance de la satisfaction que j'ai d'avoir pû répondre à la confiance que vous m'avez témoignée, & les sentimens avec lesquels j'ai l'honneur d'être &..

C. CRAMER

Addressed: A Monsieur / Monsieur franklin Ministre / plenipotentiaire des Etats / unis d'Amerique / à Passy.

6. At M. Marignac's brother's country place, Gachet: see BFB's letter of July 27. In 1782, Geneva was a republic separate from Switzerland. It did not become a Swiss canton until 1814: Paul Guichonnet, ed., *Histoire de Genève* (Toulouse and Lausanne, 1974), p. 278.

From Gérard de Rayneval

AL (draft):[7] Archives du Ministère des affaires étrangères

à Vles. le 12. avril 1782

J'ai mis Sous les yeux de M. le Cte. de Vergennes, M, les differentes letres que M Hartley vous a écrites,[8] ainsi que votre projet de rèponse;[9] ce Ministre a donné une entiére aprobation à la manière dont vous vous exprimez. Je joins ici un postscriptum concernant M. forth; M. le Cte. de Vergennes, qui en a pris lecture, trouve que vous pouvez sans inconvénient le transmettre à votre correspondant.

M. franklin

P.S. Apostille fournie à M. franklin le 12. avril 1782. a écrire à M. Hartley.[1]

Depuis ma lettre écrite, M, j'ai pezé de nouveau les différentes ouvertures qu'elle renferme. Selon vous l'ancien ministère anglois desiroit sincèrement une reconciliation avec nous, et il nous proposoit dans cette vüe une paix Séparée. Tandis que vous me transmettiez ce vœu du Ld North, cet ex-ministre avoit ici un émissaire chargé de Sonder le ministere françois Sur Ses dispositions pacifiques, et de lui faire des propositions fort avantageuses.[2] Vous pouvez juger par là, M, de l'opinion que je dois avoir des intentions du Ld North et de Ses Collègues. Pour vous convaincre de la vérité de la notion que je vous transmets, je vous confiérai que l'emissaire étoit un M. forth;[3] et qu'on l'a chargé ici de rèpondre aux ministres anglois, que le Roi De france desiroit

---

7. WTF published the now-missing recipient's copy in *Memoirs*, II, 301–2.

8. BF enclosed letters he had received from Hartley with his March 22 letter to Gérard de Rayneval, above.

9. BF's draft is missing. It included at least one sentence that Rayneval in his suggested revision (the postscript to this letter) did not retain. BF quoted it to JA on April 13, below. BF already had been told about Louis XVI's response to Forth (see BF to Livingston, April 8), but Rayneval here provides further details.

1. BF adopted this response with minor variations. The English version he sent to Hartley on April 13 is below.

2. At this point Rayneval wrote but then deleted the following phrase, "pour l'engager à toutes abandonner Les Etats-Unis."

3. Rayneval here deleted "qu'il a offert à la france l'uti posseditis et

la paix autant que le Roi d'angre. [Angleterre], qu'il s'y prêteroit
des qu'il le pourroit avec dignité et sûreté; mais qu'il importe
avant tout à S. M. T. C.[4] de savoir si la Cour de Londres etoit disposée a traiter ègalement avec les alliés de la france.[5] M. forth est
parti avec cette réponse pour Londres; mais il y a aparence qu'il
ne sera arrivé qu'après la retraite des Ministres qui l'avoient envoyé. Vous pourrez, M, Sans aucun inconvénient faire usage de
ces détails, Si vous le jugez à propos: ils feront connaître au Ministere actüel les principes de la Cour de france, et ils le convain-
cront, jespère, que le projet de nous desunir seroit aussi illusoire
qu'il nous seroit injurieux. Quant au probleme remis à M. forth,
je ne Saurois prévoir, (Si les nouveaux Ministres en sont instruits) de quelle maniére ils croiront devoir le resoudre: S'ils
aiment La paix, comme ils l'ont persuadé à la nation anglaise et
à toute l'Europe, ils ne doivent pas être embarassés: la france leur
a ouvert une voie qu'ils peuvent, selon moi, suivre sans blesser
la dignité de leur maître; s'ils ne la suivent pas, ils se flattent sans
doute que le Sort des armes procurera à L'angre. des succès qu'il
leur a refusé jusquà present: ce Sera à La providence à couron-
ner ou a frustrer leurs espérances./.

To John Adams

LS:[6] Massachusetts Historical Society; copy: Library of Congress

Sir,   Passy April 13th. 1782.
Inclosed with this I send to your Excellency the Pacquet of
Correspondence between Mr Hartley and me which I promised

---

d'autres avantages". The *uti posseditis* was retention of the territories currently held by the competing parties; the other advantages, as Vergennes told
La Luzerne on March 23, were the removal of the English commissioner at
Dunkirk and advantages in India (although elsewhere Vergennes described
the proposed concessions in India as minimal): Giunta, *Emerging Nation*, I,
320; *JCC*, XXII, 303–4; Vergennes to Montmorin, March 16 (AAE).
4. Sa Majesté Très Chrétienne.
5. Vergennes gave La Luzerne a similar account of the King's response;
see our annotation of BF to Livingston, April 8.
6. In WTF's hand. BF added the postscript, which is not on the copy.

in my last.[7] You will see that we have held nearly the same Language[8] which gives me Pleasure.

While Mr Hartley was making Propositions to me, with the Approbation or Privity of Lord North, to treat separately from France, that Minister had an Emissary here, a Mr Forth, formerly a Secretary of Lord Stormonts, making Proposals to induce this Court to treat with [without] us. I understand that several Sacrifices were offer'd to be made, and among the Rest Canada to be given up to France.[9] The Substance of the Answer appears in my last Letter to Mr Hartley. But there is a Sentence omitted in that Letter which I much liked, viz: "that whenever the two Crowns should come to treat, his most Christian Majesty would shew how much the Engagements he might enter into were to be rely'd on by his exact observance of those he already had with his present Allies."[1]

If you have received anything in consequence of your Answer by Digges, you will oblige me by communicating it. The Ministers here were much pleased with the Account given them of your Interview, by the Ambassador.[2]

With great Respect, I am, Sir, Your most obedient & most humble Servant.   B FRANKLIN

7. Of March 31, above.

8. As JA had held with Digges.

9. We do not know the source of BF's information, but we doubt Forth made an offer concerning Canada. Vergennes made no mention of it in his letters to La Luzerne and Montmorin, cited in our annotation of Gérard de Rayneval to BF, April 12. Forth's mission provoked a number of rumors: Richard B. Morris, *The Peacemakers: the Great Powers and American Independence* (New York, Evanston, and London, 1965), p. 254. Vergennes had asked Ambassador La Vauguyon to inform JA about the Forth mission under condition of secrecy: Vergennes to La Vauguyon, April 4, 1782 (AAE).

1. The letter to Hartley is immediately below. BF was following Gérard de Rayneval's suggested draft; see Rayneval's letter of April 12. The omitted sentence was used, however, by Vergennes in a May 9 interview with Thomas Grenville; see BF's journal of the peace negotiations.

2. La Vauguyon to Vergennes, March 27, 1782 (AAE), gives full details provided by JA about his meeting with Digges.

You will be so good as to return me the Papers when you have a good Opportunity.

His Exy J. Adams Esqre

Endorsed: Dr Franklin. Ap. 13. 1782

To David Hartley[3]

Copies: Library of Congress, William L. Clements Library[4]

Dear Sir, Passy April 13. 1782.

Since mine of the 5th. I have thought farther of the Subject of our late Letters. You were of Opinion that the late Ministry desired sincerily a Reconciliation with America, and with that View a separate Peace with us was proposed. It happened that at the same time Lord North had an Emissary here, employ'd to sound the French Ministers with regard to Peace and to make them very advantageous Propositions, in Case they would abandon us. You may judge from hence, my dear Friend, what opinion I must have formed of the Intentions of your Ministers. To convince you of the Truth of this, I may acquaint you that the Emissary was a Mr. Forth; and that the Answer given him to carry back to the English Ministers was, *que le Roi de France desiroit la Paix autant que le Roi d'Angleterre; qu'il s'y prêteroit dès qu'il le pourroit avec Dignité et Sureté; mais qu'il importoit avant tout à S.M.T.C. de savoir Si la Cour de Londres étoit disposée à traiter égalalement avec les Alliés de la France.* Forth went off with this Answer for London, but probably did not arrive till after the Dismission of the Ministers that sent him. You may make any use of this Information that you judge proper. The new Ministry may see by it the Principles that govern this Court; and it will convince them, I hope, that the Project of dividing us is as vain, as it would be to us injurious. I can-

---

3. This letter follows the suggestions of Gérard de Rayneval's letter of the previous day (above), except for BF's addition of the final sentence before the complimentary close.

4. This copy is with the papers of the Earl of Shelburne and is in Hartley's hand. It contains several minor differences in wording from the letterbook copy in L'Air de Lamotte's hand from which we print.

not judge what they will think or do in Consequence of the Answer sent by Mr. Forth (if they have seen it). If they love Peace, as they have persuaded the English Nation and all Europe to believe, they can [*be*] under no Difficulty. France has opened a Path which in my Opinion they may use, without hurting the Dignity of their Master or the Honour of the Nation. If they do not chuse it they doubtless flatter themselves that War may still produce Success, in favour of England, that have hitherto been witheld. The Crowning or frustrating of such Hopes belongs to divine Providence. May God send us all more Wisdom. I am ever, my dear Friend, Yours most affectionately

D. Hartley Esqe.

To Mary Hewson

Reprinted from Stan V. Henkels, Catalogue No. 1262 (July 1, 1920), item 31; and American Art Association, Sale Catalogue (April 22–4, 1924), item 295.[5]

My dear dear Friend,   Passy, April 13, 1782.
    I received your kind Letter of the 23d of December.[6] I rejoice always to hear of your & your good Mother's Welfare, tho' I can write but Seldom, Safe Opportunities are Scarce. Looking over some old Papers I find the rough Draft of a Letter which I wrote to you 15 Months ago, and which probably miscarried, or your Answer miscarried, as I never receiv'd any. I enclose it, as the Spring is coming on and the same Proposition will now again be in Season and easily executed if you should approve of it.[7] You mention Mr. Viny's being with you. What is his present Situation? I think he might do well with his Wheel-Business in this Country. By your Newspapers Jacob seems to have taken it to

    5. A photograph of the second page of the now-missing ALS, beginning "her Lowness of Spirits," was published in the American Art Association sale catalogue. We print our own transcription of that portion, and reprint the Henkels catalogue transcript of the first page.
    6. XXXVI, 287–9.
    7. BF is probably referring to his letter of Jan. 10, 1780, in which he proposed that Hewson and her mother and children come to Passy. The only extant version of that letter is a draft marked "Sent": XXXI, 360–2.

himself.[8] Could he not make up a good Coach with the latest Useful improvements, & bring you all in it? It would serve here as a Specimen of his Abilities, if he chose to stay; or would sell well if he chose to return. I hope Your Mother has got over her Lowness of Spirits about the Dropsey. It is common for aged People to have at times swell'd Ancles towards Evening; but it is a temporary Disorder, which goes off of itself, & has no Consequences.— My tender Love to her.

If you have an Opportunity of sending to Geneva, I like well enough your sending the Books thither for my Grandson, who goes on well there.—[9] You do well to keep my Grandaughter[1] without Stays. God bless her, and all of you.—

You may imagine that I begin to grow happy in my Prospects. I should be quite so, if I could see Peace & Good Will restored between our Countries; for I enjoy Health, Competence, Friends & Reputation; *Peace* is the only Ingredient wanting to my Felicity.

Adieu, my dear Friend, and believe me ever Yours most affectionately　　　　　　　　　　　　　　　　　B FRANKLIN

Addressed:[2] To / Mrs Hewson / at Cheam / in Surrey.

To William Hodgson　Incomplete copy:[3] Sheffield Central Library

Sir　　　　　　　　　　　　　　　　　Passy Apl 13th 1782

On looking over the Letters you have favored me with, I see several particulars, that have been hitherto unanswered, thro the Multiplicity of Affairs which devour my Time & distract my attention;

8. The wheel-manufacturing firm operated by John Viny (XVII, 72n) and Joseph Jacob went bankrupt in 1778. Jacob held the patent for an innovation that Viny claimed had been developed primarily by himself and BF; a legal battle ensued: XX, 157–8n.

9. BF had instructed Hewson to purchase matching books for her son and BFB; see XXXVI, 287n.

1. BF perpetuates the running joke that Hewson's daughter, Elizabeth, would one day marry BFB: XXXVI, 288n.

2. The address sheet is no longer with this letter. Mary Hewson drafted part of her reply of May 1, below, on the verso.

3. In Hodgson's hand.

You hinted your Willingness to come over hither, in case the Journey cou'd be made usefull to the publick;[4] I did not at that Time see any Probability of it— But the Change of Sentiments respecting America, and the consequent Change of Ministry, render it possible; If therefore you continue of the same Mind, & it wou'd not now be more inconvenient to your Private Affairs— I wish you wou'd wait on Lord Camden[5] or Lord Shelburne, acquaint them with your Intention that you possess my fullest Confidence, & that if they desire any Propositions or even Ideas, to be communicated to me, tending to the good End we ought all to have in View, Peace, they may safely convey them by you, a Passport from this Court is not necessary to enter the Kingdom. Englishmen arrive here daily without any & are not questioned, and I shou'd be very happy indeed to see you.[6]

Extract from a Letter Dr. F. to. W.H—

From John Adams   AL (draft): Massachusetts Historical Society

Sir   Amsterdam April 13. 1782

I have the Honour to inform you that I have this day drawn upon you, a sett of 2 Bills of Exchange, at one usance, in favour of Messrs Fizeaux Grand & Co, for Six hundred and twenty five Pounds sterling being my Salary for one Quarter, computed in the Bill at four Thousands seven hundred and thirty three Crowns, Ten Sols and nine Deniers, of Sixty Sous the Crown, which you will please to charge to the United States of America according to the Resolution of Congress.[7]

I have the Honour &c

Mr Franklin

4. See XXXVI, 278, as well as Hodgson's letter of March 22 (above).

5. BF's old friend Charles Pratt, Lord Camden (XXI, 322n), became president of the Council in the Rockingham administration: Sir F. Maurice Powicke and E. B. Fryde, eds., *Handbook of British Chronology* (2nd ed., London, 1961), p. 138.

6. On April 14, Richard Oswald arrived in Paris, making it unnecessary to seek another British emissary; see our headnote to BF to Vergennes, April 15.

7. The resolution ordered BF to pay the salaries of JA and his secretary:

From John Bondfield

ALS: American Philosophical Society

Sir   Bordeaux 13 April 1782

We have advices from Edenton in No. Carolina so late as the 14th March brought by a Vessel arrived at this port the 9th. One of my Letters contains "It is reported an Attack against Charles Town is preparing by General Green 2000 Militia of this State are orderd imediately to join him and all the Troops from Virginia have marchd up"—[8] The Captain informs me a Number of Transports were arrived at Charles Town the English and their Emissaries gave out they had Troops on board. They had certain intelligence to the contrary that they arrived in Ballast and was to wait the event that in case of Nessessity the British Army in Charles Town might have the means to retreat to New York or Jamaica— By a packet arrived at Couronna from the Havanah we have advice of the arrival of Comodore Gillon at that Port with five rich homeward bound Jamaica Men;[9] A fortunate Event as it will ease the State of South Carolina from the Heavy expence of the Outfits of that Expedition and reimburss the Engagements enterd into by Mr Gillon in Europe on that Account.

We are at a loss to construe the Intentions of the British Ministry in stoping the Issuing of Commissions against American Vessels and calling in them that are out. Under these Circumstances should a Vessel of mine be sent into England by a Privateer or other Commissiond vessel of Great Britain not having a Commission against America but only against France and the other Beligert. [Belligerent] Powers in Europe is it your opinion that being reclaimd by my Agent as my property under your Commission or Register she would be recoverd. I shoud be obliged to you for your sentiments on this head.

XXX, 543; *JCC,* XVII, 476. BF had promised his compliance and JA elected to draw on Horneca, Fizeaux & Cie., now Fizeaux, Grand & Cie.: XXXIII, 379; XXXIV, 91; XXXV, 82n; XXXVI, 26.

8. Actually, at this time Greene admitted his forces were "incompetent . . . to any great operation": Richard K. Showman *et al.,* eds., *The Papers of General Nathanael Greene* (12 vols. to date, Chapel Hill, 1976–), X, 471, 495n.

9. For Gillon's successful cruise see Barclay to BF, April 11.

With due respect I have the Honor to be Sir Your most Obedient Humble Servant   JOHN BONDFIELD

To His Exellency Benj Franklin Esqr

Addressed: A Son Excellence / Benj Franklin Esqr / Ministre
Plenipotenre / des Etats Unies / de lAmerique / a / Paris

From Hilliard d'Auberteuil

ALS: University of Pennsylvania Library

Monsieur   Paris ce 13e. avril 1782.

Je vous envoye une seconde épreuve de mes Essais et vous
prie de me Renvoyer la premiere si vous l'avez lue.[1]

J'aurais été rendre mes devoirs à votre excellence ces jours ci
si j'avais été moins indisposé.

Je suis avec la plus respectueuse Consideration de votre Excellence Le très humble & très Obéissant Serviteur
    HILLIARD D'AUBERTEUIL
    Rue st. Louis Au marais vis avis celle des 12 portes

Notation: Dauberteuil 13. avril 1782.

From Daniel Hopkins[2]

ALS: American Philosophical Society

Hond. Sir,   Salem April 13th. 1782.

Tho' the Eye of your Country is upon you, and you are engaged in great Matters, yet I take the freedom to call your Attention to an Object which demands that Humanity which ever
possesses great Minds: it is the American prisoners confin'd in
that Land of Slavery, Great Britain.

A Number belonging to this Town are among those miserable

1. In the second signature of part 3, Hilliard recounted the arrest and imprisonment of WF, "fils unique du célèbre docteur Franklin." *Essais historiques
et politiques* . . . , II, pp. 20–21.
2. Pastor of a church in Salem: XXVII, 615n.

Men. The distressed Friends look with Expectation to Doc. Franklin for their Liberation.— Since the Capture of Lord Corn'—— their Hopes are raised. Doubt not but you will do all in your power to effect the desired Ends— I have more especially now in view, at this Time, Capt. Gideon Henfield, who is confind in Mill prison.—[3] He deserves the attention of every Friend to Mankind.

Should be much obliged to you, Sir, if you would use your Endeavour to effect his Discharge.

Any Money, expended to this End, shall be refunded, upon Sight of your Order.—

If Capt. Hamilton[4] could bear him company, it would add to my Obligation. I cannot tell in which prison he is confined.— I once wrote you upon the Subject of prisoners and received your agreeable answer.[5]

Wishing you long to continue a Blessing to your Country, am, with much Esteem, Hond. Sir, your most humle Servant,

DANIEL HOPKINS

Doctor Franklin.

Addressed: Honle. Benjamin Franklin Esqr. / Paris.

From Lafayette   L: University of Pennsylvania Library

a Versailles Ce 13. Avril 1782

Le Mis De la fayette a l'honneur de presenter Son Respect à Monsieur franklin, et comme il ne doit Voir qu'a onze heures la personne interessée dans la petite affaire dont il la Chargé hier, il pense que le depart d'aujourd'huy pourroit être differé jusqu'a demain au point du jour. Dès qu'il y aura une Réponse Le Mis De la fayette aura lhonneur d'en faire part a Monsieur franklin.

3. The commander of the *Roebuck* was committed to Mill Prison on Jan. 16, 1781. In November, 1782, after being exchanged, he accepted the command of the *Friendship:* Claghorn, *Naval Officers,* p. 148.

4. Charles Hamilton of Salem, commander of the *Jason,* was captured in October, 1781: *ibid.,* p. 135; Kaminkow, *Mariners,* p. 227.

5. See XXVII, 615.

From Antoine-Laurent Lavoisier

ALS: American Philosophical Society

a lacademie Ce Samedy. [April 13, 1782?][6]

Monsieur et tres respectable Confrere

M. Le Roy veut bien Se charger de vous faire passer Ce billet et nous nous reunissons pour vous prier de venir diner avec nous a l'arsenal apres demain lundy. Nous aurons M. Magellan et quelques academiciens; nous esperons que Mr votre petit fils voudra bien vous accompagner.

J'ay lhonneur detre avec lattachement le plus respectueux Monsieur et tres respectable Confrere Votre tres humble et tres obeissant serviteur LAVOISIER

Addressed: A Monsieur / Monsieur francklin ministre / des etats unis de lamerique / A Passy.

Notation: Lavoisier

From Jean-Hyacinthe de Magellan

ALS: American Philosophical Society

Hotel de Savon, Rue de l'Université, this 13 April—82

My dear Dr & Respected friend

I here send you the original Letter of Mr. Nairne about the acident of the House of industry at Heckingham, which was struck by lightning on last June, tho' furnished with 8 Conductors, on account of being wrongly set up, without proper Communication with the earth or water &a.[7] I have made an extract

---

6. The only clues to dating this invitation are the inclusion of Magellan in the dinner party and the way in which BF is addressed. Magellan was in Paris in June, 1778 (XXVI, 380n, 663–4), and may have returned at any time thereafter. The next visit of which we have evidence, however, was in April, 1782; see Magellan's letter immediately below. Of the two possibilities, 1782 is the more attractive because Lavoisier here addresses BF as minister; this he did not do—although others did—in his few surviving letters while BF was still a commissioner.

7. Richard Price had written to BF about this lightning strike in early January, when the Royal Society appointed Nairne and Charles Blagden, ac-

of this letter to be read to the Royal academy of Sciences, and to be inserted in the Roziers journal,[8] but I did not name Mr. Nairne that the *wise* Council of the Royal Socy. of London may not find it any ways Against their *punctilio* for Communicating, what he had inspected by their order, and of which a Report was Communicated to the same Royal Society. You may keep this Letter if you like, as I have excerpted from it the particulars of the Case for public advantage: Viz that of not lessening the trust that electrical Conductors deserve for discharging the lightning without any damage: And that of being Careful how to erect them properly, in order to obtain the desired effect.

I'll set off to Bruxelles and from thence to London with the smallest delay (of 2 or 3 days at Bruxelles) on tuesday next: and if you have any letter or Commands to England, I hope you know enough my readiness & dispositions &a.

Our good friend Dr. Begue du Presle will soon deliver to you the Compleate work of Miller (of the Linnean system with fine prints &a.) which our late friend Dr. Fothergill desired to be forwarded by you to Pensylvany, or to the Philosal. Socy. in America.[9] The deficiencies were filled up by his sister viz. at her expense: she not allowing me to pay for them, & saying, that it being the intention of her Brother to make this present to the American Socy., she was very willing to pay for the remainder &a. Miss Fothergill added her hearty wishes for your well-fare and of the general interest of the people you have so gloriously espoused, and which I hope to see very soon Crown'ded with Success, as I heartily join in the same sentiments, and ever am, My good Respected Sir, Your most obedt., hble., and faithfull servt.

JOHN-HYACINTH DE MAGELLAN

---

companied by a draftsman, to investigate: XXXVI, 407. Their extensive report was published, along with twelve detailed engravings of the building and its lightning rods, in *Phil. Trans.*, LXXII (1782), 355–78. Nairne's letter to Magellan summarizing their findings is dated March 5 (APS).

8. Magellan sent his extract to the Academy of Sciences in a March 28 letter from Brussels. It was read to the Academy on May 14 and published the following month in Rozier's *Jour. de physique*, XIX (1782), 471–4.

9. John Miller, *Illustratio systematis sexualis Linnaei* (London, 1777). Fothergill's presentation copy is still in the library of the APS.

To David Hartley

ALS: British Library; copy: William L. Clements Library

Dear Sir, Passy, April 14. 1782

The Bearer having been detain'd here,[1] I add this Line to suggest, that if the new Ministry are dispos'd to enter into a General Treaty of Peace, Mr Laurens being set intirely at Liberty may receive such Propositions as they shall think fit to make relative to Time, Place, or any other Particulars, and come hither with them. He is acquainted that we have full Powers to treat & conclude, and that the Congress promise in our Commission to ratify and confirm, &c.—[2] I am ever, Yours most affectionately

B Franklin

Addressed: To / David Hartley Esqe / Golden Square / London

Endorsed: D F Ap 14 1782

From William Hodgson

ALS: American Philosophical Society

Dear sir London 14 April 1782

I am still deprived of any of your favors, tho' very anxious for your next Letters, having wrote you several, since the late happy Change, in the Administration of this Country.[3]

I now enclose you, the Sketch of an Agreement (if it meets yr Ideas) relative to the exchange, of the American prisoners, [*in the margin:* in Agitation betwixt me & Mr Nepean under Secretary] in Conformity to the Propositions, which you, empowered me to make, in your last,[4] as well as in former Letters, the Clause, relative to the furnishing Provisions to the Brittish Troops

---

1. Moses Young, who carried BF's April 12 letter to Henry Laurens, did not leave Passy until April 14: Laurens to BF, April 30, below; annotation of Young to BF, July 10, below.

2. BF sent a copy of the peace commissioners' commission with his April 12 letter to Laurens. See xxxv, 165, for Congress' promise to ratify what they signed.

3. Only a week earlier Hodgson had acknowledged receiving BF's letter of March 31: letter (I), April 9, above.

4. BF to Hodgson, March 31.

home, at the Expence of America, I consented to, not only, as being reasonable & fair in itself, but, in the last Conversation, I had with Mr Laurens, he seemed to think, it ought to be complied with, it will be expected, either, that you sign the Agreement yourself, or that, you do, in a particular manner, authorise me, to do it for you, in such Manner & Form, as you shall judge proper, to have full Effect.

I have, further to inform you, that, the Transports, to take the Prisoners on board, will be ready, in a short Time; therefore, no Time shou'd be lost, in finishing the business;[5] Goverment propose, to allow, Two Ton to each man, therefore, as there are, about Eleven hundred Men, Passports, for Eight or Nine Ships, may be required & you will please to send me, so many; leaving the proper blanks, to be filled up, as the Circumstances may require & you will please to let them be full & adequate to the purpose, for which they are intended, there are Seventy men, arrived from Ireland, at Plymo, a few days ago & alltho, the Propositions agreed upon, do not mention Ireland, yet, I have been assured, that a Vessell shall call at Kinsale, to take on board, the Prisoners, that remain there.

I am obliged, to write in a hurry, to avail myself of this opportunity, of conveyance, & cannot wait to see, if the mail (which is just arrived) brings me, any thing from you, as the Letters, will not be delivered, till to morrow— I am with the greatest Esteem & Respect— Dr sir yours most sincerely

WILLIAM HODGSON

P.S. Will it not be proper, for you to Write per the Cartel Ships now going, to acquaint Congress, with the Terms of the exchange, or otherwise, they may not be apprized of what has been done, & I presume, you may send me, any Dispatches, you may have & that, there can be, no objection, to their being forwarded, by that Conveyance.

---

5. On May 8, Shelburne ordered that the prisoners be put on the transports hitherto intended to carry 2,700 recruits to America: David Syrett, *Shipping and the American War 1775–83: a Study of British Transport Organization* (London, 1970), p. 235.

Conditions of the exchange of Prisoners with America

The American Prisoners now in Forton & Mill Prisons, are to be sent forthwith to America in Transports, provided for that purpose & to be supplyed with Provisions for their Subsistence during the passage at the expence of Goverment; The Prisoners who belong to massachusets Bay & the Colonies adjacent, to be conveyed to Boston & those belonging to the southern Colonies to be conveyed to the Chesapeak or Philadelphia, The Prisoners are not upon any acc't to be allowed to proceed from hence to any other Country but America, & in case they shoud take possession of the Vessells on board of which they may be embarked & carry them to France, it is expected they are not to be sufferred to remain there, but to be ordered immediately to the places of their Destination in America— The Master of the Transport on board which the Prisoners may be embarked is to be furnished with a Certificate of the Number he receives from such agent as may be appointed to superintend their Embarkation & upon such Certificate being produced by the Commander in chief of his Majestys Forces in North America the like Number of Brittish Seamen, soldiers or Marines, as are specified in the said certificate, who have been made Prisoners by the Americans, shall be immediately released, from such particular Corps, & be delivered up at such of the ports in the Possession of his Majestys Forces, as the Commander in Chief in North America shall determine.

In case the Commander in Chief of his Majestys Forces in America shou'd wish to have in Exchange any of the Soldiers of Lord Cornwallis' late Army now in Virginia, or elsewhere, it is expected that the Transports which are to receive them on board are to be furnished with a proper Proportion of Provisions for the Subsistence of the Brittish Troops so exchanged during the Time of their passage from Virginia to the place fixed upon for their delivery at the Expence of America— The Transports on board which the American Prisoners may be embarked, as well on their passage to America, as during the Time they have on board the Kings Troops exchanged in the manner before mentioned, are to be protected from the interruption of any of the Subjects of any State at present at War with Great Brittain.

From ———— Landrin   ALS: American Philosophical Society

Monsieur   Ce Dimanche 14 avril 1782
    Nayant point Lhonneur destre Connu de vous Jay esté tres
Surpris de voir vôtre Nom Ecrit Sur ma porte de cette facon;
Docteur franclin a 3. heures, Je vous ay attendu et personne nes
venu, jay pensé que quelquun en conversant avec vous vous aura
parlé par hazards parlé de mes ouvrages Mecaniques, ce qui a put
vous Exiter a me procurer l'honneur de votre Connoisance au
reste le mal nest pas grand, Cy joint est un petit memoire de mon
Mecanique.[6]
    Jay lhonneur destre avec Consideration et une parfaite Estime
Monsieur Vostre tres humble et obeissant Serviteur
                    LANDRIN
                    faubourg Saint Martin chez
                    Mr Bertrant Mrd. Mercier au Troisieme

Addressed: A Monsieur / Monsieur le Docteur franclin / Duputé
de la Republique / des Colonies de La Merique / A Passy les
Paris

Notation: Bertrand 14 Août 1782.

To the Comte de Vergennes

ALS: Archives du Ministère des affaires étrangères; press copy of ALS,
and copy:[7] Library of Congress; transcripts: Massachusetts Historical
Society, National Archives

On Sunday, April 14, Shelburne's representative Richard Oswald, accompanied by Franklin's old friend Caleb Whitefoord,[8] arrived in

----

6. The memoir states that, after years of trying, Landrin has finally perfected a device that allows one man, without tiring himself, to turn between
four and eight grist mills that use millstones measuring three feet in diameter. A single man "sans se fatiguer" could also operate a sugar cane mill in
place of the 16 mules that are customarily needed. Landrin would explain the
details in person. APS.
    7. The copy and transcripts are in BF's journal of the peace negotiations.
    8. Whitefoord, as Shelburne surely knew, had been BF's neighbor on
Craven Street and an intimate friend: X, 171–2n. He remained in Paris through-

Paris bearing Shelburne's April 6 letter. That evening Whitefoord traveled to Passy on his own and arranged for Franklin to meet with Oswald at eleven o'clock the next morning.

In the present letter Franklin informs Vergennes of the substance of that meeting. He wrote a somewhat fuller account in his journal of the peace negotiations. Oswald wrote a far more detailed set of "minutes" for Shelburne on April 18, before returning to London. His account fills four folio manuscript pages and, while agreeing with Franklin's distilled assessment, includes many details that Franklin did not record. What follows here is a summary of Oswald's account.[9]

Once Whitefoord had introduced Oswald, he left the room. Oswald presented letters of introduction from Shelburne and Laurens. Franklin offered Oswald the opportunity to reread the one from Shelburne, and expressed his "great Regard" for the earl based on a "long acquaintance" in former and happier times. He said he would be glad to hear any proposition Oswald had to offer. Oswald replied that he had no particular instructions from Shelburne and no commission beyond delivering the letter. As Shelburne had trusted his discretion, however, he volunteered to offer his own personal opinions about public affairs.

Oswald began by saying he believed his court desired peace, was glad that Franklin and the other American commissioners were equally well disposed, and wondered whether the commissioners' powers were absolute and unlimited. Franklin assured him that they were, Congress wanting to "save time in putting an end to the Miseries of Mankind." Oswald allowed that Franklin must know of the resolution of the House of Commons ordering the cessation of offensive operations in North America. He then presented Franklin with a copy of a bill (given to him by Shelburne) which had passed the House of Commons empowering the King to dispense with and annul every Parliamentary act concerning the American colonies.[1] Franklin read it, and said he had heard that there was another act pending that would

---

out the peace negotiations, serving as Oswald's secretary: W. A. S. Hewins, ed., *The Whitefoord Papers* . . . (Oxford, 1898), pp. xxiii, 193–4.

9. Journal of Richard Oswald, April 18[–19], 1782 (Public Record Office). The journal covers Oswald's entire visit, beginning with his departure from London on April 7. It is partially printed in Giunta, *Emerging Nation*, I, 344–52.

1. This bill was the so-called Enabling Act, although Oswald exaggerated its progress; see our annotation of BF to Livingston, March 30. The rest of this paragraph, concerning the exchange of American prisoners, summarizes a paragraph omitted from Giunta, *Emerging Nation*.

remove the charge of high treason against the American prisoners and allow them to be exchanged.[2] Oswald replied that the bill had been passed, and produced a copy that Shelburne had likewise provided. Franklin said "it would be very pleasing to the Americans" and would lead to Britain's recovering an equal number of prisoners. Shelburne had assured Oswald that the King intended to place all the prisoners on board transports and send them to America.[3]

Oswald then raised the issue of a separate peace, saying that, in his private view, the English people wanted and expected it. Franklin replied that this was "impracticable" and that they could neither proceed nor conclude anything except in communication with the French foreign minister. Oswald wondered whether it might not be possible to frame "some particular points seperately regarding Great Britain" in order to prevent France from taking too great an advantage of the current situation. Setting reasonable bounds on the demands of France would prevent further trouble and bloodshed, since Britain would never submit to conditions she considered dishonorable or unfavorable to her interests. Oswald speculated that if necessary the British people might agree to a substantial tax on the annual income of all persons of estate. Franklin replied, "perhaps it would not be the worse for them." Oswald said that with reduced spending on a land war in North America, the British could use their surplus funds on the navy and France might come to tire of the war and wish she had been moderate in her demands, particularly as she might not continue to have a quiet time on the continent of Europe. She would have all the more reason to be moderate assuming America gained independence, this being her goal in entering the war. The Americans, too, would have gained their objective and would have no reason to see England sustain any further loss.

Oswald then repeated his "just & natural expectation" that the American commissioners would consider the matter and help forestall any demands that would be too unreasonable for England to accept. Oswald said he did not know the extent of their commitments to France and whether they were obliged to guarantee France's conquests. Oswald mentioned the sugar islands but did not pursue the

2. Burke's bill to which the King had given his assent on March 25; see our annotation of Hodgson to BF, March 22.

3. Oswald here noted, "On this occasion there Seemed to be a ray of Complacency flashing over the Doctors Features which I could not but value the more that it proceeded from a Countenance not liable to the impulse of common fluctuation & I was charitable enough to Suppose that his feelings were So Liberal as not to be Confined to any particular Side of the question."

subject, fearing Franklin would raise the question of Grenada and the other islands Britain acquired at the Peace of Paris of 1763.[4] Franklin told him that the Americans "had been much obliged to France," and that he could do nothing without consulting Vergennes. He was going to Versailles the next day and would lay before the minister Shelburne's and Laurens' letters and the two copies of the Acts of Parliament. Franklin would call on Oswald the following morning to take him to meet Vergennes, if Oswald had no objections. Franklin described Vergennes as "a Candid moderate Man" whose secretary could translate if necessary. Oswald said that he understood French but could not speak it properly.

Franklin then said he did not imagine the French would make unreasonable demands as they were primarily concerned with their safety, not in extending their dominions. He speculated that they might insist on an article concerning Dunkirk as a point of honor and that the Dutch might expect indemnification for their losses. He mentioned having heard that the British had recently approached the Dutch with peace proposals.[5]

Oswald's final assessment was that Franklin was cordial, though "Sparing of his words," and was sincere in wishing the war concluded. When it was, Franklin said, "we Should all be good friends," and he predicted that Britain would have a large share of America's commerce.[6]

Sir,   Passy, April 15. 1782.

An English Nobleman, Lord Cholmondely, lately returning from Italy, called upon me here at the time when we receiv'd the News of the first Resolutions of the House of Commons relating to America. In Conversation he said that he knew his Friend Lord Shelburne had a great Regard for me; that it would be pleasing to him to hear of my Welfare and to receive a Line from me, of which he, Lord Cholmondeley should like to be the Bearer; adding that if there should be a Change of Ministry, he believ'd Lord Shelburne would be employ'd. I thereupon wrote

---

4. Toward the end of the journal entry Oswald noted that he specifically avoided mentioning Canada, Nova Scotia, Newfoundland, or Florida.

5. Fox's proposal to Simolin, for which see BF to Livingston, April 12.

6. On an earlier occasion BF had predicted to Vergennes (with considerably less accuracy) the progressive increase of American trade with France: XXXV, 228–9.

a few Lines, of which I enclose a Copy.[7] This Day I receiv'd an Answer, which I also enclose, together with another Letter from Mr Laurens. They both, as your Excellency will see, recommend the Bearer, Mr Oswald, as a very honest sensible Man. I have had a little Conversation with him. He tells me, that there has been a Desire of making a separate Peace with America, and of continuing the War with France and Spain; but that now all wise People give up that Idea as impracticable, and it is his private Opinion that the Ministry do sincerely desire a *General Peace,* and that they will readily come into it, provided France does not insist upon Conditions too humiliating for England, in which case she will make great and violent Efforts rather than submit to them, and that much is still in her Power, &c.— I told the Gentleman, that I could not enter into Particulars with him but in concert with the Ministers of this Court, and I propos'd introducing him to your Excellency, (after communicating to you the Letters he had brought me) in case you should think fit to see him; with which he appear'd to be pleas'd. I intend waiting on you to-morrow, when you will please to acquaint me with your Intentions, and favour me with your Counsels.—[8] He had heard nothing of Forth's Mission, and imagines the Old Ministry had not acquainted the New with that Transaction. Mr Laurens came over with him in the same Pacquet-Boat, and went from Ostend to Holland.[9] With great Respect I am, Sir, Your Excellency's most obedient and most humble Servant,   B FRANKLIN

His Excelly the Count de Vergennes.

From Dumas   ALS: American Philosophical Society

Monsieur,   Amsterdam 15e. Avril 1782

Enfin j'ai le plaisir de vous féliciter, avec une certitude parfaite, de la reconnoissance de l'Indépendance Américaine par

---

7. BF to Shelburne, March 22, above. For Cholmondeley's visit see his March 21 letter to BF.

8. Vergennes agreed to meet Oswald the following day, Wednesday; see BF's journal of the peace negotiations.

9. To meet with JA; see Laurens to BF, April 7.

cette République: car je ne puis plus douter de la Résolution de la Gueldre conforme à celles que j'ai en mains des 6 autres Provinces.[1] Je puis dire avec vérité que *non tanta molis erat Romanam condere gentem*.[2] Initié depuis longtemps dans tout le mystere de la marche des bien intentionnés, je me suis prescrit la plus rigoureuse discrétion, en travaillant journellement avec eux dans le secret & dans le silence. Je savois que l'on eût ouvert mes Lettres à la Poste, & que les espérances, même générales, que j'y aurois fait paroître, eussent tiré en conséquence de ma part plus que de toute autre. J'ai donc pris le parti de me taire, & de n'écrire à personne; espérant qu'en faveur du succès, dont je ne suis sûr d'ailleurs que depuis peu de semaines, obtiendra mon pardon de votre part & de la part de tous ceux avec qui j'ai gardé ce silence forcé.

Je repars après-demain pour La Haie, tant pour y faire sentinelle jusqu'à-ce qu'il soit temps d'y appeller Mr. Adams, que pour prendre possession le 1er. de May au nom de Mr. Adams de l'Hôtel américain, & le mettre en état de le recevoir. Je suis tout fier d'avoir ménagé cet article aussi si à propos. Cette fierté est pardonnable; c'est même une vertu: car elle est analogue à celle que j'ai de pouvoir compter sur votre Amitié, que je suis sûr de mériter toujours par le respectueux dévouement avec lequel je suis pour la vie Monsieur Votre très humble & très obéissant serviteur DUMAS

P.S. J'espere, Monsieur, que vous avez bien reçu le paquet que je vous ai envoyé dernierement par Mr. Boers Avocat de la Compe. des Indes Hollandoises[3] qui m'a promis de vous le remettre en mains propres.

Ayez la bonté, Monsieur, de cacheter & acheminer l'Incluse le plutôt possible, & d'y mettre même une seconde Envelope avec

---

1. On April 17, Gelderland (Guelders) voted to recognize JA. It was the last of the seven Dutch provinces to do so: Wharton, *Diplomatic Correspondence*, v, 318.

2. "Tantae molis erat Romanam condere gentum" (So vast was the struggle to found the race of Rome): Virgil, *Aeneid*, 1, 33. H. Rushton Fairclough, trans., *Virgil* (2 vols., Cambridge, Mass., and London, 1978), 1, 242–3.

3. Frederik Willem Boers (1743–1815): *NNBW*, IV, 185. The packet accompanied Dumas' letter of March 29, above.

la même adresse afin que la Lettre souffre moins d'un frottement dans le trajet, auquel la finesse de mon enveloppe ne résisteroit pas.

Passy à Son Excellence Mr. Franklin

From John Adams

AL (draft): Massachusetts Historical Society; copy:[4] Library of Congress; transcripts: National Archives, Massachusetts Historical Society

Sir   Amsterdam April 16. 1782

Yesterday noon, Mr William Vaughan[5] of London, came to my House, with Mr Laurens, the son of the President,[6] and brought me a Line from the latter, and told me, that the President was at Harlem, and desired to See me.— I went out to Haarlem and found, my old Friend at the golden Lyon.

He told me that he was come partly for his Health and the Pleasure of seeing me and partly, to converse with me and see if he had at present just Ideas and Views of Things, at least to see if We agreed in Sentiment, and having been desired by Several of the new Ministry to do so.[7]

I asked him if he was at Liberty? He said no, that he was still under Parole but at Liberty to say what he pleased to me.

I told him that I could not communicate to him, being a Prisoner, even his own Instructions, nor enter into any Consultations with him as one of our Colleagues in the Commission for Peace. That all I should Say to him would be as one private Citizen conversing with another. But that upon all such occasions I Should reserve a right to communicate whatever Should pass to our Colleagues and Allies.

He Said that Lord Shelburne and others of the new Ministers,

4. The copy and transcripts are in BF's journal of the peace negotiations.

5. One of Benjamin Vaughan's younger brothers: XXII, 71n; *DNB*.

6. Henry Laurens, Jr.: XXVII, 370n. His father had been president of Congress from November, 1777, to December, 1778.

7. For Laurens' account of the meeting see *Laurens Papers*, XV, 402, 486–9.

were anxious to know whether, there was any authority to treat of a Seperate Peace, and whether there could be an Accommodation, upon any Terms short of Independance.— That he had ever answd them, that nothing short of an express or tacit Acknowledgement of our Independence, in his opinion would ever be accepted, and that no Treaty ever would or could be made Seperate from France. He asked me if his answers had been right? I told him I was fully of that opinion.

He Said that the new Ministers had received Digges Report, but his Character was such that they did not choose to depend upon it.— That a Person, by the Name of Oswald I think set off for Paris to see you, about the same time, that he came away to see me.

I desired him, between him and me to consider, without Saying any thing of it to the Ministry whether We could ever have a real Peace with Canada or Nova Scotia in the Hands of the English? And whether, We ought not to insist, at least upon a Stipulation that they should keep no standing Army or regular Troops, nor erect any fortifications, upon the frontiers of either. That at present I saw no Motive that We had to be anxious for a Peace, and if the nation was not ripe for it, upon proper terms, We might wait patiently till they should be so.

I found the old Gentleman, perfectly sound in his system of Politiques. He has a very poor opinion both of the Integrity and abilities of the new Ministry as well as the old.— He thinks they knew not what they are about.— That they are Spoiled by the same Insincerity, Duplicity, Falshood, and Corruption, with the former. Ld Shelburne still flatters the King with Ideas of Conciliation and seperate Peace &c— Yet the Nation and the best Men in it, are for an universal Peace and an express Acknowledgment of American Independence, and many of the best are for giving up Canada and Nova Scotia.

His Design seemed to be, solely, to know how far Diggs's Report was true. After an hour or two of Conversation, I returned to Amsterdam and left him to return to London.

These are all but Artifices to raise the stocks, and if you think of any Method to put a stop to them, I will chearfully concur with you.— They now know sufficiently, that our Commission is to treat of a general Peace, and with Persons vested with equal

Powers—and if you agree to it, I will never to see another Messenger that is not a Plenipotentiary. It is expected that the Seventh Province, Guelderland will this day Acknowledge American Independence.— I think, We are in such a Situation now that We ought not, upon any Consideration to think of a Truce, or any Thing short of an express Acknowledgement of the Souvereignty of the United States. I Should be glad however to know your sentiments upon this Point.

I have the Honor to be

Dr Franklin

From Richard Oswald

Copy:[8] Library of Congress; transcripts: Massachusetts Historical Society, National Archives

Sir,   Paris 16th April 1782.

I have the honour of yours[9] by the Bearer and shall be sure to wait of you tomorrow at half past Eight—and am with much Respect—Sir, Your most obedient humble servant

RICHARD OSWALD

From Robert Morris

LS:[1] Historical Society of Pennsylvania, University of Pennsylvania Library; copy: Library of Congress

Sir,   Office of Finance, Philadelphia, April 17th., 1782.

In consequence of the communications made to me by his Excellency the Chevalier de La Luzerne since his return from

---

8. The copy and transcripts are in BF's journal of the peace negotiations.

9. A now-missing invitation to accompany BF to meet Vergennes; see our annotation of BF to Vergennes, April 15, as well as BF's journal of the peace negotiations.

1. The body of each LS is written in the cipher discussed in our annotation to Morris' April 8 letter. We reproduce here the decipher interlined by WTF on the first LS.

Virga.,[2] I shall proceed to draw Bills upon Monsieur Grand to the Extent of Livs. five hund: thousd. monthly; so that Computing the Months of Jany., Feby., March, and Apl., I have now to draw for two Millions of Livs.; as I hope and expect that the Livres 500,000 already drawn may be provided for out of the ballance due on the dutch Loan. This Supply Comes most seasonably, and at a more leisure moment you will be charged with the proper Acknowledement to the Court. I must however repeat that the Sum requested for the service of this year,[3] will be necessary to enable me to support the Campaign and perfect my arrangements; it will be my constant study to draw forth our own resources and lessen our demands on France, but these things require time. I find it will be advantageous to draw upon Holland and Cadiz as well as on Paris, and therefore I request that you will desire mr. Grand to give immediate Orders to Messieurs Fizeaux Grand & Co. in Amsterdam, to honour any Bills I may draw on them, with directions to take their reimbursement on him, for account of the United States. He must also give similar Orders to Messieurs Harrison & Company of Cadiz,[4] and I shall furnish Mr Grand with regular Advice of every Bill I draw, whether on himself or either of those housses; my Bills in the whole wil not exceed the sums to which I am limited, and the Commission those Houses charge will be paid by mr. Grand, I expect it will not exceed a half per Cent respecting which I shall write to them.[5] I am induced to draw on those places because the sale of Bills will thereby be extended and the price better supported. I have the honour to be, your Excellency's most obedient & most humble Servant   ROBT MORRIS

His Excellency Benjamin Franklin Esquire Minister, &ca

Endorsed: Mr Morris April 17. 1782. Money & Drafts

2. La Luzerne returned on April 12 and met with Morris the next day, and again on April 16. These discussions were most likely Morris' first notification of the French loan for 1782: *Morris Papers*, IV, 570; V, 3–4.

3. 12,000,000 *l.t.;* see Morris' April 8 letter.

4. Headed by Richard Harrison, the firm was associated with Hooe & Harrison of Alexandria, Va. Morris repeated these instructions in his May 17 letter to Grand: *Morris Papers*, V, 207, 259n.

5. He proposed this rate in his May 25 letter to Harrison & Co.: *Morris Papers*, V, 259.

To the Earl of Shelburne

LS:[6] Public Record Office; press copy of LS, and copy:[7] Library of Congress; transcripts: Massachusetts Historical Society, National Archives

My Lord,   Passy Apl. 18. 1782.

I have received the Letter your Lordship did me the honour of writing to me the 6th. Instant. I congratulate you on your new Appointment to the honourable & important Office you formerly filled so worthily;[8] an Office which must be so far pleasing to you as it affords you more Opportunities of doing Good, and of serving your Country essentially in its great Concerns.— I have conversed a good deal with Mr Oswald, & am much pleased with him. He appears to me a Wise & honest Man. I acquainted him that I was commission'd with others to treat of and conclude a Peace. That full Powers were given us for that purpose, and that the Congress promised in good Faith to ratify, confirm, & cause to be faithfully observed the Treaty we should make; but that we could not treat separately from France; and I proposed introducing him to M. le Comte de Vergennes,[9] to whom I communicated your Lordship's Letter containing Mr. Oswald's Character, as a Foundation for the Interview. He will acquaint you that the Assurance he gave of his Britannic Majesty's good Dispositions towards Peace, was well received, and assurances returned of the same good Dispositions in his most Christian Majesty.—[1] With regard to Circumstances rela-

6. In wtf's hand except for the last six words of the complimentary close and the line "Rt. Honourable Earl of Shelburne", which are in bf's hand. There is a French translation at the AAE.

7. On the press copy bf noted "Answer to Lord Shelburne April 18. 1782". The copy and the transcripts are in bf's journal of the peace negotiations.

8. Shelburne's former position as secretary of state for the southern department (July 30, 1766, to Oct. 19, 1768) entailed responsibilities different from those of his new office of secretary of state for the home department: Sir F. Maurice Powicke and E. B. Fryde, comps., *Handbook of British Chronology* (2nd ed., London, 1961), pp. 114–15. bf here acknowledges that American matters will be handled by Shelburne in his new capacity (as they had been, under far different conditions, in his old).

9. Oswald's account of this conversation is summarized in the headnote to bf's April 15 letter to Vergennes.

1. On April 17, Oswald and bf met with Gérard de Rayneval, who then

tive to a Treaty, M. de Vergennes observed, that the Kings Engagements were such as that he could not treat without the Concurrence of his Allies; that the Treaty should therefore be for a *general* not a *partial* Peace; that if the Parties were disposed to finish the War speedily by themselves, it would perhaps be best to treat at Paris, as an Ambassador from Spain was already there,[2] and the Commissioners from America might easily and soon be assembled there. Or if they chose to make use of the proposed Mediation,[3] they might treat at Vienna: But that the King was so truly willing to put a speedy End to the War;[4] that he would agree to any Place the King of England should think proper. I leave the rest of the Conversation to be related to your Lordship by Mr. Oswald; and that he might do it more easily and fully than he could by Letter, I was of Opinion with him that it would be best he should return immediately and do it *vivâ voce*.[5] Being myself but one of the four Persons now in Europe, commission'd by the Congress to treat of Peace, I can make no Proposition of much Importance without them; I can only express my Wish, that if Mr Oswald returns hither, he may bring with him the Agreement of your Court to treat for a General Peace, and the Proposal of Place and Time; that I may immedi-

---

brought them to Vergennes. Oswald's account of these meetings (Richard Oswald's Journal, April 18[–19], 1782, Public Record Office) is published in Giunta, *Emerging Nation*, I, 348–51.

2. The conde de Aranda, who in fact would play a critical role in the making of peace.

3. The proposed mediation was that of Russia and Austria: XXXIV, 350n. Vergennes reported to Montmorin that Britain seemed opposed to it. A translation of his April 18 letter, recounting this meeting, is in Giunta, *Emerging Nation*, I, 352–5.

4. Vergennes stressed that peace should be made "solidement" and BF repeated the phrase: Giunta, *Emerging Nation*, I, 350.

5. Oswald's proposal that BF negotiate a truce with Great Britain was rejected by both Vergennes and BF (Oswald wrote that he had already proposed this privately to BF), but all parties agreed that they ardently desired an end to hostilities: Oswald's Journal, in Giunta, *Emerging Nation*, I, 349–50. A paragraph omitted in *Emerging Nation* described how Vergennes assured Oswald that France would not insist on articles of humiliation, or any kind of retribution, in a treaty with Britain.

ately write to Messrs. Adams, Lawrens & Jay. I suppose that in this Case your Lordship will think it proper to have Mr Lawrens discharged from the Engagements he enter'd into when he was admitted to bail. I desire no other Channel of Communication between us than that of Mr Oswald, which I think your Lordship has chosen with much Judgment. He will be Witness of my acting with all the Simplicity & Good Faith which you do me the honour to expect from me; and if he is enabled when he returns hither to communicate more fully your Lordships Mind on the Principal Points to be settled, I think it may contribute much to expedite the blessed Work our Hearts are engaged in.

By the Act of Parliament relative to American Prisoners, I see the King is empower'd to exchange them. I hope those you have in England & Ireland may be sent home soon to their Country in Flag's of Truce, and exchanged for an equal Number of your People: Permit me to add, that I think some Kindness mix'd in such a Transaction would have good Effects in America. Those poor unfortunate People have been long absent from their Families & Friends, & rather hardly treated.

With great & sincere Respect, I have the honour to be, My Lord, Your Lordship's most obedient and most humble Servant

B FRANKLIN

Rt. Honourable Earl of Shelburne

Endorsed: No. 2 18 April 1782 Dr. Franklin

From Castries

LS: Library of Congress

Versailles le 18 avril 1782.

J'ai l'honneur Monsieur, de Vous envoyer une liste de trois americains pris sur batimens de cette Nation et qui sont revenus d'angleterre sur le Paquebot anglois la Molly arrivé à Cherbourg. Le commissaire de Plymouth demandant en échange trois anglois dont les noms sont portés sur la même liste j'ai cru devoir vous envoyer cette piece.[6]

6. The prisoners, captured aboard the *Essex,* were Bryant Newcomb, Job Field, and Edward Savile, all of whom had been committed to Mill Prison on

J'ai l'honneur d'etre avec la considération la plus distinguée, Monsieur, Votre trés humble et trés obeïssant serviteur

CASTRIES

Mr. franklin ministre des Etats unis de l'amerique, à Paris.

From Jonathan Williams, Jr.

ALS: American Philosophical Society; copy: Yale University Library

Dear & hond sir.   Nantes April 18. 1782

I cannot account for the delay of the seeds; in order to get them expeditiously to you I addressed them to a Mr Goddard at the Bureau de la messagerie at Versailles, and desired him to send them to you without going into Paris, this precaution Billy desired me to take: If they are not arrived when you receive this please to send to Mr Goddard & you will certainly hear of them.[7] I yesterday heard of another Case of seeds which came to your address in the Nonesuch & of which I had no advice,[8] I have sent it to the Messagerie which goes off tomorrow; this I have addressed directly to you & hope you will receive it without delay.

I am preparing a long Letter for you, with a detail of Obstacles in the way of american Commerce in this place & others in this part of the Kingdom many of these must be removed if the French think our Trade worth keeping at a Peace; I shall delay this Letter a few Days in order to make the Information com-

---

July 21, 1781, and pardoned for exchange on Feb. 6: Kaminkow, *Mariners*, pp. 65, 140, 167. They were to be exchanged for Joseph Newman, James Miggins, and Edward Ashley. This list was signed by William Cowdry, warden of Mill Prison (XXX, 526n).

7. For these seeds see JW to BF, March 19. JW told Goddard in a covering letter (March 22, Yale University Library) that there were two cases, which means that this was the shipment from Boston, via the *Betsey*, and included one case for Barbançon and the gift box for BF (XXXVI, 186n).

8. RB sent the second of Barbançon's cases on the *Nonesuch* and the third on the *St. Helena*, both sailing from Philadelphia: RB to WTF, Jan. 5, 1782 (Musée de Blérancourt). By the beginning of March, the *Nonesuch* had arrived at Nantes and the *St. Helena* at Lorient: JW to Harrison & Co., March 4, 1782 (Yale University Library).

pleat.[9] I have not met with the difficulty I apprehended about the Comte de Grasse, so shall not trouble you. You have not yet answered my Letter of the 26th & the Prisoners are still at Board at my Expence.

I am as ever Your dutifull & affectionate Kinsman

JONA WILLIAMS J

P.S. You have often talked of coming hither to see the salt Pitts at the mouth of the River.[1] The season is now advancing, and I should be happy if you would put your design into Execution, I have a large House & can accomodate you very well, I am sure a Journey would be beneficial to your Health.

Notation: Williams M Jona. Apl. 18 1782.

Franklin: Notes for a Conversation with Oswald

Copies:[2] Library of Congress (two), William L. Clements Library; transcripts: Massachusetts Historical Society, National Archives

[on or before April 19, 1782][3]
Notes of Conversation.

To make a Peace durable, what may give Occasion for future Wars, should, if practicable, be removed.

9. BF's request for this memoir is missing, but JW described it in an April 24 letter to the Bordeaux firm V. & P. French & Nephew: BF had desired "a memoire setting forth what disadvantages the American Commerce suffers from the laws & regulations of the Customs &c. & what remedies would be of service." JW asked the firm to send their views relating specifically to their port. Yale University Library. JW's memoir is below, June 15.

1. BF had wanted to view the salt works ever since arriving in France: XXIV, 357, 375. The shortage of salt in America meant that European methods of production were of particular interest: XXIV, 420; XXV, 455; XXVII, 463–4. The French system of moving sea water through a network of channels and evaporating basins is still used in the salt fields northwest of the Loire estuary. These methods are described and illustrated in Pierre Lemonnier, *Paludiers de Guérande* (Paris, 1984).

2. We publish the copy in WTF's hand. The other Library of Congress copy and the transcripts are in BF's journal of the peace negotiations.

3. After dining with Oswald on April 18 at Passy and giving him Vergennes' passport for Calais, BF asked whether Oswald would delay his de-

The Territory of the United States, and that of Canada, by long extended Frontiers touch each other.

The Settlers on the Frontiers of the American Provinces are generally the most disorderly of the People, who being far removed from the Eye & Controll of their respective Governments, are more bold in committing Offences against Neighbours,[4] and are forever occasioning Complaints and furnishing Matter for fresh Differences between their States.

By the late Debates in Parliament, & publick Writings, it appears that Britain desires a *Reconciliation* with the Americans. It is a sweet Word. It means much more than a mere Peace, & what is heartily to be wish'd for. Nations may make a Peace whenever they are both weary of making War. But if one of them has made War upon the other unjustly, and has wantonly and unnecessarily done it great Injuries, and refuses Reparation; tho' there may for the present be Peace, the Resentment of those Injuries will remain, and will break out again in Vengeance, when Occasions offer. These Occasions will be watch'd for by one side, fear'd by the other; and the Peace will never be secure; nor can any Cordiality subsist between them.

Many Houses & Villages have been burnt in America by the English and their Allies the Indians. I do not know that the Americans will insist on Reparation. Perhaps they may. But would it not be better for England to offer it? Nothing could have a greater Tendenccy to conciliate? And much of the future Commerce & returning Intercourse between the two Countries may depend on the Reconciliation. Would not the Advantage of Reconciliation by such means be greater than the Expence?

If then a Way can be proposed which may tend to efface the

---

parture the following morning to accommodate one final visit. BF wanted to deliver a letter for Shelburne (above, April 18) and have "some farther Conversation." They met for breakfast the following morning and spent about an hour in what Oswald characterized as a "familiar" exchange. Oswald left for London around noon, convinced of BF's trust in him: Richard Oswald's Journal, in Giunta, *Emerging Nation*, I, 351. See also BF's journal of the peace negotiations.

4. BF had used the same argument in his Canada pamphlet of 1760: IX, 65. Four years later he had occasion to condemn such an offense, the massacre of Christian Indians by Pa. frontiersmen: XI, 42–69.

Memory of Injuries, at the same time that it takes away the Occasions of fresh Quarrel & Mischief, will it not be worth considering, especially if it can be done not only without Expence but be a means of saving?

Britain possesses Canada. Her chief Advantage from that Possession consists in the Trade for Peltry. Her Expences in Governing and Defending that Settlement must be considerable. It might be humiliating to her to give it up on the Demand of America. Perhaps America will not demand it: Some of her politic Rulers may consider the fear of Such a Neighbour as a Means of keeping the 13 States more united among themselves, and more attentive to Military Discipline.[5] But on the Minds of the People in general, would it not have an excellent Effect, if Britain Should voluntarily offer to give up this Province; tho' on these Conditions, that she shall in all times coming have & enjoy the Right of Free Trade thither, unincumbered with any Duties whatsoever; and that so much of the vacant Lands there shall be sold, as will raise a Sum sufficient to pay for the Houses burnt by the British Troops and their Indians;[6] and also to indemnify the Royalists for the Confiscation of their Estates.[7]

5. A point James Logan had made years earlier: Joseph E. Johnson, "A Quaker Imperalist's View of the British Colonies in America: 1732," *PMHB*, LX (1936), 128; Gerald Stourzh, *Benjamin Franklin and American Foreign Policy* (2nd ed., Chicago and London, 1969), p. 209.

6. This suggestion (although not the one which follows) resembles one BF had made to the British four years earlier: XXV, 562–3.

7. Congress would not have been pleased to learn that BF had made such an offer (see XXXVI, 128–9), and he realized his mistake almost immediately; see BF's journal of the peace negotiations. It was not only his reputation in Congress that he put at risk. By hinting at an offer which the peace commissioners would not have the inclination to grant, he risked losing Shelburne's trust. In fact Shelburne *was* encouraged to raise the question of compensation for the loyalists during the negotiations and this issue proved extremely difficult to resolve. BF's suggestion that Britain cede Canada also was imprudent, particularly since he gave Oswald notes outlining the offer. Even made informally, it could be considered a violation of his instructions, recently repeated to Oswald before Vergennes, to undertake nothing without the concurrence of the French government. Such a violation was not something to be done lightly, given America's continued economic dependence on France; had Shelburne leaked the proposal to the French government, it might well have damaged the French government's trust in BF. Fortunately,

This is mere Conversation-matter between Mr. O. & Mr. F. as the former is not impower'd to make Propositions, and the latter cannot make any without the Concurrence of his Colleagues.—[8]

To Silas Deane

 LS:[9] Mrs. Archibald M. Crossley, Princeton, N.J. (1955)

Sir,   Passy, April 19. 1782.

I received the Letter you did me the honour to write to me the 30th. past, and will write to the purpose you desire respecting your Accounts.[1] I hope the Method you propose for settling any disputable points in them will be approved and ordered. I received also your very long political Letter.[2] The Multiplicity of Business on my Hands, on which Account you are so good as to excuse my not answering it, really makes it impossible for me to enter into the voluminous Discussions that would be necessary to do it fully. I can only say at present that I am not convinced; that perhaps my answer would not convince you; but that I think Time will. I am really sorry on your Account that you have written so much of the same kind to America. The Publication of those Letters has done great Prejudice to your Character there, and necessarily diminish'd much of the Regard your Friends had for you. You are now considered as having abandoned the Cause of your Country, and as having with Arnold espoused that of its Enemies. To me it appears that your Resentments and Passions

---

Shelburne kept it secret: Richard B. Morris, *The Peacemakers: the Great Powers and American Independence* (New York, London, and Evanston, 1965), p. 264; Edward E. Hale and Edward E. Hale, Jr., *Franklin in France . . .* (2 vols., Boston, 1887–88), II, 51.

8. According to BF's journal he used that conversation as a way of learning about Shelburne's thinking. Conversely Oswald hoped to use it to further the negotiations: Richard Oswald's Journal, in Giunta, *Emerging Nation*, I, 351. For further details about the conversation see BF to JA, April 20.

9. In L'Air de Lamotte's hand.

1. BF did not do so until Dec. 14, when he mentioned Deane's accounts in a letter to Robert Morris. By then Morris had received them from Barclay via the *Heer Adams: Morris Papers*, VI, 353n, 418; VII, 204.

2. XXXVI, 507–25.

have overcome your Reason and Judgment; and tho' my ancient Esteem & Affection for you induce me to make all the Allowances possible, in considering the Circumstances that have attended you since you first left France, yet the Lengths you have gone in endeavouring to discourage and diminish the Number of the Friends of our Country and Cause in Europe and America, and to encourage our Enemies, by those Letters, make it impossible for me to say with the same Truth & Cordiality as formerly that I am, Your Affectionate Friend & humble Servant.

B FRANKLIN

Honble. Silas Deane Esqe.

To Margaret Stevenson and Mary Hewson

ALS: Yale University Library

Paris, April 19. 1782

I wrote to you, my dear dear Friends, very lately,[3] and directed my Letter to Cheem in Surrey. Mr Whitefoord tells me that you are removed to Kensington Square, and I fear that my Letter may therefore not find you. I sent it under Cover to Mr William Hodgson, Mercht in Coleman street, which I mention that in case it has not come to hand, you may there enquire for it; tho' it continues [contains] little worth the Trouble, as it only expresses what you always knew, that I love you both, very much and very sincerely. Mr Whitefoord will inform you how I live,[4] & that I am very well, as happy as the Situation of public Affairs will permit, only capable of being made more so if you were here with me; being ever your truly affectionate Friend

B FRANKLIN

Mrs Stevenson & Mrs Hewson

Endorsed: Paris Apr 19—82 37

3. On April 13, above.
4. Whitefoord and Oswald left Paris on April 19. BF called on them early that morning and must have brought Whitefoord this letter to deliver; see our annotation of BF's notes for a conversation with Oswald, [on or before April 19].

From Franklin Read[5]

ALS: American Philosophical Society

Hond. Sir   Cape Francoys[6] Aprill 19th. 1782—

I have not had it in my Power to give You aney Acount of my Procedings relative to what you recomended me when I had the Honour of your Favour (untle now). I found on my Return home that my Business was dull and as I had gained Experience in the Sea way that it was much more to my Advantage to follow it. It would be a great Satisfaction for me to Stay at home with my Famely, but as Cercomstances are I find it quite Imposible. I have been something unfortunate this War but am now in a fairer way. I have just Come up from Jaimaica on Parole. I was Prisoner near three Months, but Expect to be Exchanged in a day or too, and shall Return home Imediately where I Shall have a good birth in a Ship of twenty Guns and Bound to Europe. If I have the Fortune to go Safe will I hope make amends for my past misfortune. I hope you will forgive me for my not Writing to you before as I never have had an Oppertunty mostly being from home. I beg to be Remember'd to Young Mr Bache & Mr Temple and Bilieve me your Afectionate Nephew

FRANKLIN READ

Benj'n Franklin Esqr.

Endorsed: Franklin Read Cape François 19th. April 1782

From John Wright[7]

ALS: University of Pennsylvania Library

Dear Friend   London 19th of 4th mo (April) 1782

I embrace with Satisfaction the opportunity which offers of writing to thee whom for many years I have been used to con-

5. A son of BF's brother-in-law John Read. Franklin (b. 1749) entered the Philadelphia Academy in 1762 and was commissioned a lieutenant of marines in 1776: VII, 203n; Francis J. Dallett, "Doctor Franklin's In-Laws," *Pa. Geneal. Mag.*, XXI (1960), chart following p. 302; Claghorn, *Naval Officers*, p. 253. This is the first of only two extant letters from BF's nephew; no replies have been found.

6. Cap Français, on the northern coast of Saint Domingue.

7. BF's former banker and friend, member of the London firm Smith, Wright & Gray: X, 350–1; XI, 179–80.

sider as a valuable sincere friend to myself in particular and to mankind in general and have often regretted the Cause of thy Seperation the unhappy cause which has so long deprived this once happy & beloved Country of thy presence assistance & advice. But I trouble thee now chiefly to beg leave to introduce to thy notice the bearer William Rawle[8] Son of the late Francis Rawle of Philadelphia[9] who has been here to finish his Studies & is returning home to whom I doubt not thy giving thy kind countenance & protection.

Suppose thou mayst have heard that our old ffrds Brown Collinson & Trittons House have failed to the surprise & Injury of many though our house is happily quite Clear. Its yet uncertain how their affairs will turn out— Hope thou hast no Concern but if thou hast I beg leave to tender our service to exhibit the proof of Debt &c. James Brown the son of Hinton Brown has been deceased abot. 12 mos. so my poor relation Ths. Collinson & his nephew Tritton Grandson of Hinton are left to endure the Storm of affliction & trouble.[1] T. C. brot. a hansome fortune with him to that House which with all that the House was once or was supposed possessed of is sunk & gone through some un-

8. Rawle (1759–1836), born into a prominent Philadelphia Quaker family, fled with his Loyalist stepfather, Samuel Shoemaker, to New York City in 1778, where he began studying law. He sailed to England in the summer of 1781 and continued legal studies at the Middle Temple, London. After returning to Philadelphia in 1783 he was admitted to the bar. He became a member of the APS in 1786 and later joined the state legislature. BF arranged for his membership in the Society for Political Inquiries, and in 1787 Rawle was named a counselor of the Pa. Abolition Society of which BF was president. In 1791, George Washington appointed him American attorney for Pennsylvania. Rawle was indirectly responsible for preserving what sections survive of BF's "Plan of Conduct" (I, 99). *DAB;* William B. Rawle, "Laurel Hill and Some Colonial Dames Who Once Lived There," *PMHB,* xxxv (1911), 389–90, 392–4.

9. Francis Rawle (1729–1761) was a prosperous Quaker merchant and generous contributor to the Pennsylvania Hospital. Shortly before his death, he was named a director of the Philadelphia Contributionship: Whitfield J. Bell, Jr., *Patriot-Improvers: Biographical Sketches of Members of the American Philosophical Society* (2 vols. to date, Philadelphia, 1997–), I, 203–5.

1. BF had last drawn on this London firm in 1780: XXXI, 360. James Brown had died on Feb. 16, 1781, leaving Thomas Collinson and John Henry Tritton: *Gent. Mag.,* LI (1781), 95.

accountable Conduct owing principally it seems to the Credulity & weakness of the late James Brown in trusting people with unwarrantable sums particularly one House viz Rabone & Crinzo's for £140.000 who stopped on the 6th. & that obliged them to Stop on the 7th. Ultimo[2] So much for this unpleasant subject.

As to publick matters they wear a more agreable aspect It is thought. The new ministry appear determined to proceed on true Constitutional principles & the K—— seem most cordially to enter into the Idea which I hope Will have the most salutary effects & that peace & prosperity may in due time insue.

I trust in thy former indulgence to excuse this freedom & if there is any impropriety in writing after this manner under present circumstances it may not be deemed impertinent but rather attributd. to want of knowledge. I should esteem a letter a favr from thee & also to receive thy Commands but permit me to say that seeing thee here again would afford the highest satisfaction & pleasure to abundance of thy ffrds as well in the highest as lower departments of life and to None more than to me in particular who am with great Esteem Thy Respectful Friend

JOHN WRIGHT

Dr. Benjamin Franklin

Addressed: Dr. Benjamin Franklin / at / Paris / per favr. of William Rawle

Endorsed: Hotel de Montgomery Rue de Colombier[3]

Notation: John Wright, London 19. April 1782.

2. The bankruptcies of Brown & Collinson and of William Rabone and Lewis Benjamin Crinsoz of Thames Street were announced in the May, 1782, issue of the *Gent. Mag.* (p. 264).

3. Where Rawle was staying. The street is now known as rue du Vieux-Colombier: Hillairet, *Rues de Paris,* II, 642. Rawle arrived in Paris on April 30 and stayed until May 8, when BF issued him a passport (below): Journal of William Rawle, Hist. Soc. of Pa.

To John Adams

LS:[4] Massachusetts Historical Society; copy: Library of Congress; transcript: National Archives

Sir, Passy, April 20th. 1782.

I hope your Excellency received the Copy of our Instructions which I sent by the Courier from Versailles some Weeks since.[5] I wrote to you on the 13th. to go by Capt. Smedly and sent a Pacquet of Correspondence with Mr. Hartley. Smedly did not leave Paris so soon as I expected: but you should have it by this time. With this I send a fresh Correspondence which I have been drawn into, viz:[6] 1. A Letter I sent to Lord Shelburne before he was Minister. 2. His Ansr. since he was Minister by Mr Oswald. 3. A Letter from Mr Lawrens. 4. My Letter to M. de Vergennes. 5. My Ansr to Lord Shelburne. 6. My Answer to Mr Lawrens, 7th Copy of Digges's Report.[7] These Papers will inform you pretty well of what pass'd between me and Mr Oswald, except that in a Conversation at parting I mention'd to him, that I observed they spoke much in England of obtaining a *Reconciliation* with the Colonies; that this was more than a mere *Peace;* that the latter might possibly be obtained without the former; that the cruel Injuries wantonly done us by burning our Towns &ca. had made deep Impressions of Resentment which would long remain; that much of the Advantage to the Commerce of England from a

---

4. In WTF's hand. BF added the postscript, which does not appear on the copy and transcript (both of which are in BF's journal of the peace negotiations).

5. BF promised to do so on March 31 (above).

6. The first six letters, all published in this volume, are dated March 22, April 6, 7, 15, 18, and 20.

7. The memorandum Digges had drawn up for Shelburne on March 30 describing his March 22 meeting with JA. BF must have received a copy from Oswald. (He already knew the substance of the meeting from Digges's letter of March 22[–26] and JA's of March 26, both above.) Shelburne sent Digges's report to George III who himself made a copy and commented that it had only served as "a melancholy confirmation of the American dependency on France." Fortescue, *Correspondence of George Third*, v, 430–3. A copy of the memorandum made for BF by Josiah Flagg when he copied the journal of the peace negotiations is at the Library of Congress. The text is published in Elias and Finch, *Letters of Digges*, pp. 365–6.

Peace would depend on a *Reconciliation;* that the Peace without a Reconciliation would probably not be durable; that after a Quarrel between Friends, nothing tended so much to *conciliate,* as Offers made by the Aggressor, of Reparation for Injuries done by him in his Passion. And I hinted that if England should make us a *Voluntary Offer* of Canada expressly for that purpose, it might have a good Effect. Mr Oswald liked much the Idea, said they were too much straiten'd for Money to make us pecuniary Reparation, but he should endeavour to persuade their doing it in this Way. He is furnish'd with a Passport to go and return by Calais, and I expect him back in ten or twelve Days. I wish you and Mr Lawrens could be here when he arrives; for I shall much want your Advice, & cannot act without your Concurrence. If the present Crisis of your Affairs prevents your coming, I hope at least Mr Lawrens will be here, and we must communicate with you by Expresses, for your Letters to me per Post are generally open'd. I shall write pr. next Post requesting Mr Jay to be here also as soon as possible.

I received your Letter advising of your Draft on me for a Quarter's Salary, which will be duly honour'd.[8]

With great Esteem, I have the honour to be, Sir, Your Excellency's most obedient & most humble Sert.   B FRANKLIN

If Mr Laurens has left Holland, please to seal his Letter with a Wafer and let it follow him.—

I shall be glad to have again all the Papers of this and the former Packet; but you can keep Copies of any you may think worth the Trouble—

His Exy J. Adams Esqre.

Endorsed: Dr Franklin. 20. April 1782 ansd May 2. recd May 1.

8. JA to BF, April 13, above. Ferdinand Grand honored the bill on May 27, paying 14,199 *l.t.* 10 *s.* 9 *d.:* Account XXVII (XXXII, 4).

To Henry Laurens

LS:[9] South Carolina Historical Society; copy:[1] Library of Congress; transcript: National Archives

Sir,   Passy, April 20th. 1782.

I received by Mr Oswald the Letter you did me the honour of writing to me the 7th Inst. He brought me also a Letter from Lord Shelburne,[2] which gave him the same good Character that you do, adding, "He is fully appriz'd of my Mind, and you may give full Credit to every thing he assures you of." Mr Oswald, however, could give me no other Particulars of his Lordships Mind, but that he was sincerely disposed to Peace. As the Message seem'd therefore rather intended to procure or receive Propositions than to make any, I told Mr Oswald that I could make none but in Concurrence with my Colleagues in the Commission; and that if we were together we should not treat but in Conjunction with France; and I proposed introducing him to M. De Vergennes, which he accepted.[3] He made to that Minister the same Declaration of the Disposition of England to Peace; who reply'd that France had assuredly the same good Dispositions; that a Treaty might be immediately begun, but it must be for a *general*, not *a particular* Peace. That as to the Place, he thought Paris might be the most convenient, as Spain had here already an Ambassador, and the American Commissioners could easily be assembled here; this upon the Supposition of the Parties treating directly with each other, without the Intervention of Mediators: But if the Mediation was to be used, it might be at Vienna. The King his Master however was so truly disposed to Peace, that he would agree to any Place that the King of England should chuse: and would at the Treaty give Proof of the Confidence that might be placed in any Engagements he should then enter into, by the Fidelity & Exactitude with which he should observe those he already had with his present allies.[4] Mr Oswald is returned with

---

9. In WTF's hand.
1. The copy and transcript are in BF's journal of the peace negotiations.
2. April 6, above.
3. For the conversation described below see BF to Shelburne, April 18.
4. The same reply supposedly was given to Forth: BF to JA, April 13, above.

these general Answers, by the Way of Calais, and expects to be here again in a few Days. I wish it might be convenient for you and Mr Adams to be here at the same time. But if the present critical Situation of Affairs there make his being in Holland necessary just now, I hope you may nevertheless be here, bringing with you his Opinion & Advice. I have proposed to Lord Shelburne to discharge you from the Obligations you enter'd into at the time of your Enlargement, that you may act more freely in the Treaty he desires.[5] I had done myself the Honour of writing to you a few days before the Arrival of Mr Oswald.[6] My Letter went by Mr Young, your Secretary, and inclosed a Copy of our Commission, with an Offer of Money if you had occassion for any. Hoping that you will not return to England before you have been at Paris, I forbear enlarging on the State of our Affairs here and in Spain. M. de Vergennes told me he should be very glad to see you here. I found Mr Oswald to answer perfectly the Character you gave me of him, & was much pleased with him.

I have the honour to be with great Esteem, Sir, Your Excellency's most obedient & most humble Servant   B FRANKLIN

His Exy. Hy. Lawrens Esqre

Endorsed: Recd. 10th. May—by H L junr who arriv'd in London the Night of the 9th.[7] Answd. Ostend 17th. May see Copy.—

Notation: Doctor Franklin—Passy 20th April 1782.

From Vergennes

L and transcript: National Archives

Vlles le 20. Avril 1782.

M. le Cte. de Vergennes a l'honneur d'envoyer à Monsieur franklin un Memoire qui lui a été adressé par l'ambassadeur du

5. In his April 18 letter.
6. Above, April 12.
7. Henry Laurens, Jr., had been in the Netherlands, leaving Amsterdam on or just after May 2: JA to BF, April 16 (above) and May 2 (below). His father returned to London on April 23 and met with Shelburne the following day: *Laurens Papers,* xv, xxxvii, 491–3.

Roi en Suisse.[8] Il le prie de vouloir bien lui faire parvenir dans le temps la reponse dont il le croira susceptible.

To John Adams

LS[9] and transcript:[1] Massachusetts Historical Society; copy: Library of Congress; transcript: National Archives

Sir,   Passy April 21. 1782.

I have just received the Honour of yours dated the 16th. Instant, acquainting me with the Interview between your Excellency and Mr Lawrens. I am glad to learn that his political Sentiments coincide with ours; and that there is a Disposition in England to give us up Canada and Nova Scotia.

I like your Idea of seeing no more Messengers that are not Plenipotentiaries; But I cannot refuse seeing again Mr Oswald, as the Minister here consider'd the Letter to me from Lord Shelburne as a kind of Authentication given that Messenger, and expects his Return with some explicit Propositions. I shall keep you advised of whatever passes.

The late Act of Parliament for Exchanging American Prisoners as *Prisoners of War* according to the Law of Nations, *any thing in their Commitments notwithstanding,* seems to me a Renunciation of the British Pretensions to try our People as Subjects guilty of High Treason, and to be a kind of tacit Acknowl-

8. The memoir, addressed to "Son Excellence Sir Franklin," is an appeal from Jean-Jacques Vallier (or Wallier) dated March 28 from Solothurn, Switzerland. Vallier and his younger brother Jean had been staying in Edenton, N.C., at the home of François La Fond, when the brother died of a fever. The attending physician, French naval surgeon Dominique Pambrun, signed a death certificate on Feb. 14, 1781 (the text of which is provided), but, being in French, it could not be certified as legal by the Edenton officials. Vallier was unable to procure an English version before joining the ship *Washington,* which was captured by the British off St. Eustatius. Now recovering from an illness contracted at sea, he asks BF's help in procuring a valid death certificate from the Edenton authorities so that he can claim his brother's estate. The vicomte de Polignac, French ambassador in Solothurn (XXVIII, 80n), has agreed to forward this appeal. This memoir and an English translation are both at the National Archives.

9. In WTF's hand.

1. The transcripts and copy are in BF's journal of the peace negotiations.

edgement of our Independency. Having taken this Step, it will be less difficult for them to acknowledge it expressly. They are now preparing Transports to send the Prisoners home. I yesterday sent the Pass-ports desir'd of me.[2]

Sir George Grand shows me a Letter from Mr Fizeaux, in which he says, that if Advantage is taken of the present Enthusiasm in favour of America, a Loan might be obtained in Holland of Five or Six Millions of Florins for America, and if their House[3] is impower'd to open it he has no doubt of Success; but that no time is to be lost. I earnestly recommend this Matter to you, as extreamly necessary to the Operations of our Financier Mr Morris, who not knowing that the greatest Part of the last Five Millions had been consumed by Purchaces of Goods &ca in Europe, writes me Advice of large Drafts, that he shall be obliged to make upon me this Summer.[4] This Court has granted us Six Millions of Livres for the current Year;[5] but it will fall vastly short of our Occasions, there being large Orders to fulfill, and near two Millions & an half to pay M. Beaumarchais,[6] besides the Interest Bills &ca. The House of Fizeaux & Grand is now appointed Banker for France by a special Commission from the King,[7] and will on that as well as on other Accounts be in my Opinion the fitter for this Operation. Your Excellency being on the Spot can better judge of the Terms, &ca. and manage with that House the whole Business, in which I should be glad to have no other Concern, than that of receiving Assistance from it when press'd by the dreaded Drafts.

With great Respect, I am, Sir, Your Excellency's most obedient and most humble Sert   B FRANKLIN

His Exy. J. Adams Esqr.

Endorsed: Dr Franklin April 21 1782

2. Probably with a now-missing covering letter to William Hodgson; see BF to Hodgson, April 26.

3. Fizeaux, Grand & Cie.

4. See XXXVI, 154–5, 190–1, 403, 580.

5. For which see BF to Jay, March 16.

6. See BF to Morris, March 30.

7. The firm was notified on April 16. The honor was in recognition of its work in managing the French government's 5,000,000 f. loan in the Netherlands on behalf of the United States: Lüthy, *Banque protestante*, II, 616–17.

From Francis Coffyn

ALS: American Philosophical Society

Monsieur   Dunkerque ce 21 avril 1782.

J'ai l'honneur de vous écrire la presente qui vous sera remise par les nommés Whipple Crow & Binjamin Hocum[8] tous deux americains qui ont été pris sur le navire brign la Polly de Rhode Island et conduits a Bristol d'ou ils se Sont sauvés des prisons & sont arrivés ici manquant de tout, comme ils cherchent a retourner en Amerique, Je leurs ai fourni pour le Compte de votre Excellence une somme de £.144[9] pour payer les frais de leur route suivant leur récépicé.

Je suis avec un tres profond respect Monsieur Votre tres humble & tres obeissant Serviteur   F. COFFYN

Addressed: A Son / Excellence M. Bn Franklin / Ministre plenipotentiaire des Etats unis / de l'amerique Septentrionale a la / cour de france / a Passi pres Paris

Notation: Coffyn Dunkerque 21. avril 1782.

From Henry Wyld

ALS: American Philosophical Society

Most Excellent sir   Hatherlow 21st. April 1782

I recd. your kind reply to the requests of the Company by mine to forward the things which were thought to be sufficient for our passage, are very sorry to hear that your Authority for granting such things is recalled, for the reasons assigned in my last, we having wholly fixed, and given up our imployments in pursuance of such things. To impose upon your excellency we should think ourselves to have forfeited all human Confidence, If you think the Hazard so great we must comply, always making our resolves (however detrimental) subserviant to superior Judgment, joined to experience, therefore we desire you will give us the most early account of a prospect to emigrate, as we

---

8. We have no record of Crow's visiting Passy, but Benjamin Slocum signed a promissory note on April 27. See the Editorial Note on Promissory Notes.

9. On March 7: Account XXVII (XXXII, 4).

ernestly desire, to be the first persons who may arrive there in the Capacity of Manufacturers in our Branches, and we are fully satisfied that our abilities are such as would gain the notice and esteem of any state where such manufactores are wanted.

Your assurances of serving us with your abilities give new life to our undertaking, and in hopes of which and satisfying you that we are every thing we pretend to be I am for myself and Friends your excellencies most obliged and very humble Servant

HENRY WYLD

Addressed: To his Excellency Benjm. Franklin / LLD. Minister plenipotentiary / from the United states of America / at Passey near Paris / France

Notation: H. Wyld 21 April 1782.

"Supplement to the Boston Independent Chronicle"

Passy, second edition, printed by Benjamin Franklin, 1782[1]

When Franklin saw that serious peace negotiations were possible, his rage at the cruelties of the war resurfaced. He had heard that Great Britain desired a reconciliation. The cessation of hostilities was not the same as a reconciliation, he maintained, and peace without reconciliation would never be durable. It would take more than a "mere Peace" to erase the memory of the atrocities that innocent Americans had suffered at the hands of the British and their Indian allies. As he insisted to Oswald on April 19 (just hours before Oswald returned to London), Great Britain should offer reparations.[2]

---

1. As we explain in the headnote, BF printed two editions, one an expanded version of the other. We print the fuller text. Examples of both are at the APS and the Library of Congress. They are both described, and the first edition illustrated, in Luther S. Livingston, *Franklin and his Press at Passy* (New York, 1914), pp. 58–67.
2. See BF's notes for a conversation with Oswald, [on or before April 19], and his journal of the peace negotiations. BF had earlier used a similar argument to press for a prisoner exchange; see his letter to Hodgson, March 31, and to Hartley, April 5.

SUPPLEMENT
TO THE BOSTON
INDEPENDENT CHRONICLE.

BOSTON, March 12.

Extract of a Letter from Capt. Gerrish, of the New-England Militia, dated Albany, March 7.

THE Peltry taken in the Expedition [*See the Account of the Expedition in Oswegatchie on the River St. Laurence, in our Paper of the 1st Instant.*] will as you see amount to a good deal of Money. The Possession of this Booty at first gave us Pleasure; but we were struck with Horror to find among the Packages, 8 large ones containing SCALPS of our unhappy Country-folks, taken in the three last Years by the Senneka Indians from the Inhabitants of the Frontiers of New-York, New-Jersey, Pennsylvania, and Virginia, and sent by them as a Present to Col. Haldimand, Governor of Canada, in order to be by him transmitted to England. They were accompanied by the following curious Letter to that Gentleman.

May it please your Excellency, Teoga, Jan. 3d, 1782.

"At the Request of the Senneka Chiefs I send herewith to your Excellency, under the Care of James Boyd, eight Packs of Scalps, cured, dried, hooped and painted, with all the Indian triumphal Marks, of which the following is Invoice and Explanation.

No. 1. Containing 43 Scalps of Congress Soldiers killed in different Skirmishes; these are stretched on black Hoops, 4 Inches diameter; the inside of the Skin painted red, with a small black Spot to note their being killed with bullets. Also 62 of Farmers, killed in their Houses; the Hoops red; the Skin painted brown, and marked with a Hoe; a black Circle all round, to denote their being surprised in the Night; and a black Hatchet in the Middle, signifying their being killed with that Weapon.

No. 2. Containing 98 of Farmers killed in their Houses; Hoops red; Figure of a Hoe, to mark their Profession; great white Circle and Sun, to shew they were surprised in the Day-time; a little red Foot, to shew they stood upon their Defence, and died fighting for their Lives and Families.

No. 3. Containing 97 of Farmers; Hoops green, to shew they were killed in their Fields; a large white Circle with a little round Mark on it for the Sun, to shew that it was in the Day-time; black Bullet-mark on some, Hatchet on others.

No. 4. Containing 102 of Farmers, mixed of the several Marks above; only 18 marked with a little yellow Flame, to denote their being of Prisoners burnt alive, after being scalped, their Nails pulled out by the Roots, and other Torments; one of these latter supposed to be of a rebel Clergyman, his Band being fixed to the Hoop of his Scalp. Most of the Farmers appear by the Hair to have been young or middle-aged Men; there being but 67 very grey Heads among them all, which makes the Service more essential.

No. 5. Containing 88 Scalps of Women; Hair long, braided in the Indian Fashion, to shew they were Mothers; Hoops blue; Skin yellow Ground, with little red Tadpoles to represent, by way of Triumph, the Tears or Grief occasioned to their Relations; a black scalping Knife or Hatchet at the Bottom, to mark their being killed with those Instruments. 17 others, Hair very grey; black Hoops; plain brown Colour; no Mark but the short Club or Cassetête, to shew they were knocked down dead, or had their Brains beat out.

No. 6. Containing 193 Boys' Scalps, of various Ages; small green Hoops; whitish Ground on the Skin, with red Tears in the Middle, and black Bullet-marks, Knife, Hatchet, or Club, as their Deaths happened.

No. 7. 211 Girls' Scalps, big and little; small yellow Hoops; white Ground; Tears; Hatchet, Club, scalping Knife, &c.

No. 8. This Package is a Mixture of all the Varieties above-mention'd, to the Number of 122; with a Box of Birch Bark, containing 29 little Infants' Scalps of various Sizes; small white Hoops; white Ground; no Tears; and only a little black Knife in the Middle, to shew they were ript out of their Mothers' Bellies.

With these Packs, the Chiefs send to your Excellency the following Speech, delivered by Conejogatchie in Council, interpreted by the elder Moore, the Trader, and taken down by me in Writing.

Father,

We send you herewith many Scalps, that you may see we are not idle Friends. *A blue Belt.*

Father,

We wish you to send these Scalps over the Water to the great King, that he may regard them and be refreshed; and that he may see our faithfulness in destroying his Enemies, and be convinced that his Presents have not been made to ungrateful People. *A blue and white Belt with red Tassels.*

Father,

Attend to what I am now going to say: it is a Matter of much Weight. The great King's Enemies are many, and they grow fast in Number. They were formerly like young Panthers: they could nei-

---

ther bite nor scratch: we could play with them safely: we feared nothing they could do to us. But now their Bodies are become big as the Elk, and strong as the Buffalo: they have also got great and sharp Claws. They have driven us out of our Country for taking Part in your Quarrel. We expect the great King will give us another Country, that our Children may live after us, and be his Friends and Children, as we are. Say this for us to the great King. To enforce it we give this Belt. *A great white Belt with blue Tassels.*

Father,

We have only to say farther that your Traders exact more than ever for their Goods: and our Hunting is lessened by the War, so that we have fewer Skins to give for them. This ruins us. Think of some Remedy. We are poor: and you have Plenty of every Thing. We know you will send us Powder and Guns, and Knives and Hatchets: but we also want Shirts and Blankets. *A little white Belt.*

I do not doubt but that your Excellency will think it proper to give some farther Encouragement to those honest People. The high Prices they complain of, are the necessary Effect of the War. Whatever Presents may be sent for them through my Hands, shall be distributed with Prudence and Fidelity. I have the Honour of being

Your Excellency's most obedient

And most humble Servant,

JAMES CRAUFURD."

It was at first proposed to bury these Scalps: but Lieutenant Fitzgerald, who you know has got Leave of Absence to go for Ireland on his private Affairs, said he thought it better they should proceed to their Destination; and if they were given to him, he would undertake to carry them to England, and hang them all up in some dark Night on the Trees in St. James's Park, where they could be seen from the King and Queen's Palaces in the Morning; for that the Sight of them might perhaps strike Mrs. Haldimand (as he called her) with some Compunction of Conscience. They were accordingly delivered to Fitz, and he has brought them safe hither. To-morrow they go with his Baggage, in a Waggon for Boston, and will probably be there in a few Days after this Letter.

I am, &c.

SAMUEL GERRISH.

BOSTON, March 20.

Monday last arrived here Lieutenant Fitzgerald abovementioned, and yesterday the Waggon with the Scalps. Thousands of People are flocking to see them this Morning, and all Mouths are full of Execrations. Fixing them to the Trees is not approved. It is now proposed to make them up in decent little Packets, seal and direct them, one to the King, containing a Sample of every Sort for his Museum, one to the Queen, with some of Women and little Children; the Rest to be distributed among both Houses of Parliament; a double Quantity to the Bishops.

Mr. Willis,

Please to insert in your useful Paper the following Copy of a Letter, from Commodore Jones, directed

To Sir Joseph York, Ambassador from the King of England to the States-general of the United Provinces.

SIR, Ipswich, New-England,
March 7, 1781.

I Have lately seen a memorial, said to have been presented by your Excellency to their High Mightinesses the States-general, in which you are pleased to qualify me with the title of *pirate*.

A pirate is defined to be *hostis humani generis*, [an enemy to all mankind]. It happens, Sir, that I am an enemy to no part of mankind, except your nation, the English; which nation at the same time comes much more within the definition; being actually an enemy to, and at war with, one whole quarter of the world, America, considerable parts of Asia and Africa, a great part of Europe, and in a fair way of being at war with the rest.

A pirate makes war for the sake of *rapine*. This is not the kind of war I am engaged in against England. Our's is a war in defence of *liberty*, . . . the most just of all wars; and of our *properties*, which your nation would have taken from us, without our consent, in violation of our rights, and by an armed force. Your's, therefore, is a war of *rapine*; of course, a piratical war: and those who approve of it, and are engaged in it, more justly deserve the name of pirates, which you bestow on me. It is, indeed, a war that coincides with the general spirit of your nation. Your common people in their ale-houses sing the twenty-four songs of Robin Hood, and applaud his deer-stealing and his robberies on the highway: those who have just learning enough to read, are delighted with your histories of the Pirates and of the buccaniers; and even your scholars, in the universities, study Quintus Curtius; and are taught to admire Alexander for what they call his conquests in the Indies. Severe laws and the hangman keep down the effects of this spirit among yourselves, (though you little regard you laws, for example, in more highway robberies than in these words than the resolution of Europe put together): but so far as to carry on your piratical war with America, the manners of your fleets, and the owners of your privateers were animated against us by the act of your parliament, which repealed the law of God—"Thou shalt not steal,"—by declaring it lawful for them to rob us of all our property they could meet with on the Ocean. This act too had a retrospect, and, going beyond bulls of pardon, declared that all the robberies you had committed, previous to the act, should be deemed just and lawful. Your soldiers too were promised the plunder of our citizens and your officers were flattered with the division of our lands. You had even the baseness to corrupt our servants, the sailors employed by us, and encourage them to rob their masters, and bring to you the ships and goods they were entrusted with. Is there any society of pirates on the sea or land, who, in declaring wrong to be right, and right wrong, have less authority than your parliament? Do any of them more justly than your parliament deserve the title you bestow on me?

You will tell me that we forfeited all our estates by our refusal to pay the taxes your nation would have imposed on us, without the consent of our colony parliaments. Have you then forgot the incontestible principle, which was the foundation of Hambden's glorious law-suit with Charles the first, that "what an English king has no right to demand, an English subject has a right to refuse?" But you cannot so soon have forgotten the instructions of your late honourable father, who, being himself a sound Whig, taught you certainly the principles of the Revolution, and that, "if subjects might in some cases forfeit their property, kings also might forfeit their title, and all claim to the allegiance of their subjects." I must then suppose you well acquainted with those Whig principles, on which permit me, Sir, to ask a few questions.

Is not protection as justly due from a king to his people, as obedience from the people to their king?

If then a king declares his people to be out of his protection—

If he violates and deprives them of their constitutional rights—

If he wages war against them—

If he plunders their merchants, ravages their coasts, burns their towns, and destroys their lives—

If he hires foreign mercenaries to help him in their destruction—

If he engages savages to murder their defenceless farmers, women and children—

If he cruelly forces such of his subjects as fall into his hands, to bear arms against their country, and become executioners of their friends and brethren—

If he sells others of them into bondage, in Africa and the East Indies—

If he excites domestic insurrections among their servants, and encourages servants to murder their masters—

Does not so atrocious a conduct towards his subjects, dissolve their allegiance?

If not,—please to say how or by what means it can possibly be dissolved?

All this horrible wickedness and barbarity has been and

daily is practised by the king your master (as you call him in your memorial) upon the Americans, whom he is still pleased to claim as his subjects.

During these six years past, he has destroyed not less than forty thousand of those subjects, by battles on land or sea, or by starving them, or poisoning them to death, in the unwholesome air, with the unwholesome food of his prisons. And he has wasted the lives of at least an equal number of his own soldiers and sailors; many of whom have been forced into that odious service, and dragged from their families and friends, by the outrageous violence of his illegal press-gangs. You are a gentleman of letters, and have read history: do you recollect any instance of any tyrant, since the beginning of the world, who, in the course of so few years, had done so much mischief, by murdering so many of his own people? Let us view one of the worst and blackest of them, Nero. He put to death a few of his courtiers, placemen and pensioners, and among the rest his tutor. Had George the third done the same, and no more, his crime, though detestable, as an act of lawless power, might have been as useful to his nation, as that of Nero was hurtful to Rome; considering the different characters and merits of the sufferers. Nero indeed wished that the people of Rome had but one neck, that he might behead them all by one stroke: but this was a simple wish. George is carrying it with as much as he can into execution; and, by continuing in his present course a few years longer, will have destroyed more of the British people than Nero could have found inhabitants in Rome. Hence, the expression of Milton, in speaking of Charles the first, that he was "sanguine nocentior," is still more applicable to George the third. Like Nero and all other tyrants, while they lived, he indeed has his flatterers, his addressers, his applauders; Pensions, places, and hopes of preferment, can bribe even bishops to approve his conduct: but, when those infamous, purchased addresses and panegyrics are sunk and lost in oblivion or contempt, impartial history will step forth, speak honest truth, and rank him among public calamities. The only difference will be, that plagues, pestilences, and famines are of this world, and arise from the nature of things: but voluntary malice, mischief, and murder are from Hell: and this king will, therefore, stand foremost in the list of diabolical, bloody, and execrable tyrants. His base-bought parliaments too, who fell him their souls, and extort from the people the money with which they aid his destructive purposes, as they share his guilt, will share his infamy,—parliaments, who to please him, have repeatedly, by different votes year after year, dipped their hands in human blood, insomuch that methinks I see it dried and caked so thick upon them, that if they could wash it off in the Thames which flows under their windows, the whole river would run red to the Ocean.

One is provoked by enormous wickedness; but one is ashamed and humbuazed at the view of human baseness. It afflicts me, therefore, to see a gentleman of Sir Joseph York's education and talents, for the sake of a red ribband and a paltry stipend, mean enough to stile such a monster his master, wear his livery, and hold himself ready at his command even to cut the throats of fellow-subjects. This makes it impossible for me to end my letter with the civility of a compliment, and obliges me to subscribe myself simply,

JOHN PAUL JONES,

whom you are pleased to stile a Pirate.

"Supplement to the Boston Independent Chronicle," verso

By April 22, Franklin had printed this hoax, a purported supplement to a Boston newspaper. Not since he and Lafayette had drawn up a "List of British Cruelties" in 1779 had he written in such detail about the savage acts visited upon American citizens.[3] If Franklin could get the articles reprinted in England, he wrote John Adams, "it might make them a little asham'd of themselves."[4] It might also influence public opinion as the peace negotiations got under way.

Franklin printed two versions of the "Supplement." The preliminary one, which we have no evidence of his having circulated, consisted only of the one-page purported letter from a Capt. Samuel Gerrish. We suspect that he wrote this piece in the days following Oswald's departure, though the lack of any manuscript versions of these pieces renders our speculations tentative. He filled the remaining space with five fictitious advertisements. Franklin then decided to add an additional article, the purported letter from John Paul Jones to Sir Joseph Yorke, and thus take advantage of the second side of the sheet. It is not known whether he drafted this piece anew or printed something he had written earlier. In any case, he removed the advertisements and replaced them with the beginning of the Jones letter, continuing that letter on the verso. To fill out the second page, he reinstated the first two of the original five advertisements. This double-sided version was the one Franklin sent to Adams on April 22, to John Jay on April 24, to Dumas on May 3, and to James Hutton in July.[5]

The form of the hoax was nearly perfect, from the newspaper's number (No. 705 of Boston's actual *Independent Chronicle and Universal Advertiser* was issued in March, 1782) down to the convincingly worded notices of land for sale in Medford and of a missing horse in Salem. The typography would attract no attention except to the most discerning reader, who might have noticed that the type was French rather than English. When he added the John Paul Jones letter, however, Franklin could not resist a subtle clue that would have piqued the curiosity of any printer: he set several elements in the unique italic script that Fournier had cut exclusively for him, and which, unbeknownst to the British, was a hallmark of his Passy Press.[6]

3. The list is in XXIX, 590–3. BF may also have written the list of bounties to be paid for atrocities, a 1778 satire published in the *Affaires de l'Angleterre et de l'Amérique:* XXVIII, 256–9.

4. BF to JA, April 22, below.

5. BF's letter to JA makes a specific allusion to the John Paul Jones letter, although the others do not. Hutton acknowledged receipt of the paper on July 23; BF may have enclosed it with his letter of July 7.

6. The Jones letter was set in cicero, or 12-point, which accommodated the

Horace Walpole needed no such typographic trickery to guess the identity of the author when the hoax (or part of it) found its way into the British press five months later. "Have you seen in the papers the excellent letter of Paul Jones to Sir Joseph Yorke?" Walpole wrote to a friend on October 1. *"Elle nous dit bien des vérités!* I doubt poor Sir Joseph cannot answer them! Dr. Franklin himself I should think was the author."[7] The Jones letter had appeared on September 27 in *The Public Advertiser*, where the publisher speculated that if the piece had not been written by Jones himself, its "contemptuous insolence" proved that it was "the Production of some such *audacious Rebel.*" The *Public Advertiser* did not print the first item, the letter from "Capt. Gerrish" quoting one from "James Craufurd." The publisher may have felt, as James Hutton did, that the news it reported was so exaggerated as to be inconceivable, even by the barbaric standards of this war.[8] Most of the piece, however, ending with Craufurd's signature, appeared in *The Remembrancer; or Impartial Repository of Public Events* for 1782, part II, pp. 135–6, where it was attributed to the *Boston Chronicle*.

[before April 22, 1782]

Numb. 705.
SUPPLEMENT
TO THE BOSTON
INDEPENDENT CHRONICLE.

BOSTON, March 12.
Extract of a Letter from Capt. Gerrish, *of the* New-England *Militia, dated* Albany, March 7.

THE Peltry taken in the Expedition [*See the Account of the Expedition to* Oswegatchie *on the River St.* Laurence, *in our Paper of the 1st Instant.*] will as you see amount to a good deal of Money. The Possession of this Booty at first gave us Pleasure; but we

---

fancy italic: XXXIII, 105n. It was used for "Mr. Willis," the two-line address to Sir Joseph Yorke, "Nerone Neronior," and, following Jones's signature, the final word "Pirate."

7. Lewis, *Walpole Correspondence*, XXXIII, 357–8.

8. Hutton to BF, July 23. For the common practice of scalping in 18th-century America see James Axtell, "Scalping: the Ethnohistory of a Moral Question," in James Axtell, *The European and the Indian: Essays in the Ethnohistory of Colonial North America* (New York and Oxford, 1981), pp. 207–41.

were struck with Horror to find among the Packages, 8 large ones containing SCALPS of our unhappy Country-folks, taken in the three last Years by the Senneka Indians from the Inhabitants of the Frontiers of New-York, New-Jersey, Pennsylvania, and Virginia, and sent by them as a Present to Col. Haldimand,[9] Governor of Canada, in order to be by him transmitted to England. They were accompanied by the following curious Letter to that Gentleman.

May it please your Excellency,   *Teoga, Jan. 3d, 1782.*
"At the Request of the Senneka Chiefs I send herewith to your Excellency, under the Care of James Boyd, eight Packs of Scalps, cured, dried, hooped and painted, with all the Indian triumphal Marks, of which the following is Invoice and Explanation.

No. 1. Containing 43 Scalps of Congress Soldiers killed in different Skirmishes; these are stretched on black Hoops, 4 Inches diameter; the inside of the Skin painted red, with a small black Spot to note their being killed with Bullets. Also 62 of Farmers, killed in their Houses; the Hoops red; the Skin painted brown, and marked with a Hoe; a black Circle all round, to denote their being surprised in the Night; and a black Hatchet in the Middle, signifying their being killed with that Weapon.

No. 2. Containing 98 of Farmers killed in their Houses; Hoops red; Figure of a Hoe, to mark their Profession; great white Circle and Sun, to shew they were surprised in the Day-time; a little red Foot, to shew they stood upon their Defence, and died fighting for their Lives and Families.

No. 3. Containing 97 of Farmers; Hoops green, to shew they were killed in their Fields; a large white Circle with a little round Mark on it for the Sun, to shew that it was in the Day-time; black Bullet-mark on some, Hatchet on others.

No. 4. Containing 102 of Farmers, mixed of the several Marks above; only 18 marked with a little yellow Flame, to de-

9. Sir Frederick Haldimand, who served as governor of Canada from 1778 to 1784. *DNB.*

note their being of Prisoners burnt alive, after being scalped, their Nails pulled out by the Roots and other Torments: one of these latter supposed to be of a rebel Clergyman, his Band being fixed to the Hoop of his Scalp. Most of the Farmers appear by the Hair to have been young or middle-aged Men; there being but 67 very grey Heads among them all; which makes the Service more essential.

No. 5. Containing 88 Scalps of Women; Hair long, braided in the Indian Fashion, to shew they were Mothers; Hoops blue; Skin yellow Ground, with little red Tadpoles to represent, by way of Triumph, the Tears or Grief occasioned to their Relations; a black scalping Knife or Hatchet at the Bottom to mark their being killed with those Instruments. 17 others, Hair very grey; black Hoops; plain brown Colour; no Mark but the short Club or Cassetete, to shew they were knocked down dead, or had their Brains beat out.

No. 6. Containing 193 Boys' Scalps, of various Ages; small green Hoops; whitish Ground on the Skin, with red Tears in the Middle, and black Bullet-marks, Knife, Hatchet, or Club, as their Deaths happened.

No. 7. 211 Girls' Scalps, big and little; small yellow Hoops; white Ground; Tears; Hatchet, Club, scalping Knife, &c.

No. 8. This Package is a Mixture of all the Varieties above-mention'd, to the Number of 122; with a Box of Birch Bark, containing 29 little Infants' Scalps of various Sizes; small white Hoops; white Ground; no Tears; and only a little black Knife in the Middle, to shew they were ript out of their Mothers' Bellies.

With these Packs, the Chiefs send to your Excellency the following Speech, delivered by Conejogatchie in Council, interpreted by the elder Moore, the Trader, and taken down by me in Writing.

Father,

We send you herewith many Scalps, that you may see we are not idle Friends.   *A blue Belt.*

Father,

We wish you to send these Scalps over the Water to the great King, that he may regard them and be refreshed; and that he may see our faithfulness in destroying his Enemies, and be convinced that his Presents have not been made to ungrateful People.

A blue and white Belt with red Tassels.

Father,

Attend to what I am now going to say: it is a Matter of much Weight. The great King's Enemies are many, and they grow fast in Number. They were formerly like young Panthers: they could neither bite nor scratch: we could play with them safely: we feared nothing they could do to us. But now their Bodies are become big as the Elk, and strong as the Buffalo: they have also got great and sharp Claws. They have driven us out of our Country for taking Part in your Quarrel. We expect the great King will give us another Country, that our Children may live after us, and be his Friends and Children, as we are. Say this for us to the great King. To enforce it we give this Belt.

A great white Belt with blue Tassels.

Father,

We have only to say farther that your Traders exact more than ever for their Goods: and our Hunting is lessened by the War, so that we have fewer Skins to give for them. This ruins us. Think of some Remedy. We are poor: and you have Plenty of every Thing. We know you will send us Powder and Guns, and Knives and Hatchets: but we also want Shirts and Blankets.

A little white Belt.

I do not doubt but that your Excellency will think it proper to give some farther Encouragement to those honest People. The high Prices they complain of, are the necessary Effect of the War. Whatever Presents may be sent for them through my Hands, shall be distributed with Prudence and Fidelity. I have the Honour of being

Your Excellency's most obedient And most humble Servant,
JAMES CRAUFURD."

It was at first proposed to bury these Scalps: but Lieutenant Fitzgerald, who you know has got Leave of Absence to go for Ireland on his private Affairs, said he thought it better they should proceed to their Destination; and if they were given to him, he would undertake to carry them to England, and hang them all up in some dark Night on the Trees in St. James's Park, where they could be seen from the King and Queen's Palaces in the Morning: for that the Sight of them might perhaps strike Muley Ishmael (as he called him)[1] with some Compunction of Conscience. They were accordingly delivered to Fitz, and he has brought them safe hither. To-morrow they go with his Baggage in a Waggon for Boston, and will probably be there in a few Days after this Letter.

I am, &c.   SAMUEL GERRISH.

BOSTON, March 20.

Monday last arrived here Lieutenant Fitzgerald abovementioned, and Yesterday the Waggon with the Scalps. Thousands of People are flocking to see them this Morning, and all Mouths are full of Execrations. Fixing them to the Trees is not approved. It is now proposed to make them up in decent little Packets, seal and direct them; one to the King, containing a Sample of every Sort for his Museum; one to the Queen, with some of Women and little Children: the Rest to be distributed among both Houses of Parliament; a double Quantity to the Bishops.

Mr. Willis,

Please to insert in your useful Paper the following Copy of a Letter, from Commodore Jones, directed

To Sir Joseph York, Ambassador from the King of England to the States-general of the United Provinces.

1. Sultan of Morocco Muley Ismail (1646–1727), whose use of Christian prisoners for forced labor gave him a reputation in Europe for cruelty: Lewis, *Walpole Correspondence*, XI, 207n; Nevill Barbour, "North West Africa from the 15th to 19th Centuries," in Hans J. Kissling *et al.*, *The Last Great Muslim Empires* . . . (Princeton, 1996), pp. 107–8.

SIR, *Ipswich, New-England, March 7, 1781.*
I Have lately seen a memorial, said to have been presented by your Excellency to their High Mightinesses the States-general, in which you are pleased to qualify me with the title of *pirate.*[2]
A pirate is defined to be *hostis humani generis*, [an enemy to all mankind]. It happens, Sir, that I am an enemy to no part of mankind, except your nation, the English; which nation at the same time comes much more within the definition; being actually an enemy to, and at war with, one whole quarter of the world, America, considerable parts of Asia and Africa, a great part of Europe, and in a fair way of being at war with the rest.
A pirate makes war for the sake of *rapine.* This is not the kind of war I am engaged in against England. Our's is a war in defence of *liberty.* . . . .the most just of all wars; and of our *properties,* which your nation would have taken from us, without our consent, in violation of our rights, and by an armed force. Your's, therefore, is a war of *rapine;* of course, a piratical war: and those who approve of it, and are engaged in it, more justly deserve the name of pirates, which you bestow on me. It is, indeed, a war that coincides with the general spirit of your nation. Your common people in their ale-houses sing the twenty-four songs of Robin Hood, and applaud his deer-stealing and his robberies on the highway:[3] those who have just learning enough to

2. BF must have seen one of two such memorials calling for British seizure of the two prizes Jones had brought into the Texel in October, 1779. The first, dated Oct. 8, was quoted in the *London Chronicle* of Oct. 19–21, 1779. Yorke justified his request by stating that Jones, "according to treaties and laws of war, falls under the class of rebels or pirates." The second, dated Oct. 29, came after the States General had denied his request. This time Yorke was more emphatic, referring to "the pirate Paul Jones of Scotland, who is a rebel subject, and a criminal of the State": *Annual Register* for 1779, p. 430.
3. Anthologies of Robin Hood ballads had been widely available since the 1660s as chapbooks entitled *Robin Hood's Garland.* The number of songs they contain ranges from 16 to 27. In his *Apology for Printers* BF mentioned selling great quantities of *Robin Hood's Songs* in Philadelphia; it is likely that he meant these chapbooks (I, 195). The first critical edition of the ballads, published in 1795 from both printed and manuscript sources, contained 27 songs: R. B. Dobson and J. Taylor, *Rymes of Robyn Hood* (rev. ed., Gloucestershire, England, 1997), pp. 51–2; Joseph Ritson, *Robin Hood: a Collection of all the Ancient Poems, Songs, and Ballads, now extant, Relative to that Celebrated English Outlaw* (2 vols., London, 1795).

read, are delighted with your histories of the pirates and of the buccaniers: and even your scholars, in the universities, study Quintus Curtius;[4] and are taught to admire Alexander, for what they call "his conquests in the Indies." Severe laws and the hangmen keep down the effects of this spirit somewhat among yourselves, (though in your little island you have, nevertheless, more highway robberies than there are in all the rest of Europe put together): but a foreign war gives it full scope. It is then that, with infinite pleasure, it lets itself loose to strip of their property honest merchants, employed in the innocent and useful occupation of supplying the mutual wants of mankind. Hence, having lately no war with your ancient enemies, rather than be without a war, you chose to make one upon your friends. In this your piratical war with America, the mariners of your fleets, and the owners of your privateers were animated against us by the act of your parliament, which repealed the law of God— "Thou shalt not steal,"—by declaring it lawful for them to rob us of all our property that they could meet with on the Ocean.[5] This act too had a retrospect, and, going beyond bulls of pardon, declared that all the robberies you *had committed*, previous to the act, should be *deemed just and lawful.* Your soldiers too were promised the plunder of our cities: and your officers were flattered with the division of our lands. You had even the baseness to corrupt our servants, the sailors employed by us, and encourage them to rob their masters, and bring to you the ships and goods they were entrusted with. Is there any society of pirates on the sea or land, who, in declaring wrong to be right, and right wrong, have less authority than your parliament? Do any of them more justly than your parliament deserve the *title* you bestow on me?

You will tell me that we forfeited all our estates by our refusal to pay the taxes your nation would have imposed on us, without the consent of our colony parliaments. Have you then forgot the incontestible principle, which was the foundation of Hambden's[6] glorious lawsuit with Charles the first, that "what an Eng-

4. Quintus Curtius Rufus (fl. 41–54), author of a biography of Alexander the Great and a history of Alexander's wars.
5. For BF's earlier outrage at this see XXII, 388–9.
6. John Hampden (*DNB*).

lish king has no right to demand, an English subject has a right to refuse?" But you cannot so soon have forgotten the instructions of your late honourable father,[7] who, being himself a sound Whig, taught you certainly the principles of the Revolution, and that, "if subjects might in some cases forfeit their property, kings also might forfeit their title, and all claim to the allegiance of their subjects." I must then suppose you well acquainted with those Whig principles, on which permit me, Sir, to ask a few questions.

Is not protection as justly due from a king to his people, as obedience from the people to their king?

If then a king declares his people to be out of his protection:
If he violates and deprives them of their constitutional rights:
If he wages war against them:
If he plunders their merchants, ravages their coasts, burns their towns, and destroys their lives:
If he hires foreign mercenaries to help him in their destruction:
If he engages savages to murder their defenceless farmers, women, and children:
If he cruelly forces such of his subjects as fall into his hands, to bear arms against their country, and become executioners of their friends and brethren:
If he sells others of them into bondage, in Africa and the East Indies:
If he excites domestic insurrections among their servants, and encourages servants to murder their masters:———

Does not so atrocious a conduct towards his subjects, dissolve their allegiance?

If not,—please to say how or by what means it can possibly be dissolved?

All this horrible wickedness and barbarity has been and daily is practised by the king *your master* (as you call him in your memorial) upon the Americans, whom he is still pleased to claim as his subjects.

During these six years past, he has destroyed not less than forty thousand of those subjects, by battles on land or sea, or by

7. Lord Chancellor Philip Yorke, Earl of Hardwicke (*DNB*).

starving them, or poisoning them to death, in the unwholesome air, with the unwholesome food of his prisons. And he has wasted the lives of at least an equal number of his own soldiers and sailors: many of whom have been *forced* into this odious service, and *dragged* from their families and friends, by the outrageous violence of his illegal press-gangs. You are a gentleman of letters, and have read history: do you recollect any instance of any tyrant, since the beginning of the world, who, in the course of so few years, had done so much mischief, by murdering so many of his own people? Let us view one of the worst and blackest of them, Nero. He put to death a few of his courtiers, placemen, and pensioners, and among the rest his *tutor*. Had George the third done the same, and no more, his crime, though detestable, as an act of lawless power, might have been as useful to his nation, as that of Nero was hurtful to Rome; considering the different characters and merits of the sufferers.[8] Nero indeed wished that the people of Rome had but one neck, that he might behead them all by one stroke: but this was a simple wish. George is carrying the wish as fast as he can into execution; and, by continuing in his present course a few years longer, will have destroyed more of the British people than Nero could have found inhabitants in Rome. Hence, the expression of Milton, in speaking of Charles the first, that he was "*Nerone Neronior*,"[9] is still more applicable to George the third. Like Nero and all other tyrants, while they lived, he indeed has his flatterers, his addressers, his applauders. Pensions, places, and hopes of preferment, can bribe even bishops to approve his conduct: but, when those fulsome, purchased addresses and panegyrics are sunk and lost in oblivion or contempt, impartial history will step forth, speak honest truth, and rank him among public calamities. The only difference will be, that plagues, pestilences, and famines are of this world, and arise from the nature of things: but voluntary malice, mischief, and murder are from Hell: and this king will,

8. George III's tutor was the hated Earl of Bute, prime minister from 1762 to 1763.

9. "More Nero than Nero." JA had earlier used the expression to describe George III: *Adams Papers*, IV, 57. For its usage see Michele Valerie Ronnick, "The Phrase '*Nerone Neronior*' in Walter of Châtillon, John Milton, and John Adams," *Notes and Queries*, CCXXXIX (1994), 169–70.

therefore, stand foremost in the list of diabolical, bloody, and execrable tyrants. His base-bought parliaments too, who sell him their souls, and extort from the people the money with which they aid his destructive purposes, as they share his guilt, will share his infamy,—parliaments, who to please him, have repeatedly, by different votes year after year, dipped their hands in human blood, insomuch that methinks I see it dried and caked so thick upon them, that if they could wash it off in the Thames which flows under their windows, the whole river would run red to the Ocean.

One is provoked by enormous wickedness: but one is ashamed and humiliated at the view of human baseness. It afflicts me, therefore, to see a gentleman of Sir Joseph York's education and talents, for the sake of a red riband and a paltry stipend, mean enough to stile such a monster *his master,* wear his livery, and hold himself ready at his command even to cut the throats of fellow-subjects. This makes it impossible for me to end my letter with the civility of a compliment, and obliges me to subscribe myself simply,

JOHN PAUL JONES,
whom you are pleased to stile a *Pirate.*

TO BE SOLD,

A CONVENIENT TAN-YARD, LYING IN MEDFIELD, on the Post Road, Half a Mile from the Meeting-House, with a good Dwelling-House and Barn, and about 20 Acres of Land, consisting of Mowing, Plowing, and Pasturing, and an excellent Orchard. For further Particulars enquire of Adam Peters, on the Premises.

TO BE SOLD,

A LARGE TRACT OF LAND, LYING PARTLY IN Oxford, and partly in Charlton, in the County of Worcester. It is situated on a great Country Road, about Half a Mile from Charlton Meeting-House, and is capable of making a Number of fine Settlements. For further Particulars enquire of Joseph Blaney, of Salem, or Doctor Samuel Danforth, of Boston.

[*Advertisements from the first edition, not included in the second:*]

ALL PERSONS INDEBTED TO, OR THAT HAVE ANY Demands on, the Estate of Richard Greenleaf, late of Newbury-Port, Esq; deceased, are requested to bring in their Accounts to Moses Frazier and Mary Greenleaf, Executors to the last Will and Testament of the deceased, for an immediate Settlement.

TO BE SOLD,

A SMALL NEW BRICK HOUSE, TWO ROOMS on a Floor, at the South Part of the Town.— Enquire of the Printer.

STRAYED OR STOLEN FROM THE SUBSCRIBER, living in Salem, a Bay Horse, about seven Years old, a stocky well set Horse, marked I. C. on his off Thigh, trots all. Whoever shall take up said Horse and return him to the Owner, shall be handsomely rewarded.   HENRY WHITE.

To John Adams   LS:[1] Massachusetts Historical Society

Sir,   Passy, April 22. 1782.

Messrs. Fizeaux and Grand have lately sent me two Accounts of which they desire my Approbation.[2] As they relate to Payments made by those Gentlemen of your acceptances of Bills of Exchange, your Approbation must be of more Importance than mine, you having more certain Knowledge of the affair. I therefore send them enclos'd to you, and request you would be pleas'd to compare them with your List of Acceptations, and return them to me with your Opinion, as they will be my Justification for advancing the money.[3]

---

1. In L'Air de Lamotte's hand, except for the last six words of the complimentary close, which are in BF's hand.

2. Their letter and enclosures have not been found.

3. On May 24, JA drafted a letter to BF acknowledging receipt of the present letter and one of May 8 (below) and promising to examine the accounts when his secretary John Thaxter, Jr., presently ill with a fever, was able to assist him. At the bottom of the draft, however, he wrote "not sent", perhaps

I am very happy to hear of the rapid Progress of your Affairs. They fear in England that the States will make with us an alliance offensive and deffensive; and the public Funds which they had puff'd up 4 or 5 per Cent, by the Hope of a separate Peace with Holland, are falling again. They fill their Papers continually with Lies to raise and fall the Stocks. It is not amiss that they should thus be left to ruin one another, for they have been very mischievous to the Rest of Mankind. I send enclosed a Paper,[4] of the Veracity of which I have some doubt, as to the Form, but none as to the Substance, for I believe the Number of People actually scalp'd in this murdering War by the Indians to exceed what is mention'd in the Invoice, and that Muley Istmael (a happy Name for a Prince as obstinate as a Mule) is full as black a Tyrant as he is represented in Paul Jones's pretended Letter: These being *substantial* Truths, the *Form* is to be considered as Paper and Packthread. If it were re-publish'd in England it might make them a little asham'd of themselves. I am very respectfully Your Excellency's most obedient and most humble Servant   B FRANKLIN

His Excy. John Adams Esqre.

Endorsed: Dr Franklin Ap. 22 ansd July 23. 1782

To William Alexander

ALS (draft): American Philosophical Society

Dear Sir,   Passy, April 22. 1782
I am much oblig'd by the Confidence you place in me by communicating your Plan, & by your kind Intentions in it of serving America.[5] Please to accept my thankful Acknowledgements, and excuse my declining to engage in the Scheme, for Reasons that I will some time or other give you. If you think fit to pro-

---

because his letter also contained criticisms of Shelburne that were too risky to entrust to the mail. Mass. Hist. Soc.

4. "Supplement to the Boston Independent Chronicle," immediately above.

5. We know nothing further of Alexander's plan, except what he says in his response to this letter (below, April 24).

pose it to this Court, I would advise your conferring on it[6] with Mr Grand, whose Opinion if he should approve of it, would have weight with the Ministry, as would also that of his Brother Sir George Grand, lately commission'd by the King as Banker to France in Holland, at present in Paris.[7] I return'd the Papers enclos'd, & am ever, dear Sir, Yours most affectionately   B F.—

Mr Alexander

To John Jay

LS:[8] Royal Archives, Windsor Castle

Dear Sir,   Passy, April 22. 1782.

I have undertaken to pay all the Bills of your Acceptance that have come to my knowledge, and I hope in God no more will be drawn upon us, but when Funds are first provided. In that Case your constant Residence at Madrid is no longer so necessary. You may make a Journey either for Health or Pleasure without retarding the Progress of a Negociation not yet begun. Here you are greatly wanted, for Messengers begin to come & go, and there is much talk of a Treaty proposed, but I can neither make or agree to Propositions of Peace without the Assistance of my Colleagues. Mr. Adams I am afraid cannot just now leave Holland; Mr Jefferson is not in Europe, and Mr Lawrens is a Prisoner, tho' abroad on Parole. I wish therefore that you would resolve upon the Journey, and render yourself here as soon as possible. You would be of infinite Service. Spain has taken four Years to consider whether she should treat with us or not. Give her Forty. And let us in the mean time mind our own Business. I have much to communicate to you but chuse rather to do it *vivâ voce*, than trust it to Letters.— I am ever, my Dear Friend, Yours most affectionately   B FRANKLIN

His Exy. J. Jay Esqre

Addressed: A Monsieur / Monsieur Jay, Minister Pleni- / poten-

6. These last three words replace "engaging in it".
7. See BF to JA, April 21.
8. In WTF's hand.

tiaire des Etats Unis de / l Amerique a la Cour d'Espagne / à Madrid

Endorsed: Doct Franklin 22 Ap. 1782 Recd 3 May Do. and [answered] 8 Do / Recd 3 May 1782

From Thomas Barclay   ALS: American Philosophical Society

Sir   Amsterdam 22 April 1782

I had the honour to write Your Excellency the 11th. since which nothing of any Consequence has happen'd. The Ship is not yet arrived and as the premium of Insurance against the risk of the sea will not be above one or one and an half per Cent I have given orders to have her Cover'd— I was principaly induced to do this, as I have never received your Excellencys approbation or An approbation of the purchase.

The half of the Vessell belonging to Congress will be filled with their goods, the other half shall excepting about 30 or 40 Tons be likewise taken up with the public stores. The freight to be adjusted and paid in America by the Agent of Congress on the Customary terms. I expect every day the Cloathing, it Consists of about 3400 suites for Privates, Sergeants, Drummers and Corporals, the Amount will be under £2400 Sterg. But when I receive them I shall Value on you for that sum, as the ship will require some Disbursement here.

I Cou'd purchase about 1000 suites more at 10 s/(?) for the privates but I have declined it, as I beleive I may be able to make better terms. I expect to hear from Ostend on the subject in a few posts. These goods are lying there. It wou'd gratify me much to have your Excellencys sentiments of this Engagement. Mr Adams had his Audience of the States General at the Hague the day before Yesterday.[9]

---

9. JA presented his credentials on April 20, the day after the States General had resolved to receive him as American envoy: *Gaz. de Leyde*, April 23 and 26 (sup.), 1782; Wharton, *Diplomatic Correspondence*, V, 318–19; *Adams Correspondence*, IV, 312–13n.

I have the honour to be with great respect Sir your Excellencys most obedt Servant   THOS. BARCLAY

His Excellency Benjamin Franklin Esq. at Passy

Endorsed: April 22.

From Anne Ogle[1]

ALS:[2] Archives du Ministère des affaires étrangères

Sr.   Boulogne Sur Mer April 22d 1782

I hope you will excuse the liberty I take in applying to you to procure an order for my grand[son][3] to be permitted to reside with me at Boulogne—he is [the] son of Mr Ridout of Maryland and came with me to [Eng]land Nine years ago for his education and is soon to [ret]urn to America, thus circumstanced, I do not imagin the [men] in power here would refuse to admit him, but I wish [not] to aske any favours of them, if my Nephew Mr Lowndes[4] [be] included in the order it will be more agreable.

I am Sr. your Most Obediant Servant[5]   ANNE OGLE

Addressed: A Monsieur / Monsieur Franklin / Ministre Plenipotentiaire / des Estats Unis de L'Amerique / A Passy / prés Paris

1. Identified in XXXI, 238n. For a history of the family, including a portrait of Anne Ogle, see Shirley V. Baltz, *A Chronicle of Belair* (Bowie, Md., 1984).
2. The manuscript is now in a tightly bound book. We supply in brackets our guesses as to the text written in the left margin, not visible in our photostat.
3. Samuel Ridout (*c.* 1766–1840) was the son of Mary Ogle and BF's acquaintance John Ridout. He had been enrolled at the Harrow School: XXXI, 238; Baltz, *Belair,* pp. 43 (first pagination), 1–2 (second pagination).
4. Francis Lowndes, son of Christopher Lowndes and Anne Ogle's sister, Elizabeth Tasker: XXXV, 179–80n; Christopher Johnston, "The Lowndes Family," *Md. Hist. Mag.,* II (1907), 277.
5. Having received no reply, Anne Ogle repeated her request on May 21. Both youths had finished their schooling in England and would return to America after perfecting their French. She needed official permission for them to stay with her. Hist. Soc. of Pa.

From the Baron de Thun[6]

ALS: University of Pennsylvania Library

Monsieur   a Paris ce 22 Avril 1782

Le Sr. Gleich, Caissier de M. le Comte de Puckler, Grand Chambellan du Sme. Duc de Wirtemberg, s'est évadé, en emportant 3000 florins de sa caisse et en y laissant un vuide de 7000.

On dit qu'il est allé a Paris, et qu'il compte passer Monsieur sous vos auspices en Amérique. Je suis chargé de vous envoyer le signalement ci-joint,[7] de vous prier s'il se présente, de le faire arrêter, de saisir l'argent comptant et les papiers qu'il aura sur lui, de le livrer a la police, et de vouloir bien m'en informer. Je viens de faire la même démarche auprès de Monsieur le Lieutenant General de Police.

J'ai l'honneur d'être avec les sentimens les plus sincers et les plus distingués Monsieur votre très humble et très obeissant serviteur   LE BARON DE THUN
                Ministre Plenipotentiaire de Wirtemberg

Notation: Le Baron de Thun 22. avril 1782

To John Jay

ALS: Columbia University Library

Dear Sir,   Versailles, April 23. 1782.

I wrote a few Lines to you from Passy[8] to go by the Post of this Day, pressing you to come hither as soon as possible. I have just mention'd it to M de Vergennes, who is of Opinion it will be proper to leave Mr. Carmichael there, that it may not seem as if we abandon'd that Court. As I understand a Courier is just set-

---

6. Identified in xxxv, 274–5n.

7. The enclosure described Gleich in detail. He had a dark complexion, black hair, gray eyes, a large mouth, good teeth, a large stomach, and big feet. A deformity in his left foot caused him to limp, and he carried a silver-topped cane and a hunting knife embellished with silver. He was about 45 years old, spoke French and German with a Swabian accent, wore a coat of green or brown cloth, and was a heavy user of tobacco. BF wrote across the top of the sheet, "Put this up in the Bureau".

8. Dated April 22, above.

ting out from hence for Madrid, I add this Line to inform you of this particular, having great regard to the Judgment of this Minister. Let me know by a previous Line if you conclude to come, & if, as I hope, Mrs Jay will accompany you, that I may provide for you proper Lodgings. I am, with great & sincere Esteem, Dear Sir, Your most obedient & most humble Servant

B FRANKLIN

His Excelly. J. Jay Esqe.

Endorsed: Dr Franklin 23 Ap. 1782 Recd 1 May Do and [answered] 8 Do

From Francis Coffyn

ALS: American Philosophical Society

Monsieur Dunkerque ce 23 avril 1782.

J'ai l'honneur de vous ecrire la presente, laquelle vous Sera remise par les Sieurs John Kemp & Alexr. findals tous deux americains; le premier Capitaine & l'autre pr. Lieutenant de la goelette le Greyhound sur laquelle ils ont été pris par la fregate le Rawley, et conduits en Angletterre, d'ou ils se sont sauvés des prisons, et sont arrivés ici manquant de tout.[9] Et comme ils Desirent de retourner en Amerique, Je leurs ai fourni pour le Compte de votre Excellence une Somme de Deux Cent seize livres pour payer les frais de leur route, suivant leur Double reçû.

Je suis avec un tres profond respect Monsieur Votre tres humble & tres obeissant Serviteur[1] F. COFFYN

9. Kemp, of Maryland, and Tindall (Tindill, Tindale) had each made previous escape attempts from Mill Prison that landed them in the black hole. In one of his more dramatic attempts, Tindall took the place of a corpse leaving the prison in a coffin. The two men finally escaped together on April 2: Claghorn, *Naval Officers*, p. 173; Kaminkow, *Mariners*, p. 104; Sheldon S. Cohen, *Yankee Sailors in British Gaols: Prisoners of War at Forton and Mill, 1777–1783* (Newark, Del., and London, 1995), pp. 183, 186, 221; Charles Francis Jenkins, "John Claypoole's Memorandum-Book," *PMHB*, XVI (1892), 179, 189.

1. On April 29, Kemp presented BF with an order for 550 *l.t.* drawn on Jonathan Nesbitt & Co. of Lorient. BF sent this to Grand, who remitted the sum to Kemp. Grand then drew on the account of JW, who drew on Williams,

APRIL 23, 1782

Addressed: A Son / Excellence Monsr. Bn Franklin / Ministre plenipotentiaire des etats unis de / l'amerique Septentrionale a la Cour de / France / a Passi pres Paris

Notation: Coffyn Dunkerque 23. April 1782.

From Aimé (Amé)-Ambrose-Joseph Feutry[2]

ALS: American Philosophical Society

Monsieur   ce 23 avril, 1782.

J'ai osé espérer, d'après toutes vos bontés pour moi, que vous voudriez bien rendre le Service, à une Mere respectable, de faire parvenir la Lettre, ci-jointe, à Son Fils, à Boston. Je vais partir, Monsieur, pour ma retraite de châtillon-Sur loing, Le 10 mai, au plus tard.[3] J'aurai, certes, L'honneur d'aller prendre congé de vous, et de vous renouveller Les témoignages sinceres de la vive reconnoissance, et du respect mérité, avec lesquels Je serai toute ma vie, Monsieur, votre très humble et très obeissant serviteur

FEUTRY

Notation: Feutry 3. avril 1782.

Moore & Co. When that firm presented the bill to Nesbitt & Co. on May 23, it was protested. On July 17, BF paid the protest fee of 3 *l.t.* 15 *s.:* Memorandum of ———— Ollivier and Th. Le Guéval, May 24, 1782 (APS); Account XVII (xxvi, 3); Account XXVII (xxxii, 4).

2. This is the last extant letter from a writer who was a devoted member of BF's circle at Passy. In 1786, at BF's suggestion, he was elected to membership in the APS. He hanged himself in 1789, after a long struggle with depression: "List of Persons to be Recommended for Members of P. Society," [*c.* July 21, 1786], APS; *DBF.*

3. Feutry's return to Paris was occasioned by the illness of his friend and patron, the marquis de Puységur, who died on Feb. 28: xxxvi, 626, 675.

From Vergennes

LS: Library of Congress; copy[4] and transcript: National Archives; copy: Archives du Ministère des affaires étrangères

À Versailles le 23 Avril 1782.

Monsieur le Bon. de Bloôme, Monsieur, vint de m'addresser le mémoire ci-joint,[5] et le Seul usage que je puis en faire, c'est de vous le communiquer, dans la persuasion que vous voudrez bien le faire parvenir au Congrès.

J'ai l'honneur d'être très sincèrement, Monsieur, Votre très-humble et très-obeissant Serviteur./.   DE VERGENNES

Mr. franklin./.

To the Comte de Creutz,[6] with Franklin's Account of Their Conversation

ALS (draft): Library of Congress

Sir,   Passy, April 24. 1782.—

I find that I have Powers to treat and conclude in the Affair you did me the honour yesterday of proposing to me.[7] I am

---

4. In the hand of L'Air de Lamotte, this is the one BF sent to Congress (BF to Livingston, June 25, below). An English translation is also at the National Archives.

5. The "Note," in French, outlines the Danish Court's protest over the capture of the *Providence* of Christiania (Oslo), on its way from London to St. Thomas, by the American privateer *Hendrick*, Capt. Thomas Benson. The prize was sent to a New England port under the pretense that its cargo might be English property. The Danish Court asks Vergennes to obtain prompt and complete restitution of the ship and its cargo, as well as reimbursement for damages, and to see that American privateers are ordered not to disturb the navigation and commerce of Denmark. The Danish court has the right to expect compliance since the Americans enjoy free access to Danish ports in the West Indies, a privilege which will continue as long as the Americans behave amicably toward Danish ships. For the *Hendrick*, 18, see Allen, *Mass. Privateers*, pp. 173–4.

6. Gustaf Philip, Graf von Creutz, the Swedish ambassador to the court of France: XXVII, 84n.

7. As BF explained to Livingston on June 25, below, these powers were granted to the first American commissioners. Apparently he is referring to a congressional resolution of Oct. 16, 1776 (XXII, 629–30).

ready therefore to confer with your Excellency on the Subject at any Time and Place you shall please to appoint. With great & sincere Esteem & Respect I have the honour to be Sir, Your Excellency's most obedient & most humble Servant

B FRANKLIN

Answer to the Question put to me yesterday at Court by the Swedish Ambassador, whether I had Powers enabling me to make a Treaty with Sweden of Commerce &c.[8] He told me the King his Master[9] was very desirous of it, and had charg'd him to tell me, that it would be particularly pleasing to him, to make the Treaty with me, *un homme si,* &c and desir'd it might be taken notice of in favour of Sweden that it was the first Power not at War with England that had sought our Alliance.

His Excelly the Count de Creutz Ambassador from Sweden

To John Jay

LS:[1] Royal Archives, Windsor Castle

Dear Sir   Passy, Apl. 24. 1782.
    The Prince de Massaran,[2] being so good as to desire carrying a Letter to you, I sit down to write you a few Lines, tho' I hope soon to see you.

8. It is likely that the Swedish government was motivated by the impending recognition of JA by their commercial rivals the States General of the Netherlands, which presaged a commercial agreement between the United States and the Netherlands. Formal discussions between BF and Creutz did not begin, however, until after the peace commissioners reached a preliminary agreement with the British: Wharton, *Diplomatic Correspondence,* VI, 113–14.

9. Gustavus III.

1. In WTF's hand, except for the last seven words of the complimentary close and the postscript, which are in BF's hand. Someone (possibly Jay's son William, who edited his father's papers) crossed out the fourth paragraph and the postscript. They do not appear in either William Jay, *The Life of John Jay: With Selections from His Correspondence and Miscellaneous Papers* (2 vols., New York, 1833), II, 95, or in early editions of BF's writings, beginning with Sparks, *Works,* IX, 212–13.

2. Felípe Ferrero de Fiesco, prince de Masserano (XXXIII, 188n). He was returning to Spain to participate in the siege of Gibraltar: Morris, *Jay: Peace,* p. 165.

Enclosed I send a Copy of one of Mr. Deanes Letters.[3] I shall show you more when you come.

In consequence of a Proposition I sent over, the Parliament of Britain have just passed an Act for exchanging American Prisoners. They have near 1100 in the Goals of England & Ireland, all committed as charged with high Treason. The Act is to impower the King, notwithstanding such Commitments to consider them as Prisoners of War according to the Law of Nations, and exchange them as such. This seems to be giving up their Pretensions of considering us as rebellious Subjects, and is a kind of Acknowledgment of our Independence. Transports are now taking up to carry back to their Country the poor brave Fellows who have borne for Years their cruel Captivity, rather than serve our Enemies; and an equal Number of English are to be deliver'd in Return. I have upon Desire furnish'd Passports for the Vessels.

I believe you will find the Marquis D'Yranda the *surest* Friend upon Occasion; and his Connection with our Banker here,[4] makes the Money Transactions more easy than with another. But I hope those perplexing Affairs are over. You will be right in taking the Arrangements with the Marquis which you mention in yours of March 29.

Our Affairs in Holland are *en bon Train,* we have some Prospect of another Loan there; and all goes well here.

The Proposal to us of a separate Peace with England, has been rejected in the manner you wish, and I am pretty certain they will now enter into a General Treaty. I wrote you a few Lines by last Post, and on the same Day a few more by the Court Courier.[5] They were chiefly to press your coming hither to assist in the Affair.

With great & sincere Esteem, I am ever, Dear Sir, Your most obedient and most humble Servant   B FRANKLIN

I inclose what I suspect to be a pretended American Paper,[6]

---

3. Probably Deane's lengthy self-justification (XXXVI, 507–25). His latest letter to BF is above, March 30.

4. Ferdinand Grand; see XXXI, 512n.

5. The earlier letters are above, April 22 and 23.

6. BF's "Supplement to the Boston Independent Chronicle," [before April 22], above.

which, however, tho' it should be found fictitious as to the *Form*, is undoubtedly true as to the *Substance*. For The English cannot deny such a Number of Murders having been really committed by their Instigation.

His Exy. J. Jay Esqre.

Endorsed: Doct Franklin 24 Ap 1782 Recd 9 May 1782

To De Thun[7]   ALS: University of Pennsylvania Library

Sir,   Passy, April 24. 1782.

No Person of the Description given has hitherto applied to me. If he appears here, I shall certainly cause him to be arrested, and give you immediate Notice.—

With sincere Respect I have the honour to be Sir, Your most obedient and most humble Servant   B FRANKLIN

M. le Baron de Thun.

From William Alexander[8]   ALS: American Philosophical Society

My Dear Sir   st Germain 24 april 1782

I thank you for your Attention in returng my papers So early, and have no doubt but you have solid reasons for declining the Execution of the plan, without pretending even to Conjecture what they may be, It is obvious that a Commonwealth shoud be Governd by different Maxims from a Monarchy.

I am exceedingly obliged to you for Suggesting to me the most likely means of rendering it Successfull Elsewhere but I shall not think of trying them for the present. The Men you indicate woud I doubt not be ready enough to adopt it— But I am Satisfied that such a Confidence woud very Essentialy Affect the Success, for

---

7. In answer to his of April 22, above.
8. In response to BF's letter of April 22, above.

it may not be Improper to Inform you that one of Them viz the Dutch Man[9] is as thorough a Jobber as is in the Alley.

Their Information might be taken without Impropriety in answering General questions that woud serve to decide The Rationality of the Enterprize, But the Man who relies upon others for forming his Judgments, when the facts are Ascertaind will be Continualy a dupe in Business to their Interrested policy— One of my Girls[1] will deliver you this. Two of Them go to town to morrow. One of Them to pass a week at the Tuileries with Madme de La Marke[2] a Lady whom it may be usefull for you or your Son to know—the other passes Some days wt Madme Helvetius— I am with the most sincere Attachment Dear Sir Your most obt hble ser W: ALEXANDER

Addressed: To His Excellency / Ben: Franklin Esqre / Passy

From Edmund Clegg

ALS: American Philosophical Society

No 2 Wilks Street Spitalfields
Hond Sir London Apl: 24: 1782

I am favourd with a coppy of your Letter to Mr Wyld of the 31st Ulto and Note the contents— I am very sorry the ardor of

9. Ferdinand Grand's brother Georges, who resided in Amsterdam.

1. The three daughters still living at home were Bethia, Christine, and Jane: XXIX, 534.

2. There were two ladies known by this title. The one whom Mme du Deffand described as knowing everyone and "reigning" in Saint-Germain was Marie-Anne-Françoise de Noailles (1719–1793), a great-aunt of the marquise de Lafayette and the second wife and widow of Louis-Engelbert, comte de La Marck: Lewis, *Walpole Correspondence*, V, 337n; VI, 397–8; *DBF*, XIX, 472; *Dictionnaire de la noblesse*, XIII, 201–2; XIV, 989. On the comte's death in 1773, his titles and property passed to his grandson (by his first wife) Auguste-Marie-Raymond de Ligne. The young comte de La Marck's wife, Marie-Françoise-Augustine-Ursule Le Danois de Cernay (1757–1810), was a friend of the marquise de Lafayette, and both these women were sympathetic to the Alexanders' case against Walpole. The younger comtesse is associated with the present letter in Price, *France and the Chesapeake*, II, 699, 1070n; see also *DBF*, XIX, 469–70, 472–3; *Dictionnaire de la noblesse*, XII, 113; Idzerda, *Lafayette Papers*, III, 9, 10n.

Bethia was probably the daughter who stayed with her; see our annotation of Rouaix to BF, May 12, and her own letter of June 9.

your good wishes towards our undertaking was damp'd, by the delay in the payment of the Bill upon me. My Circumstances were too Narrow to pay it without the Remittance; and the Country People, are not sencible of the delicate honor required in Paper transactions. This is the only appology I can make, for it is the truth of the matter.

All the Persons in the Neighbourhood of M-nch—r have gone too far in ending their Concerns to stop short now & Mr W—d says, Your Letter has thrown them into the greatest distress & Confusion: But as the Postcript of Yours, give us hopes something may yet be done to purpose— I humbly beg Your Aid, as far as the Circumstances you mention, will admit, in favour of our Voyage— And for the rest we are willing to cast ourselves upon the kindness of an Almighty Providence, which is able to carry us through all dangers & difficulties, though we are not so enthusiastic as to neglect any moral means for our safety which we hope to have through Your favour, as far as may now be granted.

My Country friends in my opinion must try to go over at all events, from the Situation they have put themselves into, for that purpose. If we get safe over we shall be able, without any material obstruction to perform more than you can as yet Conceive and with respect to the silk Manufactory If the Country can yeild a Sufficient quantity of Raw silks We can make it as independant upon Europe for those Goods: As I hope it will soon be owned to be Independant of all the World in its Government— If a Sufficient quantity of Silks can't be produced upon the Spot— I hope the Italian & East India Markets may be open'd in the mean time; I hope by the favour of your reply to my former, to Judge with more accuracy upon this Subject when Mr H—ds—ns[3] dispatches arrive, for which I would have waited, had not the Situation of my Country friends been so Pressing.

If it should so fall out that they don't go this season I should wish to go with my two sons as soon as Possible and as an inducement to You to Notice my request I will State to you what We three can Perform— We can Perform the silk Manufactory thro' both in Plain & Figured Goods both broads and Narrow—

3. William Hodgson served as BF's intermediary with this group.

but chiefly the former— I am short however in the Dying of most fancy Colours— But can Perform properly all Common Colrs. as Whites, Yellows, Oranges, Scarlets, Crimsons, Blacks & some others— And also we can perfect the whole of the other Branches laid before you—but not so expeditiously as the Country frds for their abilities will upon tryal be found to be great tho' I know not of any thing they know more than me except the Management of that Cotton Carding Machine of which you saw a Model.[4]

Having said thus much I beg leave to tell You that I had for Many Years the Conducting of a Large Manufactory in Manch—r and afterwards in Company with two others returnd for more than 6 Years £40,000 a Year In the silk Branch— But this Wicked American War has uniformly attackd every thing I have set my hand to since it Commenced, and left me scarcely able to get a Living—[5] Also I farther inform You that I have for many Years—full more than 20—set my h[eart?] on America— In order to be usefull there— I have obtaind every kind of Knowledge in my Power to be as complete a Mechanic & Manufacturer as Possible—and if that happy time should arrive to try my abilities in the much desired Country—I have not the Shaddow of a Doubt—but we shou'd daily grow in happiness, by Seeing our labours Crown'd with success— With respect to Political Matters I dare say little—but I think all the real Liberty now, or hearafter enjoy'd in this Island may be with great Justice attributed to the Noble heroes of No America— I wait

4. Unless Wyld had shown a model to BF in January, which seems unlikely, Clegg may be referring to one of the cotton carding machines that the Manchester émigré James Milne had constructed in France; see XXXII, 395–6, where the first of these machines, made for Holker, is noted in annotation. According to one of Milne's undated memoirs (Hist. Soc. of Pa.), he had constructed one carding machine near Rouen when he arrived in 1779 (presumably the one cited above) and in 1780 constructed another one in Paris by order of the government. This, he said, was approved by the Academy of Sciences. He then constructed in Neuville a machine to card and spin cotton, and established a manufactory with François Perret of Lyon.

5. The political and economic motivations of these would-be emigrants are discussed in Robert Glen, "Industrial Wayfarers: Benjamin Franklin and a Case of Machine Smuggling in the 1780s," *Business History*, XXIII (1981), 310–11.

anxiously for your kind Notice of my former Letter per Mr
H-ds-n— As I have not time to recoppy this beg You'll excuse
mistakes and inaccuricies— I am with the highest reguard Your
Excellencys—very obt. & mo: H Sert   EDMD: CLEGG

His Excellency B Franklin L L D &c &c

Addressed: Monsr à / Monsr Franklin / Passi

Notation: Ed. Clegg London April 24 1782.

From Jan Ingenhousz   ALS: American Philosophical Society

Dear Sir   Vienna in Austria. april 24th 1782
   When you consider, how long time I had the honour of enjoying your friendship, you can easily concieve, who much I am
affected by having not recieved a single word from you in answer
to So many letters, and instanty made by several hands. I doe not
know by which way I may have forfeited your friendship. But as
I am Conscious of having by no means deserved the loss of a
friendship I have allways highly estiemed and of which I was allways and will be allways proud of, I doe not apprehend that you
have withdraw'n your friendhip from me, but I think still that
your silence has been occasion'd by your wighty occupations. It
would have been a great satisfaction to me to be informed by you
of what you thaught of the experiment upon the conducting
quality of heat of different metals. I have waited for a word of
answer upon it either from you, your clerk or from Dr. le Begue,
and I have retarded for this answer more than a year the publication of the book, of which I send you a copy.[6] The fransch
original edition has been likewise retarded for the same reason,
and God knows, when it will now come to light. You will find a

---

6. The present letter and a copy of Ingenhousz' *Vermischte Schriften phy-
sisch-medizinischen Inhalts* were delivered to BF by Francesco Favi on June 15;
see his letter of that date, below. BF had indeed been dilatory in answering
Ingenhousz' previous letters. He started a reply on Oct. 2, 1781, but only
finished it on June 21, 1782. The entire answer appears in XXXV, 544–51; see
that letter and its annotation for the topics and publications mentioned here.

polemical dissertation at the beginning of the book which the translator ãsked me leave to place in it. I gave him leave for it under condition he should use no expressions, which could offend my friend Dr. Priestley. But he seems to me to have been reather heated on the subject. Dr. Priestley in my opinion has been in the wrong to attack me without the least provocation, finding at the same time nothing in my book worth his recommendation but that it gave him satisfaction of having found my assiduous attention on the subject of plants; at least smothering in silence every article by which he could be instructed but in one article, which is that leaves of plants retain their life longer, than he thaught; but even this he says he might have learned from mr. Bonnet. (Priestley vol. v. p. 29 & 30). I got letters from England, by which I was informed that Dr. Priestley's V volum, was so far derogatory to my book, that my whole doctrine seems overturn'd by it, and that a second edition of my book would not Sell. The critical revew of Septemb. 1781. pag. 180 draws from Dr. Priestleys book a still more humiliating consequence In regard to my book. However I will not quarel with him about it. I have facts so convincing that I can confound him and his whole manner of thinking about the manner, in which the vegetables are subservient to the animal creation.

I am indeed very sorry that neither you, your son, or mr. Bankroft have not answered me a single word about mr. samuel wharton, who has employed more than a thousand pound St of my money in trade which he took with him, and of which I have not yet got the least intelligence, though he solemnly pledged his word of honour, that I should be the first, to whom he should write as soon as he should arrive at Philadelphia. You can concieve, what uneasiness such strange behaviour of mr. Wharton must give me, which uneasiness is increased by the silence of Dr. Bankroft. Let me beg you once more the favour of an answer from you.

In this expectation I am respectfully dear sir your obedient humble servant INGEN HOUSZ

I begg the favour of forwarding the inclosed to mr. samuel Wharton at Philadelphia by the first oportunity to Mr. Benj. Franklin ministre Plenip. of the congress to the Court of France

Addressed: a Son Excellence / Mons. Benjamin Franklin / Ministre plenipotentiaire de la Republique / des Provinces unies de l'Amerique / à la Cour de France / a Passy

Endorsed: April 24. 82

From Thomas Barclay   ALS: American Philosophical Society

Sir   Amsterdam 25 april 1782
    I gave your Excellency the trouble of a letter last post,[7] and I have Now the pleasure of informing You that the ship from Ostend[8] is at length arrived— Captain Smedley who is to take the Command of her will, I hope, be able to Examin her Compleatly tomorrow, and the day following I shall begin to load.— I am very much indisposed with a fever and Cold, and therefore must beg leave to Conclude, Sir Your Excellencys Most Obedient Huml Servt.   THOS BARCLAY

His Excellency Benjn. Franklin Esqe. Passy.

Endorsed: April 25. 82

From Mary Hewson   ALS: American Philosophical Society

Dear Sir   Kensington Ap. 25. 1782
    We this day received your kind favour by Mr Whitefoord. After a silence of more than a year we hardly expected ever to hear from you again.[9] We are always happy to learn you are well, which Mr W. assures us you were when he saw you. I was much

7. That of April 22, above.
8. The *Heer Adams.*
9. Whitefoord conveyed BF's April 19 letter (above), the first Hewson had received from BF since his of Dec. 7, 1780 (XXXIV, 134).

surprised to find you did not know of our removal to this place, as Mr Alexander[1] saw us here in Feby. last. He slipt away without paying us a second visit, or we should have sent you a letter by him.

Mr Whitefoord gives us a pleasing description of your situation and so flattering an invitation from you, that we could almost resolve to undertake the journey. My mother sees no obstacles; but I confess the expence we must incur and the difficulties we must incounter in travelling so far through a foreign land without a friend to assist us on the way are considerations which make me shrink from the attempt. My mother has of late been much out of health, & her spirits are bad; I believe indeed nothing could do her so much good as being with you; I wish there were no obstacles in our way, for I have no doubt but I should be well pleased at the end of the journey. But I hope you will come to us, and that will be better.

I and my children thank God! are well. My boys are still at Cheam, I know of no better school. My girl remains with me.[2] She has begun to learn French of a woman whom Hutton[3] recommends. She learnt to write a little while before we left Cheam, and I intend she shall have music & dancing very soon, the rest I take upon myself. A trip to France would certainly compleat her.

I must dispatch my letter immediately so cannot add more than that I am as ever your obliged & affecte   MARY HEWSON

Addressed: Dr Franklin

From Lenoir   LS: American Philosophical Society

a Paris Ce 25. avril 1782.

Je Fais passer à l'inspecteur de la douane, Monsieur, la permission, que vous desirez, pour que les livres, que vous devez y en-

---

1. William Alexander. The family was still in Cheam in late December: XXXVI, 287.

2. For the children see XXXIV, 524n.

3. James Hutton.

voyer pour être plombés et conduits à Rochefort,[4] ne Soient point assujetis à la visite de la chambre Syndicale des Libraires de Paris.

Je vous prie de recevoir de nouvelles assurances du respectueux attachement, avec lequel je suis, Monsieur, votre très humble et tres obéissant Serviteur. LENOIR

M Franklin.

Notation: Le Noir 25 avril 1782.

Jacques-Donatien Le Ray de Chaumont and Franklin: An Exchange About Accounts

(I) Copy:[5] Historical Society of Pennsylvania; (II) AL (draft):[6] American Philosophical Society; copy: University of Pennsylvania Library

Franklin received Robert Morris' request for copies of the public accounts in September, 1781.[7] He assumed that Thomas Barclay would examine them, but Barclay—who finally reached Europe in November—was detained in Holland for longer than he expected. In February, 1782, when Barclay's arrival in Paris seemed imminent, Franklin approached Matthew Ridley about assisting in the accounts' examination.[8] On March 4, with Barclay still delayed, Franklin sent to Morris an unverified copy of at least some of the public accounts (probably his account with the French government, kept by Ferdinand Grand).[9] He must also have asked Chaumont to review the account that he had drawn up and signed on July 1, 1781, for transactions between Chaumont and the American commission.[1]

4. BF was shipping books to both Livingston and Morris; see his March 30 letters to each of them.

5. In the hand of L'Air de Lamotte. This account is one of the items in Account XXVI (XXXII, 3).

6. Part of Account XIX (XXVIII, 3).

7. XXXV, 265–6, 465.

8. XXXVI, 557; *Morris Papers,* IV, 244. Barclay did not return to Paris until the end of August: Klingelhofer, "Matthew Ridley's Diary," p. 103.

9. See XXXVI, 651.

1. Two versions of this account survive as part of Account XIX. The fair

Trying to settle Chaumont's account proved to be an infuriating process, and one that occupied Franklin sporadically from April through July. Chaumont submitted multiple versions of his claims, altering them seemingly at whim, and refused to be bound by the decisions of the arbitrators he himself helped select.[2] Understanding their dispute—which Franklin let drop in July, and only picked up again in May, 1784—requires a close examination of the individual undated documents that comprise Accounts XIX and XXVI, as well as alternate versions of those items and other related material now scattered in various public and private archives.[3] Nine of the key documents bear the numbers that Ferdinand Grand assigned them as he reviewed the stages of the dispute and tried to bring both parties into agreement. Grand's descriptive list of these items, entitled "Etat des pieces Concernant Le Compte de Mr De Chaumont," has assisted us in putting these documents in order.[4] We offer below an overview of these financial negotiations.

The account that Franklin signed on July 1, 1781, labeled by Grand "No. 1", began by citing an unpaid draft on Chaumont for repairs to his ill-fated packet *La Mère Bobie*. Jonathan Williams, Jr., had sent the draft to Passy on June 12, 1777,[5] and (according to the account entry) Franklin gave it to Chaumont on October 8, 1779. Also from 1779 were two bills of exchange totaling 50,000 *l.t.* In 1780, Franklin ordered Grand to issue Chaumont 750,000 *l.t.* in three equal installments, and on November 10 he loaned Chaumont another 200,000 *l.t.* toward freighting the *Marquis de Lafayette*. In the first quarter of 1781,

copy, in French and signed by BF, is in the hand of Gurdon Mumford. It is headed, "Doit— Monsieur Le Ray de Chaumont son Compte Courant avec B Franklin." The working copy, primarily in the hand of L'Air de Lamotte, was reviewed by JW, who added the final entry of July 1 (for interest to that date) and attested that it was "Sauf Erreurs ou Omissions ce 1re Juillet 1781."

BF had been trying to settle his account with Chaumont since December, 1780. See XXXIV, 36–8 (for Chaumont's disastrous financial situation), 173, and 190–1.

2. BF complained about this erratic behavior to JW on June 13 (below).

3. Account XIX, two groups of manuscripts at the APS, is loosely described in XXVIII, 3. Account XXVI, two groups of manuscripts at the Hist. Soc. of Pa. that relate to Account XIX, is introduced in XXXII, 3. We said there that Account XXVI was signed on July 9, 1782. More precisely, one of Chaumont's several versions was signed by Chaumont on that date but not endorsed by BF. Excerpts from it are published under July 9, below.

4. Grand's list is in Account XIX, though many of the items on that list are not.

5. See XXIV, 3–4, 153.

Franklin paid twenty different drafts drawn on Chaumont by both Jonathan Williams, Jr., and Fizeaux, Grand & Cie., for which he had not yet been reimbursed. Along with the interest that had accrued on these expenditures (a separate list of which is labeled by Grand "No. 2"), Franklin totaled Chaumont's debt as approximately 1,530,812 *l.t.* Deducting four items from that sum—the drafts that Jonathan Williams, Jr., drew on Chaumont during 1780; the cloth Chaumont purchased that same year by drafts on Congress; the value of officers' uniforms supplied in January, 1781; and the 240,000 *l.t.* that Jonathan Williams., Jr., owed Chaumont for freighting the *Marquis de Lafayette* on May 23, 1781—Franklin figured that Chaumont owed him 95,415 *l.t.* 15 *s.* 10 *d.*

Chaumont disagreed. His version of their account, document (I), below, acknowledged receipt of only six of the nine sums Franklin claimed to have furnished, and he debited Franklin for fifteen items as compared to the four Franklin had listed. Of those four, Chaumont left three as they were, but inflated one (the amount owed him for supplying uniforms to the American army) by adding on a hefty commission. According to Chaumont's calculations, Franklin owed him 91,733 *l.t.* 18 *s.* 6 *d.*

Franklin reviewed the new claims carefully, first sketching out his responses under the heading "Articles charged by M. de Chaumont qui ne sont pas dans ma Compte." He then delivered to Chaumont an item-by-item reply (labeled by Grand "No. 4") consisting of brief but polite statements. With one exception (the 600 copies of an engraving) Franklin either disallowed the charges altogether or requested further explanation or documentation.[6] Chaumont countered with a new version of credits (now missing) that included two additional items, bringing their number to seventeen. It evidently provided some of the explanatory material Franklin requested, but demanded more detailed explanations for the expenses Franklin was disallowing. Franklin's response to this new version is document (II), below, which Grand labeled "No. 5."

At this point, Franklin and Chaumont evidently agreed to submit their paperwork to Ferdinand Grand. On April 26, Grand's son told

---

6. BF's draft of his response is at the APS. A copy of the actual reply, in L'Air de Lamotte's hand and numbered by Grand, is at the Hist. Soc. of Pa. Both documents are in French.

The item Grand labeled "No. 3", according to his descriptive list, was Deane's account with Chaumont, which (according to Grand) "on ne produit que pour fair voir que Mr de Chaumont exigeoit des Interrets".

Matthew Ridley that his father was trying to settle this dispute, in which each man claimed that the other owed him a balance.[7] Grand completed his report, we believe, on May 7; the "award," as Franklin called it, is published below under that date.[8] Chaumont, however, refused to comply with this award, which settled matters in Franklin's favor. He eventually accepted Franklin's suggestion of adding a second arbitrator whom Chaumont could select,[9] and on July 7 the two men signed an agreement for arbitration by Grand and Dangirard (below). There is evidence that Franklin prepared a revised account on July 1, though that manuscript has been lost.[1] Chaumont revised his version of what Franklin owed him on July 9, dropping certain items but inflating others. We publish excerpts from that revision below, as well as Franklin's exasperated private reactions.

Rather than submit these revised accounts to arbitration, however, Franklin simply let the matter drop. Chaumont's financial desperation was driving him to increasing levels of irrationality, and to press things further would have been embarrassing and, ultimately, counterproductive. Besides, having just learned of Shelburne's appointment as prime minister, Franklin needed to focus on the negotiations. It was not until the spring of 1784 that he attempted a final settlement. Explaining to Chaumont that he had desisted from pressing his advantage out of friendship, he gently proposed that they now try to settle their account amicably.[2] This time it worked. With Grand's guidance, the two men signed an agreement on May 28, 1784. What they approved, in fact, was the very account that Grand had drawn up on May 7, 1782, with an adjustment for the subsequent two years' rent. Franklin endorsed his copy, "Mr Grand's Award May 1782 and the Acceptance of it May, 1784".

7. Matthew Ridley's journal, entry of April 26, 1782 (Mass. Hist. Soc.).
8. In Grand's list, this is "No. 8", called "Rapport de Mr Grand". The ninth and final item, a letter from jw, has not been identified.
9. See BF to jw, June 13.
1. On a worksheet of calculations dated May 10, 1784, BF compared the figures of his account against Chaumont of July 1, 1782, with Chaumont's account of July 9. This single sheet is in Account XIX.
2. BF to Chaumont, May 2, 1784 (APS).

I. Chaumont's Initial Claim

[before April 26, 1782][3]
Monsieur le Docteur Franklin son Compte
avec M. Le Ray de Chaumont à Passy,

DOIT,

Pour Solde du précédant Compte avec les Deputes du Congrès lequel a été remis à M. Deane qui est encore à l'arrêter	3849.13.1.
Payé le 5 Avril 1780. à Rogé pour frais de course de Passy à Nantes	193.10.
Idem le 9. dit pour 600 Exemplaires d'une planche representant un Sujet Americain[4]	63.—
Tenu Compte à Bersolle de Brest le 22 may dit pour frais à 11. Balles de Toile à voile et 100 Ballots d'Habillemens chargés dans le Navire le petit Cousin Capitaine Carouge[5]	1803. 9.3.
Idem le 5. Juillet dit pour frais à la Reception et Expedition de 239. Ballots Habillemens[6]	5847.16.6.
Pour prix de 11. Balles de Draps achetées par M. Jon Williams de Nantes et cédées pour l'habillement des officiers de l'Armée américaine suivant les deux factures du dit Sieur des 3 Juillet et 26 Septembre 1780.[7]	25970. 6.
Pour escompte au payement des dites deux factures et commission sur icelles	626. 2.5.
Pour indemnité au Sujet du Paquebot la Mere	

3. The date on which Henry Grand told Ridley that his father had undertaken to settle the dispute between BF and Chaumont over their accounts; see the headnote.

4. For this engraving see XXXII, 66n.

5. For the shipment of these uniforms see XXXII, 269, 360.

6. For the assembling and shipping of the uniforms mentioned in this and subsequent entries see, for example, XXXIII, 88–9, 160–1.

7. This is one of the items BF had listed on his July 1, 1781, account. The entry, dated Jan. 22, 1781, reads, "Pour montant des Habillemens d'Officiers qu'il m'a cedé." See also XXXIV, 309.

Bobie Capne. Charles Glayo de la Chenaye
qui a été renvoyé en France sur son Lest par
le Congrès pour y apporter ses Depeches la
dite indemnité reglée à   12000.—
Pour le montant des Traites faites sur moi
par M Jon. Williams de Nantes pour
compte de l'habillement des Troupes
Américaines[8]
Commission à ½ pour cent sur   741095.18.4.⎫
649322.1.2 payés par les mains   ⎬744342.10.7.
de Banquier   3246.12.3.⎭
Pour la traite à mon ordre de M. Jon. Williams
de Nantes du 19. Decembre 1780 à 10 Jours de
vue sur M. Franklin pour le prix des Draperies
cedées au Congrès[9]   428330. 2.8.
Pour la traite à mon ordre de M. Jon. Williams
à Nantes du 24 may dernier à vue sur M. le
Dr. Franklin pour le montant du fret du
Vaisseau le Marquis de Lafayette envoyé à
l'Amerique Septentrionale[1]   240000.—
Payé à M. Grand pour frais de courtage a
⅛% sur les 400,000 l.t. ci contre suivant
sa reconnoissance du 22. Décembre 1780.[2]   500.—
Pour [blank] années de loyer de la maison qu'il
occupe depuis le [blank] jusqu'au [blank] à
raison de [blank] par prix convenu
Pour Commission de Banque a ½ pour Cent
sur les 25970 l.t. 6 s. de traites de M.

---

8. BF had included this exact sum in his July 1, 1781, account. His entry
reads: "Pour montant des Traittes de Mr. Williams de Nantes sur lui a diverse
Epoques depuis le mois de Fevrier jusqu'au mois de Sept. 1780, pour Compte
du Congres." For his response to Chaumont's addition of a commission see
document (II).

9. BF included this sum in his July 1, 1781, account, dating the entry Sept.
1, 1780. JW sent Chaumont the draft on BF for this amount on Dec. 19, 1780:
XXXIV, 185.

1. BF included this sum in his July 1, 1781, account, dating the entry May
23, 1781.

2. See XXXIV, 48–9.

Williams de Nantes en remboursement
des deux factures de Draps d'officiers
cédés au prix coutant   129.17.
Pour le prix des Marchandises livrées par le
    Capitaine Maniville au général Lincoln et la
    valeur de 10. Caisses et 2 Barils médicamens
    portés par le Navire le petit Cousin Capitaine
    Carrouge dès le Commencement de l'Année
    1780. le payement desquels objets a été sollicité
    par M. Holker fils auprès du Congrès qui n'y
    a point satisfait, par les Raisons annoncées dans
    sa Lettre dont l'original est en mes Mains[3]   70000.——
                                                        1533656. 7.6.
                                                        1441922.19.
                                                          91733.18.6.

AVOIR,

Reçu de M. Le Docteur Franklin son mandat
    sur M. Grand du 19. Mars 1780.   250000.——
Idem du [blank] Juillet dit   250000.——
Idem du 20 Septembre 1780. pble. 15 Novbre.
    du susdit   250000.——
Reçu de M. Grand sur ma reconnoissance du 4
    Decbre. 1780.   400000.——
Pour mes acceptations aux traites de M.
    Jon. Williams de Nantes pour Compte de
    l'habillement des Troupes Americaines qui
    ont été acceptées par M. Grand qui aura à
    me les remettre   91922.19.
Mes Traites du 10. Novembre 1780. à 4
    u/ces à mon ordre sur M. Franklin à
    valoir sur le fret du Vaisseau le Marquis
    de la Fayette pour l'Amerique Septentrion.[4]   200000.——
                                                       £1,441,922.19.

3. See XXXII, 201–2.
4. See XXXIV, 168–70.

II. Franklin's Reply to Chaumont's Answer[5]

[before May 7, 1782][6]

Mr Franklin's Reply to Mr Chaumont's Answer, respecting the Observations of Mr Franklin on his Account.—

Article 1. The Charge of 3189.13.4. *l.t.* Ballance of Mr. Deane's Acct. with M. de Chaumont.

Mr F. has seen two Copies of this Account, in which the Ballance differs widely. It does not appear by any Evidence produc'd in Writing or otherwise that Mr Deane has been acquainted with and approv'd of this Demand against him. On the contrary he has told Mr F. that M. de Chaumont owed him a considerable Sum of Money, which from the then present Situation of Mr. C's Affairs could not be obtained, & which oblig'd him to ask a Loan of Money from Mr F.— And as Mr F. finds in the said account against Mr Deane many Articles which appear to him to relate to particular Speculations & Adventures in Business between M. de Chaumont & him, that do not at all concern the Public: and it farther appears that the Sums actually credited in that Account as paid to Mr de Chaumont by Mr Deane & Mr Franklin as Commissioners of Congress exceed the Value of the Supplies charg'd therein as furnish'd for the Congress; Mr. F. conceives that the

5. As we state in the headnote, BF responded to document (I) with an item-by-item answer. Chaumont countered with a now-missing response (expanding the original 15 articles to 17), which in turn elicited this document. BF here justifies at greater length his objections to several of Chaumont's claims, while allowing others based on whatever justifications Chaumont had provided. We supply BF's earlier article-by-article responses in our annotation below.

6. Because so many of BF's responses state that he will abide by whatever Grand decides, we assume that BF wrote this document before Grand made his May 7 award. That award, however, is based on Chaumont's original claim (to judge by the totals) rather than the expanded one. We speculate that Chaumont withdrew his revised account and submitted his original claim to Grand's judgment. This may explain why Chaumont's revised account is not mentioned on Grand's list of items relating to the dispute (cited in the headnote), and why it is no longer among BF's papers.

Charge of the Ballance in Question is not well placed in an Account against the United States; and that he cannot without Authority from Mr Deane undertake to settle the private Part of Mr Chaumont's Account against him or to admit that the said Ballance is due from him. Mr Deane resides at Ghent, and Mr C. may settle the Matter with him by Writing.[7]

Art. 2.	193. 1.0. *l.t.*	Mr. F. cannot understand this without seeing the Account.[8]
Art. 3.	63	Is just.[9]
— 4.	1803. 9.3.	Allow'd[1]
— 5.	5847.16.6.	Allow'd.[2]
— 6.	25970. 6.0.	Allow'd.[3]
— 7.	626. 2.5.	Allow'd[4]
Art. 8.	12,000.	*Indemnité sur la mere Bobie.* This Charge appears to me very high. I do not think it right to estimate it by Tobacco; there being none at Boston to be shipp'd on such Terms. They were allow'd from Maryland, but the Risque there was greater. I leave this however to the Judgment of Mr Grand.[5]
Art. 9.	741,095..16..4.	Allow'd.[6]
2d. Art. 9.	3246.12.3.	pour Commission, &c. Submit-

7. BF had earlier responded: "Il n'y a que Mr. Deane qui puisse arreter ce Compte, il n'y a aussi que lui qui puisse le payer, ainsi c'est à lui qu'il faut s'addresser."

8. "Il faut sçavoir qui elle regarde."

9. In his earlier response BF had not written anything about this item, though in his sketch of the present reply he had written "bon".

1. "Il faut fournir le Compte de Bersolle à ce Sujet pour en charger ceux que cet Envoy regarde."

2. "De même".

3. "Mr. De Chaumont en est credité."

4. "Si ces fraix sont convenus il faut en donner le compte."

5. "Pour la fixer il faut connoitre en quoi elle consiste et sur quoi elle doit porter."

6. "Mr. De Chaumont en est credité."

		ted to the Judgment of Mr Grand.[7]
Art. 10.	428,330..2..8.	Allow'd[8]
Art. 11.	240,000. 0.0.	Allow'd[9]
Art. 12.	500. 0.0.	Courtage submitted to Mr Grand— M. Franklin not understanding the Answer of M. de Chaumont concerning the Exchange.[1]
Art. 13.	Rent.	Mr Franklin leaves this intirely to M. Grand, and shall be content if fix'd as M. Chaumont propos'd to him.[2]
Art. 14.		To be decided by Mr Grand[3]
Art. 15.	70,000.	Mr Franklin had never intimated to Congress that M. Chaumont owed him any thing. It seems therefore unintelligible to him that they should give Mr Holker such a Reason for not paying. Mr Holker might however have obtain'd their Drafts on Mr Franklin if they had approv'd of the Account. Genl. Lincoln

7. "Cette Partie supporte déjà une Commission et ne peut en supporter deux."

8. "Mr. de Chaumont en est credité."

9. "Idem."

1. "Les 400,000 *l.t.* ayant été payées par anticipation Les fraix qui en resultent ne doivent pas être à la Charge de Mr. Franklin."

2. "Pour Loyer de maison pour 5 années Mr. de Chaumont propose 20,000 *l.t.* & quil [*one word illegible*] à Mr. Franklin qui observe que la partie qu'il occupe actuellement n'étoit pas apprêtée que longtems après son Arrivée." BF had at first occupied a garden pavilion on Chaumont's property, beginning in February, 1777, but moved to a wing of the main house sometime after February, 1779: XXIII, 244–6; Thomas J. Schaeper, *France and America in the Revolutionary Era: the Life of Jacques-Donatien Leray de Chaumont, 1725–1803* (Providence, R.I., and Oxford, 1995), p. 103.

3. "Il ne paroit pas dû de Commission sur le Payement d'une facture de draps à qui l'on a fait déjà supporter 626 *l.t.* 2.5. Article 7."

might have purchas'd the Goods
partly on the public Account, &
partly for himself & officers. Mr
F. knows nothing of the Matter,
has receiv'd no Orders relating to
it, And he thinks that Persons in
one Department, especially at so
great a Distance, should not be
apply'd to for Payment of Debts
contracted by those in another.[4]

Art. 16[5]   Mr F. does not understand this,
and leaves it to Mr Grd.

Art. 17.   This also is for the same reason
left to the Judgmt of Mr Grand,
with which Mr F. will be satisfied.

To Leopold Caldani[6]

Facsimile of ALS in Heinrich Lempertz, comp., *Bilder-Hefte zur Geschichte des Bücherhandels und der mit demselben verwandten Künste und
Gewerbe* (Cologne, 1853–65), p. 46; AL (draft):[7] University of Pennsylvania Library

Sir   Passy, April 26. 1782

I am extreamly sensible of the Honour done my [me] by your
Academy, in admitting me one of its Foreign Members, and I beg
they would accept my thankful Acknowledgements: Your City
has been famous many Ages for its successful Cultivation of the
Sciences, & for the Number of Great Men it has produced. This

4. "Si le Congrès n'a pas voulu les rembourser Mr. Franklin ne peut prendre sur lui de le faire sans ordre, puisqu'il se compromettroit par là, et s'ex-
poseroit à n'en être pas remboursé."

5. Articles 16 and 17 were added by Chaumont to his revised account and
later dropped. We have found no trace of what they claimed.

6. President of the Academy of Sciences, Letters and Arts of Padua:
XXXVI, 273. See Delfino's letter of April 6, and BF's reply which immediately
follows it.

7. BF used the same draft as the basis for his acceptance to the Société

augments the Honour of being associated to its Academy. I wish it may be in my Power to promote in any degree the Design of their very laudable Institution. I shall be able however to communicate to the new World the Lights they may furnish by the Publication of their Memoirs;— and if when I return thither I can be useful to any of the Members by Informations relating to our Natural History, or by sending Specimens, Seeds, &c. or in any other manner, it will give me infinite Pleasure.

With great Respect, I have the honour of being, Sir, Your most obedient and most humble Servant   B FRANKLIN

To Edmund Clegg

LS:[8] Elisha K. Kane, Kane, Pennsylvania (1956)

Sir,   Passy, April 26. 1782.

Your Letter dated April 4. came to my hands but a few Days since. I apprehend from some Passages in it, that there has been a Misunderstanding between Mr. Wyld and me, or that he has misrepresented what passed between us. I certainly never undertook to provide a Vessel to carry him and his Friends over, and therefore could have no occasion to "send a special Messenger to acquaint them when all things were ready". On the contrary, I advised their not attempting to go till Peace should be established. Or if they were resolved to go in time of War, that they should send to Ireland some Person acquainted with such Business, to hire and victual a Vessel for them there. He inform'd me they were People of Substance sufficient to bear their own Expences. I should certainly have great Pleasure in seeing a Set of honest industrious People as your Company is describ'd to be, made happy by a Settlement to their Minds in our new Country, but I have no Orders to advance any publick Money for the Purpose of conveying them thither; and indeed if it had

---

royale de physique, d'histoire naturelle et des arts d'Orléans on July 9, 1785. He interlined changes and in the margin wrote "Change for Answer to Orleans."

8. In the hand of L'Air de Lamotte, except for the last seven words of the complimentary close, which are in BF's hand.

ever been the Practice to give that assistance to New Comers, which it has not, the immense Charge of the War would at this time forbid it. The particular Recommendations and Passports you desire I should give you willingly if I had a List of the Names Characters &c. But if you are all determin'd to go Suddenly there may not be time, and in that Case, I would have you apply to Mr. Laurens and request them of him. You would also do well to ask and take his Advice with regard to the whole of your Proceedings. I send you enclos'd a general Recommendation to the Government of Pennsylvania, requesting they would favour your Establishment; and also a Passport for the Company and their Effects;[9] advising you withal to be careful not to attempt sheltering under that Passport any English Goods sent over by others for Sale, all the Manufactures of England being at present prohibited there and seizable: and such an Attempt would hurt you exceedingly.

As to the Silk produced in America, concerning which you desire Information, I take it to be much the same with that which you have from Savoy. When I was in London I had several Trunks of it consign'd to me for sale, and I remember it fetched at a publick Sale as high a Price within 6d. in the pound weight, as the Italian sold at the same time.[1] I think you will do right to take with you some of the Chains you mention. As to the Reeds if you cannot easily take them, I believe you may get them made there. I wish you Success, but fear you are too hasty; and think that if one of your Company had first gone over to inspect the State of things, obtain the proper Informations, send you his Advice & prepare for your Reception, the Operation would have had a better Chance of Succeeding, and been attended with less Inconvenience.

I am, Sir, Your most obedient and most humble Servant

B Franklin

Mr. Edmund Clegg.

9. Wyld destroyed these documents when his group was apprehended: Edmund Clegg to William Livingston, April 21, 1784 (Mass. Hist. Soc.).

1. BF knew a great deal about the silk industry. He had encouraged silk production in America since the late 1750s and had educated himself in many aspects of its cultivation; see, for example, VII, 156n; X, 321; XVI, 200–1; XVIII, 31–2. The sale he mentions here took place in 1772: XIX, 134–9.

To William Hodgson

Dear Sir   Passy April 26. 1782.

Your two Favours of the 9th Instant came to my hands but a few days since. I had written so fully to you by the preceeding Post, sending at the same time the Passports and Powers you had demanded, which I hope will be sufficient, that I find little left to answer.[2]

I am much pleas'd with the memorial you presented respecting the Prisoners, and thank you heartily for the Pains you have so kindly taken in that affair.

As to the Expence of the Transports and Provisions, I would just remark, that a great Number of our People, made Prisoners in America, instead of being exchanged there, were cruelly and unnecessarily sent by Admiral Rodney to England in Irons, & pack'd together in the unwholesome Holds of the Ships, which kill'd many.[3] The Provisions for those taken in these Seas, should I think in Justice be compensated by an equal Quantity delivered in America to the Prisoners we shall give in Exchange to be returned in Europe. The Transport Vessels would perhaps go in their Ballast, as they will be wanted probably in America to recieve the exchanged Men, or to remove their Garrisons; & if your Government will accept my first Proposition, and deliver our men to me here,[4] I would save it the Expence of hiring Ships for transporting them to America, as I could easily find the Means of doing it in our own or French Ships.

Having mentioned these Ideas, I confide the whole Transaction to your Judgement and Equity, and shall be satisfied with any Agreement you make, for I know you will do what is right and obtain for us every Advantage we ought to expect. Lord

2. BF sent his now-missing letter and passports on April 20: BF to JA, April 21, above.

3. In 1780, Admiral Rodney, who characterized the American prisoners as unprincipled pirates, converted the hospital ship *Jersey* into a prison ship on which thousands of Americans died: *Letter-Books and Order-Book of George, Lord Rodney, Admiral of the White Squadron, 1780–1782* (2 vols., New York, 1932), I, 55–6; Thomas Dring, *Recollections of the Jersey Prison-Ship . . .* (Providence, 1829).

4. As BF had proposed in November, 1781: XXXVI, 62–3.

Shelburne's intended Kindness to the Prisoners, so as to render their Voyage comfortable, gives me great Pleasure, not so much on Account of an Expence to be saved by that means, but because I know it will have an excellent Effect in America, by its Tendency to *conciliate;* which I think a material Point that merits the attention of both Sides at present: for a Peace may be made by merely agreeing to cease fighting; and that may be without *Reconciliation;* in which Case the Peace will be less advantageous & of a short Duration. Whatever Allowance his Lordship makes for the Purpose abovementioned to the Prisoners in England, I suppose he will extend also to those in Ireland.— If not, I request you will desire your Friends at Kinsale to furnish it, and I will pay the Account upon Sight. Be so good as to present my best Respects and Thanks to his Lordship, for this Instance of his Humanity & Benevolence towards our poor People, and assure him I shall always retain a gratefull Sense of it.

With great Esteem I have the honor to be, Dear Sir, &c. &c.

B. FRANKLIN.

Mr. Hodgson.

Copy of a Letter from Dr. B. Franklin to Mr Hodgson. dated Passy, April 26. 1782. (Copy)

From Margaret Stewart   ALS: American Philosophical Society

London 26 April 1782

I longe Since, hoped; & expected; to have the honor of hearing from Your Excellency; particularly, as Mr Ray of Ostend; wrot me that he Sent You, the Copy of my Brothers Work, in Decr last,[5] I flatered myself that by Your protection; & recomendation, it cou'd not fail of Sucess; as You was so good to Writ; me in the Year Seventy four;[6] that You wou'd be happy at any time, to render me any Service; I never Wanted asistance More than at

---

5. BF received John Stewart's *The Senator's Remembrancer* on Dec. 15: XXXVI, 410n.
6. Missing; see XXIII, 302n.

present; for an Expencive Law Suit,[7] & a Longe illness; has reduced me Much; I had the honor of writing to Your Excellency in Janr last;[8] but Suppose that affairs of consequence prevented my having an enswere; but earnestly beg I may now & that You will, give me Some asistantance & have the honor to be Your Excellency's Obliged humble Servant   M STEWART

PS please to direct for me No 26 union Street Near great Tichfeild Street

Addressed: Son Excellance Dr Franklin / a Passy Pres / de Paris

Notation: Stwart Mr. M. London 26. apl. 1782.

From the Comte de Barbançon[9]

ALS: American Philosophical Society

A Varennes par Noyon ce 27. avril 1782.

On ne sorait ètre, Monsieur, plus reconoisant que je le suis de la bonté que vous avez bien voulu avoir de me faire venir un tresor imanse des Grenes les plus rares,[1] Je ne puis assé vous exprimer conbien je suis sensible a tout la grace que vous y aves mis, je regrete infiniment, Monsieur, que Mon séjour a la campagne me prive du double aventage d'aller vous en remercier de vif voix et de cultiver votre connoissance; je vous prie d'en être bien persuadé, ainsi que des sentiments d'attachement les plus sinceres avec les quels j'ay l'honneur d'être Monsieur, Votre très humble et très obéissant serviteur   LE CTE. DE BARBANÇON

Notation: Comte de Barbançon Varennes 27 Avril 1782

7. She had already described it: xxxv, 636.

8. XXXVI, 410–11.

9. Amateur botanist Augustin-Jean-Louis-Antoine du Prat, comte de Barbançon (1750–1797), had been commander of the infantry regiment of Orléans since 1775. Later he would represent the nobility of Villers-Cotterêts at the Estates General. *DBF.* WTF, who ordered seeds for him from America, described him as "a Gentleman of the first Rank and Merit in this Country, who employs most of his Time in Cultivation" (WTF to RB, Feb. 24, 1781, Library of Congress).

1. For these long-awaited seeds see JW to BF, March 19 and April 18.

From the Comte d'Estaing

L: American Philosophical Society

à Passy ce samedi 27. avril 1782.

Mr. D'Estaing est si accoutumé a devoir des Remercîments à Monsieur franklin, et il a tant de plaisir a les lui faire, qu'il a eû L'honneur d'aller hier chez lui pour former sa Demande de graine. Il lui Renvoye l'Etat[2] qu'il a eû la Bonté de lui Confier. Les articles marqués d'une Croix sont Ceux qu'il desire. La Confiance de Mr. D'Estaing est une excuse de son indiscretion.

Si Monsieur franklin est visible aujourd'hui a une heure après-midi, Mr. D'Estaing aura L'honneur de lui Rendre ses devoirs, et de s'assûrer de la possibilité, et du succès de sa Demande.

Notation: Mr. Destaing 27. avril 1782.

From Johann Reinhold Forster[3]

ALS: American Philosophical Society

Halle in the Dutchy of Magdeburg April the 27th. 1782.
Sir.

Permit me to introduce to Your acquaintance the Bearer Mr. Loder, first Physician to the Duke of Saxe Weimar a Man remarkable for his natural & acquired talents & one of the first Anatomists of our Germany.[4] The happy moments which my

---

2. Either a list of the contents of the case of seeds BF had recently received (see the preceding document), or a list that might have accompanied it for future orders. WTF had suggested to RB that if John Bartram, Jr., or any other botanist wished to establish a "Commerce of Seeds, [he] could easily find them a Correspondent here of the Same Profession": Feb. 24, 1781 (Library of Congress). See also XXIV, 88, 89; XXXII, 55n.

3. For this famous German naturalist see XV, 147–8, and XXVII, 181–2.

4. Justus Christian von Loder (1753–1832) was named professor of anatomy, surgery, and obstetrics at Jena in 1778 and in 1781 became the personal physician to Karl August, Duke of Saxe-Weimar. He made a study trip to Paris, London, and the Netherlands in 1782–83 and went on to have a distinguished medical career in both Germany and Moscow: *Deutsche Biographische Enzyklopädie* (12 vols., Munich, New Providence, and London, 1995), VI, 435–6; *Neue Deutsche Biographie* (20 vols. to date, Berlin, 1953–), XV, 7–10.

Son[5] has passed in Yr. company & the civilities You honoured him with as well as the condescendence & Kindness You are used to treat with, all Men of talents & Science let me hope a favourable reception for my Friend Loder, & will serve as An Apology, for the Liberty I presume to take on this occasion.

Give me leave at the same time to congratulate You, on the happy prospect of seeing Your Country at last acknowledged as independent by all Europe & Great Britain itself. The Satisfaction of seeing this great work so near a Conclusion at a general Pacification, must naturally contribute to Yr. happiness, who have had So great a share in the delivering Your Country from the Oppressions of a Set of despotick Men, then at the head of the British Administration. May providence shower down on You the choicest of her Blessings; is the sincere wish, together with the most respectuous regard, of Sir Your most obedt. humble Servant   FORSTER.

His Excellency. Benj. Franklin. Esqr.

Notation: Foster, April 27. 1782.

From Anthony Barons and Alexander Cummings

ALS: American Philosophical Society

Au haver De Grase Aprele the 28 17[82?]

Sir this Is the humble petiton of seventeen Americans now in this plase in A very Low Condition Jus come from england wheair wee have had the most long and sevear imprisonment that the subgects of Any cuntry has Been this war for the want of Cloaths and every necary of Life now wee your humbl Petitioners and Cuntrymen mak as Bold to aqueant you of our needsisity at this time hoping that you will Look upon your Cuntrymen that has Been fighting for our Cuntry and has Been ther Most of us in prison tow years and some mor But few of us Looss when wee arived hear wee had Passports for Luriant and Differant ports of france but not Being able to persed on our Journy we

5. Johann Georg Adam Forster: XXVII, 181.

was obliged to Continue in this plas And the will not Lett us hav a pass to go to Sea In any ship without paying the money that wee have received from them wee hae Been advised to aquent you of our Condition And the Consell told us that hee maid no Doubt but you would help us in the Low Sitation that wee ar now in the most of us hav got wives and familis in America And hav paid [?]ats and Evrything Acord to our stayton And it is very hard if wee can Not bee Rileved out of our Distress by our Contry wee must go to parts of the worled upon tha Acount of not being sent home that very posible wee never shall Bee able to geet home tow our wives Any mor or forevr and Wee hope that thiss Letter will put you Remembrance of your poore Contrymen, And If the power is invested in you to help them to Some Little money you And in so Doing you will hav the thanks of your humbl petitinors And their prayres Likways

ANTHONY BARONS
ALEXER CUMMINGS

Addressed: Son Excellence / Monseigneur francklin / ministre des Etats unis de / L'amerique septentrionalle / en Son hotel / à / Paris

From François-Félix Nogaret, with a Note from Elisabeth Nogaret   ALS: American Philosophical Society

Monsieur et bon ami   [on or after April 28, 1782]
    Vous trouverés cy Joint une Lettre que mon ministre ma fait le plaisir d'ecrire pour moi à M. Le Mis. de Serent de qui dépend une place de *Lecteur de Mgr Le Duc de Berry* que je demande.[6] M Le Mis. de Castellanne et M. Le Mis. de Montbel qui ont de même ecrit pour moi,[7] m'ont donné un fort bon Conseil: comme

6. Nogaret enclosed a copy of a letter dated April 28, 1782, from Antoine-Jean Amelot de Chaillou (XXIX, 285n). Chaillou recommended his *commis* Nogaret to Armand-Louis, marquis de Sérent, *maréchal des camps et armées du roi* and governor of the comte d'Artois' three children. The youngest of these was Charles-Ferdinand d'Artois, duc de Berry (b. 1778): *Dictionnaire de la noblesse*, VIII, 594; XVIII, 532.
    7. Esprit-François-Henri de Castellane-Novejan, *dit* marquis de Castel-

cette place exige des connaissances, ils m'ont dit que Je ferais bien de me faire recommander aussi par des gens de Lettres: Je demande a M. de Buffon par cet ordinaire d'ecrire pour moi, et je Suis sûr de lui. Rendés moi je vous prie et à ma femme le service de temoigner par ecrit *à M. Le Mis. de Serent* que vous prenés à nous quelqu'interêt; je vous en serai sensiblement obligè. Le plutot que vous Le pourrés faire sera Le mieux: Je vous demande en grace d'ecrire *de votre main et en anglais.* M de Serent scait cette Langue. Votre Lettre peut être mise à la poste.

Ma femme vous presente son respect. Agrées je vous prie les assûrances du mien et pardonnés La liberté avec laquelle J'ose me dire, Monsieur et bon ami votre très humble et très obeissant Serviteur FELIX NOGARET

[*In the hand of Elisabeth Nogaret:*] Md nogaret prie bien monsieur Le docteur de vouloir bien obliger son mari pour Cette place qui ne donne guerre qu'un titre honnorable Car pour de Largent il ny en a guerre[8]

Notation: Nogaret.

From the Earl of Shelburne[9]

Copies:[1] Massachusetts Historical Society, Library of Congress; AL (draft): Public Record Office; press copy of copy: Library of Congress; transcripts: Massachusetts Historical Society, National Archives

Shelburne House 28th. April 1782.
I have received much Satisfaction in being assured by you, that the Qualifications of Wisdom & Integrity which induced me to

---

lane (Castelanne), was *maréchal de camp* and *chevalier d'honneur* to Mme Sophie, the King's aunt: *Dictionnaire de la noblesse*, IV, 811; *Almanach royal* for 1782, pp. 140, 155. The comte de Montbel was *premier maître d'hôtel* to the comtesse d'Artois: *ibid.*, p. 136.

8. BF obliged: Nogaret to BF, May 24 (below) and April 1, 1783 (APS). BF's letter to the marquis de Sérent has not been located.

9. In answer to BF's of April 18. This letter was delivered by Oswald when he returned to Paris on May 4; see BF's journal of the peace negotiations.

1. The copy we print, made by WTF, was sent to JA on May 8. (BF's ac-

make Choice of Mr. Oswald, as the fittest Instrument for the renewal of our Friendly Intercourse, have also recommended him so effectually to your Approbation & Esteem. I most heartily wish that the Influence of this first communication of our mutual Sentiments may be extended to a happy Conclusion of all our Public Differences.—

The Candour, with which Monsieur le Comte de Vergennes expresses his most Christian Majesty's Sentiments and Wishes on the Subject of a speedy Pacification is a pleasing Omen of its accomplishment. His Majesty is not less decided in the same Sentiments & Wishes, and it confirms his Majesty's Ministers in their Intention to act in like manner, as most consonant to the true Dignity of a great Nation.[2]

In consequence of these Reciprocal Advances Mr. Oswald is sent back to Paris for the purpose of arranging & settling with you the preliminaries of Time and Place, and I have the Pleasure to tell you, that Mr Laurens is already discharged from those Engagements, which he enter'd into, when he was admitted to Bail.[3]

It is also determined that Mr Fox, from whose Department[4]

---

companying letter of that date is below.) The press copy at the Library of Congress was made from this version and retained by BF. The original may have been given to Vergennes; there is a French translation at the AAE. The other copy and transcripts are in BF's journal of the peace negotiations, where they were misdated April 20.

2. The Cabinet met on the evening of April 25 and recommended to the King "that Mr. Oswald shall return to Paris with authority to name Paris as the Place, and to settle with Dr. Franklin the most convenient time for setting on Foot a Negotiation for a General Peace,—and to represent to him that the principal points in contemplation are the allowance of Independence to America, upon Great Britain being restored to the situation she was placed in by the Treaty of 1763, and that Mr. Fox shall submit to the consideration of the King a proper person to make a similar communication to Monsr. de Vergennes." The next morning Shelburne forwarded the minutes of their meeting to the King. On April 27, he told the King that Oswald could leave the next day and sent a draft of the present letter for approval. George replied immediately that it "would be perfectly safe . . . to send it without any alteration." Fortescue, *Correspondence of George Third*, V, 488, 492, 494.

3. *I.e.*, to appear before the Court of King's Bench. On April 26, Shelburne released him from the obligation: XXXVI, 372n; *Laurens Papers*, XV, 397, 401, 494.

4. As Foreign Secretary.

that Communication is necessarily to proceed, shall send a proper Person, who may confer and settle immediately with Monsr de Vergennes the further Measures and Proceedings, which may be judg'd proper to adopt towards advancing the Prosecution of this Important Business. In the mean time Mr Oswald is instructed to communicate to you my Thoughts upon the principal Objects to be settled.

Transports are actually preparing for the purpose of conveying your Prisoners to America to be there exchanged, and we trust, that you will learn, that due Attention has not been wanting to their accommodation & good treatment.—

I have the honour to be with very sincere Respect, Dear Sir, Your faithful & obedient humble Servant   SHELBURNE

From Benjamin West   ALS: American Philosophical Society

Dear Sir   London April 28th. 1782.

Your friendly remmbrences of me by the bearer of this is so flattering, I could not permit his return to you without making my Acknowlegments by letter for so pleasing a marke of your esteem,[5] It allways gave me and Mrs. West the greatest satisfaction to hear of your health—a confirmation of which I have not only recived by our friend, but have now before in a Bust; which he procured two or three days past, the likeness is strong and time seems to have made but little impression on the Origenal (as he apeared some years past in Craven Street) but in my family he has rought great changes since you ware with us— My Eldest son now in his Sixteenth year has increased in hight two inches above his father; and the Other (your Godson) now in his tenth year, bids faire to do the Same, they with Mrs. West are in health and desire to be most affectionately remmembred to you—[6] My Eldest has greatly improved in painting, and I have determined to do my utmost to cultivate those talents which

5. BF must have sent a now-missing letter via Caleb Whitefoord, who also delivered one to Mary Stevenson and Mary Hewson dated April 19, above.

6. For the West family see XXXIII, 196–7. The elder son, Raphael Lamar, had been a schoolmate of WTF: West to BF, Sept. 7, 1783 (APS).

apear in him; that they may some day I hope be an Orniment to the profession, my Other son is at school, and shews great phicility in larning; what is to be his lott or profession is not yet determined; In reguard to my own Situation our mutual friend Mr. Whiteford can best discribe, in his interview with you—his arrend is to me a pleasing one, and I pray every blessing may attend it, and your joint endavours to affect the wished for end— my kind complts to your Nephew—and be Assured I am with great reguard and respect Dear Sir Your Obliged and Obedt. Humble Servant   BENJN. WEST

Dr. Franklin—

Notation: West Benjamin, London apl. 28. 1782.

From Thomas Barclay   ALS: American Philosophical Society

Sir   29 april 1782. Amsterdam
    Since I had the honour of addressing Your Excellency last post[7] I heard from Mr. Adams that a Cartel is settled for the Exchange of Seamen between America and Great Britain, and that some ships are getting ready in England to Transport the prisoners that are Now there. As we shall be in great want of some to Man the Ship that is going out, I wish it were possible to get about forty or fifty of them either to Ostend or this place. I have already written to Dunkirk and Ostend to Collect and send hither all that are there, but an addition of either of the above Numbers wou'd Accommodate Us Compleately. I am not Clear in the practicability of the Measure, but I thought I wou'd submit it to your Excellencys Consideration. We shall want a Commission to intitle Captain Samuel Smedley to make prize of any of the Enemys vessells that possibly may fall in his way, which I will be obliged to you to send and if it is Necessary to go through any forms here I shall do it. The ship is Now Called the *Heer Adams*, Burthen 250 Ton, American built, and will sail with Six-

7. Above, April 25.

teen guns and about Sixty Men. Mr. Peter Le Pool[8] of this place requests me to write to your Excellency for such an other Commission for his Brigantine General Green, Edward Bacon Master,[9] will Carry 10 Guns & 30 men. Perhaps the short way wou'd be to send some to Mr. Adams to be deliver'd when wanted.

I have the honour to be with great respect Sir Your Excellencys Most Obed   THOS BARCLAY

Endorsed: April 29. 82

From Monsieur and Madame de Baussan[1]

AL: University of Pennsylvania Library

Ce 29 avril [1782][2]

Mr et Me de Baussan espere que la résolution du papa pour ne point diner a paris n'est pas encore bien préte et quil Voudra bien Leur faire l'honneur de Venir diner chès eux avec Monsieur Son petit fils lundy prochain 6 may. Si M. et Me Caillot[3] Se trouvoit

8. Pieter Le Poole, whose family was from Leiden, had been for a brief period a landowner and merchant in South Carolina: *Laurens Papers,* VIII, 405–6, 536n; P. J. Van Winter, *Het aandeel van den Amsterdamschen handel aan den opbouw van het Amerikaansche Gemeenebest* (2 vols., The Hague, 1927–33), I, 14, 31, 96; II, 429; W. Robert Higgins, "Charles Town Merchants and Factors Dealing in the External Negro Trade, 1735–1775," *S.C. Hist. Mag.,* LXV (1964), 212; R. Nicholas Olsberg, comp., "Ship Registers in the South Carolina Archives, 1734–1780," *S.C. Hist. Mag.,* LXXIV (1973), 275.

9. Perhaps Edward Bacon, Jr., of Barnstable, Mass.: Claghorn, *Naval Officers,* p. 11.

1. This is the first of several invitations (all in the hand of the wife) for dinner at the Paris house of a couple we surmise are the marquis and marquise de Baussan. The marquis N. de Baussan, a cavalry officer and *maréchal-de-camp,* was from a family of magistrates and high administrative officials: Jean-Baptiste-Pierre Julien de Courcelles, comp., *Dictionnaire historique et biographique des généraux français* (9 vols., Paris, 1820–23); *Dictionnaire de la noblesse,* II, 571; *État militaire* for 1781, p. 98; Michel Antoine, *Le Gouvernement et l'administration sous Louis XV: Dictionnaire biographique* (Paris, 1978), pp. 22–3.

2. The only year during BF's French mission when May 6 fell on a Monday.

3. BF's neighbors, the actor and his young wife.

libre et que le tres bon papa Voulut les ammener M. et Me de Baussan seroit ravis de les voir, ils ont l'honneur doffrir leur Tendre hommage a Ce tres aimable papa.

Addressed: A Monsieur / Monsieur francklin ministre / plénipotentiaire des états unis de lamérique / a passy

From Michael Hillegas als: American Philosophical Society

Dr Sir   Philada. April 29. 1782.

Your favour of the 17th. June last introducing Mr. Beyerle,[4] was handed me about 10 or 12 days ago by that Gentleman immediately after his arrival at this place— It gave me great pleasure to hear of your health— And I pray God may continue you in the same whilst on Earth, and to grant you everlasting happiness in the World to come.— As to Mr. Beyerlé, you may rest assured, I shall give him that attention which your reccommendation and the great esteem I have for you, entitle him to.

Altho' I am sencible of your time being so very much taken up in public business, yet knowing the goodness of your Heart I am prevailed on by a poor Widow of this City[5] to request the favour of your endeavours some way or other to obtain the Releasement or Exchange of her Son John Claypoole, who was taken Prisoner on Board the Ship called the Luzerne commanded by Captain Bell Bound from L'Orient for this place, (on Board of which he was in the Character of Steward) was carried into Ireland and from thence to England and committed to Mill Prison near Plymouth.[6] I understand he is a clever fellow, and

4. XXXV, 171–2.

5. Elizabeth Hall Claypoole (1718–1805) had been a widow since 1779: Rebecca Irwin Graff, comp., *Genealogy of the Claypoole Family of Philadelphia 1588–1893* (Philadelphia, 1893), p. 65.

6. Claypoole (1752–1817) served initially in the army, where he was wounded at the Battle of Germantown in the fall of 1777. He was captured at sea on April 4, 1781, and remained in Mill Prison until the general exchange of American prisoners in the summer of 1782. Upon his return to Philadelphia Claypoole had to inform his lifelong friend Betsy Ross that her husband, also incarcerated in Mill, had died in prison. Ross and Claypoole married in

was the only support of his Mother—his liberation would therefore be an Act of Charity.

A very particular friend of mine has requested me to solicit you to inform me, For what Sum, A Compleat set of the Encyclopædia can be purchased in France? *of the best Edition* in handsome binding.— Also whether the Work entituled *Histoire des Arts et Mettiers,* differs materially from the Encyclopædia— And at what price they are to be procured in bindings similar to those above described.[7]

I am with the most profound respect & esteem Your most Obedient and most humble Servant   M. HILLEGAS

P.S. Mrs. Hillegas requests me to present you with her best Respects.

His Excellency Benja. Franklin Esqr.

Addressed: His Excellency / Benjamin Franklin Esquire / Embassador from the United States of / America at the Court of Versailes / Passy

From Francis Hopkinson   ALS: Historical Society of Pennsylvania

Dear sir.   Philada. April 29th. 1782

I am told there is a most valuable Work in the Press at Paris, entitled *Encyclopædia Methodique,* to be published in yearly Volumes, & that the Subscription will in the whole amount to about 100 Dollars.[8] I am very desirous of having this Com-

---

May, 1783, and had five children: Charles Francis Jenkins, ed., "John Claypoole's Memorandum-Book," *PMHB,* XVI (1892), 178–90. See also Graff, *Claypoole Genealogy,* pp. 65, 68–75.

7. The friend was Matthew Clarkson (1733–1800), who in 1772 was a member of a Library Company committee that directed BF to order Diderot's *Encyclopédie:* Hillegas to BF, Jan. 6, 1783 (APS); XIX, 117–18; *Biographical Directory of the American Congress 1774–1961...* (Washington, D.C., 1961), p. 702. BF had subscribed to the Neuchâtel edition of *Descriptions des arts et métiers* in 1779: XXXI, 4n; XXXII, 117n, 300n.

8. The colossal project to redesign and rewrite Diderot's *Encyclopédie,* now under the direction of Parisian publisher Charles-Joseph Panckoucke,

pendium of human Knowledge, & request the favour of you to enter me as a Subscriber. If you will be so good as to advance the first Deposit for me I will repay it to Mr. Bache or otherwise as you shall direct; or my friend Mr. Barclay will make the necessary Advance which I will repay to any of his Correspondents here.

I am, dear Sir Your ever affectionate　　　　FR. HOPKINSON

Honb. Dr. Franklin

Addressed: To The Honourable / Doctor Franklin / at Passy / near Paris

Notation: F. Hopkinson 29. April 1782.

From Freegift Arnold[9]　　ALS: American Philosophical Society

Honoured Sir　　　　　　　　L'Orient 30th Apl. 1782

I must take the liberty to claim your Honours attention while I relate my unhappy Situation: not doubting but the singular circumstances with which it is Attended, will, in some Measure apologize for my troubling your Honour at this time.

I have been an Officer in the service of the Congress since the

------

was announced in December, 1781, with a prospectus for subscribers. The *Encyclopédie méthodique* (conceived at this point as 26 dictionaries and seven volumes of plates) would contain a systematic and fully cross-referenced compendium of knowledge arranged by subject rather than alphabetically. Each finely printed volume would be written by a leading expert in the field. Both the quarto edition (42 vols.) and the octavo (84 vols.) were offered to the public at the same subscription price of 672 *l.t.* The subscription would close on July 1, 1782, after which the price would be 798 *l.t.* The entire series was to be completed in five years.

The failure of this prospectus to attract subscribers induced Panckoucke in March, 1782, to abandon the octavo edition, shorten the subscription period, change the financial terms, and issue a new prospectus. This time he generated a frenzy of interest, and the project was able to move forward. The tortured history of the *Méthodique* is detailed in Robert Darnton, *The Business of Enlightenment* (Cambridge, Mass., and London, 1979), pp. 395–519.

9. An American sailor whose story is confirmed by British prison records: Kaminkow, *Mariners,* p. 6; Claghorn, *Naval Officers,* p. 7.

commencement of the present War was a Midshipman in the Alfred with Capt Hinman[1] when at this place in 1777. was taken in sd Ship in March 1778. immediately after obtaining my liberty & ariving at Boston which was 1st Octr. 1778, I went on board the Alliance frigate Capt Landais. & sailed from this port in Augt 1779 in Compy. Capt Jones &Ca. on a Cruize, was put on board a prize 5th Sept. & on the 18th was taken Prisoner & carried to Forton Prison, where I remained untill the 5th Inst. when I found means to effect my escape, after having Experienced more than 30 Mo. imprisonment attended with all the Distresses & Cruelties which a Barbarous & Inhuman Enemy could inflict—

Previous to the Sailing of the Alliance I empowered Mr. Moylen to receive what Prize Money might become due to me, & at the same time received a trifling sum from him: on my arrival here was informed that, (notwithstanding several of our Prises were sold here) not a farthing had been paid; Mr. Moylan being absent, & no American Vessels in want of Seamen was under the necessity to take lodgings in hopes of receiving some assistance from Mr. Moylen on his return; but being infomed from him that he cannot assist me without your Honours Orders, and being not only indebted to Mr. Moylen the sum of Seventy Livers, but also for three weeks subsistence since my arival at this place, and not having a farthing of Money, must beg the favour of your Honour to Order me a trifling Sum, to be deducted out of my Wages should there be no prize Money Due, which will be esteemed a particular favour confered on—Hond Sir Your most Obt Hbl Servt.   FREEGIFT. ARNOLD

Honble. B. Franklin Esqr.

Addressed: The Honble. B. Franklin Esqr / Minister Plenipotentiary / from the United States of / America / at / Passey— / prés Paris

Notation: Arnold Freeight, L'orient 30. Apl. 1782.

---

1. Elisha Hinman, who corresponded with BF after his escape from captivity: XXVII, 276.

From Henry Laurens

L:[2] Historical Society of Pennsylvania; copies: Library of Congress,[3] South Carolina Historical Society; transcript: National Archives

Sir,   London 30th April 1782

I writ to you on the 7th. Inst: by Mr Oswald, since which, that is to say, on the 28th. I was honored by the receipt of your letter of the 12th. inclosing a copy of the Commission for treating for Peace, by the hands of Mr Young.

The Recognizance exacted from me by the late Ministry has been vacated & done away by the present, these have been pleased to enlarge me without formal conditions; but as I would not consent the United States of America should be outdone in Generosity, however late the Marks appeared on this side, I took upon me to assure Lord Shelburne in a letter of Acknowledgment for the part which his Lordship had taken in obtaining my release, that Congress would not fail to make a just and adequate return—[4] the only return in my View is Lieutenant General Lord Cornwallis; Congress were pleased to offer some time ago a British Lieutenant General for my ransom,[5] and as I am informed the special Exchange of Lord Cornwallis for the same Subject was lately in contemplation it would afford me very great satisfaction to know that you will join me in cancelling the debt of honor which we have impliedly incurred by discharging his Lordship from the Obligations of his Parole, for my own part, tho' not a bold Adventurer, I think I shall not commit myself to the risque of censure by acting conjunctly with you in such a Bargain; I entreat you Sir, at least to reflect on this Matter, I shall take the liberty of requesting your determination when I reach the Continent, which will probably happen in a few Days.[6]

Lord Cornwallis in a late conversation with me put the fol-

2. In the hand of Henry Laurens, Jr., with an insertion by his father (noted below).

3. Both this copy and the transcript are in BF's journal of the peace negotiations, where they are misdated April 20.

4. *Laurens Papers*, xv, 476–8.

5. Burgoyne; see Laurens' April 7 letter.

6. Laurens left London on May 10: *Laurens Papers*, xv, xxxvii.

lowing case— Suppose, said his Lordship it shall have been agreed in America, that Lord Cornwallis should be offered in Exchange for Mr Laurens, don't you think although you are now discharged, that I ought to reap the intended Benefit? A reply from the feelings of my heart, as I love fair play, was prompt; undoubtedly My Lord, you ought to be, & shall be in such case discharged, and I will venture to take the Burthen upon myself. Certain legal forms, I apprehend rendered the discharge of me without condition unavoidable; but I had previously refused to accept of myself for nothing, and what I now aim at was understood as an adequate return, it is not to be doubted his Lordship's Question was built upon this Ground.[7]

I had uniformly & explicitly declared to the people here, people in the first rank of Importance, that nothing short of Independence in terms of our Treaty of Alliance, could induce America to treat for truce or peace, and that no Treaty could be had without the consent of our Ally first obtained, in a Word, if you mean to have Peace, you must seek for a general Peace; The Doctrine was ill relished, especially by those whose Power only, could set the Machine in motion; but having, since my return from Harlaem, asserted in very positive terms that I was confirmed in my former opinions, the late obduracy has been more than a little softened, as you will soon learn from the worthy friend,[8] by whom I address'd you on the 7th. who, two days ago

7. At this point Henry Laurens, Sr., added, "I shewd this part of my Letter to Lord Shelburne who remarked that it was all very fair & true.—but his Lordship when reading the following Lines did not seem well pleased with the part marked * he nevertheless confirmed the fact." (Laurens added asterisks before and after the expression "the late obduracy has been more than a little softened" in the following paragraph.) On his retained copy (in Moses Young's hand: S.C. Hist. Soc.) Laurens expanded this note. He had shown the letter to Cornwallis on April 30 and to Shelburne on May 1. Shelburne "expressed himself very well pleased with the parts relative to Ld. Cornwallis, said it was all right & very generos. &ca. but His Ldship was silent & appeared dissatisfied with the paragraph x to x [the entire following paragraph] which he had first asked if he should read—I had intended only the foregoing part for his perusal, but when he asked—I replied, 'by all means My Lord' & he read the whole." Laurens actually met with Cornwallis on April 29: *Laurens Papers*, xv, 503n.

8. Richard Oswald.

set out on his return to Passy & Versailles, with, (as I believe) a more permanent Commission than the former.

Accept my thanks Sir, for the kind Offer of a supply of Money. I know too well how much you have been harrased for that Article, and too well how low our American Finances in Europe are, therefore, if I can possibly avoid it, I will not further trouble you nor impoverish them, or not 'till the last Extremity; hitherto I have supported myself without borrowing from any body, and I am determined to continue living upon my own stock while it lasts; the stock is indeed small, my Expences have been, & shall be in a suitably modest stile.

I pray God to bless you, & I have the honor to be Sir, Your most obedient humble Servant   (signed)HENRY LAURENS.

P.S. I judged it proper not only to shew the Peace Commission to Lord Shelburne, but to give his Lordship a copy of it, from an Opinion that it would work no Evil, being shewn elsewhere—

(Copy)

Notation: H. Laurens, London 30. April 1782.

From Jonathan Williams, Jr.

ALS: American Philosophical Society; copy: Yale University Library

Dear & hond sir   Nantes April 30. 1782.

Mr James Moore Brother to Mr Philip Moore of Philadelphia has been some Time in this Town. He came hither from Scotland intending for America, but finding that through his Brothers Connexions he can fix himself advantageously in Business here he has determined to stay & enter into the american Trade.[9]

9. Philip and James Moore, sons of the wealthy merchant Sir James Moore of the Isle of Man, had established independent business ventures, Philip in Philadelphia and James in Glasgow. JW had long been friendly with Philip. James, whose fortunes had suffered during the war, had been with JW in Nantes since early February. He made such a favorable impression that JW decided to take him and his brother into partnership. On May 10, 1782, they established the firm of Williams, Moore & Co., and James Moore promptly left for Lorient where he would anchor the firm's operations. JW to William

I advised him first to take the Oath of Allegiance to the United States which he had not the smallest Objection to do, & would have set off immediately for Paris to take it in your Presence, but I apprehended the signing one before Witness might answer the Purpose, I therefore send it inclosed & request to know if it is sufficient because otherwise he will go to Paris immediately.[1] I shall write you more fully respecting this Gentleman in a few days & request your Friendship for him. I have not yet recd your Answer about the Prisoners who are on Board here at my Expence, I have done nothing more than their necessities require & I doubt not you will think this a Charge rather on the Public than me.

I am as ever Your dutifull & affectionate Kinsman

JONA WILLIAMS J

have the seeds at last come to hand?

Notation: Jona. Williams 30 Apl. 1782.

From Jean-Pierre Blanchard[2]

ALS: American Philosophical Society

Monsieur   ce jeudy soir [*c.* April, 1782][3]

Monsieur de sarsfield m'ayant annoncè que vous me feriez l'honneur de venir voir mon vaisseau Volant dèmain.[4] J'ay l'hon-

---

Alexander, May 10, 1782; JW to Williams, Moore & Co., Aug. 1, 1782 (Yale University Library).

1. The undated oath, written and signed by Moore and witnessed by JW, is among BF's papers at the APS.

2. Blanchard (1750–1809), whose name is sometimes given as "François," had spent 12 years trying to construct a flying machine. Though these various "vaisseaux volants" were unsuccessful, Blanchard established his place in the history of aeronautics by completing, with the American John Jeffries, the first balloon crossing of the English Channel and by pioneering the parachute: *DBF; Encyclopædia Britannica; Jour. de Paris,* Aug. 28, 1781.

3. Blanchard initially issued tickets for a public demonstration of his flying machine to be held on Sunday, April 28; he then rescheduled for the following Sunday, May 5: *Jour. de Paris,* May 1, 1782. The present letter seems to date from a time when he was engaged in the final construction tasks.

4. Parisians had been visiting Blanchard's workshop ever since the inven-

neur de vous donner avis, qu'ayant commencé a faire mettre la couverture de carton vous ne verrez absolument rien d'interessant la meccanique etant enfermée par cette envelope. Je ne pouray percer la place des Glaces et en ouvrir la porte que dans environ 8 jours, alors Monsieur sy a cette époque vous vouliez choisir un jour et une heure jauray l'honneur de vous recevoir, j'ay celuy dêtre très parfaitement Monsieur Votre très humble serviteur   BLANCHARD

Addressed: A Monsieur / Monsieur franklin / a Passy / Blanchard

From ———— Richard   ALS: American Philosophical Society

Monsieur,   [before May 1, 1782][5]
   Sans avoir l'honneur d'être connu de vous, j'ose prendre la liberté de vous envoyer un éxemplaire d'une pièce que j'ai faite

---

tor aroused public curiosity and debate by describing his project in the *Jour. de Paris* on Aug. 28, 1781. The "vaisseau volant" was at that time shaped like a small boat, four feet long by two feet wide, that could hold two people. Two pairs of ten-foot-long wings would create a parasol 20 feet in diameter; the mechanics of locomotion were not detailed. Blanchard later modified that design, adding an outer layer to the body, the "couverture de carton" that he alludes to in the present letter. A witness at the May 5 viewing observed this covering (with a window and door cut in it) and described the vessel as resembling the body of a bird, with the bow shaped like a beak and the tiller, a tail. There were now six wings in all. Fore and aft wings would levitate the vessel, and two pairs of side wings would propel it. Certain lingering design flaws prevented Blanchard from demonstrating the machine to the enormous crowd that turned out, despite terrible weather, at the home of his patron the abbé de Vienné on May 5. He needed three more weeks, he said, during which no one would be allowed to visit the atelier. Despite large financial incentives promised by the comte d'Artois and the duc de Chartres if the "vaisseau" were to fly, Blanchard's project failed, and it was rumored that he fled Paris with a substantial sum of the abbé's money: *Jour. de Paris,* Jan. 14, April 4 (and issues cited there), and April 27, 1782; Bachaumont, *Mémoires secrets,* XX, 142, 229–30, 232–4, 237; Métra, *Correspondance secrète,* XIII, 100.
   5. This is the first of several letters from a student who was bold enough to send BF poems and fortunate enough to receive from him a degree of encouragement. BF's responses are missing, but we publish this undated letter on the basis of Richard's next one, May 1, below.

au nom de l'université de Paris, sur la naissance de Monseigneur. le Dauphin. C'est un hommage du à vos profondes lumières. D'ailleurs, Monsieur, ce qui pourroit encore excuser ma témérité, c'est que, dans ma pièce, il y á un endroit, ou je chante les héros de Boston, et Surtout le fameux Wasingthon dont la valeur dirigée par vos conseils ne tardera pas à affermir entiêrement cette précieuse Liberté dont vous avez jetté les premiêres Racines dans votre courageuse patrie. Au reste, l'accueil favorable que le Roi et la Reine ont bien voulu faire à ma pièce, l'orsque je la leur ai presenté,[6] me fait espérer que vous ne dédaignerez pas d'y jetter un coup d'oeil dans vos moments de loisir. Pardonnez, monsieur, si j'interromps le cours de tant d'affaires importantes qui vous occupent. Je me trouverai trop heureux; si vous ne blamez pas mon Zêle, et si ma pièce peut obtenir un Sourire de la part d'un personnage qui fait l'admiration de l'europe entiêre par ses vertus, soit civiles, soit politiques.

J'ai l'honneur d'être avec le plus profond respect, Monsieur, Votre trés humble et trés obeissant serviteur,

RICHARD
vétéran de Rhétorique[7] au college de Lizieux,
dans l'université de Paris

Notation: Richard

6. Probably at one of the public ceremonies in honor of the dauphin's birth during the King and Queen's visit to Paris in January: XXXV, 638–9n; XXXVI, 442n.

7. A student in his second year of rhetoric.

From Charles James Fox[8]

Copy:[9] Library of Congress; AL (draft): Public Record Office; transcripts: Massachusetts Historical Society, National Archives (two)

Sir,   St. James's 1. May 1782

Though Mr. Oswald will no doubt have informed you of the nature of Mr. Grenville's Commission,[1] yet I can not refrain from making use of the opportunity his going offers me, to assure you of the esteem and Respect which I have borne to your character, and to beg you to believe that no change in my situation has made any in those ardent wishes for reconciliation which I have invariably felt from the very beginning of this unhappy Contest. Mr. Grenville is fully acquainted with my sentiments upon this subject, and with the sanguine hopes which I have conceived that those with whom we are contending are too reasonable to continue a contest[2] which has no longer any object either real or even imaginary.——

8. Who was more concerned at the moment with preventing Shelburne's gaining control over the French negotiations than with gaining a footing in the American negotiations, given BF's recent endorsement of Shelburne's man Oswald as a negotiating partner: Fox to Richard Fitzpatrick, April 28, in Lord John Russell, ed., *Memorials and Correspondence of Charles James Fox* (4 vols., London, 1853–57), I, 316.

9. Made from the original under BF's supervision, this copy is a more accurate text than the draft, which lacks a dateline, salutation, and complimentary close, and varies slightly in wording. This copy is in BF's journal of the peace negotiations, as are two of the transcripts.

1. Fox sent his representative Thomas Grenville (for whom see our headnote to Shelburne's letter of April 6) to Paris not only to negotiate with Vergennes, but also to open a channel of communication with BF in case negotiations with France failed. He was not given full powers and Fox's instructions left him the option of speaking privately or officially; in either case he was to inform both Vergennes and BF about the cabinet's terms for peace with America. In essence, Britain would acknowledge American independence, evacuate New York, Charleston, and Savannah, return to France the islands of St. Pierre, Miquelon, and St. Lucia, and restore India to its prewar condition if France returned all her conquests: Fox's instructions to Grenville, April 30, 1782, in Giunta, *Emerging Nation*, I, 367–9. Grenville's letter of introduction to Vergennes is published in Lord John Russell, ed., *Memorials and Correspondence of Charles James Fox* (4 vols., London, 1853–57), IV, 178–9.

2. Fox here drafted but deleted "of which the object is at length entirely gone".

I know your liberality of mind too well to be afraid lest any prejudices against Mr. Grenville's *Name*[3] may prevent you from esteeming those excellent qualities of heart and head which belong to him, or from giving the fullest credit to the sincerity of his wishes for Peace in which no Man in either country goes beyond him. I am with great truth and Regard, Sir, your most obedient humble Servant   C. J. Fox

Benjamin Franklin Esq.

From David Hartley

Transcripts:[4]National Archives, Massachusetts Historical Society

My dear Friend,   London, May 1st. 1782.

I have received a Packet from you containing several Letters of various Dates. As I shall probably have a safe Opportunity of Conveyance to you when Mr. Laurens leaves this Country, I am now sitting down to write to you an *omnium* Kind of a Letter, of various Matters as they occur. The late Ministry being departed, I may now speak of Things past more freely. I will take a Sentence in one of your Letters for my Text. Vide yours of April 13th. 1782, in which you say— "You was of Opinion that the late Ministry desired *sincerely* a Reconciliation with America, and, with that view, a separate Peace with us was proposed." I must qualify this Sentence much, before I can adopt it as my Opinion. As to *Reconciliation,* I never gave them much Credit for that Wish. "It is a sweet expression; it certainly means *more* than Peace."[5] The utmost that I ever gave the late Ministry Credit for, was a Wish for *Peace.* And I still believe that the wisest amongst them grew from Day to Day more disposed to Peace (or an

3. Thomas Grenville was a son of the late George Grenville, who as prime minister had been responsible for the passage of the Stamp Act and other legislation unpopular in America.

4. In BF's journal of the peace negotiations, where this letter is included under May 26, the date BF received it.

5. He is quoting phrases (in reverse order) from BF's April 5 letter to him, above.

Abatement of the War,) in Proportion as they became more alarmed for their own Situations, and their Responsibility. Had the War been more successful, I should not have expected much relenting towards Peace or Reconciliation. That this has always been the Measure of my Opinion of them, I refer you to some Words in a Letter from me to you, dated Jany: 5th: 1780 for Proof.— "But for the Point of Sincerty? Why,—as to that, I have not much to say. I have at least expected some Hold upon their *Prudence*. My Argument runs thus— It is a *Bargain* for *you* (Ministers) to be sincere *now*. Common Prudence may hint you to look to yourselves. It has amazed me beyond Measure, that this principle of common selfish *Prudence* has not had the Effect which I expected."[6] I have not been disposed to be deceived by any conciliatory Professions, which I considered only as arising from Prudence; and I hope that I have not led you into any Deception, having so fully explained myself to you on that Head. Had the american War been more prosperous on the Part of the late Ministry, I do not believe the late Resignation would have taken place, but it is evident, from the Proposition to the Court of France, which you have communicated to me, (and which I have communicated to the present Ministry, with your Letter) that even to the last Hour, some Part of the late Ministry were still set upon the american War, to the last Extremity: and, probably another, more *prudent* Part of the Ministry would proceed no farther; which, if it be so, may reasonably be imputed as the Cause of the Dissolution of the Late Ministry. These are the Arguments, which I have always driven, and insisted upon, with the greatest Expectation of Success, vizt. *prudential* Arguments; from the total Impracticability of the War— Responsibility, &c. &c. I have been astonished, beyond Measure, that these Arguments have not had their Effect sooner. If I could give you an Idea of many Conferences, which I have had upon the Subject, I should tell you that many Times, *Felix has trembled*.[7] When re-

6. XXXI, 343.
7. Felix was the governor of Caesarea before whom the apostle Paul was brought. "And as he reasoned of righteousness, temperance, and judgement to come, Felix trembled": *Acts of the Apostles*, 24:25. The other transcript does not include the word "has."

duced by the Terror of Responsibility, either to renounce the american War, or to relinquish their Places, they have chosen the latter: which is a most wretched and contemptible Retribution, either to their Country, or to Mankind, for the Desolation in which they have involved every Nation that they have ever been connected with. *Peace*, they would not leave behind them! Their Legacy to their Country and to Mankind has been, Let Darkness be the Burier of the Dead!

As to the Proposal of a *separate* Peace, arising from a Desire of *Reconciliation*, it certainly was so, on the Part of the People of England, but, on the Part of the late Ministry, it probably arose from the Hopes of suggesting to France Ideas of some Infidelity, on the Part of America, towards them. If you should ask me why I have *seemed* to conspire with this, my Answer is very plain. In the first Place, if I could have prevailed with the late Ministry to have actually made an irrevocable Offer, *on their own Part*, of a *separate* Peace to America, that very Offer would in the same Instant have become, *on their Part* also a Consent to a *general* Peace; because *they* never had any Wish to a separate Contest with France, and America being out of the Question, *they* would have thought of Nothing after that, but a general Peace. But I never could bring them even to this. *They* wished that *America* should make the Offer of a separate Treaty; (for obvious Views.[8]) *My* Proposal was, that *they* should offer irrevocable Terms of peace to America. If they had really meant what they pretended, and what the People of England did really desire, they would have adopted that Proposition. Then the Question would have come forward upon the fair and honorable Construction of a Treaty between France and America, the *essential and direct End* of which was fully accomplished.—When I speak of great Britain offering irrevocable Terms of Peace to America, I mean such Terms as would effectually have satisfied the Provision of the Treaty; vizt. *tacit* Independence. I send you a Paper intitled a Breviate, which I laid before the late Ministry: and their not having acted upon it, was a Proof, to me, that the Disposition of their Heart to America was not altered, but that all their relenting arose from the Impracticability of that War, & their Want of

---

8. The other transcript has this word as "reasons."

Success in it. But, desponding as they were at last, it was not in-consistent with my Expectations of their Conduct, that they should make great Offers to France to abandon America: it was the only Weapon left in their Hands. In Course of negotiating with the said Ministry, I perceived their Courage drooping from Time to Time, for the last three or four years; and it was upon that Ground that I gave them Credit for an increasing Disposi-tion towards Peace. Some dropt off—others sunk under the Load of Folly—and, at last, they all failed.

My Argument *ad homines* to the late Ministry, might be stated thus, respecting the american War. "*If you don't kill them, they will kill you.*"— "But the War is impracticable *on your part—Ergo*, the best Thing you can do, *for your own Sakes*, is to make Peace."— This was reasoning to *Men;* and, *through* Men to *Things*. But there is no Measure of Rage in Pride and Disap-pointment.

> Spicula cœca relinquant
> Affixe venis, animasq in vulnere ponunt.[9]

So much for the Argument of the Breviate, as far as it re-spected the late Ministry. It was a Test, which proved that *they* were not Sincere in their Pretensions. If they had been in earnest to have given the War a Turn towards the House of Bourbon, and to have dropt the american War, a plain Road lay before them. The Sentiment of the People of England was conformable to the Argument of that Breviate: or rather, I should say what is the real Truth, that the Argument of the Breviate was dictated by the Notoriety of that Sentiment in the People of England. My Object and Wish always has been to strike at the Root of the Evil, the American War. If the british Nation have Jealousies and Resentments against the House of Bourbon; yet still, the first Step, in every Case, should be to recind the American War; and not to keep it lurking in the Rear, to become hereafter, in Case of certain Events, a *reversionary* War with America for uncondi-

---

9. A description of the rage of injured bees from Virgil's *Georgics*, 4:237–8, "in thy veins their darts invisible cling / and they leave them there, even life unto vengeance surrendering." Arthur S. Way, trans., *The Georgics of Virgil in English Verse* (London, 1912), pp. 100–1.

tional Terms. This reversionary War was never the Object of
the People of England; therefore the Argument of the Breviate
was calculated, *bonâ fide*, to accomplish their Views; and to dis-
criminate the fallacious Pretenses of the late Administration
from the real Wishes of the Country, as expressed in the circular Resolutions of many Counties, in the year 1780, first moved
at York on March 28th 1780.[1] Every other Principle and Mode of
conduct only implies, as you very justly express it, a secret Hope
that War may still produce Successes, and *then* &c. &c. &c. The
Designs which have been lurking under this Pretext could not
mean any Thing else than this— "Who knows but we may still
talk to America at last?"— The only Test of clear Intentions
would have been this, to have cut up the american War, and all
possible return to it, for any Cause, or under any Pretext. I am
confident that the Sentiment of the People of England is, and always has been, to procure Peace and Reconciliation with America, and to vindicate the national Honor in the Contest with the
House of Bourbon. If this Intention had been pursued in a simple and direct Manner, I am confident that the Honor and Safety
of the British Nation would long ago, have been established, in
a *general* Peace with all the Belligerant Powers.

These are the Sentiments to which I have always acted in
those Negotiations which I have had on the Subject of Peace,
with the late Ministry; Reconciliation with America, and Peace
with all the World, upon Terms consistent with the Honor and
Safety of my own Country. Peace must be sought in such Ways
as promise the greatest Degree of Practicability. The Sentiments
of Individuals, as Philanthropists, may be overborne by the
Powers of ancient Prejudices, which too frequently prevail in the
Aggregates of Nations. In such Cases, the Philanthropist, who
wishes the good of his own Country and of Mankind, must be
the Bulrush bending to the Storm, and not the sturdy Oak, un-
availingly resisting. National Prejudices are, I hope, generally
upon the Decline. Reason and Humanity gain Ground every

---

1. This petition called the war "most expensive and unfortunate" and
asked the House of Commons "to correct the gross abuses in expenditure
of public money": *The Annual Register for the Year 1780* (London, 1781),
pp. 338–9 of the first pagination.

day, against their *natural* Enemies, Folly & Injustice. The ideas of Nations being *natural* Enemies to each other, are generally reprobated. But still *jealousies* and ancient *Rivalships* remain, which obstruct the Road to Peace among Men. If one belligerant Nation will entertain a standing Force of three or four hundred thousand fighting Men, other Nations must have defended Frontiers and barrier Towns; and the Barrier of a neighboring Island, whose Constitution does not allow a standing military Force, must consist in a Superiority at Sea: it is necessary for her own Defence. If all Nations will, by mutual Consent, reduce their *offensive* Powers (which they only claim under the Pretext of necessary *Defence*) and bring forward the Reign of the Millennium, then, away with your Frontiers and Barriers! Your Gibralters, and the Key of the Baltic! And all the hostile Array of Nations!

Aspera compositis mitescant sœcula bellis![2]

These must be the Sentiments of every Philanthropist in his interior Thoughts. But, if we are not to seek Peace by some practicable Method, accommodated to the remaining Prejudices of the Multitude, we shall not, I fear, in our Time, see that happy Day. If Great Britain and France are ancient Rivals, then (until the Reign of the Millennium shall approach) arrange that Rivalship upon equitable Terms: As the two leading Nations of Europe, set them in Balance to each other, the one by Land, the other by Sea. Give to France her elevated Rank among the Nations of Europe: Give to Great Britain the honor of her Flag, and the Security of her Island by her wooden Walls; and there would be no Obstruction to general and perpetual Peace.

The Prejudices of Disrespect between Nations, prevail only among the inferior Ranks. Believe me, for one, at least, I have the highest Sentiments of Respect for the Nation of France. I have no other Sentiment of Hostility, but what is honorable towards them, and which, as a Member of a rival State at War with

---

2. The passage, from the *Aeneid,* 1:291, should read, "Aspera tum positis mitescent saecula bellis": "Then wars shall cease, and the rude age grow mild." Charles J. Billson, trans., *The Aeneid of Virgil* (2 vols., London, 1906), 1, 18–19.

them, constitutes the Duty of Vigilance which I owe to the Honor and Interests of my own Country. I am not conscious of a Word or, a Thought, which, *on the Point of Honor*, I would wish to have concealed from a french Minister. In the Mode which I have proposed, of unravelling the present Subjects of Jealousy & Contest, I would make my Proposals openly to France herself. Let America be free and enjoy Happiness & Peace forever.— If France and Great Britain have Jealousies and Rivalships between themselves as European Nations, I would then say to France— Let us settle those Points between ourselves, if unfortunately, we shall not be able, by honorable Negotiation, to compromise the indispensable Points of national Honor and Safety. This would be my Language to France, open and undisguised. In the mean Time I desire you to observe, that it would not be with Reluctance that I should offer eternal Freedom, Happiness and Peace to America. You know my Thoughts too well to suspect that. I speak only as in a State of War, desirous to arrange the complicated Interests, and to secure the respective Honor of Nations. My Wishes are, and always have been, for the Peace, Liberty and Safety of Mankind. In the Pursuit of those blessed Objects, not only this Country and America, but France herself and the House of Bourbon, may justly claim the conspiring Exertions of every free and liberal Mind, even among their temporary Enemies & Rivals.

I am, Sir, Your affecte. Friend.   D. HARTLEY.

Breviate. Feby. 7th. 1782.

It is stated that America is disposed to enter into a Negotiation of Peace with Great Britain without requiring any formal Recognition of Independence always understood that they are to act in Conjunction with their Allies conformable to Treaties.

It is therefore recommended to give for Reply that the Ministers of Great Britain are likewise disposed to enter into a Negotiation for Peace, and that they are ready to open a general Treaty for that Purpose.

If the british Ministers should see any Objection to a general Treaty, but should still be disposed to enter into a separate Treaty with America, it is then recommended to them to offer such Terms to America as shall induce her to apply to her Allies for their Consent that she should be permitted to enter into a separate Treaty with Great Britain. The Condition of which, being the consent of Allies no Proposition of any Breach of Faith can be understood to be required of them by the Requisition of a separate Treaty.

The british Ministers are free to make any Propositions to America which they may think proper provided they be not dishonorable in themselves, which, in the present Case, is barred by the Supposition of Consent being obtained. In this Case, therefore, if they should be inclined to offer a separate Treaty, it is recommended to them to offer such Terms to America as should induce her to be desirous of closing with the Proposal of a separate Treaty on the Grounds of national Security and Interests, and likewise such as may constitute to them a Case of Reason & Justice, upon which they may make Requisition to their Allies for their Consent. It is suggested that the Offer to America of a Truce of sufficient Length, together with the Removal of the british Troops, would be equivalent to that Case, which is provided for in the Treaty of February the 6th: 1778 between America, and France viz. tacit Independence; and the declard Ends of that Alliance being accomplished, it would not be reasonable that America should be dragged on by their Allies in a War, the Continuance of which between France and Great Britain could only be caused by separate european jealousies and Resentments (if, unfortunately for the public Peace, any such should arise) between themselves independent and unconnected with the american Cause.

It is to be presumed that France would not in Point of Honor to their Allies, refuse their Consent so requested as any rivalship, or Punctilios between her and Great Britain, as European Nations (principles which too often disturb the Peace of Mankind) could not be considered as *Casus Fœderis*[3] of the american Alliance; and their Pride as a belligerant Nation would not permit them to claim the Assistance of America as necessary to their

3. A case of the treaty, *i.e.*, something which would activate the Franco-American Treaty of Alliance.

Support, thereby proclaiming their Nation unequal to the Contest in Case of the Continuance of a War with Great Britain after the Settlement and Pacification with America. Their Consent, therefore, is to be presumed. But, if they should demur upon this Point, if Great Britain should be disposed to concede *tacit* Independence to America by a long Truce and the Removal of the Troops, and if the Obstruction should evidently occur on the Part of France, under any equivocal or captious Construction of a *defensive* Treaty of Alliance between America and France, Great Britain would from thence forward, stand upon advantageous Ground, either in any Negotiation with America, or in the Continuance of a War, including America, but not arising from any farther Resentments of Great Britain towards America, but imposed reluctantly upon both Parties by the Conduct of the Court of France.

These Thoughts are not suggested with any View of giving any Opinion of Preference in Favor of a separate Treaty above a general Treaty, or above any Plan of separate, but concommitant Treaties, like the Treaties of munster and Osnabrug,[4] but only to draw out the Line of negotiating a separate Treaty, in Case the British Ministry should think it necessary to adhere to that Mode. But, in all Cases, it should seem indispensable to express some Disposition of the Part of Great Britain, to adopt either one Mode or the other. An absolute Refusal to treat at all, must necessarily drive America into the closest Connection with France and all other foreign hostile Powers, who would take that Advantage for making every possible Stipulation to the future Disadvantage of british Interests, and, above all Things, would probably stipulate that America should never make Peace with Great Britain without the most formal and explicit Recognition of their Independence, absolute and unlimited.

4. These two treaties, concluded on Oct. 24, 1648, are known collectively as the Treaty of Westphalia.

From Mary Hewson

ALS: University of Pennsylvania Library; incomplete AL (draft):[5] American Philosophical Society; incomplete AL (draft): James S. Bradford, Philadelphia (1956)

Dear Sir   Kensington May. 1: 1782

I yesterday received yours of the 13th April, and as Mr Hodgson, in the note which inclosed it, offers to forward an answer I sit down to write one, tho' I wrote to you last saturday by Mr W. to acknowledge that which he brought us from you.[6] I sent some of the books, but as I left him free to refuse taking them if they would incumber him, I am not certain you will have more than one by him, that one I desired him not to refuse. I selected that as being peculiarly adapted to please and interest your grandson, from this circumstance among others, that he will there find your name frequently mentioned. I judge so from the effect it had on my young folks, for if ever they opened the book where they found your name that passage was sure to be read with delight, as something which nearly concerned them. I have still money in hand for my young men's libraries,[7] so the rest of Mr Bache's books I will send to Geneva, if I can convey them thither more conveniently than to Paris, but perhaps that may not now be the case. I am obliged to you for intending the persian tales for my son.[8] He learns French at Mr Gilpin's,[9] and as far as I can judge

5. Hewson drafted her letter on several pages, which were later separated. One of these was an address sheet written by BF, probably that of his April 13 letter to her, above. The surviving draft sheets lack only the closing paragraph and two sentences from the first paragraph.

6. Caleb Whitefoord carried BF's April 19 letter and returned to Passy with Hewson's reply, dated April 25 (a Thursday). Both are above.

7. The volume singled out here is most likely Thomas Percival's *A Father's Instructions.* For this work and other titles already chosen by Hewson for BFB and her son William see XXXVI, 288. Hewson probably also purchased at that time Percival's *A Socratic Discourse on Truth and Faithfulness . . .* , for which see Percival to BF, May 12.

8. BF offered William a five-volume edition of *Les Mille et un jours, contes persans,* translated by François Pétis de La Croix: XXXI, 361–2.

9. Probably William Gilpin (c. 1757–1848), the son of an educational reformer, minister, and author of the same name. Around 1778, the younger Gilpin took over his father's position at the Cheam school attended by William and Thomas Hewson. *DNB* under William Gilpin (1724–1804).

is a tolerable proficient in it. I had my boys at home a fort-night at Easter, and during that time I gave them every amusement that I thought would contribute to open and improve their minds; and I had the satisfaction of seeing them set off on their return to school without a murmur, or even a look of discontent. As they were very sorrowful when I left Cheam[1] I feared they would not have behaved so heroically at leaving me. I came to this place purely to gratify my mother,[2] who found Cheam so extremely dull that it lowered her spirits; my heart is still there, but as I have great confidence in those whose care my sons are under, and as I have here better opportunities of keeping up connections, I flatter myself that my removal will, upon the whole, be beneficial to the dear children. They are all very good (and very clever too). My girl was highly pleased with your telling me I do right to keep her without stays. Her reflection upon it when she was going to bed last night was. "It is very curious Grandmama should want me to wear stays when her best friend, the one she thinks most of, says you do right to keep me without."

I thank you for inclosing the copy of the old letter, for that letter never came to me, and so I lose the sight of what you tell me would shew I have already some character in France: this loss is a mortification to my vanity. Your invitation is flattering; Prudence alone keeps me from accepting it. This has already been to me a year of expence and loss; moving from Cheam has cost me some money, I have here a higher rented house with many other charges, and I had upwards of £500 in Collinson's house at the time of the bankruptcy.[3] Now, tho (I thank God) all these things my pocket and my temper can very well bear, they have made sufficient impression to oblige me to think what I can afford.

Our friends from Black Friars[4] dined with us last Sunday. His business now is making common wheels, and repairing car-

1. Sometime between late December, 1781, and the end of February, 1782: Hewson to BF, April 25, above.

2. Margaret Stevenson.

3. The London banking firm Brown, Collinson & Tritton failed in March: John Wright to BF, April 19, above.

4. John Viny and his wife. Viny's wheel manufactory was located on Black Friar's Road: XIX, 39; Viny to BF, May 21, 1783 (APS).

riages. We delivered to him the verbal message we received by Mr W. which was not exactly what you wrote, for we understood that you meant the carriage for yourself. Mr V. says he knows of a coach that was built purposely for travelling, has a set of his wheels to it, and has never been used, which will be sold for at least one third less than it cost, if you wish to have it he would purchase it for you.

My mother talks of visiting you this summer, and if she can get a companion I believe she will. I rejoice in the prospect of Peace; if it should be restored between the countries, we probably may meet. I am Dear Sir Your ever affectionate

MARY HEWSON

Notation: Henry Hewson May 1. 1782.

From John Jay

AL (draft): Columbia University Library

Dr Sir   Madrid 1 May 1782

I have this Day drawn upon your Exy three Sets of Bills in Favor of the Marqs D Yranda

for £ 4600

4400

4297.10.6

13297.10.6[5] being the Ballance of principal and Interest due to him on the Sum of one Million seven hundred and Eighty thousand eight hundred and sixty seven Reals of Vellon and twenty six Marevodis, borrowed of him by me on the 11 April 1781 for the purpose of paying a number of Bills of Exchange drawn upon me by order of Congress, payable about that June.

I have the honor to be with great Regard & Esteem Dr Sir Your obliged & obt Servt

His Exy Doctr Franklin

To Dr Franklin 1 May 1782 advisg the dr. of Bills to pay Marqs. D Yranda

---

5. The sum is in *livres tournois*. Ferdinand Grand honored the bills on Aug. 9: Account XXVII (XXXII, 4).

ALS: American Philosophical Society

Monsieur   Paris Le 1. mai 1782.

La Lettre que vous m'avez fait l'honneur de m'écrire, en réponse à l'envoi de ma piéce sur la naissance de Monseigneur le Dauphin,[6] est Sans-doute le prix le plus flatteur que je pouvois éspérer de mon travail. Mais il est un autre avantage dont je Serois bien jaloux, et que vous Seul pouvez me procurer: ce Seroit de pouvoir me vanter un jour d'avoir vu celui qui fait l'admiration des deux-mondes. Vous me pardonnerez ma témérité en faveur de mon âge, et j'ose me flatter d'avance que vous me permettrez D'aller vous rendre mon hommage un de ces jours de congé ou l'on à Coutume de nous mener en promenade á Passy. Cependant j'attendrai vos ordres, aimant mieux sacrifier l'envie que j'ai de vous voir, à la crainte de vous déplaire par une démarche imprudente.

Derniérement Le professeur de Rhétorique de mon collége Nous à rapporté un vers Latin qui vous á été appliqué trés heureusement. Le voici:

Eripuit cœlo fulmen, Sceptrumque Tyrannis.[7]

Il a proposé une récompense à celui qui Le rendroit Le mieux en françois. Animé par un Zêle ardent je n'ai pas eu de peine à remporter La palme dans ce nouveau genre de Combat. Vous me permettrez, Monsieur, de vous rapporter ma traduction.

Dystique.
à L'olympe Surpris il arracha La foudre,
et d'un Tyran barbare il mit le Sceptre en poudre.

Vous m'avez dit, Monsieur, dans votre Lettre que le plus bel emploi de la poësie étoit *de chanter Les choses utiles à L'humanité, et Les hommes qui les exécutent.*[8] J'ose me vanter d'avoir rempli aujourd'hui ce devoir, dans toute son étenduë: heureux Si ce

6. Richard's letter, [before May 1], is above. BF's reply is missing.
7. BF received several translations of this verse, the most famous line of Turgot's sestet, but this is the only evidence we have of its use as a school exercise: XXVI, 670–1n; XXXIV, 419n, 450–1.
8. BF had used nearly identical terms to praise the literary efforts of another correspondent: XXXVI, 607–8.

foible témoignage de ma Reconnoissance peut vous convaincre du profond respect avec lequel j'ai L'honneur d'être, Monsieur Votre trés humble et très obèissant Serviteur

RICHARD

en Rhétor. au collége de Lizieux./.

Notation: Richard 1 May 1782.

From John Adams

AL (draft): Massachusetts Historical Society; copy:[9] Library of Congress; transcripts: Massachusetts Historical Society, National Archives

Sir   Amsterdam May 2d. 1782

I am honoured with your Favour of the 20 of April, and Mr Lawrens's Son proposes to carry the Letter to his father forthwith.[1] The Instructions by the Courier from Versailles came Safe, as all other Dispatches by that Channell, no doubt will do.— The Correspondence by Mr Hartly I recd by Capt Smedley, and will take the first good opportunity by a private Hand, to return it, as well as that with the E. of S.[2]

Mr Laurens and Mr Jay will, I hope be able to meet at Paris, but when it will be in my Power to go, I know not.— Your present Negotiation about Peace falls in, very well to aid a Proposition which I am instructed to make, as soon as the Court of Versaills shall judge proper of a tripple or quadruple Alliance.—[3] This matter, the Treaty of Commerce which is now under deliberation, and the Loan will render it improper for me to quit this station, unless in Case of Necessity.— If there is a real Dissposition to permit Canada to acceed to the American association I should think there could be no great difficulty in adjusting all things between England and America, provided our allies are contented too. In a former Letter I hinted that I thought an ex-

9. The copy and transcripts are in BF's journal of the peace negotiations.
1. BF to Laurens, April 20, above.
2. Earl of Shelburne.
3. For a military alliance consisting of France, the United States, the Netherlands, and possibly Spain, but only for the duration of the present war: *JCC*, XXI, 877–8.

press Acknowledgment of our Independence might now be insisted on:[4] but I did not mean that We should insist upon Such an Article in the Treaty. If they make a Treaty of Peace with the United States of America, this is Acknowledgment enough for me.— The affair of a Loan gives me much Anxiety and Fatigue.—[5] It is true I may open a Loan for five millions,[6] but I confess I have no hopes of obtaining so much. The Money is not to be had. Cash is not infinite in this Country. Their Profits by Trade have been ruined for two or three Years: and there are Loans open for France, Spain, England, Russia, Sweeden, Denmark and Several other Powers as well as their own national, provincial and collegiate Loans. The Under takers are already loaded with Burthens greater than they can bear, and all the Brokers in the Republick are so engaged, that there is Scarcely a Ducat to be lent but what is promised.

This is the true Cause why We shall not Succeed; Yet they will Seek an hundred other Pretences.— It is considered Such an honour and Such an Introduction to American Trade to be the House, that the Eagerness to obtain the Title of American Banker is prodigious. Various Houses have Pretensions, which they set up very high, and let me choose which I will, I am Sure of a Cry & a Clamour. I have taken some measures to endeavour to callm the Heat and give general Satisfaction, but have as yet Small hopes of success. I would Strike with any House that would insure the Money, but none will undertake it, now it is offered although Several were very ready to affirm that they could, when it began to be talked of.— Upon Enquiry they dont find, the Money easy to obtain which I could have told them before. It is to me personally perfectly indifferent which is the House, and the only Question is, which will be able to do best for the Interest of the United States. This question however Simple is not easy to answer.— But I think it clear, after very painfull

4. JA to BF, April 16, above.

5. On the previous day JA had opened a loan with John Hodshon & Son. This produced an outcry because the firm was regarded as sympathetic to Britain, and he was forced to suspend the loan: James H. Hutson, *John Adams and the Diplomacy of the American Revolution* (Lexington, Ky., 1980), p. 114.

6. Florins (or guilders), the amount which he sought when he reopened the loan: Ferguson, *Power of the Purse*, p. 128.

and laborious Enquiries for a Year and an half, that no House Whatever, will be able to do much.— Enthusiasm, at some times and in some Countries, may do a great deal: but there has as yet been no Enthusiasm in this Country, for America, Strong enough to untie many Purses.— Another Year, if the War should continue, perhaps We may do better.

I have the Honour to be, Sir your most obedient and most humble sert

Dr Franklin

From Thomas Ruston: Two Letters

(I) ALS: American Philosophical Society; AL (draft): New-York Historical Society; copy:[7] Historical Society of Pennsylvania; (II) ALS: American Philosophical Society; AL (draft): New-York Historical Society

I.

Dear Sir   Exeter May 2d: 1782.

Your favour of the 9th: of October 1780,[8] gave me great pleasure. The Scheme of a Bank, which you was pleased to say you would forward to a friend in Congress, I presume was sent to Mr Morris, as I have since seen a resolve of Congress to approve of a Scheme of his, and giving him ample powers to carry it into execution; tho the Scheme as published, I cannot help observing, seems to me to be defective in sundry very material respects.[9] I am therefore very uncertain how far it may have succeeded, and could have wished to have known the opinion of Congress on the plan sent to you, in order that every particular might have been adjusted, with the greatest exactness, previous to its being carried into execution. Any attempt of that kind failing, must render it the more difficult to execute afterwards. The Congress

7. In Ruston's hand and apparently an intermediate stage between the draft and ALS.

8. XXXIII, 390–2.

9. For Congress' resolutions, passed on May 26, 1781, see *JCC*, XX, 546–8. Morris' plan is in *Morris Papers*, I, 66–74.

Paper I am told is entirely laid aside, but if the bank Scheme has been fortunate enough to meet with any degree of success,[1] it is not impossible but it may still be improved so as to be followed with the most desirable effects. The Bank of England went on heavily for the first two or three years. The reflexions upon Finance, I presume, must have suggested the Idea of the utility of procuring coin, as a sure resource, even tho credit should fail. In the mean time I have a thing to propose, which I am convinced will be of mutual advantage both to England and America. Perhaps I am somewhat premature, as it cannot well be carried into execution, before there is either a peace or a truce, but I think it should be made a condition of either, and therefore it should be known before hand. What I mean is, that America shall be at liberty to institute a Loan in England.[2]

I am well aware that it has hitherto been a maxim with the English Government, not to suffer forreigners to institute loans with them, because they have had so much occasion to borrow money themselves, but I see very good reasons why this should be made an exception to the general rule. If America is to become independent, which nobody seems to doubt, however averse many may be to the thought, then the next most desirable óbject for England undoubtedly is, to cultivate the strictest friendship and intimacy between the two countries by a mutual exchange of good offices, and can there be a closer bond of union formed than by means of the loan I have just now mentioned. Can we wish for a stronger proof of this than the great friendship, so long subsisting, between England and Holland, cemented by this means. I have sounded several people in London upon this subject, all of whom seemed pleased with the Idea. A

1. The national bank opened on Jan. 7, 1782: XXXVI, 405.

2. Evidently this was not the first time he had broached the subject with BF. On the draft of the present letter, Ruston tried out the following opening paragraph: "When last in London I took the liberty of troubling you with some thoughts on the subject of finance and at the same time hinted at a loan to be instituted in London for the use of America as an expedient that might be made use of as a bond to bring the two countries together, by the strongest tye that subsists between nations namely mutual interest. I could not help fancying that the Idea seemd to strike you, and therefore tooke the liberty of requesting that you would revolve it in your mind."

very old friend of yours and a Financier, who has easy access to one of the Secretaries of State, was struck with it, tho the thought seemed quite new to him. A Person of great note in that line of life, who has negotiated perhaps as many millions in the English funds as any man in the kingdom, has promised me that he will chearfully lend his assistance, should such a measure be adopted. The multitude of people in this country, who are upon the wing, and only wait for the era of peace, to transport themselves to America, would be happy to have such an oppertunity of conveying their property thither. I only wait to know your sentiments upon it, before I mention it to the other Secretiary of State, whose disposition I believe to be such, that in all probability he will in due time give it his hearty approbation.

Before this step could be finally taken, it would be necessary to know what kind of security America could give, that is, whether the Congress, or the several particular States, shall become security. And it would likewise be of use to know, upon what terms loans have been instituted already in other countries. The sum necessary to be borrowed ought also to be made another matter w[*torn:* orthy] of consideration. I have not mentioned any particular sum. In any commission that might be given, that ought to be limited. Though this country seems nearly exhausted with respect to men, yet her resources with regard to money seem almost inexhaustible. How this comes to pass, is a subject of curious disquisition, I could wish for the pleasure of some conversation with you upon it, and would not grudge even a Journey to Paris for that purpose. A line directed to me, at Exeter, under cover to Mr Thos Powell Mercht Philpot Lane, London, would oblige Yr obedt humble Servt

Thos: Ruston

Addressed: His Excellency / Doctr: Franklin / Paris

Notation: Ruston, Exeter May 2. 1782.

II.

Dear Sir   Exeter May 2d: 1782.

The bearer hereof, Major Van Braam, is a native of Holland. He has been in the English service these thirty years and was sent hostage by General Washington to Canada in the beginning of the last War. Not liking the present American service, he quited it about two years ago having obtained liberty to sell out, and retired to this place where I had the pleasure of becoming first acquainted with him. He is now determined to remove to France with his Family in order to seek a peacable retreat.[3] He will be very happy to have the honour of paying his respects to you. I am Dr Sr your obliged and obedt humble servt

THOS RUSTON

Addressed: His Excellency / Dr: Franklin / Paris

To Dumas   Transcript: National Archives

Dear Sir   Passy. May 3. 1782.
I receiv'd yours of the 15th past and perus'd the contents with great Pleasure. I had before receiv'd your Pacquet by Mr. Boers, and forwarded it immediately.

Inclos'd I send you a few copies of a Paper that places in a striking Light the English Barbarities in America, particularly those committed by the Savages at their Instigation.[4] The *Form* may perhaps not be genuine but the *Substance* is Truth; the Number of our People of all Kinds and Ages murdered & Scalp'd by these being Known to exceed that of the Invoice.— Make any use of them you may think proper to shame your Anglomanes but do not let it be Known thro' what hands they come. I am ever Yours affectionately   B. FRANKLIN

3. Jacob Van Braam (1725–1784) arrived in America in 1752, served briefly as George Washington's interpreter, and, after the Fort Necessity defeat in 1754, was imprisoned in Canada by the French until 1760. He settled in Wales but returned to service in America in 1775, finally selling his commission in 1779. By December, 1783, Van Braam was residing at the château de Rouville near Malesherbes, enjoying the civilities of its owner Chrétien-Guillaume de Lamoignon de Malesherbes (XXXV, 518n): W. W. Abbot *et al.*, eds., *The Papers of George Washington:* Colonial Series (10 vols., Charlottesville, Va., 1983–95), I, 80; Donald Jackson *et al.*, eds., *The Diaries of George Washington* (6 vols., Charlottesville, Va., 1976–79), I, 174–5n; Jacob Van Braam to George Washington, Dec. 20, 1783 (Library of Congress).

4. BF's fictitious "Supplement to the Boston Independent Chronicle," above, [before April 22].

My Respects & Congratulations to Mr. A.—[5]

From David Hartley

Transcripts:[6] National Archives, Massachusetts Historical Society

My Dear Friend,   London, May 3rd. 1782.

I write to you only one Line just to inform you that a general Order is issued, by our Government, for the release of all the american Prisoners every where. I have had this from Lord Shelburne, who informed me that the Order was not partial or conditional, but general and absolute. I heartily congratulate you upon this first Step towards *sweet Reconciliation*. I hope other Things will follow. I have had a long Conversation with Lord Shelburne relating to America, in which he expressed himself in most favourable Terms. I shall have the Honor of seeing and conversing with him again. But at present as you know certain Matters are depending from your Side of the Water.— Mr: Laurens is entirely at Liberty. I see him very frequently; and when you see him he will tell you many Things from me, which have occurred to me in the course of my poor Endeavors to promote the Cause of Peace.— Da pacem Domine in diebus nostris.[7]

Your affecte.   D. H.

5. Dumas' letter of April 15 reported on JA's impending recognition.
6. In BF's journal of the peace negotiations.
7. "Give peace in our time, O Lord," a quotation from the morning prayer (Mattins) of *The Book of Common Prayer*.

To Vergennes

ALS: Archives du Ministère des affaires étrangères; copy:[8] Library of Congress; transcripts: Massachusetts Historical Society, National Archives

Sir,   Passy, May 4. 1782.

I have the honour to acquaint your Excellency, that Mr Oswald is just returned from London and now with me.[9] He has deliver'd me a Letter from Lord Shelburne, which I enclose for your Perusal, together with a Copy of my Letter to which it is an Answer.[1] He tells me, that it has been agreed in Council to treat at Paris, and to treat of a *General Peace:* and that as it is more particularly in the Department of Mr Fox to regulate the Circumstantials, a Gentleman (Mr Grenville) to be sent by him for that purpose, may be daily expected here. Mr Oswald will wait on your Excellency whenever you shall think fit to receive him. I am, with Respect, Sir Your Excellency's most obedient and most humble Servant   B FRANKLIN

His Excelly. the Count de Vergennes.

From Alice Freeborn   LS: American Philosophical Society

Sir   Newport Rhode Island May 4th. 1782

I hope your Excellancy, will Excuse the liberty I take, in beging your assistance, to relieve my Newphew, who is now Closely confin'd in Forton Prison in England— His Name is Isaac Allen son of my Brother William Allen and Grandson to the late James Franklin your Excellancies Brother—[2] He in the early part of the present War, enterd the cause of his Country, and Remained some time on Board the American Navey, after which he sailed,

---

8. The copy and transcripts are in BF's journal of the peace negotiations.

9. For BF's discussions with Oswald see BF to JA, May 8, and BF's journal of the peace negotiations.

1. BF to Shelburne, April 18, and Shelburne's reply, April 28 (both above).

2. I, lix–lx. Catharine Greene had already written BF about Allen, on his aunt's behalf, in October: XXXV, 570–1. Allen had recently escaped from Forton; see the petition from Daniel Edwards *et al.*, April 8.

an officer of the Morning Starr, a Private Shipp of War, from Philadelphia, in which he was taken by the Enemy, and carried to Charles Town South Carolina, where he was confined, some time, from whence, he was carried to New York, and there Lodged, on Board a Prison Shipp, after which he with several others, were taken on Board a Man of War, and Carried to England— He was absent from New York, several Months, before we had any official accounts of his situation, while I received, his Letter of the 23d. of November 1781, giving an Account, of his Being confind, in England after suffering, very much with the Enemy as his Zeal for his Country, occasiond his Experiencing many distinguished markes of Indignity.

His Excellancy Govenor Greene is so obliging, as to forward this Letter, and I hope as he has sufferd, an Imprisonment, of near two Years, your Excellancy, will consider his situation and if possible relieve him from his long confinement. Relying on your goodness to excuse the Liberty, I have taken— I am Sir Your most Obediant and mo. hum. Servant   ALICE FREEBORN

His Excellancy Benjamin Franklin Esqr.

From Vergennes

Copy:[3] Library of Congress

A Versailles le 5. May 1782.
J'ai reçu, Monsieur, la lettre que vous m'avez fait l'honneur de m'écrire le 4. de ce mois, ainsi que celles qui'y étoient jointes, je vous verrai avec plaisir avec vôtre ami demain matin a onze heures.[4]

J'ai l honneur d'ètre très sincerement Monsieur, vôtre très humble et très Obeissant Serviteur   (signé) DE VERGENNES.

M. Franklin.

3. In BF's journal of the peace negotiations.
4. For BF's account of Oswald's discussions with Vergennes see BF's journal of the peace negotiations. According to Vergennes, Oswald announced unofficially that George III was disposed to treat of a general peace, that he preferred negotiations be established in Paris, that the independence of the United States would not be an obstacle, and that Fox's emissary would soon arrive to confirm all he had said: Vergennes to Montmorin, May 11, 1782, in Giunta, *Emerging Nation*, 1, 385.

From William Allcock[5]

ALS: American Philosophical Society

Sir   Amnear [Amiens] May the 6th. day 1782

This Comes to Enform you that I have Come from americay from Newborn [New Bern] Department in Northcarolina age 32 I further Inform you that I have servd in americay Service at the head of a company I first was a recruting Officer to the tenth Redgment at kingstown [Kinston] in Northcarolina Raised in the year 1777 Commanded by Corronal Sheperd[6] I futher inform you that I have Servd five years all most in the Contanettal and meleshe [militia] amerecan Servise I further inform you that I was under Genrall Retherford near the affair at Brear Creek[7] I further Inform you that I was in gates Defeat[8] and many others Ingagements that I was in and I had Retired home and Come to Eadontown [Edenton] to See my frends and tuck a noshon to go a voige to See to Refresh my Self in the Brig frends Commanded By Capten John Norcom Bound to Sentomases [Saint Thomas] left Northcarolina March the 13th. day on the 26th day to the

5. This is the first extant letter in a correspondence concerning Allcock and his companions that began some days earlier. Allcock, as he says here, landed at Calais on April 26. Having obtained a loan and a pass to travel to Paris, he got as far as Amiens before running out of money. BF evidently received word, from both Calais and the Amiens merchant N. Leleu l'aîné, that the Americans needed assistance. Discrepancies in the stories aroused his suspicions, however, and he expressed them to Leleu in a letter of May 3 (now missing). Leleu received BF's letter on May 6. He may then have counseled Allcock to write the present account, which he forwarded to BF on May 7 along with his own letter of that date and one from Thomas Price vouching for the sailors' honesty (both below). Allcock and his fellow seamen, as well as Capt. John Norcom of the *Friends* (whom he mentions below), received aid from BF when they arrived at Passy: Editorial Note on Promissory Notes, above.

6. Allcock enlisted as a private in the 10th North Carolina Regiment of the American army under Col. Abraham Shepard on Aug. 31, 1777, and deserted about five months later: William L. Saunders, Walter Clark, *et al.*, eds., *The Colonial and State Records of North Carolina* (30 vols., Raleigh, 1886–1914), XVI, 1006.

7. In March, 1779, N.C. Brig. Gen. Griffith Rutherford was posted a short distance from Briar Creek, S.C., where a detachment of Gen. Lincoln's troops were defeated: Mark Mayo Boatner III, *Encyclopedia of the American Revolution* (New York, 1966), p. 953.

8. Gates had some 2,000 N.C. militia under his command during the disastrous Camden campaign in August, 1780: *ibid.*, pp. 161–70.

Eastord of Permudus twelve aclock at Nite I was made A pris-
nor by a letermark from Santlezey [Saint Lucia] Bound to liverpool Commanded By Capten Jorge Brown on the 27th day she
Brought a dun too from Sandecruce Bound to ostend she was a
Brig Commanded By Mr. Capten Vaile which she put my self
and ten more on Bord the Dean [Dane?]⁹ Aprill the 26th day we
landed at Celles [Calais] I heir Obtained a pass to travell to parress I further Inform you that I Receivd four guineas which was
to carey me In a carriage to parress which having my Money and
Clothes taken from me By the Inglish which Caused me to make
use of Part of my Money for Neaseareys that I could not Do with
Out which Obliged me to under take to walk which Could travil
no further than Bullin [Boulogne] I their Payd Very Dear for a
carrage to Amnear which I am in Veary Disagreable situation
and I beg that you would not forget a distressed amerecan in a
strainge Cuntray as I have not Money to Cary me any further
and I hope when I see your Onour I shall be able to give a full
account of my Self like wise the offairs of americay so no more
at Preasent so I remain your frend to Serve

WILLIAM ALLCOCK

May the 6th day 1782

[*Note by Thomas Price:*]¹ These men where taken prisoneurs &
brought to Callis along with mr. Wm. Allcock the writer of this
Letter.

James Tew Born'd at Eadenton in north Caroline Bread a

farmer.			aged 19
Zakeriah Webb	from the same place		22
Thomas Britton²	do	do	21.
Robert Dolison	do	do	24.
Thomas Simons	do	do	22

Notation: William Allcock

9. According to Leleu's May 7 letter, the Americans were deposited at
Calais by a Danish vessel to which the letter of marque had transferred them.
1. See Price's letter of May 7, below.
2. Probably the Thomas Britten of Edenton who became a North Carolina citizen on Jan. 23, 1779: Saunders and Clark, *North Carolina Records*,
XIII, 654.

From ———— Didelot ALS: Historical Society of Pennsylvania

Monsieur   Paris le 6 May 1782.

Le sr Didelot après avoir fait des expériences sans nombre[3] s'est decidé a en faire une en grand sur la seine vis-avis de la place Louis 15. sur un ponton de 30 pieds de long orné de son mat et de ses voiles bien goudronnés et sera enflammé par 2. bouches à feu l'une avec un tonneau qui a contenu de la thérébentine et l'autre du goudron après il allumera un boulet d'une composition nouvelle que l'eau ne peut eteindre il espere avec sa liqueur de l'anéantir, en outre, il sera allumé deux Chaudiere de goudron dont une sera eteinte avec sa Liqueur et l'autre on l'esseyera avec de l'eau simple, il laissera en flammes le Ponton jusqu'à la moitié.

Cette experience se fera Lundi 6. may entre 11 hres. et midi,[4] Je vous prie, Monsieur, sil vous fait plaisir de m'honorer de votre présence.

J'ai l'honneur d'être avec respect Monsieur Votre très humble et obéissant serviteur   DIDELOT

From Matthew Ridley ALS: American Philosophical Society

Sir   Hotel d'Vauban May 6h: 1782.

Monsieur Midy de la Grainerais of Rouen[5] being desirous of seeing you to ask some Questions relative to a deed of a Mr. Shaffre's for Lands in Pensylvania, has begd of me to give him

3. After having demonstrated in December the effectiveness of a liquid with flame-retardant properties, the result of twenty years' research, Didelot was encouraged by La Blancherie's Assemblée to conduct experiments on a larger scale: XXXVI, 357–8, 386–7.

4. The experiment was announced in the *Jour. de Paris* of May 1 and 5. It was a great success. Castries immediately authorized Didelot to go to Brest to test his anticombustible on an even larger scale, presumably a ship: Bachaumont, *Mémoires secrets*, XX, 234–5.

5. Most likely Auguste-Louis-Eugène Midy de la Grainerais, a member of an important outfitter-merchant family established at Rouen since the beginning of the century: Pierre Dardel, *Commerce, industrie et navigation à Rouen et au Havre au XVIIIème siècle* (Rouen, 1966), pp. 148, 208. A summary of this letter in Ridley's letterbook specified that he was with "La Maison Midy frères" (Mass. Hist. Soc.).

a Letter to you for the purpose.—[6] I have told him I doubted much your power of giving him any Information: but he still wishes to see you—

Monsieur de la Grainerais has been introduced to me as a person of strict Honor & considerable Fortune—

I have the Honor to be Sir Your most Obed sert

MATT: RIDLEY

Addressed: A Son Excellence / Son Excellence B. Franklin Esq / a / Passy

Notation: Ridley May 6. 1782.

From Madame de Baussan   ALS: American Philosophical Society

Mardy 7 [May, 1782][7]

Ce Voyage a Versailles nous a bien chagriné,[8] tres cher papa, nous avions Calculé, le diné amériquain du dimanche, le Voyage a la Cour ordinairement le Mardy, et nous nous Croyons assurés du plaisir de vous posseder avec monsieur votre petit-fils, a qui je dois bien quelques reproches pour son oubli. Nous avions donné rendés vous après diné a 2 italiens qui vous auroient amusé par leurs tours, leurs grimaces, et leur musique, Ce Maudit Voyage de Versailles nous a fait grand tort; il n'est pas si aisé de vous déterminer a venir diner a une lieue, et puis Me Brilion qui arive incessamment[9] voudra vous avoir tout a elle, enfin, je vous suplie tres bon papa de vous souvenir que vous vous engagés a me dédomager un autre jour, jirai si je puis vous le de-

6. In October, 1781, the unfortunate John Shaffer had persuaded BF to certify the form of this deed, which he was trying to use as security for his release from prison: XXXV, 531–2, 588–9, and *passim.*

7. The day after the Baussans expected BF and WTF for dinner; see their letter to BF, April 29.

8. The arrival of Richard Oswald was the occasion for BF's unexpected trip to Versailles. See Vergennes' letter of May 5 and BF's journal of the peace negotiations.

9. The Brillons, returning from their winter stay at Nice, were detained at Tonneins, southeast of Bordeaux, for two weeks by M. Brillon's gout: Louis Le Veillard fils to WTF, May 4, 1782 (APS).

mander un Matin a l'heure du Thé,[1] et vous offrir l'hommage du sincer attachement avec lequel jay l'honneur dêtre votre tres humble et tres obeissante servante   N. BAUSSAN

Addressed: A Monsieur / Monsieur francklin ministre / plenipotentiaire des états unis / a passy

Endorsed: Baussan

From N. Leleu l'aîné[2]

ALS: American Philosophical Society

Monsieur   a Amiens Le 7 mai 1782

La Lettre dont vous m'avez honnoré Le 3 de ce mois ne m'est parvenüe qu'hier.[3] Vous aurez pu remarquer une sorte de contradiction entre ce qui vous a ete marqué de Calais au sujet des six americains en question, et ce que je vous ai mandé quils avoient beaucoup souffert en angleterre. Ils n'y ont point eté conduits. Mon erreur sur ce point provient de ce que L'on ne m'a fait voir que le passeport de L'officier d'infanterie et non ceux des cinq matelots, et comme L'interprete me dit quils avoient beaucoup souffert de la dureté des anglois qui les avoient dépoüillés, Javois conçu qu'ils avoient eté conduits en angleterre. Mais La Verité est certainement qu'ils ont eté tous pris a bord du meme navire americain par le Corsaire de ste Lucie qui les a remis au navire Danois et que ce dernier les a deposés a Calais. Je me suis encore mieux assuré de ces circonstances en faisant interroger ces americains par un homme tres veridique et intelligent qui a Lhonneur d'etre connu de vous Monsieur; C'est le Sieur Preis[4] anglois cy devant negociant a Londres et qui est depuis dix ans a la tete d'une manufacture en cette ville. Voicy sa Lettre qui vous Le certifie. Vous pouvez donc etre a labry de

1. The next day ("Mercredy 8") she sent by M. Caillot an invitation proposing dinner on Sunday, May 19. APS.

2. One of the principal merchants of Amiens: XXVII, 27; *Almanach des marchands*, p. 24.

3. BF's letter is missing; see our annotation to William Allcock's letter of May 6.

4. Thomas Price, whose May 7 letter is below.

tout soupcon que ces etrangers soient des anglois deguisés qui cherchent a nous surprendre. La candeur qui regne sur Leur phisionomie atteste Le contraire.

J'ai Lhonneur de vous remettre aussy une Lettre de L'officier Thoms Elves qui vous donnera Les details que vous demandez sur Leur compte.[5]

J'attendrai donc Monsieur que vous me fassiez connoitre vos intentions, et vous prie, autant que cela se pourra, que votre Lettre soit en francois.

Je suis avec beaucoup de respect Monsieur Votre tres humble et tres obeissant serviteur[6]　　　　N. LELEU L'AISNÉ

Mr. franklin a Passy

Notation: Leleu, 7 May 1782

From Thomas Price[7]　　　ALS: American Philosophical Society

Honner'd Sir　　　　　　　　Amiens 7 may 1782

The Letter you honour'd Mr Lew[8] the Gentleman who wrote you on the Subject of these unhapy Americans—beg'd me to Interprit it. That Gentleman was mistaken when he told you They came from the prisons in England, as they can prouve the Contrary.— I doubt not but when your Exellencey Shall be propperly Satisfied of the facts, that your humanity will Imediately order them the necessary.

The many Cheats of this Sort is a Sufficient Reason for the precaution you have taken. I have the honour to be Sir Your most Obedient & Very hmble Servt.　　　　THOS. PRICE

The honourable Docter Franklin

Notation: Tho: Price—Amiens May 7 1782.

5. Missing.
6. Leleu's May 16 bill for disbursements for six Americans, totaling 383 *l.t.* 18 *s.*, was paid by Grand on June 12: Account XXVII (XXXII, 4).
7. A textile manufacturer in Amiens: Ronald Hubscher, ed., *Histoire d'Amiens* (Toulouse, 1986), p. 156.
8. Leleu; see his letter immediately above.

From Matthew Ridley

ALS: American Philosophical Society

Hotel de Vauban ce May 7h: 1782.

Mr. Ridley has the Honor to present his Respects to Mr. Franklin & incloses him 14 Bills numbered as underneath which he begs the favor of him to accept & return with the Letter intended for Holland.[9]

No.   48 ———— 12
      302 ———— 18
      187 ———— 300
      180 ———— 18
    2571 ———— 24
     661 ———— <u>120</u> 492 Dollars[1]

Addressed: A Son Excellence / Son Excellence B Franklin Esq / Passy / Mr Ridley begs the reception of this Letter may be acknowledged in case Mr F. is not at home by Mr. La Motte.

9. Most probably BF's May 8 letter to JA. Ridley left Paris for the Netherlands on May 9: Matthew Ridley's journal (Mass. Hist. Soc.).

1. Ridley's letterbook (Mass. Hist. Soc.) contains copies of covering letters for six more sets of bills sent to BF for acceptance: 16 bills worth 6,160 *l.t.* on July 7, five bills worth 990 *l.t.* on July 22, eight bills worth 1,920 *l.t.* on July 25, 28 bills worth 11,340 *l.t.* on Aug. 20, 41 bills worth 3,420 *l.t.* on Sept. 24, and seven bills worth 1,200 *l.t.* on Jan. 21, 1783. These copies, in French, are in the hand of Nicolas Darcel, a clerk whom Ridley had hired and had left behind in Paris to handle his correspondence: Ridley's journal, entries of Jan. 31 and May 9, 1782.

One of the bills presented on July 7 was not properly endorsed, so BF drafted an undated bond of indemnity for Ridley to sign: "I do hereby promise to make good any Damage that may arise to Benjamin Franklin or to the United States of America, from his Acceptance and Payment of a Bill drawn by M. Hillegas the 18th of December 1781, No 1335 for Thirty-six Dollars in favour of Lee and Jones, the said Bill not being by them endorsed. Witness my hand this   Day of   1782." APS.

Ferdinand Grand's Report on Chaumont's Account
with Franklin

DS: Historical Society of Pennsylvania

[May 7, 1782][2]

Le Compte que m'a remis Monsieur
  De Chaumont rend Monsieur Le
  Docteur Franklin son Débiteur de   £[*l.t.*] 91733. 8. 6
  Mais par l'Examen & le Dépouillement
  que jai fait de tous les Papiers & pieces,
  je trouve qu'il faut en déduire les parties
  suivantes
1° Le Solde du Compte de M.
  Dean qui ne regarde point M. Franklin
  qui n'a nulle Vocation pour le payer   3849.13.1
2 La partie du Général Lincoln de même   70000.
3 Ses Billets à lordre de
  Mr. Franklin de £30000
            £20000   50000.
4 Ses fraix de Circulation
  pour procurer 400,000 *l.t.*
  à M. de Chaumont & qu'il
  a sollicité   19188.9[3]
5 fraix de Courtage pour le
  même   500.
6 Commission sur £ 649322.12
  de traites de M. Williams de
  Nantes faites Sur M. de
  Chaumont, cetoit un double
  Employ, le Congres ne peut
  pas en payer deux pour le
  même objet & comme cette

---

2. Grand wrote this date in the entry for BF's rent, in what had been a blank space left by the secretary. We indicate that insertion by italics, and we assume that this is when Grand signed the document.

3. A worksheet itemizing the various costs resulting in this sum was generated by Grand's office and is in Account XIX, as is a copy by L'Air de Lamotte. A second version made in Grand's office is filed separately at the APS. BF endorsed it, "Note of the Charges occasioned by Drawing & Redrawing to furnish M. de Chaumont with 400,000 Livres".

Operation a produit des
Jouissances à M. de Chaumont,
lun doit compenser lautre   3246.12.3

7 La traite de Williams de
Nantes pour réparations &
fraix faits pour la Mere Boby   450.12.7

8 Difference sur £ 91922.17
bonifiés par M. Chaumont au lieu
de £ 91925..13.2 d'Interventions
payées pour lui   2.14.2

Commission de Banque sur les
Draps d'officiers   129.17   147,367.18 .1

£ 55634. 9.7

à déduire les Loyers qui lui reviennent   20000.

Reste Débiteur à M. Franklin   £ 35634. 9.7

Le Compte que m'a remis Monsieur
Franklin rend Monsieur de Chaumont
son Débiteur de   £ 95415.15.10

Mais par lexamen & le Depouillement
que jai fait de tous les Papiers & pieces
je trouve qu'il faut en déduire les parties
suivantes

1 Le Loyer de lAppartement qu'occupe
M. Franklin jusques au *7 May 1782*   15000.

2 Je crois que le Congrès doit une
Bonification à M. de Chaumont, pour
les fraix & Dépenses en tous Genres
qu'il a faites pour loger à la fois tous
les Commissionaires, & jusques à des
Ameriquains de leurs amis   5000.

3 pour fraix d'un Courrier à Nantes le
5 Avril 1780   193.10

4 Pour une Planche de Gravure Allégorique 63.

5 fraix de réception & Expédition à des
marchandises suivant le Compte de Bersolle
de Brest   1803. 9.3

6 Mêmes fraix à 239 Ballots de Draps   5847.16.6

7 pour fraix d Escompte & de Commission

sur 11 Balles de Draps, achettés par
M. Williams à prix coutant & que ces
fraix existoient avant la Cession suivant
lexposé de M Chaumont   626. 2.5
8 Indemnité pour le retour en France sur
son Lest du Navire La Mère Boby frétée
en Dépeche & qui me paroit fondée   12000.
9 pour Compte d'Interet, je crois qu'il
nen doit point être passé de part ni   19247. 8.1
d'autre a déduire du solde ci dessus   59781. 6. 3
Il revient pour solde à M. Franklin   £ 35634. 9. 7

Si je me Suis trompé dans les résultats de ces Comptes ce ne peut
être que manque de plus de renseignemens, car je ne crois pas
avoir erré Sur ceux qui m'ont été donné: Si dans les Marchés ou
cessions qui ont eu lieu, il y a eu des conditions particulieres ou
Verbales je les ignore, ce dont je Suis bien sur c'est qu'à cela près
que dans un Arbitrage il est permis de mitiger la severité de la
rigueur pour opérer un Accomodement amiable. Il n'est pas possible d'apporter plus de Soin & d'Impartialité que je lai fait dans
ce travail; qui ne doit au reste être envisagé que comme celui
d'un Ami commun.   GRAND

Endorsed: Mr. Grand's Award May 1782 And the Acceptance of
it May 1784

To John Adams

 LS:[4] Massachusetts Historical Society; copy:[5] Library of Congress; transcripts: National Archives, Massachusetts Historical Society

Sir,   Passy, May 8. 1782
   Mr Oswald, whom I mention'd in a former letter which I find
you have received,[6] is returned and brought me another Letter
from Lord Shelburne of which the above is a Copy.[7] It says

4. In WTF's hand.
5. The copy and transcripts are in BF's journal of the peace negotiations.
6. On May 2, JA acknowledged receiving BF's letter of April 20. Both letters are above.
7. The present letter is written below a copy of Shelburne to BF, April 28.

Mr Oswald is instructed to communicate to me his Lordships Thoughts. He is however very sparing of such Communication. All I have got from him, is that the Ministry have in Contemplation, the allowing Independence to America on Condition of Britains being "put again into the State she was left in by the Peace of 1763"[8] which I suppose means being put again in Possession of the Islands France has taken from her. This seems to me a Proposition of selling to us a Thing that is already our own, and making France pay the Price they are pleased to ask for it. Mr. Grenville who is sent by Mr. Fox is expected here Daily; Mr Oswald tells me that Mr Lawrens will soon be here also. Yours of the 2d Inst is just come to hand. I shall write you on this Affair hereafter by the Court Couriers, for I am certain your Letters to me are open'd at the Post-Office either here or in Holland, and I suppose mine to you are treated in the same manner. I inclose the Cover of your last that you may see the Seal.— With great Respect, I am, Sir, Your Excellency's most obedient & most humble Servant.

B FRANKLIN

8. This is a paraphrase of a passage in the minutes of the cabinet meeting of April 25, for which see our annotation of Shelburne's letter of April 28. Shelburne told Oswald on April 28 to show but not give BF a copy of the minutes. He ordered Oswald to insist that as a condition of independence the United States have "No secret, tacit or ostensible connection with France." Shelburne also responded to the notes that BF gave Oswald (above, [before April 19]) by rejecting the request for Canada as indemnification. He further ordered Oswald to "Make early and strict conditions not only to secure all debts whatever due to British subjects, but likewise to restore the loyalists to a full enjoyment of their rights and privileges. And their indemnification to be considered. . . . No independence to be acknowledged without their being taken care of. A compensation expected for New York, Charleston, and Savannah. Penobscott to be always kept." Oswald was to sound BF in greatest confidence about the idea of a federal union between Great Britain and the United States, warning him that "the country at large is no way reconciled to Independence" and that should negotiations fail Britain was prepared to resume the war "with the utmost vigor." Shelburne did indicate a willingness to correspond more particularly with BF and to grant Oswald whatever title BF desired: Edward E. Hale and Edward E. Hale, Jr., *Franklin in France* . . . (2 vols., Boston, 1887–88), II, 51–4; Harlow, *Second British Empire*, I, 251; Fitzmaurice, *Life of Shelburne*, II, 136–7. For Oswald's conversations with BF see also BF's journal of the peace negotiations.

NOUS Benjamin Franklin, Ecuyer, Ministre Plénipotentiaire des Etats-Unis de l'Amérique, près Sa Majesté Très-Chrétienne,

PRIONS tous ceux qui sont à prier, de vouloir bien laisser sûrement & librement passer *Messieurs Rawle et Walker, allant à Ostende,* sans *leur* donner ni permettre qu'il *leur* soit donné aucun empéchement, mais au contraire de *leur* accorder toutes sortes d'aide & d'assistance, comme nous ferions en pareil cas, pour tous ceux qui nous seroient recommandés.

EN FOI DE QUOI nous *leur* avons délivré le présent Passe-port, valable pour *quinze jours* signé de notre main, contre-signé par l'un de nos Secretaires, & au bas duquel est l'empreinte de nos Armes.

DONNÉ à Passy, en notre Hôtel, le *8 May* mil sept cent quatre-vingt *deux*

B Franklin

Par Ordre du Min. Plen.

W T Franklin sec

Gratis.

M Walker embarqué à Calais dans l'Aurora le 13 May 1782

Passport for William Rawle and ——— Walker

[*In Franklin's hand:*] When you write per Post please to put your Letter under Cover to Mr Grand

His Exy. J. Adams Esqr.

Endorsed: Dr Franklin. May 8. 1782.

Passport for William Rawle and ——— Walker[9]

Printed form, signed, with MS insertions:[1] Historical Society of Pennsylvania

May 8, 1782

NOUS Benjamin Franklin, Ecuyer, Ministre Plénipotentiaire des Etats-Unis de l'Amérique, près Sa Majesté Très-Chrétienne,

PRIONS tous ceux qui sont à prier, de vouloir bien laisser surement & librement passer *Messieurs Rawle et Walker, allant à Ostende,*

sans *leur* donner ni permettre qu'il *leur* soit donné aucun empêchement, mais au contraire de *leur* accorder toutes sortes d'aide & d'assistance, comme nous ferions en pareil cas, pour tous ceux qui nous seroient recommandés.

EN FOI DE QUOI nous *leur* avons délivré le présent Passeport, valable pour *quinze Jours* signé de notre main, contre-signé par l'un de nos Secretaires, & au bas duquel est l'empreinte de nos Armes.

9. Rawle was introduced by John Wright in a letter of April 19, above. His travelling companion may have been Joseph Walker, introduced to BF in John Thornton's letter of April 6, above. While Rawle intended to sail for America, Walker was returning to London (Rawle to WTF, June 26, APS).

For a list of passports BF issued during the period covered by this volume see XXXVI, 379–80.

1. This is the earliest of four surviving passports BF printed in the 52-point script type cut for him by Fournier le jeune; see XXX, 346–7; XXXII, 349–50, 362–3. The type itself was clearly intended to imitate handwriting, but BF's method of printing enhanced that effect by producing letters that intersected. This could only have been achieved by printing the sheets in two passes, each time printing alternate lines. See the illustration on the facing page.

DONNÈ à Passy, en notre Hotel, le *8 May* mil sept cent
quatre-vingt *deux*   B Franklin
                                          Par Ordre du Min. Plen.
                                          W T Franklin sece.
Gratis.

[*Notations in different hands:*] M. Walker embarqué a Calais Pour
Douvres Le 13 may 1782.[2] / Passport from Dr. Franklin May 10,
1782

To John Thornton

Reprinted from Jared Sparks, ed., *The Works of Benjamin Franklin* (10
vols., Philadelphia, 1840), IX, 221.

Sir,   Passy, 8 May, 1782.
I received the letter you did me the honour of writing me,[3]
and am much obliged by your kind present of a book. The relish for reading poetry had long since left me; but there is something so new in the manner, so easy, and yet so correct in the language, so clear in the expression, yet concise, and so just in the
sentiments, that I have read the whole with great pleasure, and
some of the pieces more than once. I beg you to accept my thankful acknowledgments, and to present my respects to the author.[4]

I shall take care to forward the letters to America, and shall be
glad of any other opportunity of doing what may be agreeable
to you, being, with great respect for your character, your most
obedient humble servant,   B. Franklin.

2. Rawle and Walker arrived in Calais on May 12. Rawle reached Ostend
on May 15 and traveled between there and Bruges several times before settling in Boulogne in mid-June: Journal of William Rawle, Hist. Soc. of Pa.
    3. Above, April 6.
    4. William Cowper was elated by BF's compliments, and sent copies of this
letter to William Unwin on May 27, 1782, and Joseph Hill on Feb. 20, 1783:
Mark Van Doren, ed., *The Selected Letters of William Cowper* (New York,
1951), pp. 93–4; Thomas Wright, ed., *The Correspondence of William Cowper . . .* (4 vols., New York and London, 1904), II, 46.

To Vergennes

L:[5] Archives du Ministère des affaires étrangères

Passy 8 May 1782.

Mr Franklin presents his respectful Compliments to Count De Vergennes & has the honour of acquainting him with the Arrival of Mr Grenville; who is desirous of knowing when his Excellency will be pleased to admit him to the honour of a Conference.

Endorsed: Rec. le meme jour

From Catharine Greene

ALS: American Philosophical Society

My Very Dear friend   Warwick May the 8th 1782

I do my Self the Pleasure to write you though I know of no opportunity to Send it. But a few days a go the inclosed[6] was Sent to be forwade to you and as Im fond of writing to My Dear friend I have taken the incloseing of it upon my Self I Some Since wrote you of the Same Person by his mothers Request which if it has Come to hand Doubt not but you have taken Care about him.[7] I have a favor to ask of the Same Nature Sister Hubbarts yongest Son a Lad of about 13 years old is a Prisoner in Ireland taken with Capt Rathbone from Boston Poor Child we Should be Glad to have him Restord again he is Very yong to go into the World.[8]

Your Dear Sister I Visited yesterday She injoys great health for a Person of her age But She has met with a Shock in the Death of Mrs Greene who Died of a Short Consumption about 4 weeks a go[9] that we did not expeckt She would have Survived but a Very little while her anxtiety was So great for her but She bears it beyond what we expeckted She left 3 Children the yonget a bout 8 or 10 weeks old at Nurs the name Jane the other 2 fine

5. In WTF's hand.
6. Alice Freeborn's letter of May 4, above.
7. Greene wrote about Isaac Allen the previous October: XXXV, 570–1.
8. Judith Ray Hubbart's son Samuel had been transferred to Mill Prison; see his letter of March 20, above.
9. Jane Mecom had turned 70 shortly before her granddaughter Jane Flagg Greene died on April 6, 1782: I, lxi.

Children at home Sally and Franklin[1] Poor Girl we all lovd and lament her.

My Spoues and Children are well that are at home we expeckt Ray from Colledge in a few days he is under Doctr Stiles they Say he is a good Scholar and behaves well[2] our yongest Son at lattin School a bout Seven miles from home our eldest Daughter has 2 of the finest boys you would wish to See our yongest lives with us Single as a good girl oght to do[3] except all there love with mine and Best wishes for yr health and hapiness and a Safe Return to America. The last letter I was favord with from you was Recomending the two Jermin Colonels[4] we Sent them a kind invitation to our house but they was So attentive to there Regiments that they never did us the Pleasure of there Company I hope there good mama will have them Restord to her again they are Spoke of in Newport as Very Worthy officers So are the whole army from the Generalls to the Privats they are heartily wisht for again.

How does our Dear Temple and Beney do Sister Mecom and my Self talke of them Some times and wish to know of there improvements but more to See them but the Dear Lady tis So long Since She has had a line from you that She Can Scarcely Speak of you with out a tear She does not Doubt but you have wrote but tis more than 12 months Since She has Receivd a line from you but from you throw Mr Willms a Very handsom Present which was Very acceptable as She had with the Rest of us lost by Paper money[5] the family are Very tender of her She is So fond of the

1. Sally was four years old, and Franklin would be two in September: XXXIV, 202n.

2. Ray was at Yale College, where Ezra Stiles was president: XXXIV, 218n.

3. The Greenes' youngest son was Samuel. The eldest daughter, Phebe Ward, had sons William and Samuel. The Greenes' youngest daughter was Celia: XXXVI, 202n; Catharine Greene to BF, [June 25], below.

4. BF's letter has not been found. It concerned Christian and Guillaume, comtes de Deux-Ponts, the sons of the duchesse douairière de Deux-Ponts: XXXV, 188.

5. BF had instructed JW in December, 1780, to send Mecom a package of items she could sell; see XXXV, 666n. It consisted of "Silk for Cloaks &c. Gauze, Lace Ribbon, Linnen, & Cambrick": JW to WTF, March 2, 1782 (APS).

Children that I fear it will be a Disadvantage to both She thinks She Cant leave them to Visit us Scarcely.

Mr Elery[6] writes Mr Greene when there is any letters from you and how well and Strong yr facultis Continue. Pray Shew us by a few lines you dont know what a New Spring it would give us when is this Cruel War to be at an end you know you used to be a Conjurer— You are Willing by this I Should Subcribe my Self your Very affectionate friend   CATY GREENE

Doctr Franklin

From Thomas Grenville[7]

AL and copy:[8] Library of Congress; transcripts: Massachusetts Historical Society, National Archives

rue de Richelieu Wednesday Night. [May 8, 1782]
Mr Grenville presents his Compliments to Mr Franklin, and will certainly do himself the honour of waiting upon Mr Franklin to-morrow morning at eight o'clock.

Endorsed: May 8 the Day of his Arrival

6. William Ellery (*ANB*) was at that time a congressional delegate representing Rhode Island: Smith, *Letters*, XVIII, xxii.

7. Who had just arrived in France bearing Fox's May 1 letter of introduction, above. Oswald introduced him to BF who, finding that he had not first called on Vergennes, sent word to the minister (May 8, above). Vergennes' answer, setting an appointment for the following day, arrived at 9:00 P.M. The present letter is Grenville's answer to BF's now-missing note inviting him to have breakfast at Passy before traveling to Versailles. BF relates these events, as well as his initial conversation with Grenville, in his journal of the peace negotiations.

8. The copy and transcripts are in BF's journal of the peace negotiations.

From John Jay

ALS: University of Pennsylvania Library; AL (draft): Columbia University Library

Dear Sir   Madrid 8th. May 1782

I have recd. your Favor of the 22 & 23 Ult. They have determined me to set out for Paris. I shall leave this Place the latter End of next Week. Mrs. Jay & my Nephew go with me.[9] Be pleased to take Lodgings for me, and to inform me of them,[1] by a Line to Mr Delap or Mr Bondfield at Bordeaux.

The Embassador of France does not dislike this Step,[2] and the Count de Florida Blanca will refer the Instructions intended for Mr. Del Campo,[3] to the Count de Aranda at Paris.

I am Dear Sir with great Regard & Esteem Your obliged & obedt. Servant   JOHN JAY

His Exy Doctr Franklin

Notation: J. Jay 8. May 1782

9. The Jays and their nephew Peter Jay Munro left Madrid on May 21: Morris, *Jay: Revolutionary,* p. 651; Morris, *Jay: Peace,* pp. 20, 31.

1. WTF wrote Jay on June 5 that he had found a place at the Hôtel de la Chine, rue Neuve-des-Petits-Champs, for 25 *louis* per month: Henry P. Johnston, ed., *The Correspondence and Public Papers of John Jay . . .* (4 vols., New York and London, 1890–93), II, 308.

2. Jay wrote Montmorin on May 1 to ask his advice: *ibid.,* II, 300–1. Montmorin predicted in a personal letter to Vergennes of May 5 that Jay would come soon to Paris (AAE).

3. Bernardo del Campo was Floridablanca's representative, with whom Jay had been negotiating futilely for a Spanish-American treaty: XXXVI, 83n.

From ————[4]

AL: South Carolina Historical Society; copy:[5] Massachusetts Historical Society

Ghent 8 May 1782

If your Excellency will reffer for No. 3——to the extract of the letter sent from Holland[6] you will find the danger express'd therein, nearly realized (by that Nation's enthusiasm for America's Cooling) and if not particularly attended to before too late, the best fruits of that connection will be lost, with the Confidence of the Nation, which might have been to America (what it has long been to England) a Gold mine! Sure it requir'd no depth of Judgment to preserve it, when it had been almost forced upon us the Union plan'd and establish'd between the two republicks was the sole work of Baron Van der Capellen,[7] and his friends—and 'tis too new yet for to change Systems, whatever policy may here after dictate. Baron Van de Capelle &c. are more than ever the dearest objects of the Nation, and 'tis not only ingratitude, but madness to disregard them now the main object is gain'd—& the fault that has been just committed ought to be immediately retrieved, for the disgust he has shewn, by preventing his friends &c. to sign in the Inteded loan[8] evidently shews what will be the Consequence, As the intoxication of the people for [America?] may be otherways of short duration— Nothing could damp more American credit here than the last foolish step of Mr. Adams, nor no one else could have been so gull'd by a rascal of John Hodshon's Character— As the trick he played of last winter, is too recent, to have been yet forgot, when to gloss over an infamous Character against America from the beginning, he petition'd the States general for leave to fit out two frigates from Amsterdam to America which he was to load with Cordage, &

4. The author of this letter remains a mystery. The handwriting does not match that of "W. R.," who wrote on Jan. 31, ostensibly from Amsterdam. Neither is it that of Edmund Jenings, whom Laurens accused of writing anonymous letters against JA: XXXVI, 499–501.

5. In JA's hand.

6. Not found.

7. The pro-American aristocrat Joan Derk van der Capellen tot den Pol (XXVI, 349n).

8. The loan JA attempted to raise using John Hodshon & Son.

Sail Cloth, and saying all he could therein to prevent its being granted; but by a manoeuvre of his opponents who let out the Cat out of the bag, wondering their H——— M———[9] should think J Hodgson (the rankest Tory here) should turn a renegado,—got the petition'd granted; but Hodshons was not to be outwitted, for the frigates were never thought of more; and if America was remember'd 'twas only to wish it might be damned.

It would have been [*several words illegible*] if Mr. Adams had not had his faculties impaired by his fever which makes him sometimes fancy himself a Missionary sent out to make Converts—of which he prides himself on having made several namely the Scotch parson who after having long preach'd here against the Rebels, was advis'd to turn Spy against Adams &c. &c.—and by his getting a dinner from him now and then thot. the business was Compleated— But the series of blunders would be endless, and of no Consequence, were not the Credit of America ruin'd by it— No. 3 will at least have pointed out the blunder which nought but obstinacy and madness would have pursued a similar plan is now follow'd with another, but it will again be the biter bit.— For Hodshon (satan like) when he found the general detestation (except a few Courtiers) all combined to prevent his succeeding with the loan was the first to damn its Success, with any one else (finding several still disposed notwithstanding to get Adams out of the Scrape) he gives out that this ones powers are not ample enough to secure to the lenders the loan or Interest and that he must have further powers from Congress, notwithstanding Mr. A's saying that he is now the Arbiter of peace and the umpire of all our Ministers (but as lying Dick his word is not now currently taken)— Verily Congress injurd themselves and him in not Confining his talents to their forte as a legislator and lawyer in his lucid Intervals; his abilities may be still great—but he Wants most of those requisite for a Minister—and some so essential, that if continued here, more injury than good will result from it, for he had already caused such disgust before the acknowledgement of the independance that had it not been a Measure of which he Knew not all the springs of—his conduct would if not wholly pre-

9. High Mightinesses, *i.e.*, the States General of the Netherlands: XXXIII, 447.

Passy, May 9th 1782

As since the Change of Ministry in England, some serious Professions have been made of their Disposition to Peace, and of their Readiness to enter into a general Treaty for that purpose; and as the Concerns and Claims of five Nations are to be discuss'd in that Treaty, which must therefore be interesting to the present Age and to Posterity, I am inclin'd to keep a Journal of the Proceedings, as far as they come to my Knowledge, and to make it more compleat will first endeavour to recollect what has already past.

Great Affairs sometimes take their Rise from small Circumstances. My good Friend and Neighbour Madame Brillon, being at Nice all last Winter for her Health, with her very amiable Family, wrote to me that they had met with some English Gentry there, whose Acquaintance prov'd agreable; among them she nam'd Lord Cholmondely, who she said had promis'd to call in his Return to England, and drink Tea with us at Passy. He left Nice sooner than he suppos'd, and came to Paris long before her. On the 21st. of March I receiv'd the following Note.

Lord Cholmondeley's compliments to Dr. Frank

Franklin's Journal of the Peace Negotiations

vented it, at least would have retarded it much— May you avert the dangers threatend from the injury our Credit will receive If not prevented &c

No. 5

Addressed: His Excellency / Doctr. Franklin / Minister plenipo. —at the / Court of Versailles / at Passy / near Paris

Franklin: Journal of the Peace Negotiations

Copy:[1] Library of Congress; transcripts:[2] National Archives, Massachusetts Historical Society

Passy May 9th.[–July 1] 1782

As since the Change of Ministry in England, some serious Professions have been made of their Disposition to Peace, and of

1. This copy was made for BF in the spring of 1786 by his 25-year-old grandnephew Josiah Flagg (I, lxi), whom BF hired to copy a number of important documents: BF to Flagg, Feb. 9, 1786 (Library of Congress); BF to Jane Mecom, May 26, 1786 (printed in Van Doren, *Franklin-Mecom*, pp. 264–6). Among those were BF's 1775 journal of negotiations in London (XXI, 540–99, where the identity of the copyist was not yet known; see pp. 540–1n). In the present case, as with the 1775 journal, BF's draft indicated places where letters which he had organized and numbered were to be inserted into the copy. In both cases BF carefully reviewed and corrected the copy. Unlike the former case, however, where both BF's draft and Flagg's meticulous copy have survived, here the draft has been lost. We therefore publish Flagg's text, lightly corrected by BF. In a few instances noted below, the inserted letters are copies by someone other than Flagg. An unidentified secretary also wrote on slips of paper two queries about the location of certain inserts. Those slips of paper are now part of the manuscript, which was assembled and bound for the collector Henry Stevens in 1882; Stevens described his collection, now at the Library of Congress, in *Franklin: A Bibliographical Essay* (London, 1881).

As with the 1775 journal, we summarize briefly the substance of the incorporated documents, but readers will find the full texts published under their individual dates. In cases where the original letters are missing (were they with BF's lost draft?), this copy and the transcripts are our primary sources for their texts. In these cases, as with the text of the journal itself, we privilege Flagg's copy over the transcripts because it was made under BF's supervision.

2. The transcript at the National Archives may have been based on the

their Readiness to enter into a general Treaty for that purpose; and as the Concerns and Claims of five Nations[3] are to be discuss'd in that Treaty, which must therefore be interesting to the present Age and to Posterity, I am inclin'd to keep a Journal of the Proceedings, as far as they come to my Knowledge, and to make it more compleat will first endeavour to recollect what has already past.

Great Affairs sometimes take their Rise from small Circumstances. My good Friend and Neighbour Madame Brillon, being at Nice all last Winter for her Health, with her very amiable Family, wrote to me that they had met with some English Gentry there, whose Acquaintance prov'd agreable; among them she nam'd Lord Cholmondely, who she said had promis'd to call in his Return to England, and drink Tea with us at Passy.[4] He left Nice sooner than she suppos'd, and came to Paris long before her. On the 21st. of March I receiv'd the following Note.

⟨March 21: Cholmondely wishes to see him for five minutes before returning to London and requests an appointment the following morning.⟩

I wrote for Answer that I should be at home all the next Morning, and glad to see his Lordship if he did me the honour of calling upon me. He came accordingly. I had before no personal Knowledge of this Nobleman. We talk'd of our Friends whom he left at Nice, then of Affairs in England, and the late Resolutions of the Commons on Mr. Conway's Motion. He told me that he knew Lord Shelburne had a great Regard for me, that he was sure his Lordship would be pleas'd to hear from me, and that if

---

now-missing copy of the journal that BF sent to Congress with his letter of Dec. 5[–14], 1782: Wharton, *Diplomatic Correspondence*, VI, 110–14. There he explained that it was only "the first Part of a Journal, which Accidents and a long severe Illness interrupted, but which from Notes I have by me may be continued, if thought proper. In its present State it is hardly fit for the Inspection of Congress, certainly not for Public View." BF's notes for the continuation have not survived, and he never finished this account.

The second transcript listed here is in the hand of Francis Dana.

3. Great Britain, the United States, France, Spain, and the Netherlands, the five combatants.

4. XXXVI, 458.

I would write a Line he should have a Pleasure in carrying it. On which I wrote the following.

⟨March 22: Franklin sends Shelburne his respects and congratulates him on the resolutions recently passed by the House of Commons.⟩

Soon after this we heard from England that a total Change had taken Place in the Ministry, and that Lord Shelburne was come in as Secretary of State. But I thought no more of my Letter, till an old Friend and near Neighbour of mine many Years in London,[5] appear'd at Passy, and introduc'd a Mr. Oswald whom he said had a great desire to see me, and Mr. Oswald after some little Conversation gave me the following Letters from Lord Shelburne, and Mr. Laurens.[6]

⟨April 6: Shelburne would be glad to discuss the means of promoting the happiness of mankind and introduces Mr. Oswald, who speaks for him.⟩

⟨April 7: Laurens also testifies to Oswald's good character.⟩

I enter'd into Conversation with Mr. Oswald. He was represented in the Letter as fully appriz'd of Lord Shelburne's Mind, and I was desirous of knowing it. All I could learn was, that the new Ministry sincerely wish'd for Peace; that they considered the Object of the War to France and America as obtain'd. That if the Independence of the United States was agreed to, there was no other Point in Dispute, and therefore nothing left to hinder a Pacification. That they were ready to treat of *Peace*, but intimated that if France should insist upon Terms too humiliating to England, they could still continue the War, having yet great Strength and many Resources left. I let him know that America would not treat but in Concert with France, and that my Colleagues not being here, I could do nothing of Importance in the Affair; but that if he pleas'd I would present him to M. de Vergennes, Secretary of State for Foreign Affairs. He consenting I wrote and sent the following Letter,

5. Caleb Whitefoord.
6. Oswald's conversation with BF is discussed in our headnote to BF to Vergennes, April 15.

⟨April 15: Franklin sends Vergennes copies of correspondence relating to Oswald and describes their conversation.⟩

The next day being at Court with the Foreign Ministers as usual on Tuesdays, I saw M. de Vergennes, who acquainted me that he had caus'd the Letters to be translated, had considerd the Contents, and should like to see Mr. Oswald. We agreed that the Interview should be on Wednesday at 10 o Clock.

Immediately on my Return home I wrote to Mr. Oswald, acquainted him with what had pass'd at Versailles, and proposing that he should be with me at ½ past 8 the next Morning, in order to proceed thither.—

I receiv'd from him the following Answer—

⟨April 16: Oswald accepts Franklin's invitation.⟩

He came accordingly, and we arriv'd at Versailles punctually.— M. de Vergennes receiv'd him with much Civility. Mr. Oswald not being ready in speaking French, Mr. de Raynevall interpreted. The Conversation continued near an Hour.[7] Mr. Oswald first thought of sending an Express with an Account of it, and was offer'd a Passport, but finally concluded to go himself; and I wrote the next day to Lord Shelburne the Letter following,

⟨April 18: Franklin congratulates Shelburne on his cabinet appointment, praises Oswald, and discusses his conversation with Vergennes.⟩

To the Account contain'd in this Letter of what pass'd in the Conversation with the Minister, I should add his frank Declaration, that as the Foundation of a good and durable Peace should be laid in Justice, whenever a Treaty was enter'd upon, he had several Demands to make of Justice from England. Of this, say's he, I give you previous Notice. What these Demands were he did not particularly say; One occur'd to me, viz, Reparation for the Injury done in Taking a Number of French Ships by Surprize before the Declaration of the preceding War, contrary to the Law of Nations.—[8] Mr. Oswald seem'd to wish obtaining some

7. See our annotation of BF to Shelburne, April 18.
8. Without a declaration of war the British government on Aug. 6, 1755, ordered Vice Adm. Edward Hawke to seize "all French ships and vessels, as

Propositions to carry back with him, but Mr. Vergennes said to him very properly, There are four Nations engag'd in the War against you, who cannot till they have consulted and know each others Minds, be ready to make Propositions. Your Court being without Allies, and alone, knowing its own Mind, can express it immediately. It is therefore more natural to expect the first Propositions from you.—

On our Return from Versailles Mr. Oswald took Occasion to impress me with Ideas, that the present Weakness of the Government in England with regard to continuing the War, was owing chiefly to the Division of Sentiments about it. That in case France should make Demands too humiliating for England to submit to, the Spirit of the Nation would be rous'd, Unanimity would prevail, and Resources would not be wanting. He said there was no Want of Money in the Nation; that the chief Difficulty lay in the finding out new Taxes to raise it: and perhaps those Difficulties might be avoided by Shutting up the Exchequer, stopping the Payment of the Interest of the Public Funds, and applying that Money to the Support of the War.— I made no Reply to this; for I did not desire to discourage their stopping Payment, which I considered as cutting the throat of their Public Credit, and a Means of adding fresh Exasperation against them with the Neighbouring Nations: Such Menaces were besides an Encouragement with me, remembring the Adage, that *they who threaten are afraid.*

The Next Morning when I had written the above Letter to Lord Shelburne, I went with it to Mr. Oswald's Lodgings, and gave it him to read before I seal'd it, that in case any thing might be in it with which he was not sattisfied, it might be corrected: but he express'd himself much pleas'd. In going to him, I had also in View the Entering into a Conversation, which might draw out something of the Mind of his Court on the Subject of Canada and Nova-Scotia. I had thrown some loose Thoughts on Paper, which I intended to serve as Memorandums for my Discourse, but without a fix'd Intention of showing them to him. On his saying that he was oblig'd to me for the good Opinion I had

---

well men of war and privateers as merchantmen": Ruddock F. Mackay, *Admiral Hawke* (Oxford, 1965), p. 128.

express'd of him to Lord Shelburne in my Letter, and assuring that he had entertain'd the same of me, I observ'd that I perceiv'd Lord S. plac'd great Confidence in him, and as we had happily the same in each other, we might possibly by a free Communication of Sentiments, and a previous settling our own Minds on some of the important Points, be the Means of great Good, by impressing our Sentiments on the Minds of those with whom they might have Influence, and where their being received might be of Importance. I then remark'd that his Nation seem'd to desire Reconciliation with America; that I heartily wish'd the same thing, that a mere Peace would not produce half its Advantages if not attended with a sincere Reconciliation; that to obtain this the Party which had been the Agressor and had cruelly treated the other, should show some Mark of Concern for what was past, and some Disposition to make Reparation; that perhaps there were things which America might demand by way of Reparation and which England might yield, but that the Effect would be vastly greater if they appeared to be voluntary, and to spring from returning Goodwill; that I therefore wish'd England would think of offering something to relieve those who had suffer'd by its scalping and Burning Parties; Lives indeed could not be restor'd nor compensated, but the Villages and Houses wantonly destroy'd might be rebuilt, &c. I then touch'd upon the Affair of Canada, and as in a former Conversation he had mention'd his Opinion that the giving up of that Country to the English at the last Peace had been a politic Act in France, for that it had weaken'd the Ties between England and her Colonies, and that he himself had predicted from it the late Revolution, I spoke of the Occasions of future Quarrels that might be produc'd by her continuing to hold it, hinting at the same time but not expressing too plainly that such a Situation, to us so dangerous, would necessarily oblige us to cultivate and strengthen our Union with France. He appear'd much struck with my Discourse; and as I frequently look'd at my Paper, he desired to see it; the following is an exact Copy.

⟨[on or before April 19:] Franklin's notes for a conversation suggesting that Britain give Canada to the United States.⟩

He then told me, that nothing in his Judgment could be clearer, more sattisfactory and convincing than the Reasonings in that Paper; that he would do his utmost to impress Lord Shelburne with them; that as his Memory might not do them Justice, and it would be impossible for him to express them so well or state them so clearly as I had written them, he begg'd I would let him take the Paper with him, assuring me that he would return it safely into my hands. I at length comply'd with this Request also. We parted exceeding good Friends, and he set out for London.—

By the first Opportunity after his Departure, I wrote the following Letter to Mr. Adams, and sent the Papers therein mentioned that he might be fully appriz'd of the Proceedings, I omitted only the Paper of Notes for Conversation with Mr. Oswald, but gave the substance as appears in the Letter. The Reason of my omitting it was, that on Reflection, I was not pleas'd with my having hinted a Reparation to the Tories for their forfeited Estates; and I was a little asham'd of my Weakness in permitting the Paper to go out of my hands.

⟨April 20: Franklin sends Adams various letters relating to the negotiation and describes his conversation with Oswald about Canada.⟩

Supposing Mr. Laurens to be in Holland with Mr. Adams, I at the same time wrote to him the following Letter vizt,

⟨April 20: Franklin describes his conversation with Oswald and invites Laurens to Paris.⟩

Just after I had dispatch'd these Letters I receiv'd the following from Mr. Adams.

⟨April 16: Adams describes Laurens' visit and their conversation.⟩

To the above I immediately wrote the following Answer.

⟨April 21: Franklin reports to Adams on the impending British release of American prisoners and forwards Georges Grand's suggestion of raising a loan in the Netherlands.⟩

For Reply to this Mr. Adams wrote to me as follows.

⟨May 2: Adams says he does not know when it will be in his power to join the other peace commissioners in Paris and complains of his difficulties in raising a loan.⟩

During Mr. Oswald's Absence I receiv'd the following from Mr. Laurens.

⟨April 30: Laurens reports he has been released from his parole and suggests Cornwallis be treated similarly.⟩

On the 4th. May Mr. Oswald return'd and brought me the following Letter from Lord Shelburne.

⟨April 28: Shelburne sends Oswald back to Paris to arrange preliminaries of time and place and announces Fox is sending someone to confer with Vergennes.⟩

Having read the Letter, I mention'd to Mr. Oswald the Part which refers me to him for his Lordship's Sentiments. He acquainted me, that they were very sincerely dispos'd to Peace: that the whole Ministry concurr'd in the same Dispositions; that a good deal of Confidence was plac'd in my Character for open honest dealing; that it was also generally believ'd I had still remaining some Part of my ancient Affection and Regard for Old England, and it was hoped it might appear on this Occasion. He then show'd me an Extract from the Minutes of Council, but did not leave the Paper with me. As well as I can remember it was to this Purpose viz.

At a Cabinet Council held April 27th. 1782

Present

Lord Rockingham
Lord Chancellor
Lord President &c &c.
Lord Camden, &c. &c.

(to the Number of 15 or 20, being all Ministers and great Officers of State.)

"It was propos'd to represent to his Majesty, that it would be well for Mr. Oswald to return to Dr. Franklin and acquaint him, that it is agreed to treat for a general Peace, and at Paris; and that the principal Points in Contemplation are, the Allowing of American Independence on condition that England be put into the same Situation that she was left in by the Peace of 1763."[9]

Mr. Oswald also inform'd me, that he had convers'd with Lord Shelburne on the Subject of my Paper of Notes relating to Reconciliation. That he had shown him the Paper, and had been prevail'd on to leave it with him a Night, but it was on his Lordship's solemn Promise of returning it, which had been comply'd with, and he now return'd it to me. That it seem'd to have made an Impression, and he had reason to believe that Matter might be settled to our Satisfaction towards the End of the Treaty;[1] but in his own Mind he wish'd it might not be mention'd at the Beginning, That his Lordship indeed said, he had not imagin'd Reparation would be expected; and he wonder'd I should not know whether it was intended to demand it. Finally Mr. Oswald acquainted me, that as the Business, now likely to be brought forward, more particularly appertain'd to the Department of the other Secretary, Mr. Fox; he was directed to announce another Agent coming from that Department; who might be expected every Day, viz. the honble. Mr. Grenville Brother of Lord Temple,[2] and Son of the famous Mr. George Grenville formerly Chancellor of the Exchequer.

I immediately wrote the following Note to Mr. le Comte de Vergennes.

⟨May 4: Franklin informs Vergennes that Oswald has returned and will call on him whenever Vergennes wishes. Fox's representative, Grenville, is expected any day.⟩

9. The cabinet meeting actually was held on April 25 and was attended by eleven officials: Fortescue, *Correspondence of George Third*, v, 488.

1. Oswald seems to be volunteering his opinion without authorization. His views contradict the tone of his instructions from Shelburne, which discourage any hope of the United States being given Canada; see our annotation of BF to JA, May 8.

2. Thomas Grenville's brother was George Nugent-Temple-Grenville, 2nd Earl Temple (1753–1813), at this time the lord lieutenant of Buckinghamshire: *DNB*.

And the next Day I receiv'd the following Answer.

⟨May 5: Vergennes replies that he will see Franklin and Oswald the next morning at 11:00.⟩

Accordingly on Monday Morning[3] I went with Mr. Oswald to Versailles, and we saw the Minister. Mr. Oswald acquainted him with the Disposition of his Court to treat for a general Peace, and at Paris; and he announced Mr. Grenville, who he said was to set out about the same time with him, but as he would probably come by way of Ostend, might be a few days longer on the Road.— Some general Conversation pass'd, agreable enough, but not of Importance.— In our Return Mr. Oswald repeated to me his Opinion, that the Affair of Canada would be settled to our satisfaction, and his Wish that it might not be mention'd, till towards the End of the Treaty. He intimated too, that it was apprehended the greatest obstructions in the Treaty might come from the Part of Spain: but said, if she was unreasonable, there were means of bringing her to Reason: That Russia was a Friend to England, had lately made great Discoveries on the back of North America, and made Establishments there,[4] and might easily transport an Army from Kamskatka to the Coast of Mexico and conquer all those Countries. This appear'd to me a little visionary at present, but I did not dispute it. On the whole I was able to draw so little from Mr. O. of the Sentiments of Lord S. who had mention'd him as intrusted with the Communication of them, that I could not but wonder at his being sent again to me, especially as Mr. Grenville was so soon to follow.

On Tuesday I was at Court as usual on that Day. M. de Vergennes asked me if Mr. Oswald had not opened himself farther to me? I acquainted him with the sight I had had of the Minute of Council, and of the loose Expressions contain'd in it of what was in Contemplation. He seem'd to think it odd that he had

3. May 6. For Vergennes' account of the ensuing conversation see our annotation of his May 5 letter to BF.

4. The first permanent Russian settlements were not established until the following year: Nikolai N. Bolkhovitinov, *The Beginnings of Russian-American Relations, 1775–1815,* trans. Elena Levin (Cambridge, Mass., and London, 1975), p. 162.

brought nothing more explicit. I suppos'd Mr. Grenville might be better furnish'd.

The next Morning I wrote the following Letter to Mr Adams—

⟨May 8: Franklin informs Adams of his discussions with Oswald and the impending arrival of Grenville.⟩

I had but just sent away this Letter, when Mr. Oswald came in, bringing with him Mr. Grenville who was just arriv'd.— He gave me the following Letter from Mr. Secretary Fox.

⟨May 1: Fox tells Franklin of his desire for reconciliation and introduces Grenville.⟩

I imagined the Gentleman had been at Versailles, as I suppos'd Mr. G. would first have waited on M. de Vergennes before he called on me. But finding in Conversation that he had not, and that he expected me to introduce him, I immediately wrote to the Minister, acquainting him that Mr. G. was arrived, and desired to know when his Excellency would think fit to receive him; and I sent an Express with my Letter. I then entered into Conversation with him, on the subject of his Mission, Mr. Fox having refer'd me to him as being fully acquainted with his Sentiments.— He said that Peace was really wish'd for by every body, if it could be obtain'd on reasonable Terms; and as the Idea of subjugating America was given up, and both France and America had thereby obtain'd what they had in View originally, it was hoped that there now remain'd no Obstacle to a Pacification. That England was willing to treat of a general Peace with all the Powers at War against her, and that the Treaty should be at Paris. I did not press him much for farther particulars, supposing they were reserv'd for our Interview with M. de Vergennes. The Gentlemen did me the honour of staying Dinner with me, on the supposition which I urg'd, that my Express might be back before we parted. This gave me an Opportunity of a good deal of general Conversation with Mr. Grenville, who appear'd to me a sensible, judicious, intelligent, good temper'd and well instructed young Man,[5] answering well the Character Mr Fox had given me of

5. This praise was echoed by Vergennes, who described Grenville to

him. They left me however about six o Clock and my Messenger did not return till near Nine. He brought me the Answer of M. le Comte de Vergennes, that he was glad to hear of Mr. Grenville's arrival, and would be ready to receive us to-morrow at ½ past 10 or 11 a Clock. I immediately inclos'd his Note in one to Mr. Grenville, requesting him to be with me at Passy by 8, that we might have time to breakfast, before we set out. I have preserv'd no Copy of these three last Notes, or I should have inserted them, as I think that tho' in themselves they seem of almost too trifling a nature, they however serve usefully some times to settle Dates, authenticate Facts, and show something of the Turn, and Manner of thinking of the Writers on particular Occasions. The Answer I receiv'd was as follows.

⟨May 8: Grenville accepts Franklin's invitation.⟩

We set out accordingly the Next Morning in my Coach, from Passy, and arriv'd punctually at M. de Vergennes's, who receiv'd Mr. Grenville in the most cordial and friendly manner, on Account of the Acquaintance and Friendship that had formerly subsisted between his Uncle and M. de Vergennes, when they were Ambassadors together at Constantinople.[6] After some lit-

---

Montmorin as displaying much spirit, wisdom, honesty, and modesty: Giunta, *Emerging Nation*, 1, 388. Grenville described in detail his conversation with BF in a May 10 letter to Fox. BF assured him that America's engagements with France were only those of the Treaty of Alliance and the Treaty of Commerce. When Grenville suggested that American independence might be sufficient gratification for France, BF replied, "it was a great deal, but that Spain might want something, he supposed would want Gibraltar, & that perhaps it would be of little use to us now we had lost Minorca & had less commerce to defend." When Grenville objected, BF replied "it was nothing to America who kept or who had Gibraltar." Grenville said that he could not help believing there was still in America a good disposition toward England. BF admitted "there were *roots*" but said "they would want a good deal of management." In order to achieve a real reconciliation he recommended Britain show kindness to American prisoners and rebuild houses in America that had been wantonly burned: Giunta, *Emerging Nation*, 1, 381–2. Shelburne claimed in a June 5 letter to British Army in America Commander Carleton and Naval Commander Digby that BF repeatedly had suggested that great effects could be obtained by some things being done "spontaneous" from England: Giunta, *Emerging Nation*, 1, 424.

6. Vergennes first was envoy and then French ambassador in Constan-

tle agreable Conversation, Mr. Grenville presented his Letter, from Mr. Secretary Fox and another I think from the Duke of Richmond.[7] When these were read, the Subject of Peace was en-tred on. What my memory retains of the Discourse amounts to little more than this, that after mutual Declarations of the good Dispositions of the two Courts, Mr. Grenville having intimated that in Case England gave America Independence, France it was expected would return the Conquests she had made of British Is-lands, receiving back those of Miquelon and St. Pierre; and that the Original Object of the War being obtained, it was supposed that France would be contented with that. The Minister seem'd to smile at the propos'd Exchange; and remark'd that the offer of giving Independence to America amounted to little: America, says he, does not ask it of you: There is Mr. Franklin, he will an-swer you as to that Point. To be sure, I said, we do not consider ourselves as under any Necessity of bargaining for a Thing that is our own, and which we have bought at the Expence of so much Blood and Treasure, and which we are in full Possession of.—— As to our being satisfied with the original Object of the War, continued he, look back to the Conduct of your Nation in for-mer Wars. In the last War, for Example, what was the Object? It was the disputed Right to some waste Lands on the Ohio and the Frontiers of Nova-Scotia. Did you content yourselves with the Recovery of those Lands? No, you retain'd at the Peace all Can-ada, all Louisiana, all Florida, Grenada and other West-India Is-lands, the greatest Part of the Northern Fisheries, with all your Conquests in Africa, and the East Indies.— Something being mention'd of its not being reasonable that a Nation after making an unprovok'd unsuccessfull War upon its Neighbours, should expect to sit down whole and have every thing restor'd which she had lost in such a War, I think Mr. Grenville remark'd that the

tinople; he resided there from 1755 to 1769. Henry Grenville (1717–1784) was British ambassador from 1762 to 1765: *Repertorium der diplomatischen Ver-treter*, II, 132, 168; Namier and Brooke, *House of Commons*, II, 545–6.

7. Charles Lennox, 3rd Duke of Richmond (XVI, 12–13n), was master gen-eral of the ordnance and a member of Rockingham's cabinet: Mackesy, *War for America*, p. 471. Vergennes himself reported that Grenville gave him let-ters from both Fox and Richmond: Doniol, *Histoire*, V, 112; Giunta, *Emerg-ing Nation*, I, 380, 385.

War had been provok'd by the Encouragement given by France to the Americans to revolt. On which M. de Vergennes grew a little warm, and declar'd firmly, that the Breach was made and our Independence declar'd long before we receiv'd the least Encouragement from France; and he defy'd the World to give the smallest Proof of the contrary. There sits, says he, Mr. Franklin who knows the Fact and will contradict me if I do not speak the Truth.[8] He repeated to Mr. Grenville what he had before said to Mr. Oswald respecting the King's Intention of treating fairly, and keeping faithfully the Convention he should enter into; of which Disposition he would give at the Treaty convincing Proofs, by the Fidelity and Exactitude with which he should observe his Engagements with his present Allies; and added that the Points which the King had chiefly in View were *Justice* and *Dignity*,[9] these he could not depart from. He acquainted Mr. Grenville that he should immediately write to Spain and Holland, communicate to those Courts what had past, and request their Answers, that in the mean time he hoped Mr. Grenville would find means of amusing himself agreably, to which he should be glad to contribute, that he would communicate what had pass'd to the King; and he invited him to come again the next day.

On our Return Mr. G. express'd himself as not quite satisfy'd with some part of M. de Vergennes Discourse, and was thought-

8. BF, who met in Philadelphia with a French representative six months before the signing of the Declaration of Independence (XXII, 310–18), knew that Vergennes was not being candid.

9. In a summary of the meeting (Doniol, *Histoire*, V, 112–13; Giunta, *Emerging Nation*, I, 380) Vergennes says he said "justice, réciproque et dignité." The summary also notes that Grenville said Paris would be the most suitable place in all regards as a site for the negotiations and declined the use of mediators. For further details see Grenville's description of the meeting to Fox and Vergennes' to Montmorin: Giunta, *Emerging Nation*, I, 382–3, 385–7. In a May 17 letter to the King, Vergennes acknowledged that the sovereign wished a just and honorable peace. He also noted, "La seule conduite sur laquelle Votre Majesté m'avait ordonné de m'expliquer affirme comme un préliminaire indispensable, était que la paix serait générale et qu'on se traiterait conjointement avec tous ses alliés et amis." Vergennes called the form of Grenville's full powers indecent because they authorized him only to treat privately with France and to take France's objections *ad referendum:* John Hardman and Munro Price, eds., *Louis XVI and the Comte de Vergennes: Correspondence 1774–1787* (Oxford, 1998), p. 305.

ful. He told me that he had brought two State Messengers with him, and perhaps after he had had another interview with the Minister, he might dispatch one of them to London: I then requested leave to answer by that Opportunity the Letters I had receiv'd from Lord Shelburne and Mr. Fox; and he kindly promis'd to acquaint me in time of the Messenger's Departure.— He did not ask me to go with him the next day to Versailles, and I did not offer it.[1]

The coming and going of these Gentlemen was observ'd, and made much Talk at Paris: And the Marquis de la Fayette having learnt something of their Business from the Ministers, discoursed with me about it. Agreable to the Resolutions of Congress, directing me to confer with him and take his Assistance in our Affairs,[2] I communicated to him what had past. He told me that during the Treaty at Paris for the last Peace, the Duke de Nivernois had been sent to reside in London, that this Court might thro' him state what was from time to time transacted, in the Light they thought best, to prevent Misrepresentations and Misunderstandings.[3] That such an Employ would be extremely agreable to him on many Accounts; that as he was now an American Citizen, spoke both Languages and was well acquainted with our Interests, he believ'd he might be useful in it; and that as Peace was likely from Appearances to take Place, his Return to America was perhaps not so immediately necessary. I lik'd the Idea and encourag'd his proposing it to the Ministry. He then wish'd I would make him acquainted with Messrs. Oswald &

1. During the meeting of the next day, May 10, Spanish Ambassador Aranda was present. Grenville repeated his contention that American independence should be sufficient to satisfy all of Britain's enemies. Grenville, who lacked powers to negotiate with Spain, agreed to write his court for instructions and Aranda agreed to do the same. Vergennes criticized the arrangements concerning India in the 1763 Treaty of Paris, which he said he could not read without shuddering: Doniol, *Histoire*, v, 113; Giunta, *Emerging Nation*, I, 381, 383–4, 387.

2. XXXVI, 124n; *JCC*, XXI, 1135.

3. The duc de Choiseul sent his old friend Louis-Jules-Barbon Mancini-Mazarini, duc de Nivernais (1716–1798) to London during the 1762 peace negotiations but personally handled the most important discussions: Lucien Perey [Clara-Adèle-Luce Herpin], *Un Petit-neveu de Mazarin, Louis Mancini-Mazarini, duc de Nivernais* (7th ed., Paris, 1899), pp. 502–37.

Grenville, and for that End propos'd meeting them at Breakfast with me, which I promis'd to contrive if I could, and endeavour to engage them for Saturday.

Friday morning the 10th. of May I went to Paris, and visited Mr. Oswald. I found him in the same friendly Dispositions, and very desirous of doing Good, and of seeing an End put to this ruinous War. But I got no farther Light as to the Sentiments of Lord S. respecting the Terms.— I told him the Marquis de la Fayette, would breakfast with me tomorrow, and as he Mr. Oswald, might have some Curiosity to see a Person who had in this War render'd himself so remarkable, I propos'd his doing me the same Honour.— He agreed to it chearfully. I came home intending to write to Mr. Grenville, whom I supposed might stay and dine at Versailles, and therefore did not call on him. But he was return'd, and I found the following Note from him.

⟨May 10: Grenville volunteers the services of his courier to carry letters for Franklin.⟩

I sat down immediately and wrote the two Short Letters following, to the two Secretaries of State viz.

⟨May 10: Franklin informs Fox he has introduced Grenville to Vergennes and assures Fox he will use his best endeavors to end the war.⟩

⟨May 10: Franklin tells Shelburne he agrees to Paris as the site for negotiations and thanks him for discharging Laurens from his parole and for his kindness to the American prisoners.⟩

and I sent them to Mr. Grenville with the following Note,

⟨May 10: Franklin accepts Grenville's offer and invites him to breakfast with Lafayette and Oswald.⟩

to which Mr. G. sent me this Answer

⟨May 10: Grenville accepts Franklin's invitation.⟩

The Gentlemen all met accordingly, had a good deal of Conversation at and after Breakfast, staid till after One o Clock, and parted much pleas'd with each other.

The Monday following I call'd to visit Mr. G. I found with him Mr. Oswald, who told me he was just about returning to London. I was a little surpriz'd at the suddeness of the Resolution he had taken, it being as he said to set out the next Morning early.[4]

I conceiv'd the Gentlemen were engag'd in Business, so I withdrew, and went to write a few Letters, among which was the following to Lord Shelburne, being really concerned at the Thought of losing so good a Man as Mr. Oswald.

⟨May 13: Franklin praises Oswald and expresses hope he will return.⟩

I went in the Evening to Mr. Oswalds Lodgings with my Letters when he inform'd me his Intention was to return immediately hither from England and to make the more Dispatch in going and returning he should leave his Carriage at Calais, as the embarking and debarking of Carriages in the Packet Boats often occasion a Tide's Delay.— I did not enquire the Reason of this Movement. We had but little Conversation, for Mr. Grenville coming in, I soon after wished him a good Journey, and retired, that I might not interrupt their Consultations.

Since his Departure Mr. Grenville has made me a Visit; and entering into a Conversation with me, exactly of the same Tenor with the Letters I formerly receiv'd from Mr. Hartley, stating Suppositions that France might insist on Points totally different from what had been the Object of our Alliance, and that in such Case he should imagine we were not at all bound to continue the War to obtain such Points for her, &c.[5] I thought I could not give him a better Answer to this kind of Discourse, than what I had given in two Letters to Mr. Hartly; and therefore calling for those Letters I read them to him.[6] He smil'd, and would have

4. The "Monday following" was May 13. Oswald and Grenville had agreed that Oswald should return to London in order to obtain further instructions, believing from their discussions with BF that if sufficiently generous peace terms were offered, America might make a separate peace. This would leave Britain free to make war against her other enemies: Harlow, *Founding of the Second British Empire*, I, 252–3.

5. Hartley frequently had argued that the American alliance with France was the chief obstacle to peace; see, for example, XXXVI, 360.

6. Probably BF's letters of Jan. 15 and Feb. 16 (XXXVI, 435–8, 583–5) in which he rejected the idea of making a separate peace from France and criticized the conditions Britain imposed on France regarding the fortifying of Dunkirk.

turn'd the Conversation: But I gave him a little more of my Sentiments on the general Subject of Benefits, Obligations and Gratitude. I said I thought People had often imperfect Notions of their Duty on those Points, and that a State of Obligation was to many so uneasy a State, that they became ingenious in finding out Reasons and Arguments to prove they had been laid under no Obligation at all, or that they had discharg'd it; and that they too easily sattisfied themselves with such Arguments. To explain clearly my Ideas on the Subject, I stated a Case. A, a Stranger to B, sees him about to be imprison'd for a Debt by a merciless Creditor. He lends him the sum necessary to preserve his Liberty. B then becomes the Debtor of A: and after sometime repays the Money. Has he then discharg'd the Obligation? No. He has discharg'd the Money Debt, but the Obligation remains, and he is a Debtor for the Kindness of A, in lending the Sum so seasonably. If B. should afterwards find A. in the same Circumstances that he B, had been in when A lent him the Money, he may then discharge this Obligation, or Debt of Kindness, *in part*, by lending him an equal Sum. *In part*, I said, and not wholly, because when A. lent B the Money, there had been no prior Benefit received to induce him to it. And therefore if A should a second time need the same Assistance, I thought B. if in his Power was in duty bound to afford it to him.— Mr. Grenville conceiv'd that it was carrying Gratitude very far, to apply this Doctrine to our Situation in respect to France, who was really the Party serv'd and oblig'd by our Separation from England, as it lessened the Power of her Rival, and relatively increas'd her own. I told him I was so strongly impress'd with the kind Assistance afforded us by France in our Distress, and the generous and noble manner in which it was granted, without exacting or stipulating for a single Privilege or particular Advantage to herself, in our Commerce or otherwise, that I could never suffer myself to think of such Reasonings for lessening the Obligation, and I hoped, and indeed did not doubt but my Country-men were all of the same Sentiments. Thus he gain'd nothing of the point he came to push; we parted however in good Humour. His Conversation is always polite and his Manner pleasing.[7]

7. On May 14, Grenville provided Fox a far different account of this con-

As he express'd a strong desire to discourse with me on the Means of a Reconciliation with America, I promis'd to consider the Subject, and appointed Saturday the first of June for our Conversation when he propos'd to call on me.

The same Day I receiv'd another Letter from my old Friend Mr. Hartley. Our former Correspondence on the Subject of Peace since the Beginning of this Year I have kept by itself, as it preceded this, was in the time of the old Ministry, and consisted wholly of Letters unmix'd with personal Conversation. This being the first Letter from him under the new Ministry, and as it may be follow'd by others which may relate to the Negociation, I insert it here with my Answer, and shall continue to insert the future Letters I may receive from him relative to the same Subject.

⟨May 3: Hartley informs Franklin of the orders for the release of American prisoners.[8]⟩

---

versation. Grenville speculated that an immediate grant of independence might make America "infinitely less likely" to support the claims of France and Spain. He continued, "Should I not however add that Mr. Franklin's conversation has at different times appeared to me to glance toward these ideas? while he was with me this morning he went so far as to say, that, when we had allowed the independance of America, the treaty she had made with France for gaining it ended, and none remained but that of commerce, which we too might make if we pleased. . . ." BF confessed ignorance of what terms France would ask but did mention Dunkirk, leading Grenville to believe America more likely to support France on the article of Dunkirk (*i.e.*, the removal of the British commissioner there) than on her claims in the East Indies. BF assured Grenville "that whatever influence he had at this Court should be used to accommodate things: he had too once before said, that in forming a Treaty, there should he thought without doubt be a difference in a Treaty between England & America, and one between England and France, that always had been at enmity: in these expressions, as well as in a former one, . . . he rested much upon the great effect that would be obtained by some things being done *spontaneously* from England": Giunta, *Emerging Nation*, I, 391–2; Lord John Russell, ed., *Memorials and Correspondence of Charles James Fox* (4 vols., London, 1853–57), IV, 187–91. Shelburne informed General Carleton and Admiral Digby, the British commanders in America, of the conversation: Giunta, *Emerging Nation*, I, 424.

8. This letter is missing from Flagg's copy of BF's journal; there is only a note in an unknown hand indicating that it should be inserted. The letter does appear in both transcripts.

⟨May 13: Franklin thanks Hartley for his letter and expresses his belief the release will tend toward reconciliation.⟩

Our Business standing still at present till the Return of Mr. Oswald, gives me a Void that I may fill up with two or three Circumstances, not at present connected with this intended Treaty, but which serve to show something of the Disposition of Courts who have or may have a Concern in it.

Mr. Jay had written to me from time to time of the unaccountable Delays he had met with since his Residence at the Court of Spain, and that he was now no nearer in the Business he had been charg'd with than when he first arriv'd. Upon the first coming of Mr. Oswald, and the apparent Prospect of a Treaty, I wrote to press his coming hither, and being a little out of Humour with that Court, I said, they have taken four Years to consider whether they should treat with us, give them forty, and let us mind our own Business: and I sent the Letter under Cover to a Person at Madrid who I hop'd would open and read it.[9] It seems to me that we have in most Instances hurt our Credit and Importance, by sending all over Europe begging Alliances, and solliciting Declarations of our Independence.[1] The Nations perhaps from thence, seem to think, that our Independence is something they have to sell, and that we dont Offer enough for it. Mr. Adams has succeeded in Holland, owing to their War with England; and a good deal to the late Votes in the Commons towards a Reconciliation; but the Ministers of the other Powers refus'd as I hear to return his Visits, because our Independence was not yet acknowledg'd by their Courts. I had heard here by good Luck, that the same Resolution was taken by several of them not to return the Visits I should make them (as they suppos'd) when I was first receiv'd here as Minister Plenipotentiary, and I disappointed their Project by Visiting none of them.[2] In my private

9. For Jay's letters see XXXVI, 89–90, 424–5, 559. BF's letter to Jay is that of April 22, above. We have no record of a covering letter, but in his letter to Jay of April 23 BF said the earlier letter had been sent by the post. It may have been sent via the banker Yranda. For BF's feelings toward Spain see also XXXVI, 452–3.

1. A longstanding opinion of BF's; see XXIII, 511; XXVII, 448.

2. The Russian minister at The Hague was surprised that JA left his call-

Opinion the first Civility is due from the old Residents to the Stranger and New-comer. My Opinion indeed is good for nothing against Custom, which I should have obeyed, but for the Circumstances, that rendred it more prudent to avoid Disputes and Affronts, tho' at the hazard of being thought rude or singular. While I am writing, something ridiculous enough on this head has happen'd to me. The Count du Nord who is Son to the Empress of Russia, arriving at Paris, order'd it seems Cards of Visit to be sent to all the foreign Ministers. One of them on which was written le Comte du Nord, and le Prince Bariatinski was brought to me.[3] It was on Monday Evening last. Being at Court the next Day, I enquir'd of an Old Minister my Friend, what was the Etiquette, and whether the Count receiv'd Visits: The Answer was, Non. *On se fait ecrire, Voilà tout.* This is done here by passing the Door, and ordering your Name to be writ in the Porters Book. Accordingly on Wednesday I pass'd the House of Prince Bariatinski Ambassador of Russia where the Count lodg'd, and left my Name on the List of each. I thought no more of the Matter. But this Day May 24. comes the Servant who brought the Card, in great Affliction, saying he was like to be ruin'd by his Mistake in bringing the Card here, and wishing to obtain from me some Paper of I know not what kind, for I did not see him. In the Afternoon came my Friend Mr. le Roy, who is also a Friend of the Prince's, telling me how much he the Prince was concern'd at the Accident; that both himself and the Comte had great personal Regard for me and my Character, but that our Independence not being yet acknowledg'd by the Court of Russia, it was impossible for him to permit himself to make me a Visit as Minister. I told M le Roy it was not my Custom to seek such Honours, tho' I was very sensible of them when conferr'd upon me;

---

ing card with foreign representatives rather than following BF's example: Dmitrii A. Golitsyn to Ivan A. Osterman, April 26, 1782, in Nina N. Bashkina *et al.*, eds., *The United States and Russia: the Beginning of Relations, 1765–1815* (Washington, D.C., [1980]), p. 143.

3. Ivan Sergeevich Bariatinskii (or Bariatinskoy) was the Russian envoy at the French court: XXIV, 49n. The "Comte du Nord" was the alias used by Grand Duke Paul of Russia during his and his wife's extended tour of western Europe. During their present visit to Paris they dined with the French royal family: XXXV, 551n; *Gaz. de Leyde*, May 31 (sup.) and June 7 (sup.).

that I should not have voluntarily intruded a Visit; and that in this Case I had only done what I was inform'd the Etiquette requir'd of me: But if it would be attended with any Inconvenience to Prince Bariatinski whom I much esteem'd and respected, I thought the Remedy was easy; he had only to rase my Name out of his Book of Visits receiv'd, and I would burn their Card.

All the Northern Princes are not asham'd of a little Civility committed towards an American. The King of Denmark travelling in England under an assumed Name, sent me a Card expressing in strong Terms his Esteem for me, and inviting me to dinner with him at St. James's.—⁴ And the Ambassador from the King of Sweden lately ask'd me, whether I had Powers to make a Treaty of Commerce with their Kingdom, for he said his Master was desirous of such a Treaty with the United States, had directed him to ask me the Question, and had charg'd him to tell me, that it would flatter him greatly to make it with a Person whose Character he so much esteem'd &c &c.⁵ Such Compliments might probably make me a little proud, if we Americans were not naturally as much so already as the Porter, who being told he had with his Burthen jostled the great Czar Peter (then in London, walking the Street;⁶) *Poh*, says he, *We are all Czars here.*

I did not write by Mr. Oswald to Mr. Laurens, because from some Expressions in his last to me, I expected him here, and I desir'd Mr. Oswald, if he found him still in London, or met him on the Road, to give him that Reason. I am disappointed in my Expectation, for I have now receiv'd (May 25.) the following Letter from him, viz.

⟨May 17: Laurens declines the honor of serving with the peace commission for reasons of health and announces plans to join Adams in the Netherlands.⟩

---

4. BF dined with King Christian VII of Denmark on Oct. 1, 1768: XV, 224–7.

5. See BF to the comte de Creutz, April 24.

6. Peter the Great visited London in 1698: Robert K. Massie, *Peter the Great: His Life and World* (New York, 1980), pp. 203–16.

To the Above I wrote the following Answer—

⟨May 25: Franklin expresses disappointment that the peace commission will not have Laurens' assistance and agrees to join Laurens in discharging the parole of Cornwallis.⟩

May 26. I receiv'd the following Letters and Papers from Mr. Hartley vizt.[7]

⟨May 1: Hartley discusses the dispositions of the previous ministry and encloses a memoir which he submitted to it.⟩

⟨May 13: Hartley describes his meeting with Shelburne and encloses peace terms.⟩

The same day Mr. Grenville visited me. He acquainted me that his Courier was return'd, and had brought him full Powers in form to treat for a Peace *with France and her Allies.* That he had been to Versailles and had shown his Power to M. de Vergennes, and left a Copy with him. That he had also a Letter of Credence, which he was not to deliver till France should think fit to send a Minister of the same kind to London:[8] That M. de Vergennes had told him he would lay it before the King, and had desired to see

7. These two letters from Hartley are missing from this copy of BF's journal. A note in an unknown hand indicates that they should be inserted, and adds, "What are they—No papers in either Bundle answering thereto". The letters do appear in both transcripts.

8. On May 18, the British cabinet approved the following minute: "It is humbly submitted to Your Majesty that Your Majesty will be pleased to direct Mr. Fox to order full powers to be given to Mr. Grenville to treat and conclude at Paris, and also to direct Mr. Fox to instruct Mr. Grenville to make propositions of Peace to the belligerent Powers upon the basis of Independence to the thirteen Colonies in N. America, and of the Treaty of Paris—and in case of such proposition not being accepted, to call upon Mons. de Vergennes to make some proposition on his part, which Mr. Grenville will of course report to Mr. Fox." Oswald arrived late on May 21 with the news that, as Fox told the King, BF was favorably disposed to peace even without the concurrence of France, and much more without the concurrence of Spain and Holland. The King initially refused to believe this and the courier departed for France with Grenville's full powers: Fortescue, *Correspondence of George Third*, VI, 32, 40–1. We have not located a copy of Grenville's full powers, but his May 21 instructions from the King are in Giunta, *Emerging Nation*, I, 395–8, and his letter of credence of the same date is in Russell, *Memorials and Correspondence of Fox*, IV, 199.

him again on Wednesday.[9] That Mr. Oswald had arrived in London about an hour before the Courier came away. That Mr. Fox in his Letter had charg'd him to thank me for that which I had written, and to tell me he hop'd I would never forget that he and I were of the same Country.[1] I answer'd that I should always esteem it an Honour to be ownd as a Country man by Mr. Fox.— He had requested, at our last Interview that if I saw no Impropriety in doing it, I would favour him with a Sight of the Treaty of Alliance between France and America. I acquainted him that it was printed, but that if he could not readily meet with a Copy, I would have one written for him. And as he had not been able to find one I this day gave it to him.— He lent me a London Gazette, containing Admiral Rodney's Account of his Victory over M. de Grasse, and the Accounts of other Successes in the East-Indies, assuring me however that these Events made not the least Change in the sincere desires of his Court to treat for Peace.[2]

9. Grenville's full powers did not satisfy Vergennes because they authorized Grenville to treat with France, but not with her allies. He told Grenville on May 26 that France would not treat on this basis, and Grenville agreed to take his objections *ad referendum*. The conversation ended with another disagreement on whether the combination of American independence (including the British evacuation of New York, Charleston, and Savannah) and the Treaty of Paris of 1763 was a proper basis of peace: Doniol, *Histoire*, V, 113–14; Giunta, *Emerging Nation*, I, 404–5, 408–10. The following Wednesday was May 29.

1. Fox's May 21 letter to Grenville stressed that proposing the Treaty of Paris as a basis for negotiations was designed to elicit counter proposals from France. If these proposals were exorbitant Britain could argue that France and Spain were persisting in the war for their own aggrandizement. Grenville was ordered to cultivate BF and the Dutch minister in the hope of laying the foundation for a separate peace with Holland, America, or both: Giunta, *Emerging Nation*, I, 398–400; Russell, *Memorials and Correspondence of Fox*, IV, 191–4.

2. On the morning of May 18 news arrived in London of the April 12 victory of Rodney over de Grasse off the Saintes, a group of small islands between Guadeloupe and Dominica: *London Courant, Westminster Chronicle, and Daily Advertiser*, May 20. De Grasse was captured aboard his flagship, the *Ville de Paris*, and four other French ships of the line were taken as well, disrupting French plans to invade Jamaica: W. M. James, *The British Navy in Adversity; a Study of the War of American Independence* (London, New York, and Toronto, 1926), pp. 337–53, 448–50; John Creswell, *British Admi-*

In the Afternoon the Marquis de la Fayette call'd upon me. I acquainted him with what Mr. Grenville had told me respecting his Credential Letter, and the Expectation that a Person on the Part of this Court would be sent to London with a Commission similar to his. The Marquis told me he was on his Way to Versailles, and should see M. de Vergennes.— We concluded that it would now be proper for him to make the Proposition we had before talk'd of, that he should be the Person employ'd in that Service.

On Monday the 27. I received a Letter from Mr. Jay dated the 8th. acquainting me that he had receiv'd mine of the 21st. & 22nd. past, and had concluded to set out for Paris about the 19th. so that he may be expected in a few days. I din'd this day with Count d'Estaing, and a Number of brave Marine Officers that he had invited. We were all a little dejected and chagrin'd with the News.— I mention'd by way of Encouragement the Observation of the Turkish Bashaw who was taken with his Fleet at Lepanto, by the Venetians. Ships says he, are like my Master's Beard, you may cut it but it will grow again. He has cut off from your Government all the Morea,[3] which is like a Limb that you will never recover. And his Words prov'd true.

On Tuesday I din'd at Versailles, with some Friends, so was not at home when the Marquis de la Fayette call'd to acquaint me, that M. de Vergennes had inform'd him, that the full Power receiv'd by Mr. Grenville from London, and communicated by him, related to France only, The Marquis left for me this Information, which I could not understand.

On Wednesday I was at Court, and saw the Copy of the

---

rals of the Eighteenth Century ... (London, 1972), pp. 163–77. Vergennes knew of it on May 17 when he wrote the King, "L'échec que les armes de Votre Majesté viennent d'éprouver aux Antilles est sans doute très malheureux; mais il n'est pas irréparable; il ne change rien essentiellement au fond des choses": Hardman and Price, *Louis XVI and the Comte de Vergennes*, p. 304. For Grenville's meeting with BF see also Guinta, *Emerging Nation*, I, 410.

3. The Turks had captured the Morea (or Peloponnesian peninsula) from Venice in 1460: Fernand Braudel, *The Mediterranean and the Mediterranean World in the Age of Philip II*, trans. Siân Reynolds (2 vols., New York, Evanston, and San Francisco, 1972), II, 664.

Power. It appear'd full with regard to treating with France, but mention'd not a Word of her Allies.

And as M. de Vergennes had explicitly and constantly from the Beginning declar'd to the several Messengers Mr. Forth, Mr. Oswald and Mr. Grenville, that France could only treat in Concert with her Allies, and it had in consequence been declared on the Part of the British Ministry that they consented to treat for a general Peace, and at Paris, the sending this partial Power appear'd to be insidious, and a mere Invention to occasion Delay, the Late Disaster to the French Fleet having probably given the Court of England fresh Courage and other Views. M. de Vergennes said he should see Mr. Grenville on Thursday and would speak his mind to him on the Subject very plainly: They want, says he, to treat with us for you: But this the King will not agree to. He thinks it not consistent with the Dignity of your State. You will treat for yourselves: And every one of the Powers at War with England will make its own Treaty. All that is necessary to be observ'd for our Common security is, that the Treaties go hand in hand, and are sign'd all on the same Day.—[4]

Prince Bariatinski the Russian Ambassador was particularly civil to me this Day at Court; apologiz'd for what had pass'd relating to the Visit; express'd himself as extreamly sensible of my Friendship in covering the Affair, which might have occasion'd to him very disagreable Consequences, &c. The Comte du Nord, came to Mr. Vergennes while we were drinking Coffee after Dinner. He appears lively and active, with a sensible spirited Countenance.— There was an Opera at Night for his Entertainment. The House being richly finish'd with abundance of Carving and Gilding, well Illuminated with Wax Tapers, and the Company all superbly drest, many of the Men in Cloth of Tissue, and the Ladies sparkling with Diamonds, form'd alltogether the most splendid Spectacle my Eyes ever beheld.—

I had some little Conference to day with M. M. Berkenrode Vanderpierre and Boeris, the Ambassador of Holland, and the Agents of the Dutch India Company.[5] They inform'd me that

4. This is consistent with what Vergennes had written to La Luzerne on April 9: Giunta, *Emerging Nation*, 1, 331.

5. The first of these is Dutch Ambassador Mattheus Lestevenon van

the second Letter of Mr. Fox to the Mediating Minister of Russia,[6] proposing a seperate Peace with Holland, made no more Impression than the first, and no Peace would be made but in Concurrence with France.

The Swedish Minister told me he expected Orders from his Court relative to a Treaty, &c.

I had at our last Interview given Mr. Grenville a Rendezvous for Saturday Morning, and having some other Engagements for Thursday and Friday, tho' I wish'd to speak with him on the Subject of his Power, I did not go to him, but waited his coming to me on Saturday. On Friday May 31st. Mr. Oswald call'd on me, being just return'd and brought me the following Letters from Lord Shelburne, the first of which had been written before his Arrival—

⟨May 21: Shelburne acknowledges Franklin's letter of May 10 and informs him Oswald has received the King's instructions to continue at Paris until he is ordered to return.⟩

⟨May 25:[7] Shelburne acknowledges Franklin's letter of May 13 and informs him Oswald has the King's orders to return immediately to Paris.[8]⟩

Berkenrode, for whom see BF to Livingston, April 12. The second may be van Berckel's nephew, Van de Perre (XXXII, 221n). The third is Frederik Willem Boers, for whom see Dumas to BF, April 15. The latter two were in Paris to solicit permission for the East India Company to embark in France a Swiss regiment for overseas service; Vergennes wrote them on June 3 granting it (AAE).

6. Simolin; see BF to Livingston, April 12. Fox's second letter to him was dated May 4 and is quoted in Sir Francis Piggott and G. W. T. Omond, eds., *Documentary History of the Armed Neutralities, 1780 and 1800* (London, 1919), pp. 325–6.

7. The date was copied as "May 26" in all three versions of this journal. While the original has been lost, it seems likely that Shelburne used the date (May 25) that appeared on both his drafts and the copies retained in England.

8. Shelburne also wrote Oswald on May 25. He instructed him to use all possible prudence and to give information and advice to Grenville. Shelburne expressed his regrets that Vergennes had given Britain reason to doubt the sincerity of his court's desire for peace. Should this prove to be the case he expected BF would consider himself and his constituents freed from their ties with France: Fitzmaurice, *Life of Shelburne*, II, 133–5.

I had not then time to converse much with Mr. Oswald, and he promis'd to come and breakfast with me on Monday.[9]

Saturday June 1st. Mr. Grenville came according to appointment. Our Conversation began by my acquainting him that I had seen Mr. de Vergennes, and had perus'd the Coppy left with him of the Power to treat. That after what he, Mr. Grenville, had told me, of its being to treat with France *and her Allies,* I was a little surpriz'd to find in it no mention of the Allies, and that it was only to treat with the King of France and his Ministers: That at Versailles there was some Suspicion of its being intended to occasion Delay, the profess'd Desire of speedy Peace being perhaps abated in the British Court since its late Successes; but that I imagin'd the Words relating to the Allies might have been accidentally omitted in transcribing, or that perhaps he had a special Power to treat with us distinct from the other. He answer'd that the Copy was right, and that he had no such special Power in form, but that his Instructions were full to that purpose, and that he was sure the Ministry had no Desire of Delay, nor any of excluding us from the Treaty, since the greater Part of those Instructions related to treating with me. That to convince me of the Sincerity of his Court respecting us, he would acquaint me with one of his Instructions, tho' perhaps the doing it now was premature and

9. Oswald took the following minutes: "Arrived at Paris, Friday, 31st May, nine in the morning. Called on Mr. Grenville; delivered his packets. Then went out to Passy, and delivered to Dr. Franklin the sundry letters for him, and had a good deal of conversation with him about the affairs of the peace. He thought there should be separate commissions to treat, one for France, one for the Colonies. Was not so positive as to Spain and Holland, although mentioned on several occasions. That though the treaties might go on separately, yet to be united in the final conclusion; meaning that there should be such correspondence between them that there should be no separate conclusion. That by treating separately, different interests and subjects not strictly relative to each other would not be mixed and involved in too much intricacy, and so might be separately discussed in the progress, and yet the final conclusion of the whole in one general settlement might be governed and made to be dependent upon those separate adjustments. Adding that the more we favoured them (meaning the Colonies) the more they would do for us in the conclusion of these separate treaties." Sir George Cornewall Lewis, *Essays on the Administrations of Great Britain from 1783 to 1830* . . . (London, 1864), pp. 82–3.

therefore a little inconsistent with the Character of a Politician, but he had that confidence in me, that he should not hesitate to inform me, (tho' he wish'd that at present it should go no further) He was Instructed to acknowledge the Independence of America previous to the Commencement of the Treaty.[1] And he said he could only account for the Omission of America in the Power by supposing that it was an Old Official Form copied from that given to Mr. Stanley when he came over hither before the last Peace.[2] Mr. Grenville added that he had immediately after his Interview with M. de Vergennes dispatch'd a Courier to London, and hop'd that with his Return the Difficulty would be remov'd:[3] That he was perfectly assur'd their late Successes had made no Change in the Dispositions of his Court to Peace; and that he had more Reason than M. de Vergennes to complain of Delay, since five Days

1. Fox long had been eager to make such an offer, in part no doubt because once American independence had been acknowledged, negotiations with the United States would fall to him as foreign secretary rather than to Shelburne as home secretary. Shelburne and George III, anxious to preserve some ties with America, opposed granting independence except as part of a general peace settlement. Fox was given encouragement by Oswald's reports that he and Grenville doubted BF's faithfulness to the French alliance. Moreover, the news of the victory at the Saintes bolstered the cabinet's desire to make a quick peace with America so as to take advantage of improving war prospects. (Such a peace would permit shifting British troops from New York, Charleston, and Savannah to the West Indies.) The cabinet meeting resolved on May 23 to recommend to the King "to direct Mr. Fox to instruct Mr. Grenville to propose the independency of America in the first instance, instead of making it a condition of a general treaty." Fox's victory was incomplete, however, as the cabinet also resolved to recommend that Oswald return to Paris. This in fact permitted Shelburne to reestablish his role in the negotiations when BF did not accept Grenville's offer: Giunta, *Emerging Nation*, I, 402–4; Russell, *Memorials and Correspondence of Fox*, I, 357; IV, 206–9; Fitzmaurice, *Life of Shelburne*, II, 132–3; Harlow, *Second British Empire*, I, 256–7.

2. Hans Stanley was provided a full power when he was sent to Paris in May, 1761, to negotiate with the French government: L. G. Wickham Legg, ed., *British Diplomatic Instructions 1689–1789, Volume VII: France, Part IV, 1745–1789* (London, 1934), p. 53.

3. Undoubtedly after Grenville's May 30 conference with Vergennes, which largely repeated what had been said at the conference of May 26: Doniol, *Histoire*, IV, 115–16; Giunta, *Emerging Nation*, I, 411–12; Russell, *Memorials and Correspondence of Fox*, IV, 209–13.

were spent before he could obtain a Passport for his Courier, and then that it was not to go and return by Way of Calais, but to go by Ostend which would occasion a Delay of five days longer. Mr. Grenville then Spoke much of the high opinion the present Ministry had of me and their great Esteem for me; their Desire of a perfect Reconciliation between the two Countries, and the firm and general Belief in England that no Man was so capable as myself of proposing the proper Means of bringing about such a Reconciliation; adding that if the old Ministers had formerly been too little attentive to my Counsels, the present were very differently dispos'd and he hop'd that in treating with them I would totally forget their Predecessors. The Time has been when such flattering Language as from great Men might have made me Vainer and had more Effect on my Conduct than it can at present, when I find myself so near the End of Life, as to esteem lightly all personal Interests and Concerns, except that of maintaining to the last and leaving behind me, the tolerably good Character I have hitherto supported.—

Mr. G. then discours'd of our Resolution not to treat without our Allies. This, says he, can properly only relate to France, with whom you have a Treaty of Alliance but you have none with Spain, you have none with Holland. If Spain and Holland, and even if France should insist on unreasonable Terms of Advantage to themselves, after you have obtain'd all you want, and are satisfied, can it be right that America should be dragg'd on in a War for their Interests only? He stated this Matter in various Lights and press'd it earnestly. I resolv'd from various Reasons to evade the Discussion, and therefore answer'd, that the intended Treaty not being yet begun, it appear'd unnecessary to enter at present into Considerations of that kind. The Preliminaries being once settled and the Treaty commenc'd, if any of the other Powers should make extravagant Demands on England, and insist on our continuing the War till those were comply'd with, it would then be time enough for us to consider what our Obligations were, and how far they extended.[4] The first

---

4. Grenville, disappointed at BF's failure to accept his offer of Britain's acknowledging American independence, sought an explanation. When he learned from Oswald for the first time of BF's "Notes for a Conversation"

thing necessary was for him to procure the full Powers, the next for us to assemble the Plenipotentiaries of all the bellegirent Parties, and then Propositions might be mutually made, received, considered, answer'd, or agree'd to. In the mean time I would just mention to him, that tho' we were yet under no Obligations to Spain by Treaty; we were under Obligations of Gratitude for the Assistance she had afforded us; and as Mr. Adams had some Weeks since commenc'd a Treaty in Holland, the Terms of which I was not yet acquainted with, I knew not but that we might have already some Alliance and Obligations contracted there. And perhaps we ought however to have some Consideration for Holland on this Account, that it was in Vengeance for the friendly Disposition shown by some of her People to make a Treaty of Commerce with us that England had declar'd the War against her.[5] He said it would be very hard upon England, if having given reasonable Satisfaction to one or two of her four Enemies, she could not have Peace with those till she had comply'd with what ever the others might demand; however unreasonable; for so she might be oblig'd to pay for every Article fourfold. I observ'd that when she made her Propositions, the more advantageous they were to each, the more it would be the Interest of each to prevail with the other to accept those offer'd to them. We then spoke of the Reconciliation, but his full Power not being yet come, I chose to defer entering upon that Subject at present. I told him I had thoughts of putting down in Writing the Particulars that I judg'd would conduce to that End, and of

---

(above, [on or before April 19]), he jumped to the conclusion that Oswald and Shelburne were negotiating behind his back. In a private letter of June 4 he so informed Fox and asked that both he and Oswald be replaced: Wharton, *Diplomatic Correspondence*, v, 474–7; Harlow, *Second British Empire*, I, 258–9. We can only speculate on BF's motivation. In addition to his basic caution, he seems to have come to distrust Grenville and Fox because Grenville had not been given adequate full powers. Moreover, the British offer was vague, saying nothing about such key issues as boundaries and fishing rights. Probably he wondered, too, about the firmness of the offer, given the King's reluctance to accept American independence; see BF to JA, June 2.

5. The professed reason for Britain's opening hostilities against the Netherlands was the Dutch refusal to disavow a draft commercial treaty signed by Jean de Neufville and William Lee: xxxiv, 8n, 176–7.

adding my Reasons, that this requir'd a little Time and I had been hinder'd by Accidents, which was true, for I had begun to write, but had postpon'd it on Account of his defective Power to treat: but I promis'd to finish it as soon as possible. He press'd me earnestly to do it, saying an Expression of mine in a former Conversation that there still remain'd *Roots of Goodwill* in America towards England, which if properly taken care of might produce a Reconciliation, had made a great Impression on his Mind, and given him infinite Pleasure, and he hop'd I would not neglect furnishing him with the Information of what would be necessary to nourish those Roots, and could assure me that my Advice would be greatly regarded.—

Mr. Grenville had shown me at our last Interview a Letter from the Duke of Richmond to him, requesting him to prevail with me to disengage a Capt. Macleod of the Artillery from his Parole, the Duke's Brother, Lord George Lenox being appointed to the Command of Portsmouth, and desiring to have him as his Aid de Camp.[6] I had promis'd to consider of it, and this Morning I sent him the following Letter.

⟨May 31: Franklin consents that Capt. Macleod serve in his military capacity in England only until Congress decides; he will write Congress immediately.⟩

America has been constantly befriended in Parliament by the Duke of Richmond, and I believ'd the Congress would not be displeas'd that this Opportunity was taken of obliging him, and that they would by their Approbation supply the Deficiency of my Power.— Besides, I could not well refuse it after what had pass'd between Mr. Laurens and me, and what I had promis'd to do for the Satisfaction of that Gentleman.

Sunday June 2nd.

The Marquis de la Fayette call'd and din'd with me. He is uneasy about the Delay, as he cannot resolve concerning his Voyage to America, till some Certainty appears of there being a Treaty or no Treaty.

6. George Henry Lennox was a major general: *DNB*. Macleod's first name probably was John: [Robert Mackenzie, comp.], *A List of the General and Field Officers as They Rank in the Army* . . . (London, [1777]), p. 203.

This Day I wrote the following Letter to Mr. Adams.

⟨June 2: Franklin reports on the difficulties encountered in the negotiations and predicts that if Britain does not provide full powers to negotiate with all the belligerents negotiations will be broken off.⟩

On Monday the 3d. Mr. Oswald came according to Appointment. He told me he had seen and had Conversations with Lord Shelburne, Lord Rockingham, and Mr. Fox. That their Desire of Peace continued uniformly the same, tho' he thought some of them were a little too much elated with the late Victory in the West Indies; and when observing his Coolness, they ask'd him if he did not think it a very good thing; yes says he, if you do not rate it too high.— He went on with the utmost Frankness to tell me, that Peace was absolutely necessary for them. That the Nation had been foolishly involv'd in four Wars, and could no longer raise Money to carry them on, so that if they continu'd, it would be absolutely necessary for them to stop Payment of the Interest Money on the Funds, which would ruin their future Credit. He spoke of stopping on all sums above £1000, and continuing to pay on those below; because the great Sums belong'd to the Rich, who would better bear the Delay of their Interest; and the Smaller Sums to poorer Persons who would be more hurt and make more Clamour; and that the Rich might be quieted by promising them Interest upon their Interest. All this look'd as if the Matter had been seriously thot on. Mr. Oswald has an Air of great Simplicity and Honesty; yet I could hardly take this to be merely a weak Confession of their deplorable State, and tho't it might be rather intended as a kind of Intimidation, by showing us they had still that Resource in their Power, which he said could furnish five Millions a Year. But he added our Enemies may now do what they please with us, *they have the Ball at their Foot,* was his Expression, and we hope they will show their Moderation and their Magnanimity. He then repeatedly mention'd the great Esteem the Ministers had for me, that they with all the considerate People of England look'd to and depended on me for the Means of extricating the Nation from its present desperate Situation, that perhaps no single Man had ever in his Hands an Opportunity of doing so much Good as I had at this present, with much more to that purpose. He then show'd me a Letter to him from Lord Shelburne, partly, I suppose, that I might see his Lordship's Opinion of me, which as it has some Relation to the Negotiation is here inserted. He left it with me requesting that I would communicate it to Mr. Walpole. &c

Copy of a Letter from Lord Shelburne
to Richard Oswald Esq.[7]

Sir,   Whitehall 21st, May 1782

It has reached me that Mr. Walpole esteems himself much injured by your going to Paris, and that he conceives it was a measure of mine intended to take the present Negotiation out of his Hands, which he conceives to have been previously commenced through his Channel by Mr. Fox.[8] I must desire that you will have the Goodness to call upon Mr. Walpole, and explain to him distinctly how very little Foundation there is for so unjust a Suspicion, as I knew of no such Intercourse.

Mr. Fox declares he consider'd what had pass'd between him and Mr. Walpole of a mere private Nature, not sufficiently material to mention to the King or the Cabinet, and will write to Mr. Walpole to explain this distinctly to him. But if you find the least Suspicion of this kind has reach'd Dr. Franklin or Monsr. le Comte de Vergennes, I desire this Matter may be clearly explain'd to both. I have too much Friendship for Dr. Franklin, and too much Respect for the Character of M. le Cte. de Vergennes, with which I am perfectly acquainted, to be so indifferent to the good Opinion of either, as to suffer them to believe me capable of an Intrigue, where I have both profess'd and observ'd a direct opposite Conduct. In Truth I hold it in such perfect Contempt,

---

7. A copy of this letter is at the Public Record Office. It lacks the complimentary close and adds the words "with the Court of France" after "Negotiation" in the first sentence.

8. Thomas Walpole was negotiating with the French government on behalf of British merchants whose property was captured while being transferred from St. Eustatius to England. He also was authorized to deal with the claims of French merchants arising from the British capture of the island: Fitzmaurice, *Life of Shelburne*, II, 125–6; Andrew Stockley, *Britain and France at the Birth of America: the European Powers and the Peace Negotiations of 1782–1783* (Exeter, 2001), pp. 103–4.

that however proud I may be to serve the King in my present Station or in any other, and however anxious I may be to serve my Country, I should not hesitate a Moment about retiring from any Situation which requir'd such Services. But I must do the King the Justice to say, that his Majesty abhors them, and I need not tell you that it is my fix'd Principle, that no Country in any Moment can be advantaged by them.

I am with great truth and Regard Sir, Your most obedient humble Servant (signed) SHELBURNE

In speaking farther of the Ministry's Opinion of the great Service it might be in my Power to render, Mr. Oswald said he had told them in one of his Conversations, that nothing was to be expected of me but Consistence, nothing unsuitable to my Character, or inconsistent with my Duty to my Country; I did not ask him the particular Occasion of his saying this, but thought it look'd a little as if something inconsistent with my Duty had been talk'd of or propos'd.

Mr. Oswald also gave me a Copy of a Paper of Memorandums written by Lord Shelburne, viz.[9]

1 That I am ready to correspond more particularly with Dr. Franklin if wished.
2 That the *enabling Act* is passing[1] with the Insertion of Commissioners recommended by Mr. Oswald, And on our part Commissrs. will be named, or any Character given to Mr. Oswald, which Dr. Franklin and he may judge conducive to a final Settlement of Things between G. B. and America. Which Dr. Franklin very properly says requires to be treated in a very different manner from the Peace between G. B. and France, who have been always at Enmity with each other.
3 That an Establishment for the Loyalists must always be upon Mr. Oswald's mind, as it is upermost in Lord Shelburne's besides other steps in their Favour, to influence the several

9. The copy bound into this journal is a single sheet written in an unknown hand. Oswald's own copy is also at the Library of Congress; it was dated "26 May 1782" by wtf, who had a secretary copy it (and mark it as such) when wtf was preparing the *Memoirs*.

1. It passed in mid-June; see our annotation of bf to Livingston, March 30.

States to agree to a fair Restoration or Compensation for whatever Confiscations have taken place.

4 To give Lord Shelburne's Letter about Mr. Walpole to Dr Franklin.

On perusing this Paper, I recollected that a Bill had been sometime since propos'd in Parliament *to enable his Majesty to conclude a Peace or Truce with the Revolted Colonies in America*, which I suppos'd to be the *enabling* Bill mention'd, that had hitherto slept, and not having been pass'd was perhaps the true Reason why the Colonies were not mention'd, in Mr. Grenville's Commission. Mr. Oswald thought it likely, and said that the Words, "insertion of Commissioners recommended by Mr. Oswald," related to his advising an express mention in the Bill of the Commissioners appointed by Congress to treat of Peace, instead of the vague Denominations of *any Person or Persons. &c*, in the first Draft of the Bill. As to the Loyalists, I repeated what I had said to him when first here, that their[2] Estates had been confiscated by Laws made in the particular States where the Delinquents had resided, and not by any Law of Congress, who indeed had no Power either to make such Laws, or to repeal them, or to dispense with them, and therefore could give no Power to their Commissioners to treat of a Restoration for those People: That it was an Affair appertaining to each State. That if there were Justice in Compensating them, it must be due from England rather than from America; but in my Opinion England was not under any very great Obligations to them, since it was by their Misrepresentations and bad Counsels that she had been drawn into this miserable War. And that if an Account was brought against us for their Losses, we should more than ballance it by an Account of the Ravages they had committed all along the Coasts of America. Mr. Oswald agreed to the Reasonableness of all this, and said he had before he came away told the Ministers that he thought no Recompence to those People was to be expected from us;— That he had also, in Consequence of our former Conversation on that Subject, given it as his Opinion that Canada should be given up to the United States, as it

---

2. The copyist misspelled this word as "there." Both transcripts are correct.

would prevent the Occasions of future Difference, and as the Government of such a Country was worth nothing, and of no Importance if they could have there a free Commerce that the Marquis of Rockingham and Lord Shelburne, tho' they spoke reservedly, did not seem very averse to it; but that Mr. Fox appear'd to be startled at the Proposition.[3] He was however not without Hopes that it would be agreed to.

We now came to another Article of the Note, viz, "On our part Commissioners will be named, or any Character given to Mr. Oswald which Dr. Franklin and he may judge conducive to a final Settlement of things between Great Britain and America." This he said was left entirely to me, for he had no Will in the Affair; he did not desire to be farther concern'd than to see it *en train;* he had no personal Views either of Honour or Profit. He had now seen and convers'd with Mr. Grenville, thought him a very sensible young Gentleman, and very capable of the Business; he did not therefore see any farther Occasion there was for himself; but if I thought otherwise, and conceiv'd he might be farther Useful, he was content to give his Time and Service in any Character or manner I should think proper. I said his Knowledge of America, where he had lived, and with every Part of which and of its Commerce and Circumstances he was well acquainted, made me think, that in persuading the Ministry to things Reasonable relating to that Country, he could speak or write with more Weight than Mr. Grenville; and therefore I wish'd him to continue in the Service; and I ask'd him whether he would like to be join'd in a general Commission for treating with all the Powers at War with England, or, to have a special Commission to himself for treating with America only: He said he did not chuse to be concern'd in treating with the foreign Powers, for he was not sufficiently a Master of their Affairs, or of the French Language which probably would be used in treat-

3. Fox claimed to have learned of BF's suggestion from Grenville's June 4 letter. Oswald may not have been candid with BF during this portion of the conversation, possibly in an attempt to ingratiate himself. He was correct, however, that Fox was startled to learn of the proposal; see Fox's June 10 response to Grenville: Wharton, *Diplomatic Correspondence*, V, 484–6. Subsequently, Fox made use of Grenville's letter to challenge Shelburne in the cabinet.

ing; if therefore he accepted of any Commission it should be that of treating with America. I told him I would write to Lord Shelburne on the Subject; but Mr. Grenville having some time since dispatch'd a Courier partly on Account of the Commission, who was not yet return'd, I thought it well to wait a few Days till we could see what Answer he would bring or what Measures were taken; this he approv'd of. The Truth is, he appears so good and so reasonable a Man, that tho' I have no Objection to Mr. Grenville, I should be loth to lose Mr. Oswald. He seems to have nothing at heart but the Good of Mankind, and putting a Stop to Mischief: the other a young Statesman may be suppos'd to have naturally a little Ambition of recommending himself as an able Negotiator.——[4]

4. Oswald took the following minutes: "I wanted to take my leave, having sat a considerable time, but he wished me to stay a little longer. And he fell into the subject formerly mentioned of the treaty going on by separate commissions for each party, and said he could see no objection to there being one commission for France, one for the Colonies, and perhaps one for Spain and one for Holland. That by this means, the business with each being separately discussed, they might more quickly and clearly come to a conclusion than when so many different interests must be jointly treated under the same commission. That, with respect to the Colony business, if my private affairs would allow of my absence, and that I would divert myself in the meantime, I might take up that commission. I told him, that if it was to trench on the character of Mr. Grenville's station, it would be the last thing I should incline to. That I believed him very capable and prudent, and had no doubt of his acquiring himself a reputation. As to my stay here, it was on account of various circumstances not the most agreeable. And with respect to my private affairs, they were in such situation that I should not suffer much by my attendance. At least, I should make no account of these matters if I thought that upon so critical an occasion I would be of any service to my country, &c.

The doctor replied, that he thought the commission for the Colonies would be better in my hands than in Mr. Grenville's. That I understood more of Colony business than he did, and he himself had a longer acquaintance with me than with Mr. Grenville, and could not say but he esteemed me; and therefore not only thought the Colony Commission would be left in my hands, but he wished it might be so.

I replied, that his wishing it was enough to determine, if I found it was a task I could go through with. That my coming here after the first time was entirely owing to the letters he wrote to Lord Shelburne, wherein he was pleased to express himself so favourably with respect to me, that I was ordered to return on the two succeeding occasions. That I was happy in the enjoyment of his good opinion. Was much obliged to him, &c.

In the Afternoon Mr. Boeris of Holland, call'd on me, and acquainted me that the Answer had not yet been given to the last Memorial from Russia relating to the Mediation;[5] but it was thought it would be in respectful Terms to thank her Imperial Majesty for her kind Offers, and to represent the Propriety of their Connection with France in Endeavours to obtain a general Peace, and that they conceiv'd it would be still more glorious for her Majesty, to employ her Influence in procuring a general than a particular Pacification. Mr. Boeris farther Inform'd me, that they were not well sattisfy'd in Holland with the Conduct of the Russian Court, and suspected Views of continuing the War for particular purposes. Tuesday June 4, I receivd another Packet from Mr. Hartley. It consisted of Duplicates of the former Letters and Papers already inserted, and contained nothing new but the following Letter from Colo. Hartley his Brother, viz'—

⟨May 24: Winchcombe Hartley copies and sends some of his brother's letters and papers; his main object in Parliament is to achieve a peaceful settlement of the war.⟩

Wednesday June 5. Mr. Oswald call'd again, to acquaint me that Lord Cornwallis being very anxious to be discharg'd from his Parole as soon as possible, had sent a Major Ross[6] hither to

---

From thence we turned to a more general course of conversation, when I told him I could not but congratulate him on his present happy situation. Since I considered the settlement of a peace on fair and equitable terms to be entirely in his hands. Since, to speak the truth I could not help thinking, that when they as Commissioners of the Colonies were satisfied, they had it in their power to draw the line of such reasonable termination as ought and must content the other Powers." Lewis, *Essays on the Administrations of Great Britain*, pp. 83–4.

Oswald reported this conversation to Shelburne on June 9: Giunta, *Emerging Nation*, I, 427; Russell, *Memorials and Correspondence of Fox*, IV, 215–18.

5. The latest memorial of Russia was that of April 3, which called on the Dutch to accept Fox's offers: Piggott and Omond, *Documentary History of the Armed Neutralities*, pp. 324–5.

6. Maj. Alexander Ross, an aide-de-camp of Cornwallis who had helped arrange the surrender terms at Yorktown. Ross and Cornwallis remained intimate friends, and Ross eventually became a full general in the British Army: *DNB*.

sollicit it supposing Mr. Laurens might be here with me. Mr. Oswald told me, what I had not heard before, that Mr. Laurens while Prisoner in the Tower, had propos'd obtaining the Discharge of Lord Cornwallis in exchange for himself, and had promis'd to use his utmost Endeavours to that purpose in case he was set at Liberty, not doubting of the Success.[7] I communicated to Mr. Oswald what had already pass'd between Mr. Laurens and me respecting Lord Cornwallis, which appears in the preceding Letters,[8] and told him I should have made less difficulty about the Discharge of his Parole, if Mr. Laurens had inform'd me of his being set at Liberty in consequence of such an Offer and Promise; and I wish'd him to state this in a Letter to me, that it might appear for my Justification in what I might with Mr Laurens do in the Affair, and that he would procure for me from Major Ross a Copy of the Parole, that I might be better acquainted with the Nature of it. He accordingly in the Afternoon sent me the following Letter.

⟨June 5: Oswald informs Franklin that Laurens promised that in exchange for being released upon parole he would apply to Franklin for an exchange with Cornwallis.⟩

⟨June 6: Franklin informs Oswald he is awaiting a paper drawn up by Laurens in order to discharge Cornwallis from his parole; if he does not receive it the next day he will do what he can toward liberating Cornwallis.⟩

Friday June 7th. Major Ross call'd upon me to thank me for the favourable Intentions I had express'd in my Letter to Mr. Oswald respecting Lord Cornwallis, and to assure me his Lordship would forever remember it with Gratitude &c &c. I told him it was our Duty to alleviate as much as we could the Calamities of War; that I expected Letters from Mr. Laurens relating to the Affair, after the Receipt of which, I would immediately compleat it. Or if I did not hear from Mr. Laurens I would speak to the Marquis de la Fayette, get his Approbation, and finish it without further writing.

7. Laurens wrote Oswald to this effect on Dec. 22, 1781: *Laurens Papers*, XV, 459–60.
8. Laurens to BF, May 17, and BF to Laurens, May 25.

Saturday June 8th. I receivd some Newspapers from England in one of which is the following Paragraph.

Extract from the London Ev'ning Post of May 30, 1782.

"If Reports on the Spot speak Truth, Mr. Grenville, in his first Visit to Dr. Franklin, gained a considerable Point of Information as to the Powers America had retained for treating *separately* with Great Britain, in Case her Claims or Demands were granted.

The Treaty of February 6. 1778, was made the Basis of this Conversation; and by the Spirit and meaning of this Treaty, there is no Obligation on America not to treat Separately for Peace, after She is assured England will grant her Independence, and free Commerce with all the World.

The first Article of that Treaty engages America and France to be bound to each other as long as *Circumstances* may require;[9] therefore the Granting America all that She asks of England, is breaking the Bond by which the *Circumstances* may bind America to France.

The second Article says, the meaning and direct End of the Alliance is, to insure the Freedom and Independence of America. Surely, then, when Freedom and Independence is allow'd by Britain, America, may or may not, as She chuses, put an End to the present War between England and America, and leave France to War on through all her mad Projects of reducing the Power and Greatness of England, while America feels herself possessed of what She wishes.

By the eighth Article of the Treaty, neither France or America can conclude Peace without the Assent of the other; and they engage not to lay down their Arms, untill the Independence of America is acknowledged; but this Article does not exclude America from entering into a seperate Treaty for Peace with England, and evinces more strongly than the former Articles, that America may enter into a separate Treaty with England, when she is convinced that England has insur'd to her *all that She can reasonably ask.*"

---

9. A misreading of this article of the treaty (xxv, 586).

I conjecture that this must be an Extract from a Letter of Mr. Grenvilles.[1] But It carries an Appearance as if he and I had agreed in these imaginary Discoveries of America's being at Liberty to make Peace without France, &c, whereas my whole Discourse in the strongest Terms declar'd our Determinations to the Contrary, and the Impossibility of our acting not only contrary to the Treaty, but the Duties of Gratitude and Honour, of which nothing is mention'd. This young Negotiator seems to value himself on having obtain'd from me a Copy of the Treaty. I gave it him freely, at his Request; it being not so much a secret as he imagin'd, having been printed first in all the American Papers, soon after it was made; then at London in Almon's Remembrancer,[2] which I wonder he did not know; and afterwards in a Collection of the American Constitutions publish'd by Order of Congress.—[3] As such imperfect Accounts of our Conversations find their Way into the English Papers, I must speak to this Gentleman of its Impropriety.

Sunday June 9th. Dr. Bancroft being intimately acquainted with Mr. Walpole I this day gave him Lord Shelburnes Letter to Mr. Oswald, requesting he would communicate it to that Gentleman. Dr. Bancroft said it was believ'd both Russia and the Emperor wish the continuance of the War, and aim'd at procuring for England a Peace with Holland, that England might be better able to continue it against France and Spain.

The Marquis de la Fayette having propos'd to call on me to day, I kept back the Discharge of Lord Cornwallis which was written and ready,[4] desiring to have his Approbation to it, as he had in a former Conversation advis'd it. He did not come, but late in the Evening sent me a Note acquainting me that he had been prevented by accompanying the great Duke to the Review:[5] But would breakfast with me to-morrow Morning.

1. It is not from any letter of Grenville's that we have located.
2. *The Remembrancer; or, Impartial Repository of Public Events for the Year 1778, and Beginning of 1779* (London, 1779), pp. 199–202.
3. *The Constitutions of the Several Independent States of America . . .* (Philadelphia, 1781), pp. 221–6.
4. It is published under its date, June 9.
5. The review consisted of exercises of the French Guards held on the

This day I received a Letter from Mr Dana, dated at St. Petersburgh April 29.[6] in which is the following Passage; "We yesterday receiv'd the News that the States General had on the 19th. of this Month, (NS.) acknowledged the Independence of the United States. This Event gave a Shock here, and is not well receiv'd, as they at least profess to have flatter'd themselves that the Mediation would have prevented it, and otherwise brot on a partial Peace between Britain and Holland. This Resentment will not be productive of any ill Consequences to the Dutch Republick."— It is true that while the War continues Russia feels a greater Demand for her Naval Stores, and perhaps at a higher Price: But is it possible that for such petty Interests Mankind can wish to see their Neighbours destroy each other? Or has the Project lately talk'd of, some Foundation, that Russia and the Emperor intend driving the Turks out of Europe; and do therefore wish to see France and England so weaken'd as to be unable to assist those People?

Monday June 10. The Marquis de la Fayette did not come till between 11. & 12 he brought with him Major Ross. After Breakfast, he told me, (Major Ross being gone into another Room) that he had seen Mr. Grenville lately, who asked him when he should go to America. That he had answer'd, I have staid here longer than I should otherwise have done, that I might see whether we were to have Peace or War, but as I see the Expectation of Peace is a Joke, and that you only amuse us without any real Intention of Treating, I think to stay no longer but set out in a few Days. On which Mr. Grenville assur'd him that it was no Joke; that they were very sincere in their Proposal of Treating, and that four or five Days would convince the Marquis of it. The Marquis then spoke to me about a Request of Major Ross's in Behalf of himself, Lord Chewton a Lieut. Colonel and Lieutt Haldane, who were Aids de Camps to Lord Cornwallis,[7] that they too might be

---

Champ de Mars and attended by Grand Duke Paul and his wife: *Gaz. de Leyde*, June 21 (sup.). Lafayette's note is missing.

6. It is published below, under its date in the Gregorian calendar, May 10.

7. Lt. Col. George Waldegrave, Viscount Chewton (1751–1789), and Lt. Henry Haldane, an engineer who sometimes served as an aide to Cornwal-

set at Liberty with him. I told the Marquis that he was better acquainted with the Custom in such Cases than I, and being himself one of the Generals to whom their Parole had been given, he had more Right to discharge it than I had, and that if he judg'd it a thing proper to be done, I wish'd him to do it. He went into the Bureau saying he would write something, which he accordingly did. But it was not as I expected a Discharge that he was to sign, it was for me to sign.[8] And the Major not liking that which I had drawn for Lord Cornwallis, because there was a Clause in it reserving to Congress the Approbation or Disallowance of my Act, went away without taking it. Upon which I the next morning wrote the following to Mr. Oswald.

⟨June 11: Franklin describes the paper he encloses and explains why it reserves for Congress the right to confirm or disapprove it.⟩

The following is the Paper mention'd in the above Letter.—[9]
I did not well comprehend the Major's Conduct in refusing this Paper. He was come express from London to solicit a Discharge, of Lord Cornwallis's Parole. He had said that his Lordship was very anxious to obtain that Discharge, being unhappy in his present Situation. One of his Objections to it was, that his Lordship with such a limited Discharge of his Parole could not enter into foreign Service. He declar'd it was not his Lordships Intention to return to America. He would not accept the Paper, unless the Reservation was omitted. I did not chuse to make the Alteration. And so he left it; not well pleas'd with me.—

---

lis: Namier and Brooke, *House of Commons*, III, 592; Franklin and Mary Wickwire, *Cornwallis: the American Adventure* (Boston, 1970), pp. 318, 383.

8. Lafayette's undated draft of this document is at the Library of Congress. It states that whereas BF has discharged Cornwallis of his parole until Congress' pleasure is known and whereas Cornwallis' aides-de-camp have certified that orders have been sent to America to propose their immediate exchange (which probably would be settled between General Washington and the British commander-in-chief), he, BF, discharges them from their paroles under the same restrictions as in the document relative to Cornwallis.

9. Apparently BF intended to insert the text of the discharge of Cornwallis (below, June 9), but it was not copied.

This day Tuesday June 11th. I was at Versailles and had a good deal of Conversation with M. de Rayneval, Secretary to the Council. I show'd him the Letters I had receiv'd by Mr. Oswald from Lord Shelburne, and related all the consequent Conversation I had had with Mr Oswald. I related to him also the Conversation I had had with Mr. Grenville. We concluded that the Reason of his Courier's not being return'd might be the Formalities occasioning Delay in Passing the Enabling Bill. I went down with him to the Cabinet of Mr. Vergennes, where all was repeated and explain'd. That Minister seem'd now to be almost persuaded that the English Court was sincere in its Declaration of being desirous of Peace. We spoke of all its Attempts to seperate us, and of the Prudence of our holding together, and treating in Concert. I made one Remark, that as they had shown so strong a Desire of Disuniting us, by large Offers to each particular Power, plainly in the View of dealing more advantageously with the rest, and had reluctantly agreed to make a general Treaty, it was possible that after making a Peace with all, they might pick out one of us to make War with seperately. Against which Project I thought it would not be amiss if, before the Treaties of Peace were signed, we who are at War against England should enter into another Treaty, engaging ourselves, that in such Case we should again make it a common Cause, and renew the general War.[1] Which he seem'd to approve of.— He read Lord Shelburne's Letter relating to Mr. Walpole, said that Gentleman had Attempted to open a Negociation thro' the Marquis de Castries, who told him he was come to the wrong House, and should go to M. de Vergennes. But he never had appear'd. That he was an Intriguer, knew many People about the Court, and was accustom'd to manage his Affairs by hidden roundabout Ways; but, says he, When People have any thing to propose that relates to my Employment I think they should come di-

---

1. By Article 11 of the existing Treaty of Alliance, France and the United States guaranteed American independence as well as France's possessions in "America" (presumably including the West Indies) "from the present time and forever" (xxv, 590–1), thus making the alliance permanent. Here BF implies the alliance would cease once a peace treaty was signed, unless a new agreement was signed first.

rectly to me; my Cabinet is the Place where such Affairs are to be treated. On the whole he seem'd rather pleas'd that Mr. Walpole had not come to him, appearing not to like him.— I learnt that Mr. Jay had taken leave the 17th. past of the Spanish Ministers, in order to come hither, so that he may be daily expected. But I hear nothing of Mr. Laurens or Mr. Adams.—

Wednesday June 12th.

I visited Mr. Oswald this Morning. He said he had received the Paper I had sent him relating to the Parole of Lord Cornwallis, and had by conversing with Major Ross convinc'd him of his Error in refusing it. That he saw I had done every thing that could be fairly desired of me, and said every thing in the Paper that could give weight to the temporary Discharge, and tend to prevail with the Congress to confirm and compleat it. Major Ross coming in made an Apology for not having accepted it at first, declar'd his perfect Satisfaction with it, and said he was sure Lord Cornwallis would be very sensible of the Favour. He then mention'd the Custom among military People, that in discharging the Parole of a General that of his Aids was discharg'd at the same time. I answer'd that I was a Stranger to the Customs of the Army; that I had made the most of the Authority I had for Exchanging General Burgoyne, by extending it as a Foundation for the Exchange of Lord Cornwallis; but that I had no Shadow of Authority for going farther; that the Marquis de la Fayette having been present when the Parole was given, and one of the Generals who receiv'd it, was I thought more competent to the Discharge of it than myself: and I could do nothing in it. He went then to the Marquis, who in the Afternoon sent me the Draft of a limited Discharge which he should sign, but requested my Approbation of it, of which I made no Difficulty, though I observ'd he had put into it that it was by my Advice. He appears very prudently cautious of doing any thing that may seem assuming a Power that he is not vested with.—[2]

Friday the 14th. Mr. Boers call'd again, wishing to know if Mr.

---

2. Lafayette gave the declaration to Ross: Lafayette to BF, [June 15 or 22], below. We have not located a copy of it, but it probably resembled the recommendations in Lafayette to BF, June 11, below.

Grenville's Courier was return'd and whether the Treaty was likely to go on. I could give him no Information. He told me that it was intended in Holland in answer to the late Russian Memorial, to say, that they could not now enter into a particular Treaty with England, that they thought it more glorious for her Imperial Majesty to be the Mediatrix in a general Treaty, and wish'd her to name the Place. I said to him, as you tell me that their H. M.[3] are not well satisfied with Russia, and had rather avoid her Mediation, would it not be better to omit the Proposition, at least of her Naming the Place, especially as France and England and America had already agreed to treat at Paris? He replied it might be better, but, says he, we have no Politicians among us. I advis'd him then to write and get that omitted, as I understood it would be a Week before the Answer was concluded on. He did not seem to think his Writing would be of much Importance. I have observ'd that his Colleague M. Vander Pierre has a greater Opinion by far of his own Influence and Consequence.

Saturday the 15th. June, Mr. Oswald came out to Breakfast with me. We afterwards took a Walk in the Garden, when he told me that Mr. Grenville's Courier return'd last Night: that he had receiv'd by him a Letter from Mrs. Oswald, but not a Line from the Ministry, nor had he heard a Word from them since his Arrival. Nor had he heard of any News brought by the Courier. That he should have gone to see Mr. Grenville this Morning, but had omitted it, that Gentleman being subject to Morning Head-Achs which prevented his Rising so early. I said I supposed he would go to Versailles and call upon me in his Return. We had but little farther Discourse, having no new Subject.

Mr. Oswald left me about Noon, and soon after Mr. Grenville came and acquainted me with the Return of his Courier, and that he had brought the full Powers. That he, Mr. G. had been at Versailles and left a Copy with M. de Vergennes. That the Instrument was in the same Terms with the former, except that after the Power to treat with the King of France or his Ministers, there was an Addition of Words importing a Power to treat with the Ministers of any other Prince *or State* whom it might concern.

3. Probably "High Mightinesses," the title given the States General of the Netherlands.

That M. de Vergennes had at first objected to these general Words as not being particular enough, but said he would lay it before the King, and communicate it to the Ministers of the Bellegirent Powers and that Mr. Grenville should hear from him on Monday. Mr. Grenville added, that he had farther inform'd M. de Vergennes of his being now instructed to make a Proposition, as a Basis for the intended Treaty, to wit the Peace of 1763. That the Proposition intended to be made under his first Power, not being then receiv'd was now Changed, and instead of proposing to allow the Independence of America on condition of England's being put into the Situation she was in at the Peace of 1763, he was now Authoriz'd to declare the Independence of America previous to the Treaty as a voluntary Act, and to propose seperately as a Basis the Treaty of '63. This also M. de Vergennes undertook to lay before the King, and communicate to me.[4] Mr. Grenville then said to me, he hop'd all Difficulties were now remov'd, and that we might proceed in the Good Work. I ask'd him if the Enabling Bill was passed? He said, No, It had passed the Commons, and had been committed in the House of Lords, but was not yet compleated. I remark'd that the usual Time approach'd for the Prorogation of Parliament, and possibly this Business might be omitted. He said there was no Danger of that, the Parliament would not rise this Year till the middle of July:— The India Affairs had put back other Business which must be done and would require a Prolongation of the Session till that time.[5] I then observ'd to him; That tho' we Americans considered ourselves as a distinct independent Power or State, yet as the British Government had always hitherto affected to consider us only as rebellious Subjects; and as the enabling Act was not yet pass'd; I did not think it could be fairly suppos'd that his Court intended by the general Words *any other Prince or State* to include a People whom they did not allow to be a State; and that

4. Grenville made another significant concession, telling Vergennes that the Treaty of Paris did not need to be ratified and confirmed in all its points but should serve merely as a basis for discussion: Doniol, *Histoire*, v, 116–17; Giunta, *Emerging Nation*, I, 431–2, 434.

5. Various questions relating to India occupied the attention of the House of Commons from April 15 to May 3, and the House of Lords on May 27: Cobbett, *Parliamentary History*, XXII, 1275–1333, 1411–12; XXIII, 75–6.

therefore I doubted the Sufficiency of his Power as to treating with America, tho' it might be good as to Spain and Holland. He reply'd that he himself had no doubt of the Sufficiency of his Power and was willing to act upon it.—[6] I then desir'd to have a Copy of the Power, which he accordingly promis'd me. He would have enter'd into Conversation on the Topic of Reconciliation; but I chose still to waive it, till I should find the Negociation more certainly commenc'd: and I show'd him the London Paper, containing the Article above transcrib'd, that he might see how our Conversations was misrepresented, and how hazardous it must be for me to make any Propositions of the kind at present. He seem'd to treat the Newspaper lightly as of no Consequence; but I observ'd that before he had finish'd the reading of the Article, he turn'd to the Beginning of the Paper to see the Date, which made me suspect that he doubted whether it might not have taken its rise from some of his Letters.

When he left me, I went to dine with M. de Chaumont, who had invited me to meet there Mr. Walpole at his Request. We shook hands and he observ'd that it was near two years since we had seen each other.[7] Then stepping aside, he thanked me for having communicated to him Lord Shelburne's Letter to Mr. Oswald; thought it odd that Mr. O. himself had not spoken to him about it. Said he had receiv'd a Letter from Mr. Fox upon the Affair of St. Eustatia, in which there were some general Words expressing a Desire of Peace; that he had mentioned this to M. le Marquis de Castries, who had refer'd him to M. de Vergennes, but he did not think it a sufficient Authority for him to go to that

6. Grenville, however, admitted to Fox on June 21, "I have already felt myself under some embarrassment respecting Mr Franklin, not seeing precisely how far the expression of *'Princes and States'* in the Full Power can apply to America till the independence is acknowledged, and knowing that he finds and expresses much doubt about it himself, & some disposition to ask a more explicit description." Grenville thus had been avoiding BF, although he did add that the last time he saw him BF "contented himself with observing that the sooner the independance was declared, the less would the business be retarded": Giunta, *Emerging Nation*, I, 435; Russell, *Memorials and Correspondence of Fox*, IV, 220–3.

7. Walpole had visited France in 1779–80 in conjunction with his lawsuit with William Alexander and his brother: XXX, 635n; XXXI, 117.

Minister; It was known that he had Business with the Ministers of the Marine on the other Affair, and therefore his going to him was not taken Notice of; but if he had gone to M. de Vergennes, Minister of Foreign Affairs, it would have occasion'd Speculation and much Discourse; that he therefore avoided it till he should be authoriz'd, and had written accordingly to Mr. Fox; but that in the mean time Mr. Oswald has been chosen, upon the Supposition that he, (Mr Walpole) and I were at Variance.— He spoke of Mr. Oswald as an odd kind of Man, but that indeed his Nation[8] were generally odd People, &c.— We din'd pleasantly together with the Family and parted agreably without entring into any Particulars of the Business.— Count d'Estaing was at this Dinner, and I met him again in the Evening at Madame Brillon's.— There is at present among the People, much Censure of Comte de Grasse's Conduct, and a general Wish that Comte d'Estaing had the Command in America.— I avoid meddling or ever Speaking on the Subject, as improper for me, tho' I much esteem that Commander.

Sunday the 16th, I heard nothing from Versailles. I receiv'd a Letter from Mr. Adams acquainting me he had drawn upon me for a Quarter's Salary, which he hop'd would be the last, as he now found himself in a way of getting some Money there, tho' not much; But he says not a Word in Answer to my late Letters on publick Affairs, nor have I any Line from Mr. Laurens, which I wonder at.—[9] I receiv'd also a Letter from Mr. Carmichael, dated June 5th. at Madrid. He speaks of Mr. Jay being on his Journey, and supposes he would be with me before that Letter, so that I may expect him daily. We have taken Lodgings for him at Paris.[1]

Monday the 17th. I received a Letter from Mr. Hodgson,[2] acquainting me that the American Prisoners at Portsmouth to the

8. Oswald was Scottish.

9. BF had received JA's letter of June 10 but apparently not his of June 13 (which did discuss the negotiations). The most recent extant letter from Laurens was that of May 20. All of these letters are below.

1. For the lodgings see our annotation of Jay's May 8 letter. Carmichael's letter is missing. He remained at the Spanish court as acting chargé d'affaires: Morris, *Jay: Peace*, p. 147.

2. Below, June 7.

Number of 330. were embark'd on board the Transports; that each had received 20 s. worth of Necessaries at the Expence of Government, and went on board in good Humour. That contrary Winds had prevented the Transports arriving in Time at Plymouth, but that the whole Number now there of our People, amounting to 700. with those arriv'd from Ireland, would soon be on their way home.

In the Evening the Marquis de la Fayette came to see me, and said he had seen M. de Vergennes, who was satisfied with Mr. Grenville's Powers.[3] He asked me what I thought of them; and I told him what I had said to Mr Grenville of their Imperfection with respect to us. He agreed in Opinion with me. I let him know that I propos'd waiting on M. de Vergennes to-morrow. He said he had sign'd the Paper relating to Major Ross's Parole, and hoped Congress would not take it amiss; and added, that in Conversation with the Major, he had ask'd him, why England was so backward to make Propositions? We are afraid says the Major, of offering you more than you expect or desire.

I find myself in some perplexity with regard to these two Negociators. Mr. Oswald appears to be the Choice of Lord Shelburne; Mr. Grenville that of Mr. Secretary Fox. Lord Shelburne is said to have lately acquired much of the King's Confidence:[4] Mr. Fox calls himself the Minister of the People, and it is certain his Popularity is lately much Increased. Lord S. seems to wish to have the Management of the Treaty; Mr. Fox seems to think it in his Department. I hear that the Understanding between these Ministers is not quite perfect. Mr. Grenville is clever, and seems to feel Reason as readily as Mr. Oswald, tho not so ready to own it. Mr. Oswald appears quite plain and sincere: I sometimes a little doubt Mr. Grenville. Mr. Oswald an old Man seems to have

3. On June 20, Vergennes read the Council of State a memorandum entitled "Observations relatives à la pacification," in which he said that Grenville's powers left nothing to be desired (AAE). The memorandum asked the council's advice on whether the Treaty of Paris would be acceptable as a basis for negotiation. That day Louis XVI accepted the council's advice to accept the treaty as a basis, but without confirming what was in it: Dull, *French Navy*, p. 289.

4. At this point in the manuscript there has been inserted, probably in error, an unnumbered page in BF's hand reading only "At Passy, this 21st Day".

now no Desire but that of being Useful in doing Good. Mr. Grenville a young Man naturally desirous of acquiring Reputation, seems to aim at that of being an able Negotiator. Oswald does not solicit to have any share in the Business, but submitting the Matter to Lord S. and me, expresses only his willingness to serve if we think he may be useful, and is equally willing to be excus'd if we judge there is no occasion for him. Grenville seems to think the whole Negociation committed to him, and to have no Idea of Oswald's being concern'd in it; and is therefore willing to extend the Expressions in his Commission, so as to make them comprehend America, and this beyond what I think they will bear.— I imagine we might however go on very well with either of them, tho' I should rather prefer Oswald; but I apprehend Difficulties if they are both employ'd, especially if there is any misunderstanding between their Principals. I must however write to Lord S. proposing something in consequence of his Offer of vesting Mr. Oswald with any Commission that Gentleman and I should think proper.

Tuesday the 18th. I found myself much indispos'd with a Sudden and violent Cold, attended with a Feverishness and Headach. I imagin'd it to be an Effect of the Influenza a Disorder now reigning in various Parts of Europe. This prevented my going to Versailles.

Thursday 20th. Weather Excessively hot, and my Disorder continues, but is lessen'd, the Head-ach having left me. I am however not yet able to go to Versailles.

Friday 21st, I receiv'd the following Note from the Marquis de la Fayette.—[5]

In the Ev'ning the Marquis call'd upon me, and acquainted me that Mr. Grenville had been with Comte de Vergennes, but could not inform me what had pass'd.[6]

Saturday the 22nd. Messrs. Oswald and Whitefoord came and breakfasted with me. Mr. O. had receiv'd no Letters, or Instruc-

---

5. The two transcripts here give Lafayette's letter of June 20, below, reporting on his meeting with Vergennes.

6. Vergennes informed Grenville of the King's decision to negotiate on the basis of the treaty without confirming its stipulations: Doniol, *Histoire*, v, 117–18; Giunta, *Emerging Nation*, I, 432–4.

tions. I told him I would write to Lord Shelburne respecting him, and call on him on Monday morning, to breakfast, and show him what I propos'd to write, that it might receive such Alterations as he should judge proper.

Sunday the 23d. In the Afternoon Mr. Jay arriv'd to my great Satisfaction.[7] I propos'd going with him the next Morning to Versailles, and presenting him to Mr. Vergennes.— He inform'd me that the Spanish Ministers had been much struck with the News from England respecting the Resolutions of Parliament to discontinue the War in America, &c, and that they had since been extremely civil to him, and he understood intended to send Instructions to their Ambassador at this Court to make the Long talk'd of Treaty with him here.

Monday the 24th. Wrote a Note of Excuse to Mr. Oswald, promising to see him on Wednesday,[8] and went with Mr. Jay to Versailles. M. de Vergennes acquainted us, that he had given to Mr. Grenville the Answer to his Propositions, who had immediately dispatch'd it to his Court. He read it to us, and I shall endeavour to obtain a Copy of it.[9]

M. de Vergennes informing us that a Frigate was about to be dispatch'd for America, by which we might write, and that the Courier who was to carry down the Dispatches would set off on Wednesday Morning, we concluded to omit coming to Court on Tuesday, in order to prepare our Letters.— M. de Vergennes appeared to have some doubts about the Sincerity of the British Court, and the *Bonne foi* of Mr. Grenville: but said the Return of Mr. Grenville's Courier might give Light.[1]

---

7. Jay wrote Livingston two days later, "I shall endeavor to get lodgings as near to Dr. Franklin as I can. He is in perfect good health, and his mind appears more vigorous than that of any man of his age I have known. He certainly is a valuable minister, and an agreeable companion." Wharton, *Diplomatic Correspondence*, V, 517.

8. BF's note to Oswald is no longer extant.

9. Here a slip of paper in an unknown hand has been inserted. It reads, "24th June. M. de Vergennes Answer to Mr Grenville about the 20th. June wanting". This answer, delivered orally on June 21, was based on Louis XVI's decision of June 20 to accept the Treaty of Paris as a basis for negotiation. A translation is published in Giunta, *Emerging Nation*, I, 432–3.

1. WTF's publication of this journal includes here the following paragraph: "I received the following letter from Mr. Adams, dated the Hague, June 13,

I wrote the following Letters to Mr. Secry Livingston and Mr. Morris—vizt.[2]

Wednesday 26th. I sent away my Letters, and went to see Mr. Oswald. I show'd him the Draft of a Letter to be address'd to him instead of Lord S. respecting the Commission or publick Character he might hereafter be vested with; this Draft was founded on Lord Shelburne's Memorandums which Mr. Oswald had shown to me, and this Letter was intended to be communicated by him to Lord Shelburne. Mr. Oswald lik'd the Mode; but rather chose that no mention should be made of his having shown me Lord S's Memorandums, tho' he thought they were given him for that purpose. So I struck that part out,[3] and new-model'd the Letter which I sent him next day: as follows.

⟨June 27: Franklin informs Oswald he would prefer negotiating with him rather than Grenville.[4]⟩

Friday 28th June. Mr. de Reneval call'd upon me, and acquainted me that the Ministers had receiv'd Intelligence from England, that besides the Orders given to General Carleton to propose Terms of Reunion to America, artful Emissaries were sent over to go thro' the Country, and stir up the People to call on the Congress to accept those Terms, they being similar to those now settling with Ireland.[5] That it would therefore be well

---

1782." The text of the letter follows (wtf, *Memoirs*, ii, 373–4). None of the MS copies of BF's journal contain this letter, which we publish under June 13.

2. Another inserted slip of paper reads, "24 June—2 Letters to Mr Secy Livingston & Mr Morris not in Draft a Copy not to be found". The letters to Livingston and Morris were dated June 25 and are published below. The frigate in question may have been the *Aigle;* see our annotation of BF's letter to Morris.

3. BF's draft is published below, June 26.

4. A copy of this letter in L'Air de Lamotte's hand is bound in the journal.

5. Shelburne did send his private secretary, Dr. Maurice Morgann (*DNB*), to New York to help Gen. Guy Carleton's efforts "to reconcile and reunite the Affections and Interests of Great Britain and the Colonies": Harlow, *Second British Empire*, i, 264–8. Vergennes received warnings about Carleton from La Luzerne; see, for example, his letter of May 19 in Giunta, *Emerging Nation*, i, 394. Carleton's efforts were futile; see Livingston to BF, May 22.

for Mr. Jay and me to write and caution the Congress against these Practices. He said Mr. de Vergennes wish'd also to know what I had written respecting the Negotiation, as it would be well for us to hold pretty near the same Language. I told him I did not apprehend the least Danger that such Emissaries would meet with any Success, or that the Congress would make any Treaty with General Carleton. That I would however write as he desired; and Mr. Jay coming in, promis'd the same. He said the Courier would go to-morrow. I accordingly wrote the following Letter to Mr. Secretary Livingston.—[6]

Mr. de Renneval (who is Secretary to the Council of State) calling again in the Evening, I gave him Copies of the preceding Letters[7] to peruse and show to Mr: de Vergennes; to convince them that we held no underhand dealings here. I own I had at the same time another View in it, which was that they should see I have been order'd to demand farther Aids, and had forborne to make the Demand, with my Reasons; hoping that if they could possibly help us to more Money, they might be induc'd to do it.

I had never made any Visit to Count d'Aranda, the Spanish Ambassador, for reasons before mention'd.[8] Mr. de Renneval told Mr. Jay and me this Morning, that it would be well for us to wait on him,[9] and he had Authority to assure us we should be well receiv'd. We accordingly concluded to wait on his Excellency the next Morning.

Saturday June 29.

We went together to the Spanish Ambassador's, who receiv'd us with great Civility and Politeness. He spoke with Mr. Jay

6. BF's June 29 letter to Livingston (below) was not incorporated into any of the extant versions of this journal.

7. BF may also have included his June 28 letter to Cooper, as WTF included an extract of it at this point in his printing of the journal: WTF, *Memoirs*, II, 378–9.

8. *I.e.*, so as not to risk Aranda's not returning his visit, the same reason BF had not visited other ambassadors. BF had paid Aranda a visit several years earlier in company with Arthur Lee and Silas Deane: XXIII, 89–90, 114, 173–80.

9. Upon arriving in Paris, Jay had notified Aranda of his readiness to begin negotiations: Morris, *Jay: Peace*, pp. 242–3.

on the Subject of the Treaty they were to make together, and mention'd in General as a Principle that the two Powers should consider each other's Conveniency, and accommodate and compensate each other as well as they could. That an exact Compensation might perhaps not be possible, but should be approach'd as nearly as the Nature of Things would admit. Thus says he if there is a certain Thing that would be convenient to each of us, but more convenient to one than the other, it should be given to the One to whom it would be most convenient, and Compensation be made by giving another thing to the other for the same reason. I suppose he had in View something relating to Boundaries or Territories, because he added, We will set down together with Maps in our hands, and by that means shall see our Way more clearly. I learnt from him that the Expedition against Providence[1] had sail'd, but no Advice was yet receiv'd of its Success. At our going out he took the pains himself to open the folding-doors for us, which is a high Compliment here: And he told us, he would return our Visit (*rendre son devoir*) and then fix a day with us for dining with him. I din'd with Mr. Jay and a Company of Americans at his Lodgings.

Sunday July 1st.

Mr. Grenville called on me[2]

---

1. The island of New Providence, where Nassau (the capital of the Bahamas) is located. On April 22, an expedition of 60 ships and 2,250 officers and soldiers sailed from Havana to attack it: James A. Lewis, *Neptune's Militia: the Frigate* South Carolina *during the American Revolution* (Kent, Ohio, and London, 1999), pp. 66–7.

2. When he sent this journal to Robert Livingston on Dec. 5, BF explained that "accidents and a long severe illness" interrupted his writing: Wharton, *Diplomatic Correspondence*, VI, 112.

From Johann Valentin Embser[3]

ALS: American Philosophical Society

Monsieur   aux Deux-Ponts ce 9 Mai 1782.

Nous obéissons aux ordres de Votre Excellence, en Lui faisant parvenir par le canal de Monsieur Grand à Paris les 26 volumes de la Collection complette des anciens auteurs Romains publiés jusqu'ici, & 1 volume des Grecs, pour la somme de 55 Livres de france.[4]

Nous souhaitons, que ces ouvrages puissent mériter l'approbation éclairée de Votre Excellence. Elle remarquera de la différence dans l'execution, qui vient de ce que les prémiers volumes de cette Collection ayant été faits avant l'établissement d'une imprimerie particuliere n'ont point été imprimés avec l'attention nécessaire.[5]

Nous avons jugé, que le texte d'après la meilleure édition, imprimé avec la plus exacte correction & délivré au plus bas prix possible, fait l'objet principal pour le bien de la jeunesse. Aussi n'avons nous rien négligé pour le remplir. La vie de l'auteur, une notice littéraire & un catalogue des éditions précedent chaque auteur, & nous ajoutons toûjours les index nécessaires.

Le second volume de Platon, qui est fini, n'a pu être joint à ce paquet, parceque l'estampe nous n'est pas encore parvenue. Mais ce volume sera délivré avec Quinte Curce & Lucrece, qui occupent maintenant nos presses avec le douzieme volume de Cicéron.[6]

3. In answer to BF's order of Jan. 15 (XXXVI, 433).
4. Grand paid this sum on July 24, for books shipped from Strasbourg by Hohlenfeld & Embser: Account XVII (XXVI, 3). The accounts indicate that Embser was charging 3 *l.t.* for Greek volumes, not the 4 *l.t.* he initially quoted (XXXVI, 388).
5. Evidently the "imprimerie particuliere" was established at Strasbourg. The place of publication for the *Societas bipontina* remained Zweibrücken (Deux-Ponts) until 1798, when it became Strasbourg: John Edwin Sandys, *A History of Classical Scholarship* (3 vols., Cambridge, 1908–21; reprint, New York and London, 1967), II, 396–7.
6. On Sept. 5, Grand paid 9 *l.t.* for another shipment of books from Hohlenfeld & Embser, presumably the three Latin works and the volume of Plato. An undated note in Embser's hand (APS) lists the twelfth volume of Cicero as well as several other works published in 1782, with their prices, and announces the next works to be issued.
As BF's private account with Grand makes clear, Hohlenfeld & Embser con-

Puisse le Ciel combler Votre Excellence de ses plus beaux présens! & faire fleurir jusqu'aux siècles les plus reculés le nouveau peuple de l'autre hémisphère, qui par les lumières, la sagesse et la fermeté de Votre Excellence jouit des droits les plus précieux de l'humanité!

J'ai l'honneur d'être avec le plus profond réspect de Votre Excellence le très humble & très obéissant Serviteur

EMBSER
Professeur au College Ducal

Notation: Embser, Deux-Ponts 9. May 1784

From Jonathan Shipley   ALS: Historical Society of Pennsylvania

Bolton Street May 9th.—82

It is with the utmost pleasure I feel an Hour is at last arrivd, when I can write without impropriety to my dear & respectable Friend.[7] You will be so just to me as to believe that my silence was not owing to neglect or indifference. Great caution was necessary to be observd by one of my rank & profession, who was acting in open opposition to an unsuccessful, detested & enrag'd Ministry. Even now I debar myself from the mention of any subject which concerns our publick situation, till the return of Peace which We all long for, & the Safety & Liberty that attends it. In the mean time I flatter myself with the hopes of seeing You once more & renewing those delightful Conversations that are still present to my Memory. Do You still relish your old Studies & sometimes make use of that Key to the secrets of Nature, which She seems to have trusted to your care as to her particular Favourite? But tho Science has certainly lost, America has gaind much more by your change of Employment. And after all the noblest Employment that falls to the Lot of Man is to serve our

---

tinued to supply BF with volumes even after he returned to America. The dates of their remittances are June 30, 1783; Aug. 2, 1784; April 5 and May 2, 1785; March 23 and Oct. 20, 1786; and [May?] 20, 1787. Account XVII.

7. This is the bishop of St. Asaph's first extant letter to BF in almost seven years. For the last one see XXII, 78–83.

Country & to make Men better & happier. (I have not the Vanity at this instant to think of Preaching or writing; but to do it as You have done by advantageous Treaties & wise Laws & Statutes.) As for me I have employd myself as occasion offerd in feebly supporting the same good Cause in which You left me engagd & which experience has renderd more dear to me even than Truth & Reason. I have found it not difficult to make some impression on disinterested or indifferent Men; but I must own I never was so lucky as to make a Convert of one who either had a Place or wishd for one. But my great resource has been to seek a refuge from Publick Misery in domestick Happiness. That dear Family of mine takes a pride in continuing to love & admire You.[8] Indeed they almost look upon You as something more than human.

We have now a new Ministry; with all of whom I have acquaintance & some degree of Friendship. Their present intentions are good & the People are their Friends; but I most want to see whether they have the Sense to make a right use of Power before I form my opinion.

The Bearer Mr. Laurens, who I hope will allow me to call him my Friend, is much respected here for his good Sense & every body must love him for his mild & benevolent Heart,[9]

Adieu my dear venerable Friend & let me hope that I may once more be happy in your Society Your ever obligd & affectiont   J St Asaph

Dr Franklin

Notation: Asoph 9. May 1782.

8. For his wife and their six children see XVIII, 136–7, 199–202.
9. Laurens left for the continent the following day; see our annotation of Laurens' April 30 letter to BF.

From Thomas Grenville[1]

AL and copy:[2] Library of Congress; transcripts: Massachusetts Historical Society, National Archives

Paris May 10. [1782]

Mr Grenville presents his Compliments to Mr Franklin; he proposes sending a Courier to England at 10 o'clock to-night, & will give him in charge any letters Mr Franklin may wish to send by him.

Addressed: Benjamin Franklin Esqr / &c—&c—&c / a Passy / ½ past 1. o'clock.

To Charles James Fox

LS[3] and two copies: Public Record Office; press copy of LS, and copy:[4] Library of Congress; transcripts: Massachusetts Historical Society, National Archives

Sir,   Passy, May 10th. 1782.

I received the Letter you did me the honour of writing to me by Mr Grenville,[5] whom I find to be a very sensible, judicious and amiable Gentleman. The Name I assure you does not with me lessen the Regard his excellent Qualities inspire. I introduced him as soon as possible to M. De Vergennes; he will himself give you an Account of his Reception. I hope his Coming may forward the blessed Work of Pacification, in which for the sake of Humanity no time should be lost; no reasonable Cause, as you observe, existing at present, for the continuance of this abominable War. Be assured of my best Endeavours to put an End to

1. When BF received this letter, he immediately wrote to Fox and Shelburne, below. See BF's journal of the peace negotiations.
2. The copy and transcripts are in BF's journal of the peace negotiations.
3. In WTF's hand, except for the last seven words of the complimentary close, which are in BF's hand.
4. This copy and the transcripts are in BF's journal of the peace negotiations.
5. Above, May 1.

it. I am much flatter'd by the good Opinion of a Person whom I have long highly esteem'd, and I hope it will not be lessen'd by my Conduct in the Affair that has given Rise to our Correspondence.

With great Respect, I have the honour to be, Sir, Your most obedient and most humble Servant   B FRANKLIN

Honble. C. J. Fox Esqr Secretary of State, &c

Endorsed: Passy May 10th: 1782. Dr. Franklin. R. 14th: (by Lauzun.)[6]

To Thomas Grenville

AL (draft)[7] and copy:[8] Library of Congress; transcripts: Massachusetts Historical Society, National Archives

Passy Friday Evening May 10.— [1782]
Mr Franklin presents his Compliments to Mr Grenville, with Thanks for the Information of his Courier's Departure, and his kind Offer of forwarding Mr F.'s Letters, who accepts the Favour, & encloses two.[9]

The Marquis de la Fayette & Mr Oswald will do Mr Franklin the honour of breakfasting with him to-morrow between 9 and 10 oClock. Mr Franklin will be happy to have the Company also of Mr Grenville if agreable to him. He should have waited on Mr Grenville to day at Paris, but that he imagin'd Mr G. was at Versailles.

6. Lauzun was Grenville's courier: Fox to Grenville, May 21, in Lord John Russell, *Memorials and Correspondence of Charles James Fox* (4 vols., London, 1853–57), IV, 191.

7. Drafted on the same sheet as Grenville's note written earlier in the day (above). BF marked Grenville's note "A" and this answer "B".

8. The copy and transcripts are in BF's journal of the peace negotiations.

9. His letters to Fox and Shelburne of this date.

To the Earl of Shelburne

LS:[1] Public Record Office; press copy of LS, and copy:[2] Library of Congress; transcripts: Massachusetts Historical Society, National Archives

My Lord,   Passy, May 10th. 1782.

I have received the honour of your Lordships Letter, dated the 28th past, by Mr Oswald, informing me that he is sent back to settle with me the Preliminaries of Time & Place. Paris as the Place seem'd to me Yesterday to be agreed on between Mr Grenville & M. de Vergennes, and it is perfectly agreable to me. The Time cannot well be settled 'till this Court has received Answers from Madrid and the Hague, and untill my Colleagues are arrived. I expect daily Messrs. Jay and Lawrens; Mr Adams doubts whether he can be here,[3] but that will not hinder our Proceeding.

It gave me great Pleasure to learn that Mr Lawrens is discharged entirely from the obligations he had entred into. I am much obliged by the Readiness with which your Lordship has confer'd that Favour. Please to accept my thankful Acknowledgements.

I am happy too in understanding from your Letter that Transports are actually preparing to convey our Prisoners to America, and that Attention will be paid to their Accommodation and good Treatment. Those People on their Return will be dispersed thro' every Part of America, and the Accts. they will have to give of any Marks of Kindness received by them under the *present* Ministry, will lessen much the Resentment of their Friends against the Nation, for the Hardships they suffer'd under the *past*.—

Mr Oswald rests here awhile by my Advice, as I think his Presence likely to be useful.—

With great & sincere Respect, I have the honour to be, My Lord, Your Lordship's most obedt and most humble Servant

B FRANKLIN

Rt. Honble. the Earl of Shelburne

Endorsed: 10th. May 1782 Doctr. Franklin

1. In WTF's hand, except for the last six words of the complimentary close, which are in BF's hand.
2. The copy and transcripts are in BF's journal of the peace negotiations.
3. See JA's letter of May 2.

From Edmund Clegg

ALS: American Philosophical Society

Hond Sir   London May 10: 1782

I Received a Letter from Mr Wyld dated the 29th of April, the 4th instant. I waited to have your reply to the one or other of my former ones to you, but being disappointed; I trouble you with this.

I find as I wrote before, that they are gone so far in the Country in getting ready to go over that delays will now be of very bad Consequence to them all & I am in such suspence as is in some respects inconvenient. I always advised them in my Letters, not to be over hasty: But as matters now stand with them—I do, most humbly, & earnestly beg; the utmost you can do towards their safe Passage; and proper directions as to the mode of embarking— I know if you knew their Situation—you would tenderly feel for them, & if kind Providence ever brings us safe over— I am firmly perswaded You will be so far from repenting your Patronage: that you will look forwards with pleasure to the fruit arising from the Planting of such a concern which I hope, when Wars are over, will Yeild you Prospects of promoteing the rising greatness of your country in the Arts of Peace.

It is my Judgement that the Silk business will be the first brought to perfection— But I could tell with more certainty if I knew the kinds of Silk the Country Produces— I hear some Gentlemen of Large Fortunes from the Neighbourhood of Derby are designing to go over to set up their Trade in that Country which is the throwing of Silk— I have no knowledge of them, But I think if they were to put the raisers of Silk into a Perfect Method of reeling it from the Worm—that would be a very great improvement. Neither the Assiatics nor many of the Europeans do that business as it ought to be, a very little extra, trouble and care would add near 10 per Cent to the Value of Raw silks.

I long to see the day, when we shall be able to unite in One our own Intrest and that of the Country which We have so fully set our Hearts upon—and beg leave to say expectation is upon the tiptoe for a favourable reply from you. In the mean time—I am Hond: Sir Your most obedt & most humble sert

EDMUND CLEGG

His Excellency Benjamin Franklin LLD &c

Addressed: Monsr à / Monsuir Franklin / Passi

Notation: Edmund Clegg London. may 10 1782.

From Francis Dana

Copy:[4] Massachusetts Historical Society

St: Petersbourg April 29th.

Dear Sir,   [*i.e.,* May 10,] 1782. OS.[5]

In your letter to me of the 11th. of May last,[6] which I received in Holland, you proposed the money I might have occasion for there, and shou'd take up on account of the United States, shou'd be considered as part of Mr: Grand's credit which you procured me on the house of Messrs: Strahlborn & Wolff of this city. The proposition was perfectly agreable to me, and I have governed myself accordingly. In Holland I took up Three hundred pounds sterlg: of Messrs: Fezeau & Grand. I also drew upon you for about One hundred pounds in favour of Messrs: De Neufville & Son. The sum mentioned in the letter of credit[7] has been due to me since the 15th. of last March (.N.S.). I have this day taken up of Messieurs Strahlborne & Wolff a sum which, together with what I have heretofore received of them, and the Four hundred pounds received in Holland, amounts to the sum mentioned in the letter of credit;[8] so that according to your proposition there is an end of that. I must therefore request you to furnish me with a credit for another year, as soon as may be convenient, that I may not be under a necessity of breaking in upon your arrangement with Mr: Grand. The first letter may be either cancelled as to the residue, or the second given for so much less. I shall hope for your answer by the return post, and the second letter of

---

4. Dana copied both this letter and an unsent version, dated April 27, in his letterbook. The latter has been crossed out.

5. The "Old Style" or Julian calendar used in Russia at the time differed by 11 days from the "New Style" or Gregorian calendar used in America and western Europe.

6. XXXV, 53–4.

7. £1,500 sterling: XXXV, 62.

8. In the unsent version Dana had proposed to draw for an additional £250.

credit, if convenient to you. Near two months will necessarily intervene.

We yesterday received the news that the States General had on the 19th. of April (.N.S.) acknowledged the independence of the United States.[9] This event gave a shock here; and is not well received, as they at least profess to have flattered themselves that the mediation wou'd have prevented it, and otherwise brought on a partial peace between Britain and Holland. This resentment, I believe, will not be productive of any ill consequences to the Dutch Republick. We have a report that Charlestown is evacuated by the enemy. You wou'd greatly oblige me by a communication of any news you may receive from our Country from time to time. Shou'd you be too much engaged yourself, a letter from Mr: Franklin, to whom I beg you to present my regards, wou'd be very acceptable.

I am with much esteem, Dear Sir, your most obedient & most humble Servant

Mr: Franklin

His Excellency Benj: Franklin Minister Plenipotentiary &c

By the Post of the 4th. of May[1]

From Thomas Grenville[2]

Copy:[3] Library of Congress; transcripts: Massachusetts Historical Society, National Archives

Paris Friday 10.[4] [May 10, 1782]

Mr. Grenville presents his Compliments to Mr. Franklin and will with great pleasure do himself the honour of breakfasting with

9. This initiated closer relations between Dana and Johan Isaac de Swart, the Dutch minister who delivered the news: Taylor, *J. Q. Adams Diary,* 1, 126.

1. BF received this letter on June 9: BF's journal of the peace negotiations.

2. Grenville's first letter of May 10, above, elicited an answer from BF, to which this is the response.

3. The copy and transcripts are in BF's journal of the peace negotiations.

4. The "10" is written over "Evn" (presumably for evening).

Mr. Franklin to morrow between 9 and 10 0 Clock. Mr. Grenville was at Versailles to day, and should have been sorry that Mr. Franklin should have given himself the trouble of calling at Paris this Morning. The Courier shall certainly take particular care of Mr. Franklin's Letters.

From Hilliard d'Auberteuil

ALS: University of Pennsylvania Library

Monsieur   à Paris le 10e. Mai 1782
    J'ai l'honneur de vous envoyer une épreuve de mon ouvrage, ma mauvaise santé m'a privé de rendre mes devoirs à votre excellence, et a aussi retardé l'impression, mais je vais reparer le tems que j'ai perdu malgré moi.
    Je suis avec respect de votre excellence Le très humble & très obéissant serviteur   HILLIARD D'AUBERTEUIL

Notation: Dauberteuil. 10. May 1782.

From William Hodgson   ALS: American Philosophical Society

Dear sir   London 10 May 1782
    I have duly rec'd your sundry favors to the 27th Ultimo the exchange of Prisoners I hope will take place in the course of next week— The Transports I am told are ready & there remains nothing to be settled so that as soon as the necessary Forms of Office are gone thro' I expect they will be sent away.[5]

5. On May 8, the Admiralty wrote the Commissioners for Sick and Wounded Seamen setting down the conditions for the exchange of prisoners with America. It specified that prisoners from Forton and Mill prisons were to be sent forthwith to America aboard transports provided for that purpose and were to be supplied provisions at the expense of the British government. Prisoners from New England were to be sent to Boston, others to the Chesapeake or Philadelphia. They were not to be allowed to go to any other country, and if they seized control of a transport and sailed to France they were to be sent to America. Once in America they were to be exchanged for an

Administration have at my request given directions to the Navy Agents, at the several ports of embarkation, to supply such Prisoners as may stand in need with Slops to an Amount not exceeding 20 s. each Man, so that they will gt away decently & comfortably provided with necessary's for the Voyage.

You will see the necessity of not losing Time in forwarding to me such Letters as you may chuse to send to Congress or Individuals by the Cartel Vessells & perhaps it may be prudent to send duplicates by different Vessells, If I do not hear from you in Time I shall send to Mr Thompson a Copy of the Agreements into which I have entered, in order that Congress may not be uninformed on the Subject, as it may be necessary for them to give some Directions on the Occasion.[6]

I presented to the Noble Personage[7] pursuant to request your thanks for his kindness & attention to your People & Yet if the Publick form, a true Estimate of the Principles of great Men, the true kindness from Principle & Conviction lies in another Quarter of Administration[8] & as that party is the strongest I, in my own Mind have no Doubt but that every reasonable Concession will be made, so that we may indulge ourselves with the pleasing hopes of seeing Peace in our Days upon solid & permanent Principles.

I had the pleasure some little Time ago of dining with your Friends, Dr Priestley, Dr Price, Mr Jones & Mr Paradise, who all desired to be remembred to you in the kindest manner. Mr Jones in particular seemed to fear he had not rec'd a Letter from you, which he believed you had honoured him with.[9]

Mr Grand has not remitted me, I believe my disburse will

---

equal number of imprisoned British seamen, soldiers, or marines, who were to be sent to whatever post was selected by the British commander in chief in America. If soldiers from Cornwallis' army were exchanged, provisions should be provided for them at American expense. The transports were to be given safe passage from any state presently at war with Britain: "Conditions of the Exchange of Prisoners with America," May 8, 1782 (APS).

6. On June 6, Hodgson sent Secretary of Congress Charles Thomson a copy of the conditions, noting that they had been agreed upon by him and Shelburne's representative Evan Nepean. National Archives.

7. Shelburne.

8. Presumably the other secretary of state, Fox.

9. William Jones wrote as much to BF on March 5: XXXVI, 655.

amount to about £280— I am not quite certain, but when the Prisoners are gone I will make up the Acco't, & if more convenient for me to draw, than you to Remitt I shall act in Conformity, the disburse at present is no Inconvenience to me.[1]

I return you my best thanks for your kind Communication,[2] not a little mortified, that I am deprived of the pleasure of paying my Respects to you on an Occasion at once so honorable & agreable—however I hope the Business will be as effectually done by those in whose hands it is at present.— May I trespass so far on your Friendship as to request you wou'd give me the earliest Information of the apparent Conclusion of the Business one way or the other, I mean when it comes to the Point, that there either *will or will not* be a Congress to Treat on Terms of Pacification, if on such an Occasion you wou'd be Kind enough to dispatch a special Messenger, I will pay his Expences & satisfy him for his Trouble directing him to come in the most expeditious Way possible because the common post will not give Time enough the Information that may be of use, so soon *as Secretarys Secretarys* will receive it with the greatest Esteem & Respect I remain Dr sir yrs Sincerely WILLIAM HODGSON

Benj. Franklin Esqr

From Edmund Clegg

ALS: American Philosophical Society

Hond Sir London May: 11: 1782

I this day recd Your Packet enclosing—two Letters one for me—A Coppy of one sent Mr Wyld the 31 March with another now with the Pass—& the other two Letters of Recommendation—[3] I find both by Yours & Mr Wylds, that We have Misunderstood the Conference betwixt him and You— I wrote by Mr Hodgsons Conveyance last night, and yet I thought it my duty to own the rect: of Your Papers for which I return you my most humble thanks.— I have another reason for troubling you with

1. For Hodgson's accounts see our annotation of his March 22 letter.
2. Of April 13, above.
3. BF's letter to Clegg is above, April 26. His March 31 letter to Wyld is also above, but the other documents mentioned here are missing.

this viz The ignorance of my Country frds in attempting to take over any English Manufactured Goods for now they are informed of their danger it will not only be the highest folly for their own sakes—but an insult upon your Patronage— I Purpose therefore to set out with the Papers to morrow night by the Coach—to set them right in that matter, and to Perswade them if they can now by any means do it, to wait for a Peace; as I did always earnestly advise them— I do not think Mr Wyld Capable of a design'd deception, but having seen little of the great World, and having been very little conversant with men of high rank—I think his ready admittance to so high a Character as I have the Pleasure and honor now to address—may have made him a little too sanguin and impatient to be gone at all events. However he has set me quite right as to the expences of the Voyage— His representation of the Company being Persons of Property was also very Just, except a very few which the rest will assist— Indeed I find no fault with them but that of being too Precipitate in their Resolution of going now at all events & as it is so, I design to run all hazards with them, if I find they really can no way will avoid going this summer, on acct: of the steps they have taken, when I get down.

I have taken much pains to see Mr Laurens—and was this morning able to see him for the first time. He recd me with Polite kindness but the event was Just as I expected. "He told me he had, had many Applications, but his Situation did not allow him to attend to them—as he would not committ a transgression"— I reply'd I was affraid before I waited upon him—that the delicacy of his Situation, would not allow a more favourable attention. I had his promise of some Notice at a future time.

I am so anxious to be on the other side the Atlantic—and at the same time, to have my frds act with the best Prospects before them, they can—considering, how they have push'd themselves forward, that I don't know any thing I could have done more to prevent hasty steps hurting them and again acknowledge our obligations to you to put us, as far as you can out of danger.

I am Hond: sir Your most obt & Very Humble Sert
EDMUND CLEGG

His Excellency B: Franklin Pleny &c &c

Addressed: Monsuer à / Monsr Franklin / Passi

Notation: Edmund Clegg London. 11. May 1782.

From Hilliard d'Auberteuil   ALS: American Philosophical Society

Monsieur   Paris ce 11. Mai 1782.
J'ai l'honneur d'envoyer à votre excellence quatre nouvelles épreuves.[4] J'espere que cette 3e. partie pourra être achevée d'imprimer la semaine prochaine.
Je suis avec respect de votre excellence Le très humble & très obéist. servr.   HILLIARD D'AUBERTEUIL

From John Foulke[5]   ALS: University of Pennsylvania Library

Sir   Paris May 12th. 82
I have the honor to enclose to your Excelly. your letter upon the little insect Ephemere which miss Alexander put into my hands to copy for her with the request to forward it immediately to your Excelly.[6]

---

4. These may have included the fourth signature (feuille D), which contained an extensive passage about BF: his early career, his arrival in France, his appearance and reputation. He never went to Paris except when accompanied by an entourage of people, some of them brilliant; his simple attire and noble bearing excited curiosity and respect; he attended meetings of the Académie des sciences and the Académie française, hearings at the Parlement, exhibitions at the Salon, and events at the Société libre d'émulation and the lodge of the Nine Sisters. *Essais historiques et politiques . . .* , II, 60–5.

5. Foulke had gone to Leipzig in the fall of 1781, and in January wrote WTF that he planned to go to Berlin and Dresden in about two months, and then return to Paris: XXXV, 585–6; Foulke to WTF, Jan. 12, 1782 (APS).

6. BF circulated manuscript copies of his letter written to Mme Brillon and known as "The Ephemera" long after its composition in 1778. He eventually printed the piece as part of his collection of bagatelles; see XXVII, 430–5. The Alexander daughter who was at this time visiting Paris was Bethia; see our annotation of William Alexander to BF, April 24, and Rouaix to BF, May 12.

I have the honor to be with the most profound respect Your obliged & sincere friend & very Hl sert.— JOHN FOULKE

His Excelly. Doctr Franklin Passy

Addressed: His Excellency / Benjamin Franklin Esqr. / Minister Plenipotentiary / from the United states of / North America / Passy near / Paris—

From Thomas Percival

AL: American Philosophical Society

Manchester May 12. 1782.
Doctor Percival requests the honour of Doctor Franklin's acceptance of the inclosed Volumes, as Memorials of his cordial Esteem and respect.—[7]

From ——— Rouaix[8]

ALS: American Philosophical Society

Monsieur   Toulouse ce 12e mai 1782
    Je viens d'apprendre par une lettre du superieur général de nôtre congrégation,[9] que vous avés bien voulu accepter la dédi-

7. This is Percival's first extant letter since January, 1775: XXI, 446. The volumes he enclosed were probably his *A Father's Instructions* (for which see XXXVI, 288n) and the first edition of its sequel, *A Socratic Discourse on Truth and Faithfulness* . . . (Warrington, 1781).
8. Rouaix (*c.* 1744–1825) was a member of the Congrégation des Pères de la Doctrine chrétienne, a teaching and preaching order founded during the Counter-Reformation: Pierre Genevray, *L'Administration et la vie ecclésiastiques dans le grand diocèse de Toulouse* . . . (Paris and Toulouse, 1940), pp. 466, 485; Georges Baccrabère, "Le Renouveau catholique (fin XVIe siècle–1715)" in *Le Diocèse de Toulouse,* ed. Philippe Wolff (Paris, 1983), pp. 129–30.
9. Pierre Bonnefoux, whose first letter to BF is below, May 22. Evidently Bethia Alexander had intervened on his behalf and persuaded BF to accept the dedication of this thesis. Bonnefoux thanked her in an undated letter addressed to "Mademoiselle Alexandre chès Madame la Comtesse de la Marck Cour des princes Aux thuileries" (University of Pa. Library). He went on to request an imprint of BF's seal bearing his coat of arms and a list of the titles

cace d'une these générale de philosophie dans nôtre college;[1] et je m'empresse de vous temoigner, combien je suis flatté de rendre un hommage public a un des plus grands physiciens de ce siecle, et au representant D'un peuple, qui fixe L'attention de L'univers entier. Je regarde cette circonstance comme la plus glorieuse de ma vie; et je croirai avoir assés fait pour ma gloire si cet hommage est digne de vous.

Je suis avec respect Monsieur vôtre très humble et très obeissant serviteur

ROUAIX

professeur de philosophie au college de Lesquile[2]

Notation: Rouaix, Toulouse 12 May 1782.

To David Hartley

LS:[3] American Philosophical Society; copy:[4] Library of Congress; transcripts: Massachusetts Historical Society, National Archives

My dear Friend,   Passy, May 13. 1782.

I have just received your Favour of the 3d. Instant. I thank you much for the good News you give me, that "an Order is issued

---

BF used on public occasions. BF was also to ask the Académie des sciences of Toulouse to represent him at the ceremony. The abbé de La Roche drafted a letter to the Académie from BF; it is filed with Bonnefoux's letter to Bethia Alexander.

The Académie royale des sciences, inscriptions et belles-lettres, its full title, was constituted in 1746 and comprised several older learned societies: Michel Taillefer, *Une Académie interprète des lumières: L'Académie des Sciences, Inscriptions et Belles-Lettres de Toulouse au XVIIIe siècle* (Paris, 1984), pp. 5–15.

1. The more usual practice for secondary students in their last year was to dedicate a thesis to a member of the Académie of Toulouse and defend it before several of its members: Taillefer, *Une Académie interprète des lumières,* pp. 127–8.

2. The Esquile (Esquille) was run by the Congrégation, or *Doctrinaires* as they were usually called: Baccrabère, "Le Renouveau catholique," pp. 136, 297; Marcel Marion, *Dictionnaire des institutions de la France aux XVIIe et XVIIIe siècles* (Paris, 1923; reprint, New York, 1968), p. 209.

3. In L'Air de Lamotte's hand.

4. The copy and transcripts are in BF's journal of the peace negotiations.

by your Government for the Release of all the American Prisoners *everywhere*, an Order not *partial* or *conditional*, but *general* and *absolute*." I rejoice with you in this Step, not only on Account of the unhappy Captives who by it will be set at Liberty and restor'd to their Friends and Families, but as I think it will tend greatly towards a Reconciliation, on which alone the hope of a durable Peace can be founded. I am much indebted to your good Brother for a very kind and obliging Letter, which was mislaid when it should have been answered.[5] I beg you would present to him my thankful Acknowledgments, and my very Sincere Respects. I join with you most heartily in the Prayer that ends your Letter, *Da pacem, Domine, in Diebus nostris!*

I am ever, my dear Friend, Your most affectionately

B FRANKLIN

D. Hartley Esqe

Addressed: To / David Hartley Esqe / Golden Square / London

Endorsed: D F Ap 13 1782

To Mary Hewson

ALS: American Philosophical Society

My dear dear Friend Passy, May 13. 1782

I received your very kind Letter by Mr. Whitefoord, with the Books,[6] which I think a judicious Collection, and hope the Reading of them by my Grandson may have a good Effect, in rendring him more worthy of the Happiness you are providing for him, in the Education of your Daughter. I suppose the Letter I had sent to you before Mr Whitefoord came here the first time, got to hand, tho' you do not mention it.[7] I submit to your Reasonings & Judgment on the Subject of the Proposition I made. I remember Dr Hawkesworth's Saying, that you had the most

5. XXXVI, 624–6.
6. Caleb Whitefoord delivered Hewson's letter of April 25, above. The books were for BFB; see Hewson to BF, May 1.
7. BF to Hewson, April 13, above.

logical Head of any Woman he ever knew.[8] In this Affair I now doubt my own Head, and suspect it was rather a Project of my Heart. The Truth is, I love you both very much, and wish to be with you any where:—but I dread exposing my good old Friend to the Fatigues and Inconveniencies of such a Journey, and therefore say no more of it *at present*. Embrace my Godson[9] for me, and my Grand-daughter-in-law. My Love to them all, and believe me ever, my dear Friend, Yours most affectionately

B FRANKLIN

Mrs Hewson

Notation: Passy May 13— 82.

To the Earl of Shelburne

ALS and two copies: Public Record Office; copy:[1] Library of Congress; transcripts: Massachusetts Historical Society, National Archives

Passy, May 13. 1782

I did myself the honour of Writing to your Lordship a few days since by Mr Grenville's Courier,[2] acknowledging the Receipt of yours of the 28th past by Mr Oswald. I then hoped that Gentleman would have remain'd here some time; but his Affairs it seems recall him sooner than he imagin'd. I hope he will return again, as I esteem him more the more I am acquainted with him; and his Moderation, prudent Counsels, & sound Judgment, may contribute much, not only to the speedy Conclusion of a Peace, but to the framing such a Peace as may be firm and long-lasting.

With great Respect, I am, My Lord, Your Lordships most obedient and most humble Servant   B FRANKLIN

Rt. honble. the Earl of Shelburne

8. John Hawkesworth, who died in 1773, had been a close friend of Hewson's: IX, 265–6n.

9. Hewson's son William: XIX, 43n.

1. This copy and the transcripts are in BF's journal of the peace negotiations.

2. Above, May 10.

Endorsed: Passy 13th May 1782 Benjn: Franklin Esqr. Rx. 22d by Mr. Oswald In Mr. Oswald's 21 May 1782.

From Silas Deane

Copy: National Archives

Sir   Ghent May 13th, 1782.

The Letter which you did me the honor to write to me on the 19th. ultimo, did not come to hand untill last evening— I pray you to accept of my thanks for your attention to Mine of the 30th, of March, and I can but flatter myself that Congress will be induced by your Letters to take decisive measures, on the subject of my acco'ts. As I did not expect an answer to my long political Letter,[3] I shall not make any observations on your short one; further than to say that I am free to join with you in an appeal to Time & Experiance to determine whether independant Sovereignty, in the hands of a Democracy, ought to be preferred by the United States, to the British Constitution free'd from the Innovations, & coruptions which have in the course of Time crept into it.— After all the clamor raised on account of my intercepted Letters, & the harsh Epithets which have been so lavishly bestowed on me, both in Europe, & America, the whole rests on the above question, which it is possible that we may both of us live to see determined, & then & not before can it be said whether my resentments, & passions, got the better of my reason, & judgment in the Letters which I wrote, & which were in part intercepted by the Enemy, & a part of them betrayed by persons in whom I had placed an unlimited, but I now find, a mistaken confidence.—[4] The present age is unquestionable the most enlighten'd of any, of which the History, has come to our Knowledge, & it stands indebted to you, for many of the most useful discoveries, & Improvements, & I have the satisfaction to find from your writings, & history, that however widely we may differ at present, yet for more than 50 years of your long & use-

---

3. XXXVI, 507–25.

4. Actually Deane had furnished the letters to the British government, which pretended to intercept them: XXXIV, 548n.

ful Life, your sentiments on Civil Government, & on the true Interest of America, were no way materially different from those which I expressed in my Letters.— But it is immaterial at present to enquire what your, or my political sentiments formerly were, the great object before us, is to secure the peace, Liberty & safety of our Country in the best manner, & on the most solid Basis possible.—& so far as either of us, suffer our resentments, & passions to get the better of our reason & judgment, on the important Question, we shall justly become the subjects, of public censure.— You believe that the peace, Liberty & happiness of our Country, will be best secured, & supported, by a close alliance with France & the House of Bourbon, & under an independant Democracy; I have the misfortune to think differently & to believe that America as she was formerly the most happy & free Country in the World, whilst under the British Constitution, though far from being then enjoyed in its purity, so that if now remitted, to that parent State under the same Constitution, modified to local circumstances & reformed of every abuse or defect complained of, our Country would enjoy greater Liberty, peace & safety, than can be hoped for, under any other Constitution whatever— A great part, perhaps the majority of our Countrymen are on your side the question, & time & Experience alone can determine which of us is right, but in the meantime it is both cruel, & unjust in us to treat each other, as Enemies, on this acco't, you say that I am considered, as having abandoned the cause, of my Country, & as having with Arnold espoused that of its Enemies— I take these to be sentiments transmitted to you from America, I am confident that they can not be yours; since it is well Known, that I have not betrayed any public trust, & that I have ever condemned the conduct of Arnold[5] as freely, as I from the first condemned that of those violent Demagarques[6] who improved every circumstance, & accident of his life to push him into desperate measures.

My case therefore in every point of view differ from his.— I have neither correspondance, or interest, or the prospect of any

---

5. Deane did criticize Arnold in an Oct. 20, 1781, letter to Benjamin Tall-madge: *Deane Papers*, IV, 494.
6. A copyist's mistranscription of "demagogues": *Deane Papers*, V, 90.

in G. Britain—the small remains of my fortune, the most of my Friends, & Family, & all my future hopes, & prospects, are in America, I have therefore every motive, to make me wish for the liberty, & happiness of my Country, & I can with great sincerity declare, that if America shall on experiment find herself happier, & more free under the present system, than she ever was, or could expect to be under the other, however modified, & reformed, that I shall rejoyce, to find that I have Judged erroneously, & that I have both written, & spoken at least imprudently, on this subject.— I will not trespass farther on your Time, than to assure you, that however greatly your sentiments may have been changed, that I retain the same respect, & Esteem for you, as when I had the honor to be numbered among your Friends.

I have the honor to be the greatest degree of both sir Yours &c S,D,

Hon, B Franklin Esqr,

From David Hartley

Transcripts:[7] National Archives, Massachusetts Historical Society

My dear Friend, London, May 13[–17]th. 1782.

I wrote you a long Letter dated May 1st. 1782. by Mr. Laurens, who left London on Saturday last, but I will add a few Lines now by a Conveyance, which I believe will overtake him, just to tell you two or three Things, which, I believe, I omitted in my last.[8] Perhaps they may not be of any Consequence; but, as they relate to my own Conduct, I could wish to have you understand them.

After several Conferences with the late Ministry, I gave in the Paper called the Breviate, on the 7th. of February;[9] but I never received any Answer from them. They resigned on the 20th. of

7. In BF's journal of the peace negotiations.
8. Hartley wrote a brief letter on May 3 but probably refers here to his letter of May 1; both are above.
9. Hartley copied this as a postscript to his May 1 letter.

March.— Upon the Accession of the new Ministry I heard Nothing from them upon the Subject; nor indeed did I apply to them. I did not know whether that Paper would not come into their Hands by Succession; and I doubted whether it might not be more proper for me to wait till I heard from them. While I remained doubtful about this, I received your Letters,[1] which determined me to go to Lord Shelburne. (This was about the Beginning of the present Month) I communicated to him some Extracts, such as those about the Prisoners, &c. and likewise the whole of your Letter of April 13th: containing the Offer of the late Ministry, the King of France's Answer, together with your Reflections in the Conclusion, respecting Peace. As you had given me a general Permission, I left with him a Copy of the whole Letter.

Upon the Occasion of this Interview, Lord Shelburne told me, that he had made much Enquiry in the Offices for the Correspondences and Papers which had passed between the late Ministry and me; but that he could not meet with them. He expressed a Regret that he had not conversed with me at an earlier Day; with many Civilities of that Kind. In Short, I had been backward to intrude myself, and he expressed Regret that he had not sent to me. Upon this Opening, on his Part, I stated to him the Substance of what had passed between the late Ministry and myself, and I left a copy of the Breviate with him. He gave me a very attentive Audience, and I took that Opportunity of stating my Sentiments to him as far as I could upon every View of the Question. Upon his expressing Regret that he had not seen me sooner, I told him that I always had been, and always shall be, most ready to give any Assistance in my Power towards the Work of Peace. I say the same to you.

I do not believe that there is any Difference of Sentiment between you and me, *personally*, in our own Minds upon Independence, &c. &c.— But we belong to different Communities, and the Right of Judgment, or of Consent and Dissent, is vested in the Community. Divide Independence into six Millions of Shares, and you should have been heartily welcome to *my* Share from the Beginning of the War. Divide Canada into six Millions

1. BF's letters during this period are above, March 31, April 5, 13, and 14.

of Shares, I could find a better Method of disposing of *my* Share than by offering it to France to abandon America. Divide the Rock of Gilbralter into six Millions of Pieces— I can only answer for one Portion. Let Reason & Justice decide in any such Case, as universal Umpires between contending Parties, and those who wish well to the permanent Peace of Mankind, will not refuse to give and to receive equal Justice. I agree with you that the equitable and the philosophical principles of Politics can alone form a solid Foundation of permanent Peace; and that the Contraries to them (though highly patronised by Nations themselves and their Ministers,) are no better than vulgar Errors: but Nations are slow to Convictions from the personal Arguments of Individuals.— "They are jealous in Honor, seeking the *Bubble Reputation*, even in the Cannon's Mouth."—[2] But until a confirmed Millennium, founded upon wiser Principles, shall be generally established, the *Reputation* of Nations is not merely a *Bubble*. It forms their real Security.— To apply all this, in one Word, let all Nations agree with one accord, to beat their Swords into plough-Shares, and their Spears into Pruning-Hooks— or—Give me wooden Walls to Great Britain!

I have nothing further to add. My Reason for writing this was just to communicate to you in what Position I had delivered over my Conferences and Arguments with the late Ministry, into the Hands of the present. And I will conclude with your own Words, may God send us all more Wisdom.

I am ever most affectly. Yours   D. HARTLEY

P.S. 17th. may 1782. Since writing the above, I have likewise left a Copy of the enclosed Preliminaries with Lord Shelburne.

May 1782.
Preliminaries.
1. That the british Troops shall be withdrawn from the thirteen Provinces of North America, and a Truce made between Great Britain and the said Provinces, for [*blank*] Years. (suppose 10 or 20 Years)
2. That a Negotiation for Peace shall *bonâ fide* be opened between Great Britain and the Allies of America.

---

2. *As You Like It*, Act II, Scene vii, lines 151–3.

3. If the proposed Negotiation between Great Britain and the Allies of America, should not succeed so far as to produce Peace; but that War should continue between the said Parties; That America should act; and be treated as a neutral Nation.

4. That whenever Peace shall take Place between Great Britain and the Allies of America; the Truce between Great Britain and America shall be converted into a perpetual Peace, the Independence of America shall be admitted and guarrantied by Great Britain, and a commercial Treaty settled between them.

5. That these Propositions shall be made to the Court of France, for Communication to the american Commissioners, and for an Answer to the Court of Great Britain.

From Thomas Pownall

ALS: American Philosophical Society; press copy of copy:[3] Library of Congress

Dr Sir.   Richmond Surrey May. 13. 82.

I have long been seeking an oportunity of doing what I have long desired to do. The Sending you on the poor Widow Barry's Account. Mr Almon's Acct of the Publication & Sale of my Topographical Description of America with the enlarged & corrected Map annexed—[4] The Following is Copy of the Account deliverd to me by him. The Ballance of which is made up by the Copies of that Work delivered in at the same time.

Copy. State of the Account of Gov Pownall's Description of America.

1776 April 6. Printing 17 Sheets at £2 pr Sheet
    Number 1,000 . . . . 34 : 0 : 0

---

3. This copy appears to be in BFB's hand and may have been enclosed in a letter from BF to Pownall, March 1, 1785 (Library of Congress), which contained another enclosure in the same hand.

4. Since at least 1779, BF and Pownall had been trying to help Amelia Barry secure proceeds from John Almon's publication of the map made by her father, Lewis Evans. Pownall had arranged the publication of the edition and contributed text to it: XXXI, 302; XXXVI, 101–2, 208n.

Paper for Do 34 Rhms. at 16/................. 27 : 4 : 0
12 Sheets of the Impression burnt in the fire at the
Savoy .... 43 : 4
Old Plate repeatedly altering & engraving the new
Plate .... 53 : 10 : 0
Paper for the Plates .... 7 : 4 : 0
Printing the Plates. .... 10 : 0 : 0
Colouring & joining the Maps at 9d. .... 37 : 10 : 0
Sewing 900 in blue paper at 6d .... 22 : 10 : 0
5 Rhms of hand-bills for sewing in different
Magazines .... 15 : 10 : 0
Advertisements in the Country Papers viz Norwich
Hereford Leicester &c &c..................... 22 : 10 : 0
Advertisements in the London Papers .... 27 : 9 : 0

$$300 : 11 : 0$$

June 81 *   96 Copies Delivd to Gov' Pownall
April 82—112 not sewed
          12 to Mr S Wharton.
          14 in hand
          776[5] sold at 8/6 .... 312 : 16 : 0

*N.B. from these 96 I took out for presents 8 & three more
which I have in my own hands. TP

I have gott packed up this day 75 Copies Sewed & 112 un-
sewed—. Which Mr Bridgen of Pater Noster Row will forward
to Mr Bowen[6] as You desired—& I hope he will give you advice
thereof— I hope Events will once more open by peace the Communications & Correspondence of Friends. I was in hopes to
have had legal authority to have communicated with You on this
Subject of Peace But as there is one Person who always objects
to me I now see I shall never be employed in Europe. I must not
therefore venture to write either what steps I took or what the
operation & effect of the steps I took in consequence of your

5. Below this number BF inserted a rule and, below it, "1010", the total of
the column of numbers.
6. François Bowens.

Letter which I communicated to his Majestys Ministers.[7] I am Dr Sir Your very humble Servant & I hope that Peace between our Countries will again before either You or I dye permett me to say how much I have been Your old invariable friend of four or five & twenty Years Standing[8]   T POWNALL.

P.S. I am puzzled about sending the Plate. I don't care to venture it in the Package with the Printed Copies I do not know how farr it may endanger their Safety in the passage

From John Bondfield   ALS: University of Pennsylvania Library

Sir   Bordeaux 14 May 1782

By an Express which past thro' this City on Sunday and by all the Letters by Yesterdays post from Spain we are informd America has declared War against Portugal and Hostilities are commenct by the Capture of Six rich Brazil Ships which they name. Captain Paul Jones is said to be the Hero. The portuguese Consul at Bayonne has sent orders to all Captains at this Port sailing under portuguese Colours to wait Instructions from Lisbon. Premiums on Portuguese Vessels have risen from 4¼ to 30 per Ct. This information is said to be brought by an American schooner arrived in Spain. This intelegence I think it my duty to Inform you.

I have the Honor to be with due respect Sr. your most Obedient Humble Servant   JOHN BONDFIELD

To His Excellency B Franklin Esqr

Addressed: Son Excellence / Benjamin Franklin Esqr / Ministre Des Etats Unies de l'Amerique / Paris

Notation: J. Bondfield 14 May 1782.

---

7. For BF's letter of November 23, 1781, and Pownall's subsequent actions see XXXVI, 101–2; Pownall to BF, July 5, below.

8. On the back of this letter BF multiplied 776 (the number of copies sold) by 8 s. 6 p. (the price per copy), arriving at a total of £329 16 s.—not the £312 16 s. listed in the account.

From Dumas

ALS: American Philosophical Society

Monsieur   La Haie 14e. May 1782

J'ai bien reçu la respectée votre du 3 court. avec les Imprimés, dont je vous suis très redevable.

Son Exc. M. l'Ambassadeur[9] ayant eu la bonté de nous faire avertir qu'il expédie un Courier ce soir, & la bonté de me permettre qu'il emporte avec lui ce paquet pour Vous, je n'ai que peu de moments pour vous écrire ce mot, & vous prier de vouloir bien cacheter l'incluse pour le Congrès, après en avoir lu le contenu.—[1] Personne, Monsieur, n'a plus constamment connu que vous mes services, mon zele & mon sincere attachement aux Intérêts des Etats. J'ose esperer de votre constante bienveillance pour moi, que vous voudrez bien accompagner ma Lettre pour Mr. Livingston d'une des votre, pour témoignage respectable de mes services, & pour appuyer ce dont il est question à mon égard. Le temps ne me permet pas d'ajouter rien autre, sinon, les assurances de mon respectueux attachement pour la vie, Monsieur Votre très-humble & très obéissant serviteur   DUMAS

Vous voudrez bien avoir la bonté, Monsieur, de faire passer l'incluse à Mr. Carmichael le plus surement & le plus promptement possible.

Paris à S. E. Mr. B. Franklin

9. French Ambassador La Vauguyon.

1. Most probably Dumas to Livingston, May 10[–12], and quite likely JA to Dumas, May 2: Wharton, *Diplomatic Correspondence*, V, 392–3, 408–10. JA was recommending to Congress that Dumas be appointed secretary and chargé d'affaires of the American legation in the Netherlands.

From Jacob Gerhard Dircks[2] AL: American Philosophical Society

Paris 15 may [1782][3] Hotel dù Parc Royal
rùe de Tournon fb: St: germain

Colonel Diriks Respectfull Compliments to the Minister of America and shall be oblig'd to his Excellency to inform him if there is an oportunity for Boston to send Some letters by, the Colonel would have given him self the honor to pay his respects to his Excell: in person, but an severe cold has prevented him from going out, and begs to accept his warmest Congratulation of that happy Event so glorieus finish'd between his Country and the american States.

His Excellency B: Franklin Esqr

Addressed: Son Excellence / Monsieur Franklin Ecuyer / Ministre Plénipotentiaire des Etats- / Unis de L'Amérique, près sa Majesté / Três-chrêtienne / A Passy

Notation: Dircks

From Francis Coffyn ALS: University of Pennsylvania Library

Monsieur Dunkerque ce 16 may 1782.

J'ai l'honneur de vous ecrire la presente laquelle vous sera remise par les nommés William Stevenson Et George Cabot[4] tous deux matelots Americains pris sur differens navires et conduits en Angletterre d'ou ils se sont sauvés des prisons, et sont arrivés ici manquant de tout, comme ils cherchent a retourner en

2. Dircks, or Diriks, was a former officer in the American army who had tried without success to raise a loan for the United States in the Netherlands. He recently had returned to Paris: XXVIII, 223, 334n; XXIX, 605, 729, 782; XXX, 402; XXXVI, 271. This is his only extant letter to BF.

3. The year is based on Dircks' congratulations, which must refer to recognition of JA by the States General of the Netherlands.

4. According to the promissory note he signed on May 22 (APS), Stephenson was a native of Massachusetts who was taken in the *Lion,* commanded by John Green of Philadelphia. The *Lion* was captured in June, 1781: Kaminkow, *Mariners,* p. 228. Cabot ("Cabit") also received money from BF on May 22; see the Editorial Note on Promissory Notes.

leur patrie, je leurs ai fourni pour le Compte de votre Excellance une Somme de £.120—pour payer les frais de leur route Suivant leur double reçû.

J'ai l'honneur d'etre tres respectueusement Monsieur Votre tres humble & tres obeissant Serviteur F. COFFYN

Addressed: A Son / Excellence Monsieur B. Franklin / Ministre plénipotentiaire des Etats unis / de l'amerique Septentrionale a la cour / de france / a Passi pres Paris

Notation: Coffyn 16. May 1782

From Hilliard d'Auberteuil

ALS: University of Pennsylvania Library

Monsieur   Paris le 16e. may 1782.

Je prie votre excellence de vouloir bien me renvoyer sans retard, les épreuves que j'ai pris la liberté de lui adresser, parceque le retard gêne les imprimeurs, qui n'ont pas assés de caracteres pour attendre plus longtems.

J'ai l'honneur de lui envoyer les feuilles K L & M, dont j'ai deja lu de premieres épreuves.[5]

Je suis avec la consideration la plus respectueuse de votre excellence Le très humble & très obeissant serviteur

HILLIARD D'AUBERTEUIL

Notation: Dauberteuil 16. May 1782.

5. These sections concluded Hilliard's specific examination of the state constitutions: *Essais historiques et politiques . . .* , II, 145–92. Part 3 ended with one more signature (feuille N), which contained a comparison of the American constitutions with the laws of France and England.

From Jonathan Williams, Jr.

ALS: American Philosophical Society

Dear & hond sir.   Nantes May 16. 1782.

It is current on Change to day that the Americans have declared War against Portugal. I can not conceive how this accot
can come yet every body seems certain it is true. I beg if there is
anything in it that you will let me have a Commn for the Spry[6]
to cruise against the Portuguese. She may pick up a rich Prize on
her Way home.

I shall be obliged to you if you will answer my Letter of the
26 March about the Prisoners I put to Board the Expence will run
high if something is not done & I surely ought not to lose it.

A Vessell from martinique is just arrived with News of a
bloody Engagement between Mr de Grasse & Mr Rodney & the
Fleets were left repairing in sight of each other, it is said the advantage was on the side of the French but there does not appear
any decisive Accot.[7]

A Vessell is arrived at L'Orient from Boston I have Letters as
late as the 15 April but no news.

I am with the greatest Respect & affection yours most dutifully & Affectionately   J WILLIAMS J

Capt Jona Coffin of Nantucket[8] is now with me & desires to be
respectfully remembered to you he has brot me 135 hhds of Tobacco.

Addressed: His Excellency / Doctor Franklin

---

6. The brig JW had purchased in early March: XXXVI, 676. She was now
ready to sail, and on May 11 JW wrote WTF to ask BF for any dispatches he
wanted sent, and for information on the Brest convoy (APS). The *Spry* sailed
for Philadelphia in mid-July: JW to Hebre de St. Clement, Aug. 31, 1782 (Yale
University Library).

7. News of Rodney's victory over de Grasse reached Vergennes by May
17; see our annotation of the May 26 entry in BF's journal of the peace negotiations.

8. Captain of the *Unity*, which reached Brest by late April: JW to Thurnin-
ger, April 29 (Yale University Library).

From Henry Laurens

Copy: Library of Congress; draft:[9] University of South Carolina Library; two transcripts:[1] National Archives

Sir,   Ostend 17th May 1782.

I had the honour of addressing you under the 30th Ulto. by Post, a duplicate of which will accompany this, in order to guard against the Effect of a Miscarriage in the first Instance and I beg leave to refer to the contents.

On the 10th. Current, and no sooner your very obliging favour of the 20th. preceding reach'd me in London. Being then on the point of leaving that Place I defer'd a Reply untill my Arrival on this side; this happen'd yesterday too late to catch the Post of the day, except by a single Letter, put into my hands, I believe, by Doctor Price, which I sent forward.[2]

I sincerely and heartily thank you Sir, for the cordial contents of your last letter, but from the most mature reflection and taking into consideration my present very infirm state of health, I have resolved to decline accepting the honor intended me by Congress in the Commission for treating with Great Britain, and I find the less difficulty in coming to this determination from a persuasion in my own mind that my assistance is not essential,

---

9. This is the first of several letters to BF that Laurens evidently dictated to his son, who served as his amanuensis during this period. (The others in this volume are dated June 24 and Aug. 7.) Laurens reviewed these drafts and in his own hand revised occasional words or phrases; he then redated them by writing over the relevant numeral. In this letter, for example, he seems to have written a "7" over the "6" of "16." These corrected dates are ambiguous, however, and have caused confusion in cases where the fair copies have not survived. The present letter is published under May 16 in *Laurens Papers*, XV, 501–4. The texts appearing in the surviving versions of BF's journal of the peace negotiations, however, cite the date as "May 17," which is how both sender and recipient subsequently refer to it; see BF to Laurens, May 25, and Laurens to BF, June 24. We are publishing this letter from the copy of BF's journal made by Josiah Flagg and corrected by BF, assuming that the differences in paragraphing and wording reflect the text as sent in the now-missing fair copy.

1. One of which is in BF's journal of the peace negotiations.

2. We have found no letter from Price, but Jonathan Shipley's May 9 letter (above) was entrusted to Laurens, and BF told Laurens on May 25 that he had received it.

and that it was not the view or expectation of our Constituents that every one named in the Commission should act. I purpose to repair to or near to Mr. Adams and enquire of him whether I may yet be serviceable under the Commission to which I had been first appointed, that, for borrowing Money for the Use of the United States,[3] if he speaks in the Affirmative I shall, tho' much against my own grain, as is well known at our little Court, proceed in the Mission with diligence and fidelity, otherwise I shall take a convenient opportunity of returning to give an account there, of having, in the course of two Years and upwards, done nothing excepting only, the making a great number of Rebels in the Enemy's Country and reconciling thousands to the Doctrine of absolute and unlimited Independence—a Doctrine which I asserted and maintain'd with as much freedom in the Tower of London as ever I had done in the State House at Philadelphia and having contentedly submitted to the loss of my Estate, and being ready to lay down my life in support of it, I had the satisfaction of perceiving the coming in of Converts every day. I must not however conclude this head without assuring you, that should you think proper to ask questions respecting American Commerce or the Interest of any particular State I will answer with Candour and the best Judgment I am possess'd of, but of that judgment I sincerely protest I have the utmost diffidence. God prosper your proceedings in the great work, you shall be called Blessed[4] by all the grateful of the present Generation and your Name will be celebrated by Posterity. I feel myself happy in reflecting that in the great outlines for Treaty, our opinions exactly coincide, that we shall not want the countenance and assistance of our great and good Ally and that you have so honest a Man as Mr. Oswald to deal with for preliminaries,[5] I know him to be superior to all chicanery and am sure he will not defile his Mind by attempting any dirty thing.

I intreat you Sir, to present my humble respects to M. de Ver-

---

3. He was traveling to the Netherlands on this mission when he was captured by the British: XXXII, 192n; XXXIII, 362–3.

4. "Blessed are the peacemakers: for they shall be called the children of God": Matthew 5:9.

5. See Laurens to BF, April 7.

gennes and thank his Excellency for his polite Expressions respecting me, and be so good as to say all that shall appear necessary in excuse for my non appearance at his Court.

Lord Cornwallis call'd on me the day before I left London, and was as you may suppose, very anxious to know when he might probably hear from me on the subject of his Release, let me therefore request your opinion in Answer to what I had the honour of writing in my last[6] concerning that affair; I wish it may prove satisfactory to His Lordship, by enabling me with your consent and concurrence to cancel a debt which does not set easy upon me, and which cannot, with honour to our Country, remain unpaid. I think we shall not, 'tis impossible we should, incur displeasure by doing an act of common justice,[7] and our authority may be fairly implied.

His Lordship declares he has no intention of returning to America, but desires to be reinstated in his Legislative and Military Characters in his own Country; and I am of opinion that in the former Station he will rather be friendly to us than otherwise.[8] For my own part, if the War continues, I should not be uneasy if His Lordship were to go to Chesapeak again.

I have a thousand Compliments and goods wishes to present you from Friends in England, where, Males and Females, I am sure you have at least so many; your own remembrance will lead you to individuals of your old acquaintance. To morrow I intend to proceed for Brussels and thence probably to Hague and Amsterdam, my movements must unavoidably be as slow as Water Carriage. My weak under limbs cannot bear continual thumping on the Pavement in the Rough Machines of this Country, and the feebleness of my Pocket will not admit the indulgence of a more convenient vehicle. I beg Sir, you will write to me at the house of Mr. Edward Jennings,[9] or under the protection of any other

6. Above, April 30.

7. Laurens' prediction was inaccurate; see our annotation of Laurens to BF, Aug. 7.

8. Cornwallis, a member of the House of Lords since 1762 (and earlier of the House of Commons) was regarded before the war as pro-American: *DNB*.

9. After meeting with JA, Laurens stayed with Edmund Jenings and became convinced he was a troublemaker: James H. Hutson, ed., *Letters from*

friend in that City that will be at the trouble of finding out a Voyageur, who is at all times and in all places with the highest Esteem and Respect.

Sir, Your most Obedient and most humble Servant

HENRY LAURENS

His Excellency Benjamin Franklin Esq. Passy

From Robert Morris

Two LS:[1] Historical Society of Pennsylvania; copy: Library of Congress

Sir   Office of Finance May 17th. 1782.

In the Letter which I had the Honor to write to your Excellency on the seventeenth of last Month I mentioned the Communications of his Excellency the Minister of France here by which I was empowered to draw to the Amount of six Millions in monthly Installments of half a Million each. He has since informed me[2] that no Monies will be paid by his Court except on my Drafts and in a Letter of the thirtieth April[3] on the same Subject he says. "Il me paroit Monsieur, que vous pouvez regarder les Fonds des mois deja ècoulés comme ètant à votre Disposition; cependant comme on ne me le mande pas positivement, je desire que vous mettiez le Dr. Franklin en etat d'informer, quelques semaines d'avance, le Ministre des Finances du montant des Fonds d'ont il aura besoin. Il me paroit que cette Operation seroit simplifie a notre Egard, si vous tiriez sur M. le Dr. Franklin douze Lettres de Change que vous lui adresserez a lui meme et dont il. touchera le montant aux Epoques indiques. Il s'arangera ensuite avec votre Correspondant pour le payement de vos traites particulieres."— It is in Consequence of this that I have drawn the

---

a Distinguished American: Twelve Essays by John Adams on American Foreign Policy, 1780 (Washington, D.C., 1978), pp. 54–6.

1. The letter that we do not publish is marked "third" and bears an endorsement similar to the one reproduced below.

2. In his April 22 letter to Morris: *Morris Papers,* V, 37–40.

3. *Morris Papers,* V, 86–8.

Bills contained in the enclosed Letter to Mr. Grand[4] which is left open for your Perusal— Your Excellency will be pleased to arrange this Matter with Mr. Grand so as best to answer the purposes intended.— You will also be pleased Sir to pay over to Mr. Grand on my Account such Monies belonging to the United States as may be in Europe distinct from those to be advanced by the Court for the current Year. I am extremely desirious of having a State of these Matters so as to know what Dependance can be made on the Funds which are at our Command. You would therefore confer upon me a very particular Obligation by transmitting the best state in your power.[5] I mentioned to your Excellency in a former Letter that I would write to you on the Subject of your Salary more particularly than I then did but I have since spoken and written to Mr. Livingston with Relation to those Matters[6] and he will I expect write you and to all our foreign Ministers very fully— We have not yet heard any Thing of the Alliance and therefore conclude that she must have been delayed in Europe.— I hope this may have been the Case for if she sailed on the first of March according to my Orders she must have met with some unfortunate Accident.—[7] I hope soon to hear from your Excellency indeed I perswade myself that in the very critical Situation of Affairs at present we cannot be long without receiving very important Intelligence.

I have the Honor to be with great Respect & Esteem Sir your Excellency's most obedient and humble Servant ROBT MORRIS

4. Dated May 17, it contained 12 bills of exchange on BF for 500,000 *l.t.* each: *Morris Papers*, V, 207–8.

5. In a March 4 letter not yet received by Morris, BF had sent a sketch of Congress' accounts with France for 1781: XXXVI, 649.

6. We find no previous reference to BF's salary in the extant correspondence between Morris and BF. Morris wrote Livingston on April 27 for information about the salaries of public servants living abroad. On May 8, Livingston sent an account to Morris, who immediately forwarded it to the President of Congress. The following day Livingston delivered to Morris a corrected list and a related report for Congress: *Morris Papers*, V, 69–70, 126, 134, 135.

7. The *Alliance* departed France on March 16 and reached New London on May 13: XXXVI, 692n.

His Excellency Benjamin Franklin Esquire Minister plenipo of the United States of America at Passey near Paris

Second

Endorsed: Mr Morris   May 17. 82   He has drawn on me for Six Millions   Letter from Mr de la Luzerne to him   Orders all Money in my Hands to be paid to Mr Grand.— Desires a State of our Accts.

From Robert Morris: Two Letters

(I) two LS:[8] Historical Society of Pennsylvania; copy: Library of Congress; (II) two LS:[9] Historical Society of Pennsylvania; copy: Library of Congress

I.

Sir.   Office of Finance 18th May 1782

I have left the enclosed Letter open for your Excellency's Perusal and am to request that you will be Pleased to apply to the Court and learn what Opportunities may Offer for making the Shippments of Money within directed.[1] The Alliance was Spoken with twenty seven Days ago off the Banks of Newfoundland being then bound for this Port. If she has not changed her distination I have very little hopes of her arrival as there are now no less than seven Ships of the Enemy in our Bay. But I am not without hopes that she may arrive in Boston altho she must run the Gauntlet to do even that as there are two Ships one of them of fifty Guns now cruizing in Boston Bay— Indeed the Vigilance of the Enemies numerous Cruizers is so great and they are so much unchecked by any Apprehensions that it must be by a kind of Miracle if any Vessel escapes them—[2]

---

8. The LS that we do not reproduce is marked "third" and also bears the endorsement "Mr Morris".

9. We reproduce the endorsed letter. The other is marked "Second".

1. Morris enclosed his May 18 letter to Ferdinand Grand requesting 1,800,000 *l.t.* specie by three conveyances, or 1,200,000 by one: *Morris Papers*, V, 220–1.

2. During the spring and summer of 1782, the eastern seaboard endured

I am with perfect Respect & Esteem Sir Your Excellencys
Most Obedient and humble Servant   ROBT MORRIS

P.S. Enclosed is a List of the Bills drawn on you in favor of Mr
Grand—

His Excellency Benjamin Franklin Esqr. Minister plenipoy. of
the Unted States

Second

Endorsed: Mr Morris

II.

Sir.   Office of Finance 18th. May 1782—
   I am to pray your Excellency to take Charge of the enclosed
Letter to Messrs. le Couteulx and Co.[3] You will remember Sir
that the Court by their Minister here empowered me to draw
twelve hundred thousand Livres, I drew only for Eleven hundred and ninety five thousand Livres intending the Remainder
to be in Part Payment of the Bankers Commissions and Charges.
I have some Reason to believe the Court have only paid the Sum
drawn for which your Excellency can know from Messrs le Couteulx. If they have paid no more I must request of you Sir, to procure the remaining five thousand Livres from the Court for
Messr le Couteulx and I must farther pray you to inform Mr.
Grand of the Result as I have given him eventual orders for Payment of their Account.[4]
   I have the Honor to be with perfect Esteem & Respect Sir
Your most obedient and humble Servant.   ROBT MORRIS

---

the tightest British naval blockade of the war. The commercially important
Delaware region was the target of particularly intense pressure: Richard
Buel, Jr., *In Irons: Britain's Naval Supremacy and the American Revolutionary Economy* (New Haven and London, 1998), pp. 219–22.
   3. Dated May 18, it informed the banking firm of the procedure by which
fees owed them would be paid, and explained the decision to employ Grand
as banker in the future: *Morris Papers,* V, 222–3.
   4. Morris wrote Grand the same day, instructing him to pay only the company's balance (1,100–1,200 *l.t.*) in excess of the 5,000 mentioned here; if,
however, BF failed to procure the sum, Grand was to pay the whole: *Morris
Papers,* V, 224.

His Excellency Benjm. Franklin Esqr. Minister Plenipoy. of the United States.

third

Endorsed: Mr Morris

From Jean-Louis Giraud Soulavie

ALS: University of Pennsylvania Library

Monsieur [before May 20, 1782][5]

Je n'ai pas voulu me distraire; mais j'ai L'honneur de vous adresser par ecrit vos profondes meditations. Laissant en blanc Les lieux & mesures, car on imprime dans Ce moment lobjet de ces questions et je desirerois Si vous l'agrées de publier vos observations à coté.[6]

Je suis penetré de veneration la plus Tendre pour vous & me felicite d'avoir vu le philosophe incomparable qui traite egale-

5. At the conclusion of Soulavie's account of his 1781 conversation with BF (XXXV, 354–60) he mentioned delivering to Vergennes a memoir revealing British activities in the south of France that he and BF thought ought to be published: XXXV, 360–1n. The present letter, written after Vergennes' receptive response, predates Soulavie's submission of his findings to the *Jour. de Paris;* see the document immediately below. The *Jour. de Paris* published Soulavie's work in four installments, beginning on May 20 and continuing on June 6, 24, and 26. It consisted primarily of a catalogue raisonné of 44 pieces documenting his discoveries. See also Soulavie's undated letter published in XXXV, 360.

6. Soulavie was at this time preparing the fifth volume of his *Histoire naturelle de la France méridionale* (Paris, 1784). He intended to include in it an account of the 1781 conversation with BF cited above, or at least the portion of it that pertained to geology: Soulavie to BF, Oct. 21, 1782 (University of Pa. Library). While the account Soulavie enclosed with the present letter is now missing, it evidently misrepresented BF's views. On Sept. 22, BF sent Soulavie a corrected version of his theories (Hist. Soc. of Pa.). For reasons that remain obscure, the conversation with BF did not appear in vol. V of *Histoire naturelle . . . .* When it was published in 1801, however, in *Mémoires historiques et politiques du règne de Louis XVI*, the observations Soulavie attributed to BF (XXXV, 356–7) accorded with BF's corrected version.

ment les secrets de la nature & les interets De leurope et de l'amerique: Mr. De Vergennes ne m'a pas ordonnè de publier mes recherches sur nos rebellions fomentées par les Anglois, il ne me l'a pas defendu; mais il me dit de choses Très flateuses; Si vous jugès que je doive m'en occuper je quitterai tout genre de Travail par le seul zéle que j'ai pour Le Bienfaiteur de L'humanité qui sera Toute ma vie l'objet de mes hommages, que la seule posterité pourra juger, a qui on dressera des statues ou des autels et que je me crois heureux d'avoir vu.

Je suis penetré du profond respect avec lequel je me dis Monsieur Votre tres humble & tres obeissant serviteur

L'ABBÉ SOULAVIE

Notation: L'abbé Soulavie

Soulavie: Account of a Conversation with Franklin

Reprinted from Jean-Louis Giraud Soulavie, *Mémoires historiques et politiques du règne de Louis XVI* (6 vols., Paris, 1801), v, 189–97.

In 1801, Soulavie published accounts of two conversations he had with Franklin on the nature of geological and political upheaval. At the conclusion of their first conversation in August, 1781,[7] Franklin suggested that the abbé send Vergennes an account of his discovery that the British had fomented unrest among Protestants of the southern regions of France. This is the topic to which Franklin and the abbé returned in 1782.

[before May 20, 1782][8]

. . . L'année suivante (1782) M. Francklin désira la publication de ces découvertes. Il s'était formé dans le sein de la France un parti contraire à la guerre de l'Amérique et cette publication, suivant M. Francklin, devait persuader à ce parti la nécessité de représailles.[9] *Le journal de Paris,* disait-il, *adoptera un article aussi*

7. XXXV, 354–60.
8. The date of the first installment of Soulavie's article in the *Jour. de Paris,* the subject of this narrative. See our annotation to the preceding document.
9. We have found only one allusion to domestic opposition to the war in

curieux, écrit de manière qu'en observant tout ce qui est dû à la vérité de l'histoire, les protestans ne puissent s'en offenser.[1]

SOULAVIE. Je consens de publier une note sur les pièces (*précitées*) plutôt que mon opinion; mais je pense que le gouvernement français est trop instruit pour ne pas connaître les situations relatives des deux nations. Cette publication ne changera ni les projets de l'Angleterre ni les destinées du royaume. Suivant le clergé, suivant les politiques, des catastrophes semblent se préparer en France, les anglais n'y sont pas étrangers. Ils se vengeront de ce que nous vous avons aidé en secret à secouer leur joug. Observez en France quels sont les esprits qui désirent les catastrophes et ceux qui les redoutent. Les uns et les autres persistent également à nous en menacer; les derniers nous en avertissent chaque jour. Vous ne lisez pas l'année littéraire.[2] C'est un journal trop méprisé. Il renferme cependant les craintes de l'archevêque de Paris; dont le conseil est le point central des affaires du clergé du royaume, auquel on porte de toutes parts de vives plaintes sur la chûte insensible des sentimens religieux, et sur la formation graduée d'un esprit d'indépendance républicaine. Ceux qui craignent le plus une catastrophe, sont des fana-

---

the contemporary press: a letter to the *Jour. de Paris* which alludes to "tous nos frondeurs Anglomanes" and "quelques mauvais François . . . sans cesse les detracteurs de leur nation," quoted in a June 5 article entitled "Patriotisme." Opposition to the American war had lost its chief spokesman with Necker's forced resignation in May, 1781. Even France's naval defeat at the Battle of the Saintes did not alter official support for the war: John Hardman, *Louis XVI* (New Haven and London, 1993), pp. 62–8, 70–1; John Hardman and Munro Price, eds., *Louis XVI and the Comte de Vergennes: Correspondence 1774–1787* (Oxford, 1998), pp. 304–6. Evidently wishing to defuse any intrigues, Vergennes was responsible for the silence of the press on domestic opposition to the war: Hardman, *Louis XVI*, p. 68; Jeremy D. Popkin, "The *Gazette de Leyde* and French Politics Under Louis XVI" in *Press and Politics in Pre-Revolutionary France*, ed. Jack R. Censer and Jeremy D. Popkin (Berkeley, Los Angeles, and London, 1987), pp. 95–6.

1. Soulavie provided this rationale in a letter to the editor which was published with his catalogue raisonné of manuscripts: *Jour. de Paris*, May 20, 1782.

2. *L'Année littéraire*, a journal founded by Elie-Catherine Fréron and inherited by his son Louis-Stanislas, was known for its traditionalist and anti-philosophe views: Claude Bellanger *et al.*, eds., *Histoire générale de la presse française* (5 vols., Paris, 1969–76), I, 262–8.

tiques qui persécutent même les paisibles observateurs des évè-
nemens, et ceux qui la désirent, me croyant du complot, me prendront pour un faux frère qui le dévoile au public. L'Angleterre,
suivant les diplomates les plus instruits, est l'amie, l'alliée naturelle de nos philosophes, et elle punit quiconque ose en France
la contrarier dans ses vues et ses plans. Elle pousse le fanatisme
de ses intérêts et de son patriotisme au point de perdre quand elle
le peut, tout français qui a des sentimens de dévouement au roi,
quand ce sentiment lui porte quelque préjudice; et on ajoute que
le ministre français qui a mis en avant un bon sujet, l'abandonne
dans le péril où il l'a mis, et le laisse devenir à Paris, la victime
secrète de la puissance britannique. On assure que la politique
française est la même à l'égard de l'Autriche. Si cela est vrai, cette
politique dénaturée et dégradée, est bien dans le cas de jeter la
France dans un état d'apathie, parce que l'astuce et l'énergie des
cabinets de Londres et de Vienne, sont les deux premières qualités de leur diplomatie. Quoiqu'il en soit, je vais rédiger l'article
tel qu'il doit être publié dans le journal de Paris, je connais Cadet
Devaux qui l'insérera,[3] et je m'y porterai avec d'autant d'empressement, qu'à côté du tableau des bouleversemens répu-
blicains et politiques que l'Angleterre se propose d'opérer en
France, vous approuverez tout comme moi la publication des
remèdes moraux qu'un état sage et prudent oppose aux dégats
des révolutions et de l'anarchie, dont nous avertissent à l'envi, le
clergé et les philosophes.

Extrait du journal de Paris, du mercredi 26 juin 1782, no. 177,
pag. 715, *sur les anciens projets des anglais de changer en république
nos provinces méridionales protestantes.*[4]

"M. de Voltaire et les historiens de Louis XIV n'ont point
suivi le détail des opérations clandestines de la Grande-Bretagne
pour fomenter la rebellion et pour changer nos provinces en
république; c'était le projet du cabinet de Londres. Le haut Usé-

---

3. Antoine-Alexis Cadet de Vaux was the director of the *Jour. de Paris:*
XXVII, 52on. Soulavie's name appeared frequently in the journal during the
spring of 1782, either as the author of letters on geological observations, or
in announcements or reviews of his published works.

4. The following piece appeared at the conclusion of Soulavie's catalogue
raisonné, without a title. In reprinting it, Soulavie made certain changes
which we note below. His claim that BF co-authored it cannot be verified.

geois, le Vivarais, le Velay, le Gévaudan, devaient former une république défendue par des rochers la plupart inaccessibles: le pays n'était pas encore percé de ces magnifiques et somptueux grands chemins que les états de Languedoc ont fait construire. Ce projet de la cour de Londres a été suivi pendant plus d'un siècle. Louis XIII, ayant fait la paix avec elle en 1629, réserva la publication de ce traité pour le camp de Privas, ville qu'il vint assiéger avec le cardinal de Richelieu. En la proclamant, le roi fit déclarer aux habitans que le parti n'aurait désormais aucun secours à attendre de cette nation; malgré les traités de paix, l'Angleterre suivit toujours le même systême, surtout sous la reine Anne; elle soudoya les révoltés qui se soulevèrent cinq fois sous Louis XIV. Elle eut des correspondances secrètes avec les seigneurs mécontens; et elle eut des caissiers à portée des rebelles. J'ai entre les mains un état des sommes que la reine Anne a employées à cette opération.[5] Les détails de cette histoire secrète sont encore ignorés, on sait seulement que Louis XIV agréa le traité conclu par ses officiers avec le trop fameux Cavalier[6] qui demanda, pour se soumettre, d'enrégimenter ses troupes, qui obtint des grades militaires et des pensions, et qui finit ses jours en Angleterre.

"La bonne intelligence qui régna entre la France et la Grande-Bretagne sous le régent, termina les dissentions. Tous ces pays livrés, dans des tems plus modernes et plus heureux, aux soins politiques de M. le maréchal duc de Richelieu, de M. le prince de Beauvau, de M. le comte de Périgord, ont changé totalement de face.[7] MM. de Saint-Priest, intendans, père et fils, ont beaucoup

5. Soulavie alludes here to the Camisard uprisings in the Cévennes, during Queen Anne's reign (1702–1714). In Soulavie's telling, BF had encouraged him to write about British interference in French internal affairs: xxxv, 358–60; Soulavie, *Mémoires historiques et politiques du règne de Louis XVI* (6 vols., Paris, 1801), v, 187–9. For British assistance to the rebels see Ernest Lavisse, *Histoire de France illustrée depuis les origines jusqu'à la Révolution* (9 vols. in 18, Paris, 1911), VIII, part 1, 378–83; J. H. Owen, *War at Sea under Queen Anne, 1702–1708* (Cambridge, 1938), pp. 50-1.
The document Soulavie mentions here was not found among his papers. Not all Soulavie's claims can be verified: Albin Mazon, *Histoire de Soulavie (naturaliste, diplomate, historien)* (2 vols., Paris, 1893), I, 23–4.

6. xxxv, 360n.

7. Richelieu (XXXII, 56n) was *lieutenant-général* of the Languedoc from

contribué à cette révolution qui s'est faite d'une manière paisible et insensible.[8] Les académies établis dans les villes principales, ont permis aux connaissances cultivées dans la capitale, de refluer dans nos provinces. Les arts, les manufactures, protégés singulièrement par MM. les archevêques de Narbonne, de Toulouse et d'Aix qui président aux états de ces provinces, ont favorisé une heureuse diversion; le commerce et l'agriculture fleurissent dans les montagnes Cévenoles moins élevées et dans la plaine: le fanatisme n'y existe plus. Les ennemis de la nation ne pourront jamais se servir de ce malheureux instrument pour opérer la révolte; et les têtes méridionales n'ont plus d'énergie que pour la défense de la patrie et la gloire du roi, contre les ennemis de l'état; on a aimé Louis XV et on y adore Louis XVI.

Lorsque je publierai mon *Histoire de l'établissement et des progrès du protestantisme en France et en Europe,*[9] mon tems n'aura point été entièrement perdu si je parviens à résoudre le problême politique que j'expose de la sorte.

Lorsqu'une portion d'une puissante monarchie s'est abandonnée aux troubles domestiques et aux guerres religieuses, pendant plusieurs siècles, et que la rébellion s'est soutenue dans l'état et a résisté à un monarque, quels sont les moyens politiques les plus sages et les plus conformes à l'humanité, que la raison et l'expérience ordonnent pour rétablir la tranquillité publique? *Signé,* Soulavie."[1]

1738 to 1755. His moderation toward the Protestants of the region gave some the occasion to question his Catholicism, but throughout his administration the region remained peaceful: Dominique de La Barre de Raillicourt, *Richelieu le maréchal libertin* ([Paris], 1991), pp. 182–3, 236; Elisabeth Porquerol, ed., *Véritable vie privée du Maréchal de Richelieu . . .* (Paris, 1996), p. 11.

René-François de Beauvau (1664–1739) was archbishop first of Toulouse (1713) and then of Narbonne (1719). *DBF.*

Gabriel-Marie de Talleyrand, comte de Périgord (1726–1795), was *commandant-général* of the Languedoc: *Etat militaire* for 1781, p. 38; Larousse.

8. Jean-Emmanuel Guignard de Saint-Priest (1714–1785) served as intendant from 1751 until a few months before his death. Marie-Joseph-Emmanuel Guignard de Saint-Priest (1732–1794) served as adjoint intendant from 1764 to 1786: Michel Antoine, *Le Gouvernement et l'administration sous Louis XV: Dictionnaire biographique* (Paris, 1978), p. 123.

9. A work he wrote but never published: Mazon, *Histoire de Soulavie*, II, 121. In the *Jour. de Paris* Soulavie implied that this work was unfinished and did not refer to it by name.

1. In the *Jour. de Paris* there appeared one final paragraph in which Sou-

L'article, concerté entre M. Francklin et l'auteur de ces mémoires, parut tel qu'on le publie ici, sauf l'article des remèdes politiques pour dissiper l'anarchie. En effet, le journal de Paris renvoya la note sur les moyens politiques d'apaiser les troubles d'un état, en observant que la France n'avait jamais été plus paisible, ni dans une situation plus éloignée des révolutions, ce qui rendait, disait-on, cette épisode étrangère au journal. Je vais indiquer ici ces moyens d'étouffer l'anarchie destinés à paraître dans le journal de Paris à la fin de la note précédente.

La diversion est le seul moïen de tempérer les troubles d'un état. Elle consiste à

Occuper les esprits d'un genre de littérature opposé aux séditions; aux écrits polémiques et aux factions: peste publique dans un état.

Les occuper du commerce en grand.

Les occuper du beau idéal dans les arts.

Les occuper des plus grandes entreprises en édifices nationaux.

Les occuper du persiflage des excès et des erreurs passées, soit politiques, soit religieuses (mais avec de grandes précautions).

Les occuper de plaisirs, de fêtes, d'amusemens, de modes, de danses et de luxe.

Amollir les caractères turbulens; s'assurer par toutes les voies, des chefs qui survivent; mais s'en assurer par négociation.

M. Francklin avouait que la diversion était le seul moyen de tempérer l'esprit séditieux des peuples, après les catastrophes.

M. Francklin n'accordait point une entière approbation au dernier des moyens relatif à l'amolissement des mœurs. Il disait que les sociétés établies en Europe étaient trop amolies. Il avouait cependant que le fanatisme, l'anarchie et les vices qui ont de l'im-

---

lavie summarized his intentions in publishing the "notice" of the manuscripts: to present the sources of anecdotes essential to the national history, to reveal the foundation of his work on the history of the provinces, to thank those who had assisted him, and to note his journeys in the provinces he has described.

pétuosité, proviennent d'un égarement d'esprit, que la violence et la force irritent, au lieu de corriger. Il dit que le moyen principal de tempérer les citoyens qui en étaient tourmentés, consistait à négocier avec les factions; mais il pensait que l'amour des rois et l'amour de la liberté républicaine étaient deux sentimens énergiques et louables qui avaient fait de très-grandes choses, et tandis que dans sa patrie les deux partis opposés en étaient venus aux mains pour décider quel parti, royal, ou républicain, l'emporterait; il était pénétré d'une vénération sentimentale pour Louis XVI, qu'il regardait comme le premier fondateur des Etats-Unis.

From Richard Bache

ALS: American Philosophical Society

Dear & Hond: Sir   Philadelphia May 20th. 1782.

We have had no Arrivals from France lately, therefore could not possibly hear from you— Your last Letter is dated in January, and was handed us by Mr. Vaughan, who had the misfortune of being taken on our Coast, and carried into Newyork; whence he came here on Parole—[2] Our Coast has for some time past, been lined with British Cruizers, which have done infinite Injury to our Trade, our port is at present intirely blocked up by them, so that nothing can get in or out; this Stroke of the British, we feel more than any hitherto experienced; it has caused a general Stagnation of Business among us, and I am afraid the consequences will be fatal to many in Trade.—[3]

We have just received very disagreeable Reports from the Westindies, of a Victory obtained over the French Fleet, which, if true, will in all probability frustrate the intended Expedition against Jamaica; there are some grounds for doubting these reports, but our fears on this occasion seem to overcome our doubts—[4]

2. BF's letter of Jan. 19, 1782, recommended John Vaughan. On April 25, a British frigate captured the ship transporting him: XXXVI, 450.

3. For the spring blockade see our annotation to Robert Morris' first May 18 letter to BF.

4. For Rodney's April 12 victory over de Grasse see our annotation to BF's

There is no possability of sending you the papers by this conveyance, as the Letters are to be carried by the post to some other port, whence they will be conveyed, I believe, by a Frigate, but this circumstance is kept secret—

I have the pleasure to inform you that Sally & the Children are well, I purpose sending them into the Country for a couple of Months during the Summer, to avoid the disorders, which you know young Children are subject to, at that Season in Town—[5] We all join in Love & Duty to yourself— With affectionate regards we also desire to be remembred to Temple & Ben.

I am ever Dear & Hond. Sir Your affectionate Son

RICH: BACHE

Dr. Franklin

Addressed: His Excellency / Dr. Benjamin Franklin / Minister Plenipoy: from the United States / of No: America at / Passy

Notations in different hands: receiv'd & forwarded by your humble St L'orient 2. augt. 1782. Jonatn. Nesbitt &c. / Rich: Bache Philadelphia May 20th. 1782.

From Hilliard d'Auberteuil

ALS: University of Pennsylvania Library

Monsieur   Paris le 20e. mai 1782.

J'ai l'honneur d'envoyer à votre excellence les feuilles Y & Z.[6] Mon imprimeur ayant imprudemment mis le papier à tremper, mon negre attendra, si vous le permettez, que vous les ayez lues.

---

journal of the peace negotiations, under May 26. Philadelphians received conflicting accounts of the battle throughout May: Livingston to BF, May 30, below.

5. William was almost nine, Elizabeth four, Louis almost two and a half, and Deborah almost eight months. The younger children had been removed for the same reason in past summers: I, lxiii–lxiv; XXVII, 603; XXXIII, 99, 271; XXXV, 278.

6. These were from Part 4 of the *Essais historiques et politiques....*

Je vous remercie de la bonté que vous avez eue de me prêter les actes du congrès[7] et je vous les renvoye par cette occasion.

Le peuple parle beaucoup de paix; je la desire, et cet évenement mettrait le comble à votre gloire s'il était possible d'y ajouter encore.

J'ai l'honneur d'etre avec une vénération profonde Monsieur de votre excellence Le tres humble & très Obéissant Serviteur

HILLIARD D'AUBERTEUIL

Addressed: A Monsieur / Monsieur Franklin / Ambassadeur des Etats unis de / L'Amerique / en son hotel / A Passy

Notation: Hillard d'Auberteuil 20. May 1782.

From Henry Laurens

ALS: American Philosophical Society

Ostend 20th. May 1782

The Letters inclosed under Cover with this[8] were detained in order to have been forwarded by Mr. Young for whom I have been waiting some days, he is now arrived & determined to proceed to Hague, therefore I embrace the opportunity of Mr. Bacon[9] who has promised care of the Packet & to deliver it without delay. HENRY LAURENS.

Notation: H. Laurens.

7. In an appendix Hilliard printed translations of the June 15, 1775, act of Congress electing Washington commander of the American army, and Washington's speech of acceptance the next day. He also included the act of Congress paying tribute to Richard Montgomery on Jan. 25, 1776, and the epitaphs of Maj. Gen. Joseph Warren, Brig. Gen. Hugh Mercer (by an act of April 8, 1777), Maj. Gen. David Wooster (by an act of June 17, 1777), and Brig. Gen. Francis Nash (by an act of Nov. 4, 1775): *Essais historiques et politiques* . . . , II, 403–12.

8. Among the enclosures may have been his letter to BF of May 17, and the duplicate of his April 30 letter. Both are above.

9. Probably the same person who, with his wife, received from BF a passport to Lorient on June 3: XXXVI, 379.

From Richard Price

ALS: University of Pennsylvania Library

Dear Sir   Newington-Green May 20th: 1782

May I take the liberty to introduce to you the two Gentlemen who will attend upon you with this note? Any notice, however slight, that you will take of them, they will reckon an honour. One of them, Mr Milford, is a young gentleman of good character, the son of a considerable merchant at *Exeter,* whose views are to amuse himself by an excursion on the continent. His companion, Mr Brown has different views. He is quitting this country entirely and going over to America. His Brother Set the example four or five years ago, and has been for Some time a Surgeon in the army under General Washington. You kindly assisted him, but this probably you may not recollect—[1] A great Revolution has at last taken place in this country. The opposers of the late measures have now the direction of our affairs. God grant they may Succeed in extricating this country and Shew themselves the friends of public liberty and justice; and may the bloodshed and havock of this war be soon terminated by an equitable and general peace. I am afraid I am too often troublesome to you, but I rely on your friendship, and am, with the greatest regard and affection, ever yours.   RICHD: PRICE

Addressed: Dr Franklin

Notation: R. Price, May 20. 1782.

From ———— Coppens fils[2] LS: American Philosophical Society

Mÿ lord   Dunkirk the 21th. Maÿ 1782.

Captain John Moultson[3] native of America has Crused sev-

---

1. Price had introduced a Mr. Brown in 1777: XXIV, 285. Surgeons by that name serving in the American army are listed in Louis J. Duncan, *Medical Men in the American Revolution, 1775–1783* (Carlisle Barracks, Pa., 1931), pp. 385–6.

2. Probably a relative of Robert Coppens, the outfitter of a privateer in Dunkirk in 1759: Henri Malo, *Les Derniers corsaires Dunkerque (1715–1815)* (Paris, 1925), p. 165.

3. Moultson (Moulton), most likely the Boston native (b. 1753) who was

eral times With the Privateers the subtle and the Victorÿ Which both I have fitted out. I am just readÿ to send him on a new Cruise with the Schooner the Sophia mounting twelve Carriage guns four pounders and Seventÿ men. The news being brought in town the War Was declared bÿ the United States of america against Portugal, I Take the libertÿ of requesting your Excellencÿ to give me a Commission of War for Captain Moultson that he maÿ with the Said schooner the sophia cruise under American Colours, & against the Ennemÿs of the united States, I hope your Excellencÿ Will not refuse such a favour, if I offer to deliver either in your hands or to the admiraltÿ office of Dunkirk a bail of guarrantee for Such an expedition, I shall Look as a dutÿ to give your Excellencÿ notice of the successes of the Sophia.[4]

I am With Great Respect Mÿlord Your Excellencÿ's Most Obedient humble servant   COPPENS FILS.

From the Earl of Shelburne

AL (draft) and two copies: William L. Clements Library; L (draft) and three copies: Public Record Office; two copies:[5] Library of Congress; transcripts: Massachusetts Historical Society, National Archives

Sir   Whitehall 21st May 1782.

I am honour'd with your Letter of the 1oh Inst. and am very glad to find that the conduct which the King has empower'd me

---

captured in 1778 while commanding the sloop *Royal Louis*, became one of the half dozen American captains to command French privateers out of Dunkirk. He remained in France after the war and enjoyed a distinguished career in the French navy. He rose from *sous-lieutenant de vaisseau* in 1786, to *capitaine de vaisseau* and commandant of a division of ships in 1792–93. In 1802, he was named *chef de division:* Claghorn, *Naval Officers,* p. 214; Malo, *Les Derniers corsaires,* pp. 128–30, 207–9, 219, 234, 279.

4. We have no record of a response from BF. Reports of the *Sophia's* successful cruise describe the schooner as a French privateer: *Courier de l'Europe,* XII (1782), 87, 99.

5. One of the copies and both transcripts are in BF's journal of the peace negotiations. The journal states that this letter was brought to Passy by Oswald.

to observe towards Mr. Laurens and the American Prisoners has
given you pleasure.

I have signified to Mr. Oswald His Majesty's pleasure that he
shall continue at Paris till he receives orders from hence to return.

In the present State of this business, there is nothing left for
me to add, but—my sincere Wishes for a Happy Issue, and to repeat my Assurances, that nothing shall be wanting on my part,
that can contribute to it.

From Pierre Bonnefoux[6]   ALS: Historical Society of Pennsylvania

Monsieur   paris le 22 mai 1782

Notre professeur de philosophie, dont vous avés bien voulu
accepter la dedicace, vient de me marquer qu'il a eu l'honneur de
vous écrire pour vous en remercier.[7] Il me parle en meme tems
de l'academie des sciences de Toulouse que je vous avois in-
diquée pour vous representer[8] et il m'observe que lorsque la
thèse Sera Soutenue le plus grand nombre des membres de Cette
Compagnie Sera à la Campagne.[9] Comme il desire de donner
tout l'éclat possible à un acte public qui doit être Soutenu Sous
vos auspices, il desireroit que vous voulussiés bien écrire à Mr.
le marquis de grammont, qui est à la tête des magistrats Munici-
paux de Toulouse, pour le prier de vous representer.[1] Avec cette

6. Bonnefoux, who had been *professeur de philosophie* at the collège de
l'Esquile and *agrégé* of the University of Toulouse, became *supérieur* of his
order in 1778. He had been a member of the Académie royale des sciences,
inscriptions et belles-lettres of Toulouse since 1770: Michel Taillefer, *Une
Académie interprète des lumières: L'Académie des Sciences, Inscriptions et
Belles-Lettres de Toulouse au XVIIIe siècle* (Paris, 1984), pp. 62, 170, 191,
257.

7. Père Rouaix thanked BF on May 12, above.

8. For Bonnefoux's earlier requests see our annotation to Rouaix's letter.

9. Religious instruction of people living in the countryside was funda-
mental to the *Doctrinaires'* rule: Hillairet, *Rues de Paris*, I, 272.

1. WTF wrote a note at the top of this letter begging the abbé de La
Roche to draft this new letter requested of BF by Bonnefoux. On a separate
sheet La Roche wrote the following: "Monsieur, Le Superieur general de la

lettre, que Vous auriés la bonté de M'envoyer meme Sans y mettre d'adresse, il Se charge d'avoir une assemblée très brillante.
Comptant Sur votre complaisance à cet egard, il a retenu la lettre que vous aviés écrite à l'academie et il la Suprimera. Je Suis
bien faché, Monsieur, de vous donner encore cet embaras; mais
je me flate que vous ne desaprouverés pas le Zele du professeur
qui ayant l'honneur de vous avoir pour mecene, ne veut rien
épargner pour donner de l'eclat à Son exercice. Mr. le marquis
de Grammont Sera très flaté de la preferance que vous lui don-
nerés et il rassemblera avec lui tout ce qu'il y a de plus distingué
à Toulouse, pour faire les honneurs de la these. J'espere que vous
voudrés bien M'envoyer Cette lettre le plutôt qu'il vous Sera
possible, à la Doctrine chretienne rue des fossés St. Victor à
Paris.

J'ai l'honneur d'être avec un très profond respect Monsieur
Votre très humble et très obéissant Serviteur

BONNEFOUX
Superieur-général

Notation: Bonnefoux 22 May 1782.

From J. F. Frin & Co.

LS: American Philosophical Society

Monsieur   Paris 22 mai 1782

Nous avons l'honneur de vous remettre ci joint une 4e. de
change en votre propre Traite du 23 Juillet 1781 à 10 jours de vue
sur M Richard Backe [Bache] de Philadelphie laquelle, ainsi
qu'il est dit au dos d'icelle, doit etre payée en france; nous vous
prions, Monsieur, de vouloir bien l'accepter & de nous la faire
repasser ensuite; Cette Te [Traite] est de 600 *l.t.* à l'ordre de M
Thomassin qui nous a chargés d'y faire remplir cette formalité.[2]

Doctrine chretienne desirant de me voir accepter la Dédicace d'une Thèse
de Philosophie d'un de leurs Professeurs de Toulouse, oserois-je attendre,
Monsieur de votre complaisance et de votre honnêteté de vouloir bien me
representer dans ces acte public. Je vous en devrai beaucoup de reconnoissance. J'ai l'honneur d'être avec estime et consideration M."

2. Grand reimbursed the banking firm the 600 *l.t.* from BF's private account on May 31: Account XVII (XXVI, 3). The money was for Lt. Thomassin, an officer in Rochambeau's army: XXXV, 13; France, Ministère des affaires

Nous avons l'honneur d'etre avec la considération qui vous est due Monsieur Vos trés humbles et trés obéissans serviteurs

J. F. FRIN ET COMPE.
Banquiers Ruë Du Carouzel

M le Dteur Francklin à Passy./.

Addressed: A Monsieur / Monsieur Le Docteur Francklin / A Passy

Notations in different hands: J. F Frin 22 May 1782. / Repe le 26.

From Robert R. Livingston

LS: American Philosophical Society, Historical Society of Pennsylvania, University of Pennsylvania Library; AL (draft): New-York Historical Society; copy and transcript: National Archives

Dear sir   Philadelphia, 22d. May 1782

I had expected to have written you a long Letter, more particularly as it is some time since you have received any information from this Country, the enemy having effectually blocked up our ports for some time past,[3] but find myself so extremely hurried that I have hardly leisure to write this, the Vessel by whom it is to be sent going sooner than I apprehended.[4]

You will receive herewith a Letter to his most Christian Majesty, which you will present & a copy which you will be pleased to deliver to the Count de Vergennes—[5] This, I believe,

---

étrangères, *Les Combattants français de la guerre Américaine 1778–1783* (Paris, 1903), p. 315.

3. For the British blockade see Robert Morris' first letter to BF of May 18.

4. According to a notation which appears on both the copy and transcript, the original of this letter was sent by express to the Chesapeake, the duplicate was carried from Boston by the ship *Intrepid* (for which see Claghorn, *Naval Officers*, pp. 37–8, under Moses Brown), and the triplicate was sent to Baltimore.

5. This May 20 letter from Congress (*JCC*, XXII, 278–9) congratulates Louis XVI on the birth of the dauphin. An LS is at the APS; copies by a congressional secretary are at the University of Pa. Library and the Hist. Soc. of Pa.

is the usual form— You will also receive in the enclosed papers an account of the marks of respect and pleasure with which the Annunciation of the birth of the Dauphin was received—[6] These are of some importance at a time when Great Britain is endeavouring to represent us as weary of our alliance, & anxiously wishing to return to our connection with them— It is probable that the late changes in the British administration & the conciliatory measures they propose may excite apprehensions of our firmness, I have the pleasure of assuring you that it has not produced the least effect—all orders of the people seem to agree that it should redouble our vigilance, & while it argues the weakness of the enemy serve as a spring to our exertion— Sir Guy Carleton shortly after his arrival, wrote a complimentary Letter to Genl Washington, sending him an account of his appointment & the prints which contained the parliamentary debates, and requesting leave to send his Secretary with dispatches to Congress—[7] The General refused the passport till he had the sense of Congress thereon, & upon Sir Guy's letter being laid before them, they came to the Resolution marked No.2—[8] The papers I send you contain also resolutions of the state of Maryland &

6. The enclosed newspapers have not survived, but see Cooper to BF, June 15.

7. Guy Carleton, the former governor of Quebec, was named on Feb. 23 to replace Clinton as commander in chief in America. He arrived in New York on May 5: *DNB*. Two days later he wrote Washington: Jared Sparks, ed., *The Writings of George Washington* . . . (12 vols., Boston, 1834–37), VIII, 536–7. A copy of his letter is with BF's papers at the University of Pa. Library; an extract, in Benjamin Vaughan's hand, is with BF's papers at the Library of Congress.

8. In the draft Livingston here wrote but then deleted, "You may assure his Majestie's ministers that they have nothing to apprehend." Washington wrote Carleton on May 10 that he could not send the passport without consulting Congress; a copy of this letter is with BF's papers at the University of Pa. Library. Four days later Congress resolved "That the Commander in Chief be, and hereby is, directed to refuse the request of Sir Guy Carleton, of a passport for Mr. Morgan to bring despatches to Philadelphia." Washington so informed Carleton on May 21: Fitzpatrick, *Writings of Washington*, XXIV, 241–2, 270; *JCC*, XXII, 263. Shelburne's secretary Maurice Morgann had been sent to assist Carleton; see our annotation of BF's journal of the peace negotiations. There are two copies of the congressional resolution with BF's papers at the Hist. Soc. of Pa.

of the executive council of Pennsylvania which I believe, speak the language of all the states, who will I doubt not make similar declarations, when their Legislatures shall be convened—[9] So that you may safely assure his Majesty's ministers, that no act which Great Britain can put in practice, will have the least influence in lessening the attachment of the people of this country to the principles of the alliance— It is true their expectations of powerful assistance this campaign are very high— They saw with some pain that the fleet was withdrawn last year when the Enemy were absolutely at their feet, & when one month's stay would have reduced either New York or Charlestown— They look eagerly for the return of the fleet, & they generally believe this to be the last campaign in America—[1] There is no knowing what effect a disappointment in this hope would have; I believe, from the present view of things they would bear it with fortitude; but I should be sorry to see it put to the trial.

Our trade has suffered astonishingly of late— The influence which this will have upon our internal resources is much to be apprehended. It is to be wished that France would see the great advantages she would derive from keeping a Superiority on this coast where her fleets would be maintained extremely cheaply,

9. The Maryland House of Delegates unanimously resolved on May 15 "that War with all its Calamities, is to be preferred to national dishonour, and that it is the Sentiment of this House that any negotiation for Peace or Truce, not agreeable to the Alliance with France is inadmissable": Extract from the *Maryland Gazette*, May 16, 1782 (Public Record Office). On July 9, Grenville told Shelburne that BF had read the resolution to him: Giunta, *Emerging Nation*, I, 460. The Pa. Supreme Executive Council unanimously resolved on May 21 "that any propositions which may be made by the Court of Great Britain, in any manner whatsoever, tending to violate the treaty subsisting between us and our illustrious Ally, ought to be treated with every mark of indignity and contempt": *Pa.Arch.*, 1st ser., XIII (*Minutes of the Supreme Executive Council of Pennsylvania*), 286–8.

1. A council of war held at Saint Domingue (where some 40 French and Spanish ships of the line assembled after the French defeat at the Saintes) did decide to send the best of the French ships to North America to obtain provisions and materiel: Dull, *French Navy*, p. 284. Louis-Philippe de Rigaud, marquis de Vaudreuil, who assumed command of the French fleet after de Grasse's capture, wrote Castries on May 19 that he planned to sail to Boston around June 10 with about 15 ships of the line: Archives de la Marine, B⁴CCVI, 181–2.

while they protected our commerce, & compelled England either to risque her army, or to keep an equal fleet here at five times their expence— Enclosed is a state of our trade drawn by Mr Morris, you are requested to communicate this to the court of Versailles & to use every means in your power to bring the Court to concur in adopting it—[2] I also enclose a resolution of Congress to request you to apply for the prisoners due to us, in order that they may be sent here & exchanged for our seamen who are confined without the hopes of relief—[3] Is it impossible to devise some means for the enlargement of those who are confined in England can no cartel be settled, or no means devised for sending them here to be exchanged?— Their case is really pitiable.

I have the honor to be, Sir with great respect & esteem Your most obedt humble servt.   ROBT R LIVINGSTON

You will oblige me by forwarding the enclose from Majr Duponseau[4] who complains that his letters have suffered Losses very unfortunate.

No. 11.

Honble. B Franklin, Esqr.

Endorsed: Mr Secy Livingston May 22. 1782

2. By congressional resolution of May 14, Livingston was ordered to transmit to BF Morris' "State of American Commerce and Plan for Protecting It," which called for French naval assistance: *JCC,* XXII, 263–74; *Morris Papers,* V, 145–57.

3. This May 7 resolution directed BF to apply to the French court so that orders would be given to the French fleet in the West Indies to send to an American port British prisoners owed to the United States. This would permit the exchange of Americans being held in New York: *JCC,* XXII, 245–6. Copies of the resolution are with BF's papers at the Hist. Soc. of Pa. and the University of Pa. Library.

4. Under Secretary for Foreign Affairs Pierre-Etienne Du Ponceau (XXXVI, 581–2n).

From Jonathan Williams, Jr.

ALS: American Philosophical Society; copy: Yale University Library

Dear & hond Sir   Nantes May. 22. 1782.

I have seen the Comissary[5] relative to a ship.— There is some misunderstanding between Mr de Castries and you for the Minister gives no other directions to the Commissary than to give me his assistance, while it appears by your Letter[6] that the whole Transaction is to be his and I am only to inform him of any Vessell I may know. This is what the Minister says. "Je suis informé, Monsieur, que M. Williams commissaire americain doit freter a Nantes pour le Service des Etats Unis un Nre de 600 Tonneaux Je vous prie de lui procurer toutes les facilités qui dependront de vous pour l'armement de ce Batiment, & pour accelerer son Expedition."

I will make all enquiry I can & inform you but as you give me no Powers to engage & the Commissary will do nothing, I shall not be able to make any Conclusive Agreement 'till I have your further Orders, at present I do not know of any Vessell but my next shall carry you the success of my Enquiries.

I am as ever most dutifully & affectionately Yours

J WILLIAMS J

I beg you will decide something about the Amn Prisoners that have been so long living at my Expence.[7] JWJ

Notation: Williams M. Jona. May 22. 1782.

5. The *commissaire* at Nantes was named Sourdeval.

6. See BF's letter of March 23.

7. JW also had been asking WTF to remind BF about reimbursing the money JW was lending to escaped prisoners. JW had described these expenses in his letter to BF of March 26. On May 27, JW sent WTF a copy of that letter, adding that there were now several more prisoners receiving his aid. He also reported that there were no prospects of getting a merchant ship for at least two months: JW to WTF, May 16, 18, 27 (APS).

From Mary Hewson

ALS: American Philosophical Society

Dear Sir   Kensington May 23. 1782

We rejoice in these frequent opportunities of hearing from you. Mr Oswald brought your letter to day;[8] I had not the pleasure of seeing him, but my mother had. As he offered to take an answer, I sit down just to give you a line to tell you we are all well; my mother has been very ill since I wrote last, but is quite recovered. I think she seems to have given up the thought of visiting you, tho', I believe, not convinced that my logic is good. I received your letter by Mr Hodgson, and returned an answer, which I hope you have received.[9] I have not time to say much now. I am glad you approve the books, and I hope your grandson will find pleasure in them.[1] I will send more by the first opportunity.

Adieu! Believe me ever your affectionate   MARY HEWSON

Addressed: Dr Franklin

From the Comte de Lacepède[2]

ALS: American Philosophical Society

Monsieur   A agen en guienne le 23 mai 1782

Je suis parti de paris avec un grand regret, celui de n'avoir pas pu vous rendre mes devoirs chez vous. M le roi, Monsieur, a bien voulu se charger de vous le peindre, et de vous prier de m'honorer toujours de vos bontés. Pardonnez moi, Monsieur, de vous en entretenir aussi, et de chercher à me dédommager de la peine que j'ai eue, en vous en parlant. Le premier volume de ma physique va paroître incessamment;[3] on aura l'honneur de vous en présenter de ma part, un exemplaire. Puisse mon ouvrage,

---

8. Richard Oswald carried BF's May 13 letter, above.
9. BF's April 13 letter and Hewson's May 1 reply are above.
1. The books were for BFB: Hewson to BF, May 1, above.
2. Identified in xxv, 355–6n.
3. The work eventually comprised two volumes: Lacepède, *Physique générale et particulière* (2 vols., Paris, 1782–84). BF already had in his library Lacepède's essay on electricity; see xxxv, 4.

Monsieur, plaire au grand homme qui a rendu de si grands services à toutes les connaissances physiques, et qui en fondant un nouvel empire a créé la science sur laquelle je me suis déja essayé. Je suis avec le dévouement le plus tendre, et toute l'admiration et toute la vénération possibles Monsieur Vôtre très humble et très obéissant serviteur   LE CTE. DE LA CEPÈDE

Notation: Le Comte de la Cépede Agen le 23 May 1782.

From Robert Morris: Two Letters

(I) Three LS:[4] Historical Society of Pennsylvania; copy: Library of Congress; (II) LS:[5] American Philosophical Society, Historical Society of Pennsylvania, University of Pennsylvania Library; copy: Library of Congress

I.

Dear Sir,   Office of Finance, 23d. May, 1782.

I received last Evening your Letters by the Alliance, Captain Barry,[6] who having come within our Capes, was chased out again by a Ship of the Line. She arrived at New-London. I have only Time to acknowlege, but not to answer yours. Captain Barry's Orders were such that he was right not to stay longer than he did in France, and therefore I must pray you to excuse his Inattention to your Requests.[7] The Express is just going off. I have written you[8] by the Opportunity which is to carry this Letter, and have only Time to add, that I am, with great Respect and Esteem, Sir, your most obedient & humble Servant

ROBT MORRIS

---

4. We print the endorsed letter. One of the others is marked "third".

5. We print the endorsed letter. The letter at the University of Pa. Library is marked "second".

6. John Barry probably carried BF's March 4 and 9 letters; the former contained copies of two Jan. 28 letters and of a Jan. 30 letter, all from BF to Morris: XXXVI, 649, 672, 692.

7. BF wanted Barry to transport some of Congress' goods stranded at Brest: XXXVI, 470, 557–8, 658.

8. We cannot be certain which correspondence he refers to, but for the letters received concurrently with this one see BF's Aug. 12 letter to Morris.

His Excellency Benjamin Franklin Esquire, Minister plenipotentiary of the United States of America.

Second

Endorsed: Mr Morris   May 23. 82   Arrival of the Alliance.

II.

Sir   Office of Finance 23d. May 1782

The Minister[9] has been so kind as to delay his Express until I could write this Letter. You mention in yours of the fourth of March[1] that on Friday (then) last the Minister[2] informed you we should have six Millions paid quarterly, &c and that you should now be able to face the Loan Office and other Bills and your Acceptances in favor of Mr. Beaumarchais. You are not unacquainted with the Disputes which have subsisted with Respect to Mr. Beaumarchais Demand.[3] Whether or not the Monies were originally advanced to him by the Court is not at present to be brought into question by me because it involves many Things which are better adjusted by the Court themselves than by any Communications to or with others. I am only to observe that if the very considerable Sum[4] which is now payable to that Gentleman forms a Deduction from the pecuniary Aid afforded us the Remainder will be extremely incompetent to the Purposes intended by it. There can be no Doubt that your Acceptances must be paid but I have always expected that you would have been enabled to do it by a special Grant for that Purpose or by an Assumption of the Payment on the Part of the Court. I shall not enter into the Mode of arranging this Business but I must not refrain from observing that the great Object *now* is to prosecute the War, that the Articles which may have been furnished for the Sum payable to Mr Beaumarchais must long since have been applied and expended, that our Necessities *now* are as pressing as

9. La Luzerne.

1. XXXVI, 649–52.

2. Vergennes.

3. BF most recently wrote about the disputes to Jean-Baptiste Durival in June, 1781: XXXV, 151–3. For more on Beaumarchais' claim see BF's Aug. 12 reply to Morris.

4. 2,400,000 *l.t.:* BF to Morris, March 30, above.

they possibly can be, and that every Thing which adds to their weight is extremely distressful.

You will have observed Sir that I have already made my Dispositions as to the six Millions granted for the current Year.[5] I shall go on to draw as Occasion Offers for all the Monies which may be in Mr. Grand's Possession making Allowance for the Shipments of Money directed in my Letter to him.[6] If therefore any Part of this Sum should be otherwise disposed of it might produce the most dangerous Consequences.

With great Respect and Esteem I am Sir your most obedient and humble Servant   ROBT MORRIS

His Excellency Benjamin Franklin Esqr. Minister plenipotentiary of the United States of America

Copy

Endorsed: Office of Finance   May 23. 1782

From Edward Newenham[7]

ALS: Historical Society of Pennsylvania

Sir—   Neuchatel (en Swisse) 23th of May 1782
According to my fathers orders I take the liberty of sending to your Excellency the enclosed Irish papers; by which, & his letters to me, it seems that Ireland will soon be as free & independant a nation as England,[8] & that England will soon recover her ancient glory.

With the sincerest wishes for the preservation of your Excellency's health & happiness I have the Honor to be your most obt: & very humble Servant.   ED: NEWENHAM

5. In Morris to BF, April 17 and May 17, both above.
6. For which see Morris' first May 18 letter to BF.
7. The eldest son of Sir Edward Newenham: XXXIII, 504.
8. For these events see our annotation of BF to Livingston, June 25.

From Madame de Baussan ALS: American Philosophical Society

[before May 24, 1782][9]

Voila, tres cher papa, un diné qui a bien de la peine a Saranger, vous avès la bonté de Moffrir vendredy, prochain, les ouvriers dont ma maison est pleine me demandoient jusqu'a dimanche pour me livrer une Salle a Manger, ou je pusse avoir l'honneur de vous recevoir Convenablement. Ce dimanche est le jour destiné a vos Compatriotes, et le vendredy me paroit être Celuy que Vous préferés, il faut donc, cher papa quelqu'impatience que jaye de vous recevoir vous demander de remettre a Celuy de la semaine prochaine qui sera le 24 de Ce Moy, la faveur que vous voulès bien me faire de Venir diner chès Moy avec Monsieur votre petit fils jespere que nous pourons engager Me Brillon et toute son aimable famille a vous accompanger et Ce sera pour Moy une grande joye que de vous reunir, ne moublies pas je vous prie, vous chagrineries bien fort le sincere attachement que vous Mavès inspiré et avec lequel jay l'honneur dêtre, Votre tres humble et tres obeissante   N. BAUSSAN

M. de Baussan et Mr de Mâchault,[1] Veulent que je vous présente l'hommage de leur Souvenir.

Addressed: A Monsieur / Monsieur franklin ministre plénipotentaire / des états unis de lamérique / a passy

9. The month and year are based on the invitation extended in this letter and in her earlier ones of April 29 and May 7, above. May 24 fell on a Friday in 1782.

1. Probably Armand-Hilaire de Machault, comte d'Arnouville (b. 1739), who had been promoted to *maréchal de camp* the same day as Baussan. Both men came from distinguished families of magistrates and high government officials: Jean-Baptiste-Pierre Julien de Courcelles, comp., *Dictionnaire historique et biographique des généraux français* (9 vols., Paris, 1820–23); *Etat militaire* for 1781, pp. 99, 430; *Dictionnaire de la noblesse*, XII, 698–9; J. François Bluche, *L'Origine des magistrats du Parlement de Paris au XVIIIe siècle . . .* (Fédération des sociétés historiques et archéologiques de Paris et de l'Ile-de-France, *Mémoires*, V–VI, Paris, 1956), 291–2.

To Anne Ogle

ALS: Mrs. Frederick G. Richards, Annapolis (1956)

Madam,   Passy May 24. 1782

I received the Letter you did me the Honour of writing to me some time since, and did apply for the Permission you desired, which was promised me. Having heard nothing farther of it, I imagined it had been sent directly to Boulogne. I have just received your second Letter, of the 21st Instant, and shall immediately apply again.[2] I suppose it has been forgotten, as I cannot imagine that there is any Objection to it, and I have no doubt of obtaining it.

I am, with Respect Madam, Your most obedient and most humble Servant   B Franklin

M. Ogle.—

Addressed: A Madame / Madame A. Ogle Dame / angloise, / a Boulogne-sur-mer.

Notation: B. Franklin

From Humbert Gerbier de Werchamp[3]

ALS: American Philosophical Society

Monsieur   à franconvile ce 24 may 1782.

Un mien Cousin de Nantes, de mon nom, m'ecrit pour m'engager à chercher quelque protection auprès de vous, à l'effet de

2. For both letters see Ogle's initial request of April 22, which BF had evidently forwarded to Vergennes, as it is archived at the AAE. Vergennes answered BF's renewed request in an undated letter published below, [on or after May 24].

3. This letter and a thank-you note that followed it on May 29 (APS) comprise the only extant letters from a man who, judging by his tone here, already knew BF well. We assume he is the "M. Humbert Gerbier M.D." whom BF would later nominate for membership in the APS: "List of Persons to be recommended for Members of P. Society," [*c.* July 21, 1786], APS. Humbert Gerbier de Werchamp (1727–1795), physician to the comte de Provence and author of *Lettres et observations de M. Gerbier,* . . . *au sujet de deux nouveaux remèdes contre les maladies squirrheuses, cancereuses, &c* (Geneva, 1777) and *Quatrième lettre de M. Gerbier,* . . . (for which see XXXVI, 333n), was a prominent freemason and had helped establish the Grand Orient de France: Daniel Ligou, ed., *Dictionnaire de la franc-maçonnerie* (Paris, 1991), p. 511.

vous demander une grace. Comme je crois monsieur que la meilleure protection auprés de vous, est vous même, et que la bonté de votre cœur ne vous laisse jamais refuser, ce quil vous est possible d'accorder, je vais vous presenter moi même la Supplique de mon cousin et j'ai la confiance que vous l'accueillerez favorablement.

M. Gerbier à fait construire à nantes un petit navire quil à été obligé de mettre sous Pavillon Portuguais depuis la guerre.

Ce navire est dans ce moment chargé en vivres, farine, salaisons, beure, huile, savon toiles et autres choses de premiere necessité pour St. Domingue. En un mot il n'a que des marchandises innocentes. C'est de l'agrement des deux ministres de la Marine et de la finance que le chargement à été fait.[4]

Pour parer à tous risques de la part des anglo-Americains, Gerbier demande une lettre de Protection qui ne Sera montrée qu'en cas de rencontre par les Americains, et dans le Seul cas de necessité.

Voila Monsieur ce que mon Cousin vous Supplie de lui accorder. Je n'en Scais pas assez long je vous l'avoue, pour juger de l'importance ou de la difficulté d'obtenir ce Passeport. Il me semble qu'étant le ministre d'une nation amie et alliée de la notre, vous ne pouvez qu'acceuillir avec empressement une entreprise dont l'objet est de porter dans une de nos Colonies, des secours de premiere necessité.

Mais grace ou justice, je vous supplie de ne pas refuser mon parent qui me paroit mettre une grande importance à obtenir de vous ce Passeport. C'est un brave et honnête négociant qui

4. Gerbier enclosed copies of the letters from Castries and Joly de Fleury, dated March 20 and 19, respectively. The enclosed memoir states that the two ministers granted permission for the vessel, *La Nossa Senhora das Chagas & San Joaõ*, to sail in March, but that its departure had been delayed by reports that the Americans had taken several Portuguese ships. Rumors that America had taken action against Portugal circulated in April and May; see BF to Livingston, April 12. The *Gaz. de Leyde* for May 28 reported that BF had dismissed the rumors saying he did not believe "qu'au moment où l'Amerique voyoit la Paix s'avancer sur ses bords, au moment qu'elle alloit enfin consolider l'Indépendance & le repos, pour lesquels elle a combattu, le Congrès voulût reculer tant de jouissances, en se donnant un nouvel Ennemi." Portugal joined the League of Armed Neutrality on July 24: Madariaga, *Harris's Mission*, p. 381.

joüiroit de vos bontés et de votre estime sil avoit lhoneur d'etre connu de vous. Vous avez paru Monsieur m'accorder ces sentimens toutes les fois que j'ai eu le bonheur de vous rencontrer chez ma niece.[5] Permettez que j'en reclame l'effet dans cet instant pour un de mes plus chers et des plus dignes parens. Je partagerai avec lui toute ma vie la reconnoissance que lui inspirera cette grace.

Je suis avec respect Monsieur Votre trés humble et trés obeissant serviteur GERBIER

Le Navire se nomme *La nostra Signora d'achagat et st. joao Capitne. Je. Raymundo*[6]

From Winchcombe Henry Hartley

Copy:[7] Library of Congress

Dear Sir   Soho Square May 24th. 1782
It is with the greatest pleasure I take up my pen to acknowledge your remembrance of me in yours to my Brother[8] and to thank you for those expressions of regard which I can assure you are mutual. My brother has desired me to copy some letters and papers by way of sending you Duplicates. I am particularly happy at the employment because the greatest object of my Parliamentary life[9] has been to cooperate with him in his endeav-

---

5. Most likely the comtesse Channaleille (d. 1835), daughter of the renowned barrister, Pierre-Jean-Baptiste Gerbier (*DBF*): Christine Favre-Lejeune, *Les Secrétaires du Roi de la grande chancellerie de France* . . . (2 vols., Paris, 1986), I, 618. BF received announcements of the daughter's wedding, undated, from the families of both the bride and the groom (APS). On July 5, 1782, the *Jour. de Paris* announced the sale of an engraved portrait of Gerbier, dedicated to the comtesse, his daughter.

6. See BF's draft of the passport, [after May 24].

7. A separate sheet, in an unknown hand, inserted in BF's journal of the peace negotiations.

8. Above, May 13.

9. He had represented Berkshire since Feb. 21, 1776: Namier and Brooke, *House of Commons*, II, 594.

ours to put a period to this destructive War & forward the blessed work of peace.

I hope to see him again in that situation where he can so well serve his Country with credit to himself, and while I have the honor of being in Parliament, my attention will be continued to promote the effects which will naturally flow from those principles of freedom and Philanthropy you have both so much supported. While I copy his words my own feelings & judgement are truly in union, and I have but to add the most ardent wish that peace and happiness may crown the honest endeavours towards so desirable an end.

I am Dear sir with the greatest respect and esteem Yours sincerely   W. H. HARTLEY

Dr. Franklin

From Nogaret

ALS: University of Pennsylvania Library

Compiegne Le 24 May [1782]

Sage Docteur! homme pour qui c'est peu d'etre en général utile au monde; Je vous dois des remercimens, et je vais vous demander une nouvelle faveur.[1] Laissez nous ma femme [2] et moi vous marquer notre reconnaissance par une preuve de notre veneration pour vous. Ma femme, depuis Longtems, me persecute pour que j'obtienne de vous la permission de vous laisser peindre en miniature: Elle desire vous avoir en médaillon pendu à son Col. Comme elle n'est pas jeune et que ses respectueux sentimens vous sont connus, quel inconvenient verriés vous à accorder cette grace à celle qui vous voit avec la tendresse d'une fille pour son Pere, et l'admiration?.. Je me tais de peur de vous deplaire en disant quelque chose de plus. J'ai un peintre qui a le merite de saisir parfaitement la ressemblance:[3] Je viens de lui faire faire, il

1. His earlier request is above, [on or after April 28].
2. Elisabeth Guillochin, the daughter of a successful haberdasher of Versailles, married Nogaret in 1769: Paul Fromageot, "Félix Nogaret (1740–1831)," in *Revue de l'histoire de Versailles et de Seine-et-Oise,* VI (1904), 3.
3. The painter was Castrique, a miniaturist about whom almost nothing is

y a quinze jours Le portrait de notre nouvel Archevêque M. de Juigné;[4] Je lui ai fait peindre Made. La Comtesse d'artois et Les Princes: je suis sûr de son talent, et je voudrais profiter du moment où je puis disposer de lui. On ne vous volera pas plus de deux heures de votre tems; c'est beaucoup; Mais qu'est-ce que cela pour repondre au voeu de deux personnes dont le coeur est penetré de sensibilité? Qu'est-ce que cela pour repondre au desir pressant d'une femme jalouse de faire voir, par cette enseigne, qu'elle vous a gravé dans son esprit et dans son coeur? N'allez pas lui faire un refus dans l'intention de menager sa bourse. Le peintre me doit son etat, il me presse depuis longtems de lui fournir quelque occasion de nous marquer sa reconnaissance: il se trouvera heureux de Saisir cette circonstance d'obliger ma femme; et il n'aura jamais aussi bien travaillé, ni d'aussi bon coeur.

Je suis à cette heure à Compiegne près de mon fils qui etudie au college Royal de cette ville. Je serai à Versailles Le 20 Juin: J'aurai L'honneur de vous aller presenter mes hommages en passant. Vous me dirés quel jour enfin vous voulez bien prendre pour sceller chez moi notre connaissance le verre en main. Vous me dirés si vous permettés que Le peintre se rende chez vous quelque jour, et l'heure de votre commodité.

Accordés à ma femme ce qu'elle desire, et je m'engage à porter la reconnaissance jusqu'à ne vous rien demander Jamais que la continuation d'un attachement, qui nous honore beaucoup sans doute, Mais qui, j'ose dire, est pourtant du à l'affection

---

known. He is said to have employed a "fine stroke technique" and grayish tones: Sellers, *Franklin in Portraiture*, pp. 166–7; Leo R. Schidlof, *La Miniature en Europe aux 16e, 17e, 18e et 19e siècles* (4 vols., Graz, 1964), I, 139. BF honored this request; see Nogaret's letter published at the end of July.

4. Antoine-Eléonor-Léon Le Clerc de Juigné de Neuchelles, peer of the realm, bishop of Châlons-sur-Marne, and *proviseur* of the Sorbonne (1728–1811), succeeded Christophe de Beaumont, to whose funeral BF was invited: XXXVI, 283. The naming of a successor had been the occasion for much jockeying. Louis XVI reportedly insisted that "il conviendrait que l'archevêque de Paris crût en Dieu" before he named Juigné on Dec. 23, but it was the fact that Juigné was Vergennes' cousin which determined his selection: *DBF* under "Juigné"; *Dictionnaire de la noblesse*, v, 824; John Hardman, *Louis XVI* (New Haven and London, 1993), pp. 88–9; *Gaz. de Leyde*, Jan. 4, 1782 (sup.).

et au respect avec lesquels j'ai l'honneur d'être, in nomine amborum, totus tuus fidelis, et beneficiorum memor[5]

FELIX NOGARET

au College Royal de Compiegne

Vous n'auriez peutêtre jamais pensé qu'un crapaud pût se priser. J'en ai pourtant tué un qui l'était de maniere que je n'ai pu consoler son maitre qu'en faisant son epitaphe. Quoiqu'elle ne vaille rien, je vous l'envoye pour la Singularité: le fait est interessant pour un naturaliste.

Je joins encore ici une Lettre imprimée dans laquelle je me suis permis de parler de vous page 12.[6]

Endorsed: Felix Nogaret

From [Vergennes]

L:[7] American Philosophical Society

[on or after May 24, 1782][8]

Si les deux jeunes gens qui doivent joindre Made. Ogle sont américains, et s'ils ne sont pas au service de l'angre. [angleterre], ils pourront sans inconvénient habiter Boulogne; le Commandant de cette Ville est deja prèvenu.

Made. Newenham n'a pas besoin de passeport pour entrer en france;[9] Elle aura seulement l'attention de ne point faire son séjour dans un port de mer.

Addressed: A Monsieur / Monsieur franklin, Ministre / plénipre. des Etats-unis / de Vergennes.

Notation: Madme. Newenham

---

5. "In the name of both of us, wholly faithful to you, and mindful of your favors."

6. We have not located the epitaph of the toad or the letter mentioning BF.

7. In the hand of Gérard de Rayneval.

8. Dated on the basis of BF's letter to Anne Ogle, May 24.

9. Edward Newenham had written a year earlier that he and his wife in-

Franklin: Passport for a Portuguese Vessel[1]

D (draft):[2] American Philosophical Society

[after May 24, 1782]

Having seen & examined certain Authentic *official* Papers which shew that the Ship La Nostra Signora d'achagat et St Joao a Portuguese Vessel of about one hundred and eighty Tons, Commanded by Capt. Jozé Raymundo, is by the *special* Permission of his most Christian Majesty, destined to St Domingo, loaded with Provisions, Wine, Flour, & other necessary Commodities for the sd Island, and that the Ship & Cargo appertain to the Subjects of his sd most Christian Majesty, *our good Friend & Ally;* I *do* hereby Certify the same to all Captains & Commanders of Vessels of War, Privateers & Letters of Marque belonging to the United States of America: & Request them *not to impede the said Ship, but* to afford her in her *intended* Voyage every Assistance she may stand in need of.[3]

---

tended to visit Paris: XXXIV, 417. On July 13, below, he wrote that their journey was imminent; they were only waiting for passports to arrive. Newenham there implies that BF had sent one that had miscarried. We have no trace of either the passport or the letter requesting it. This response from Vergennes is our only indication that BF had discussed the matter with the French ministry.

1. Gerbier de Werchamp requested this passport in his letter of May 24, above. On May 29, he thanked BF for having sent it, adding that he looked forward to seeing him soon at his niece's. APS.

2. In WTF's hand with interlineations by BF. We indicate BF's additions in italic.

3. Filed with this passport at the APS is a scrap of paper on which BF wrote, "Brigantine Elizabeth 140 Tons 14 Carriage Guns W Stewart, Capt". This may have been the same brigantine on which Thomas Barclay shipped shirts and blankets; see his letters to BF of June 27 and July 17.

To Henry Laurens

LS:[4] South Carolina Historical Society; copy:[5] Library of Congress; transcript: National Archives

Sir,   Passy, May 25. 1782

I am now honour'd with yours of the 17th. I had before received one of the 17th.[6] which remain'd unanswer'd, because from the Words in it, "when I reach the Continent, which will probably happen in a few Days," I flatter'd myself with the Pleasure of seeing you here. That Hope is disappointed by your last, in which you tell me you are determined not to act in the Commission for treating of Peace with Britain. I regret your taking this Resolution, principally because I am persuaded your Assistance must have been of great Service to our Country. But I have besides some private or particular Reasons that relate to myself. To encourage me in the arduous Task, you kindly tell me I shall be called *Blessed, &c.* I have never yet known of a Peace made, that did not occasion a great deal of popular Discontent, Clamour and Censure on both Sides. This is perhaps owing to the usual Management of the Ministers and Leaders of the contending Nations, who to keep up the Spirits of their People for continuing the War, generally represent the State of their own Affairs, in a better Light, and that of the Enemy in a worse, than is consistent with the Truth: Hence the Populace on each Side expect better Terms than really can be obtained; and are apt to ascribe their Disappointment to Treachery. Thus the Peace of Utrecht, and that of Aix la Chapelle[7] were said in England to have been influenc'd by French Gold, and in France by English Guineas. Even the last Peace, the most advantageous and glorious for England that ever she made,[8] was you may remember violently decry'd, and the makers as violently abus'd. So that the Blessing promis'd

---

4. In L'Air de Lamotte's hand, except for the last seven words of the complimentary close, which are in BF's hand.

5. The copy and transcript are in BF's journal of the peace negotiations.

6. Laurens marked this date with an "x" keyed to his note in the margin, "a Mistake in this quotation of date it should have been the   April." Laurens' letter is above, April 30.

7. In 1713 and 1748, respectively.

8. A restatement of his opinion at the time: X, 236.

to Peace Makers, I fancy relates to the next World, for in this they seem to have a greater Chance of being curst. And as another Text observes, that *in the Multitude of Counsellors there is Safety,*[9] which I think may mean Safety to the Counsellors as well as to the Counselled, because if they commit a Fault in Counselling, the Blame does not fall on one or a few, but is devided among many, and the Share of each is so much the lighter, or perhaps because when a Number of honest Men are concern'd the Suspicion of their being byas'd is weaker as being more improbable; or because *defendit Numerus;*[1] for all these Reasons, but especially for the Support your established Character of Integrity would afford me against the Attacks of my Enemies, if this Treaty takes Place, and I am to act in it, I wish for your Presence, & for the Presence of as many of the Commissioners as possible, and I hope you will reconsider and change your Resolution. In the meantime as you have had Opportunities of conversing with the new Ministers and other leading People in England, and of learning their Sentiments relating to Terms of Peace &c. I request you would inform me by Letter of what you think important; Letters from you will come safer by the Court Courier than by the Post; and I desire you would, if you should continue determined not to act, communicate to me your Ideas of the Terms to be insisted on, and the Points to be attended to, respecting Commerce, Fisheries, Boundaries, & every other material Circumstance, that may be of Importance to all or any of the United States.

Lord Shelburne having written to me on the Subject of the wish'd for Peace, I acquainted him in my Answer sent by our Friend Mr. Oswald, that you were one of the Commissioners appointed by Congress to treat with Britain, and that I imagin'd his Lordship would therefore think it proper to discharge you intirely from the Obligations you enter'd into when you were admitted to Bail, that you might be at Liberty to act freely in the Commission. He wrote to me in Reply that you were accordingly discharg'd immediately.[2] His Lordship mention'd nothing

9. Proverbs 11:14.
1. "There is safety in numbers."
2. These letters are Shelburne to BF, April 6; BF to Shelburne, April 18; and Shelburne to BF, April 28, all of which are above.

of any Exchange being expected for you. Nevertheless I honour your Sensibility on the Point, and your Concern for the Credit of America that She should not be out-done in Generosity by Britain, and will chearfully join with you in any act that you may think proper, to discharge in Return the Parole of Lord Cornwallis, as far as in our Power may lie; but as we have no express Authority for that Purpose and the Congress may possibly in the meantime have made some other Arrangement relative to his Exchange, I conceive that our Act should contain a Clause reserving to Congress the final Approbation or disallowance of the Proceeding. And I have some doubt whether Lord Cornwallis will think himself well freed from his Engagement and at Liberty to exercise his military Employments, by Virtue of any Concession in his Favour made by Persons who are not vested with authority for that Purpose. So that on the whole perhaps the best and surest way will be our writing immediately to Congress and strongly recommending the Measure, However I will do what you shall think best.

I heartily wish you Success in any Endeavours you may use in Holland for raising a loan of Money. We have press'd rather too hard on this Court, and we still want more than they can conveniently spare us. But I am sorry that too scrupulous a Regard to our Wants and Difficulties, should induce you, under the present Infirmity of your lower Limbs, to deny yourself the necessary Comfort of an easy Carriage, rather than make any use of the public assistance, when the Public must be much in your Debt. I beg you would get over that Difficulty and take of me what you may have Occasion for.

The Letter you forwarded to me, was from America's constant Friend the good Bishop of St Asaph. He speaks of you in Terms of the highest Esteem & Respect.[3]

Mr. Oswald is gone back again to London, but intended to return immediately. Mr. Grenville remains here, and has received Power to treat, but no farther Steps can be taken till Spain & Holland have impower'd Ministers for the same Purpose.— I shall inform you and Mr. Adams (if he does not come) of the Pro-

---

3. Jonathan Shipley to BF, May 9, above.

ceedings from time to time, and request your Counsels in Cases of any Difficulty.

I hope you will not think of hazarding a Return to America before a Peace, if we find any hopes of its being soon obtained. And that if you do not find you can be useful in the manner you wish in Holland, you will make me happy by your Company & Counsels here.

With great & sincere Esteem, I have the honour to be, Sir, Your most obedient and most humble Servant   B FRANKLIN

Mr. President Laurens

Endorsed: Doctor Franklin 25th. May 1782. Recd at Bruxelles from Amsterdam 8th. June Answd. Lyon 24th.

From [David Hartley]

> Reprinted from William Temple Franklin, ed., *Memoirs of the Life and Writings of Benjamin Franklin* . . . (3 vols., 4to, London, 1817–18), II, 349–50.

My Dear Friend,   London, May 25, 1782.

Yours of the 13th instant I received by Mr. Oswald.[4] I did not doubt but that the news of a general and absolute release of the American prisoners which Lord Shelburne was so good to communicate to me, in answer to that part of your letter of the 5th of April in which you speak so pathetically of *sweet reconciliation,* would give you much sincere and heartfelt pleasure. God send that it may be the happy omen of final *reconciliation* and *durable peace.* I should be very happy to hear that good news from you, and in any way to contribute to it. Having on that subject communicated, the preliminaries dated May 1782, to Lord Shelburne,[5] you may be assured that I have no reservations upon that head respecting America, in any circumstances or condition

---

4. Oswald arrived in London for consultations late on May 21; see our annotation of BF's journal of the peace negotiations.

5. These preliminaries are the postscript of Hartley's letter of May 13[–17]. WTF, *Memoirs,* printed them immediately following the present document.

whatever. You know all my thoughts upon that subject, and the principles upon which they are founded, and therefore that they are not changeable.

It would give me the greatest pleasure if I could hope for any opportunity of seeing you. I could say many things which are otherwise incommunicable, and which perhaps would contribute to facilitate the road to peace. I think I see, in many parts, much matter to work with, out of which a peace, honourable to all parties, and upon durable principles, might be established.—*No degrading or mortifying conditions, to shorten peace and rekindle war.* Perhaps I might not say too much if I were to add that simply the adoption of *reason* among nations, and the mere rectification of obsolete and gothic absurdities, which carry no gratification, would afford a fund of remuneration to all parties for renouncing those objects of mutual contention, which, *in the eye of reason,* are no better than creatures of passion, jealousy and false pride. Until the principles of *reason* and equity shall be adopted in national transactions, peace will not be durable amongst men.

These are reflections general to all nations. As to the mutual concerns between G.B. and N.A., *reconciliation* is the touchstone to prove those hearts which are without alloy. If I can be of any assistance to you in any communications or explanations conducive to peace, you may command my utmost services. Even if a French minister were to over hear such an offer, let him not take it in jealous part. Zealously and affectionately attached to my own country and to America, I am nevertheless most perfectly of accord with you, that justice and honour should be observed towards all nations. Mr. Oswald will do me the favour to convey this to you. I heartily wish him success in his pacific embassy. Yours ever most affectionately,   G. B.[6]

6. Hartley had occasionally used these initials ever since his first extant letter to BF in 1775: XXII, 128–30.

From Hilliard d'Auberteuil

ALS: American Philosophical Society

Ce Mardi 25e mai 1782.

Je saisis avec empressement l'occasion d'assurer monsieur franklin de mon respect et de mon attachement sincere et suis de son excellence Le très humble & très obeissant serviteur

HILLIARD D'AUBERTEUIL

P.S. Je desire que le petit monument que j'ai voulu ériger à la mémoire de la pauvre mis Mac Rea,[7] Paraisse agréable à lui et à ses amis

DL

Addressed: A Monsieur / Monsieur Franklin / Ambassadeur des états unis / de l'amerique. / A Passy

From Anne Ogle

ALS: Historical Society of Pennsylvania

Sr.   Boulogne Sur Mer 25th May 1782

In consequence of your most Obliging application, two days ago I received a Visit from the Commandant of this place—to inform me he had an order from the Minister to Cross examine me, I think I must call it.[8] I told him Mr. Franklin knew my fam-

---

7. Following his account of Burgoyne's 1777 campaign in New York, and a general mention of Indian atrocities against Americans, Hilliard inserted the tragic and (by then) infamous story of the murder of Jane McCrea. The daughter of a New York merchant, in Hilliard's version, McCrea had fallen in love with a young British officer who was serving under Burgoyne and camping close to where her family was living. McCrea, joined by two servants, left home to join her lover. Indians guarding the camp assaulted and scalped her, triumphantly displaying her long hair before the English army and her lover: *Essais historiques et politiques . . . ,* II, 282–3.

News of the murder spread quickly. Private citizens and military officers on both sides of the conflict were horrified, and Burke even used the incident to argue in the House of Commons against Britain's use of Indian allies. Hilliard later turned the story into a novella, entitled *Mis Mac Rea, roman historique* (Philadelphia, 1784), which drew on his own recollections of New York. For a modern edition, with a critical introduction by Lewis Leary, see *Miss McCrea (1784): A Novel of the American Revolution, a facsimile reproduction together with a translation from the French,* trans. Eric LaGuardia (Gainesville, Fla., 1958).

8. See BF to Ogle, May 24, and Vergennes to BF, [on or after May 24].

ily tho' I had not the honour of being personaly known to him—
our conference ended with his saying—he would immediatly
write and as soon as he got an answer acquaint me with the determination—be it how it will be asured Sr. I shall always think
myself greatly indebted to you for your polite atention to me—
believe me to be with great respect Sr. your most Obedient and
much Obliged servant   A OGLE

From the Earl of Shelburne

AL (draft)[9] and three copies: Public Record Office; AL (draft) and copy:
William L. Clements Library; three copies:[1] Library of Congress; transcripts: Massachusetts Historical Society, National Archives

Sir   Whitehall 25 May 1782
I have the Honor to receive your Letter of the 13th. of May
by Mr. Oswald.

It gives me great Pleasure to find my opinion of the Moderation, Prudence & Judgement of that Gentleman confirm'd by
your Concurrence.— For I am glad to assure you that we likewise concur in hoping that those Qualities may enable him to
contribute to the speedy Conclusion of a Peace, and such a Peace
as may be firm and long lasting. With that View he has The
King's orders to return immediately to Paris,[2] and you will find
him I trust properly instructed to co-operate to so desireable an
Object.

May 25 1782 To Dr. Franklin

9. This was probably the draft Shelburne submitted to George III for his
approval at 5:30 P.M. on May 25. The King granted that approval 40 minutes
later: Fortescue, *Correspondence of George Third*, VI, 44–5.

1. One of these copies is in Oswald's hand and is dated May 26. Another
of the Library of Congress copies and the two transcripts (all three dated
May 26) are in BF's journal of the peace negotiations.

2. See BF's journal of the peace negotiations for the decision to have Oswald return to Paris. At this point in the rough draft (William L. Clements
Library) Shelburne wrote but deleted, "I trust I shall not be disappointed in
the pleasure of seeing you once more in this Country and in this House as a
Friend of Both."

To William Hodgson[3]

Copy: Public Record Office

Dear Sir, Passy, May 27th: 1782.

You mention that Administration have at your request given Directions to the Navy agents at the several Ports of Embarkation to supply the Prisoners with Slops to the Value of 20 s. each.— Please to inform me whether this is the Goodness of Government, or whether you have engaged to pay it?

I have been so incessantly occupied, as not to be able to write by those Transports, your Letters directed to Mr. Thomson,[4] with a Copy of the Agreement, and a Copy of my Letter impowering you to make it, will be sufficient. And I have no doubt that the Congress part of the Engagement will be honourably executed.

When you happen to see again those Friends of mine whom you mention, be so good as to assure them that I love them much, and wish the more for Peace, as it may afford me another opportunity before I die of enjoying their Sweet Society.

I hope you have received the 200£ that by mistake had fallen into the hands of your Namesake in Aldersgate Street.[5]

You may rely on my complying punctually with your Request contained in yours of the 10th: Instant.— You certainly merit from me every thing that can afford you any kind of Satisfaction.

With great & Sincere Esteem, I am, &c: B FRANKLIN.

Mr: Hodgson.

(Copy)

Notation: Copy of a Letter from Dr. B. Franklin, to Mr. Hodgson, dated Passy May 27th: 1782.

3. In answer to Hodgson's of May 10, above.
4. Secretary of the Continental Congress Charles Thomson.
5. On Sept. 4, 1781, Hodgson had warned against sending letters by accident to his namesake: XXXV, 440.

From David Barclay

ALS: University of Pennsylvania Library

Respected Friend.   London 27th: of 5th: mo: 1782.

I embrace the opportunity of my Friend Baron Dimsdale[6] to convey to Thee two attempts on the Character of our late valuable Friend Doctor Fothergill,[7] another more at large is in the press—

   I am—Thy respectful Friend.   DAVID BARCLAY.

Addressed: Dr. Franklin

Notation: David Barclay 27. May 1782.

From William Strahan

ALS: American Philosophical Society; two copies:[8] Yale University Library

Dear Sir   London May 27. 1782.

I was favoured with yours of the 4th. December,[9] and immediately delivered the Letter enclosed to Mrs. Strange, which she has no doubt long since told you.

I remember perfectly well receiving from you some Copies of Tully on Old Age printed in Philadelphia, but have totally forgot what became of them. Becket, into whose Hands I think they were put, can recollect nothing of them. He became a Bankrupt some time ago, so that had any remained unsold, they must have

---

6. The Quaker physician Thomas Dimsdale, for whom see the *DNB* and Namier and Brooke, *House of Commons,* II, 325–6.

7. Fothergill died on Dec. 26, 1780: XXXIV, 260. We do not know what Barclay enclosed. An account of Fothergill's life appeared in John Elliot, ed., *A Complete Collection of the Medical and Philosophical Works of John Fothergill* . . . (London, 1781), pp. i–xx. Tributes to Fothergill by Dr. William Hird and Dr. Gilbert Thompson were published in 1781 and 1782, while in 1783 Dimsdale printed privately his *Tribute of Friendship to the Memory of Dr. Fothergill:* R. Hingston Fox, *Dr. John Fothergill and His Friends* . . . (London, 1919), pp. 416–17.

8. Both in the hand of William Duane. One summarizes the sixth paragraph but does not reproduce it.

9. XXXVI, 192–3.

appeared in the general Sale of his Stock.[1] However, on my Enquiry among the Trade, I found on Sale an Edition of the Book,
seemingly printed from yours, which I sent you;[2] and this, I
hope, will answer your present Purpose.

I am happy to hear there is so great an Emulation upon the
Continent for the Improvement of the Art of Printing, and I
hope it will continue. Here all our Pressmen are spoilt by the
hasty and slovenly Manner in which our numerous Newspapers
and Magazines are printed; nor is there the least Encouragement
for any one to carry the Art to any farther Degree of Perfection.
I am now too far advanced in Life to think of it; but I shall be
much obliged to receive from you a Sample of Didot's Perfor-
mances in that Way, as you kindly promise me.

I rejoice to see that you do me the Honour still to retain a Remembrance of our antient private Friendship, and in the present
Prospect that Public Circumstances will not much longer divide
us. That Event I long for, I will own, with no small degree of Impatience; sincerely hoping, that no Success on either Side, however flattering, will induce us to protract this unnatural War,
which tends only to strengthen the Hands of our mutual Enemies, who are at the same time Enemies to the Liberties, civil and
religious, of all Mankind.

Inclosed I send you a Copy of the Bill to enable His Majesty
to conclude a Peace, &c. with the Amendments, as it passed the
House of Commons last Friday. These Amendments, if I am not
misinformed, were suggested by yourself;[3] so it is plain that here

1. For BF's edition of *Cato Major* and for bookseller Thomas Becket see
XXXVI, 192–3n. Becket appeared on a list of bankrupts published in March,
1779: *Gent. Mag.*, XLIX (1779), 160.

2. Strahan entrusted the book to Robert Strange: XXXVI, 627. It was probably the 1778 London reprint produced for Fielding & Walker: Edwin Wolf
2nd, unpublished catalogue of books and pamphlets in BF's library (XXXVI,
331n).

3. The May 24 reading of the Enabling Act before the House of Commons
was in fact only a second preliminary one. The act would not officially pass
Parliament until June, when it was approved by the House of Lords without
any amendments; see our annotation to BF's March 30 letter to Robert R. Livingston, and *Journals of the House of Commons* (51 vols., reprint, London,
1803), XXXVIII, 1022, 1028, 1060. The amendments may have concerned in
part a rewording which would have enabled the King to treat expressly with

is no Impediment to the accomplishing so necessary and so desireable a Work. Of the good Disposition of his Majesty's present Ministers, you have already had ample Testimony.

The Person who I hope will have the Honour of to put this into your Hands, is a very valuable young Relation of mine, Miss Sally Beckwith, Daughter of General Beckwith, and Granddaughter of the venerable Dr Wishart,[4] who, in consequence of some Misunderstanding with her Father, in which I think her blameless (for Particulars I beg leave to refer you to herself) hath taken the Resolution of emancipating herself from his Authority and trying her Fortune in N. America. She is really an accomplished young Woman; and laying aside all Consideration of her Birth, she is desirous of doing what she is extremely well qualified for, of superintending the Education of young Ladies either in a public or a private Way, or of following the Business of a Milliner, in which she has a very good Taste. She would indeed be a Jewel in any genteel Family that wanted such a Person. In short, she is one who will soon, if I am not much mistaken, attract your Notice and secure your Friendship. I have desired her to open her whole Mind to you, which you will find to be stored with all those Qualities you most admire in a Woman.[5]

After what I have said of this amiable but at present distressed young Creature, and after you yourself have seen her, I am sure I need add nothing to obtain her your Patronage, which will be of infinite Service to her where she is going, and I will venture to say you will have the Thanks of the Community for honouring her with your Introduction; such firm Dependence have I on

---

those commissioned by Congress, rather than with "any person or persons whatever," as originally stated (XXXVI, 688n). BF criticized this part of the initial act in his March 30 letter to Livingston and later mentioned such a proposed alteration; see the June 3 entry of BF's journal of the peace negotiations.

4. For Maj. Gen. John Beckwith and Dr. George Wishart, a prominent minister, see X, 329n. In 1779, the general visited BF and offered to serve in the American Army: XXIX, 447–8, 506–7.

5. Sally Beckwith forwarded the present letter with hers of July 17, below. She did indeed immigrate to America, where she established a school for girls near Philadelphia: SB to BF, Jan. 24 (two letters) and June 1, 1783, APS.

her Virtues, her Accomplishments, and in her Powers of Pleasing.

I begin now to flatter myself that we shall soon meet again. Mean while you have my best Thanks for your good Wishes, so kindly expressed in your last, towards my Family, who are all well (my Wife excepted who is now at Bath for the Recovery of her Health) and remember you with wonted Esteem and Affection. You will find your Wife the same plain honest Girl she was when she made choise of you above 20 Years ago,[6] and myself writing at the same Desk where you first found me at a still more distant Period.

With farther Particulars I will not now trouble you, hoping soon to have an Opportunity of writing again.

I remain, with the greatest Esteem and Respect Dear Sir Your most obedient, and affectionate humble Servant

WILL: STRAHAN

B. Franklin Esqr.

From Robert Morris

Four LS:[7] American Philosophical Society (two), Historical Society of Pennsylvania (two);[8] copies: Historical Society of Pennsylvania,[9] Library of Congress (two)

Dr. Sir—   Office of Finance, 29th. May 1782—

I do myself the Honor to enclose you Copies of two Acts of Congress one of the fifth of June, and the other of the eighteenth of June 1779 relating to the affairs of Mr: de beaumarchais.[1] You will observe Sir that you was authorized to Pledge the faith of

6. Margaret Strahan Spottiswoode, William Strahan's daughter, whom BF had called his "little Wife": XXXI, 404n.
7. We publish the only one that is not encoded. The other three are written in the cipher described in our annotation to Morris' April 8 letter.
8. BF interlined a decipher on one of these, marked "second".
9. In WTF's hand.
1. The acts ordered that bills of exchange be drawn on BF to pay Beaumarchais 2,400,000 *l.t.* principal (on June 15, 1782) plus 432,000 *l.t.* interest: XXIX, 707–8.

the United States to the Court of Versailles for obtaining money or Credit to honor the Drafts on you— There is a misteriousness in this Transaction arising from the very nature of it which will not admit of Explanation here, neither can you go fully into an Explanation with the Court. Mr. de beaumarchais certainly had not funds of his own to make such considerable Expenditures neither is there any reason to beleive that he had Credit. If the Court advanced money it must be a Secret. But there would be no Difficulty in giving an order in your favor for the Sum necessary to Pay those Bills and thereupon measures might be taken to obtain from him the Reimbursment of any Sums he might have received— Consequently there would be no Actual advance of money made as the whole might be managed by the Passing of proper Receipts from you to the Court from Mr de beaumarchais to you, and from the Court to him. I wish that you would Apply on this Subject, and get it adjusted. The diverting from a Loan for the Service of the Current Year, so considerable a Part as that due to Mr de beaumarchais will defeat the Object for which it was granted. It ought not therefore to be done if possible to be avoided.

I have the honor to be sir Your most Obedt & most humble Servant ROBT MORRIS

To His Excy Benjn. Franklin Esqr.

Endorsed: Office of Finance May 29. 1782

From Dumas

ALS: American Philosophical Society

Monsieur La haie 30e. May 1782.

Le porteur de la présente, Mr. De Berenger, Chargé d'Affaires de France à la Haie depuis cinq ans, allant faire un voyage à Paris,[2] veut bien me faire la double faveur de le présen-

2. Laurent Bérenger (xxv, 375n) has appeared frequently in Dumas' correspondence. We do not know how long he was in Paris, but on Nov. 29, 1782, he took charge of the French embassy in the Netherlands when La Vauguyon went on leave: Bérenger to Vergennes, Nov. 29, 1782 (AAE); *Repertorium der diplomatischen Vertreter*, III, 126.

ter, & de le présenter à vous: & il m'est bien agréable de vous le faire connoître comme aussi parfaitement bien intentionné pour la cause Américaine, que zélé pour le service & pour la gloire du Roi son Maître. C'est, Monsieur de Berenger qui communiqua en 1778 la déclaration de la Reconnoissance de l'Indépendance des Etats unis de la part de S.M.T.Chr.[Sa Majesté Très Chrétienne] à L.H.P. [Leurs Hautes Puissances], & qui, se trouvant le lendemain chez le Chev. York, qui lui reprocha d'avoir violé sa fille, lui répondit, qu'elle étoit émancipée, & qu'on ne lui avoit fait que ce qu'elle avoit demandé, pour lui faire plaisir.[3]

Jamais je n'ai servi les Etats Unis avec plus de zele & de succès, que depuis 6 mois; & jamais je n'ai pu moins entrer dans les détails là-dessus, surtout sur le papier. Ce dont je puis en tout temps me glorifier plus hautement, c'est le sincere & respectueux attachement avec lequel je suis toujours & pour toujours, Monsieur Votre très humble & très obéissant serviteur

DUMAS

Passy à S.E. Mr. Franklin, &c.

Addressed: à Son Excellence / Monsieur Franklin, Esqr. / Min. Plenipo: des Et. Un. / &c. &c. / à Passy./.

From Robert R. Livingston

ALS and two LS:[4] University of Pennsylvania Library; AL (draft): New-York Historical Society; copy and transcript: National Archives

Dear Sir   Philadelphia 30th. May 1782
Since my last of the   instant,[5] I have been honoured with yours of the 30th. March together with a copy of Mr. Adam's Letter to you & the English papers—for all of which I am ex-

3. Dumas already had told BF the story about Bérenger and former British Ambassador Yorke: XXVI, 162–3.

4. According to notations on the copy and transcript, the ALS was sent from Boston on the ship *Intrepid*, the duplicate was sent to Baltimore, and the triplicate was delivered to La Luzerne.

5. The duplicate and triplicate read, "22d. instant." Livingston's May 22 letter is above.

treamly obliged to you. I am not at all disappointed at the manner in which the British administration have declared their wish for peace or at the reluctance they shew in parting with this country. To a proud nation the loss of three million of subjects must be mortifying. Every journyman weaver, in every petty village in England, conceived himself a sovereign even while working for the slaves of his supposed subjects. It requires a degree of magnanimity of which they are incapable, to surrender with dignity what they can no longer hold. They must suppose the politicks of the rest of the world to move upon weaker principles than their own if they imagine any offers they can make in their present debilitated situation, will detach the bellegerent powers from each other till all the objects of their union are attained. Of what avail would the cessions they offer to make in the west Indies be to France if by our reunion with England her naval power was restored what security would she have for those cessions or even for the rest of her Islands? What she has offered Spain I know not. To us she has offered nothing which I have yet heard of, but her friendship & the blessings of her government. A seven years emnity has extinguished our desire for the first. And the present apparent happiness of the people of England & Ireland has enabled us to form a just estimate of the last.

I have told you that we have nothing to apprehend here from the offers of Britain.[6] I have had no reason since to change that opinion, the way however to put it out of doubt is to enable us to expel the enimy from the continent this summer, the task is not difficult & the object is sufficiently important not to let it depend on other operations.

I am instructed by congress to prepare a memorial to the court of Versailles on the subject of the money due to the Americans who sailed with Capt. Jones[7]—continual complaints are made here on that subject. Surely sufficient time has been allowed[8]

6. See Livingston's May 22 letter.

7. We find no such instructions in the *JCC*, but Livingston also mentioned them in an April 20 letter to John Paul Jones (Bradford, *Jones Papers*, reel 7, no. 1392).

8. The duplicate and triplicate read, "Surely Mr. Chaumont has had sufficient time".

to settle this business. I must beg the favors of you to press it, & to draw & present a memorial to the Court if it can not otherwise be accomplished. Mr. Barclay will have orders to receive the money for them.[9] I enclose an extract of a Letter from Capt Jones to me on that subject together with a list of the Ships & their force agreeable to which the divission should be made.[1] I also enclose his account of the detention of the Brigantine Berkenbosh, together with a copy of Capt De Nefs certificate that the property belonged to british owners this is at first view a sufficient justification of his conduct[2] & I hope will be deemed satisfactory, when it is considered that our courts are open for a further prosecution of the inquiry, if any injury has been unjustly sustained. I shall take the earliest opportunity to enquire into the other cases you mention. If I am rightly informed the insult to the coast of Norway is already avenged the vessels who are said to have committed it having been lost at sea, this puts a stop to any further inquiries about it.[3] I shall however get this fact more fully assertained & write to you again on the subject.

I wish to know on what principle these applications are made to the court of France? If the powers who suppose themselves injured consider us as independant they should address themselves directly to the Ministers of Congress, if they think us the subjects of Great Britain they should apply to the court of London for redress— I am happy to find that you have not lost sight

9. Livingston sent Barclay those orders on May 31 (National Archives). The same letter told Barclay that a number of dispatches for BF, JA, and Jay were enclosed and asked him to forward them as soon as possible.

1. The extract was of Jones's letter to Livingston, May 10, 1782 (reproduced in Bradford, *Jones Papers*, reel 7, no. 1398). The ship list might have been the Aug. 13, 1779, list of ships in the *Bonhomme Richard* squadron (XXX, 223n).

2. Jones's account is in the extract of his May 10 letter. The Jan. 9, 1780, certificate from Capt. Ary de Neef of the *Berkenbosch* (for whose capture see XXXI, 389–90, and subsequent volumes) is reproduced in Bradford, *Jones Papers*, reel 7, no. 1399. Ary de Neef's deposition of Aug. 4, 1780, is in *ibid.*, no. 1392.

3. The insult was by three American ships operating together: XXXVI, 610n, 638, 644.

of the prizes detained by the danish court,[4] & that you so happily availed yourself of the opportunity they afforded you to renew your application. This object ought to be pushed, not so much on account of the value of the vessels, as to shew that we know what is due to ourselves—

Enclosed is a resolution of Congress on the subject of accounts, which you will be pleased to take the earliest opportunity to carry into execution.[5] You draw an agreeable picture of the french court, & of their favourable dispositions.[6] They stand very high in the esteem of this country, & tho' we entertain the hope of repaying by our commerce & alliance the frienship they have shewn us, we are not on that account the less sensible of our obligation to them. The distrusts, & jealousies, which secret enimies endeavoured to excite have died away, one succesful exertion in our favor will secure to them forever the affections of this country.

I take such an interest in the happiness of the Marquis De Lafayette as makes me learn with great pleasure the reception he has met with—[7] No man is more worthy of the esteem he enjoys both here & at home— I have foreborn to write him for some time past, in expectation that he was upon his way, the same reason restrains me now. Should any extraordinary event have de-

4. Three of the *Alliance*'s prizes were returned to the British by the Danish government, prompting a protest from BF: XXXI, 261–5.

5. A May 28 resolution, "That the minister plenipotentiary of the United States at the Court of Versailles, be instructed to take immediate measures for liquidating the accounts subsisting between the said states and the said Court, and report a state thereof to Congress": *JCC*, XXII, 305–6. This resolution was in response to a request by La Luzerne, who wished BF to be authorized to fix terms of reimbursement to France: *Morris Papers*, V, 37–40, 126–9. Among BF's papers at the APS, Hist. Soc. of Pa., and University of Pa. Library are copies of both this resolution and another of the same day (*JCC*, XXII, 306), "that a commissioner be appointed to liquidate and finally settle the accounts of all the servants of the United States, who have been entrusted with the expenditure of public monies in Europe." At the Hist. Soc. of Pa. are also resolutions of May 29 authorizing public servants to draw quarterly on Morris for funds and ordering that S.C. delegates be furnished documents relating to Capt. Alexander Gillon: *JCC*, XXII, 308–9.

6. See XXXVI, 645–6.

7. See XXXVI, 644.

tained him, you will be so obliging as to mention this to him as my appology.

I am charmed with your idea of the medal to perpetuate the memory of York & Saraytoga the design is simple, elegant, & strikingly expressive of the subject.[8] I can not however but flatter myself that before it can be executed your Hercules will have tasked your invention for a new emblem. I enclose a number of Letters that have passed between Genl. Washington & Genl. Clinton Robinson & Carleton chiefly on the subject of Capt Huddy who having been taken prisoner & confined for some time at New York was carried by a capt. Limpencut & a party of soldiers to the Jersey shore and there hanged without the least pretence. You will see an account of the whole transaction in some of the papers sent you. The Genl. in pursuance of his determination has ordered the lott to be cast. It has fallen upon Capt. Asgil of the guards who is now on his way to camp, a friend of his capt. Ludlow is gone to New York with the permission of the Secretary at war to see if Carleton can be persuaded to give satisfaction for the murder. It is a melancholy case but the repeated cruelties of the British has rendered some retaliation absolutely necessary how much soever they may hurt our feelings.[9]

We are yet totally ignorant of the event of the battle in the

8. See XXXVI, 644.

9. Joshua Huddy, a militia captain of artillery, was hanged by Loyalists on April 12. Washington demanded that Clinton deliver to him the Loyalist officer believed responsible, Capt. Richard Lippincott. When Clinton refused, a British prisoner, Capt. Charles Asgill (who had served under Cornwallis), was selected by lot to be hanged in retaliation. Eventually Asgill was spared when Vergennes intervened on his behalf at the request of Asgill's mother: Freeman, *Washington*, V, 412–14, 419–20, 425; Wharton, *Diplomatic Correspondence*, V, 634–6; VI, 3–4; *JCC*, XXIII, 715. Among BF's papers at the Hist. Soc. of Pa. are copies, in a secretarial hand, of the following documents relating to this incident: the label attached to the breast of Capt. Huddy (for which see Freeman, *Washington*, V, 413); letters to Washington from Clinton on April 25 and Maj. Gen. James Robertson on May 1 (*The Remembrancer . . . For the Year 1782*. Part II [London, 1782], pp. 156–7); a congressional resolution of April 29 (*JCC*, XXII, 217–18); Washington's May 4 reply to Robertson and May 10 letter to the President of Congress (Fitzpatrick, *Writings of Washington*, XXIV, 220–1, 243–4).

west Indies which was fought the 12th. of April. You will see various & contradictory accounts in our papers[1]—you will probably have better information in Europe— The Island of providence is taken by the Spaniards, Gillon commanded the fleet as is said upon that expedition. He yesterday arrived here with a number of vessels from the Havanah for whom we were in great pains, as this port had been closely blocked up for some time—[2] I have the honor to be sir with great esteem & respect Your Most obt hum Servt   ROBT R LIVINGSTON

No.12

His Excellency Benjamin Franklin Esqr.

Endorsed: Secretary Livingston No 12 May 30. 1782 recd. Augt. 6.— Money due to Ce. Jone's Crews Dutch Vessel.— Danish Affair. Medal. Marquis de la Fayette. Lippincut. Gillon's Arrival

To Thomas Grenville[3]

Copy:[4] Library of Congress; transcripts: Massachusetts Historical Society, National Archives

Sir,   Passy May 31st. 1782.
    I do not find that I have any express Authority to absolve a Parole given by an English Officer in America. But desirous of Complying with a Request of the Duke of Richmond as far as may be in my Power, and being confident that the Congress will

1. At this time reports of the Battle of the Saintes were still sketchy; see Wharton, *Diplomatic Correspondence*, v, 447–8.
2. The *South Carolina*, commanded by Commodore Alexander Gillon of the S.C. Navy, participated in the capture of New Providence, which capitulated on May 8. Six days later Gillon sailed for Philadelphia with a convoy of American ships which had participated in the operation: James A. Lewis, *Neptune's Militia: the Frigate* South Carolina *during the American Revolution* (Kent, Ohio, and London, 1999), pp. 65–78.
3. In answer to a verbal request made by Grenville on May 26, on behalf of the Duke of Richmond; see the June 1 entry in BF's journal of the peace negotiations.
4. The copy and transcripts are in BF's journal of the peace negotiations.

be pleased with whatever may oblige a Personage they so much Respect. I do hereby consent that Capt. Macleod serve in his military Capacity, in England, only, till the pleasure of the Congress is known, to whom I will write immediately,[5] and who I make no doubt will discharge him entirely.— I have the honour to be Sir,

Mr Grenville

To John Adams

LS:[6] Massachusetts Historical Society; copy:[7] Library of Congress; transcripts: Massachusetts Historical Society, National Archives

Sir,   Passy, June 2d. 1782.

Since mine of May 8th I have not had any thing material to communicate to your Excellency. Mr Grenville indeed arriv'd just after I had dispatch'd that Letter, and I introduc'd him to M. De Vergennes; but as his Mission seem'd only a Repetition of that by Mr Oswald, the same Declarations of the King of England's sincere Desire of Peace, and willingness to treat of a General Pacification with all the Powers at War, and to treat at Paris, which were answer'd by the same Declarations of the good Dispositions of this Court; and that it could not treat without the Concurrence of its Allies, I omitted writing till something should be produc'd from a kind of Agreement that Mr Vergennes would acquaint Spain & Holland with the Overture and that Mr. Grenville would write for full Powers to treat & make Propositions &ca, nothing of Importance being in the meantime to be transacted.

Mr. Grenville accordingly dispatch'd a Messenger for London, who return'd in about 12 Days. Mr. G. call'd on me after having been at Versailles and acquainted me that he had received the Power, and had left a Copy of it with M. de Vergennes, &

---

5. We have found no indication that he did so.

6. In WTF's hand.

7. The copy and the transcripts are in BF's journal of the peace negotiations, which discusses the various events here mentioned.

that he was thereby authoris'd to treat with France and her *Allies*. The next time I went to Versailles, I desired to see that Copy, and was surpris'd to find in it no mention of the Allies of France or any one of them; and on speaking with M. De Vergennes about it I found he began to look upon the whole as a Piece of Artifice to amuse us & gain Time; since he had uniformly declar'd to every Agent who had appear'd here, viz: to Forth, Oswald, & Grenville, that the King would not treat without the Concurrence of his Allies, and yet England had given a Power to treat with France only, which shew'd that she did not intend to treat at all, but meant to continue the War. I had not 'till Yesterday an Opportunity of talking with Mr. Grenville on the Subject, and expressing my Wonder, after what he told me, that there should be no mention made of our States in his Commission: He could not explain this to my Satisfaction; but said he believ'd the Omission was occasioned by their Copying an old Commission given to Mr. Stanly at the last Treaty of Peace, for that he was sure the Intention was that he should treat with us, his Instructions being fully to that purpose. I acquainted him that I thought a special Commission was necessary, without which we could not conceive him authoris'd and therefore could not treat with him.— I imagine that there is a Reluctance in their King to take this first Step, as the giving such a Commission would itself be a kind of Acknowledgment of our Independence; their late Success against Count de Grasse may also have given them Hopes that by Delay & more Successes they may make that Acknowledgment & a Peace less necessary.

Mr. Grenville has written to his Court for farther Instructions. We shall see what the Return of his Courier will produce. If full Power to treat with each of the Powers at War against England does not appear, I imagine the Negociation will be broken off. Mr. G. in his Conversations with me insists much on our being under no Engagements not to make Peace without Holland. I have answer'd him that I know not but you may have enter'd into some, and that if there should be none, a general Pacification made at the same time, would be best for us all, & that I believ'd neither Holland nor we could be prevail'd on to abandon our Friends. What happens farther shall be immediately communi-

435

cated. Be pleased to present my Respects to Mr Lawrens to whom I wrote some Days since.[8] Mr Jay I suppose is on his Way hither.

With great Respect, I have the honour to be, Sir, Your Excellency's most obedient & most humble Servant   B FRANKLIN

His Exy: Jn. Adams Esqr

Endorsed: Dr Franklin June 2. 1782 Ansd 13. recd 11th.—

From Charles-Etienne Gaucher[9]

Printed invitation, signed, with MS insertions: American Philosophical Society

[before June 3, 1782]

VERITE∴ UNION∴ FORCE∴

T∴ C∴ F∴[1]

L∴ R∴ L∴ des Neuf Sœurs, Est convoquée pour le *lundi 3* du *4e.* mois D∴ L∴ D∴ L∴ V∴ L∴ 5782, en son local, rue Coquéron, à *5* heures précises. *Il y aura prestation de Serment par les officiers nouvellement Elu, & Reception au 2d. et 3eme. Grade.*[2]

Vous êtes prié d'y venir augmenter les douceurs de l'union Fraternelle.

Je suis par les N∴ C∴ D∴ V∴ M∴ V∴ T∴ H∴[3] & affectionné Frere,   GAUCHER

2e Secretaire de la R∴ L∴ des IX. Sœurs.

---

8. Above, May 25.

9. The engraver and newly elected second secretary of the Neuf Sœurs: XXXIII, xxvii; XXXVI, 461; *DBF.* His famous engraving of the crowning of the bust of Voltaire was announced in the *Jour. de Paris* on March 25, and duly praised when it was issued on July 4.

1. Très Cher Frère. The two abbreviations in the next paragraph stand for La Respectable Loge and De L'année De La Vraie Lumière 5782. The masonic year began on March 1.

2. The Neuf Sœurs held elections for new officers in May.

3. Probably, Nombres Connus Des Vénérables Maîtres Vôtre Très Humble.

L'adresse de la Loge est à M. GAUCHER, des Académies de Londres, &c. rue S. Jacques, porte cochére, vis-à-vis Saint-Yves.

Addressed: A Monsieur / Monsieur Le Docteur / franklin / A Passy / N∴ S∴

From François-Pierre de Séqueville

AL: American Philosophical Society

[before June 4, 1782][4]
Le Roy recevra Messieurs les ambassadeurs et Ministres Etrangers, Le Samedi 8 Juin au lieu du Mardi, 4.

Addressed: A Monsieur / Monsieur francklin Ministre / plenipre. des provinces unies de / l'amérique Septentrionale / A Passy. / De Séqueville

From Tench Coxe[5]

ALS and LS:[6] American Philosophical Society

Sir   Philadelphia June 4th. 1782
    I take the liberty of troubling your Excellency with information of an accident which lately happened to some Bills of Exchange drawn by the Commissioner for the time being at the Court of Versailles.

---

4. During BF's mission to France, June 4 fell on Tuesday only during 1782.
    5. This is the first extant letter from Coxe (1755–1824), a Philadelphia merchant and early promoter of American industrialization. In 1775, Coxe joined the United Company of Philadelphia for Promoting American Manufactures, and the following year he became a partner in his father's firm of Coxe, Furman & Coxe. During the war Coxe sympathized with the British and was charged with treason but avoided conviction. This is his only surviving communication with BF until 1786; the following year the two men served together in the Pa. Society for Promoting the Abolition of Slavery, and the Philadelphia Society for Political Inquiries. Coxe achieved greatest prominence as a political economist and publicist. *ANB;* Jacob E. Cooke, *Tench Coxe and the Early Republic* (Chapel Hill, N.C., 1978), pp. 93, 99.
    6. On which BF wrote "Receivd Jan 31 1783".

The *fourth* Bills of four sets were delivered to a gentleman in Philada. to be taken to Borden Town in order to procure a continuation of the set as it was feared the others were lost. This gentleman has unluckily dropt them in our Streets & every proper Step has been made use of to regain them. Under these Circumstances your Excellency will excuse the freedom I take in writing to you to apprize you of the accident— The Bills are as follow—

4th. of one set of Bills N.539. 12 drs. 26th. Feb. 82 to
Wm DeHart[7] mark KL
do of 1   do.   N. 11. 30 drs. 5th April. 82 to
Mary Henry mark PK—
do of 1   do.   . 94. 300 drs. 12th Sepr. 81 to
Jno Stevens senr. mark YW[8]
do of 1   do.   . 23. 300 drs. 8th. Jany. 82 to
Peter Schenck[9] mark ..do.

The two last were drawn by Mr. Hopkinson for interest & the two first by Mr. Hillegas for the same. *All* countersigned by Mr. Borden—[1] N.94 was endorsed to Messrs. Nesbitt & Co mentioning *I think* in the endorsement for Account of Mr. James Abercrombie[2] & the other three vizt. N.539 N.11 & N.23 were endorsed to Messrs Sigourney Ingraham & Bromfield Merchts.

7. Possibly William D'Hart (d. 1801), a major and lieutenant-colonel in, respectively, the 1st and 2nd N.J. Regiments. He resigned in 1781: Heitman, *Register of Officers*, p. 153.

8. Here BF wrote "2d Accep'd 2d May 82". Stevens was probably John Stevens, Sr. (1716–1792), a N.J. merchant who served in the Continental Congress and as president of his state's convention ratifying the Constitution: Maxine N. Lurie and Joanne R. Walroth, eds., *The Minutes of the Board of Proprietors of the Eastern Division of New Jersey . . .* (4 vols., Newark, N. J., 1949–85), IV, 474.

9. Possibly the man of this name of Millstone, N.J.: Lurie and Walroth, eds., *The Minutes of the Board of Proprietors,* IV, 248.

1. Joseph Borden, Jr. (1755–1788), the Continental loan officer for New Jersey: *Morris Papers,* I, 201n.

2. Possibly the man of this name living on Pine Street in Philadelphia by 1785: [John] Macpherson, *Macpherson's Directory, for the City and Suburbs of Philadelphia* (Philadelphia, 1785), p. [1].

of Amsterdam—[3] purporting I *think* to be for value in account with Me—

As these are all *fourth* Bills I have determined that they shall not be forwarded from hence by Me, so that if they should be presented to your Excellency for payment, I ask the favor of their being refused payment and the proper Steps taken— Unless it should be thought proper on detection of the Bills to pay the Money to the respectable houses in whose favor the genuine endorsements (under the hand of the payees) are.

I have the honor to be with very great Respect yr. Excellency's mo. obedient & mo. humble Servt.   TENCH COXE

His Excelly. Benj. Franklin Esqr.

Addressed: His Excellency / Benjamin Franklin Esqr. / Minister Penipotentiary / of the United States of Ameri / ca— / Paris / via Baltimore

Notation by William Temple Franklin: No 94—for 300 Drs. was accepd the 2d May 82—presented by Mr Chaumont

3d: No 23, accepd the 24 Augt 82. being regularly indorsed to Sigourney, Ingraham & Bromfield & presented by them, thro Messrs. Mallet le Royer—[4]

The 3d of No 11. in the same Case.

The 3d. of No 539. Do.[5]

3. For the firm see XXXVI, 119–20, and Butterfield, *John Adams Diary*, II, 453–4n.

4. The Paris banking firm of Mallet, Le Royer & Mallet fils: XXX, 570.

5. The bills to DeHart, Henry, and Schenck are listed on page 27 of BF's ledger of loan office bills dated Jan. 8 to Sept. 12, 1782 (APS). Grand accepted them at an exchange rate of 5 *l.t.* per dollar.

From ———— Jaubert fils

ALS: University of Pennsylvania Library

Monsieur   Dunkerque Le 4 Juin 1782.

Si jen dois croire Les bruits public j'aurois lieu desperer une commission en guerre contre les portugais et les anglais; armateur en cette ville, je desirerais armer en course contre ces deux nations si reellement les etats unis on declaré la guerre a cette premiere, je vous prie monsieur de me faire informer sur mon incertitude et si je puis obtenir de vous au nom des etats unis une lettre de marque pour mon projet.[6]

J'ai L'honneur d'etre tres respectueusement Monsieur Votre très humble Et très obeissant serviteur   JAUBERT FILS

Notation: Jaubert 4 Juin 1782

From Richard Oswald[7]

Copies: University of South Carolina Library (two),[8] Library of Congress (three),[9] Massachusetts Historical Society

Sir,   [June 5, 1782]

Mr Lawrens while under Confinement in England, proposed that, upon his being liberated upon his Parole, he would apply to you for an Exchange in favour of My Lord Cornwallis, by a Discharge of his Lps. [Lordship's] Parole granted upon the Surrendry of his Garrison at the Village of York in Virginia; and in Case of your being under any Difficulty in making such Ex-

---

6. For these rumors see our annotation of Gerbier to BF, May 24.

7. Written at BF's request, after Oswald had communicated its contents verbally. See the June 5 entry in BF's journal of the peace negotiations.

8. We print from the one in WTF's hand; the other is incomplete.

9. One of which, written in an unknown hand, was interleaved in BF's journal of the peace negotiations. It contains the alternate postscript, "Major Ross has got no copy of Ld. C's parole. He says it was in the common form, as in like Cases". The other two and the copy at the Mass. Hist. Soc. were made (possibly around September, 1783) by L'Air de Lamotte in three similar letterbooks consisting of documents relating to the peace negotiations.

change, he undertook to write to the Congress, and to request it of that Assembly, and made no Doubt of obtaining a favourable Answer, without Loss of Time.

This Proposal signed by Mr Lawrens's Hand, I carried and deliver'd, I think in the Month of December last, to the then Secretarys of State. Which was duly attended to; and in Consequence thereof, Mr. Lawrens was soon after set at full Liberty. And though not as a Prisoner upon Parole, yet it is to be hoped, a variation in the Mode of Discharge will not be supposed of any essential Difference. And with respect to Mr. Lawrens I am satisfied he will consider himself as much interested in the Success of this Application, as if his own Discharge had been obtained under the form proposed by the Representation which I deliver'd to his Majesty's Secretaries of State. And I make no doubt will join Lord Cornwallis in an Acknowledgement of your favour & good Offices, in granting his Lordp. a full Discharge of his Parole, as abovementioned.— I have the honour to be, Sir, Your most obedient, humble Servant,

(signed) RICHARD OSWALD

P.S. Since writing the above I recollect I was under a Mistake as if the Proposal of Exchange came from Mr. Lawrens—Whereas it was made by his Majesty's Secretaries of State to me—[1] That Mr. Laurens should endeavour to procure the Exchange of Lord Cornwallis—so as to be discharged himself. Which Proposal I carried to Mr. Laurens, & had from him the Obligation abovementioned—Upon which the Mode of his Discharge was settled.—[2] (signed) R. O.

Copy of a Letter from R. Oswald Esqr to B. Franklin Esqr dated 5th. June 1782, at Paris.

1. The British government in turn may have acted in response to Laurens' Dec. 1 petition to the House of Commons. Laurens concluded by promising that if released he would obtain in exchange the release of an equivalent British officer or other British subject or subjects imprisoned in America. This promise was dropped by the time the petition was presented, but it had been in the draft which Laurens gave Edmund Burke: *Laurens Papers*, XV, 456–8.

2. See Laurens to Oswald, Dec. 22, *Laurens Papers*, XV, 459–60.

To Richard Oswald

Copy:[3] Library of Congress

Sir   Passy, June 6th. 1782

I received the letter you did me the honor of writing to me, respecting the Parole of Lord Cornwallis. You are acquainted with what I wrote sometime since to Mr. Laurens.[4] Tomorrow is Post-day from Holland, when possibly I may receive an Answer, with a paper drawn up by him for the purpose of discharging that Parole, to be signed by us jointly. I suppose the being at Paris another day will not be very inconvenient to Major Ross;[5] and if I do not hear tomorrow from Mr. Laurens, I will immediately, in Complyance with your request, do what I can towards the Liberation of Lord Cornwallis. I have the honor to be with great Respect Sir Your most obedient Humble Servant   B. Franklin

Richd: Oswald Esqr.

From Fizeaux, Grand & Cie.

LS: University of Pennsylvania Library

Monsieur   Amsterdam le 6 Juin 1782

Pour nous rembourser des acceptations de M. Adams à nôtre domicile que nous acquitons conformement à vos ordres, & dont vous avéz la notte, nous avons pris la liberté de tirer aujourd'hui sur Vôtre Excellence

écus 2200. ⎫
  " 2300. ⎬ à 3 usances à notre ordre

écus 4500 ensemble dont nous creditons le Compte des Etats unis de l'amerique au Che. de 53 ⅞ en B f. 6032.\6.— dans la persuasion que vous voudrés bien accueillir nos traittes.[6]

---

3. In a hand we do not recognize, interleaved in BF's journal of the peace negotiations.

4. Above, May 25. See also the June 5 entry in BF's journal of the peace negotiations.

5. Identified in the journal entry cited above.

6. The bankers were drawing on BF for 4,500 écus (13,500 l.t.), exchanged for 6,032 florins 6 schellings bank money. The exchange rate was 53 ⅞ grooten

Nous avons l'honneur d'être avec une parfaite Consideration, Monsieur Vos trés humbles & tres obeissans Serviteurs

FIZEAUX GRAND COMP

S. E. Monsieur Francklin, à Passi.

Notation: Fizeaux Grand & Co. 6. Juin 1782.

William Temple Franklin to ——— Cabaret

L: American Philosophical Society

le 6 Juin 1782

Pour M. Franklin

Une Rame de Papier même Grandeur de ce ci—mais sans etre coupé et sans etre Gommé: enfin, propre pour imprimer dessus, et de la meme Espece qu'on vend aux Imprimeurs pour cet Effet—[7]

Addressed: M. Cabaret, Md de Papier / au Griffon, / Rue de Bussy / fbg St. Germains

---

per *écu,* roughly similar to the rate for a transaction in October, 1780: XXXIII, 36on, 36in. (There were 40 *grooten* in a guilder or florin: John J. McCusker, *Money and Exchange in Europe and America, 1600–1775: a Handbook* [Chapel Hill, N.C., 1978], p. 44.) Grand paid the 13,500 *l.t.* on Sept. 15: Account XXVII (XXXII, 4).

7. An undated answer from Cabaret, signed "Votre Md de papier", asked WTF for clarification. Should the sheets be full size, or cut according to what Cabaret had previously supplied? He would fill the order the following day. APS. Cabaret's bill for the period June 6 through July 26, 1782 (APS) indicates that on June 6 the stationer supplied a ream of "grand papier" for printing, at a cost of 9 *l.t.*

WTF's stationery order of July 26 is also at the APS. It requests ink, pens, and a bone folder.

To Joseph Priestley AL (draft)[8] and copy: Library of Congress

Dear Sir, Passy, near Paris, June 7. 1782.

I received your kind Letter of the 7th of April, also one of the 3d of May.[9] I have always great Pleasure in hearing from you, in learning that you are well, and that you continue your Experiments. I should rejoice much if I could once more recover the Leisure to search with you into the Works of Nature, I mean the inanimate, not the animate or moral Part of them. The more I discover'd of the former, the more I admir'd them; the more I know of the latter, the more I am disgusted with them. Men I find to be a Sort of Beings very badly constructed, as they are generally more easily provok'd than reconcil'd, more dispos'd to do Mischief to each other than to make Reparation, much more easily deceiv'd than undeceiv'd, and having more Pride & even Pleasure in killing than in begetting one another, for without a Blush they assemble in great Armies at Noon Day to destroy, and when they have kill'd as many as they can, they exaggerate the Number to augment the fancied Glory; but they creep into Corners or cover themselves with the Darkness of Night, when they mean to beget, as being asham'd of a virtuous Action.[1] A virtuous Action it would be, and a vicious one the killing of them, if the Species were really worth producing or preserving; but of this I begin to doubt. I know you have no such Doubts, because in your Zeal for their Welfare, you are taking a great deal of Pains to save their Souls. Perhaps as you grow older you may

8. BF began this letter on May 31 but the draft shows that he changed the date when, on June 7, he added the final paragraph. On the verso of the second page appears a three-inch sketch resembling a thick, double-headed arrow.

9. Neither has been found.

1. BF evidently paraphrases the following passage from Montaigne's essay "On Some Verses of Virgil": "Every one avoids seeing a Man born, every one runs to see him die. To destroy a Man, a spacious Field is sought out, and in the Face of the Sun; but to make him, we creep into as dark and private a Corner as we can. 'Tis a Man's Duty to withdraw himself from the Light to do it; but 'tis Glory, and the Fountain of many Vertues, to know how to destroy what we have done: The one is Injury, the other Favour." Robert Newcomb, "Benjamin Franklin and Montaigne," *Modern Language Notes*, LXXII (1957), 489–90.

look upon this as a hopeless Project, or an idle Amusement, repent of having murdered in mephitic Air so many honest harmless Mice, and wish that to prevent Mischief you had used Boys and Girls instead of them. In what light we are view'd by superior Beings, may be gather'd from a Piece of late West India News, which possibly has not yet reach'd you. A young Angel of Distinction being sent down to this World on some Business for the first time, had an old Courier-Spirit assign'd him as a Guide. They arriv'd over the Seas of Martinico in the middle of the long Day of obstinate Fights between the Fleets of Rodney & DeGrasse. When thro' the Clouds of Smoke he saw the Fire of the Guns, the Decks cover'd with mangled Limbs, & Bodies dead or dying, the Ships sinking, burning, or blown into the Air, and the Quantity of Pain, Misery, and Destruction the Crews yet alive were thus with so much Eagerness dealing round to one another; he turn'd angrily to his Guide, & said, You blundering Blockhead, you are ignorant of your Business; you undertook to conduct me to the Earth, and you have brought me into Hell!— No, Sir, says the Guide; I have made no Mistake; this is really the Earth, and these are Men. Devils never treat one another in this cruel manner; they have more Sense, and more of what Men (vainly) call *Humanity!*

But to be serious, my dear old Friend, I love you as much as ever, and I love all the honest Souls that meet at the London Coffeehouse.[2] I only wonder how it happen'd that they and my other Friends in England, came to be such good Creatures in the midst of so perverse a Generation. I long to see them and you once more, and I labour for Peace with more earnestness, that I may again be happy in your sweet Society.

I show'd your Letter to the Duke de Rochefoucault,[3] who thinks with me that the new Experiments you have made are extreamly curious; and he has given me thereupon a Note which I inclose, and I request you would furnish me with the Answer desired.

Yesterday the Count du Nord was at the Academy of Sciences, when sundry Experiments were exhibited for his Enter-

2. The Club of Honest Whigs: XI, 98n.
3. La Rochefoucauld.

tainment; among them one by M. Lavoisier, to show that the strongest Fire we yet know, is made in a Charcoal blown upon with dephlogisticated Air. In a Heat so produc'd he melted Platina presently, the Fire being much more powerful than that of the strongest burning Mirror.[4]

Adieu, and believe me ever, Yours most affectionately.

Reverend Dr Priestly

From William Hodgson   ALS: American Philosophical Society

Dear sir   London 7 June 1782

I have recd your favor of the 27th Ultimo & your preeceeding Letter with an Acc't of a Bill you intended for me having been recd by a Namesake of mine for £200—[5] I have rec'd the Money from him tho a good deal alarmed at first at the Circumstances.

Administration have given Clothing at their expence to the amount of 20s each man[6] indeed I cou'd not have that myself justifiable in running to such an Expence without orders, the allowance I look upon as fully sufficient for the purpose & the Men appear well satisfied with what has been done for them & I have had many handsome Letters from sundry Prisoners expressing their thankfullness at what has been done & I hope it will have

---

4. Grand Duke Paul of Russia and his wife, known in Paris as the comte and comtesse du Nord, were being entertained all over the city. At the meeting of the Academy of Sciences on June 5, they heard a number of papers, witnessed demonstrations by Lavoisier and others, and were presented with a piece of ivory carved in 1717 by Czar Peter I during his visit to France: *Jour. politique, ou Gaz. des gazettes,* July, 1782, p. 52. Lavoisier's memoir describing his technique, submitted to the Academy in November, 1782, is "Mémoire sur un Moyen d'augmenter considérablement l'action du Feu & de la Chaleur, dans les Opérations chimiques": *Histoire de L'Académie royale des sciences* for 1782, pp. 457–65.

5. The £200 is mentioned in BF's May 27 letter, but we have not found a preceding letter discussing it.

6. The order was issued at the end of May: Sheldon S. Cohen, *Yankee Sailors in British Gaols: Prisoners of War at Forton and Mill, 1777–1783* (Newark, Del., and London, 1995), pp. 173, 253.

its effect to do away in some degree the bitterness that has prevailed in the minds of Americans in general.

The Prisoners from Portsmo to the amount of 330 are gone;— Last week the Commissioners of Sick & Hurt informed me of very alarming apprehensions their Agents were filled with relative to the prisoners meditating to set fire to their prison & that they were become so riotous & ungovernable that they feared on embarkation some mischeif wou'd ensue— I happened to see the Duke of Richmond in the Evening I recd this Acct—(he had the week before been at Forton & behaved with great kindness to the prisoners)— I communicated to his Grace the Information I had recd he was much concerned at it & inded alarmed & said If I coud possibly spare Time he wou'd wish me to go to Portsmo to endeavour to pacify the Men if any thing was wrong assuring me that I might depend whatever I did he wou'd bear me out in— I accordingly set out post immediately & was agreably surprised on my Arrival to find all peace & good order & a total inability to discover the least foundation for the surmise—the Men embarked with all the good Temper imaginable not a disorderly sound or Gesture from any one nor a Man disguised in Liquor.

The wind having been contrary the Transports for the Plymo prisoners were not arrived, but I imagine they are by this Time— I had previous to the reception of your last Letter, written to Congress (per Mr Thomson) just in the manner you recommend, & have no doubt but they will do what is just & right on their part in the Business[7]—there will be upwards of 700 Prisoners from Plymo—the greatest part of those from Kinsale being arrived at Plymo[8]—some few sick will remain so that another Vessell will be required as a Cartel in a short Time.

I am very much obliged to you for your obliging assurance of a compliance wit my request of the 10th Ultimo, & hope you will

7. For Hodgson's letter to Thomson see our annotation of Hodgson to BF, May 10.

8. On June 24, some 400 American prisoners from Mill Prison in Plymouth (including 70 or 80 transferred from Kinsale) embarked aboard the cartel ship *Lady's Adventure:* Cohen, *Yankee Sailors,* p. 203.

be pleased to remember that to be usefull it must be special in dispatch I am with the greatest Respect Dr sir yrs most Sincerely

WILLIAM HODGSON

P.S. I am more & more convinced every day that what I surmised in my last Letter⁹ respecting the friendly disposition of certain persons more than others, is wellfounded, & I am further convinced that if any obstacles occurr, which cannot well be got over in the common form, that if you give me a hint to guide them it will be attended to—for I seriously believe they mean to walk fairly & uprightly.

Addressed: To / His Excellency Benj. Franklin Esqr

From Benjamin Vaughan   ALS: American Philosophical Society

My dearest sir,   London, June 7th:, 1782.

Mr Bowen has by this time received your books, directed to Ostend.—¹ May you go on with the work of peace for which you are so gloriously prepared by the spirit of sweet humanity & an enlarged mind. I think I may venture to say from a knowledge of characters that no liberality YOU introduce herein, will meet with a repulse; on the contrary, that it will meet with a most willing acceptance. I must look therefore to *you* on this occasion for some generous precedent in favor of human rights; and as you labored so meritoriously to prevent a senseless war,² I hope you will now adopt hints in your peace, framed upon some of those liberal doctrines with which your mind & writings are so conspicuously marked. A philosopher of your stamp should do nothing which is not novel & pregnant; and I *know* that more may [*be*] done in this line than you suspect, both in the form of [*torn*]erous language & humane measures, with which therefore I hope to hear your terms are marked and tinctured throughout.— You are too wise to let this hint displease or escape you,

9. Above, May 10.
1. For these books, see BF to Vaughan, July 10.
2. See particularly XXI, 540–99.

knowing from what opportunities I speak.— If the sugar refiners press our West India people, in addition to the admission of sugars from all our captured islands, I shall not be surprised if we get neutral colors to go to all our islands, so as to make for us a maritime peace, & thus lessen the horrors of war to individuals.

At present I am as much hurried as yourself, but I thought this hint of too much magnitude to your glory & that of mankind to omit it.

Mr Oswald perhaps may tell you of Mr Laurens's strange behavior here.[3] As I thought he might ask to see my first letter about him to you, I made it very civil.[4]

I am, my dearest sir, ever yours most devotedly, gratefully, & affect[*torn*]   B V——N.

I have given orders for shipping £6000 in goods to America.— A number of people are beginning to emigrate but none of much conseq[*torn*] I think many amiable people will go from our islands, & with conside[*torn*]

From James Moylan   ALS: American Philosophical Society

Honord Sir   L'Orient 8th. June 1782

Mr. Henry Mitchell[5] of Boston who arrived here in the ship Alexander from Virginia, thinks it necessary to have a Letter of introduction to your Excellency, and notwithstanding I am con-

---

3. Oswald had discussed with BF Laurens' attempts to procure his exchange, but we do not know whether this is the "strange behavior" in question: Oswald to BF, June 5, and BF's journal of the peace negotiations, under the same date. Vaughan had been involved in a dispute with Laurens over the latter's supposed ill-treatment of Vaughan's brother William: *Laurens Papers*, XV, 563n.

4. Vaughan had discussed Laurens in several letters written to BF before Oswald's appointment: XXXVI, 59, 371–2, 414, 543–4.

5. BF had furnished Mitchell with a passport in March, 1780: XXXI, 365n. He was the owner of the *Alexander:* Charles Henry Lincoln, comp., *Naval Records of the American Revolution, 1775–1788* (Washington, D.C., 1906), p. 223. On June 18, BF gave him a pass to travel to Amsterdam: XXXVI, 380.

vincd that an American Subject do's not stand in need of any to your Excellency, yet to gratify Mr. Mitchells desire I have freely consented to recommend him to your civilities. He is a very particular friend & nearly connected with Mr. Thomas Barclay, who, as well as myself will acknowlege any obligation this introduction may lay us under to your Excellency. I have the Honor to be with the utmost respect Hond. Sir Your most hl st
JAMES MOYLAN

His Excellency B. Franklin Esqr. Passÿ

Addressed: His Excellency / Benj: Franklin Esqr. / American Ambassador / at the Court of Versailles / Passy

Notation: James Moylan 8. June 1782.

From Schweighauser & Dobrée

ALS: Historical Society of Pennsylvania

Sir!   Nantes 8 June 1782.
We have had the honor of writing to your Excellency the 18 dec. last informing you of the decease of our Worthy Parent Mr Schweighauser[6] and are Since without any of your esteemed favors. The chief purpost of this Serves to acquaint You that the King's Officer has obliged us instantly to remove all the articles of the Arsenal[7] in another Magazine in order to make Baracks of the former, we have made every representation in our power to save this expence but to no purpose, we are now employed to this desagreable work as Soon as it is finished we will Send your Excellency a note of our charges together with an account of money paid to Americans escaped from prison—at this occasion permit us once more to request you would fix the exact allowance to be given them— We have constant applications from Brest, Morlaix & St: Malo & are obliged to leave these letters unan-

6. Their letter has not been found. The late senior partner of the firm was Jean-Daniel Schweighauser (XXII, 314–15n).

7. The firm was still responsible for the United States' arsenal in the port. JW had turned it over to Schweighauser in 1778: XXVII, 455–6; Thomas Barclay to BF, July 28, 1783 (AAE).

swered— Our Correspondents have occasionally afforded Some Assistance to those who have landed in the above ports & drawn the amount on us which we have regularly honoured.

In our last we requested your Excellency would remind our advances for the Alliance—[8] Our partners in the house en *Commandite* of Puchelberg & C in L'Orient insisted on arresting this frigate during her last Stay in that port—*but we absolutely forbidded it;* not doubting but Congress in its Equity & Justice will soon remit us our due with usual Interest especially if your Excellency will be please to represent our case when next you write which would be most greatfully acknowledged by us & our Co-heirs.

Mr Arnous[9] a Capital Merchant of this place having desired us to sell him two Anchors of the Arsenal we have promised to Sollicit that permission of your Excellency.

We have the honor to be Your Excellency's Most humble & most obt servants   SCHWEIGHAUSER & DOBRÉE

To his Excellency Benjamin franklin Esqr Minister plenipotentiary of the united States of America Passy

Notation: Schweighauser et Dobré 8. Juin 1782.

Franklin: Discharge of Cornwallis from His Parole

Press copy of LS, copy and transcript:[1] National Archives; copies: William L. Clements Library,[2] South Carolina Historical Society

Given at Passy, this 9th Day of June 1782.
The Congress having by a Resolution of the 14th. of June last, impower'd me to offer an Exchange of General Burgoyne for the

---

8. These were unauthorized: XXXIII, 171–4. The principal of the firm had appealed directly to Congress for payment on Nov. 30, 1780: *JCC*, XX, 590.

9. For whom see our annotation of JW to BF, June 14.

1. The LS is in WTF's hand. The copy, made by L'Air de Lamotte, was received by Congress on Sept. 18. According to a notation, it was referred to a committee consisting of delegates Ezekiel Cornell, James Madison, and John Rutledge.

2. Which is in Shelburne's papers along with a memorandum of Oswald's (summarized in our annotation of BF to Oswald, June 11).

honourable Mr Lawrens then a Prisoner in the Tower of London, & whose Liberty they much desired to obtain;[3] which Exchange tho' proposed by me according to the said Resolutions,[4] had not been accepted or executed, when Advice was received that General Burgoyne was exchang'd in virtue of another Agreement[5] and Mr Lawrens having thereupon proposed another Lieutenant General, viz Lord Cornwallis, as an Exchange for himself, promising that if set at Liberty he would do his utmost to obtain a Confirmation of that Proposal:[6] And Mr Lawrens being soon after discharged and having since urged me earnestly in several Letters, to join with him in absolving the Parole of that General,[7] which appears to be a Thing just and equitble in itself, and for the honour therefore of our Country; I do hereby as far as in my Power lies, in virtue of the abovementioned Resolution or otherwise, absolve and discharge the Parole of Lord Cornwallis given by him in Virginia; setting him at intire Liberty to act in his Civil or Military Capacity, untill the Pleasure of Congress shall be known, to whom is reserved the Confirmation or Disapprobation of this Discharge, in Case they have made or shall intend to make, a different Disposition.

B FRANKLIN
Minister Plenipotentiary from the United States of America at the Court of France.

From Bethia Alexander   ALS: University of Pennsylvania Library

St: Germain Ce 9 Juin 1782

La peste, mon cher Docteur a derangée tous les projets du Philosophe de Toulouse—[8] il n'y aura ni Thèse ni dedicace— ainsi nous voila quitte de tous ces embarras là.— Je voudrois

---

3. XXXV, 221–2; *JCC*, XX, 647–8.
4. XXXV, 594. See also XXXVI, 13, 279n, 300–2, 326–7, 371, 621n.
5. See Laurens to BF, April 7.
6. See Oswald to BF, June 5.
7. Laurens to BF, April 30 and May 17, above.
8. Bonnefoux's letter to BF of June 16, below, describes the epidemic at Toulouse.

savoir si vous avez fait une visite à Madame la Comtesse de la Mark[9] comme vous me l'avez promis—si vous l'avez oublier vous meritrez que J'aille à Paris exprès pour vous Gronder—si vous l'avez fait Je desirois y aller pour vous remercier, de tout façon Je meure d'envie de vous voir—mais Je ne sais pas comment m'y prendre— Je n'est pas de voiture—si vous m'aimez autant que Je vous aime vous tacherez d'arranger tout cela avec mon Pere.— Le Pere General vous ecrit il vous expliquera pourquoi son Philosophe n'a plus besoin de vous.—[1] Adieu Docteur ingrat Docteur car Je suis sure que vous ne pensez non plus a moi qui si Je n'etois plus au nombre des vivans—ecrivez moi que J'ai tort si vous l'osez.— Votre affectionnée

BETHIA ALEXANDER

Il y a ici une Dame qui desire savoir si vos cheminées à la Franklin—epargne du Bois—donne plus de chaleur que les autres; et ce qu'elles coutent[2]

Apropos mon Pere parle d'aller en angleterre souvenez vous de votre promesse et n'aller pas engager une autre menagere— Mes Compliments à mon Petit Cousin.—

Addressed: His Excellence B. Franklin Esqr: / at / Passy

Notation: Mlle Alexander. 9. Juin 1782.

From Hilliard d'Auberteuil

ALS: University of Pennsylvania Library

Monsieur   Paris ce 9 Juin 1782.
    Vous avez bien raison, Mais sur dix noms Anglais nos imprimeurs font neuf fautes, cela engage à éviter de les répéter; d'ailleurs l'usage a établi ces traductions de noms à tel point dans

---

9. For the comtesse see our annotation to William Alexander's letter to BF of April 24.

1. Bonnefoux's title was *supérieur-général;* his explanation is below, June 16.

2. Possibly Mme de Poterat, whose letter thanking BF for information about the stove is in XXXV, 576–7.

ce pays ci, que je m'apercois à peine moi même de leur irregularité; tout le monde dit ici le nouveau Jersey et jamais *New Jersey* &ca.[3] J'ai à ce sujet des altercations journalieres avec l'ingenieur geographe qui dirige la gravure de mes cartes,[4] Il traduit la moitié des noms, & me cite toujours l'autorité de ses predecesseurs et de ses confreres, en sorte que le lecteur cherchant sur les cartes telle ville qu'il aura remarquée dans le livre, aura quelques fois de la peine à la trouver. Je tacherai pourtant d'éviter cet inconvenient autant qu'il dépendra de moi.

Je suis infiniment reconnaissant de votre attention et j'ai profité de votre avis relativement au gué de *Chadd* &ca.[5]

Je suis avec la plus respectueuse consideration, Monsieur de votre Excellence Le très humble & très obéissant serviteur

HILLIARD D'AUBERTEUIL

3. Inconsistent renderings and outright misspellings of American place names can be found throughout Hilliard's volumes, even on the same page. "New" and "Nouveau" (or "Nouvelle," for New York/Yorck) were interchangeable. Rhode Island, which variously appeared with hyphens, apostrophes, and a dropped "e," was occasionally rendered as "l'île de Rhodes."

4. The maps for both volumes were being engraved by Louis Brion de la Tour, *géographe du roi*, based on English originals and were available for sale individually or as a set. The first group of six maps was advertised in the *Jour. de Paris* on July 30. The remaining two maps were announced on Oct. 19, along with the rest of the illustrative material. Four historical prints, drawn by Barbier and engraved by Messrs. Halbou, Patas, and Ponce, could be purchased separately for 3 *l.t.* apiece. The three portraits—Hancock, William Pitt, and BF—were 2 *l.t.* apiece. The octavo edition of *Essais historiques et politiques . . .* , including all plates, was offered at 21 *l.t.;* without plates, the volumes were sold for 12 *l.t.* Both books and plates were available from Hilliard. For Brion de la Tour (1756–1823) see Ronald Vere Tooley, *Tooley's Dictionary of Mapmakers* (Tring, England, 1979), pp. 81–2.

5. Though Hilliard usually referred to Chadd's Ford as "gué de Chadd," BF may have been responsible for his adding a gloss to the term "Chadd'sfort" on p. 256.

From Georgiana Shipley

ALS: American Philosophical Society

My dear Doctor Franklin,   Bolton Street June the 9th. 1782

As Mr Jones[6] is so obliging as to promise he will convey my letter to Passy, I can not resist this good & safe opportunity of writing to assure my very best friend, that among all the events which may possibly arise from the late changes in our Administration, there is no one can give me half so much pleasure as the flattering idea of seeing you once more in England & again renewing those delightful hours, I have formerly spent in your valued society— I hope you have received a letter & parcel I intrusted to Mr Alexander, which contained the shades you requested;[7] the resemblance is so imperfect, I fear you will be scarce able to trace the likeness of any one of your young friends.

Next week we begin our long journey to St Asaph; we are all weary of London & wish to enjoy good country-air, but we have been detained here beyond the usual time by an epidemic disorder, which none of us have escaped; indeed it has prevailed universally, altho: it has been far more severe in the metropolis & its environs than in any other part of the Kingdom.

I have been so unfortunate as seldom to have seen Doctor Price during the winter— Doctor Priestley was in town for about six weeks & is returned to Birmingham; we propose dining with him there, in our way to St Asaph.

I am in a great hurry of business, but would not omit an occasion of assuring you, my dear Doctor Franklin, with how great respect & esteem, I am Your obliged & affecate Friend.

G: SHIPLEY

Addressed: Doctor Franklin / Passy

---

6. William Jones.

7. BF requested the silhouettes in February, 1781, and almost certainly received them in early March, 1782, when William Alexander returned to Paris from England: XXXIV, 347, 410; XXXV, 34; XXXVI, lxv, 257. We cannot identify the letter entrusted to Alexander.

From Joseph Smith[8]

ALS: American Philosophical Society

at Cape St Nicelaw [Nicolas]

Dear Sir   Hispanola June 9th 1782

As a true Subject to the States of ammerecia and our Worthy Alleys I would take the Liberty haveing this Oppertunity to acquaint your honner of a Case which hes bentride [has been tried] in this Iseland and is now Left to your honnors determination that on or About the 25 of febury I being in a Crusing brig Cauled the Lady Greene duly Commisned by Congress to Crueze against the Enemise of Unitd States of Ammerica being of the West End of this Iland I fell in with a Sloop Cauled the St Thomas under danish Colours I brot her two & upon Examing her papers I found a burgers breefe and a Clearance from the Custom house in Kingston in Jamaica Shee had Sundry Merchantdise on board I thot it my duty to Carry her in to port for Trial I carryed her into the Port of Jeremee [Jérémie] wher Shee was Tryed and Condemnd as A Good prise to the Captors the Judgment of the admeltry was Sent to the Cape and their Ratifide by the General and Intendant as a Good prize to mee and the Neat proseads Ordred to bee deposd in the hands of the Tresery untill Judgment Should bee determined by the dupetyse [deputies] from Congress I Expectd to have arrivd at the Cape before the Convoy Saild I Expet the papers will Come to your hands by this Convoy if they are Sent if they are not I Shall forward them as Soon as possibell. You will Sir See Every Paper that was onbord of Hur and you may depend that the Sloop is Three Quarters Oned in Jamaica and one Quarter Oned in the Cape.

As I have Sence bentaken and Carryed to Jamaica and was Credebly Informd I hope your honour when Seing the papers and the Judgment of the Courts of this Iland which I have Inclosd a Coppy[9] would take the matter into your most Srus [serious] Consideration and finding her to bee a Good prise would

---

8. A veteran ship captain from Middletown, Conn., Smith was at this time commander of the brigantine *Lady Greene*, 14: Claghorn, *Naval Officers*, p. 286; Louis F. Middlebrook, *History of Maritime Connecticut during the American Revolution, 1775–1783* (2 vols., Salem, Mass., 1925), II, 71, 142–3.

9. The enclosure was a rough translation of the Admiralty court's judgment, in Smith's hand.

Order the money to bee paid to the Captors as I make no dout
but I Shall have Justes done me and am Sir with due Respect your
most Obediant Humbl Servant   JOSEPH SMITH
                                Comd of Lady Greene

To the Right Onnerabe Mr Franklin imbassedor for the United
States of America now Residing in Parris

To Jonathan Shipley

LS:[1] Yale University Library; AL (draft) and copy: Library of Congress

Passy June 10th. 1782.

I received and read the Letter from my dear and much respected
Friend[2] with infinite Pleasure. After so long a silence, and the
long Continuance of its unfortunate Causes, a Line from you
was a Prognostic of happier Times approaching, when we might
converse and communicate freely, without Danger from the
malevolence of Men enraged by the ill Success of their distracted
Projects.

I long with you for the Return of Peace, on the general Principles of Humanity. The Hope of being able to pass a few more
of my last Days happily in the sweet Conversations & Company
I once enjoy'd at Twyford,[3] is a particular Motive that adds
Strength to the general Wish, and quickens my Industry to procure that best of Blessings. After much Occasion to consider the
Folly and Mischiefs of a State of Warfare, and the little or no
Advantage obtained even by those Nations who have conducted
it with the most Success, I have been apt to think that there has
never been or ever will be any such Thing as a good War or a
bad Peace.[4]

---

1. In WTF's hand.

2. Above, May 9.

3. For BF's visits to Twyford see *Autobiog.*, pp. 22–3, illustration between
pp. 44 and 45; Van Doren, *Franklin*, pp. 413–17.

4. For an earlier expression of this sentiment see XXXI, 437. In the margin
of the draft BF wrote but crossed out, "tho' there may have been a difference
in degree yet [*word illegible*]".

You ask if I still relish my old Studies? I relish them, but I cannot pursue them. My Time is engross'd unhappily with other Concerns. I requested of the Congress last Year my Discharge from this Publick Station, that I might enjoy a little Leisure in the Evening of a long Life of Business: But it was refused me;[5] and I have been obliged to drudge on a little longer.

You are happy as your Years come on in having that Dear & most amiable Family about you. Four Daughters[6]—how rich!— I have but one, and she necessarily detained from me at 1000 Leagues Distance. I feel the Want of that tender Care of me which might be expected from a Daughter, and would give the World for one. Your Shades[7] are all placed in a Row over my Fire place, so that I not only have you always in my Mind, but constantly before my Eyes.

The Cause of Liberty and America has been greatly obliged to you. I hope you will live long to see that Country flourish under its new Constitution, which I am sure will give you great Pleasure. Will you permit me to express another Hope, that now your Friends are in Power they will take the first Opportunity of shewing the Sense they ought to have of your Virtues and your Merit.

Please to make my best Respects acceptable to Mrs. Shipley, and embrace for me tenderly all our dear Children. With the utmost Esteem, Respect & Veneration, I am ever my dear Friend, Yours most affectionately.   B FRANKLIN

Bishop of St Asaph.

From John Adams

AL (draft): Massachusetts Historical Society

Sir   Amsterdam June 10. 1782

I have the Honour to inform you, that I have this day drawn upon you, in favour of Messrs Fizeau Grand & Co for the

5. XXXIV, 446–7; XXXV, 174–5.

6. One of his five daughters, Amelia, was married and no longer living at home: XVIII, 199–202.

7. The silhouettes drawn by Shipley's daughter Georgiana, for which see her letter of June 9.

Amount of Six hundred and twenty five Pounds sterling being for my Salary, for one Quarter of a Year, which you will please to charge to the United States, according to the Resolutions of Congress.[8] I hope I shall not have occasion to draw upon your Excellency for any further Sums for my Salary, because although I have no Sanguine Hopes of obtaining a Loan very Suddenly, for any very large sum, yet I am led to expect some what.

I have the Honour &c

His Excellency Benjamin Franklin Esq.

From Edward Bridgen

ALS: American Philosophical Society

My Dear Sir London June 10 1782
  This letter will be delivered into your hands by Mr Foy[9] a particular & worthy Friend of Mine who is going to Switzerland but intending to make some little Stay in the Neighbourhood of Paris in order to perfect himself in the French Language wishes for the honour of being introduced to you Sir which I now take the liberty of doing and to recommend him to your kind Notice & Advice if wanting and whatever civillities you Are So good to Shew him I shall esteem as done to Dr Sir Your Affectionate Friend and Obliged Hum: Servt: EDWD: BRIDGEN

Benjn: Franklin Esqr

[*In Foy's hand:*] Mr Foy Hotel de Saxe Rue de Columbier.

Addressed: Benjn. Franklin Esqr / at Passy / near Paris / by favour of Sidney Hollis Foy Esqr

Endorsed: E Bridgen 10 June 82

---

8. Ferdinand Grand paid the bill on July 20: Account XXVII (XXXII, 4).
    9. Foy was from Dorsetshire. He died at Caen early in 1784: *Gent. Mag.*, LIV (1784), 150.

From Seth Jaquà[1]

ALS: Historical Society of Pennsylvania

My Lord.   Lisbon 10th, June 1782.

I eagerly embrace this opportunity of informing your Excellency that I am an American, born in Salisbury, had the Honr. of serving Two years and Six Months as a Lieutenant in Colonel Brown's Corps and acted as Commissary to Genl. Sullivan's Camp, had the Misfortune to be taken by a party of the Indians, who lay in ambush on our march to fort Stanwix, Commanded by the inhuman & unfeeling Colonel Butler, from whom, & from the merciless, & blood thirsty Indians acting under him, I recd. the most cruel and shocking Treatmt. marched quite naked thro Swamps woods, & wildernesses, for sevl. days, witht. any Nourishment, but what was hardly sufficient to sustain nature, words cannot express the miseries & torments I was daily exposed to, was confined in Jail in Quebeck for two years & odd days, on a half Starving allowance of provisions. At the expiration of sd. Time was sent on board an English Transport bound to London, but being drove by contrary winds into Beerhaven in the South west part of Ireland where I got an opportunity of escaping from their hands into the Country, from which place I in six Months time procured a Passage on board of a Portugueze Vessel bound to this Port, thro' the Generosity & goodness of an Irish Young Man, who sailed in the same Vessel, Paid five Guineas for my Passage, & was my best friend both here & in Ireland on every occasion his name is Mr. Thornton. I would have suffered a great deal here, being destitute of Cloaths, money, or necessaries, had it not been for the humanity of the French Agent[2] residing here, The American Gentleman[3] who

---

1. Though many of the officers mentioned in this letter are well-known (and Maj. John Butler was indeed notorious for his cruelty), Jaquà's chronology of events does not conform with any accounts we located.

2. Most likely either Jean-Baptiste Pecquet or a M. Mazaret, who had been aiding Americans in Lisbon: XXXIII, 517; XXXVI, 628n.

3. He may be referring to Arnold Henry Dohrmann, a Dutchman, who had been named American agent in Portugal in 1780. In August, 1781, BF asked John Jay to appoint a new American agent in Lisbon after Dohrmann went bankrupt. As far as we know, no American replaced Dohrmann: XXVI, 211n; XXXV, 381, 397–8.

succours distressed men in my Situation being not at Home, I arrived here the 7th. Inst.

I humbly request that your Excellency will be so Kind as to remit me in behalf of the Continental Congress, by the return of the Packet, a Sum sufficient for buying me a couple Suits of Cloths, for paying what I owe to Mr. Thornton, for defraying my Expences here & for paying my travelling Expences & Passage to America by the way of Cadiz, as it is the nearest place where I expect a Vessel. I remain with due esteem your Excellencies most obedient & most humble Servant   SETH JAQUÀ

His Excellency Dr. Franklin Ambassador at the Court of Paris in behalf of the free & Independent united States of North America.

From Robert Morris

LS: American Philosophical Society; copy: Library of Congress

Sir,   Office of Finance Philada. June 10th. 1782

The Annexed is Copy of a Letter which was written to you on the 22d. March last by the Baron D'arndt[4] who had the misfortune to be Captured and carried into New York, he is come out on Parole and informs me that he lost the original Letter wherefore I furnish him with a Copy and hereby Confirm the Contents.

I am Sir Your most obedient humble Servant.

ROBT MORRIS

His Excellency Benjm. Franklin Esqr.

Notation: Robt. Morris March 22. 1782

4. The letter, printed above, was actually from Morris; d'Arendt was its intended bearer. The copy that accompanied the present letter is at the APS.

From Matthew Ridley

ALS: American Philosophical Society

Sir   Amsterdam June 1oh: 1782.

A Vessell is arrived here from Baltimore. She brings Letters dated as late as the 15h: April.— Got out of the Capes the 7th. May— It appears Mons de La Luzerne's House at Philadelphia had been struck in the Month of April with Lightning— From the account given of it—The House appears in a manner to rent in pieces—some Furniture inside the House burnt & a French Officer much scorch'd but fortunately no Lives lost.— They impute the accident to the want of *Dr. Franklin's* lightning Rods.—[5] Genl. Washington had appointed Genl. Knox & Mr Governeur Morris to negotiate an exchange of prisoners.—[6] Mr Gadsden had been elected Governor of South Carolina but declined serving—[7] British property in that state was confiscated. The Reason given the having sequestered American property by the British & the savage manner in which Lord Cornwallis had conducted the War.—[8] Their Government seems to be acquiring some consistancy: And it is expected they will raise their Quota of Troops— They held their Assembly within 30 miles of Charles Town.—[9] The following Action in the Delaware I think deserves to be noticed.

The Merchants of Philadelphia fitted out a Vessell called the Hyder-Aly for the protection of the River. She mounted 10 six & six nine pounders had 125 Men & was commanded by Captain: J. Barney.— She went down with a number of Vessells outward bound & was laying at Anchor at the Capes when the General Monk Sloop of War & the Fair American Lately taken by

---

5. La Luzerne's residence, which lacked lightning rods, was struck by lightning on March 27; the injured French officer, Lt. Albert-Rémy de Meaux (b. 1753), died on April 30: Bodinier, *Dictionnaire* (under Meaux).

6. They were appointed on March 11, but their negotiations failed: Fitzpatrick, *Writings of Washington*, XXIV, 53–9, 186–7.

7. Christopher Gadsden declined for reasons of health and age: *ANB*.

8. On Feb. 26, the S.C. legislature authorized seizure of the property of a number of Loyalists: Richard K. Showman *et al.*, eds., *The Papers of General Nathanael Greene* (12 vols. to date, Chapel Hill, N.C., and London, 1976–), X, 415n, 458–9n.

9. The S.C. legislature met at Jacksonborough (Jacksonboro), west of Charleston: *ibid.*, 48n.

the English made their appearance. At their approach most of the Vessells push'd up the River—two or three attempted to push out & are supposed to be taken by the Fair American. The General Monk or rather the Captain of her judging from the appearance of the Hyder-Aly that she was an easey prize fired a single Gun to bring her to, in action. Capt: Barney raked him with a Broad side which killed & wounded almost every Officer & a number of Men— He gave a second equally as well directed & after an Action of 28 minutes the General Monk struck & was as my Letter says at Phila.—she is coppered, mounts 18 nine pounders & have 125 Men.— The Hyder-Aly had 4 Men killed & 11 wounded— The General Monk 53 killed & wounded.[1]

I have not yet been able to learn any other particulars— If I do that should be worth communicating I will write again—

The Vessell that arrived was chased off the Texel by part of Lord Howes fleet—[2] The Captain says he counted 16. Sail.

Since being here I have been attacked with a violent disorder called by some the Influenza. With Bleeding &c. I am got better— Every American here has had it & many of the Dutch.—[3] Mr Barclay is just getting about after having had it. He desires his respects. I beg you will accept mine with kind remembrance to Mr Wm Franklin & that you will believe me respectfully.

Your Excellencys Most Obedient servant   MATT: RIDLEY

Notation: Ridley 10 June 1782

---

1. The *Hyder-Ally*, commanded by Joshua Barney (xxxv, 427n), captured the *General Monk* (formerly the American privateer *General Washington*) on April 8. She was taken into service by the Pa. State Navy, renamed the *General Washington*, and placed under Barney's command, but soon was converted into a packet boat: Hulbert Footner, *Sailor of Fortune: the Life and Adventures of Commodore Barney, U.S.N.* (New York and London, 1940), pp. 101, 104–8, 116, 125.

2. On May 10, Adm. Richard Howe sailed with nine ships of the line to cruise off the Dutch coast: David Syrett, *The Royal Navy in European Waters during the American Revolutionary War* (Columbia, S.C., 1998), p. 156.

3. Both JA and Thaxter had what JA called influenza: *Adams Correspondence*, IV, 324.

To Richard Oswald

LS:[4] William L. Clements Library; copy:[5] Library of Congress, transcript: National Archives

Sir,   Passy, June 11. 1782.

I did intend to have waited on you this Morning, to enquire after your Health, and deliver the enclos'd Paper relating to the Parole of Lord Cornwallis;[6] but being oblig'd to go to Versailles I must postpone my Visit till tomorow. I do not conceive that I have any Authority in Virtue of my office here to absolve that Parole, in any Degree: I have therefore endeavoured to found it as well as I could on the express Power given me by Congress to exchange Gen. Burgoyne for Mr. Laurens. A Reservation is made, of Confirmation or Disapprobation by Congress, not from any Desire in me to restrain the entire Liberty of that General; but because I think it decent and my Duty, to make such Reservation, and that I might otherwise be blam'd as assuming a Power not given me, if I undertook to discharge absolutely a Parole given to Congress without any Authority from them for so doing. With great Esteem and Respect, I have the honour to be, Sir, Your most obedient and most humble Servant

B Franklin

I have receiv'd no answer from Mr. Laurens.[7]

R. Oswald Esqe.

Endorsed: Doctr Franklins Letter to Mr Oswald on the Subject of Ld Cornwallis's Parole 11— June 1782

---

4. In L'Air de Lamotte's hand, except for the last seven words of the complimentary close, which are in BF's hand.

5. The copy and transcript are in BF's journal of the peace negotiations.

6. BF's declaration conditionally releasing Cornwallis from his parole, above, June 9. Oswald made a copy to which he appended a memorandum, presumably for Shelburne as it is among the latter's papers (William L. Clements Library). The memorandum asserted that in spite of the conditional nature of the parole, Congress would not dare rescind it; hence, Cornwallis need have no concern. Oswald believed it would have been improper to insist on alterations as the document was "abundantly Sufficient." See also the June 12 entry in BF's journal of the peace negotiations.

7. An answer to BF's May 25 letter to Laurens, above.

Notation: Passy. 11th. June 1782 Dr. Franklin to Mr. Oswald. on Lord Cornwallis's Parole. In Mr Oswald's of 11th. June.[8]

From Lafayette   ALS: Library of Congress

My Dear Sir   Paris june 11h 1782[9]

Major Ross Having Called Upon me this Morning, and Having said that in the Mean while You Give His Lordship's Conditional Disharge it was Your Opinion I should Give that of the Aids de Camp at the Bottom of which you will Express Your Approbation of the Measure, I Request You will please to Have the Piece drawn up in the Way that Appears to You the Most properly Expressed—[1]

When General Lincoln Has Been Released his family were Exchanged With Him, and it May serve as a precedent, particularly Now that Negotiations *are said* to Be likely to take place.[2]

Congress are so very strict, and General Washington so very Cautious Upon the Exclusive Rights of Governement *Alone* in

8. As this letter is with Shelburne's papers, presumably it was enclosed in a June 11 letter from Oswald to Shelburne. On the following day Oswald wrote Shelburne that he had thanked BF for the generous way he had treated Cornwallis: Guinta, *Emerging Nation,* I, 428–9.

9. Our best reading of the date; Idzerda, *Lafayette Papers,* V, 39 gives it as "June 12h."

1. In his journal of the peace negotiations (entries of June 9–12), BF relates the process by which discharges from parole were drafted for Cornwallis and his aides-de-camp. On June 10, Lafayette went to Passy with Ross. There they saw the discharge for Cornwallis that BF had drafted on June 9 (above), but Ross also wanted discharges for the aides-de-camp. BF told Lafayette to write the document; Lafayette, instead, drafted something for BF to sign. BF refused (entry of June 10). In the present document Lafayette seems to agree that he will sign a discharge if BF drafts it. On the afternoon of June 12, Lafayette sent BF his own draft of the discharge, which BF approved. In the meantime, BF had sent his discharge for Cornwallis to Oswald on June 11 (above).

2. Lincoln's "family" refers to his military family, *i.e.,* his aides. They and Lincoln were exchanged in November, 1780, five months after being released on parole: Fitzpatrick, *Writings of Washington,* XX, 322–3; Idzerda, *Lafayette Papers,* III, 260n; David B. Mattern, *Benjamin Lincoln and the American Revolution* (Columbia, S.C., 1995), pp. 110, 114.

settling all Exchanges[3] that I Cannot take Great deal Upon Myself— I am without Instructions whatsoever, and Have no Powers of Any kind— But Congress know My Intentions are Good, and I Cannot Be Accused of a Propensity towards the British Nation— I think therefore that if I Am Authorised By your Advice I May Concur with You in Releasing the family of the General you Have disharged, Provided it is in the same Conditional Way—that is in Case the Exchange is Immediately Made By Congress, or Has been Agreed to Even Before We write this peace— Be pleased therefore, My dear sir, to Have it drawn up in the Way that Appears Most Convenient to Every party, Provided it does not Commit Either You or Me (for you know that in our American Governement one Must be Cautious) and after it is writen fair, Leave a place for My Name to Be put in and Be pleased to write You think the Conditional exchange of these Gentlemen (so far as you know it) Consistent with the sense of Congress, and that you Advise me to Agree to the Measure, or any thing that Appears to You will Answer the purpose.

Most Respectfully and Affectionately Yours   LAFAYETTE

I think with you, My dear sir, we must in this Moment do every thing we Can to show our good dispositions, so as to let the Ennemy Have the Blame in every miscarriage of Negotiations— and personally I wish to Act politely By lord Cornwallis

From Jonathan Williams, Sr.

ALS: Historical Society of Pennsylvania

Dear sr   Boston June 11th. 1782

Your favour of the 7 June 81 was handed me a few days ago. I understand the Gentleman Mr: Beyerle you recommended Landed at Rhod Island & went to the southward[4] had he Come

---

3. See Fitzpatrick, *Writings of Washington*, XIX, 148–9.

4. BF's letter has not been found. It was almost certainly a duplicate of the recommendation of John Francis de Beÿerlé that BF sent to Michael Hillegas on June 17, 1781: XXXV, 171–2. Beÿerlé reached Philadelphia in April: Hillegas to BF, April 29, above.

to Boston your Letter would have intitled him to every Assistance in my power & Given me pleasure.

Aunt Mecom paid us a Visit in the Spring & was so fourtunate as to receive your present wilest she was here & indeed apear'd as happy as I ever new her, but by a Late Letter from her I find she is sadly afflicted with the Death of her most Amiable G——Daughter Mrs Green.[5]

We all have Our Trobles my Only Brother[6] a few days ago Died allso but as Death is the Condition of human life we have no reason to Complain.

The Inclos'd Letter I recd from your Sister.

Bilive me ever your dutifull Nephew & most Hble Servant

JONA WMS

N.B. my Wife & Children are all well Desire their Duty

Our Oldest Daughter Betsy is the mother of a Very fine Daughter Nam'd after her mother[7]

Doctr Benja Franklin

Addressed: His Excellency / Benjamin Franklin Esqe. / Passy / near / Paris

From Ingenhousz

ALS: American Philosophical Society

Dear Sir   Vienna in Austria Juin. 12th. 1782

I hope you have recieved in du time my last dated april 24 togeather with the Copy of a book in the German language. Mr. le

---

5. Jane Mecom received BF's gift, described in our annotation to her June 17 letter, below, during a visit the preceding fall, not spring: XXXV, 666. Jane Flagg Greene died in April: Catharine Greene to BF, May 8, above.

6. John Williams (I, lviiin), whom we erroneously placed in Europe until the end of the war: XII, 193n; JW to John Williams, Sr., June 9, 1782; JW to Jonathan Williams & Son, Sept. 3, 1782 (both at Yale University Library).

7. Elizabeth (XIV, 289n) gave birth to Grace Williams Eaton on Feb. 15: *A Report of the Record Commissioners of the City of Boston, Containing Boston Births from A.D. 1700 to A.D. 1800* (Boston, 1894), p. 331. She had married Joshua Eaton on April 24, 1781; Van Doren, *Franklin-Mecom*, p. 215.

Begue has the original frensh Manuscript in hands, but does not goe on with the printing of it.

I take the liberty of begging the favour to peruse with attention the inclosed lettre to mr. Samuel wharton, (of which a duplicate is joined to it to go by a different vessel for securities sake) and after you and your son have perused it, to put a cover over each with a propre direction and to send them both, but in different vessels, to philadelphia.[8] You would oblige me very much if you would be so good as to recommend, in the cover, my intrest to Mr. Wharton.[9] The perusal of the inclosed will furnish you an idea of my situation and particular intrest in mr. Wharton's honesty, of which I Should very much like to have your opinion for my own tranquillity. I am sur you can not approove of his behaviour towards me. I am not rich enough to bear such a great loss, if mr. Wharton should proove to be a dishonest man, Which I can not believe, tho mr. Coffyn seems still to suspect him to be soo. I hope you will let me know that this letter is recieved and the two inclosed forwarded to mr Wharton, and that allso the former I did send with the book has been allready forwarded to philadelphia. This intelligence will make me more quiet.

If you had som american newspapers, which you doe not want, I should be Glad to have them. I could even send them back by the way of Count Mercy,[1] to whom you may give any lettre or paquet you Should have a mind to Send me.

---

8. BF retained the duplicate, also dated June 12, which is filed with the present letter at the APS. Ingenhousz complains that he has heard nothing from Wharton about their two 1780 mercantile projects—one, a 40,000 *l.t.* consignment to be shared with Wharton, Bancroft, and Coffyn; the other, an 8,000 *l.t.* contribution to a venture that he shared with Wharton. Ingenhousz has learned from Coffyn that most of the goods arrived safely, and that Coffyn has received two payments from Wharton. The second of these is destined for Ingenhousz, but Coffyn was retaining part of it as payment for a loan he issued Wharton. Ingenhousz demands an explanation and wonders why Wharton has not remitted the full amount through BF, as they had agreed? Bancroft has not answered any of Ingenhousz' inquiries. For background on these transactions see XXXIV, 124n, 163–4.

9. BF's cover letter, of which he sent a copy to Ingenhousz, is now missing: Ingenhousz to BF, Aug. 20, 1782 (APS).

1. The comte de Mercy-Argenteau, imperial ambassador to France, had offered to convey BF's letters to Ingenhousz: XXXV, 549.

The Emperour does not seem to give up all hopes of seing you here as ministre on the ensuing general Congress; but nobody wishes more sincerely for such meeting as I. Let me hear from you weather our hopes are grounded, and weather Lord Shelburn and mr. Fox will declare you a free people. I hope you are content with my country men.

Mr. Le Begue informes me he has seen a lettre you wrote to me but not finish'd. But, pray, send it to me as it is, if you should not have time to finish it.[2] Let me have some thing to tell from you to my Imperial Master, who often askes me news about you. Lettres delivred to Count Mercy will surely Come to hand.

I expect the new English Ministers will soon become as haughty as the former if succes attends the national armies, as this caracter is that of the whole nation.

Give my best Compliments to your son, and doe not entirely forget your old and faithfull friend.   J. INGEN HOUSZ

to his Excellency Mr. Benj. Franklin minister plenipot. from the Congress to the Frensh Court.

Endorsed: June 12. 1782

From Stephen Sayre[3]   ALS: Historical Society of Pennsylvania

Sir   Paris 12th. June 1782—

As the English Commissioners of peace may probably demand the Island of Porto Rico, either as a preliminary article, or endeavour to obtain it in the course of negotiation;[4] I beg leave to offer the following Idea to your Excellency's consideration.

Whether you cannot, with the aid of the French Minister who

2. BF finished it on June 21. The entire letter, begun on Oct. 2, 1781, is published in XXXV, 544–51.

3. Who spent most of 1782 in Paris: John R. Alden, *Stephen Sayre: American Revolutionary Adventurer* (Baton Rouge, La., and London, 1983), pp. 132–6. We have no record of a response to the present letter, Sayre's last to BF as far as we know.

4. The Spanish island eventually did figure in the negotiations. Shelburne suggested it as a partial equivalent for Gibraltar: Dull, *French Navy,* p. 321.

must see, clearly, the national Interest greatly benefited, turn this object so as to let the Island, hereafter become free, & open to a commerce with all the world.

If the powers in treaty say to England "we cannot suffer this Island to be monopolized by you; but we have no objections to your profiting by its Market &c &c." The object remains still extremely important to her & worth her pursuit.

I need not state any arguments as to the advantages America would gain by such a measure. We all know them to be of high importance. Your Excellency may be assured of having the thanks & praise of every person now living, & of all posterity for opening such a profitable Market for us.

It is an object of so much weight, that I am persuaded your Excellency will do well to write for Instructions respecting it; should there be time for them, even before a definitive Treaty.

I hope you will not impute this Letter to any impatient desire of medling in public affairs, but to the ardent desire of serving my Country. *If you please—myself:* for if adopted, I should hope to have your Excellency's support in recommending me to the Government of it—most certainly, there is some merit in promoteing an Affair, by which, all the world must be benefited: for even Spain will not be injured by it.

I am with great Respect & Consideration your Excellency's most obedient Servant STEPHEN SAYRE

To his Excellency Benjamin Franklin Esqr &c &c

To Mary Hewson

ALS: Yale University Library

My dear Child, Passy, June 13. 1782

I received your pleasing Letter of the 1st of May thro' the hands of Mr Hodgson, and one since by Mr Oswald.[5] You cannot be more pleas'd in talking about your Children, your Methods of Instructing them, and the Progress they make, than I am in hearing it; and in finding, that instead of following the idle

---

5. William Hodgson conveyed the first letter; Richard Oswald forwarded one dated May 23. Both are above.

Amusements, which both your Fortune & the Custom of the Age might have led you into, your Delight and your Duty go together, by employing your Time in the Education of your Offspring. This is following Nature and Reason instead of Fashion, than which nothing is more becoming the Character of a Woman of Sense & Virtue. We have here a Female Writer on Education, who has lately publish'd three Volumes, that are much talk'd of. I will send them to you by the first Opportunity. They are much talk'd of, prais'd & much censur'd. The Author, Madame la Comtesse de Genlis, is made, in consequence of her writing that Work, *Governor* of the Children of the Duc de Chartres, who is Son of the Duke of Orleans.[6] Perhaps you may not find much in it that can be of use to you, but you may find something. I enclose another Piece on the same Subject, written by another Comtesse, Madame de Forbach, who does me the honour of calling me her Friend, by which means I have a Copy, it not being publish'd.—[7] When you have Leisure I shall like to see your Remarks.

Do not send any Books to Geneva. The Troubles of that City have driven the School and my Boy out of it, and I have thoughts of sending for him home.[8] Perhaps I may put him for a while un-

---

6. The comtesse, Caroline-Stéphanie-Félicité Ducrest de Saint-Aubin, later marquise de Sillery-Genlis (1746–1830), wrote didactic plays and novels. She shared some of the philosophes' ideas but believed that religion should also play a role in education. Governess to the duke's twin daughters since 1779, she was named governor of his sons in January, 1782, an unprecedented appointment for a woman: *DBF;* Gabriel de Broglie, *Madame de Genlis* (Paris, 1985), pp. 104–9, 117–8; Lewis, *Walpole Correspondence,* XXXIII, 483–4n. For the ensuing public debate see Bachaumont, *Mémoires secrets,* XX, 27–8.

The three volumes, *Adèle et Théodore, ou lettres sur l'éducation* (Paris, 1782), presented Genlis' educational plan for girls and boys in the form of an epistolary novel. For discussion of the work's merits see *Jour. de Paris,* issues of March 21, 22, 27, and 30, 1782; Métra, *Correspondance secrète,* XII, 266, 347–9, 372–4, 407; Bachaumont, *Mémoires secrets,* XX, 75–6, 92–4.

7. Mme de Forbach had promised BF that she would devise a plan for the education of girls: XXVI, 459.

8. For the political background to the disturbances in Geneva see XXXIV, 486. During the upheaval BFB resided at the country home of schoolmaster Marignac's brother: BFB to BF, July 27, below.

der your Care to recover his English in the same School with
your Sons.

I hope with you that there may be a Peace, & that we may once
more meet. Remember me kindly to Mr & Mrs Vining.[9] I do not
at present want a Carriage. Embrace your good Mother for me
with much Affection, and believe me to be, my dear dear Friend
Yours ever   B FRANKLIN

Endorsed: B Franklin June 13. 1782

To [Richard Price][1]

ALS: American Philosophical Society; copy: Library of Congress

Dear Sir,   Passy, June 13. 1782
I received a few Days since your kind Letter of the 27th past,
by Messrs. Milford & Brown.[2] It gave me great Pleasure to hear
of your Welfare. All that come with a Line from you are welcome.

I congratulate you on the late Revolution in your Public
Affairs. Much Good may arise from it, tho' possibly not all that
good Men, and even the new Ministers themselves may have
wished or expected. The Change however in the Sentiments of
the Nation, in which I see evident Effects of your Writings, with
those of our deceas'd Friend Mr Burgh, and others of our valuable Club, should encourage you to proceed.[3] The ancient Roman and Greek Orators could only speak to the Number of Citizens capable of being assembled within the Reach of their
Voice: Their Writings had little Effect because the Bulk of the
People could not read. Now by the Press we can speak to Nations; and good Books & well written Pamphlets have great and
general Influence. The Facility with which the same Truths may

9. John and R. W. Viny.
1. His name is specified on the copy.
2. Price's letter was actually dated May 20 (above).
3. James Burgh, author of *Political Disquisitions* (3 vols., London, 1774–
75) and fellow member of the Club of Honest Whigs, had died in 1775: XI,
98n, 100n.

be repeatedly enforc'd by placing them daily in different Lights, in Newspapers which are every where read, gives a great Chance of establishing them. And we now find that it is not only right to strike while the Iron is hot, but that it is very practicable to heat it by continual Striking.— I suppose we may now correspond with more Freedom, and I shall be glad to hear from you as often as may be convenient to you. Please to present my best Respects to our good old Friends of the London Coffeehouse.[4] I often figure to my self the Pleasure I should have in being once more seated among them. With the greatest & most sincere Esteem an Affection, I am, my dear Friend, Yours ever

B FRANKLIN

Endorsed: Dr. Franklin 1782

To Jonathan Williams, Jr.

AL (draft): American Philosophical Society

Dear Jonathan   Passy, June 13. 1782

I have never yet been able to settle my Account with M. de Chaumont. I got Mr. Grand to endeavour it, but he is on the Point of giving it up as impracticable.[5] One is never sure of having finish'd any thing [*with*] Mr C. He is forever renewing old Demands or inventing new ones. He now refuses to allow me Interest on the 50,000 livres he kept so long in his Hands,[6] or on any other Article of my Account, and yet as you know, charges it on every one of his. And he says if I charge Interest he will charge me for I know not how many 100 Tons of Freight in the Marquis de la Fayette more than he was paid for.[7] He refuses to

4. Where the Club of Honest Whigs met: XI, 98n.
5. For an overview of the dispute see the Exchange About Accounts, [before April 26]. Grand had drawn up a settlement on May 7 (above), but Chaumont refused to abide by it.
6. This sum was from 1779; see the headnote to the Exchange About Accounts, [before April 26]. For further explanations of this and the following points BF raises see JW's answer, June 18.
7. The price per ton, but not the capacity, was fixed by the charterparty signed on Aug. 30, 1780, by Chaumont and JW (APS).

allow the Charge of Exchange &c that arose on paying him for his Clothes here instead of paying it in America, and says if I insist on that he will be paid 25, and sometimes he talks of 50 per cent Advantage he should have made by being paid for the Cloth in America either by Cash or Bills on me,[8] an Advantage of which I cannot form the least Conception. Thus the bad Situation of his Affairs forces him upon the Use of all Sorts of Chicanery to evade a Settlement & doing Justice to his Creditors. When you see a Man naturally honest thus driven into Knavery by the Effect of imprudent Speculations, let it be a Warning to you how you venture out of your Depth, in hope of Gain, to the hazard of your Virtue, which ought to be dearer to you than any Fortune, as being in itself more valuable & affording more Comfort. Mr Grand has considered all his Pleas, and even a private Memoir which he desired might not be shown me (I suppose lest I should answer it) wherein he makes a sort of Account of all his Losses in American Transactions, & even of all his Civilities to me or any of my Friends.— Mr Grand has given an Award which he will not submit to, tho' he had agreed to his being the Arbitrator:[9]—and now I have proposed that he should chuse another to be join'd with Mr Grand, and that if they do not agree they may chuse a third, whose Decision shall be final.—[1] In case this takes place, I shall want your Information in what manner & by whom the Tonnage was settled, and what you understood to be the Agreement relative to the Payment for the Cloths. By what I can recollect or gather from the Memorandum written by him,[2] it was to this purpose, that to encourage me to buy the Cloth when I objected my want of Money, he propos'd to take his Pay in America, or if the Congress could not pay him in Cash he would take their Bills on me for the Sum, which as it would

8. When Chaumont submitted a revised version of his account on July 9 (below), he indeed added this as a new item. He charged a 25 percent commission on the bills that BF furnished him on Congress for the final shipment of cloth, evidently believing that he was owed this benefit according to the scheme worked out by Necker and Grand in November, 1780: XXXIV, 36–7.

9. The "award" is published above, May 7.

1. Chaumont chose the banker Dangirard. Chaumont and BF signed an agreement for arbitration by Grand and Dangirard on July 7 (below).

2. Dated Nov. 26, 1780: XXXIV, 73–5.

be some time before they could return & be payable here, would be equivalent to giving me so long Credit. If I am wrong, pray set me right; and do not delay writing, because I want much to finish the Affair. I am ever Your affectionate Uncle

P.S. I wish also to know whether you have not, as I think you told me, some reasons to believe that Salt or other Goods were shipt in that Vessel without your Knowledge or Consent. Also I would have your Opinion of the Damage we suffer'd by the Delay of the Vessels coming to l'Orient by the Operations of his Creditors, and by her not being in time to sail with the Convoy. For as he brings all sorts of Artillery to bear against us, we are oblig'd to muster what Arms we can to defeat its Effects.

Letter B Franklin to Mr Williams June 13 1782 Mr de Chaumont's Chicanery Questions about the Clothing &c

From John Adams[3]   AL (draft): Massachusetts Historical Society

Sir   The Hague June 13. 1782
  I had Yesterday, at Amsterdam, the Honour of receiving your Excellencys Letter of June 2d.
  The Discovery that Mr Grenvilles Power, was only to treat with France does not Surprize me, at all. The British Ministry, are too much divided among themselves, and have too formidable an opposition against them, in the King and the old Ministers, and are possessed of too little of the Confidence of the Nation, to have the Courage to make Concessions, of any Sort, especially Since the News of their Successes in the East and West Indies.
  What their Pride will end in, God only knows.— For my own Part, I cannot See, a Probability, that they will ever make Peace,

---

3. A version of this letter is printed as part of BF's journal of the peace negotiations in WTF, *Memoirs*, II, 373–5. Presumably that version was based on the now-missing recipient's copy, but as *Memoirs* is an unreliable source of accurate texts, we cannot judge whether the discrepancies (some of which are noted below) were original or introduced.

untill their Financies are ruined and Such Distresses brought upon them as will work up their Parties into a civil War.

I wish their Ennemies could by any means be persuaded to carry on the War against them in Places where they might be sure of Triumphs, instead of insisting upon pursuing it, where they are Sure of Defeats.— But We must take Patience, and wait for Time to do, what Wisdom might easily and soon do.

I have not as yet taken any Engagements with the Dutch not to make a Peace without them, but I will take such Engagements, in a moment if the Dutch will take them, and I believe they will chearfully.— I shall not propose it however untill I have the Concurrence of the Duke de la Vauguion who will do nothing without the Instructions of his Court.[4] I would not delay it, a moment from any Expectation that the English, will acknowledge our Independence and make Peace with Us, because I have no such Expectations.— I confess, it would be with infinite Reluctance that I should see a Peace made between England and any of her Ennemies, unless it is made with all.— If France, Spain and America should make Peace with England, and leave Holland alone at War, she would be at Mercy, and she would find the tenderest of it, Cruelty.[5]

The permanent and lasting Friendship of the Dutch, may be easily obtained by the United States; that of England never. It is gone with the days before the Flood.— If We ever enjoy the Smallest degree of Sincere Friendship again from England I am totally incapable of Seeing the Character of a Nation or the Connections of Things, which however may be the Case, for what I know. They have brought themselves by their Frenzy into Such a Situation. Spain has such Pretensions, Holland has Such Pretensions, America has Such Pretensions, the Armed Neutrality has Such Pretensions, that where is the English Minister,

4. On June 17, La Vauguyon informed Vergennes that once a Dutch-American commercial treaty had been signed, JA wished to invite the Dutch to join the American-French Treaty of Alliance. In response, Vergennes ordered La Vauguyon to discourage such a move: James H. Hutson, *John Adams and the Diplomacy of the American Revolution* (Lexington, Ky., 1980), p. 114; Giunta, *Emerging Nation*, 1, 436–7.

5. The preceding two sentences do not appear in WTF's version of this letter.

or Member of Parliament that dares to vote for the Concession to them? The Pretensions of France I believe would be so moderate that possibly, they might be acceeded to.— But I fear that Spain who deserves the least will demand the most. In Short the Work of Peace appears so impracticable, that I am happy in being restrained to this Country by my Duty and by this means excused from troubling my Head much about it.— I have a Letter from America which informed me that Mr Jay had refused to Act in the Commission for Peace: but if he is on his way to Paris, as you suppose I presume, my Information must be a Mistake, which I am very glad of. Mr Laurens, did me the Honour of a very short Visit, in his Way to France, but I was very Sorry to learn from him, that in a Letter to your Excellency[6] he had declined Serving in the Commission for Peace. I had vast Pleasure in his Conversation, for I found him possessed of the most exact Judgment respecting our Ennemies, and of the Same noble Sentiments in all Things, which I Saw in him in Congress.

What is the System of Russia? Does she Suppose that England has too many Ennemies upon her, and that their demands and Pretensions are too high? Does she Seek to embroil affairs and to light up a general War in Europe? Is Denmark in Concert with her, or any other Power? Her Conduct is a Phenomenon.— Is there any Secret Negotiation or Intrigue on Foot, to form a Party for England among the Powers of Europe, and to make a Ballance, against the Power of the Ennemies of England?

The States of Holland and several other Provinces have taken the Resolution, against the Mediation for a Separate Peace, and this nation seems to be well fixed in its System and in the common Cause.[7]

My best Respects and Affections to my old friend Mr Jay, if you please.

6. WTF's version here adds the words "from Ostend". That letter was Laurens' of May 17, above. In late May, Laurens met with JA at The Hague to offer to help raise money but was rebuffed: *Gaz. de Leyde*, May 31, sup.; *Laurens Papers*, XV, 508, 521–2; James H. Hutson, ed., *Letters from a Distinguished American: Twelve Essays by John Adams on American Foreign Policy, 1780* (Washington, 1978), p. 54.

7. On July 1, the States General of the Netherlands rejected the idea of a separate peace with Britain: Dull, *French Navy*, pp. 285–6.

From Benjamin Putnam

ALS: American Philosophical Society

Cape Nichola Mole
Honorable Sir,   June 13th. 1782.— Hispaniola

Least by any Accident, I should fail of a safe Arrival at France, I wish to inform you, that, I have not relinquished the Idea, or by any means, quitted my Resolution but too long since form'd, of waiting on your Excellency on the subject of the two Vessels which some months since I had the honor to represent to your Excellency thro Mr. Lovell, & by my own Letters.[8]

I am in the Flora Frigate, commanded by Capt Henry Johnson, in which, I left Boston, Jany last, bound to Bourdeaux: But the misfortunes of being dismasted, & an unusual long Passage, together with the great Difficulty of procuring Masts & other necessary Materials for our refitting, have long protracted our sailing, & caus'd this tedious Delay.

We shall sail the 15th. Inst in Company with a French Bregantine, by which, I have the honor of addressing your Excellency with this Advice, and am Sir, with profound Respects Your Excellency's most Obedient & most Hble Servant

BENJ. PUTNAM

His Excy, Doctor Franklin—

Addressed: His Excellency Doctor B. Franklin / American Minister at the Court / of France— / Paris

Notation: Colonies

From Jonathan Williams, Jr.

ALS: American Philosophical Society; copy: Yale University Library

Dr & hond Sir.   Nantes June. 13. 1782.

Inclosed are 2 Letters from Major Franks one for you[9] & one for Mr Jay. The Bills mentioned I have sent to Mr

8. XXXIV, 369–70; XXXV, 78, 477; XXXVI, 239–40.
9. Missing. David Franks, returned from Spain, was in Nantes by mid-May awaiting passage for America: XXXVI, 551n; Franks to WTF, May 22 and 26 (APS).

Grand.—[1] What is to be done about sending out the public Stores? There are here two large american Ships now here which will want Freight one of them the Cato of 300 Tons to my address, but these Ships belong to the Northward & cannot take Freight to go South of Boston.— There is a fine new french Ship just launched which is to be coppered burthen about 300 Tons, she may be ready in two months, but the owner will not freight her under £300 per Ton measurement on Goods. I do not for my own part think a good Ship can be had for less. If you can consent to send to the Northward the american Ships might answer, but if not you must depend on french ones. Please to inform me what I am to do.

I am as ever most dutifully & affectionately Yours.

J WILLIAMS JR

Doctor Franklin.

From Jonathan Williams, Jr.

ALS: American Philosophical Society; copy: Yale University Library

Dear & hond sir.   Nantes June 14. 1782.

I wrote you last Post relative to a ship of 300 Tons which is offered for Freight to take out the public Stores. The proprietor of this Ship is Mr Arnoux one of our principal Merchants here[2] & his son in Law Mr Mitchel[3] will call on you to talk on the sub-

---

1. Franks' June 10 bill for 1,148 *l.t.* was paid by Grand on July 15: Account XXVII (XXXII, 4).

2. Nicolas Arnous III (1719–1807), in addition to being one of the principal merchants and shipowners of Nantes, was a *conseiller secrétaire du Roi* and a former *juge-consul:* Yvonne Arnous Rivière, *Nantes et ses messieurs les Arnous* (Chabris, 1994), pp. 135, 137, 451; Villiers, *Commerce colonial*, pp. 193, 404; Jean Meyer, *L'Armament nantais dans la deuxième moitié du XVIIIe siècle* (Paris, 1969), p. 265.

3. Gabriel-Augustin Michel de Tharon (b. 1753), scion of a prominent Nantais merchant family, married Marie-Suzanne Arnous in 1778, when he was a deputy mayor of the city: Arnous Rivière, *Les Arnous*, pp. 102, 136–7.

ject whatever you do with him therefore will be conclusive on Mr Arnoux & I will take Care of the Execution here.

I am as ever most dutifully & affectionately Yours

JONA WILLIAMS J

The Prisoners I wrote about on the 26 March are gone at last & left me to pay my Engagements for their Board &c. This Letter has never been answered but I hope you will not let me suffer a Loss which certainly ought to be a charge of State more especialy as the Men have arrears due. JW

From Samuel Cooper

ALS: American Philosophical Society

Sir, Boston June 15th. 1782.

I never was more pleased with the Spirit of my Country than upon a late general Apprehension that Sr. Guy Carleton had come from the Court of London with a Design to create Divisions in these States and sow Jealousies between us and our great and good Ally, by Propositions particularly for some separate Negotiations. The Indignity and Contempt with which such an Idea was every where received, even among People who feel most the Burdens of the War, and the public Testimonies of this in the Newspapers and in the express Declarations of a Number of the States which this Occasion has already drawn forth, in which the Massachusetts will soon join,[4] must effectually dash all the Hopes of our Enemies, if they have entertained any upon such a Plan. Tho I cannot find that Sr. Guy has yet made any such Propositions, I am not sorry for the general Apprehension prevailing among us that it was Part of his Errand, since this has afforded an Opportunity of displaying in so full and clear a Light

4. For declarations already made by Pennsylvania and Maryland see Livingston to BF, May 22. On July 4, the Mass. General Court resolved that "every idea of deviating from the treaty of the *United States* with his *Most Christian Majesty* in the smallest article, or of listning to proposals of accommodation with the Court of *Great Britain* in a partial and separate capacity, shall forever be rejected by us with the greatest abhorrence and detestation": *Resolves of the General Court of the Commonwealth of Massachusetts in New-England . . .* (Boston, 1782), p. 40.

the Sentiments of the Continent upon such a Design. These Sentiments appear to be what the warmest Friends to our happy Alliance must wish; and are founded not only in a clear Understanding of our own Interest, but also in a Sense of Fidelity Friendship and Honour, that can be no Disadvantage to the Character of this rising Nation, and will not induce a Blush upon the Face of it's Friends and Ministers abroad. Upon this and other Occasions I have continued to exert my small Abilities in my little Sphere for advancing a Cause in which I was early engaged, and for establishing a Revolution of which I shall say with my latest Breath, *Esto perpetua.*[5]

The Birth of a Dauphin has but very lately been officially announced to the States: And the Demonstrations of Joy upon this auspicious Occasion have been what we call brilliant; they certainly flowed from very warm and friendly Hearts. Nothing could be more elegant, pertinent, and affecting than the Speech of the Chevalier de la Luzerne to Congress;[6] it has had every where a very happy Effect: and indeed His Excellency has upon every Occasion cultivated the public Friendship with particular Felicity. In this Town, I can say with Truth, the public Tokens of Joy far exceeded any Thing ever known here upon the Birth of a Prince of Wales, or the Birth Day of any British King.[7]

5. "May she live forever."

6. On May 13, La Luzerne delivered to Congress a letter from the King (written on Oct. 22, 1781) announcing the birth of his son and warmly renewing his assurance of continued friendship. La Luzerne extended those assurances to future generations in his own speech: "The prince who is just born will one day be the friend and ally of the United States. He will, in his turn, support them with all his power, and while in his dominions he shall be the father and protector of his people, he will be here the supporter of your children, and the guarantee of their freedom." *JCC,* xxii, 261–2.

7. Over 30 celebrations of the dauphin's birth took place in America during the summer. Boston's event occurred on June 12. Cooper wrote an account of it, which appeared in various newspapers. The day began with the ringing of church bells and firing of ships' cannons, followed by an afternoon of toasting in the Senate. The evening featured the illumination of ships and prominent homes, a fireworks display, and more cannon blasts. William C. Stinchcombe, "Americans Celebrate the Birth of the Dauphin," in Ronald Hoffman and Peter J. Albert, eds., *Diplomacy and Revolution: the Franco-American Alliance of 1778* (Charlottesville, Va., 1981), pp. 57, 65; *The Boston Evening-Post,* issue of June 15, 1782.

Sr. Guy Carlton is in a complete Dilemma bequeathed him by Genl. Clinton. Genl. Washington has demanded of him to deliver up Lippencut the Ringleader of the Refugees in N. York who murderously hung Col. Huddy, one of our brave Officers, Prisoner in that City; and has ordered a Lot to be drawn by the British Officers Prisoners among us for a Victim in Case of a final Refusal. The Lot has found out Capt. Asgill of distinguished Family, and who is said to have been particularly cruel towards our People at the Southwards. The Refugees in N. York say they will lay down their Arms if the Demand is complied with; the British Officers insist upon it's being performed. The Uneasiness runs high between them; our General is determined, and let Carlton take what Part he will, he is sure mortally to offend a great Party in his own Army.[8]

The Army of the united States is every day increasing, and now looked upon as one of the best disciplined in the World. Ways and Means to support it are the Object that at present employs the Attention of the States. We have now a Committee from Congress to confer with this and the other Eastern States upon this important Affair. I hope our Efforts will surmount all Obstacles many and great as they are.—[9] Dr Thomas Leverett, a Descendant from Govr. Leverett was taken in an armed Ship of this State the Protector, Capt. John Foster Williams, carried to England in July 1781. where he is supposed to remain in Mill Prison: I have also a Kinsman, William Cooper, in the same Sit-

8. For the affair involving Richard Lippincott, Joshua Huddy, and Charles Asgill see Livingston's letter of May 30. For Carleton's negotiation of this conflict between the Loyalists and the British army that involved wf as president of the Board of Associated Loyalists, which may have sanctioned Lippincott's actions, see Sheila L. Skemp, *William Franklin: Son of a Patriot, Servant of a King* (New York and Oxford, 1990), pp. 261–2.

9. On May 22, a committee informed Congress that the states had not effectively complied with requisitions for funding the army. Concluding that a circular letter to the states would be ineffectual, Congress instead appointed two teams to visit the states and urge compliance. The first team was assigned the states south of Philadelphia, and the second, consisting of Joseph Montgomery and Jesse Root, was sent to the states east of Philadelphia: *JCC*, XXII, 289.

uation.[1] Perhaps a Change of Ministry may facilitate Measures for a General Release of Prisoners.

I very sensibly feel my Obligations to you for your kind Regard to my little Grandson now at Geneva. I wish he may well improve his own Genius and present Opportunities. His Father Col Johonnot, I am just told, is arrived at Baltimore in a Ship from France.[2] I am anxious to have this News confirmed, as the British Cruizers since the Spring have taken almost every Thing upon the American Coast. We expect soon to see a French Armament in it; and shall be well prepared I hope to cooperate with it; and the more vigorously from the late Check we have received in the W. Indies.

I am Sir, with the greatest Esteem, and the most constant Affection, Your obedt humble Servant   SAML: COOPER.

His Excellency Benjn. Franklin Esqr.

From Francesco Favi   ALS: American Philosophical Society

Monsieur   Paris ce 15 Juin 1782

J'ai L'honneur de vous envoyer un Livre avec une Lettre de M. Inghenhousz, qui m'ont etè remis pour vous Les faire venir.[3] Si vous avès une reponse à Lui faire je vous prie de m'envoyer votre Lettre rue de Seine a l'hôtel de Mirabeau; je la Lui ferai parvenir exactement.

J'ai L'honneur d'etre avec respect Monsieur Votre trés humble, et trés Obeissant Serviteur   FAVI

Notation: Favi 5. Juin 1782.

1. Thomas Leverett (1758–1784), the great-great-great grandson of Gov. John Leverett (*ANB*), was the surgeon on board the *Protector* when she was captured in May, 1781. Leverett was committed to Mill Prison on July 21. Samuel Cooper's nephew William was committed to Mill exactly four months later: XXXV, 411; XXXVI, 660; [Charles E. Leverett], *A Memoir, Biographical and Genealogical, of Sir John Leverett . . . and of the Family Generally* (Boston, 1856), p. [192]; Kaminkow, *Mariners*, pp. 44, 116.
2. Gabriel Johonnot, the father of Samuel Cooper Johonnot, had arrived in France in March, 1781, and departed for America about a year later: XXXV, 39n; XXXVI, 578.
3. See Ingenhousz to BF, April 24.

From Lafayette : American Philosophical Society

Saturday Morning [June 15 or 22, 1782][4]
Will You Please, My dear sir, to let me Have a Copy of the Paper I gave to Major Ross, that I May Enclose it to General Washington and get His approbation of the Measure?

The Moment You get the Bill[5] be pleased to Communicate it— I will do the same on my part, and am Very Anxious to see How that Piece is Manufactured.

Notation: La Fayette

From Jonathan Williams, Jr.

Copy:[6] Archives du Ministère des affaires étrangères; AL (draft):[7] Indiana University Library, Bloomington

Dear & hond. Sir, Nantes June 15, 1782[8]
In consequence of your Desire to be informed what Facilitys or Disadvantages the American Commerce enjoyed or suffered in this Place,[9] I sit down to give you a few outlines on the Subject, which may serve to give you a general Idea, and what Questions you may have to ask afterwards, I will answer as particuly as I can.

---

4. The two Saturdays between June 12, when Lafayette gave BF a draft declaration authorizing the release of Cornwallis' aides-de-camp from their parole, and June 25, when Lafayette sent George Washington a copy of the declaration. For the former see Lafayette to BF, June 11; for the latter see Idzerda, *Lafayette Papers*, V, 48–9.

5. Presumably the Enabling Act. BF asked Grenville about it on June 15; see BF's journal of the peace negotiations.

6. In the hand of L'Air de Lamotte. BF forwarded this copy to Vergennes on March 16, 1783; the cover letter and a French translation are at the AAE. We have silently corrected a few errors of spelling and punctuation based on the AL (draft).

7. Because this draft has many abbreviations and few paragraph indents, we opted to publish the copy made from the version BF received. The two differ significantly in punctuation and capitalization.

8. We supply the dateline from the AL (draft). The copy was marked simply "June 1782."

9. See JW to BF, April 18.

The Difficulties attending the commercial Regulations and Duties in this Country are of more Consequence even than the Expence of them, though this is very considerable. This Difficulty is in some Measure unavoidable under the present System. The Farmers General naturally endeavour to make as much annual Revenue as they can; and their Officers are so tied down to rule, that the least trifling Circumstance which renders Goods seizable or otherways perplexes Commerce, is as bad to the Merchant as the most palpable Fraud; for not a Director in any Seaport has the least discretionary Power. If a Sailor steals half a dozen Pound of Tobacco and clandestinely sells it, it on discovery causes as much Trouble to the Merchant, as perhaps the Management of the whole Ship, & the Director can give no relief; So Petitions must be sent to Paris, and the greatest Favour ever obtained is to be let off; by giving a Gratification to the Officers who have been the most troublesome, because that encourages them to trouble us again; Tho' it very often happens that a heavy Fine is inflicted.

There is an another Regulation which often produces Vexation & is in itself impracticable, The *Arrêts du Conseil* obliges a Declaration of the Weight and Kind of all Goods to be declared before they are examined and weigh'd; if after Declaration is made there should be any difference in the Quality, or short Weight, they are at once confiscated; if the Declaration be over Weight, the Duty on the Surplus is demanded, tho' the article does not exist; So that a Merchant who does not know the Weight of his Goods (which is often the Case with the French and almost always the Case with us) must declare what he is sure is *more*, for fear of Confiscation by declaring too little, and as it is a Matter of Guess Work it is generaly much over.

In regard to Tobacco it is still worse, for an over Declaration would be as bad as a short one in other Instances; for they would then say that the surplus Quantity was really brought in, & has been smuggled into the Country, tho' the Impracticability of such Smuggling is evident from the Watch that is kept; then comes the *Procès Verbal*, & the Merchant is condemned, not only to pay the highest Value of the Surplus so supposed to be smuggled, but likewise to pay a heavy fine for being Guilty of what they know he could not do. The Hardship and absurdity however of this has induced the Farmers to allow their Directors to relax in those impossible Cases, and accept a Declaration *en attendant* a more particular one after the weight is known. But this is a Matter of Favour which must be sollicited for on every Occasion, because everything granted by the Bureau is always *sans tirer à Consequence,* and if the officer happens to be out of humour, the Merchant must let his Ship remain idle till he can procure an Order from Paris for a permit to unload. This little Sketch will give you a faint Idea of the Vexation we are liable to from the execution of the System of collecting the Revenue here; but to let you know the full extent of it, I should be obliged to write Volumes. I will now give you a few Observations on the Duties and Regulations themselves. The Freight Duty is common to all foreign Ships that navigate from any Port of the French Dominions, and the object of it is to preserve the carrying and coasting Trade to themselves, it is 5. *l.t.* per Ton & 10. *s.* per Livre which makes it amt. to 7. *l.t.* 10. *s.* per. Ton for the whole Tonnage of a Ship; and the discharging one Box makes the Ship liable for the whole. I believe however the Exemption I obtained for the Aurora about 18 Months ago has extended to all American Ships which come from the west Indies, for nothing has yet been said to me about the Ship Count de Grasse. I believe therefore I shall not trouble you with any Sollicitation on the Subject, but as the Law subsists, and as the Exemption is only a temporary Matter of Favour, this may be included in the general Application. Imports from America are subject to various Duties of which I send you a State inclosed,[1] some of these are inconsiderable in their Nature, but others are serious. That on Tobacco is a town Duty, and was laid on under the head of Medicaments, for Tobacco was never imported in this Kingdom 'till since the War, except for the Farmers (who are exempt from all Town Duties) & for medicines; this latter was so inconsiderable that ¼[2] of a Denier a hundred now would raise as much money as 29 *s.* 6. *d.* used to do. This little Duty therefore has become very considerable & I with other Merchants have paid many Thousand Livres before we were roused to an examina-

1. Missing.
2. The draft reads "⅒".

tion of the Right, we have now refused to pay any more and have petitioned the Consulat[3] here to support our Claim, in the mean time we are sued for what remains due, and Judgement will soon be obtained; we shall then appeal, & so go on 'till we can obtain Redress from Court. What makes this Duty more particularly unjust, is, that it is taken on the Weight of the Tobacco as it comes out of the Ship, and wet or dry is the same Thing. I have been obliged to pay it on Tobacco condemned to be burned; and part of what I am now sued for was a damaged Cargo which sold for only 15 *l.t.* per hundred while Good Sells for 100 *l.t.* per hund. This Tobacco Duty is only here; Bordeaux & L'Orient are exempt. I send you a Copy of our Petitions to the Consulat. All these Town Duties or Grants called *Octrois* are very impolitic, and contrary to the Interest of the Town, for it is the readiest way to turn Business to another Channel. I had a parcel of Peltry arrived here and another at L'Orient, the one cost me 5 per Ct. at least and the other nothing; & what makes the Matter absurd is, that if the Goods come in the Towns by Land the Duty is not exacted; so by Landing the Furs at another Port the Duty may be avoided, so the effect of it is only giving the Merchant the Trouble of evading it which is very shallow Policy. But it is the Duty, or Formality to avoid Duty, on the Exports, that is the most Vexatious; to give you an Idea of this, I must enter into some details which may perhaps be fatiguing, but I cannot otherwise explain myself fully. All the Manufactures & Produce of France are more or less Subject to Dutys when transported from one Province to another; these Dutys are of different Kinds, *Droits de Prevoté* which go to the Farmers, & *Droits Locaux* which go to the *Seigneurs* of the different Places over which they pass. By the following extract of a Letter I wrote to a Friend in Philadelphia some time ago, you will see my Idea on the Subject viz.

"Before I proceed any further, it will be proper to observe to you, that every Province in France exacts certain Duties on all Goods which pass through them; these are called *Droits locaux* (*Local Duties*) the Towns in general also exact Duties which are

---

3. A local tribunal which adjudicated commercial disputes: Hervé du Halgouet, *Nantes: ses relations commerciales avec les îles d'Amérique au XVIIIe siècle ses armateurs* (Rennes, 1939), pp. 269–70.

Octrois (grants) besides which the Seigneurs or Nobility are entitled to certain private Duties on all Goods which pass over their Territories; in Addition to all this, there are the Duties of the Farmers General which are indeed the only ones of Consequence, for the others are an immense Detail of trifling things. The Farmers Duty is understood to be a Duty on the Consumption in the Kingdom only, & Goods for Exportation are therefore exempt from it; but in order to obtain this exemption we are subjected to such Forms and such Restrictions as make the Trouble and disadvantage almost equivalent to the Duties themselves, and in small Shippments much more so; for Instance, if I order a Trunck of Silks from Lyons, my Correspondent must enter into a bond under Penalties of four times the Duty to return in three Months a Certificate of its Reception at the Custom House in Nantes; in order to obtain this certificate, I must enter into a Bond of the same Kind, from which I cannot be released 'till after the Custom House Officer certifies having seen the Trunk in the hold of the Ship with all its Seals entire; so that to enjoy this Exemption each Kind of goods of the several Manufactories, should be for one Mark only, and packed by themselves, without having it in my Power to know whether they are well or ill put up 'till after they arrive in America. It is true I might order Goods for ten Correspondents in one Package, and by solliciting Permissions might obtain leave to open them. It must be in the Presence of a Custom House officer that ten Packages must be made of them, and all the other formalities ten times repeated. I have no doubt however that in the Course of time, when the Importance of the American Commerce and the Necessities of giving it every Facility, are better understood, this matter will be so modified as to be less disadvantageous. I have had thoughts of Proposing to the Farmers, with several of whom I have corresponded, to abolish the Exemption of Duty so far as relates to the United States, reducing the Duties to one half or even one third of their present amount. I am confident the Revenue would gain by such a Measure they are defrauded of immense Sums by sham Exportations—smuggling Goods.

I am confident also such a Measure would be beneficial to the American Trade for a Duty, an exemption of which cannot be enjoyed—without as much Disadvantage as its worth, amounts to no exemption at all; and the Facilitys of transacting Business not subject to custom house Formality would be more than adequate to the Expence of half the Duty, but for an American to sollicit the Abolition of what is supposed to be a Priviledge would not place him in an advantageous Light among his Countrymen."

I confess I do not see how this could be satisfactorily arranged without abolishing the *Acquit à Caution* as I have mentioned, for it is an endless Trouble and Formality to keep the Identity of the Goods always certain that causes all the Difficulties, and this is so great & so vexatious that the Privilege of an Exemption from Duty is no Privilege to me, as I do not think the Duty sufficient to pay me for my Time, Trouble, Vexation, & Delay and consequently I in general pay as I go, & as I never do these things I am the Dupe of my own Honesty.

If the English mode was adopted it might be better, of granting Drawbacks on exportation about equal to the Dutys & these drawbacks to be made as simple as possible. So as the Multiplicity of Formality might not take up too much time; but this I am sure would never go down, because first they could not be made to Understand the thing; and secondly because if they did, there would be as much trouble and Vexation to prove the Shipping the Goods entitled to the Drawback as there is in the *Acquit à Caution,* and Numberless Smugglers would make sham Shipments on Ships, receive the Drawback, and the Goods would be taken on shore again, and then cheat as much as they do now; this Way of sham Clearances to exempt Goods from Duty is so much in Practice here, that one Friend Lends his Name and his Ship to another by way of Compliment, as English Members of Parliament Frank Letters. The generous and realy most advantageous way would be to set up of all the Duties at once & leave the Trade free. But the Cry would then be, where is the Revenue to come from? Any Thing but Commerce, if they mean to rise with other Nations & obtain a Preference for the American Trade. For no American will buy at a Ship that sells dear, when he can find one that sells cheap.

The French may think our Commerce worth preserving at a Peace; but if they do, they must begin to encourage it now, so as the mercantile Part of America may understand all the Advantages of trading with them before other Channels open, and being once well fixed in the habit of trading hither they will on the same Terms give a Preference. It is much more easy to fix a Trade in the Channel it is in, by making it so advantageous as not to make it worth while to change, than it is to bring it back again after it has taken another Course.

This is but an imperfect State of the Difficulties we labour under by our Custom House Formalities, for these change every day, according to the whim of the *Conseil de la Compagnie*, their officers are continually inventing New Vexations to fabricate new Places, and they seem to imagine all mankind but themselves a Set of Cheats. I must however do Justice to the officers here, particularly to the Director, who as far as has been in his Power, has appeared disposed to oblige me.[4]

From Bonnefoux

ALS: American Philosophical Society

Monsieur   paris le 16 juin 1782

Vous avés, Sans doute, entendu parler de la Maladie épidémique qui a affligé et qui afflige encore la ville de Toulouse.[5] La frayeur a été Si grande que tous les etudians de l'université ont disparu. La these dont vous aviés bien voulu accepter la dedi-

4. A wrapper sheet filed with the AL (draft) is marked "Memoirs on Trade for Doctor Franklin". The fact that "Memoirs" is plural suggests that JW may eventually have forwarded the now-missing memoir from the Bordeaux firm of V. & P. French & Nephew, which he had solicited earlier; see our annotation to JW's letter of April 18. On June 16, responding to a now-missing letter from the firm, JW declined to send them a copy of the present memoir (which largely concerned Nantes) and urged them to focus their own statement on Bordeaux, "because by preserving these distinctions it is more likely that the remedies we may procure will apply directly to the Evils complained of." Yale University Library.

5. Miliary fever, an epidemic disease characterized by fever, sweating, and the eruption of miliary vessels in the skin, had broken out the previous September in Languedoc and spread to surrounding areas, including Toulouse. A report presented at the June 4 meeting of the Société royale de médecine and published shortly thereafter attributed the resurgence of the disease to extreme temperature fluctuations around the spring equinox: *Jour. de Paris,*

casse n'aura donc pas lieu pour Cette année.[6] J'espere que vous voudrés bien nous Conserver pour un meilleur tems votre bonne volonté.

J'ai l'honneur d'être avec respect Monsieur Votre très humble et très obeissant Serviteur

BONNEFOUX
supérieur Général de la Doctrine chretienne

Notation: Bonnefoux Paris. 16. Juin 1782.

From Edmund Clegg   ALS: American Philosophical Society

Hond: Sir   London June 16: 1782

I wrote you on the 12th Ulto,[7] to own the receipt of the Papers you sent to my care for the use of the Company of adventurers, from the Neighbourhood of Manchester. I have been down to see them—and find they are gone too far in the affair to Stop— One of the Company is now in Ireland to provide a Vessel to carry them over:[8] But they have disposed of the Goods bought in for the American Markets in Consequence of your Letter— They beg me to present their most humble thanks for your very much esteemed kindness—which I now do together with my own— I am in great straits what to do in this matter— for if I go not with them—I know they will not do so well as if I did—and at same time I have always wished to defer the Voyage untill a Peace.

Your advice is also of the utmost weight with me and therefore—I presume to lay my thoughts freely before You—and shall take it as a mark of great favour at Your hands to have Your reply.

I have always since I had this project in View—looked upon America to possess a fund of produce for what I will call natural

---

June 20, 1782. BF's copy of this report, "Réflexions sur la nature et le traitement de la maladie qui regne dans le Haut-Languedoc," is at the APS.

6. See Rouaix's letter of May 12 and Bonnefoux's of May 22.

7. Actually, May 11 (above).

8. Joseph Schofield, described as a "tall, Genteel man twenty five years of age," arranged for a ship in Londonderry to transport the emigrants: William Clark to Thomas Townshend, Aug. 8, 1782 (Public Record Office).

Manufactories— Of which I esteem the silk & Cotton—as belonging to the Weaving Branch, to stand in the first Rank— The Silk Business—I am led to think will take the lead of all others— if properly Managed and Your acct: of the silks You have sold in London is a full confirmation of my Opinion— But to do things to good Purpose—I am certain more Mony will be wanted than my friends Possess— Therefore though I am not a Person of any Property, chiefly Occasioned thro' this Wicked American War— Yet having had much experience I know myself Capable of Conducting with success either the Linnen, Cotton or Silk Manufactories—or their dependant Mixtures—without any Material error— I would farther Notice that two kinds of Italian Organzines would be wanted in America for some Years to come—they are denominated Piedmonts & Bergams— I Suspect the French use them in most of their Manufactories for Warps— Nor could American Manufactories do without them—tho' I am almost certain such silks as you mention will answer well for all kind of Weft or shute silks & also for many kinds of Warps.

If I could have my Choise—I would wish to take a proper assortment of Prepared Materials such as Warps and Wefts ready Prepared—and also Reeds to Work them in. I have a Brother who resided in New York & Philadelphia some time—about the Years 1772 & 73—from whom I learn that the Reeds then used in that Country where too Coarse for the silk Business in the Proportion of 12 to 20— But by taking some ready made the Artists there would be able by a Sample to provide for future wants.

My great objects in going over there prepared are: To loose no time:— To prove what may be done:— To put forward a Spirit of self provision on that side of the Water:— To depend as little as may be upon foreign Markets—that the great object of a Balance in Commerce may be soon acquired to be in favour of the Country—with every other appendage—and the opening Perhaps of more than can now be conjectured— Indeed I am such a lover of America, that I should rejoice to see her want Nothing from foreign Nations—and to spare much for them.

All these things and many more, I wished to have laid before the Hon: Mr Laurens but wrote You before his Answer I have not been favourd with a Line from him, tho' I had his promise to send— I suppose he knows you have wrote to me which may have prevented him.

You will from what I have said, plainly see that My aim is to promote Public & private good at the same time—and if I had not these principles I should not look upon myself to be worthy of becoming an American Citizen—under Your Patronage— But I submit it to you wether—it will not be best to accomplish the end—That some Person or Persons of that Country—who are Men of Property able to carry the Undertaking through: to Join me in the Matter as Partners in the Concern— I own I should prefer this on Many Accts:—and I could like to keep my-self in reserve untill I may be favour'd with Your reply—which I most respectfully crave as soon as may be, for my Govern-ment— In the Mean time I am—with the most profound respect Hond: sir Your most obedt & most Humble Sert

EDMUND CLEGG

P.S. please excuse inaccuracies as I am pinched for time

Addressed: Monsuir à / Monsuir Flanklin / Passi

From Thomas Barclay
ALS: American Philosophical Society

Sir   Amsterdam 17th. June 1782
    Since I had the honour of Addressing your Excellency[9] I have been Very much indisposed, but as I am now better, I hope I shall be able to leave this place on my way to France in a Couple of weeks. Captain Smedleys Vessell[1] will be, I expect, fully Man'd by that time, and the last of her Cargo Might have been on board long ago if it had been found Necessary, but the Captains sick-ness and want of hands made all kind of hurry useless. Mess. De Neufvilles furnish'd Me with the inclosed Accounts a few days ago, and are Very pressing to have theirs settled. As all the ex-

9. His most recent extant letter is above, April 29.
1. The *Heer Adams;* see Barclay to BF, April 11.

pences attending the two ships that were Charterd,[2] occur'd prior to my arrival to Europe it wou'd be very improper for Me to pretend to enter in them without particular directions from you, therefore I have Consented No farther than to promise to send them to You, and to Obey such Instructions as you are pleased to give me— I know of but two ways to have the Accounts adjusted, one is by a reference of the whole of them to Congress, the other by having them liquidated here by three or four Merchants indifferently Chosen on the part of Mess. De Neufville and on that of the United states, and shou'd your Excellency think proper to adopt the later Mode, I will endeavour to end the affairs before my departure.

I had the honour to inform you some time ago that I had made proposals for some more Cloathing that was lying at Ostend—[3] It arrived here in Consequence of My offer, and is ship'd on board a Brigantine for Boston, It Consists of about 1800 suits, and will make the whole of the Cloathing purchased here about 5200 suits— I hope this will in some small degree supply the disapointment of the supplies expected from France— I shall To-morrow ship on board a Vessell that is bound to Philadelphia, under Neutral Colours, 65 Chests Containing 16350 shirts, being part of the Goods I received from Ghent in Exchange for the British Manufactures purchased by Mess. De Neufville & son. I will not leave behind Me any of the public stores if I Can help it; But if I am obliged to do it, I will deliver them over to some good House here who will take the first opportunity of shipping them to America.

I have the honour to be with the greatest respect Sir Your Excellencys Most Obedient Most Huml Serv.   THOS BARCLAY.

His Excellency Benjn. Franklin Esqre. Passy near Paris

2. The *Liberty* and *Aurora*, partly owned by Neufville & fils: XXXV, 426–7.
3. Above, April 11.

From Hilliard d'Auberteuil

ALS: University of Pennsylvania Library

Monsieur   Paris Ce 17e. Juin 1782

J'ai l'honneur d'envoyer à votre excellence les épreuves des feuilles *T* & *V.* et de vous prier de me les renvoyer le plustot possible.

Je suis avec les sentimens de la plus profonde Consideration Monsieur de votre Excellence Le très humble & très obéist. servir.   HILLIARD D'AUBERTEUIL

From Jane Mecom

ALS: American Philosophical Society

My Ever Dear Brother   warwick 17 June—1782

I wrot to you in october or Novr. Last from Boston to thank you for the grat present I then recd. throw the hands of young cousen Jonathan Williams,[4] with wich I had no Leter from my Dear Brother nor have I recved any of a Later Date than two years ago Last march,[5] since my Return home my time & atention has been fill'd with sickness & Deaths in the Famely in perticular that of my Dear Grandaughter Jenny who Died of a consumption has left three sweat babes won about too months old, a sorrofull Husband & a Distres'd Grand mother[6] I Injoy'd sweat Peace in her Pleasant conversation & grat comfort in her Dutifull & tender atention was Pleased with the hopes of the continuance of it the Remainder of my Life but those comforts are Vanish'd & a care Devovled [devolved] on me that I find my self unequel to that of the children the youngist is at nurs but the other too Require some person more lively & Paitient to watch

4. Mecom's Oct. 29 letter is in xxxv, 666–7. For BF's gift of textile goods to sell see our annotation of Catharine Greene to BF, May 8.

5. This evidently refers to a short letter (now missing) written in March, 1780, acknowledging receipt of some soap. Recently, however, Mecom had referred to it as dating from 1779: xxxIV, 200, 424; xxxV, 158, 666.

6. In the late fall of 1781, Mecom had returned to the home of Jane Flagg Greene, who died on April 6. Greene was survived by her husband, Elihu, and their children Sarah, Franklin, and Jane: xxxVI, 202; Catharine Greene to BF, May 8, above.

over them continuealy, my Dear child urged me Earnestly not to Leave them as long as I Live & tho I made her no promis I find the Request to be very Powerfull her Husband is Desierous I should continue with Him & treats me very Respectfully that I have no thoughts of Removeing at Present but circumstances may alter in Time I can't Expect it to be other ways as he is a young man but my stay in the world may be much shorter, & Life becomes Less Desierable Exept I could find a capasety to be more Usefull which growing Infermities & low spirits Prevent, my Friend Greene Tould me she wrot you soon affter my child Died[7] & I dont doubt she was more Perticular than I can be at Presant for my litle wons are Interupting me Every miniut & it is so hot I am not willing to trust them out of my sight, should not have wrot in such a hurry but at the Request of Gover'r Green in behalf of some Friend who is Prisener in England[8] whome you may do more towards Inlarging than any won Els they call for the Leter & I can add no more but that I wish for the comfort of a leter from you & am under all circumstances your affectionat sister   JANE MECOM

I began this at the Govr'rs but was fetchd home to the funeral of my Gransons Brothers wife[9] who died in the same house with us.

I Inclose the memerandom about the man

Addressed: Doctr. Franklin / at Paris / In France.

7. Above, May 8.

8. William Greene's June 25 letter to BF, below, describes the plight of captive Ezekiel Durfey.

9. Most likely Catharine Ward Greene (1752–1782), the wife of Elihu Greene's brother Christopher (1748–1830): Richard K. Showman *et al.*, eds., *The Papers of General Nathanael Greene* (12 vols. to date, Chapel Hill, N.C., and London, 1976–), I, 20n, 38n.

From Vandenyver frères[1] LS: University of Pennsylvania Library

Monsieur   Paris le 18 Juin 1782

Le Sieur henri van Eupen négotiant recommandable de la ville d'Anvers voulant envoyer à Philadelphie Sous pavillon Imperial[2] Son navire nommé le plus Ultra commandé par le Capitaine hermanus kuiebel, nous charge de Supplier votre Excellence de vouloir bien lui indiquer une maison Solide & honnête à qui il Ladresseroit, & de le favoriser d'une lettre de recommandation pour le Congrès en vertu de la quelle il put réclamer sa protection en cas de besoin; nous prions votre excellence d'accueillir favorablement la demande du dit Sieur & d'en agréer Lhommage de Sa reconnaissance, ainsi que les assurances du profond respect avec le quel nous avons Lhonneur dêtre Monsieur de votre Excellence Les très humbles & très obéissants Serviteurs

VANDEN YVER FRERES & CE

Monsieur franklin à Passi

Notation: Vandernyver 18. Juin 1782.

From Jonathan Williams, Jr.

ALS: American Philosophical Society; copy: Yale University Library

Dear & hond Sir.   Nantes June 18. 1782.

I hasten to answer your respected Favour of the 13 Inst. this moment received.—I am sorry Mr de Chaumont makes so many unjustifiable Difficulties, and agreeable to your desire I will answer your Questions in their Course to refute his ill founded arguments. He cannot avoid paying you Interest on the £50,000 Livres he has had so long in his Hands; this Money was due at the Time, 30,000 Livres of it he had orders to pay me, & the other 20,000 I paid to him myself to make up the 50,000 for

---

1. This is the last extant letter to BF from the Paris banking firm (XXVI, 659n). There is no record of a response.

2. Antwerp, like the rest of the Austrian Netherlands, was part of the Holy Roman Empire.

which he had previously accepted a Bill and he paid that Bill by two notes to prolong the Time. But his Notes would have been protested or paid at the Day of their Expiration if you had acted with rigour, it was therefore an act of Favour to let them lay over. But without all this Reasoning the very circumstance of charging Interest on one side, justifies a similar Charge on the other, unless there be some agreement to the Contrary.— He was paid for many more Tons in the Marquis de la Fayette than there were on board for the public. I paid him for 1200 Tons & that I believe to be as much as the Vessell could carry;[3] it is true the Vessell guaged 1687 Tons but then the Cabins, the Gun Deck, the forecastle magazine, & all the Store Rooms were included, & the deduction of 487 Tons was for *l'emplacement de l'equipage* agreeable to Usage & our agreement. On the Contrary if that ship had arrived in America, there would have been some very serious Deductions for Freight smuggled on board without my knowledge or Consent, and this to an amount I dare say not less than 2 or 300 Tons but this I cannot ascertain now the ship is lost. I know however that my Clerk stopped a number of Hogshead of salt from going on board, & the Officer of the ship told him there were 100 to come. I have no doubt but these were put on board afterwards.[4] Mr Gourlade acknowledges to have shipped up-

3. See XXXIV, 9n.

4. JW was correct. The first portion of the *Marquis de Lafayette*'s cargo to be auctioned in London included 20 hogsheads of salt, as well as large quantities of wine, tea, china ware, and miscellaneous foodstuffs. When BF asked JW to review the set of auction catalogues, JW annotated the cover page of that sale with a note exonerating himself of responsibility. With the exception of some wine, "I do not find anything that belonged to the public . . . all was put on board without my knowledge or Consent". Panter & Co. Sale Catalogue of the Prize Cargo of the *Marquis de Lafayette*, Oct. 11, 1781. Subsequent catalogues for sales on Jan. 29, 30, 31, Feb. 5, 6, and 7 were likewise annotated by JW, whose markings distinguished public from private goods. Among the supplies for the army (uniforms, shoes, buttons, firearms, saltpeter, etc.), were huge quantities of general clothing, fabric, notions, housewares, stationery, and luxury items. JW may have been surprised to see listings for 4,694 ostrich feathers, two leopard skins, 32 silk umbrellas, and 80 parcels of artificial flowers alongside a variety of womens' hats. On the other hand, he had engaged in clandestine trade earlier in the war; see XXXII, 155–8. This set of annotated sales catalogues is at the APS.

wards of 30,000 Livres on board on Accot of Mr de Chaumont, when you will see by the agreement that he promised not to ship anything.[5] Capt Robeson also told me that after the Capture the Marquis de la Fayette supplyed the whole Fleet with Wine, & a vast number of Casks were taken out.—[6] Now I never shipped a Cask:— 45 Cases of 50 Bottles each are all I knew went on board on Freight.— I thought it best not to enter into disputes which I could not support for want of Evidence & which would have detained the ship. But I wrote to Congress & desired that every Bale Case or Cask might be examined & those not in my List seized for the payment of the Freight.[7]

The Refusal to take the Charge of Exchange on himself is unjust,—it was to be sure a most extravagant Way to raise Money, but it was his Necessity alone that occasioned that Measure; The payment here was so far from being disadvantageous to him as he represents, that it was the Express motive for buying the Cloths *to pay for them in America*, & without that the Bargain would not have been made. You may remember sir you told me when the matter was proposed, that if the payment could be made in America or in the Way of Bills at a long date it might do, but *you would not consent to any purchase which required any advance of Cash*. And it was in consequence of this absolute Determination before the Bargain was made that the mode of drawing on America & redrawing on France was proposed by Mr de C himself & accepted by you. I am at a Loss to understand what he means by advantages he would have had by being paid in America, for the sum was to be fixed in the first Instance & it would not have increased or dimished by drawing or redrawing, unless the Payment had been prolonged longer than usual Time, in which Case he would have had a right to Interest, and it is for this Reason he should rather pay you Interest, than refuse the Loss of exchange submitted to on accot of his Necessity.

Were I to estimate the Damage sustained by the Delay of the Vessell at Bordeaux I might calculate the whole value; for I firmly believe that if the Ship had been ready at the Time fixed

5. Specified in the charterparty signed on Aug. 30, 1780: XXXIII, 336n.
6. Robeson sailed as a passenger: XXXIV, 298n.
7. See XXXIV, 478–9n.

she would not have been taken. But at least, all the army might
be supposed to suffer for want of these Cloathing for the Space
of Time, might be called the real Damge: This I am not a Judge
of. Thus I think I have gone through the Matter. If M. de Chaumont comes to Reason & allows the Accot with Interest & exclusive of the Loss on Exchange I think the affair of the Freight
should be dropped, because it was arbitrated & closed by Mr
Jauge the Banker, and I do not like the most distant appearance
of flying from a Decision; but if Mr de C brings up that matter
again it will be well to turn his own Artillery on himself. I thank
you for your Advice to me which I shall attentively follow and
am as ever your most dutifull & affectionate Kinsman

JONA WILLIAMS J

His Excellency Dr Franklin.

Endorsed: Mr Williams June 18. 1782 Answering my Questions
relating to M. de Chaumont's Objections. Stating Facts relating
to the Cloths, &c

From Jean-Baptiste Le Roy   AL: American Philosophical Society

[after June 18, 1782][8]

J'apprends dans le moment mon Illustre Docteur que vous avez
envoyé hier chez moi pour me demander de mes dragèes noires
parceque vous ètes enrhumé. J'ai compris par la que c'etoit de
mon Suc de réglisse et Je vous en envoye un pacquet. Je vous demande pardon de ce qu'il a eté entamé mais je n'en ai pas d'autre.
Jespere qu'on vous aura dit que j'ai envoyé chez vous Vendredy
pour me dédommager de ce que J'avois perdu la veille mais vous
n'etiez pas chez vous. Voulez vous de moi cette après midy. Je

8. The day BF came down with what he called a violent cold, accompanied
by fever and headache, which he feared might be influenza; see the entry of
that date in his journal of the peace negotiations. On June 10, the *Jour. de
Paris* had reported on the influenza epidemic that had swept through Europe
and was now at Paris. Symptoms included either sore throat or headache, fatigue, and a fever that usually lasted two or three days.

serai à vos ordres avec grand plaisir. Jespere bien que votre
rhume n'a rien de dangereux.

From William Hodgson ALS: American Philosophical Society

Dear Sir   Coleman St. 20 June 1782

At the Instance of a very worthy Friend, I take the liberty of
introducing to your Notice, Mr Robt. Milligan, of Cecil County
in Maryland; a young Gentleman, I am assured, of great worth
& Character, who has been for some years studying the Law in
this Country, & now designs to visit Paris on his return to America.[9]

From this discription, I am confident, he will stand in need of
no Recommendation, to entitle him to your Civilities, permit me
however, on this occasion, to assure you, I shall consider myself,
much obliged, by the Attentions, you may be pleased to show
him, as it puts me in the agreable Situation, of doing a Civility,
to a Man, I much esteem. I am with the greatest Respect Dear sir
Your most Obedt Hble servant   WILLIAM HODGSON

To His Excellency Benjn. Franklin Esqr Minister Plenipotentiary from the United States of America at the Court of France

Addressed: To / His Excellency Benjn. Franklin Esqr / Minister
Plenipotentiary from the / United States of America at / the
Court of France

9. Milligan (1754–1806) probably came to England in the summer of 1779.
By 1786, he was practicing law in Philadelphia: XXX, 621–2; Harold C. Syrett
et al., eds., *The Papers of Alexander Hamilton* (27 vols., New York, 1961–87),
III, 647n; J. Hall Pleasants, ed., "Letters of Molly and Hetty Tilghman . . . ,"
Md. Hist. Mag., XXI (1926), 238n.

From Lafayette

ALS: American Philosophical Society; transcripts:[1] National Archives, Massachusetts Historical Society

My Dear Sir   Versailles Thursday Morning [June 20, 1782][2]
    Agreable to Your Desire I Have Waited Upon Count de Vergennes and said to Him What I Had in Command from Your Excellency— He Intends taking the King's orders this Morning, and Expects He Will Be Able to propose Mr. Grenville a Meeting for to Morrow where He Will Have Him to Explain Himself Respecting france and Her Allies,[3] that He May Make an official Communication Both to the King and the Allied Minister—[4] What Count de Vergennes Can Make out of this Conversation Will Be Communicated By Him to Yo [Your] Excellency in Case You are able to Come—in the other Case I Will Wait Upon You to Morrow Evening with Every Information I Can Collect— I Have the Honor to Be very Respectfully My dear sir Your obedient servant and affectionate friend   LAFAYETTE

Notation: Mr. de La Fayette Versailles 20th. June 1782

From ——— Guilin

L: American Philosophical Society

Monseigneur,   [before June 21, 1782][5]
    C'est avec la confiance que vos bontés inspirent à tous ceux qui reclament votre protection que le nommé Guilin fruitier à Chaillot a l'honneur de réprésenter trés humblement à votre Excellence que depuis cinq ans il a celui de fournir en sa qualité de

1. In BF's journal of the peace negotiations.
2. Below Lafayette's dateline, an unknown hand wrote "20th," to which BF added "June 82".
3. For Vergennes' meeting with Grenville see our annotation of the June 21 entry in BF's journal of the peace negotiations.
4. Either Lafayette means so that Grenville may make an official communication both to George III and Oswald or, more likely, so that Vergennes may make an official communication both to Louis XVI and BF.
5. The day Campo-de-Arbe, the object of Guilin's suspicions, received his final payment as BF's maître d'hôtel; see the Editorial Headnote on Accounts. The present appeal and another one from BF's *pâtissière* Louise Lahannée, immediately below, may have occasioned his replacement.

fruitier votre maison[6] avec l'honneteté et l'exactitude possible, mais depuis un mois il ne sçait pourquoi il est privé de cet Honneur: Il a tout lieu de penser que le Sr. Campot votre maître d'hôtel l'a deservi en ce que le supliant n'a pas eu la faculté de lui prêter une Somme de 360 *l.t.;* Il auroit fait ce pret, si ses moyens lui eussent permis. Ce Considéré, MONSEIGNEUR, il a recours à vos bontès et vous supplie de lui accorder la continuation de la fourniture de votre maison qu'il servira toujours avec le même zèle & de lui procurer le payement de 10 *l.t.* 8 *s.* qu'il a fourni pour le compte du d. [*dit*] Campot. Sa profonde réconnoissance égalera l'ardeur des vœux qu'il ne cessera de former pour la conservation des jours précieux de VOTRE EXCELLENCE./.

A Son Excellence Monseigneur le Docteur Franklin

Notation: Guilen

From Louise Lahannée
L: American Philosophical Society

MONSEIGNEUR [before June 21, 1782][7]

LOUISE LAHANNÉE votre patissiere depuis plusieurs années, dans L'assurance par son attention et Son Exactitude, a ne vous avoir Laissé rien desirer dans toutes fournitures qui pouroient vous agreer par La recherche, et Le Choix qu'elle a Toujours fait d'ouvriers capables de vous contenter, Se Trouvant privée depuis quelque Temps de L'honneur de vous servir qui Luy etoit, Si Flateur, sans en pouvoir Imaginer aucuns motifs qui puissent vous Interesser ose VOUS SUPLIER TRES HUMBLEMENT MONSEIGNEUR de vouloir bien Les demander a votre Maitre d'hotel, et, de luy ordonner de luy en faire part. Comme elle aprend n'être pas la seule quil Ecarte de Votre maison par des raisons qui Luy Sont personnelles, La supliante, n'en pouvant voir a son Egard d'autres que celle de luy avoir refusé Logement pour une personne quil Simagineroit ne luy avoir pas parû plus Convenable a sa relation qu'a la sienne propre; elle ressent MONSEIGNEUR que la reconnoissance qu'elle vous doit tant de la

---

6. By early March, 1777, BF and his family had set up household in Passy: XXIII, 245.

7. For the dating see Guilin's letter, immediately above.

bonté, que vous avez eû de luy Temoigner a elle même votre satisfaction de ce qu'elle vous etoit attachée que de la Confiance, que vous avez en d'autres ouvriers de Sa famille, Exige d'elle de se justifier a vos ieux faits pour toutes Justices. Elle, est a même de s'affranchir pour ses livres de tous reproches (n'en n'ayant Jamais recû de qui que ce soit) vis avis de son adversaire, Si les memoires propres de la supliante vous parviennent Comme elle les fournit.[8] Il suplée dit-on par luy même a l'Insufisance de Ceux quil employe Nouvellement, pour les faire Valoir, Cela ne peut Inculper aucun des autres qui n'avoient pas a luy Tenir compte de sa Complaisance. Quoyqu'il en Soit La supliante, vous conjure MONSEIGNEUR de vous persuader, qu'elle n'en est pas moins ardente a faire les voeux Les plus parfaits pour La durée et La prosperité des jours DE VOTRE EXCELLENCE SI INTERESSANTS a tant d'Egards./.

A son Excellence Monseigneur Frankelein

Notation: Lahannée

To Ingenhousz[9]

AL (draft), press copy of L, and copy:[1] Library of Congress

[June 21, 1782]
An Attempt to explain the Effects of Lightning on the Vane of the Steeple of a Church in *Cremona*, August 1777. Address'd to Dr John Ingenhauss, C. & Archiat. Cæs. &c &c

1. When the subtil Fluid which we call Fire or Heat enters a

8. Her bills have not survived. Campo-de-Arbe was reimbursed for family expenses every two months (Account XXIII, xxix, 3).

9. Ever since May, 1780, BF had been promising to send Ingenhousz some thoughts on Carlo Barletti's pamphlet analyzing a lightning strike on the weathervane atop a church in Cremona: XXXII, 343n, 348; XXXV, 548. He finally finished the paper on June 21, 1782. That same day he added a final section to an ongoing letter to Ingenhousz begun on Oct. 2, 1781 (XXXV, 544–51), and enclosed this paper with that letter.

1. We publish from BF's draft since the L (in L'Air de Lamotte's hand) is flawed by numerous copying errors. The third version, a copy in Josiah Flagg's hand, was made for BF in 1786.

solid Body, it separates the Particles of which that Body consists farther from each other, and thus dilates the Body, increasing its Dimensions.

2.   A greater Proportion of Fire introduc'd separates the Parts so far from each other, that the solid Body becomes a Fluid, being melted.

3.   A still greater Quantity of Heat separates the Parts so far, that they lose their mutual Attraction & acquire a mutual Repulsion, whence they fly from each other, either gradually or suddenly with great Force, as the separating Power is introduc'd gradually or suddenly.

4.   Thus Ice becomes Water, and Water Vapour, which Vapour is said to expand to 14000 times the Space it occupied in the Form of Water, and with an explosive Force in certain Circumstances capable of producing great & violent Effects.

5.   Thus Metals expand, melt, & explode. The two first effected by the gradual Application of the separating Power, and all three in its sudden Application, by artificial Electricity, or by Lightning.

6.   That Fluid in passing thro' a Metal Rod or Wire, is generally suppos'd to occupy the whole Dimension of the Rod. If the Rod is smaller in some Places than in others, the Quantity of Fluid which is not sufficient to make any Change in the larger or thicker Part, may be sufficient to expand, melt, or explode the smaller, the Quantity of Fluid passing, being the same, and the Quantity of Matter less that is acted upon.

7.   Thus the Links of a Brass Chain, with a certain Quantity of Electricity passing thro' them, have been melted in the small Parts that form their Contact, while the rest have not been affected.

8.   Thus a Piece of Tin Foil cut in this Form, inclos'd in a Pack of Cards,

and having the Charge of a large Bottle sent thro' it, has been found unchang'd in the broadest Part between a and b. melted only in Spots between b & c, totally melted between c and d, and the Part between d and e reduc'd to Smoke by Explosion.

9. The Tinfoil melted in Spots between b and c, and that whole Space not being melted, seems to indicate that the Foil in the melted Parts had been thinner than the rest, on which thin Parts the passing Fluid had therefore a greater Effect.

10. Some Metals melt more easily than others. Tin more easily than Copper, Copper than Iron. It is suppos'd, (perhaps not yet prov'd) that those which melt with the least of the separating Power, whether that be common Fire or the electric Fluid, do also explode with less of that Power.

11. The Explosions of Metal like those of Gunpowder act in all Directions. Thus the Explosion of Gold Leaf between Plates of Glass, breaking the Glass to Pieces, will throw those Pieces into all Parts of the Room, and the Explosion of Iron or even of Water between the Joints of Stone in a Steeple, will scatter the Stones in all Directions round the Neighbourhood. But the Directions given to those Stones by the Explosion, is to be considered as different from the Direction of the Lightning, which happen'd to occasion those Explosions of the Matter it met with in its Passage between the Clouds & the Earth.

12. When Bodies positively electris'd approach Sharp Pointed Rods or thin Plates of Metal, these are more easily render'd negative by the repulsive Force of the Electric Fluid in those positively electris'd Bodies, which chases away the natural Quantity contain'd in those mince Rods or Plates, tho' it would not have Force enough to chase the same out of larger Masses. Hence such Points, Rods, & Plates, being in a negative State, draw to themselves more strongly and in greater Quantities the Electric Fluid offer'd them, than such Masses can do, which remain more nearly in their natural State. And thus a pointed Rod receives not only at its Point, tho' more visibly there, but at all Parts of its Length that are expos'd. Hence a Needle held between the Finger & Thumb, and presented to a Charg'd Prime Conductor, will draw off the Charge, more expeditiously if held near the Eye & the rest of its Length is expos'd to the Elecl. Atmosphere, than if all but ½ an Inch of the Point is conceal'd & cover'd.—

13. Lightning so differs from solid Projectiles, and from common Fluids projected with Violence, that tho' its Course is rapid, it is most easily turned to follow the Direction of good Conductors. And it is doubted whether any Experiments in Electricity have yet decisively proved that the electric Fluid in its violent Passage thro' the Air when a Battery is discharg'd has what we call a Momentum, wch would make it continue its Course in a right Line tho' a Conductor offer'd near that Course to give it a different or even contrary Direction; or that it has a Force capable of pushing forward, or overthrowing the Objects it strikes against, even tho' it sometimes pierces them. Does not this seem to indicate that the Perforation is not made by the Force of a Projectile passing thro', but rather by the Explosion or the Dilatation in passing, of a subtil Line of Fluid.

14. Such an Explosion or Dilatation of a Line of Fluid passing thro' a Card, would raise Burrs round the Hole sometimes on one side, sometimes on the other, & sometimes on both, according to the Disposition of the Parts of the Paper near the Surfaces, without any regard to the Direction of the Fluid.—

15. Great Thanks are due to the ingenious Philosopher who examined the Vane at Cremona, and who took the Pains to describe so exactly the Effects of the Lightning upon it, and to communicate that Description. The Fact is extreamly curious. It is well worth considering. He invites to that Consideration. He has fairly given his own Opinion. He will with Candour receive that of others, tho' it may happen to differ from his own. By calmly discussing rather than by warmly disputing, the Truth is most easily obtained. I shall give my Opinion freely, as it is asked, hoping it may prove the true one; and promising my self if otherwise, the Honour at least of acknowledging frankly my Error, and of being thankful to him who kindly shows it to me.

16. By the Account given of this Stroke of Lightning upon the Steeple at Cremona, it appears, that the Rod of Iron or Spindle on which the Vane turned was of about two Inches Circumference, terminating in a Cross above the Vane, and its lower End fix'd in a Marble Pedestal.

17. That the Plate of the Vane was Copper 8 or 9 Inches wide and

near twice as long. That it was about one Line thick near the Spindle, and growing thinner insensibly towards the other End, where its Thickness did not exceed three quarters of a Line; the Weight 20½ Ounces.

18. That the Copper had been tinned over.

19. That the Marble Pedestal was split by the Stroke into many Pieces, & scatter'd over the Roof, Garden & Court of a neighbouring Building, One Piece was thrown to the Distance of 40 feet. The Spindle was broken and displac'd, and the Vane thrown on the Roof of the Parsonage House 20 feet from the Steeple.

20. That the Vane was perforated in 18 Places, the Holes of irregular Forms and the Metal which had filled them push'd outwards, in some of them on one Side of the Vane in others on the other. The Copper show'd Marks of having been partly melted, and in some Places Tin and Copper melted & mingled together. There were Marks of Smoke in several Places.

21. The Ragged Parts bent outwards round each Hole, being brought back to their original flat Positition, were not tho' evidently a little thinned & dilated, sufficient to fill the Place.

22. From the Effects describ'd (19) it is clear that the Quantity of Lightning which fell on the Steeple at Cremona, was very great.

23. The Vane being a thin Plate of Copper, its Edges & Corners may be considered as a Series of Points, and being therefore sooner render'd negative by the repulsive Force of an approaching positive Cloud, than the blunt & thick Iron Cross, (12) was probably first struck; and thence became the Conductor of that great Quantity.—

24. The Plate of which the Vane was formed being thicker near the Spindle and diminishing in Thickness gradually to the other End, (17) was probably not of Copper plated by passing between Rollers, for they would have left it of equal Thickness, but of Metal plated by the Hammer. The Surface too of rolled Copper is even & plain, that of hammered is generally uneven, with Hollows occasioned by the Impressions of the Hammer.

25. In those concave Impressions the Metal is thinner than it is

around them, and probably thinnest near the center of each Impression.

26. The Lightning which in passing thro' the Vane was not sufficient to melt its thicker Parts, might be sufficient to melt the thinner, (6)(7)(8)(9) and to soften those that were in a middle State.

27. That part of the Tin (18) which covered the thinner Parts, being more easily melted and exploded than Copper, (10) might possibly be exploded when the Copper was but melted. The Smoke appearing in several Places (20) is a Proof of Explosion.

28. There might probably be more Tin in the concave Impressions of the Hammer on one Side of the Plate than on the Convex Part of those Impressions on the other. Hence stronger Explosions on the Concave side.

29. The nature of those Explosions is, to act violently in all directions, and in this Case being near the Plate, they would act against it on one side, while they acted against the Air on the other.

30. Those thin Parts of the Plate being at the same Instant partly in fusion, and partly so softned as to be near it: the softned Parts were push'd outwards, a Hole made, and some of the melted Parts blown away; hence there was not left Metal enough to refill the Vacancy, by bending back the ragged Parts to their Places.

31. The concave Impressions of the Hammer being indifferently made on both Sides of the Plate, it is natural, from (28,29,30) that the Pushing outwards of the softned Metal by the Explosions, should be on both Sides of the Plate in a proportion nearly equal.—

32. That the Force of a simple electric Explosion is very great appears from the Geneva Experiment, wherein a Spark between two Wires, under Oil in a drinking Glass, breaks the Glass, Body Stem & Foot, all to Shivers.

33. The electric Explosion of Metal acts with still more Force. A Strip of Leaf Gold no broader than a Straw, exploded between two Pieces of thick Looking Glass, will break the Glass to pieces, tho' confin'd by the Screws of a strong Press. And between two Pieces of Marble press'd together by a Weight

of 20 pounds, will lift that Weight.— Much less Force is necessary to move the melted & softened Parts of a thin Plate of Copper.

34. This Explication of the Appearances on the Vane, is drawn from what we already know of Electricity & the Effects of Lightning. The learned Author of the Account, gives a different but very ingenious one, which he draws from the Appearances themselves. The Matter push'd out of the Holes is found, that of some on one side of the Plate, & of others on the other. Hence he supposes them to be occasion'd (if I understand him rightly) by Streams or Threads of Electric Matter, of different and contrary kinds, rushing violently towards each other, and meeting with the Vane so accidentally placed, as to be found precisely in the Place of their Meeting, where it was pierc'd by all of them, they all striking on both its Sides at the same Instant. This however is so extraordinary an Accident as to be in the Author's own Opinion almost miraculous. "Passeranno (says he) forse picès ecoli prima que ritorni tralle infinitè combinazioni un caso simile a quello della banderuola, che ora abbiamo per mano. Forza é que si esaurisca una non pisi udita miniera difulmini sopra una grande città, pressoque seminata di campanili, e di banderuole, il che è rarissimo; e può ancora picè volte ciò succedere, senza che s'incontri giammai un altra banderuola tanto opportunatamenta situata tra è limiti della fulmine a Explosione."

35. But tho' the Author's Explication of these Appearances on the Vane does not satisfy me, I am not so confident of my own as to propose its being accepted without Confirmation by Experiment. Those who have strong electric Batteries may try it thus..— Form a little Vane of Paper, and spot it on both sides by attaching small Pieces of Leaf Gold or Tinfoil, not exactly opposite to each other. Then send the whole Force of the Battery thro' the Vane, entring at one End of it & going out of the other. If the Metal explodes I imagine it will be found to make Holes in the Paper, forcing the torn Parts out on the Side opposite to the Metal.— A more expensive, but perhaps more satisfactory Experiment would be, to make a new Vane as exactly as possible like that in question, in all the Particulars of its Description, and place it on a tall Mast fix'd on some Hill

subject to Strokes of Lightning, with a better Conductor to the Earth than the Wood of the Mast; If this should be struck in the Course of a few Years, & the same Effect appear upon it, it would be still more miraculous to suppose it happen'd by Accident to be exactly situated where those crossing threads of different Electricities were afterwards to meet.

36. The Perforation of Glass Bottles when over-charg'd, is I imagine a different Case, & not explicable by either of these Hypotheses.— I cannot well suppose the Breach to be occasion'd by the Passage of Electricity thro' it, since a single Bottle tho' so broken in the Discharge, always is found to send round in its usual Course the Quantity with which it was charged. Then the Breach never happens but at the Instant of the circuitous Discharge, either by the discharging Rod, or in overleaping the Borders of the Glass. Thus I have been present when a Battery of twenty Glasses was discharg'd by the discharging Rod, and produc'd the same Effect in its Circuit as if the Bottles had none of them been pierced; and yet on examining them we found no less than twelve of them in that Situation.— Now all the Bottles of the Battery being united by a Communication of all the Outsides together, and of all the Insides together, if one of them had been pierc'd by a forc'd Passage of the different kinds of Electricity to meet each other, before the Discharge by the discharging Rod, it would not only have prevented the Passage of the Electricity by the common Circuit, but it would have sav'd all the rest of its Fellows, by conducting the whole thro' its own Breach. And it is not easy to conceive that 12 Bottles in 20 should be so equally strong as to support the whole Strength of their Charge till the Circuit of their Discharge was opened, and then be so equally weak as to break all together when the Weight of that Charge was taken off from them by opening the Circuit.— At some other time I will give you my Opinion of this Effect if you desire it.—

I have taken the Acct. of this Stroke of Lightning from an Italian Piece, intitled, *Analisi d'un nuovo Fenomeno del Fulmine*, the Dedication of which is subscribed *Carlo Barletti delle Scuole Pie*, who I suppose is the Author. As I do not perfectly understand that Language, I may possibly in some things have mistaken that Philosopher's Meaning. I therefore desire, my dear Friend, that you would not permit this to be published, till you have compar'd and considered it with that original Piece, and communicated to me your Remarks and Corrections.— Nor would I in any Case have it appear with my Name, as perhaps it may occasion Disputes and I have no time to attend to them.—

From Pierre-Augustin Caron de Beaumarchais

L: University of Pennsylvania Library

ce 21— Juin 1782

Mr. de Beaumarchais présente ses très humbles complimens à Monsieur Le Docteur Franklin, et en reponse à la Lettre que M Le Ray de chaumont lui a écritte au Sujet de Mr Morice.[2] Il vient de persuader ce de[rnier][3] du peu de fondement que son opposition a[ura] entre les mains de Monsieur, Le Docteur franklin, il ne la fera pas fermer, et il n'est pas meme nécessaire d'en prevenir M Morice, si Monsieur Le Docteur franklin ne veut pas en prendre la peine.

M. de Beaumarchais vient de partir pour la Campagne et il avoit chargé l'Ecrivain de prendre ses mesures afin d'expedier la présente reponse aussitot l'explication[4]

Notation: Beaumarchais 22. Juin 1782.

---

2. We do not know what Chaumont wrote Beaumarchais, who was becoming very concerned about his credit. On June 3, Beaumarchais sent his accounts to Morris and begged for at least a partial settlement: *Morris Papers*, V, 318–28. BF made a large payment to Beaumarchais on June 25; see our annotation of BF to Morris, Aug. 12.

3. The MS is torn; we have guessed at this word and one on the following line.

4. Beaumarchais was back by July 9, when he signed a printed bond (prepared by WTF on July 8) for his frigate *Alexander* (*Alexandre*), Capt. Etienne Gregory. APS. Stephen Gregory is identified in XXXV, 433–4. This is the earliest dated example of the bond form BF printed at Passy, illustrated in Luther S. Livingston, *Franklin and his Press at Passy* (New York, 1914), fac-

From Cabaret

ALS: American Philosophical Society

Ce 21 juin 1782

Jay Lhonneur de repondre a vos ordres aiant celuy de Vous observer quil faut pour L'Execution Suivant Votre Model de tres grand papier pour Remplir L'infolio et pour Le grand in 4to il faut prendre de L'infolio Reduit par Les bouts pour former la Largeur.

Je joins a la presente 2 feuilles du papier quil faut prendre Pour Suivre Votre model.

D'après Votre definition L'Execution en sera prompte.[5]

Jay Lhonneur d'Etre en attendant vos ordres avec Le respect le plus profond Votre tres humble et tres obeissant serviteur./.

CABARET

Notation: Cabaret 21. Juin 1782.

From Antoine Court de Gébelin

ALS: American Philosophical Society

Monsieur   Rue Poupée 21e. Juin 1782

J'ai l'honneur de vous envoier une lettre que j'ai recue pour vous, de la part d'un jeune homme nommé Saussine, Ministre Protestant dans le bas Languedoc;[6] j'y joins une qui l'accompa-

---

ing p. 86. BF based his form on the one approved by Congress on May 2, 1780 (*JCC*, XVI, pp. 403–6), copying its language and imitating its typography. He was evidently unaware that a new form, with slightly modified language, had been issued by Congress in the summer of 1781. That form was in use until the end of hostilities. See *JCC*, XX, p. 645.

5. Cabaret's bill covering June 6 through July 26, 1782 (APS), indicates several orders for paper that were filled on June 28. This is one of them. Another was "une demie Rame grand Caré d'hollande" for 35 *l.t.* BF evidently found this price too high. In an undated letter, Cabaret countered the charge, asserting his integrity and begging BF to continue to patronize him. In a postscript, however, Cabaret offered to lower the price to 33 *l.t.* APS.

6. Pierre Saussine, a young minister writing from Nîmes on May 28, begs BF's help in discovering the whereabouts of an orphaned relative named Boudon, now somewhere in America. Boudon, who had a sizable inheritance, had formed a strong attachment to his tutor, but unscrupulous relations eager to secure his money had separated them. Boudon was sent first to Paris and, after a series of misfortunes, ended up in Philadelphia without

gnoit et qui etoit pour moi Signée *St Etienne* autre jeune Ministre de la meme Province, correspondant du Musèe de Paris & fils du celebre *Paul* Pasteur de Nimes.[7]

Ces lettres sont relatives à un autre jeune homme dont je connois fort les Parens & qui est actuellement dans les Etats Réunis de l'Amerique, dont on voudroit fort le faire revenir.

Ayez donc la complaisance de lire ces lettres & si vous pouvez contribuer en quelque chose à nous faire decouvrir ce jeune homme, nous vous en aurons tous la plus vive obligation.

Je suis avec un respectueux devouement Monsieur Votre très humble & très ob. Servitr.   COURT DE GEBELIN

Notation: Court de Geblin 21 Juin 1782.

---

friends or resources. If Mr. Wharton, who met Boudon in Paris, has not taken charge of him, Saussine fears the worst. The tutor, whom Court de Gébelin knows well, is also desperate with worry and is willing to do whatever BF might deem advisable. APS.

7. Jean-Paul Rabaut Saint-Etienne (1743–1793), a pastor at Nîmes who was a former student and close friend of Court de Gébelin's at Lausanne, enclosed Saussine's letter to BF in his June 3 letter to Court de Gébelin. Rabaut Saint-Etienne corroborated Saussine's story and praised him as a man of talent and genius. He revealed that the tutor, Renouard de Calvisson, was Boudon's uncle and was prepared to pay the young man's return passage to France. Rabaut Saint-Etienne asked also if Court de Gébelin could secure for Saussine a secretarial position "chez un franklin ou un Buffon," where the young minister might pursue his true calling, the study of physics, which had led him to conceive a system to explain all natural phenomena, including magnetism. APS.

In the years before the Revolution, Rabaut Saint-Etienne worked tirelessly, with Malesherbes, Lafayette, and others, to improve the civil status of Protestants, and during the Revolution, to restore to Protestants religious rights as well. He became a prominent member of the Girondins: Raymond Birn, "Religious Toleration and Freedom of Expression" in *The French Idea of Freedom: the Old Regime and the Declaration of Rights of 1789*, ed. Dale Van Kley (Stanford, Calif., 1994), pp. 267–8, 270–2, 294–7; Jean-René Surrateau and François Gendron, eds., *Dictionnaire historique de la Révolution française* (Paris, 1989), pp. 879–81.

Paul Rabaut (1718–1794), his father, studied at the Lausanne seminary founded by Court de Gébelin's father. Named pastor at Nîmes, Rabaut continued the efforts of Antoine Court to reorganize French Protestantism, in disarray since the revocation of the edict of Nantes in 1685: Larousse under Court and Rabaut.

From Lafayette

ALS: Library of Congress

My Dear Sir, Versailles june 21st [1782] friday Evening
Having Nothing New to Communicate I will Remain this day at Versailles, and will Wait on Your Excellency in the Course of to morrow's Morning— Mr. Grenville Has dined with Count de Vergennes, and is Going Again to write to London[8]—if this Goes on, at Least it Goes at A Moderate Gate— I Hope Your Health is Better, and Have the Honor to Be with Great Respect Your Affectionate ser and friend LAFAYETTE

Addressed: His Excellency / Mr. franklin A m p[9] / Passy

From Dumas

ALS: American Philosophical Society

Monsieur Lahaie 22e. Juin *1782*.
Je m'empresse de profiter du Courier que S. E. M. l'Ambassadeur[1] va dépecher dans une heure, pour vous faire parvenir l'incluse plus sûrement que par toute autre voie, vous priant, Monsieur, après l'avoir lue de vouloir bien la fermer & acheminer avec vos paquets.[2] Elle contient en Substance ce qui se passe ici de plus interessant; & cela me dispense de rien ajouter ici, sinon, que j'espere de recevoir de bonnes nouvelles, tant de votre santé, Monsieur, que de la prospérité des affaires publiques; comme aussi que Vous avez bien reçu mes Lettres antérieures.

Je suis toujours avec le respectueux attachement, qui vous est voué pour la vie, Monsieur Votre très-humble & très-obéissant serviteur DUMAS

8. Grenville wrote Fox that day about his conference with Vergennes. He confessed that in his embarrassment about the ambiguous nature of his powers he had "purposely avoided" seeing BF: Giunta, *Emerging Nation*, I, 434–5.

9. American minister plenipotentiary.

1. "Son Excellence Monsieur" La Vauguyon.

2. Undoubtedly Dumas was forwarding his June 1–20 letter to Livingston (Wharton, *Diplomatic Correspondence*, v, 466–7). He sent duplicate copies by other routes, as there are two copies at the National Archives with a brief additional entry of June 26, and a third (which contains slight variations), dated June 1–18.

Passy à S. E. Mr. Franklin

Addressed: à Son Excellence / Monsieur Franklin, Esqr., Min. / Plénipo: des Etats-Unis, &c. / à *Passy* / près *Paris*

Notations in Augustin's hand: Augustin courier de S. Exce. Le Duc De La Vauguyon Logé chez Madme. Michel rue St. martin pres la rue aux ours, repart vendredy prochain a 6 heures du matin pr La haye / au coin de la rue au ours St Martin / Michel

From Thomas Grenville

AL: Library of Congress

rue de Richelieu. Saturday. [June 22, 1782] Mr. Grenville presents his Compliments to Mr Franklin, and had proposed to himself the pleasure of calling at Passy yesterday, but was so much occupied at Versailles that he had not time to stop in returning, & has been much occupied ever since. Mr de Vergennes will doubtless shew to Mr Franklin the copy of the Power he is desirous of seeing;[3] and Mr Grenville learnt with great pleasure yesterday that Mr Franklin is enough recovered[4] to propose to go to Versailles.

Endorsed: June 22

Notation: June 22. 1782

From Jonathan Williams, Jr.: Two Letters

(I) ALS: University of Pennsylvania Library; (II) ALS: American Philosophical Society

I.

Dear & hond sir   Nantes June 22. 1782
    The Bearer Mr Tardy who has been 4 Years in my 'Counting House goes to Paris for some Family Affairs. I have directed him

---

3. Grenville's powers to negotiate, which on June 15 he had promised to provide BF; see BF's journal of the peace negotiations.
4. From the flu-like illness mentioned in the entry of June 18 in BF's journal of the peace negotiations.

to call on you. He can give you a full Accot of every thing that I know of Mr de C & by having the Letter I wrote you before him he will be able to answer any Question you may desire on the Subject.[5]

Please also to return by him an answer to my Letter of the 26 March. I shall be obliged by any Civilities you may show Mr Tardy, & You may depend he is in every Respect a discreet worthy young man for whom I have a great Esteem. I am as ever most dutifully & affecy Yours   J WILLIAMS J

His Excelly Doctr Franklin.

Notation: J. Williams June 22. 1782

II.

Dear & hond sir   Nantes June 22. 1782.

Mrs Adams is the Wife of an american Captain. She Came from England expecting her Husband would arrive here, but she now finds he is bound to Amsterdam, and she therefore goes to Paris on her Way to that City.

I shall be obliged to you if you will please to give her a Passport for the purpose of her Journey.[6] I am as ever your dutifull & affect Kinsman   JONA WILLIAMS J

Notation: J. Williams 22. Juin 1782.

From Robert R. Livingston

Two LS:[7] University of Pennsylvania Library; AL (draft): New-York Historical Society; copy and transcript: National Archives

Dear Sir   Philadelphia 23d June 1782

This will be sent with duplicates of some of my former Letters to the Southward to embrace the first opportunity that shall

5. Gabriel Tardy, JW's chief clerk, had overseen the loading of the *Marquis de Lafayette:* XXXIV, 396, 467, 494.

6. BF gave Mary Adams a pass to Ostend on June 26: XXXVI, 380.

7. The original and the duplicate. While BF received both, we print from the latter because it bears the more extensive endorsement.

offer from thence—[8] By so uncertain a conveyance you can Expect nothing particular— Nor indeed does our present situation furnish any thing that calls for your immediate attention, unless it be the unanimity with which the people of all ranks agree in determining to listen to no proposals from England which have not the alliance with France for their basis— Perhaps the joy they have discovered in celebrating the birth of the Dauphin will be considered as a proof of their sincere attachment to the present illustrious monarch of France & his family— Leslie has endeavoured to bring General Greene to agree to a suspension of arms for the southern department, to which he has very prudently refused to consent—[9] Nothing has yet been determined or rather executed with respect to Capt Asgill, the Enemy are holding a Court Martial on Lippencutt, the executioner of Capt Huddy—on their decision the life of Capt Asgill will depend, Such is the melancholy necessity which the cruelty of the enemy has imposed.[1]

You enclosed a Letter from the Count de Vergennes on the subject of the pension due to Mr Toussard—[2] Congress are too sensible of that Gentleman's merit to deprive him of it. But as it is necessary that every thing of this kind be transacted at one Office— It is proper that he direct some person as his agent to apply to the Treasury Office here & produce your certificate of

8. Notations on the copy and transcript indicate that the original was sent to Baltimore, the duplicate was delivered to La Luzerne, and the triplicate (now missing) was sent from Baltimore by the ship *Favourite*. Livingston also sent copies of his May 22 and May 30 letters (above) from Baltimore, where shipping in 1782 surpassed that of Philadelphia: Richard Buel, Jr., *In Irons: Britain's Naval Supremacy and the American Revolutionary Economy* (New Haven and London, 1998), pp. 222–4.

9. Brig. Gen. Alexander Leslie (*c.* 1740–1794) had assumed command at Charleston the previous November: Mark Mayo Boatner III, *Encyclopedia of the American Revolution* (New York, 1961), pp. 617–18. For Greene's rejection of Leslie's proposal see Richard K. Showman *et al.*, eds., *The Papers of General Nathanael Greene* (12 vols. to date, Chapel Hill, N.C., and London, 1976–), XI, 227–9, 235, 247, 263–4.

1. See Livingston to BF, May 30.

2. See XXXV, 138, 148–9. Livingston here reiterates a decision reached by Robert Morris, to whom Congress recently had referred the matter: *JCC*, XXII, 321; *Morris Papers*, V, 455.

the time to which the last payment was made—or at least transmit a state of his account, on which the ballance will be paid & his pension regularly settled with his Attorney in future.

The case of the Brigantine Eersten has been decided upon in the inferior Court & in the court of appeals— The latter have been prevailed upon at my request to give a rehearing which is not yet determined; should the determination be against the Vessel or Cargo upon a conviction that she was British property, Congress will not chuse to interfere in the execution of the sentence which the court they have instituted are competent to award—[3] I could wish to know from you what allowance you make to your private secretary & to have an accurate estimate of those contingent expences of your office which you think ought to be charged as distinct from your salary—[4] I enclose a Copy of a Letter from Deane to Govr. Trumbull with his answer which you will be pleased to forward, a copy of the answer is also enclosed—[5] I have the honor to be, sir With the highest respect & esteem Your Excellency's Most obed humble servt,

ROBT R LIVINGSTON

No. 13 Duplicate

His Excellency Benj Franklin, Esqr

Endorsed: No 13 Mr Secry. Livingston June 23. 1782 M. Toussard Brig. Eersten Private Secry.

To Bethia Alexander[6]

AL (draft): Library of Congress

Passy, June 24. 1782

I am not at all displeas'd that the Thesis and Dedication with which we were threatned are blown over, for I dislike much all

---

3. Vergennes had forwarded BF a memorial from the owners of the brig *Den Eersten*. BF sent it to Livingston: XXXVI, 446–7, 644. Congress responded to Vergennes' concern by granting a stay of execution in the case: XXXVI, 448n; *JCC,* XXII, 117–18n.

4. For BF's views on contingent expenses see XXXV, 145–6.

5. Deane to Gov. Jonathan Trumbull, Oct. 21, 1781, and Trumbull to Deane, May 15, 1782: *Deane Papers,* IV, 509–14; V, 93–7. BF had discussed Deane's correspondence in a March 4 letter to Livingston (XXXVI, 647–8).

6. In answer to her letter of June 9, above.

sorts of Mummery.— The Republic of Letters has gain'd no Reputation, whatever else it may have gain'd, by the Commerce of Dedications. I never made one, and I never desir'd that one should be made to me. When I submit[*torn:* ted to?] receive this, it was from the bad Habit I have long had of doing every thing that Ladies desire me to do. There is no refusing any thing to Madame la Marck nor to you. I have been to pay my Respects to that amiable Lady, not merely because it was a Compliment due to her, but because I love her; which induces me to excuse her not letting me in; the same Reason I should have for excusing your Faults, if you had any. I have not seen your Papa since the Receipt of your pleasing Letter, so could arrange nothing with him respecting the Carriage. During seven or eight days I shall be very busy, after that you shall hear from me, and the Carriage shall be at your Service. How could you think of writing to me about Chimneys & Fires, in such Weather as this. Now is the time for the frugal Lady you mention to save her Wood, obtain *plus de Chaleur,* and lay it up against Winter as People do Ice against Summer. Frugality is an enriching Virtue; a Virtue I never could acquire in my self: but I was once lucky enough to find it in a Wife, who thereby became a Fortune to me. Do you possess it?— If you do, and I were 20 Years younger, I would give your Father 1000 Guineas for you. I know you would be worth more to me, as a *Menagere,* but I am covetous and love good Bargains.

Adieu, dear Friend, & believe me ever Yours most affectionately

My Love to Christy & to Jenny—&c[7]

Miss Alexander

7. Bethia's sisters Christine and Jane. The "&c" no doubt includes the two other sisters, Isabella and Joanna (XXXIII, 46n), and perhaps their brothers, William (1755–1842) and Robert (1767–1841): Charles Rogers, *Memoirs of the Earl of Stirling and of the House of Alexander* (2 vols., Edinburgh, 1877), II, 34–7.

From William Alexander

ALS: Historical Society of Pennsylvania

St Germain 24 June 1782

I hope my Dear Sir you will acquit me of Impertinent Curiosity, in wishing very anxiously to know, what is likely to be the fate of an Island, in which my family yet think, they have a stake[8] because a little knowledge of this, will Affect my measures, & may Save some Expence. If there be any thing improper in the request, be So kind as let your Son tell me So, by a line, but as it can Affect no public Interest, If you can gratify me with a Single word, that it will Continue wt its Masters, or get a new one.[9] You will serve me very much, & you may relie that it shall go no further—

Supposing that my request is Improper—but that the Island is to be receded to Britain—I must request Your Attention to the wording of the Clause affecting the Islands in General, & that there be nothing to Bar a future Investigation of the Rights of British Subjects, what ever Clause may be Inserted to Insure the Native french in the benefit of decisions, they may have obtain in the french tribunals— The Importance of the Matter will I hope Excuse this trouble—and I have only to add that whilst I live, You will find me with the warmest Attachment Dear Sir Your most obt hble ser   W. ALEXANDER

P.S. My friend M Benoit who passing through Passy undertakes to deliver this will take Care of the Answer—[1] Mons Pchmeja will be of the Party to Marli & the Doctor also, provided his Patients will allow Him a few hours to himself—[2] If you will Tell

---

8. After the Seven Years' War, William Alexander and his brothers had purchased two large estates on Britain's newly acquired island of Grenada. Since William Alexander's bankruptcy in 1775, however, the family's claim had been disputed in British courts and, after the French capture of the island, in French courts: XXIX, 689n; XXXI, 242n; XXXV, 314n; XXXVI, 365n, 439–40.

9. *I.e.*, whether France would retain it when peace was made, or would return it to Great Britain.

1. This may be Pierre-Antoine Benoît, who in 1804 was mayor of Auteuil, adjacent to Saint Germain, where Alexander lived: Société Historique d'Auteuil et de Passy *Bulletin*, VII (1910), 23.

2. The writer Jean-Joseph Pechméja (1741–1785) and his close friend

521

L'abbé de La Roche to give us three days notice, I think he may depend on both & Madme Helvetius wishes much to see the Doctor

Addressed: A Son Excellence Monsieur / Monsieur Franklin / M: P: des Etats de L'americque / Passy

Notation: W. Alexander 24, June 1782.

From Thomas Grenville

AL: Library of Congress

Paris. Monday. [June 24, 1782?][3]

Mr Grenville presents his Compliments to Mr Franklin: the Enabling Bill if Mr Grenville recollects right was to be read in the H. of Lords on Friday the 14th,[4] & Mr Grenville has not received any account of it whatever since that date: Mr Grenville did not write yesterday, imagining that the post might have brought him some intelligence upon the subject.

Dr. Jean-Baptiste-Léon Dubreuil (1743–1785), both from Villefranche-de-Rouergue: Bachaumont, *Mémoires secrets,* XXXII, 161–3; David Smith *et al.,* eds., *Correspondance générale d'Helvétius* (4 vols. to date, Toronto, Buffalo, and Oxford, 1981–), IV, 95n. For the trip to Marly see Bethia Alexander's letter of [June 27].

3. Monday, June 17, seems rather early for Grenville to be surprised at not hearing London news of June 14. By Monday, July 1, he should have learned that the Enabling Act had received the royal assent on June 19 (for which see our annotation of BF's March 30 letter to Livingston).

4. It received its first reading in the House of Lords on that day and passed that house on June 17: *London Courant, Westminster Chronicle, and Daily Advertiser,* June 15 and June 18.

From Henry Laurens

Copy:[5] Library of Congress; L (draft): University of South Carolina Library

Sir,   Lyon June 24th 1782.

In pursuance of the measure which I had the honour of intimating in my last of the 17th. Ulto. I waited on Mr. Adams at Hague and made a tender of my Service in the duty first charg'd upon me by Congress, that of borrowing Money for the Use of our United States, provided I was included and Authoriz'd in the Commission transmitted to him for that purpose, informing him, the original Commission to myself had been destroy'd at the time of my Capture. Mr. Adams did not say whether my Name stood in the subsisting Commission or not,[6] but gave me to understand, that such an arrangement had been made of the business as rendred my attendance or interference unnecessary.[7] As speedily as possible therefore I retired from the Low Countries where I was in extreme bad health and commenc'd the Journey which I am now engaged in, to the South of France, partly for the recovery of health but chiefly for the purpose of visiting my much distress'd friends, a Brother, Sister in Law, and my two Daughters, from whom I have been separated upwards of seven Years.[8] Your Letter of the 25th May which now lies before me had been sent from Bruxelles to Amsterdam, passed by me on the Road and was not return'd in convenient time for me to reply to before I reached this City.

5. In the hand of Josiah Flagg, and made from the now-missing recipient's copy. See our annotation of Laurens' letter of May 17.

6. It did. JA's appointment was provisional until Laurens arrived in the Netherlands: *Adams Papers*, IX, 452–3.

7. Laurens was angry about the way JA had treated him, at least according to Edmund Jenings, with whom Laurens stayed after the meeting in early June: James H. Hutson, ed., *Letters from a Distinguished American: Twelve Essays by John Adams on American Foreign Policy, 1780* (Washington, D.C., 1978), pp. 54–5. See also Laurens' account of the meeting in his May 30 letter to President of Congress John Hanson: *Laurens Papers*, XV, 522. In a June 9 letter to Livingston, JA implied the meeting had been purely social: Wharton, *Diplomatic Correspondence*, V, 483. See also JA's June 13 letter to BF.

8. His brother James, sister-in-law Mary, and daughters Martha and Mary Eleanor were at Le Vigan in Languedoc: XXVII, 468–70.

It might be improper and impertinent to trouble you with a detail of reasons weighing with me against acting under the Commission for treating with Great Britain, the following apology which I have transmitted to Congress I hope will be satisfactory.[9]

"On the 10th Instant [May][1] I receiv'd from Dr Franklin a formal notification of my appointment in the Commission for treating with Great Britain and also a Copy of the said Commission,[2] I left London on the 11th and arriv'd at Ostend on the 15th. from whence I inform'd Doctor Franklin that I declined the honor of that Office but that I should proceed to the Hague.

I might assign various reasons all valid for this determination, the following single consideration I trust will be satisfactory to Congress.

Five persons are nominated in the Commission, not conjunctly but severally and respectively fully empowerd, whence it evidently appears Congress had not in view or expectation, that the whole would act, and certainly it is not necessary, nor would it be beneficial that the whole should act, therefore as there are three of those persons besides myself, and all of superior abilities, upon the Spot, were I to thrust myself in, merely to make a fourth figure, I should feel guilty of a species of peculation, by putting the publick to unnecessary expence, without any well grounded hopes of rendring Publick service."

Now Sir, after the most mature deliberation, taking also into consideration, all that popular discontent Clamor & censure which you say has ever been attendant upon definitive Treaties,[3] I see no cause for altering my Resolution, Nevertheless had I not been previously engag'd to make this Journey & written to my friends to expect me[4] & had I not too much reason to fear I shall scarcely end it time enough to find my Brother alive, I do assure you Sir, the desire which you express for your seeing me on your

9. This apology was part of his May 30 letter to Hanson: *Laurens Papers*, XV, 521.

1. Brackets in MS.

2. BF to Laurens, April 12, above.

3. BF to Laurens, May 25, above.

4. He had promised to meet his daughter Martha if his services were not needed in the Netherlands: *Laurens Papers*, XV, 508–9.

own Account would have hastened me to pay my respects to you at Passy, under a previous condition that I should have been as much incog: [incognito] as possible and I will still with great Pleasure wait on you there should you continue to wish it, after I have spent a few days at Vigan en Cevennes and adjusted a plan for the future Conduct of my suffering friends abovemention'd, who reside at that Place,—a Letter under direction to my eldest Daughter Madmoiselle M. Laurens, will find me there, or soon overtake me.

He was a very sensible Man and much of a Gentleman who said, if our hopes were confin'd to this Life, we should of all Men, be most miserable, he was an Ambassador too, the observation is strong but full of encouragement and with proper Modification may be fairly adopted by every honest Man of the diplomatic Corp—probably I had this in contemplation when I promised you should be Blessed,[5] but we may have hopes even in this Life, not confine them to it; popular Clamor and Censure raised with out Foundation soon vanish and leave no record, Wise and discerning Men will give just applause to Virtuous servants of the Publick and transmit to Posterity fair Accounts of their faithful and judicious Conduct.— The Circumstances of our Country cry aloud for Peace, I mean taking the Country collectively, and Blessed, here and hereafter with my Will, shall the Men be who are Instrumental in making Peace for her upon honourable terms—the Number whose Duty, being in place, will constrain them to Act is very ample, more would be too many, and let us look at the other side, we shall see the respective dividend of honour, will be larger, than it would have been if shar'd between five or four, but certainly in the latter days of my residence in England the Mouth of every Man who conversed with me was full of Blessed shall be the Peace Makers, which seem'd at that time to flow from the Abundance of the Heart.

It is true Sir, I had some opportunities of conversing with the New Ministers of the Court of London[6] and that I sedulously avoided many more which I might have had, and if they were

5. Laurens to BF, May 17, above.
6. For his conversations with Shelburne see Laurens to BF, April 30, and *Laurens Papers*, XV, 398–402, 477–8, 491–3.

sincere on their part, I could tell you what were the Sentiments of some of them, and add, that I could not comprehend the metaphysical Ideas of others, who wish'd as it seem'd to me, for somewhat of a connection between Great Britain and America like Platonic Love, something which they mumbled but could not define and which considering their good sense, created a Suspicion of their sincerity. One of the last things which the principal stickler against our Independence,[7] said to me was, "Well Mr. L. if I must part with America it will be with great reluctance, because I think it will not be for her good." Which I read, "Well Sir, after all, I perceive in the present Circumstances of this Kingdom we must have Peace at any rate, that we cannot obtain it without recognizing the Independence of America, which I have a thousand times sworn never to concede and for aught you know it was the tenure under which I obtain'd my place; but you say, 'the Peace Bill in its present Shape will prove nugatory and offensive, that Independence must be a Preliminary and an Ultimatum.' I am sorry you will not be persuaded out of your Notions, believe me they are chimerical and will certainly bring on Confusion and ruin to your Country, why wont you listen to the cordial Admonition of disinterested friends who have been heaping Acts of Kindness upon you, Year by Year, for seven Years past— If you will not be advised you must have your own way, but mark we have forewarned you of consequences &c"— To the best of my Ability I made a reply adapted to the Comment, not to the Text, the former is actually a compound of scraps of different conversations—this is a representation of what *I knew* of the sentiments of Ministers when I left England, but who can tell what changes may since have been wrought by the Affair in the West Indies;[8] *You* may be able by this time to form some judgment on that head, I am totally ignorant of what has been doing for many days; the last intelligence I pick'd up, was the City Address,[9] how dextrously and glibly do those Ad-

7. Shelburne; see *Laurens Papers*, XV, 399–400.

8. The British victory at the Saintes.

9. The congratulatory address on the British success in the West Indies which was presented to the King by the lord mayor, aldermen, and Commons of London on June 5: *Gent. Mag.*, LII (1782), 307.

dressors, term that Glorious, which erst they reprobated as unjust, the War with America is the foundation of the extended War, the War with Holland has been a thousand times cursed by them, yet these worthies now vaunt of a Glorious War without exception.— Sir George Rodney's adventitious Success has absolved him from all the Sins, "wittingly," "deliberately," "inhumanly," "wantonly," committed at St. Eustatia[1]—the Volunteer determined—Inquisitors of his mal-practices, who enter'd upon their enquiry from "pure motives of Justice and in order to wipe out a stain upon national Character" have adjourned the Inquest, *sine die,* and are become his Panegyrists—notwithstanding all this, I believe that moral honesty and disinterested Patriotism still subsists in the breasts of Individuals, but who will dare to promise for the faithfulness of New or Old Ministers and publick Bodies of Men,—in a word the little knowledge which I might have had of the sentiments of the New Ministry on the 11th. of May was all effaced by the appearance of the Gazette Extraordinary about nine days after[2] hence it is clear, I cannot speak to the general point of your enquiry and I presume Congress have given special Instructions respecting Commerce, Fisheries Boundaries &c for the guidance of the acting Commissioners.

Certainly Lord Shelburne made no Stipulation respecting Exchange in return for my enlargement; but it is equally true, that His Lordship has it from under my hand, of dates previous and subsequent to my discharge, that an adequate return would be made and also that his Lordship intimated to me, that the discharge of Ld. Cornwallis in return would be generous and acceptable, he did not say an exchange was expected, but I much misunderstood His Lordship If he did not mean it.[3] About the time of my enlargement, there appeared rather a glaring display of comingness and liberality, nothing that I propos'd for the Exchange and return to America of our fellow Citizens, Prisoners at Portsmouth & Plymouth was objected to, there was a general

1. For which see XXXIV, 465n.
2. Announcing the news of the triumph. This government publication was dated May 18.
3. See Laurens' memorandum about his April 6 conversation with Shelburne: *Laurens Papers,* XV, 477–8.

chearful acquiescence, and I left that Business in the fairest way under the auspices of our active friend Mr. Hodgson, nevertheless I understood that returns were to be made in Exchange for those Prisoners, altho' I knew of no express stipulation, having refer'd the executive part to our said friend but 'tis not to be doubted that an agreement for a fair Exchange was made, now certainly if a Cartel is fix'd for the Exchange of Men who were esteem'd only at the rate of "deluded Subjects," a proper return for the enlargement of one who was accounted by Ministry, "a, or *the*, most heinous offender" as Lord Hillsborough was pleased to stile him,[4] is expected—otherwise will not the frank discharge of the latter wear the aspect of a Bribe? and I dont know but it might at first have been so projected, it is my wish to view it in a more favourable light and to cancel the debt without delay. Before I went to meet Mr. Adams in April Lord Shelburne knew that I was appointed in the Commission to treat with Great Britain and had offer'd me an unconditional release which as I have heretofore said, I refus'd to accept,[5] nor did the discharge, such as it is, come to me, until I had declar'd to His Lordship through Mr. Oswald that I would surrender myself to the Court of King's Bench then sitting, in order to acquit my Bail and would submit my Body to the disposal of the Court.[6] Upon the whole I think Congress are in Honour bound to make an adequate return in Exchange for me, and that the British Court expect such a return will be made, the adequacy Congress have been pleas'd to settle at the Rate of a Lieutt.-General[7] and by their own management, as it appears to me, they have now only one of that Rank to offer, admit therefore that some other arrangement relative to Lord Cornwallis's Exchange shall have been made in America, no other inconvenience can result but that of our remaining unavoidably indebted for my Exchange which will neither hurt Lord Cornwallis, nor in such Case, the

4. Secretary of State Hillsborough described Laurens' offenses to Laurens' friend James Bourdieu: *Laurens Papers*, XV, 428–9. We have not located the quotation.

5. See Laurens to BF, April 30.

6. See *Laurens Papers*, XV, 394–5n, 397, 459–60.

7. By proposing the exchange of Laurens for Burgoyne: XXXV, 221–2, 363n.

subject against whom it is propos'd to set his Lordship, but if no arrangement has been made there, we shall by discharging Lord Cornwallis perform an act of Justice and please all Parties; and I am very well satisfied from the tenor of several conversations with his Lordship he will think himself effectually discharged under our joint declaration or your own singly. I have written to Congress on this subject as follows.[8]

"Within a day or two after the British Ministry had determin'd against accepting Lieutt. General Burgoyne in Exchange for me an enquiry was made of me [in the Tower][9] from them as I believ'd, whether Doctor Franklin had power to Exchange Lord Cornwallis for me, to which I could give no positive Answer and there the subject dropped.

Lord Shelburne before I had been to visit Mr. Adams propos'd to grant me a full and unconditional discharge, I replied to his Lordship that I dared not accept of myself as a Gift, that Congress would make a just and adequate return for my enlargement, that having once offer'd a British Lieut-General in Exchange for me, I was under no doubt they would give for my reason [ransom] an Officer of the same Rank and I have reason to believe that after my refusal to accept the Gift His Lordship understood and expected that such a return would be made altho' from the nature of my Commitment, it was pretended, he could not formally enter into a stipulation therefore immediately after receiving the discharge I writ to Dr. Franklin and solicited his concurrence for discharging Lt. General Lord Cornwallis, hitherto I have not received the Doctor's answer, should he concur in my opinion and join in the necessary Act for that purpose, I trust we shall receive the approbation of Congress."

From former transactions I take it for granted you are authoriz'd by Congress to make Exchange for Prisoners in general, that under that authority you would readily have consented to Exchange a British Seaman or Soldier in your possession for Mr Laurens, provided the British Ministry would have accepted of such consideration, the difficulty on your Part was, in what Rank

8. The following two paragraphs are extracted from Laurens' May 30 letter to Hanson (*Laurens Papers*, XV, 519, 521); there are some variations.
9. Brackets in MS.

to class him, this was solv'd by Congress, when they were pleas'd to ascertain that of a Lieutt. General or the highest value they were possess'd of, and to name the particular Officer to be set against me; while the intended Exchange was in a course of negotiation, Congress, possibly for good reasons, dispose of that Officer in another way,[1] but leave one of equal Rank to serve the purpose first in view—the general power of Exchange still resides in you, the Rank for Exchange is adjusted by Congress, the Offer of Lord Cornwallis is acceptable to the other Party, I therefore think, with great deference to your better Judgement, there does not remain the Shadow of a doubt that you are authoriz'd, if authoriz'd to work any Exchanges, to Exchange any British Lieutt General for me and that a clause of reservation is altogether unnecessary— "But Lord Shelburne mention'd nothing of an Exchange expected for you."[2] True, His Lordship did not expressly mention an expectation, but I know that after my refusal to accept the intended munificent Gift, His Lordship did expect, & that he does expect a proper return in Exchange. I believe he expected it even when he offer'd the Gift, and I make no doubt but at this moment he wonders at our delay. I submit my reasoning to you, determine as you may on that point, you will clearly perceive "what I think best." I much regret that I have not been able to explain myself in few words, and finally, under the encouragement which you have been pleas'd to give me, I request you will compleat my Exchange by discharging Lord Cornwallis from the Obligations of his Parole as speedily as possible, the Act you may still say is *ex post facto*, but a proper Whereas and the acceptance of the other Party will make the whole smooth and I am secure we shall incurr no displeasure at Home. Until this is done I shall feel myself in a more irksome state, than I should have been in, had I been enlarg'd upon my Parole, and shall be under continual fear that one day or other there will be diabolically trump'd up against me, an imputation of having been discharged under a Pardon, and I declare that if from casualties, there hereafter should appear a necessity for my acting under the Commission for Treating with Great Britain I

1. For Burgoyne's exchange see Laurens to BF, April 7.
2. The quotations in this paragraph are from BF to Laurens, May 25, above.

should hold myself unqualified until my Exchange was fairly and fully liquidated. You certainly judge right Sir, "We have no Authority," the Business rests, as far as, I know, with yourself alone and with you I ought to leave it, my Offer to join in the Act was made before I had been necessitated to consider the Case so fully, and was indeed intended, however improperly, as a kind of guarantee or "*defendit Numerus.*"

The Bishop of St. Asaph[3] is a good Man, he deserves the highest acknowledgements of our Country, and will always be spoken of by me in particular, in sentiments of gratitude. His Lordship unsolicited held out the offer of relief to me when he believ'd me to be in need.

I must not conclude without thanking you heartily for your repeated tender of a supply of Money. I shall certainly take the liberty of calling on you should there be real occasion, but not before, how can I do so, when you say, what indeed I too well know, that We have already press'd rather too hard upon our Ally and that we shall still want more than can be conveniently spar'd to us? At Bruxelles I accidentally met with and purchas'd a light English Post Chaise at a moderate price which has enabled me to travel these 80 Posts without very much fatigue, the warm weather has restor'd the strength of my Knees and Ankles beyond expectation, I mean to morrow to descend the Rhone par Eau and hope to make the whole intended Journey tolerably easy and to regain health, tis my present design to return to America in the Autumn maugre all hazards, when my plan is fix'd I shall take the Liberty of asking for your Commands being with the highest degree of Respectfulness.

Sir, Your most obedient and most humble servant

HENRY LAURENS

His Excellcy. Benjamin Franklin Esquire Passy

---

3. Jonathan Shipley.

From Joseph Priestley   ALS: Connecticut Historical Society

Dear Sir   Birmingham 24 June 1782.

You have made me very happy by your letter,[4] as I find by it that, notwithstanding the unpleasing state of Politicks, your usual humour and pleasantry has not forsaken you. I am only concerned that you have not mentioned the case of my friend *Mr Russell,* about which I wrote to you so particularly. But I have taken the liberty to assure him, that, notwithstanding this omission, I am as confident you have not neglected the business, as if you had given me the most express assurance of it. One line, however, informing me what you think of the case, will give me great satisfaction.[5]

Having at length got *sunshine,* I am busy in prosecuting the experiments about which I wrote to you, and shall soon draw up an account of them for the Royal Society.[6]

Please to inform the Duc De Rochefocault, whose civilities to me I remember with pleasure, that my experiments are certainly inconsistent with Mr Lavoisier's supposition, of there being no such thing as *phlogiston,* and that it is the addition of *air,* and not the loss of any thing, that coverts a metal into a calx. In their usual state calces of metals do contain air, but that may be expelled by heat; and after this I reduce them to a perfect metallic state by nothing but inflammable air, which they imbibe *in toto,* without any decomposition. I lately reduced 101 Ounces mea-

4. Of June 7, above.
5. William Russell (1740–1818), a merchant, political reformer, and staunch supporter of Priestley's, had property claims in Maryland: *DNB;* F. W. Gibbs, *Joseph Priestley: Adventurer in Science and Champion of Truth* (London and Edinburgh, 1965), pp. 139, 170. Priestley's previous letter discussing the case has not been located. On Sept. 18, 1783, Samuel Chase in London acknowledged receiving from BF a recommendation of Russell written on July 15, 1782. BF's letter had only arrived in March, 1783, however, by which time the order had already been given to sell Russell's property. According to Chase, that sale had subsequently been postponed. APS.
6. "Experiments relating to Phlogiston, and the seeming Conversion of Water into Air," *Phil. Trans.,* LXXIII (1783), 398–434. Priestley's earlier letters describing some of these experiments are missing; see BF to Priestley, June 7.

sures of this air to *two* by calx of lead, and that small remainder was still inflammable.

I explain Mr Lavoisier's experiments by supposing that *precipitate per se* contains all the phlogiston of the mercury, but in a different state; but I can shew other calces which also contain more phlogiston than the metals themselves. That mercury, in its metallic state, does contain phlogiston, or inflammable air, is evident from the production of nitrous air & by the solution of it in spirit of nitre, and I make *nitrous air* from nothing but *nitrous vapour* and *inflammable air,* so that it indisputably consists of those two ingredients.

I have already ascertained the proportion of inflammable air that enters into the composition of *lead, tin, copper,* and *silver,* and am proceeding to the other metals as fast as I can. When the whole is completed, I shall give you a farther account of it.

I am exceedingly concerned to find that it is so difficult a thing to make *peace;* but I hope that before the campaign be over all parties will have had enough of *war,* and be sensible that they will gain nothing by continuing it. If I had any voice in the business, the prospect of seeing you once more in this country would be a strong additional motive to accelerate the negotiations.

With the greatest respect, and every good wish, I am, Dear Sir yours sincerely   J PRIESTLEY

P.S. If you should think it proper, I have no objection to your sending a Copy of my former letter to *Rosier's Journal,* as a general outline of what I am doing.[7] I wish to have every new fact to be as speedily, and as generally known as possible.

Addressed: To / Doctor Franklin / Passy, / near Paris

Notation: Priestley. 24 June 1782.

7. Priestley's letter was not published in the abbé Rozier's *Jour. de physique* for either 1782 or 1783.

From Lafayette[8]

ALS: Library of Congress

My Dear Sir   St Germain tuesday [June 25, 1782]

You Have Been Acquainted that Mr. de Castries's Courier was to Go to Morrow Evening,[9] and I intend taking the same Opportunity to write to Congress and General Washington—[1] But as I want to justify My delay, Upon the trüe Motives of it, those of Public Utility, and American Wellfare, I Hope Your Excellency will please to Mention fully the Matter to Congress, and By Making them sensible of your opinion Respecting this Measure, to let them know that My services Here, for some Weeks to Come, May Be of some Use to the interest of America. I Have just Happened to Hear of Mr. jay's Arrival[2] and will wait Upon Him to Morrow Evening when I will Also Call at passy to Pay You My Respects— You will oblige me to talk with mr. jay Respecting our opinion on the subject I Have Mentioned.

With Every sentiment of Affection and Regard I Have the Honor to Be My Dear sir Your Most affectionate friend

LAFAYETTE

Endorsed: June 25. 82

To Lafayette

ALS (draft): Library of Congress

Dear Sir,   Passy, June 25. 1782

Hearing yesterday at Versailles of the Opportunity you mention,[3] I have stay'd at home to day employ'd in writing my Letters. You may depend on my doing fully what you desire.— Mr Jay is at Paris employ'd as I am, so that I do not expect to see him

---

8. This note prompted BF's response, immediately below.

9. Vergennes had informed BF of this on June 24; see the entry of that date in BF's journal of the peace negotiations.

1. Lafayette wrote Livingston and Washington on June 25: Idzerda, *Lafayette Papers*, V, 43–8, 48–9.

2. On June 23. Lafayette wrote him on June 25: Morris, *Jay: Peace*, pp. 243–4.

3. See Lafayette's letter immediately above.

till Thursday.[4] With the utmost Esteem & Affection I am ever
Yours   B Franklin

To Robert R. Livingston

LS,[5] copy, and transcript: National Archives; incomplete AL (draft):[6] Library of Congress

Sir,   Passy, June 25. 1782.

I have received your respected Letters of Jany 26 & Feby 13th.[7] The first was accompanied with the form of a Convention for the Establishment of Consuls. Mr. Barclay having been detained these 6 Months in Holland, tho' in continual Expectation of returning hither, I have yet done nothing in that Business, thinking his Presence might be of use in settling it. As soon as he arrives I shall move the Completion of it. The second enforces some Resolutions of Congress sent me with it, respecting a Loan of 12,000,000 l.t. to be demanded of France for the current Year. I had already received the Promise of six Million,[8] together with the clearest and most positive Assurances, that it was all the King could spare to us; that we must not expect more; that if Drafts & Demands came upon me beyond that Sum, it behov'd me to take Care how I accepted them, or where I should find Funds for the Payment, since I could certainly not be farther assisted out of the Royal Treasury. Under this Declaration with what Face could I ask for another six Millions? It would be say-

4. June 27. There is no entry for this date in BF's journal of the peace negotiations, but Jay was at Passy the morning of June 28, and they went together to Versailles on June 29.

A note from Jay dated only "Monday Morn" inviting BF to dinner on "Wednesday next" could have been written at any time during John and Sarah Jay's stay in Paris. Except for a vacation in Normandy and a journey to England, the Jays were there from June 23, 1782, until May 16, 1784: Morris, *Jay: Peace*, pp. 20–2.

5. In WTF's hand.

6. Consisting only of the last page, beginning with the words "more us'd to it" (the end of the first sentence of the penultimate paragraph).

7. XXXVI, 484–5, 569–72.

8. At the beginning of March: XXXVI, 650.

ing, you are not to be believ'd; you can spare more: You are able to lend me twice the Sum if you were but willing. If you read my Letter to Mr Morris of this Date,[9] I think you will be convinced how improper any Language capable of such a Construction would be to such a Friend. I hope, however, that the Loan Mr Adams has opened in Holland for three Millions of Florins, which it is said is likely to succeed, will supply the Deficiency.

By the News papers I have sent, you will see that the general Disposition of the British Nation towards us had been chang'd. Two Persons have been sent here by the new Ministers to propose treating for Peace. They had at first some Hopes of getting the belligerent Powers to treat separately one after an other; but finding that impracticable, they have after several Messengers sent to & fro, come to a Resolution of treating with all together for a general Peace; and have agreed that the Place shall be Paris.[1] Mr Grenville is now here with full Powers for that Purpose; (if they can be reckon'd full with regard to America, 'till a certain Act is compleated for enabling his Majesty to treat, &ca. which has gone thro' the Commons and has been once read in the Lords.)[2] I keep a very particular Journal of what passes every Day in the Affair, which is transcribing to be sent you.[3] I shall therefore need to say no more of it in this Letter, except that tho' I still think they were at first sincere in their Desire of Peace, yet since their Success in the West Indies, I imagine that I see Marks of their desiring rather to draw the Negotiations into length, that they may take the Chance of what the rest of the Campaign shall produce in their Favour: and as there are so many Interests to adjust, it will be prudent for us to suppose that even another Campaign may pass before all can be agreed. Something too may happen to break off the Negotiations, and we should be prepared for the worst. I hoped for the Assistance of Mr Adams and Mr

9. Immediately below.

1. This is a paraphrase of the cabinet resolution of April 27, which Oswald showed to BF on May 4; see BF's journal of the peace negotiations.

2. The Enabling Act.

3. BF did not send Congress his journal until December: Wharton, *Diplomatic Correspondence*, VI, 110–14.

Lawrens. The first is too much engag'd in Holland to come hither, and the other declines serving: but I have now the Satisfaction of being joined by Mr Jay, who happily arrived here from Madrid last Sunday. The Marquis de la Fayette is of great Use in our Affairs here, and as the Campaign is not likely to be very active in N. America, I wish I may be able to prevail with him to stay a few Weeks longer. By him you will receive the Journal abovementioned which is already pretty voluminous, and yet the Negotiations cannot be said to be open'd.

Ireland you will see has obtained all her Demands triumphantly. I meet no one from that Country who does not express some Obligation to America for their Success.[4]

Before I received your just Observations on the Subject, I had obtained from the English Ministers a Resolution to exchange all our Prisoners. They thought themselves obliged to have an Act of Parliament for authorizing the King to do it; this War being different from others, as made by an Act of Parliament declaring us Rebels, and our People being committed as for high Treason. I impower'd Mr Hodgson who was Chairman of the Committee that collected and dispens'd the charitable Subscriptions for the American Prisoners, to treat and conclude on the Terms of their Discharge, and having approved of the Draft he sent me of the Agreement,[5] I hope the Congress will see fit to order a punctual Execution of it. I have long suffer'd with those poor brave Men, who with so much Publick Virtue have endur'd 4 or 5 Years hard Imprisonment, rather than serve against their Country. I have done all I could afford towards making their Situation more comfortable; but their Numbers were so great that I could do but little for each; and that very great Villain Digges defrauded them of between three & four hundred Pounds which he drew from me on their Account. He lately wrote me a Letter in which he pretended he was coming to settle with me and to

4. Parliament was in the process of granting sweeping political and religious concessions to Ireland: R. B. McDowell, "Colonial nationalism and the winning of parliamentary independence, 1760–82," in T. W. Moody *et al.*, eds., *A New History of Ireland* (7 vols. to date, Oxford, 1976–), IV, 232–5.

5. With his letter of April 14, above.

convince me that I had been mistaken with regard to his Conduct;[6] But he never appear'd, and I hear is gone to America.[7] Beware of him, for he is very artful; and has cheated many. I hear every Day of new Rogueries committed by him in England.

The Ambassador from Sweden to this Court, applied to me lately to know if I had Powers that would authorise my making a Treaty with his Master in behalf of the United States. Recollecting a general Power that was formerly given to me with the other Commissioners, I answer'd in the Affirmative.[8] He seem'd much pleased, and said the King had directed him to ask the Question, and had charged him to tell me, that he had so great an Esteem for me, that it would be a particular Satisfaction to him to have such a Transaction with me. I have perhaps some Vanity in repeating this; but I think too, that it is right the Congress should know it, and judge if any Use may be made of the Reputation of a Citizen, for the Public Service. In Case it should be thought fit to employ me in that Business, it will be well to send a more particular Power, and proper Instructions. The Ambassador added, that it was a pleasure to him to think, and he hop'd it would be remember'd, that Sweden was the first Power in Europe, which had voluntarily offer'd its Friendship to the United States, without being sollicited. This Affair should be talk'd of as little as possible 'till compleated.

I inclose another Complaint from Denmark which I request you will lay before Congress.[9]

I am continually pester'd with Complaints from French Seamen who were with Capt. Conynham in his first Cruize from Dunkerque; from others who were in the Lexington, the Alliance &ca. being put on board Prizes that were retaken, were never afterwards able to join their respective Ships, and so have been depriv'd of the Wages, &c. due to them. It is for our National Honour that Justice should be done them if possible; and

6. Above, March 22[–26].

7. Digges did not return to America until 1798: Elias and Finch, *Letters of Digges*, pp. lxix–lxx.

8. See BF to the comte de Creutz, April 24.

9. The memorial which Vergennes enclosed with his letter of April 23, above. The matter was referred to Robert Morris: *Morris Papers*, VI, 600.

I wish you to procure an Order of Congress for enquiring into their Demands, and satisfying such as shall be found just. It may be address'd to the Consul.

I enclose a Note from M. de Vergennes to me accompany'd by a Memoire relating to a Swisse who died at Edenton.[1] If you can procure the Information desired, it will much oblige the French Ambassador in Switzerland.

I have made the Addition you directed to the Cypher: I rather prefer the old one of Dumas, perhaps because I am more us'd to it.[2] I enclose several Letters from that antient and worthy Servant of our Country. He is now employ'd as Secretary to Mr Adams and I must, from a long Experience of his Zeal and Usefulness, beg leave to recommend him warmly to the Consideration of Congress with regard to his Appointments, which have never being equal to his Merit. As Mr. Adams writes me the good News, that he shall no longer be obliged to draw on me for his Salary,[3] I suppose it will be proper to direct his paying that which shall be allow'd to Mr. Dumas.

Be pleased to present my Duty to the Congress, and believe me to be with great Esteem & Regard Sir, Your most obedient & most humble Sert.   B Franklin

Honble: Robt R. Livingston Esqre.

To Robert Morris   AL (draft): Library of Congress

Dear Sir,   Passy, June 25. 1782.

I have long waited here for a good and safe Opportunity of Writing. I have expected from Week to Week that the Departure of the Eagle with the Marquis de la Fayette would be resolv'd on, and that I should have Notice of it.[4] In the mean time some

---

1. Vergennes to BF, April 20, above.
2. Dumas had sent it in 1776 to the committee of secret correspondence, of which BF was a member: XXII, 404–5.
3. Above, June 10.
4. The *Aigle*, 40, sailed from Rochefort in company with the *Gloire* on July 15; Lafayette was not aboard, but the fair copy of this letter was. On reach-

important Affairs being on the Tapis, I omitted writing till they should be a little more advanced. Yesterday M. de Vergennes inform'd me that Dispatches would go from his Office, as to-morrow: I shall use the little time this short Notice affords me in writing to you what I can respecting our Affairs.

I have receiv'd yours of Jan. 7. and March 9.[5] these are all that have this Year come to hand from you, and are not before acknowledg'd. With this you will receive Copies of my preceding Dispatches since the Commencement of this Year. The Cargo of Mars. de la Fayette has been all replac'd, and the Goods lodg'd at Brest. Some part of it was shipt last Summer. Want of Transports to take the rest, occasion'd their being rather luckily left when the Convoy sailed that was in great part intercepted by the English.[6] I believe that tho' Part may have since been shipt, none has sail'd,[7] and that some is still in the Storehouses. M. de Castries would have had me procure Ships; but it has not been in my Power. Mr Barclay, who I hop'd from time to time would have return'd to France and assisted in such Operations, is still, I suppose necessarily, detained in Holland. He has, as he writes me, exchang'd some of the English Goods bought on our Acct by Mrs Neufville, for Shirts, &c. and he has bought 6 or 7000 Suits of Soldiers Cloaths very cheap, which he is shipping with all the other Goods from Holland.[8] If he has Orders to make such Purchases, it is very well. His large Drafts upon me, however, to pay for them & for a Ship, and to discharge other Demands, may be very inconvenient, and distressing to me before the Year is out;[9] as I have had the fullest and fairest Warning, not to expect or

---

ing the Delaware, the *Aigle* ran aground and was captured: Louis-Philippe, comte de Ségur, *Mémoires ou souvenirs et anecdotes* (3 vols., Paris, 1827), I, 294–6, 329, 338. This letter was saved and Morris forwarded it to Congress on Sept. 18: *Morris Papers*, v, 480n; vi, 393. Lafayette did not return to America until August, 1784: Idzerda, *Lafayette Papers*, v, xxiv.

5. The former letter is in xxxvi, 403–6; the latter is missing.

6. In December, 1781: xxxvi, 533n.

7. Three ships had sailed but were forced into another French port; see our annotation of BF's March 30 letter to Morris.

8. Barclay to BF, June 17, above.

9. Morris took the hint; at his request Congress ordered Barclay to desist from making such purchases: *Morris Papers*, vi, 399–400; *JCC*, xxiii, 595.

hazard the Want of more than the Six Millions promis'd us for the present Year. This indeed is duly advanc'd in quarterly Payments.[1] But I am so frequently attack'd by unforeseen Demands, that I can by no Means assure my self, of having a Sufficiency. I have acquainted Mr Grand with this Opportunity of Writing, and I suppose you will receive from him a State of our Cash, which I have requested him to send you as often as possible.— You will also have from me a Copy of the replacing Account above-mentioned,[2] if the transcribing can be finished in time.

We have not yet got clear of our miserable Affair in Holland. Capt. Gellon you have heard went away without taking under his Convoy, two vessels which he himself had hired to receive out of his Ship the Goods he had engag'd to carry in her. The Owners then stopp'd the Vessels, charg'd high Damages, & detain'd the Goods. I have receiv'd yesterday from Mr Barclay, an Account of Messrs Neufville, wherein the Charges occasion'd by that Operation of Gellon's are made to amount to near 40,000 florins.[3] Mr Barclay proposes to settle it by Arbitration. I suppose that by Right it is Gellon who should pay whatever may be awarded; but where shall we find him?— Perhaps since his Success in the West Indies, he may venture into an American Port, in which case it would be well to secure him, & make him account for the 10,000£ Sterl. he receiv'd of me in consequence of his Agreement with Col. Laurens.[4]

Your Bills for the 500,000 livres which you mention, begin to appear; one for 100,000 *l.t.* in favour of H. Hill is already accepted, with my Approbation. But you will learn these Matters best from Mr Grand.[5] We have no Money to expect as you imag-

1. BF had already received one quarterly installment: XXXVI, 650n. For subsequent payments see his July 16 contract with Vergennes.

2. *I.e.*, an account of the goods which had been replaced. BF sent it to Morris with his letter of Aug. 12, below.

3. The account was enclosed with Barclay's June 17 letter to BF.

4. Gillon's frigate, the *South Carolina*, recently had arrived in Philadelphia. Gillon was able to stall Morris but not La Luzerne and in November fled Philadelphia to avoid arrest: James A. Lewis, *Neptune's Militia: the Frigate* South Carolina *during the American Revolution* (Kent, Ohio, and London, 1999), pp. 79–84.

5. Apparently Morris mentioned the bills to BF in his now-missing letter

ined from the Sale of the Goods in Holland, they being exchanged & shipt before your Letter arrived.

With regard to my Contract for furnishing Provisions to the French Army in America, as Mr Necker had not so much Faith in its being executed as I had, and never advanced me a Livre on that Account; and as I found it would be difficult to settle Prices here as you propos'd, I have chosen not to push it.[6] It seems therefore not necessary that you put yourself to any further Trouble in that Affair. If any Quantity has been furnished by you, it is a Debt contracted with you, and of which you may expect Payment there, I being upon the Point of liquidating all our Accounts with the Government here, and giving one general Obligation for the whole Sum that the King has lent us (exclusive of Gifts or Subsidies) which Sum amounts, to 18,000,000 *l.t.*[7] By the particular Obligations I have from time to time given for separate Sums, I had engaged in behalf of the Congress that they should be paid off the first of January 1788 with the Interest at 5 per Ct. By the Terms of this general Obligation, which is in form of an Agreement or Contract between the King and the United States, his Majesty graciously considering that it may incommode the United States to pay the whole Sum at one time, is pleased to agree that it may be paid in 12 different yearly Payments, to commence with the first Year after the Peace; leaving nevertheless to our Choice & Liberty the Paymt. of any greater Proportions at more early Periods, as may be convenient to our Finances. His Majesty also kindly and generously remits all the Interest already accru'd on my former Obligations or that would have accrued thereby to the End of the War which is already a considerable Sum. With Regard to the 10,000,000 borrowed in Holland; we have that at 4 per Cent. and we are to pay the Interest annually here, on the 5th of November, the first Payment in November next: & after 5 Years we are to begin to repay the

---

of March 9. Morris had sold 500,000 *l.t.* worth of bills drawn on Ferdinand Grand: Morris to BF, April 8, above. Henry Hill was a Philadelphia merchant: *Morris Papers*, v, 481n.

6. This plan had failed largely because Washington opposed it and Morris believed it impractical: XXXIV, 36–8, 97–9.

7. See BF's July 16 contract with Vergennes.

Principal in ten Yearly Payments, so that in 15 Years that Debt will be discharged. The Charges of Commission & Banque on this Loan have been considerable, and paid by the King; these also his Majesty is pleased to remit. These repeated Instances of his Goodness towards us, make me consider and respect & love him as our Father. I shall send you a Copy of this Contract as soon as it is compleated. Perhaps the first Payment may be settled to be the third or fourth Year after the Peace. And since the King takes every Opportunity of showing his Good will to us, I dread disobliging him again, as I have already too often done, by large & repeated Demands; and therefore hope your Drafts will not exceed what I shall be able to pay.

Notwithstanding what I wrote in mine of the 30th of March, the German Troops are embark'd. Yet my Information was good at the Time. There has been[8] a Change of Orders.

Capt. Frey, whom you recommended to me,[9] had formerly taken up of me 20 Guineas on a Bill he drew upon Bordeaux. It came back protested, and he went to America. To oblige him, on Receipt of your Letter in his Favour, I paid him the Sum you mentioned as due to him, by an Order on my Banker, in whose hands he promis'd to leave the 20 Guineas he owed me. But he took the whole, left nothing, and I cannot recover it. If any thing be, as he says, still due to him there, pray stop that Sum of 20 Guineas out of it.[1]

The Books you wrote for[2] have been sent. With this you will receive a kind of Table, which is said to contain very clearly & concisely all the true Principles of Finance.[3]

Your Boys continue well.[4] Mr Ridley is still in Holland.

For what relates to War and Peace, I must refer you to Mr Livingston, to whom I write fully.[5] I will only say that tho' the English a few Months since seem'd desirous of Peace, I suspect they now intend to draw out the Negotiations into Length, till they

8. BF here wrote but deleted "in England".
9. XXXVI, 196–7.
1. For the debt see XXXVI, 690.
2. See BF to Morris, March 30.
3. Not found.
4. See BF to Morris, April 8.
5. Immediately above.

can see what this Campaign will produce. I hope our People will not be deceiv'd by fair Words, but be on their guard, ready against every Attempt that our insidious Enemies may make upon us.

With the greatest & most sincere Esteem & Affection, I am, Dear Sir

honble Robt Morris Esqe

From Edward Bridgen   ALS: Historical Society of Pennsylvania

London June 25 1782

You were so good my Dr Sir to say, in the postcript of a letter[6] last winter, that you hoped my Affairs in No: Carolina were settled to my sattisfaction, or something to that Amount; I am sorry to say, that by late letters receiv'd, that it is far otherways; and that not only my land on the Sound, in Cape Fear River, which has been in possession of my Family and Self since the Year 1736 with My Negroes, & land adjoining, since purchased by my self, and Debts owing to *Bridgen & Waller* to no inconsiderable amount; have, by some late laws of the province,[7] been all confiscated; how justly, reasonably, or *politically* I cannot devise! I therefore take the liberty to trouble you with this representation requesting your kind interference in behalf of my self & Mr Waller?

I hope that this Measure taken by the Legislature of that State, has been rather by Mistake, than design from those who are indebted to the Copartnership, as the general Interest and Honour of the State is immediately concerned in this Transaction, besides *very seriously* interesting my self & Partner.

May I, my Dr Sir, beg your kind and early representation, where it will have most weight, in our favour, which will add to the many Obligations already conferred on My Dr Sir Yr: Affectt: Friend & Hum: Servant   EDWARD BRIDGEN

Benjn: Franklin Esqr &c &c

6. BF to Caroline Edes, Dec. 13, 1781: XXXVI, 243–4.
7. A legislative act of 1779: XXXVI, 244n.

From Catharine Greene[8]   ALS: American Philosophical Society

My Very Dear Friend   [June 25, 1782]
    I wrote you a few days Since[9] of your good Sisters Tolerable health and Poor Jennies Death Particuliars of our family &c but Mr Greenes writeing I must add a kind how do you do when did you here from Benny and is temple well and when do you Come to New england, and ask when this Shocking War will be at an end the Sceenes of Misery it has occationd is beyond Discription our State has felt it Severely having So long a Sea Coast to guard but Ile not trouble you with the Disagreeables our hopes is now that the times is Just at hand when we Shall Drive them Root and Branch from our land. Our Children are Tollerable well I told you in my other letter Particulier of them that Ray was a Pretty Promising Lad at New haven Colledge Samey at lattin School 7 miles from home and that I wisht for A Peice of Beneys Drawing excuse the interlineing &c for I write hurried but beleive me your Very affectionate friend.   C Greene

I wonder if you get half the letters I write for you dont forbid me and I write again.

From William Greene   ALS: American Philosophical Society

Sir   Warwick State Rhode-Island &c. June 25th. 1782.
    I am informed that Ezekiel Durfey a small Officer on board of the Ship Tracy commanded by John B Hopkins[1] was taken and carryed to Newyork and from there to England, where he has been confined about eighteen Months, and by the last account he was in Mill Prison,[2] his Friends have very earnestly requested me

---

8. Enclosed in her husband's letter of the same date.
9. Her May 8 letter is above.
1. The *Tracy*, a Mass. privateer, was captured in September, 1780. Before assuming her command, Hopkins had been a prominent officer in the American Navy, but he was suspended in 1779 for disobeying orders: John A. McManemin, *Captains of the Continental Navy* (Ho-Ho-Kus, N.J., 1981), pp. 199–200; Kaminkow, *Mariners*, p. 235; *DAB*.
2. Durfey was committed on Jan. 16, 1781: Kaminkow, *Mariners*, p. 59.

to inform your Excellency of his distressed situation and request that you will be pleased to use your influence that he may be liberated. Being sencible of the great business you have to transact and likewise that it is very probable that you have many of those applications, it is very disagreable to ask this favour, but as his Friends have urged the necessity of this measure by assigning as a reason that they have tryed many ways to procure his liberty without the least degree of success and being sencible of your good intentions to relieve Mankind when in captivity has induced me to take this liberty.

My spous writes Postscrip,[3] my Children joins me in sending their Sincere regards and believe me to be your sincere Friend and very Humble Servt.　　　　　　　　　　　　　W. GREENE

Doctr. Franklin

From Hilliard d'Auberteuil

ALS: University of Pennsylvania Library

Monsieur　　　　　　　　　　　à Paris le 25e. Juin 1782.

Votre aprobation sur ce que je dis du traité d'amitié et de commerce, et du traité d'alliance éventuelle entre la france et les états unis de l'amerique,[4] m'aurait fait grand plaisir; mais je n'ai pas été le maitre de la meriter.

J'ai ma maniere de considerer cette grande affaire politique, et je l'avais racontée le mieux que j'avais pu, il a fallu tout changer; et voici ce que le departement des affaires étrangeres a noté sur mon manuscrit.

"Tout ceci est bien incomplet: l'auteur trouvera de quoi y supléer dans *les observations en reponse au memoire justificatif de la cour de Londres*,[5] tous les faits y sont de la plus exacte verité."

---

3. The letter immediately above.

4. *Essais historiques et politiques* . . . , II, 335–401, spanning signatures X through Cc.

5. Gérard de Rayneval's *Observations sur le Mémoire justificatif de la Cour de Londres* (Paris, 1780), a response to Edward Gibbon's *Mémoire justificatif pour servir de réponse à l'exposé, &c. de la Cour de France* (London, 1779).

Sur une autre feuille

"L'auteur ne distingue pas assés le traité d'amitié & de commerce du traité d'alliance éventuelle, encore une fois il doit s'en raporter *aux observations en reponse au memoire justificatif de la cour de Londres,* il ne peut s'en écarter sans blesser la verité."[6]

Il a donc fallu suivre mot à mot les observations en reponse au memoire justificatif de la cour de Londres, et d'après cela je prie votre excellence de m'accorder son indulgence, tout ce que j'ai dit du traité important qu'elle a conclu avec la france, est faible, timide, j'en conviens, mais ce n'est pas ma faute; on pourrait peut être même y trouver de l'erreur, mais je n'en suis pas garant. On ne m'a pas obligé à faire bien, mais à faire comme on a voulu.

Je suis avec la plus profonde consideration de votre Excellence Le très humble & très obéissant serviteur

HILLIARD D'AUBERTEUIL

Addressed: A Monsieur / Monsieur Franklin / Ambassadeur des Etats unis / de l'Amerique / en son hotel / A Passy

Notation: Hilard d'auberteuil 25. June 1782.

Rayneval's account denied that France had aided the United States before the Franco-American alliance and asserted that British aggression drew France into the war. Vergennes recently told Grenville in BF's presence that France had not assisted the United States before 1778; see the entry of May 9 in BF's journal of the peace negotiations. For the pamphlet exchanges between the governments of France and Great Britain regarding the French decision to assist the Americans see Thomas R. Adams, *The American Controversy: a Bibliographical Study of the British Pamphlets About the American Disputes, 1764–1783* (2 vols., Providence, R.I., and New York, 1980), II, 613–15, 640–3; Durand Echeverria and Everett C. Wilkie, Jr., comps., *The French Image of America* (2 vols., Metuchen, N.J., and London, 1994), I, 386–8, 391, 426.

6. Hilliard's revised account (pp. 348–9) insisted that the Treaty of Alliance was an American initiative and was signed only reluctantly by the French as a defensive measure against a perceived British threat.

From Jane Mecom

ALS: American Philosophical Society

Dear Brother   warwick 25 June 1782

I wrot you a few Days ago,[7] & at Governer Greenes Request Inclosed a memorandom concerning a Prisoner I also Informed you of the Irreparable Lose I have mett with in the Death of my Dear Grand Daughter Greene with whome I had Lived in as Perfect composeure & Tranquility as Human-Nature will admit of, she was affectionate & Respectfull to me, an affectionate & Prudent wife, & an Indulgent mother, I am still at her Dieing Request that I would not Leve her children as long as I live & the Request also of her bereved Husband with Them in the Famely, He is kind & affectionat to me but something constantly Passes that keeps alive my sorrow tho I have Plenty of all Nesesarys & the same Beautifull Prospect around me & all the season Blooming I so much mis her sosiety that it spreads a gloom over all.

Cousen Williams has made me a visit He came Partly on Busness as far as Provedence & Partly to Recrute His spirits affter the long sickness & Death of His Brother who Died much about the same time my child did, He has lost three Grand children by His son John, has won by His Daughter Bettsey (who married a mr Eaton)[8] He seems much Pleas'd with, as we all are with our litle wons, they are Realy Pleasant diverting things I seem as if I could not soport Life without mine tho they cause many sorrowfull Reflections, there Father desiers His Duty to you.

I have wrot many leters to you since I recved won I never atempt to give any acount of Publick affairs I sopose you constantly recive all from good hands I should never the less be gratified to recive some from you I give you Joy of the birth of the Prince[9] & as sinsearly of the Progres yr Granson makes in His Larning & the Honours confer'd on Him for it,[1] I hope you will Live to see him a worthy & usefull man; I Long to hear of Sturdy Bill, & the Rest of the Famely which I sopose is Increas'd

7. On June 17, above.

8. For recent events in the family of Jonathan Williams, Sr., see his letter of June 11.

9. The dauphin, whose birth was widely celebrated throughout America; see our annotation to Samuel Cooper's letter of June 15.

1. BFB won a prize in 1780 for translating a Latin passage: XXXII, 611.

since I heard from them which is more than two years, I think I have wrote twice to them since,[2] I beleve some of my leters to you miscarry, but I think they c[torn] not to them as I wrot by Post.

I am Informed yr Health is so ferm & yr spirits so good that I am not out of hopes of seeing you again in your Native Place if the War should ceace as some Imagin it will soon God grant it may for the Raveges of war are Horrible we have been Lately surprised with a considerable Fleets apearing as tho t[hey] Intended to Reposes Rhoad Island but they Passd by affter 3 or four Days Alarm, In won of my Leters I wrot my thanks for the Present you sent me throw Cousen Jonathan williams's hands[3] many of the Articles came seasonable for my own use the Rest I sould & Put the monny to Intrest; I hope I shall be so Lucky as hear this gits saif to yr hand cousen williams tells me it will go by a very good opertunity if it should let me hear from you soon & Refresh the hart of yr Ever affectionat sister   JANE MECOM

Addressed: His Excellency Benjamin Franklin Esqr / at Pasy / In / France

From Benjamin Vaughan   ALS: American Philosophical Society

My Dear sir,   London, 25 June, 1782.

I beg to introduce to your acquaintance my friend Dr. Lister,[4] whom I first became acquainted with at Edinburgh, and who was there a good deal respected for his good character and assiduity,

2. "Sturdy Bill" is William Bache, associated in past correspondence with Hercules: XXIX, 614. For the most recent known correspondence between Mecom and the Baches see XXXIV, 202n, 425n.

3. See our annotation to Mecom's June 17 letter.

4. Probably Dr. William Lister (1756–1830), who received his medical degree at the University of Edinburgh in 1781 and became a physician at St. Thomas' Hospital, London: *List of Graduates in Medicine in the University of Edinburgh from MDCCV to MDCCCLXVI* (Edinburgh, 1867), p. 16; P. J. and R. V. Wallis, comps., *Eighteenth Century Medics (subscriptions, licences, apprenticeships)* (2nd ed., Newcastle, Eng., 1988), p. 368; *The Royal Kalendar . . . for the Year 1783*, p. 222.

and who I find bears an equal character among his connections here in London. I know him to be a person of very amiable & honorable character in his private conduct, from transactions in which I have seen him engaged; and I believe that his public principles are likewise upright.— Your attentions & civility to him will not only oblige me considerably, but be very acceptable to some of your dissenting friends here; and I am convinced that you will gratify by him by your philosophy & philanthropy, as well as by the other circumstances of your character. Should you find him over-modest, you will not the less incline to admit him into your society.

I am, my dearest sir, your most obliged, devoted, & affectionate
BENJN: VAUGHAN

Addressed: A Monsr. / Monsr. Franklin, / Passy, / pres Paris.

To Sarah and Richard Bache

ALS: American Philosophical Society

Dear Son and Daughter   Passy, June 26. 1782

I have only time to write a few Lines. I am well, and your Son was well about 10 Days ago.[5] He is not in the Town of Geneva, where the Government is at present in Disorder; but is at the Master's Country-House, a few Miles distant where he goes on with his Studies. Let me know in your next what his Age is, which I have forgotten.—[6] I send enclos'd some of his Letters;[7] & am ever Your affectionate Father   B FRANKLIN

Temple presents his Duty—

5. The most recent extant letters to BF concerning BFB are Catherine Cramer's of April 9 and 12, both above.

6. BFB would turn 13 on Aug. 12: I, lxiii.

7. We have located three BFB letters from this period. He wrote to his parents on Jan. 1, 1782, expressing enthusiasm for the Yorktown victory, hope that his brother William would join him in Geneva, and pleasure at renewing his acquaintance with Robert Montgomery (APS). BFB sent a similar letter to WTF around the same time (XXXVI, 476–7n) and wrote to BF on Feb. 21 (XXXVI, 597–8).

To Richard Oswald: Unsent Draft[8]

AL (draft): Library of Congress

Dear Sir,   Passy, June 26. 1782

In the Note that you show'd me[9] it is said, that "Mr Oswald may be vested with any Character or Commission that he and Dr F. shall think proper;" or to that purpose: and you desire my Sentiments.— We should be willing to treat with such Persons as the King may think fit to appoint.— I am however very sensible of the Kindness that appears in Lord Shelburne's offering me any Appearance of Influence in that Choice, and I esteem it as a Proof of his sincere Desire of making with us a good Peace.— I can have no Objection to Mr Grenville, who is already appointed *to treat with the King of France or his Ministers, or the Ministers of any other Prince or State whom it may concern;* as he informs me:[1] And as soon as the Enabling Act is pass'd, and the *States* of America are acknowledg'd to be such,[2] I suppose the Words of that Commission may be clearly interpreted to mean & include those States, in the Understanding of your Government, with those of Spain & Holland. At present it seems dubious. And as your long Residence in America has given you a Knowledge of that Country its People, Circumstances, Commerce, &c. which added to your Experience in Business may be useful to both sides, in facilitating & expediting the Negociation, I cannot but wish that you may be join'd with Mr Grenville in the Commission, at least for the Part which relates to America; or if that Should seem in any Respect inconvenient, than that you might be, in a distinct Commission, named as Plenipotentiary to treat with the Plenipotentiaries of America particularly. This is what occurs to me. With great and sincere Esteem, I have the honour to be, Dear Sir, Your

---

8. As BF explains in the postscript and in his journal of the peace negotiations (June 26 entry), he rewrote this letter after consulting Oswald. The final version is dated June 27 (below).

9. On June 3; see the entry of that date in BF's journal. The note was from Shelburne, to whom BF wanted this letter communicated.

1. See the June 15 entry in BF's journal.

2. The Enabling Act used the expression "colonies or plantations" rather than "states": XXXVI, 688n.

This Draft being shown to Mr Oswald & he not Chusing that his Showing me Lord S's Note should be mention'd, I first cros'd it out, but afterwards new model'd the whole[3] the Draft is in red Ink

R Oswald Esqe

From David Hartley: Two Letters

(I) and (II) ALS: Library of Congress

I.

Dear Sir   London June 26 1782

I take the liberty of recommending to your acquaintance a gentleman of this Country (Mr Bowles) who has been bred to the profession of the law.[4] He has some thoughts of settling in America, I believe with a view to practise the law, or to make some other establishments there, such as he may find most suitable upon trial of the Case. He is at present making enquiries for the most practicable mode of proceeding towards his proposed settlement. I hope that the interchange and communications of persons mutually friendly to both Countries, will lay a foundation of peace & future harmony between the two nations of Great Britain and America. I am Dear Sir Your much obliged friend & most obedt Servt   D HARTLEY

To Dr Franklin &c &c &c

II.

My Dear friend   London June 26 1782

Major young who is going to Paris this morning[5] has just called upon me wch gives me but just half an hours opportunity to write to you. But indeed not having heard from you since my

---

3. BF initially bracketed and crossed out the first three sentences of this letter and deleted the fourth (except for the portion in italics).

4. Possibly John Bowles (c. 1751–1819), who became a barrister and political writer and resided in Bath: *Gent. Mag.*, LXXXIX (1819), part II, pp. 565–6.

5. In order to return to America; see his letter of July 10.

last of May 25 by Mr Oswald I have not much to add, except my anxiety for the success of the negotiations wch are now on foot for peace. As such I heartily wish them success; Tho I have had some conversations with Ld S [Shelburne] upon the subject, I am not specifically informed of the plan or particulars. I have not at all endeavored to dive into the thoughts of ministers, but as far as any thoughts or sentiments of mine cd in any way be instrumental in his hands, I have not withheld any thing. I have never made any scruple of any such disparity in the mutual communications with ministers; Not having any actual employment in the business my situation at present is limited. My office extends only to this, to state to ministers honestly and unequivocally, such principles and plan as alone seem to me to be the strait road to Peace; the execution depends upon them. I am very anxious for the result. Let me once more repeat to you (tho I hope it is not necessary to your conviction) that the utmost of my powers shall always be devoted to assist in the work of peace, in any manner in wch I may be serviceable.— Since I writ last to you I have been again chosen into Parliament for Hull.[6] God bless you Your affecte   D H

To Dr Franklin.

From Robert Morris   Copy: Library of Congress

Sir,   Office of Finance 26. June 1782.,
    The Bearer of this Letter Doctor Texier late Surgeon of Count Pulaski's Legion will shew you a Certificate for two thousand one hundred and ten dollars signed by Joseph Nourse Esquire Register of the Treasury of the United States and issued by Virtue of a Warrant of the eighth day of January last from me. This Money is on Interest at six per Cent from the fifth of

---

6. Hartley was elected unopposed in his former constituency, Kingston-upon-Hull (which he had served from 1774 to 1780), on June 6, replacing Lord Robert Manners, who had died a week earlier: Namier and Brooke, *House of Commons*, I, 434–5; II, 592–3; III, 107; *London Courant, Westminster Chronicle, and Public Advertiser*, June 10.

January 1782. and is the Balance still due after a partial Payment[7] in Consequence of an Act of Congress of the twelfth of November, a Copy of which he will also shew you.[8] Should it be perfectly convenient to you it will be a great Favor to him and agreable to me that this two thousand one hundred and ten Dollars be paid to Doctor Texier taking his Receipt in full of all Demands against the United States on the Back of the Certificate with three Copies thereof signed by him and sending them by different Opportunities. I mention two thousand one hundred and ten Dollars without noticing the Interest because in Case of Payment by you the Transaction will be substantially as if I had given him here a Bill of Exchange.

With all possible Respect I have the Honor to be Sir your most obedient and humble Servant   R M.

His Excelly. Benja. Franklin

From William Rawle

ALS: American Philosophical Society

Sir   Boulogne sur mer 26. June 1782.

It is with reluctance I give your Excellency a trouble which necessity alone could induce me to think of.

Soon after my return to Ostend from Paris,[9] I was seiz'd with a violent cold and fever, which, added to the effects of a former indisposition at London, has render'd me so exceedingly weak, that I have been prevail'd on by my friends to defer my voyage

---

7. On Jan. 8, Morris ordered Felix Texier, a Frenchman who had served under Casimir Pulaski, one-fifth of his balance "on account of Depreciation and the remainder to be put on Interest." Morris wrote the present letter in response to a June 26 visit from Texier requesting his remaining pay. On July 3, Texier applied to Morris for more money but was refused: *Morris Papers,* III, 506, 507n; V, 484, 519.

8. The mention of this act was probably a copying error, as it refers specifically to Capt. Jacob Schreiber: *JCC,* XXI, 1111–2. Morris was doubtless using as a model for this letter a similar one he had previously written to BF about Schreiber: XXXVI, 197n. Morris had also written two others, which did not mention this act but otherwise were virtually identical in wording, for the baron de Frey and the baron d'Arendt: XXXVI, 196–7; above, March 22.

9. BF furnished Rawle with a passport for Ostend on May 8, above.

to America, till I could re-establish my health; and to retire in the mean time to some place on the sea-coast; where I might enjoy the benefit of bathing; which was also strongly recommended by my physicians in England.

It was natural to prefer France to Flanders and I made choice of Boulogne on account of the agreeable society it contains, its situation on the sea and its vicinity to Ostend, from whence I propose to embark in the autumn.

As I was then ignorant of those very proper precautions, which the French government observes with regard to the residence of strangers in their sea ports, I did not trouble your Excellency for a passport or a recommendation for permission to continue here; but I now find I cannot remain without permission from Paris.[1]

I therefore take the liberty to request your Excellency's assistance on this occasion as a favor of which I shall retain a lasting remembrance.

I have the honor to be Your Excellency's most obedient and most humble servant　　　　　　　　　　　　　W: Rawle.

Addressed: His Excellency / Benjamin Franklin Esqr

Notation: W Rawle 26 June 1782.

From Jonathan Williams, Jr.

ALS: American Philosophical Society; copy: Yale University Library

Dear & hond sir.　　　　　　　　　　　　Nantes June 26. 1782.

I send inclosed Copy of a Letter I have just recvd from Brest to which I request your kind attention.[2] There cannot be a doubt

---

1. Foreigners were not permitted to stay longer than 24 hours without permission of the court. Rawle prevailed upon the *commissaire* to allow him to stay until BF sent either a letter or a passport valid for what he estimated would be eight or ten weeks: Rawle to WTF, June 26, APS. Rawle remained in Boulogne until Sept. 19 and finally sailed for America in mid-November, arriving on Jan. 10, 1783: Journal of William Rawle, Hist. Soc. of Pa.

2. The letter, dated June 17, was from Richmond Springer, a Rhode Islander who had been captured aboard the *Wexford* on Sept. 29, 1781, and im-

but the Prize in Question belongs to the Captors, or at least that whatever the Rigour of the Law may be, the Custom in such Cases is to give them up. The Ordonnances of the Marine confiscated all prises made without a Commission, but the Admiral always gives them back to the Captors. In the present Case the Ordonnances of the Marine are out of the Question, as Prises made by Americans have particular Laws relating to them. I shall be much obliged if you will please to interest your self for these men, and I am sure you cannot fail of Success. A State of the Fact to M. de Castries would answer the purpose, I would have done it myself & saved you the Trouble but it would be presuming to Act when I have no right to do.

I am as ever yours most dutifully & affectionately
JONA WILLIAMS J

Notation: Jona. Williams June 26. 1782.

From Williams, Moore & Co. Copy: Yale University Library

Honoured Sir, Nantes June 26. 1782

The present serves to hand you a Certificate from the Commandant of the Port of L'Orient[3] acknowledging the Reception of Prisoners delivered him by our House from the american Privateer Revolution[4] to our Address Ten Men from the Prize *Anne* & five from the Prize *Will*, making together fifteen men which we request you will note for Exchange in course.

---

prisoned at Kinsale. He escaped in April, he wrote, and met five other Americans in Cork, three from his own ship and two from the *Essex*. On May 5, they boarded and seized the cutter *Bourke*, which carried a load of provisions, and sailed to Brest. They engaged Pierre Rïou to write BF for help in condemning the prize but have received no answer. Enclosing a list of their names and an invoice of the cargo, they ask JW to contact BF on their behalf. APS.

3. Thévenard.

4. The *Revolution*, 20, Capt. Stephen Webb, was owned by John and Andrew Cabot of Beverly, Mass.: Charles H. Lincoln, comp., *Naval Records of the American Revolution, 1775–1788* (Washington, D.C., 1906), p. 443.

We have the honor to be with the most perfect Respect, Yours Excellys most Obedt Servants   WILLIAMS MOORE & CO

His Exy B. Franklin Esqr.

From Moses Young   ALS: American Philosophical Society

Sir   London 26th June 1782.
   The bearer of this letter is Mr. Cephas Dawes a Gentleman of a very respectable family in Pennsylvania, he was settled as a Merchant in the West Indies previous to the commencement of the war, and is a warm friend to the cause of America, which I hope will be my apology for taking this liberty with Your Excellency. Mr. Dawes will Carry with him some of the latest Newspapers.[5]
   I have the honor to be, With the highest veneration & respect Your Excellency's Most humble And most devoted Servant
                                                        MOSES YOUNG

His Excellency Benjamin Franklin Esquire

Addressed: His Excellency / Benjamin Franklin Esquire / Minister Plenepotentiary from the United States / of America at the Court of France / Passy

Notation: Young Mr. Moses—26 June 1782.

5. Dawes was in Paris by July 19, when he visited BF. The next day, writing from the Hôtel Luxembourg, rue des Petits Augustins, Dawes acknowledged that visit and sent BF another newspaper that he had just discovered in his trunk (APS). BF issued him a passport on July 24 for travel to Ostend: XXXVI, 380. Dawes may be the merchant of that name who lived at 138 Water Street, Philadelphia, in 1785, next to the prominent Quaker merchant Abijah Dawes: [John] Macpherson, *Macpherson's Directory, for the City and Suburbs of Philadelphia* (Philadelphia, 1785), p. 33; Elaine F. Crane, ed., *The Diary of Elizabeth Drinker* (3 vols., Boston, 1991), III, 2133.

To Richard Oswald[6]

LS[7] and two copies: Public Record Office; copies: William L. Clements Library, Library of Congress (two);[8] copy and transcript: Massachusetts Historical Society; transcript: National Archives

Sir,   Passy, June 27. 1782.

The Opinion I have of your Candour, Probity, good Understanding, and good Will to both Countries, made me hope that you would have been vested with the Character of Plenipotentiary to treat with those from America. When Mr. Grenville produced his first Commission which was only to treat with France,[9] I did imagine that the other to treat with us, was reserved for you, and kept back only 'till the Enabling Bill should be pass'd. Mr. Grenville has since received a second Commission, which as he informs me, has additional Words, impowering him to treat with the Ministers of any other Prince, or State whom it may concern, and he seems to understand that those general Words comprehend the United States of America. There may be no doubt that they comprehend Spain and Holland, but as there exist various Public Acts by which the Government of Britain denies us to be States, and none in which they acknowledge us to be such, it seems hardly clear that one could be intended, at the Time that Commission was given, the Enabling Act not being then pass'd. So that tho' I can have no Objection to Mr Grenville, nor right to make it if I had any, yet as your long Residence in America has given you a Knowledge of that Country, Its People, Cir-

---

6. A revised version of the letter BF drafted on June 26, above. Oswald forwarded it to Shelburne on July 8 with a covering letter describing a conversation he had with BF on July 6: after a general discussion about what issues might be raised in the negotiations, BF invited him to return on July 10, when BF would show him "a minute of some things" that he wanted to put forward anonymously. BF emphasized that "there would be no solid peace, while [Canada] remained an English colony." Lord John Russell, ed., *Memorials and Correspondence of Charles James Fox* (4 vols., London, 1853–57), IV, 228–34.

7. In WTF's hand.

8. One of the Library of Congress copies, and both transcripts, are in BF's journal of the peace negotiations.

9. Grenville presented his commission during the May 9 meeting when BF introduced him to Vergennes; see BF's journal of the peace negotiations.

cumstances, Commerce &ca. which added to your Experience in Business may be useful to both sides in facilitating and expediting the Negotiation, I cannot but hope that it is still intended to vest you with the Character abovementioned respecting the Treaty with America, either separately, or in Conjunction with Mr Grenville, as to the Wisdom of your Ministers may seem best. Be it as it may, I beg you would accept this Line as a Testimony of the sincere Esteem & Respect with which I have the honour to be, Sir, Your most obedient and most humble Servant.

B FRANKLIN

R Oswald Esqr.

Notation:[1] Doctr. Franklin to Mr. Oswald In Mr. Oswald's of the 8th. 12th. July—

From Bethia Alexander   ALS: American Philosophical Society

St. Germain Jeudy au Matin [June 27, 1782][2]
J'espere que vous n'avez pas oublié, mon cher Docteur, notre partie de Marly—la permission de manger dans les Jardins ou dans les pavillons est obtenu.—[3] Messrs: de Breuil et Pechmeja[4] vienent—et porteront avec eux une bonne provision du fruit—pour moi Je porterai la plus grande longe de veau que Je pourrois trouver à St. Germain et quelques couverts—la reste vous regarde—souvenez vous que le rendez vous est au chateau de Marly a onze heures precises—ce seroit bien aimable de votre part de nous mener mon Frere.[5]

1. In Shelburne's hand.
2. The Thursday between June 24, when William Alexander wrote BF about the outing to Marly (above), and July 3, when Bethia wrote BF after the outing had been canceled (below).
3. Marly, designed by Mansart for Louis XIV as a retreat from the formal court life, lay on the road between Saint-Germain and Versailles. On each side of a central pavilion were six smaller ones linked by arbors of jasmine and honeysuckle: Pierre de Nolhac, ed., *Souvenirs de Mme Louise-Élisabeth Vigée-Le Brun: Notes et portraits, 1755–1789* (Paris, [1910?]), pp. 31–2. For a history of Marly see Jeanne and Alfred Marie, *Marly* (Paris, 1947).
4. Introduced by William Alexander in his June 24 letter, above.
5. For her brothers see our annotation of BF's letter to her, June 24.

Parlez de moi à Madame Helvetius dites lui que J'attende Lundy avec impatience.[6] Adieu mon cher Docteur— Je vous garde votre Baiser. Votre   BETHIA ALEXANDER

Mes Complimens à votre Fils. Si il nous manque quelques choses à notre diner nous nous en prendrons à lui.

Addressed: A Monsieur / Monsieur Franklin / Passy / prés / Paris

From Thomas Barclay   LS: American Philosophical Society

Sir   Amsterdam 27th. June 1782.

Since my last Covering Messrs. De Neufvilles accounts[7] I have not had the honour of a Letter from your Excellency; Captain Smedley has I expect this day got his Vessell over the Sand Banks that interupt the Navigation of the River Y[8] and will in a few days be able to put to Sea he is tolerably well Man'd and with the assistance of a few more people who I believe he will procure in a day or two he shall proceed.

I have Ship'd on board the Brigantine Sukey Mosses Grinnell Master for Boston[9] about 2400 suits of Soldiers Cloathing, the amount of the last 33 Bales which I bought together with Two Bales of Blanketts of the Marquis De la Fayette's Cargo which I took a 5/9 sterling per Pair, Two Boxes of White Cloth which I Purchased to replace Some of the Same Kind which Messrs. De Neufville returned to us as English, and the freight per the Sukey a 12½ per Cent, amount to upwards of £2000 Sterling, and therefore of this date I have valued on you as under, favour of Messrs. Ingraham & Bromfield at 40 days Sight, for the following Sum making together 13333½ Ecus or 40 Thousand Livers—which please to honour.[1]

6. July 1, presumably the day initially planned for the outing to Marly.

7. Above, June 17.

8. Or Ij, an arm of the Zuider Zee.

9. The *Sukey,* commanded by Moses Grinnell, reached Boston safely: *Morris Papers,* VI, 418.

1. The 40,000 *l.t.* were not paid until Oct. 8: Account XXVII (XXXII, 4).

I have likewise Shiped by the Brigantine Elizabeth John Cornelieus Master for Philadelphia 63 Chests of Shirts and 30 Bales of Blanketts, this Vessell will proceed under Neutral Colours, and I have ordered £3000 Stg. Insurance to be made a 17 per Cent which is 13 per Cent under the premium paid on American Vessells, I am to pay Freight on this Vessell 12½ per Cent Value on the Shirts and 20 per Cent on the Blankets—²

I have the honour to be with the greatest respect Sir your Excellency's most obedient, most Humble Servant

THOS BARCLAY

No. 15	1333⅓ Ecus
16	1600
17	1400
18	1500
19	1200
20	1500
21	1000
22	1000
23	1000
24	1800
	13333⅓

His Excellency Benjamin Franklin Esqre

Endorsed: Barclay June 27. 82

From Favi

ALS: American Philosophical Society

Monsieur   Paris ce 27 Juin 1782/

J'ai L'honneur de vous adresser une Lettre de M. Ingenhousz;³ il seroit charmè d'avoir une reponse, que je me chargerai avec plaisir de Lui faire parvenir, si vous voulés avoir La bontè de me L'envoyer rue de *Seine a l'hôtel de Mirabeau.*

2. The *Elizabeth* was captured by the British and taken to New York: *Morris Papers*, VII, 314n.
3. Above, June 12.

J'ai L'honneur d'etre avec respect Monsieur Votre très humble, et très obeissant Serviteur   FAVI

Notation: Favi. 27 Juin 1782.

From Poreau & Cie.   ALS: University of Pennsylvania Library

Monsieur   Dunkerque le 27 Juin 1782
La bonté avec la quelle vous avez bien voulu acceuillir notre Sr. Poreau Lorsqu'il a eu l'honneur de vous presenter Ses Respects pendant son Sejour a Paris, et la promesse obligeante que vous lui avez faite de vous employer pour obtenir L'Echange du Capitaine Christophe Codner cy devant Capitaine dun de nos Corsaires, nous fait esperer que vous ne prendrez pas de mauvaise part la liberté dont nous usons en vous envoyant cy Incluse une Lettre que nous venons de recevoir de ce pauvre Garçon qui est reellement digne d'un meilleur Sort. Vous y verrez Monsieur q'un Terme de Souffrance aussi Long que celuy qu'il a deja eprouvé n'a point encore Suffit pour mettre des bornes aux Traitements farouches qu'il essuy de la part des Anglois.[4]

Nous osons esperer de votre humanité Monsieur, que vous voudrez bien prendre cette affaire a Cœur et mettre en œuvre des Moyens efficaces pour obtenir La Liberté du Capitaine Codner, qui est natif et bon Sujet de L'amerique. Nous vous serons garants de sa Reconnaissance parfaite.

Avec Tout le Respect possible Nous avons L'honneur d'etre Monsieur Vos tres humbles & tres obeissants Serviteurs[5]

POREAU & COMP

Notation: Poureau & Co. 27. Juin 1782.

4. Codner, a New Englander who commanded one of the firm's privateers, was captured in the summer of 1781. The firm soon applied to BF for help in securing his release: XXXV, 371–2. The enclosure to the present letter was undoubtedly Codner's letter of June 20, 1782, in which he details further cruelties on board the British prison ship *Greenwich* and complains of being malnourished and extremely ill. All the other Americans confined with him were sent to Forton Prison for eventual exchange. The ALS, endorsed by Poreau & Cie., also bears a notation by L'Air de Lamotte. Hist. Soc. of Pa.

5. While this is the last extant letter from the firm, they forwarded to BF a copy of Codner's next letter, dated July 26. Still aboard the *Greenwich* and

To Samuel Cooper: Extract

Reprinted from William Temple Franklin, ed., *Memoirs of the Life and Writings of Benjamin Franklin* . . . (3 vols., 4to, London, 1817–18), II, 378–9.[6]

Passy, June 28, 1782.

Our public affairs are in a good situation here. England having tried in vain to make a separate peace with each of the powers she is at war with, has at length agreed to treat for a general peace with them altogether; and at Paris. If we all continue firm in the resolution not to separate, we shall command the terms. I have no doubt of this steadiness here; and though we are told that endeavours are making on your side the water to induce America to a re-union on the terms now granting to Ireland, and that powers are sent to General Carleton for that purpose, I am persuaded the danger of this project will appear so evident, that if offered it will be immediately rejected.[7] We have no safety but in our independence. With that we shall be respected, and soon become great, and happy. Without it we shall be despised, lose all our friends, and then either be cruelly oppressed by the King who hates and is incapable of forgiving us, or having all that nation's enemies for ours, shall sink with it. I am ever, my dear friend, yours most affectionately, B. FRANKLIN.

From Dumas

ALS: American Philosophical Society

Monsieur, Lahaie 28e. Juin *1782*
J'ai profité la semaine passée d'un Courier expédié par Mr. l'Ambr. pour vous faire une de mes Lettres pour le Congrès No.

---

with no hope of release, he writes again to beg that "that Gentleman Which you mention'd in your last may be acquainted with our Situation; as it Lays in his Power to Releive us. . . ." APS.

6. WTF incorporated this extract into his printing of BF's journal of the peace negotiations.

7. BF issued this warning, like that to Livingston of the following day (below), at the request of Gérard de Rayneval; see the June 28 entry in BF's journal of the peace negotiations. The warning was not necessary; see Livingston to BF, May 22 (which BF could not yet have received).

4, laquelle j'espere que vous aurez bien reçue ainsi que mes précédente.[8] Il ne s'est rien passé ici depuis que j'aie à y ajouter. Mais après mercredi prochain,[9] les Etats d'hollde., qui se rassembleront alors, pourront me fournir matiere à une autre dépeche interessante.

En attendant, je prends la liberté, de vous adresser, Monsieur, l'incluse pour Mr. Carmichael,[1] n'étant pas sûr s'il est resté à Madrid, ou s'il a accompagné Mr. Jay, si celui-ci est allé à Paris, comme je le conjecture d'après ce que vous en avez écrit à Mr. Adams.

Comme on me demande souvent des adresses de maisons commerçantes & solides en Amérique, j'ai soin de fournir entre autres celle de Mrs Bache & Shea à Philadelphie, à nos Négocians en ce pays.[2]

Il nous tarde ici d'apprendre à quoi aboutira la Négociation du Chev. G——lle [Grenville]. A dire vrai, je n'en ai pas encore grande idée. Il est plus apparent que vous entendrez bientôt parler d'un Ministre à envoyer à Philadelphie de la part de cette rep.[3]

Je suis avec tout le respectueux attachement qui vous est connu, Monsieur, Votre très-humble & très-obéissant serviteur

DUMAS

Passy à S. E. Mr. Franklin.

8. Dumas' letter is above, June 22.

9. July 3.

1. Not found.

2. Dumas had arranged for distribution in the Netherlands of circulars for RB's firm: XXVIII, 552–3n; XXIX, 273n; XXX, 383.

3. Eventually Pieter Johan van Berckel, brother of the pensionary of Amsterdam, was selected, although he did not sail for America until the following June: Schulte Nordholt, *Dutch Republic*, pp. 252–3.

To Robert R. Livingston[4]

LS,[5] copy, and transcript: National Archives

Sir,   Passy June 29. 1782.

In mine of the 25th. Inst. I omitted mentioning, that, at the repeated earnest Instances of Mr Lawrens, who had given such Expectations to the Ministry in England, when his Parole or Securities were discharged, as that he could not think himself at Liberty to act in Publick Affairs 'till the Parole of Lord Cornwallis was absolved by me in Exchange, I sent to that Genl. the Paper of which the inclosed is a Copy;[6] and I see by the English Papers, that his Lordship immediately on the Receipt of it, appear'd at Court,[7] and has taken his Seat in the House of Peers, which he did not before think warrantable. My Authority for doing this appear'd Questionable to my self, but Mr Lawrens judg'd it deducible from that respecting General Burgoyne, and by his Letters to me seem'd so unhappy 'till it was done, that I ventur'd it, with a Clause however (as you will see) reserving to Congress the Approbation, or Disallowance of it.

The enabling Act is now said to be passed but no Copy of it is yet received here, so that as the Bill first printed has suffer'd Alterations in passing thro' Parliament, and we know not what they are, the Treaty with us is not yet commenc'd. Mr Grenville expects his Courier in a few Days, with the Answer of his Court to a Paper given him on the Part of this. That Answer will probably afford us a clearer Understanding of the Intentions of the British Ministry, which for some Weeks past have appear'd somewhat equivocal and uncertain. It looks as if since their late Success in the West Indies they a little repented of the Advances they had made in their Declarations respecting the Acknowledgement of our Independence; and we have pretty good Information that some of the Ministry still flatter the King with the Hope of re-

4. Written in response to a June 28 request by Gérard de Rayneval, for which see BF's journal of the peace negotiations.
5. In WTF's hand.
6. BF's discharge of Cornwallis from his parole: above, June 9.
7. Cornwallis met with the King on June 19 and was introduced to the Queen the following day: *London Courant, Westminster Chronicle,* and *Daily Advertiser,* June 20 and June 21, 1782.

covering his Sovereignty over us, on the same Terms as are now making with Ireland. However willing we might have been at the Commencement of this Contest to have accepted such Conditions, be assur'd that we can have no Safety in them at present. The King hates us most cordially; and his Character for Falsehood and Dissimulation is so thoroughly known, that none even of those who call themselves his Friends have any Dependance on him. If he is once admitted to any Degree of Power or Government among us, how ever limited it will soon be extended by Corruption, Artifice and Force, till we are reduced to absolute Subjection; and that the more easily, as by receiving him again for our King, we shall draw upon ourselves the Contempt of all Europe who now admire and respect us, & shall never again find a Friend to assist us. There are it is said great Divisions in the Ministry on other Points as well as this; and those who aim at engrossing the Power flatter the King with this Project of Reunion; and it is said have much Reliance on the Operation of private Agents sent into America, to dispose Minds there in favour of it, and to bring about a separate Treaty there with General Carleton. I have not the least Apprehension that Congress will give into this Scheme, it being inconsistent with our Treaties as well as with our Interest; but I think it will be well to watch these Emissaries and secure or banish immediately such as shall be found tampering & stirring up the People to call for it. The firm united Resolution of France, Spain & Holland, join'd with ours, not to treat of a particular but a general Peace, notwithstanding the separate tempting Offers to each, will in the End give us the Command of that Peace. Every one of the other Powers see clearly their Interest in this, and persist in that Resolution: the Congress I am persuaded are as clear sighted as any of them, and will not depart from the System which has been attended with so much Success, and promises to make America soon both great and happy.

I have just received a Letter from Mr Lawrens, dated at Lyons, on his Journey into the South of France for his Health.[8] Mr Jay will write also by this Opportunity.[9]

8. Above, June 24.
9. Jay wrote Livingston on June 28: Wharton, *Diplomatic Correspondence*, v, 527–8.

With great Esteem I have the honour to be Sir, Your most obedient & most humble Servt. B FRANKLIN

Honble: Robt R. Livingston Esqre

Notation: Letters 25. 29 June. 1782 Doct Franklin & Letter 25 June. Mr J. Jay 18 Sept 1782 Referred to Mr Lee & Mr Izard & Mr Duane[1]

From Williams, Moore & Co.

ALS:[2] American Philosophical Society

Sir   L'Orient 31st. June [*i.e.,* on or after June 30] 1782
   We do ourselves the honor to forward Sundry Papers respecting two Prizes brought in here by the Revolution Privateer, with which We beg you will do the needfull.[3]
   Permit us to inform that there are some Americans Confined in Jail, they experienced a long Confinement in England, escaped, & arrived in Brest, applied there for a Passage home, were sent here, fed on Bread & Water, & are refused their Liberty.
   With great Respect We remain Sir Your most Obt humble Servants[4] WILLIAMS MOORE & CO

---

1. Arthur Lee, Ralph Izard, and James Duane were members of the congressional committee which was given BF's letters to Livingston of June 25 and 29 (above), and John Jay's to Livingston of June 25 (Wharton, *Diplomatic Correspondence*, V, 516–17). They reported to Congress on Sept. 19 and then were appointed to prepare a draft treaty with Sweden (in response to BF's letter of June 25 reporting Swedish interest in such a treaty), as well as a commission and instructions: *JCC*, XXIII, 592.
2. In the hand of James Moore.
3. That is, condemn them as legal prizes. The ships were the *Anne* and *Will*, both of which were sold by Williams, Moore & Co. in August. Dossiers on their condemnation and sale, which no longer contain the prize condemnation forms BF must have signed, are at the Archives départementales de Morbihan. BF might have completed those forms on July 10, when Richard Oswald observed him in his role as "Judge Admiral" for prizes: Lord John Russell, ed., *Memorials and Correspondence of Charles James Fox* (4 vols., London, 1853–57), IV, 242.
4. On July 3, the firm wrote a brief letter enclosing the present one, which

Addressed: Monseiur / Monseiur B. Franklin / Ministre plenipotentiare des Etats Unis / de L'Amerique / a la Cour de / France a / Passy

Notations: Williams Moore 31. Juin 1782. / [*in William Temple Franklin's hand:*] Ansd 9 July

From [Philip?] Keay[5]   AL: University of Pennsylvania Library

Rue Ne. des Mathurins Friday [June, 1782?][6]
Mr. Keay presents his Respects to Mr. Franklin, & takes the liberty of enclosing the relation of the Accident at Philadelphia. The Person who mention'd it to Made. de Cheminot had seen Conductors upon the House, & had hastily concluded, that they had been put up previous to the accident, which they certainly were not— Madame de Cheminot presents her Compts. to Mr. Franklin & his Son.

From Robert Morris

LS: American Philosophical Society, Historical Society of Pennsylvania;[7] copy: Library of Congress

Sir,   Office of Finance 1 July 1782
I have deferred until this Moment my Answers to your Letters of the fourth ninth and thirtieth of March[8] in Expectation that I should have heard from you by the Marquis de la fayette.

---

their clerk had neglected to send with the ships' papers. They also reported that the *Buccaneer* had sent into Brest a prize from Quebec.

5. Keay and his *amie*, Mme de Cheminot, are identified in XXV, 725, and XXX, 165–6.

6. Matthew Ridley had received news by June 10 that La Luzerne's house in Philadelphia was struck by lightning; see his letter to BF of that date. We conjecture that the "Accident at Philadelphia" mentioned in the present letter is that same lightning strike.

7. Marked "Second", BF endorsed it "Office of Finance July 1. 1782".

8. The first two letters are in XXXVI, 649–52, 672–4; the third is above.

A Vessel now about to depart induces me to address you— I enclose an Act of Congress by which you are empowered to adjust the Public Accounts with the Court of France. I wish this may be done and the Amount transmitted hither that Arrangements may be taken for ascertaining the times and mode of Payment. You will at the same time observe that it is determined to appoint a Commissioner for Liquidating and finally adjusting the Accots. of the public Servants of Congress in Europe.[9]

The Minister here in a Letter to me of the twenty fifth of May last[1] gives the following State of Monies granted by France Viz: "These Advances have been made at the following Periods and are payable with Interest according to the Obligations and Acknowlegements of Mr Franklin

In 1778 .... 3.000.000 *l.t.*
   1779 .... 1.000.000
   1780 .... 4,000.000
   1781................................... 10.000.000
                      Total— 18.000.000

From this Sum must be deducted the
  gratuitous Subsidy of last Year....}......... 6.000.000
                   Remains 12.000,000

To this must be added—
1st The Produce of the Loan in Holland...... 10,000,000
2ly The Loan made by his Majesty for the
  current Year......................... 6.000.000

Capital of the Debt due to his Majesty by
  the United States .... 28.000.000 *l.t.* "

I think it right to send you this State on which I will make a few Observations. I could have wished that the whole of the Monies which the Court have furnished us had been what the greater Part is a *Loan*. I know that the united States will find no difficulty in making Payment and I take this Opportunity to give *you* an Assurance which is not meant for the Court that I will endeavor to provide *even now* the Means of Repayment by getting Laws passed to take Effect at a future Period or otherwise as shall

9. For these two May 28 resolutions see Livingston to BF, May 30.
1. La Luzerne's letter is in *Morris Papers*, v, 261–4.

be most convenient and agreeable to all Parties after the Amount is ascertained and the Times of Payment fixed. I wish it had *all* been a Loan because I do not think the Weight of the Debt would be so great as the Weight of an Obligation is generally found to be and the latter is of all others what I would least wish to labour under either in a public or private Capacity. A still further Reason with me is that there is less Pain in soliciting the *Aid* of a Loan when there is no Expectation that it is to be a Gift. Prompted by such Reasons I could be well content that the advances made previously to the Year 1778 were by some Means or other brought into this Account. By Mr Grands Accounts it appears that Messrs. Franklin, Deane and Lee paid him on the thirty first of January 1777. 500.000 *l.t.* on the twenty eighth of April other 500.000 *l.t.* on the fourth of June 1.000.000 *l.t.* on the third of July 500.000 *l.t.* and on the tenth of October other 500.000 *l.t.* Amounting in the whole to three Millions of Livres.[2] I suppose that these Sums were received of Private Persons in like manner with those Supplies which were obtained thro' Mr de Beaumarchais and if so they will be payable in like Manner with those Supplies— I have in a former Letter estimated the Yearly Interest on Loan Office Certificates payable in France at 2.200.000 *l.t.*[3] consequently taking in the Months intervening between September and March the Total Amount from September the tenth 1777 to March the first 1782 may be stated at 9.000.000 *l.t.* which is just one half the Supplies granted for the Years 1778. 1779 1780 and 1781. A Resolution now before Congress will I beleive direct that no more Bills be drawn for this Interest[4] but

2. The French government provided 2,000,000 *l.t.*, in four payments of 500,000 *l.t.* each, under the guise of private contributions. The other million proceeded from a tobacco contract made with the farmers general but effected through French governmental influence: XXIII, 197–9, 468–9, 514–17; XXV, 40–1. Once received, the funds were deposited with Grand. The first three credits mentioned here appear in Account X (XXIII, 22), and the last two appear in Account XI (XXIV, 3), but the July 3 payment was credited on July 5.

3. Estimated at 2,193,990 *l.t.* in his first Nov. 27, 1781, letter to BF: XXXVI, 147.

4. The July 1 resolution called instead for the interest to be paid out of impost revenues: *JCC*, XXII, 365.

Mr. Grand in his Letter of the fourth of March tells me he has paid £6.239.186 *l.t.* 13.4. in 16819 Bills from 11th February 1779. to 28th Jany 1782. His Accounts are now translating and when that is compleated I shall transmit them to the Treasury and I hope soon to have the Accounts of the Several Loan Officers in such a train of Settlement that all these Matters may finally be wound up.

Should the Court grant 6.000,000 *l.t.* more for the Service of the Current Year making 12.000.000 *l.t.* in the whole which to tell you the Truth I do expect then the Sum Total in five Years will be 40.000.000 *l.t.* or 8.000.000 *l.t.* annually. And when the Occasion of this Grant is considered the Magnitude of the Object and the Derangement of our Finances naturally to be expected in so great a Revolution I cannot think this Sum is by any Means very extraordinary. I beleive with you most perfectly in the good Dispositions of the Court but I must request you to urge those Dispositions into Effect. I consider the six Millions mentioned to me by the Minister here and afterwards in your Letters[5] as being at my Disposal. The Taxes come in so slowly that I have been Compelled and must Continue to draw Bills but I shall avoid it as much as possible. In my Letters of the twenty third and twenty ninth of May of which I enclose Copies are Contained my Sentiments as to Mr. de Beaumarchais Demand. Indeed if the Sums paid to him and others for Expenditures Previous to the Year 1778 and the Amount of the Interest Money of which the principal was also expended at that Time be deducted the remaining Sum will be considerably less than thirty Millions.

I must entreat of you Sir that all the Stores may be forwarded from Brest as soon as possible and I shall hope that the Court will take Measures to afford you the necessary Transports so as that they may come under proper Convoy. As to the Cargo of the Ship Marquis de la fayette it is true that some of it has arrived here thro' neutral Ports but it is equally true that Money was necessary to purchase it and that money is quite as scarce as any other Article. If however all the Cargo of that Ship was like

5. La Luzerne had informed Morris of the loan in mid-April: Morris to BF, April 17, above. BF's March 4 and 9 letters mentioning it probably arrived in late May: Morris to BF, May 23 (first letter), above.

some which I did procure the taking of her has been no great loss for the Cloathing was too small to go on Men's Backs. The Goods from Holland we still most anxiously expect Would to God that they had never been purchased— Mr. Gillon however is at Length arrived and I hope we shall have those Matters in which he was concerned brought to some kind of Settlement.

I have the Honor to be with perfect Esteem and Respect Sir your most obedient and humble Servant ROBT MORRIS

His Excellency Benjm. Franklin Esqr Minister Plenipotentiary at the Court of Versailles

Endorsed: answerd Oct. 14. / Office of Finance July 1. 1782

From Jean de Neufville & fils

LS: American Philosophical Society

Sir   Amsterdam July 1st 1782
By the earliest opportunity after the arrival of the Brig Fire-brand Capn. Caleb Trowbridge[6] from Boston in forty eight days. We have the honor of forwarding to your Excelly. the Letters we received to your address, we had not an opportunity of acknowledging with propriety the Letter we were favoured with, in date of 4 Feby.[7] untill all the accounts relative to the business it is upon, were furnished to the Honble Mr. Barclay, as that is now the case, and Said Gentleman informs us, he has wrote you, for the permission of paying us the ballance due to us, being satisfied of the Justice of our demands,[8] persuaded of not finding less from your Excelly. we shall be happy to see that business finally settled, by your remitting us, or permitting us to draw, at the time that shall be most convenient to your Excelly. for the Ballance.

Our Senior Mr J..D.N..[9] after having so long unremittedly

6. XXXV, 564n.

7. XXXVI, 534.

8. Barclay forwarded the accounts with his letter of June 17, above, but did not endorse the firm's claims.

9. Jean de Neufville. He emigrated to the United States in 1785 and died

laboured for the common cause with the Satisfaction of having accellerated by it, the wished for event, has thought his task fulfilled: and his Services either of no further use, or no longer wanted, he has therefore taken the resolution of Spending the remainder of his days in easy retirement, out of business, and free from every incumbrance, when his vows for the welfare & prosperity of the Twenty States will not be less fervent, nor the respect lessened, with wch. we have the honor to be Your Excellys. Most Obdt huml Servts   JOHN DE NEUFVILLE SON

His Excellency Doctr. Benjn. Franklin Passy./

Addressed: His Excellency. / Doctor Benjn Franklin / Minister plenipoty. at the court of Versailles / Passy

Notation: De Neufville & Son July 1st. 1782

From Parish & Thomson[1]

ALS: Historical Society of Pennsylvania

Sir   Hamburg 1 July 1782
    We had the honour to receive in Course your Letter of the 19 April,[2] & agreeable to the Contents, our Bills on Mr. Jay have all been paid in Paris by your Excellency's orders.[3]
    As it will always give us singular Pleasure to render You

---

in Albany in 1796: *NNBW*, VIII, 1211–14; Winslow C. Watson, ed., *Men and Times of the Revolution; or, Memoirs of Elkanah Watson* (New York, 1856), pp. 267–8. The firm was continued by his son Leendert: JW to Jean de Neufville & fils, June 16, 1782 (Yale University Library).

    1. For whom see XXXV, 404n. This is the last extant letter in their correspondence.

    2. Not found.

    3. BF had honored a number of bills drawn on Jay during the previous months: Account XXVII (XXXII, 4). In an undated letter, Henry Grand wrote BF that he was taking "the liberty to return him his order concerning Mr. Jay's acceptences, against which he will be so Kind as to exchange his approbation to the list of Bills sent by Mess Parish & Thomson to which there is to be added the charges claimed by them, according to their here inclosed Letter, which Mr. franklin is begged to return when done with." APS.

agreeable Services, we beg leave to inform You that we have at present a remarkably fine sailing American Vessel just now at No. Faro,[4] from whence she proceeds to Philda.—if you have any Letters to forward, they will be in time to go out from hence with our Dispatches to Faro in about three weeks hence.

We have the honour to be very respectfully, Honoured Sir Your most obedient, & most humble Servants

PARISH & THOMSON

The Honourable Benjamin Franklin Esqe &c, &c, &c Passy

To Henry Laurens

LS:[5] South Carolina Historical Society

Sir, Passy, July 2. 1782.

I received the Letter you did me the honour of writing to me from Lyon the 24th. past.

I wonder a little at Mr. Adams not acquainting you whether your Name was in the Commission or not. I begin to suspect from various Circumstances that the British Ministry elated perhaps too much by the Success of Admiral Rodney, are not in earnest to treat immediately, but rather wish Delay. They seem to hope that farther Success may enable them to treat more advantageously; or, as some suppose, that certain Propositions to be made to Congress by General Carleton, may render a Treaty here with us unnecessary. A little bad News, which it is possible they may yet receive from the same quarter, will contribute to set them right; and then we may enter seriously upon the Treaty; otherwise I conjecture it may not take Place till another Campaign. Mr. Jay is arrived here. M. Grenville & Mr. Oswald continue here: Mr. Oswald has yet received no Commission; & that of Mr. Grenville does not very clearly comprehend us according to British Ideas, therefore requires Explication. When I know more you shall have farther Information.

---

4. The Faeroe Islands, located between the Shetland Islands and Iceland, were part of the kingdom of Denmark.

5. In L'Air de Lamotte's hand, except for the last seven words of the complimentary close, which are in BF's hand.

Not having an immediate answer to what I wrote you concerning the Absolution of Lord Cornwallis's Parole,[6] and Major Ross coming over hither from him to press it; I gave him the Discharge you desired. Inclos'd I send you a Copy.— I hear it has proved satisfactory to him; I hope it will be so to you.

I cannot wish you to quit the fine Climate you are in, and the comfortable Society of your Brothers Family and your Children, 'till your Health is fully established; Please to present my respectful Compliments to your eldest Daughter, with whom I have had some Correspondence;[7] and believe me to be, with great Esteem, Sir, Your most obedient and most humble Servant

B FRANKLIN

Honble. Henry Laurens Esqe.

Addressed: Honble. / Henry Lawrens Esqr / &ca &ca / Vigan en Cevennes.

Endorsed: Doctr Franklin 2d July 1782 Recd 12th. Answ'd. 7th Augt.

From Bethia Alexander   ALS: University of Pennsylvania Library

St: Germain Ce 3 Juillet [1782]

Je vois bien, mon cher Docteur, qu'il faut renoncer a notre partie de Marly,[8] ou plutôt y substituer un diner chez vous—ce n'etoit pas un beau Jardin que nous desirions voir mais nos amis et Je m'imagine que nous les trouverons tous réunis a Passy— tout ce qui me chagrine c'est que mon Pere à votre priere et à celle de Mad: Helvetius avoit engagé ses deux amis ici Messrs: de Breuil et Pechmeja d'etre de notre partie et à moins que vous ne les en-

6. Above, May 25.
7. For BF's correspondence with Martha Laurens see XXXIV, 578–9; XXXVI, 52–5, 326–8, 427, 443.
8. Described in her letter of [June 27], above. A meeting with Thomas Grenville may have caused BF to withdraw from the outing to Marly planned for July 1; see BF's entry of July 1 in his journal of the peace negotiations.

gagiez a nous accompagner chez vous ils auront quelques droits de croire que nous nous sommes moqués d'eux— Nous aurons prie sur nous mes Soeurs et moi de les en prier sans vous en parler bien sure de notre pardon si nous n'avions été certain que ne pouvons [pouvant] pas dire que c'etoit de votre part on nous auroit refusé; tout ira bien pourvu que vous m'ecriviez de faire mes efforts pour vous les amener; ils seront enchantés d'aller [*chez*] vous dès l'instant qu'ils croiront ne vous pas etre importun.—
J'ai eu bien envie de lire à la Dame aux cheminées votre reponse à ses questions,[9] mais cette Dame n'entendes pas raillerie, elle se croiroit offensée et Je me serois fait une querelle pour la vie. Repondez donc Je vous prie à ces demandes.

Adieu mon cher Docteur— J'ai envie de vous assurer que Je vous aime tendrement mais il me semble que J'aurois encore plus du plaisir a vous le dire que de vous l'ecrire. Je l'aisse donc toutes ces protestations au Jour ou Je pourrois vous assurer de mes Sentimens et vous embrasser toute à mon aise.

Votre   B: ALEXANDER

Repondez moi toute de suite Je vous prie et fixé si cela se peut le Jour ou nous irons chez nous [*vous*]— Je voudrois bien que ce fût Lundy.

Addressed: A Monsieur / Monsieur Franklin / A Passy / prés / Paris

Endorsed: Miss Alexander

From Richard Bache   ALS: Historical Society of Pennsylvania

Dr. Sir—   Philada. 3d. July 1782.

Hearing this Moment of an opportunity for France, from an Eastern port[1]—I inclose you Mr. R Morris' Draft on Mons. Grand a 60 days for Lrs. 3200 Livres, being Moneys recd. from Christian Scheinder of German Town say £200. this Curry. on

9. Which he had written in his letter to Bethia Alexander of June 24, above.
1. Boston: RB to BF, July 23, below.

acct. of the Family in Germany, who sent me a power of Attorney to receive a Legacy for them from him, whose name I cannot now recollect, & being from home, cannot recur to— I paid 6/3 [6 s., 3 p.] for 5 Livres Tournois.—² The Family is well— I am in haste but great Affection D. Sir Yours &c   R BACHE

Dr. Franklin

Addressed: His Excellency / Dr. Benjn. Franklin / Minister Plenipoy. from the / United States of N. America / at Passy.

Notation: Mr. Bache Phila. 3. July 1782.

From David Jones *et al.*   L: American Philosophical Society

[after July 3, 1782?]³

Les sieurs David Jones, Williams Duglos, Benjamin hyland⁴ James Trompkins, Moriss. Wainwrigth, Mulachy Dodge, Benjamin Davis Williams Peyton et Joseph Crusman tous citoyens des Etats unis de L'Amerique

Ont Lhonneur de reclamer votre protection bienfaisante auprès de son altesse Serenissime Monseigneur Le Duc de Penthievre Amiral de france pour appuier la demande en mainlevée quils ont présentée à Ce prince du Brigantin Le London que les exposans avoient pris sur les Anglais et quils avoient Conduit dans le port de paix Ile St Domingue.

Pour prouver a Votre Excellence que la Confiscation de Ce brigantin prononcée au proffit de Monsieur L'Amiral le 3 juillet 1781 est Contraire aux ordonnances de la Marine de france et a

---

2. The draft, dated July 3, calls for the sum to be paid to RB or at his order. RB added "Pay the Contents to Dr. Benjn. Franklin on Order" and signed his name. See also *Morris Papers*, V, 529. Schneider was transferring money to Widow Höklin of Ebingen; see his letter of April 3.

3. The year is either 1781 or 1782; the memorial begins by citing the first but shifts halfway through to the second. Having been unable to locate any other references to the mutiny described here or the subsequent Admiralty decision, we speculate that the author corrected himself as he wrote.

4. Possibly the same man who received financial assistance from BF in 1780: XXXII, 7.

la decision textuelle du Congrès Americain, Les Exposans se trouvent forcés d'entrer dans quelques détails.

Le hazard les fit embarquer en 1781 au Port de la Jamaïque, en qualité de Matelôts, sur le Brigantin *Le London* armé de 12 canons, monté de 49 hommes dequipage et chargé de Sucres. Dans la traversée les Exposans reconnurent que Le Capitaine et six hommes de L'Equipage étoient Anglais. Linterêt de leur patrie, Le droit de la guerre, et la superiorité que le nombre des Exposans donnoit sur leurs ennemis, leur firent prendre la résolution de s'emparer du Capitaine, du Brigantin, et des anglois à bord.

Le 18 juin 1781 les exposans, se trouvant au vent du môle St. Nicolas éxécuterent leur resolution, se saisirent du Capitaine et conduisirent le Brigantin au port de Paix, où le sieur Giffort Americain et second Capitaine sur le dit Navire fit sa déclaration, Conformément aux ordonnances.

Mais Les officiers de L'amirauté de Ce port, non seulement saisirent le Brigantin et touttes les Marchandises dont il étoit chargé, mais même en prononcerent la Confiscation au proffit de M. L'amiral par le Jugement du 3 juillet 1782.

Votre Excellence a deja pressenti que Cette Confiscation est Contraire à tous les principes connus sur Cette matiére, et notemment à la décision donnée par le Congrès americain le 14. 8bre. 1777 résolution[5] "est il dit que tout vaisseau et Cargaison appartenant à un sujet britannique quelconque mené dans un port ou *havre de quelques états unis par le maître d'Equipage ou mariniers Seront réputés de bonne prise et le produit sera divisé entre les Capteurs dans la même proportion que sils avoient été pris par un vaisseau de guerre Continental.*"

Le Droit de la guerre qui autorisait les représailles, la decision, dont on vient de rapporter les expressions, la liberté indéfiniment donnée aux Américains *de disposer des prises ennemies, dans les ports de france, ainsi quils l'auroient fait dans leurs propres ports*[6] tout invitoit Les exposans *Américains* à se saisir du

---

5. *JCC*, IX, 802.

6. A misquotation of Article VIII of the regulations governing prizes issued by the French government. The draft regulations were sent to the American Commissioners and went into effect on Sept. 27, 1778: XXVII, 260, 648; Wharton, *Diplomatic Correspondence*, II, 686.

Brigantin *Le London* appartenant à un armateur Anglais leur *ennemi*, commandé par un Capitaine Anglais aussi leur *ennemi*. Ils devoient S'attendre à partager, dans le port de Paix des proffits que les loix americaines leur accordoient. Ils ont Cependant été frustrés de leur Espoir par la sentence du 3 juillet 1782.

Les Suplians ne se permettront sur les dispositions de Cette sentence aucune espèce de réflexion. Ils aiment à Croire que, si, on leur a enlevé Ce quils ont gagné au péril de leur vie et de leur liberté C'est parceque les Juges de L'Amirauté ont trop sévérement suivi la loi, qui prononce la Confiscation de tout vaisseau qui ne seroit pas muni d'une Commission en guerre.[7]

Mais les Exposans observent que dans Lespèce Ce deffaut de Réprésentation de la Commission en guerre, ne peut leur être opposé. Ils Sont Sujets des Etats Unis. Le hazard leur avoit donné de l'emploi Sur un vaisseau de leur ennemi. L'occasion, les loix Americaines et le droit de la guerre leur permettoient de se Saisir de leur ennemi et d'affaiblir les moyens de Nuire à L'ami commun: Ces loix, pour ainsi dire, leur dictoient à la lettre Ce quils ont si heureusement éxécuté. Ils devoient donc S'attendre à trouver dans les port de france la même protection quils auroient trouvée dans les ports de leur republique. Cest de la part des officiers de LAmirauté de Paix avoir donné aux ordonnances de la Marine francoise une extension quelles n'ont pas et quelles n'ont jamais pu avoir, puis quil etoit impossible aux exposans d'etre muni d'une Commission en guerre. Ainsi donc, loin d'etre puni de leur heureuse témérité par la Privation des proffits quils auroient retirés de leur prise, ils auroient du trouvé des protecteurs dans les Juges qui les ont si mal à propos Condamné.

Les Exposans remplis de Confiance en la justice de Monseigneur L'Amiral viennent de lui présenter leurs Suplications dans un mémoire quils ont fait passer dans les bureaux de L'Amirauté. Ils demandent la mainlevée du Brigantin, Ses aggrès apparans et Marchandises. Ils Croient, dans, Cette position, devoir Implorer votre protection bienfaisante. Ils Sollicitent en france

---

7. The same court had rendered a different decision when a group of captured American sailors had taken control of a British-owned vessel in Jamaica and carried it into Môle Saint Nicolas in July, 1779: Smith, *Letters*, XIV, 272n.

léxécution des Loix Americaines— Quel appui plus Certain pourroient ils Emploier que Celui de Votre Excellence, Le Legislateur, Lorgane et le soutien de Ces mêmes loix. Vous ne dedaignerés point de proteger Les exposans, en Soutenant leurs droits auprès de Monseigneur LAmiral. Ils ne cesseront de faire des Vœux pour la Conservation des jours du Bienfaiteur et du restaurateur de la liberté de Leur patrie./.

From Robert R. Livingston

LS: University of Pennsylvania Library; AL (draft): New-York Historical Society; transcript:[8] National Archives

Dear Sir   Philadelphia 5th. July 1782.

I have the honor to transmit you a letter from the United States in Congress to his most Christian Majesty, together with a copy for your perusal,[9] I also enclose a Resolution of Congress on the subject of Mr Lee's demands,[1] which you will see carried into effect—nothing of moment has occured, since I last wrote you, it is very long since we have heard from Europe— We wait for your dispatches with some degree of impatience— I hope they will be sufficiently particular to answer our expectations.

I have the honor to be Sir with great Respect & Esteem your most obedt. humble Servant   ROBT. R LIVINGSTON

---

8. Which notes that the first copy was delivered to La Luzerne, the duplicate was carried from Baltimore by the ship *Favourite*, the triplicate by the ship *Washington*, and the quadruplicate by the ship *Queen of France*.

9. A June 13 letter from Congress to the King expressing condolences on the death of his aunt (*JCC*, XXII, 327–8), a copy of which is with BF's papers at the APS. Sophie-Philippine-Elisabeth-Justine of France (b. 1734), a sister of the King's father, died in early March: *Dictionnaire de la noblesse*, VIII, 593; Bachaumont, *Mémoires secrets*, XX, 110.

1. The enclosure was the congressional resolution of July 2, "That the Secretary for foreign affairs inform Mr. William Lee, that he apply for payment of the monies due to him to Mr. Benjamin Franklin" (*JCC*, XXII, 369). The previous September, Congress ordered BF to pay Lee 42,189 *l.t.* plus interest (XXXVI, 155, and see *Morris Papers*, III, 291n; Smith, *Letters*, XVIII, 63n), but BF answered that he did not know where to find Lee: BF to Morris, March 30, above.

His Excellency Benjn. Franklin

No. 14. *3plicate*

Notation: Mr Franklin No. 14. 3plicate

Endorsed: No 14. Mr Secry. Livingston July 5. 1782 Wm Lee's Affair

From Robert Morris[2]

LS: American Philosophical Society; copy: Library of Congress

Sir.   Office of Finance 5th July 1782

I enclose to you the form of an acknowledgement of our Debt to the Court of France which I desire you would Seal and execute,[3] After having ascertained the Amount of the Debt, and that you will send Copies thereof thro the Office of foreign Affairs to Congress; as well as inform me of the Amount of the Debt and the Time of Settlement.

I have the Honor to be with great Respect Your most Obedient and humble Servant   ROBT. MORRIS

Benjamin Franklin Esqr. minister plenipotentiary of the United States at the Court of Versailles

Endorsed: Office de Finance   July 5. 1782   Acct with France how to be attested.—

2. Morris composed this letter and its enclosure to satisfy La Luzerne that BF was authorized to settle America's debt. Morris sent both items to the chevalier on July 5, requesting that they be forwarded: *Morris Papers,* v, 533, 536.

3. The one-page form confirmed the "full Powers and Authorities" given the signatory and specified that the payment schedule and interest were to be mutually determined by the King and America. For the full text see *Morris Papers,* v, 534–5.

From James Moylan

ALS: American Philosophical Society

Honord Sir   L'Orient 5th. July 1782

I received in course the Letter wch. Mr. Will: Franklin honor'd me with, inclosing your condemnation of the prize Mary of London captur'd by the privateer Revolution of Salem.[4] I now beg leave to trouble you with the procedure of the prize st. Pierre of st. Andere [Santander] recaptured by the Ship Carolina Cap: Newell of Philadelphia after being four days in the Enemys possission, on wch. I request your judgement to enable me to proceed in her sale &ca. as the Law directs.[5]

I have the honor to be with the utmost respect & esteem Honord Sir Your most obt hle st.   JAMES MOYLAN

The Honorable B. Franklin Esqr. American Plenepotentiary Minister at the Court of Versailles

Notation: James Moylan 5. Juillet 1782.

From Thomas Pownall

ALS: American Philosophical Society

Dear Sir.   Richmond hill July 5. 1782.

I have by my friend Mr Hobart sent You a Printed Copy of the Three Memorials which I published on the Subject of America, one addressed to the Souvereigns of Europe—& two oth-

---

4. BF's certificate condemning the *Mary*, dated June 14 and addressed to the Judges of the Admiralty of Vannes, indicates that she was captured on April 22. This certificate is from the second printing of the form described in XXX, 360–1. Since the publication of vol. 30 we have discovered ten more examples of that second printing, including this one, in the Archives départementales de Morbihan.

5. BF sent a certificate to the Judges of the Admiralty of Vannes condemning the *St. Pierre* on July 15. Identical in wording to the printed certificates, this one was written by L'Air de Lamotte and signed by BF: Archives départementales de Morbihan. For Thomas Newell see Claghorn, *Naval Officers*, p. 219.

BF issued another printed prize certificate to the Judges of the Admiralty of Vannes on July 21 for the *Auguste*, bound from Quimper to Nantes, taken first by a British privateer and recaptured on June 22 by the *Hamburg*, Capt. George Blackwell: Archives départementales de Morbihan.

ers addressd to the Souvereign of Gr Brittain.[6] And I beg your acceptance of them.

I hope you received my Letter of May 13 1782 forwarded by Mr Bridgen as also the Package containing 187 printed Copies of my Topographical Description of America with the Map. Which I sent as You desired for the Widow Barry & which Mr Bridgen was so good to forward for me by way of Ostend directed to Mr Bowen.

As it is possible You may see Mr Hobart He can inform you from me as well as of his own knowledge of the steps we took upon the ground of Your Communications to him & me "That there were Persons Authorised to treat of Peace, & that Such Persons were willing to give to reasonable measures taken to that End, every assistance in their power." He can inform you also of the circumstances which attended those Steps; & of the Effect *which they missed in the direct line;* as of the Effect *they actually had in an oblique one.* As from the beginning of this matter of trying to bring on negotiation for Peace I considered him as joined with me in our endeavors; so I have given to him a Memorandum which I made on the course of this Buisness.[7] He will communicate to You every thing which it is not improper for a Man of honor to communicate to the Minister of a People at warr with us: Nor will he abstain from communicating anything which that Minister, wishing Peace to our Country, ought to be apprized of, respecting the Effect of his friendly offerrs. He will do every thing which a Man of honor ought to do; & He will do nothing which a Man of honor ought not to do.

---

6. Presumably George Hobart forwarded Pownall's *A Memorial, Most Humbly Addressed to the Sovereigns of Europe, on the Present State of Affairs, between the Old and New World* (London, 1780), as well as his *Two Memorials . . .* (London, 1782), addressed to George III. Pownall may have already sent the first memorial the preceding fall; see xxxv, 627. BF owned two copies of it. The first, inscribed "To His Excellency Benjamin Franklin Esq LLD Minister Plenipotentiary From the United States of America Q D C—D, D, D, T Pownall," is at the APS; the second, bound with other tracts in a volume with a table of contents written by BF, is at the Library of Congress: Edwin Wolf 2nd, unpublished catalogue of books and pamphlets in BF's library (xxxvi, 331n).

7. The memorandum, dated July 2, is printed in WTF, *Memoirs,* ii, 381–5. For the matter as a whole see Pownall to BF, May 13.

I have desired him to give You a paper of Quæries respecting the *modes* & *terms* of Settling in America which People of this old world & of the old Country may in future be admitted to & receive. I am, not only for my friends, but personally, interested to gain information on that head—& as I wish that which will not deceive them or myself I apply to you.[8]

May God send Peace on Earth. I hope amongst the general blessings it will bring—; It will restore me to the communications & enjoyment of my old & long valued friendship with You. May You live to see, & have health to enjoy, the Blessings which, I hope, it may please God, to make you the Instrument of communicating to Mankind.

I am Dr Sir Yr friend & very humble Sert   T POWNALL

Notation: T Pownall 5 Jully 82

To Vergennes   ALS: Archives du Ministère des affaires étrangères

Sir,   Passy, July 6. 1782.

The State of Maryland being the last that acceded to the Confederation, & therefore esteemed by some the least hearty in the Cause, your Excellency may judge, by the Sentiments of the General Assembly of that State, as express'd in their Resolutions which I have the honour to send you enclos'd,[9] what Reception any Propositions made by General Carleton for a separate Treaty in America, are likely to meet with from Congress.

I am, with great Respect, Your Excellency's most obedient and most humble Servant   B FRANKLIN

M. le Comte de Vergennes.

Endorsed: M. franklin

---

8. The paper, in Pownall's hand and filed with the present letter, includes questions about the value of improved lands in several regions, the expense of settlement, and the necessary stock and particulars that should be brought over. Pownall also inquires if sufficient improved tracts could be purchased to accommodate a company of newcomers, and on what terms such a party would be admitted.

9. The May 15 resolution which Livingston had sent BF with his May 22 letter, above. A copy is at the AAE.

From the Comtesse de Benyowzky[1]

ALS: Historical Society of Pennsylvania

Monsieur   Passy ce 6 Juillet 1782

Pardon si je prend La liberté de vous ecrire, je vien d'apren-
dre que un nomé Graubner bourgois de paris, a eté ché vous
Monsieur, pour vous importuner par a port [par rapport] une
Lettre de change, de mon mary Le quelle a eté doné pour de l'an-
ciene déte de mon bau frére qui a été au Service du Congré,[2] je
vous demande mille excuse a La place de mon mary, qui vous a
ocasioné L'importunité, je cependant deja prevenu Le Sieur
Graubner que, Si tau [sitôt] j'en recois de mes revenu je Solderais
l'engament de mon mary, cette méme home a tenu de propos tres
Disgracieux pour moi a paris devants mes amis, ou il disait aussy,
que vous Monsieur Lui avé dit, que je dois nullement attendre,
dé L'argent ou de secours de L'amerique de mon mary, puisque
il n'est pas au Service du Congré. Permete moi Monsieur vous
avec un Caractere franche et juste ne trouvé pas mauvais q'une
ame Sensible ce Justifie au pres de vous, premierment, je n'attend point de Secours de mon mary, je Lui enverais plus tau, que
d'en récévoire, parcque un homme ne vas pas Si Loin avec L'e-
conomie q'une femme. A L'égard de L'emplois Monsieur, je
vous a vou que [j'ai] cru tout bonement que mon mary a Le bonheur de Servire au Congré, pour etre utile a Leurs defense avec
Son Sens, puisque vous mème vous m'avé fait Lhoneur de me dir
L'hiver passé que mon mary est allé Combattre La Liberté, cela
etait un raison de plus pour moi de Le Croire, et je me Suis glo-
rifié, dé dévenir une americaine;[3] depuis Monsieur je vous e toujours regarder Comme mon protecteur. Ne mé dedaigné pas
Monsieur de mé doner des eclairsisment Sur Le Sort de mon
mary, Si vous avé de nouvelle de L'amerique, a L'egard de son

---

1. The comtesse and her two young daughters met BF shortly before her
husband departed for America in January: XXXVI, 292, 355; Eufrosina
Dvoichenko-Markov, "Benjamin Franklin and Count M. A. Benyowski,"
APS *Proc.*, XCIX (1955), 410.

2. Benyowzky's brother Francis: Stephen Gál, *Hungary and the Anglo-
Saxon World* (Budapest, 1943), pp. 23–4.

3. For her husband's attempts to serve the cause of American liberty see
XXXVI, 228n.

emplois, cette un grand hardiesse de ma part j'en Convien, de vous mander cela, mais come je n'aspire que pour Le bonheur de mon mary et mes enfants, je me Console de votres indulgence.

Jay L'honeur D'etres Monsieur Votres tres humble et tres obeisante Servante COMTESSE DE BENYOWZKY

Notation: Beniousky, 6 Juillet 1782.

From Vergennes

ALS: Library of Congress

Versailles Le 6. juillet 1782

Je recois Monsieur, La Lettre de ce jour dont vous mavés honoré et La resolution de L'Etat de mary Land que vous aves bien voulu me Communiquér. Je l'ai lue avec Le plus grand plaisir et je la garde pour La montrér au Roi qui y trouvera La conviction de la Confiance quil a dans La fidelité de ses alliés Les Etats unis. Il faut Esperér qu'n langage aussi affirmatif detrompera une bonne fois pour toutes Le ministere anglois de lEspoir de divisér des alliés qui sont unis par Le Sentiment de lhonneur autant et plus que par celui de linterest.

Jai lhonneur dEtre avec un sincere attachement Monsieur, Votre tres humble et tres obeissant serviteur DE VERGENNES

To James Hutton

AL (draft): Library of Congress

My old and dear Friend   Passy, July 7. 1782

A Letter written by you to M. Bertin, Ministre d'Etat,[4] containing an Account of the abominable Murders committed by some of the frontier People on the poor Moravian Indians, has given me infinite Pain and Vexation.[5] The Dispensations of

4. Bertin had interceded with BF in Hutton's most recent request for a passport: XXXVI, 683, 691–2.

5. Hutton must have sent Bertin the text that was copied for BF by L'Air de Lamotte and entitled "American News From the New York Papers" (Library of Congress). It is a transcription of an article from the *New York Gazette and Weekly Mercury,* issue of April 29, 1782, detailing the slaughter by American frontiersmen of members of three congregations of Moravian

Providence in this World puzzle my weak Reason. I cannot comprehend why cruel Men should have been permitted thus to destroy their Fellow Creatures. Some of the Indians may be suppos'd to have committed Sins, but one cannot think the little Children had committed any worthy of Death. Why has a single Man in England, who happens to love Blood, and to hate Americans; been permitted to gratify that bad Temper, by hiring German Murderers, and joining them with his own, to destroy in a continued Course of bloody Years, near 100,000 human Creatures, many of them possessed of useful Talents, Virtues and Abilities to which he has no Pretension! It is he who has furnished the Savages with Hatchets and Scalping Knives, and engages them to fall upon our defenceless Farmers, and murder them with their Wives and Children paying for their Scalps, of which the Account kept already amounts as I have heard, to near *two Thousand*. Perhaps the People of the Frontier exasperated by the Cruelties of the Indians have in their [*torn*] been induced to kill all Indians that fall[6] into their Hands, without Distinction, so that even these horrid Murders of our poor Moravians may be laid to his Charge; And yet this Man lives, enjoys all the good Things this World can afford, and is surrounded by Flatterers, who keep even his Conscience quiet, by telling him he is the best of Princes! I wonder at this, but I cannot therefore part with the comfortable Belief of a divine Providence; and the more I see the Impossibility, from the number & Extent of his

---

Indians near the Muskingum River. Some 95 Indians, half of them women and children, were scalped and murdered. Elated by their success, the Americans vowed to send another excursion as far as the Sandusky River. A final paragraph of commentary (presumably Hutton's) reported that this information had been confirmed. For an account of the massacre, which occurred on March 7, and an analysis of its causes see Leonard Sadosky, "Rethinking the Gnadenhutten Massacre: the Contest for Power in the Public World of the Revolutionary Pennsylvania Frontier," in David C. Skaggs and Larry L. Nelson, *The Sixty Years' War for the Great Lakes, 1754–1814* (East Lansing, Mich., 2001), pp. 187–213.

At this point in the letter BF drafted but crossed out, "You know I formerly took Arms and rais'd the City in their Protection, because I believed them to be innocent and good People." See XI, 42–69.

6. We supply these three words, now torn away from the bottom of a page, from WTF, *Memoirs*, II, 38.

Crimes of giving equivalent Punishment to a wicked Man in this Life, the more I am convinc'd of a future State, in which all that here appears to be wrong shall be set right, all that is crooked made straight. In this Faith let you & I, my dear Friend, comfort ourselves. It is the only Comfort in the present dark Scene of Things, that is allow'd us.——

I shall not fail to write to the Government of America urging that effectual Care may be taken to protect & save the Remainder of those unhappy People.[7]

Since writing the above, I have received a Philadelphia Paper, containing some Account of the same horrid Transaction, a little different, and some Circumstances alledged as Excuses or Palliations, but extreamly weak & insufficient. I send it to you inclos'd.[8]

With great and sincere Esteem, I am ever, my dear Friend Yours most affectionately

Franklin and Chaumont: Agreement for Arbitration by Grand and Dangirard[9]

DS: Archives Nationales, Paris; D:[1] American Philosophical Society

Compromis 7 Juillet 1782.

Aujourdhui sont comparus pardevant les Conseillers du Roi Notaires au Chatelet de Paris Soussignés

S.E. Benjamin franklin Ministre plenipotentiaire des Etats unis de l'Amerique Septentrionale, demeurant à Passy près Paris, d'une part

7. See BF to Livingston, Aug. 12.

8. This must have been the *Pa. Evening Post, and Public Advertiser,* issue of April 16, which reported the event as revenge for the Indians having attacked white settlers. See Hutton's reply, July 23, based on this article. BF evidently also enclosed his "Supplement to the Boston Independent Chronicle," which Hutton acknowledged.

9. Either Jean-Baptiste-François (XXVII, 52n) or his older brother Louis-Jacques: Lüthy, *Banque protestante,* II, 808. At this time their firm was established at Paris as Dangirard frères: XXXVI, 617n; *Almanach royale* for 1782, p. 467.

1. In the same hand as the DS, bearing the same stamped seals, and signed by the two notaries. BF endorsed it "July 7. 1782".

Et M. Jacques Donatien Le Ray de Chaumont, demeurant pareillement à Passy près Paris, d'autre part.

Lesquels ont dit que pour terminer à l'amiable les difficultés qui Se Sont elevées entr'eux lors de la liquidation et de l'apurement des comptes courants qu'ils se doivent et de leurs prétentions respectives ils Sont convenus d'en passer par l'avis et le jugement de Mrs. Grand et Dangirard Banquiers à Paris, qu'ils ont choisi pour arbitres et amiables compositeurs; En conséquence les d. srs. Comparants ont par ces presentes donné respectivement pouvoir aux d. srs. Grand et Dangirard de juger et terminer leurs d. differend et liquider leurs prétentions reciproques, fixer les reliquats actifs et passifs des d. comptes courants, déterminer et arrêter le quantum de ce que l'un des d. srs. comparants Se trouvera définitivement devoir à l'autre, le tout Sur les nottes, pieces, registres et renseignements que les d. srs. Comparants remettront incessamment en mains des d. srs. Arbitres, a fin que ces derniers puissent donner leur avis et jugement dans trois mois de ce jour au plus tard.

Dans le cas ou les d. srs. Arbitres Se trouveraient d'avis contraire, les d. Srs. Comparants ont encore donné pouvoir aux d. srs. Grand et Dangirard de choisir et nommer tel Surarbitre qu'ils aviseront pour rendre conjointement le d. jugement au quel les Parties promettent d'acquiescer, comme à un jugement de Cour Souveraine, à peine de dix mille livres d'amende qui demeurera de plein droit encourue au profit de celui qui adherera au jugement contre celui qui refusera d'en exécuter les dispositions, Sans que cette clause puisse être reputée comminatoire, Declarant les d. srs. Comparants que Sans cette clause le present compromis n'eut point eu lieu.

Pour l'execution des presentes les d. srs. Comparants ont fait élection de Domicile en leurs demeures Sus d. Aux quels lieux nonobstant, promettant, Obligeant, Renonçant.

Fait et passé à Passy près Paris en demeures des Parties ou les Notaires soussignés se sont exprès transportés

L'an Mil Sept cent quatre vingt deux le Sept Juillet avant midi; Et ont signé. LERAY DE CHAUMONT
B FRANKLIN
DUNOR
SEMILLIARD

From Pieter Buyck[2]   LS: University of Pennsylvania Library

Son Exellence   Gand 7 Juillet 1782
    Je prends la Respectueuse liberté de Vous envoier cÿ inclus une
lettre que Je Vous prie de faire Remettre à Monsieur Laurens qui
Je Suppose Sera encore à Paris au Cas qu'il Soit deja parti ne
doutant nullement que Vous ne Sachiez ou il est Je Vous supplie
d'avoir La Complaisance de L'enveloper & La lui faire parvenir.
Si en Pareille ou toute autre occasion Je puis Vous être de quelque
utilité, daignez m'honnorer de Vos cheres Commandemens.
    J'espere que ma firme ne Vous est point inconnuë car depuis
Le Commencement & durant la presente guerre J'ai Soutenu
L'amerique audessus de mes forces & ai derechef Pris des fortes
engagemens avec Monsr. Ths. Barclay Consul & Agent General
de Nord Amerique presentement a Amsterdam pour Compte du
Congres.
    J'ai en portefëuille 5 Obligations à la charge de Monsr. Le
Commodore Alx. Gillon Authorisé des Etats de Zud Caroline
par procuration signée de Messieurs Jn. Neiger & Rawlens Lowndes[3] dont 4 de f. 15000. & une de f. 23000. ensble. f. 83000. Court.
d'hollande quel Capital J'ai fourni à Mon dit Sieur Alx. Gillon
pour Etre Remboursé Le 2 fevrier 1782.[4] Sur quoi J'ai fait fond
& me trouve maintenant en Besoin de gros fond pour L'Execution de nouvelles Entreprises. J'ose donc prendre La Confiance de
Vous demender Si Vous ne me pourriez indiquer un moÿen pour en
placer une partie ou bien Si Vous même ne Voudriez point me
faire Le Plaisir d'accepter une ou 2 de Ces obligations pour me Pre-
valoir sur Vous d'une partie du montant a 3 ou 4 mois de datte en
Ce Cas Je Vous Envoirai Celles qu'il Vous plaira de m'ordonner.
    J'Espere que Vous me fera La grace de m'honnorer de Votre
Reponse, ayant celui d'Etre avec le plus profond Respect De Son
Exellence Le plus humble & Plus Obëissant Serviteur
                                            PR. BUYCK

2. For whom see Barclay's April 11 letter.
3. For Rawlins Lowndes see XXVII, 118n.
4. An Augustine Buyck, probably the son of Pieter, took passage aboard
Gillon's frigate, the *South Carolina: James A. Lewis, *Neptune's Militia: the
Frigate* South Carolina *during the American Revolution* (Kent, Ohio, and London, 1999), pp. 36, 46, 124–5.

A Monsieur Doctor franklyn ministre Plenepetre des Etats unis de L'amerique Septentrionnal A Paris

Notation: Buyck 7. Juillet 1782.

From William Carmichael   ALS: American Philosophical Society

Dear Sir   Sn. Ildefenso 8th July 1782

On the 3d. Instant I received from the French Embassador Your Excys. obliging favor of the 11th. Ulto.[5] I should have done myself the honor of answering it the Same day by Mr Clonard the Bearer of Dispatches from the Chevalier de La Luzern & General Rochambeau,[6] Had not my whole Time been taken up in Copying letters to Mr Jay which I was afraid had been detained, as I have not had the pleasure to hear from him, & others for America, which I took this opportunity of sending free from Inspection here to the Ports of France. I am Infinitely obliged to you for the kindness with which you excused the Liberty I took in drawing upon you for my Salary, & the readiness you have shown to make me further Supplies. Your present permission to draw for another Quarter came very apropos and I have availed Myself of it, as you will see by a bill dated the 6th Inst. in favor of Messrs. Drouilhet & Company for 3600 Livres Tournois at 90 days after Date.[7] I spoke to the Marquis de Yranda, who is here at present, He had not recd any Letter from Mr. Grand authorising him to furnish me and he intimated that it was with Difficulty he found cash for the Supply of the Count de Montmorin— The last Emission of bills has increased their Depretiation to 4½ to 5 pr. Ct. and very well informed persons

5. Not found.

6. The bearer almost certainly was Robert Sutton, chevalier de Clonard (*c.* 1744–1788), a naval officer whose frigate, the *Diligente*, had been shipwrecked in February: Asa B. Gardiner, *The Order of the Cincinnati in France* . . . (n.p., 1905), p. 145; Catherine Gaziello, *L'Expédition de Lapérouse* . . . (Paris, 1984), p. 271. He returned to France via Spain, also carrying a letter from Montmorin to Vergennes: Giunta, *Emerging Nation*, I, 454.

7. The bill was honored by Grand on Aug. 7: Account XXVII (XXXII, 4). The banking firm had been used by Jay: XXXIII, 199n.

assure me it will be at 7 or 8 in two months Time. If the War Continues, This country will feel the Distress which we experienced from a paper Medium.

Permit me to thank your Excellency for the Communication you were pleased to make me on the Subject of the proposed Negotiation & your promise of future information— Be persuaded that I shall endeavour to merit your Confidence— A General knowledge on this Subject will enable me to obtain Information of particulars here, which it may not be improper for Your Excy & Mr Jay to be acquainted with— On the 3d Instant the Imperial Embassador & Russian Minister once more proposed the mediation of their Courts, and made proposals for a Congress of Ministers to assist at the Negotiation for a pacification; Alledging, among other Reasons that it would be more honorable for the United States to have their Independence acknowledged Generally, than by a particular Treaty; I have some reason to think this Offer is regarded as Officious—[8] I hear that these Ministers have not yet received an explicit answer, and I am inclined to believe that, as the Count de Kaunitz has not dispatched a courier which he talked of sending away on Saturday last— All the Neutral Ministers here are Dissatisfied with Spain & are Jealous of its being in possession of Gibraltar. Perhaps one Object of the proposed Congress may be to secure the Freedom of their Commerce in the Mediterranean should England Consent to this Cession— What ever Stipulations they may secure favorable for their Commerce, will be equally so to ours— This Affair, the seige of Gibraltar, The Death of one Infanta & the Birth of Another[9] so engage the Attention of Ct. de Florida Blanca & Mr Del Campo that Altho the Former of his own Motion desired me to see him on Saturday last, I was obliged to defer the meeting

8. The imperial (or Austrian) ambassador was Count Joseph Clemens von Kaunitz-Rietberg (XXXIV, 565n), while the Russian minister plenipotentiary was Stepan Stepanovich Zinovyev (*Repertorium der diplomatischen Vertreter*, III, 367). For their proposals see the Montmorin letter cited above.

9. María Luisa Carlota, the four-year-old second daughter of the Prince and Princess of Asturias (the King's son and daughter- in-law), died on July 2. Four days later the princess gave birth to their fourth daughter, María Luisa Vicenta Josefina: Patrick Van Kerrebrouck, *La Maison de Bourbon, 1256–1987* (Villeneuve d'Ascq, 1987), pp. 341–45.

to another Day— The Latter accompanied the Corpse of the Deceased to the Escurial— I send your Excy The last Madrid Gazette which Contains a Journal of the Operations of General Galvez & the consequent promotions.[1] I beg you to present my Compliment to Mr & Mrs Jay & your Grandson & to believe me with Great Respect & Esteem Your Excy. Obliged & Humble Sert   WM. CARMICHAEL

His Exy. B. Franklin

From Dumas

ALS: American Philosophical Society

Monsieur,   Lahaie 8e. Juillet 1782
Je continue de profiter des bontés de S.E.M. l'Ambassadeur, en vous faisant parvenir la présente par le Courier qu'il expédie ce soir.

L'Escadre du Texel est sortie enfin, & sera maîtresse à son tour dans les mers du Nord, à moins que les Anglois ne détachent une portion de la leur, suffisante pour faire rentrer dans la coquille les Hollandois.[2] Dans ce cas ce seroit une diversion des forces Brit. utile à la France & à l'Espagne; tout comme la flotte combinée de celles-ci l'est présentement pour le développement des forces de la Rep.— Vous aurez déjà appris l'interception d'une grande partie du Convoi Britannique parti pour Québec, Hallifax & la Caroline sous l'Escorte de Campbell, par la Flotte combinée.—[3] J'ai appris l'arrivée à Paris de Mr. Jay et de Made.

1. A 20-page supplement to the *Gazette* reported on the successes of Matías de Gálvez (father of Bernardo de Gálvez) in the Gulf of Honduras, including the capture of the island of Roatán; he was promoted to lieutenant general: *Courier de l'Europe*, XII (1782), 65, 81.

2. The Dutch fleet, which sailed on July 7, did dominate the North Sea until its return to the Texel on Aug. 16: Dull, *French Navy*, p. 291.

3. Adm. Luis de Córdoba y Córdoba brought 27 Spanish and five French ships of the line to Cape Ushant, capturing 18 or 19 ships from an outbound British convoy before arriving at the beginning of July. He then was joined by eight more French ships of the line for the remainder of his cruise: Dull, *French Navy*, pp. 281, 290; W. M. James, *The British Navy in Adversity: a Study of the War of American Independence* (London, New York, and To-

son Epouse. J'ignore encore, ce que je voudrois bien savoir, si Mr. Carmichael est aussi à Paris, ou s'il est resté à Madrid.

J'espere que Votre santé est parfaite, & que vous voudrez bien avoir la bonté de m'accuser la réception des diverses Lettres que j'ai eu l'honneur de vous écrire depuis quelquetemps.

J'espere aussi de pouvoir dans peu vous donner la nouvelle agréable du succès de la suite des opérations ici. Je consulterai demain ou après-demain avec un ami sur les meilleurs moyens d'aller en avant pour d'autres choses non moins importantes, sur lesquelles je pourrai m'expliquer d'avantage, à mesure qu'elles prendront de la consistance. Je suis toujours avec le plus respectueux attachement, Monsieur Votre très-humble & très-obéissant serviteur   DUMAS

Passy à S.E.M. Franklin

From David Hartley: Memorandum

Reprinted from William Temple Franklin, ed., *Memoirs of the Life and Writings of Benjamin Franklin* . . . (3 vols., 4to, London, 1817–18), II, 385–6.

July 8, 1782.

To a person who no longer thinks of American dependence, what disadvantage can there be in making its independence a fixed article (whether the treaty succeeds or no) instead of making it a first article of the treaty, and so to depend on the success of that which may miscarry. To a person indeed who looks on it as an evil, and as an evil which there are *yet some hopes* to avoid, it is a rational proceeding to provide for *all* possibilities of realizing those hopes; and the case of the treaty not succeeding is that reserved possibility. Were I treating with an enemy indeed for a barrier town (which I certainly wish to keep or to get something for), nothing I own would be so absurd as to give it up at

---

ronto, 1926), p. 368; *London Courant, Westminster Chronicle, and Daily Advertiser,* July 5. Vice Adm. John Campbell (*DNB*), who had been appointed governor and commander-in-chief in Newfoundland, accompanied the convoy.

starting, as a *fixed* article *before* the treaty, instead of making it the first article *of* a treaty, and dependent on the success of the rest. But I had rather have American independence (for one reason amongst others), because the bolder way of giving it up, will secure a greater certainty of peace, I would then be for giving it up in that bolder way, nay had I some reluctance to American independence, I should still think the smallest probability added of peace, would over-balance the whole value of a mere reserved possibility of dependence, which could only, after all, arise from the failure of the treaty.

From William Lee

ALS and copy: American Philosophical Society; AL (draft): Virginia Historical Society

Sir.   Bruxelles 8th. July 1782.

I am advised that Robt. Morris Esqr. The Superintendant General of Finance for Congress, has directed you to pay me, what is due to me from Congress out of the first money that came into your hands.[4]

I am now to request that you will please to inform me whether you have, or have not recd. such directions from Mr. Morris, & if you have, when I may draw on you for the Money.

A speedy answer will very much oblige me, who has the Honor of being with very high Respect Your Excellencies Most Obedt. & Most Hble Servt.[5]   W: LEE

His Excellency Benjamin Franklin Esq. at Passy.

Addressed: A Son Excellence / Monsieur Le Docteur B. Franklin Ecuyér / a Passy / pres Paris——

---

4. See Livingston to BF, July 5. Arthur Lee, having learned from Robert Morris in March that BF was supposed to pay William Lee, had notified his brother: *Morris Papers*, IV, 400; Ford, *Letters of William Lee*, III, 864–5.

5. Not receiving an answer, Lee sent another copy of this letter on Aug. 20 with a brief note: APS; draft at Va. Hist. Soc. He sent them to the care of Ferdinand Grand.

From Séqueville

Printed form, signed, with MS insertions: American Philosophical Society

Monsieur,   Paris, le   [before July 9, 1782][6]
    Le Roi ne verra point Mardi prochain 9— du mois, Messieurs
les Ambassadeurs et Ministres étrangers.
                    DESEQUEVILLE
                    Secrétaire ordinaire du Roi,
                    à la conduite des Ambassadeurs.

Addressed: a Monsieur / Monsieur francklin Ministre / Plenipte des Etats unis de / L'Amerique Septentrionale / A Passy / Desequeville

To the Continental Congress[7]   LS:[8] Yale University Library

                    Passy, 9th. July 1782.
From the Knowledge I have of Mr Young, by his Conduct while in my Family, writing in the Secretary's Office, and waiting the Arrival of Mr. Lawrens then expected here; I esteem him a Person of Virtue and Merit, and I recommend him and his Account to the Consideration of Congress, not thinking myself authorised to discharge it without their Order; tho' to assist him in his present Occasions, and in returning to America, I have ventured to advance him Three thousand Six hundred Livres.[1]
                    B FRANKLIN

6. Below this line BF wrote "Juillet 82".
7. A statement given to Moses Young.
8. In WTF's hand.
    1. Young had decided to go into partnership with Benjamin Vaughan and move to the Caribbean island of St. Thomas. He came to Paris on July 6 to settle his accounts, and gave BF a statement claiming £567 14 s. 2 p. for his salary as Laurens' secretary from October, 1779 to February, 1782, at £250 per annum. He added a paragraph describing his experiences since leaving Philadelphia with Laurens. After his capture and subsequent escape from Forton Prison he came to Passy; he was employed by BF from Feb. 5 until April 14, 1782, when BF consented to his going to England to rejoin Laurens. Beneath this statement Young copied an extract of Laurens' May 30 letter to the President of Congress recommending payment of his claim (*Laurens Papers*, XV, 524). Laurens himself certified the accuracy of the extract. This

Notations in different hands: Accot. against the United States —
Amsterdam 30th May 1782. / Letters of Moses Young Henry
Laurens Benjamin Franklin Benjamin Vaughan[2]

From Lafayette

Reprinted from William Temple Franklin, ed., *Memoirs of the Life and
Writings of Benjamin Franklin* ... (3 vols., 4to, London 1817–18), II,
386.

Paris, July 9, 1782.

I have the honour to inform you, my dear Sir, that Mr. Grenville's express is arrived this morning by way of Ostend.[3] The
gentleman is gone to Versailles.[4] I fancy he will wait upon you,
and will be much obliged to you, to let me know what your opinion is. I am going to Saint Germain, but if any intelligence comes
to hand will communicate it as soon as possible.[5] I rest respectfully and affectionately, yours, La Fayette.

---

sheet (Young's statement, the extract, and the certification) is filed with the
present letter; a copy in Young's hand is at the APS.

On July 8, BF replied that he did not think he had authorization to pay
Young's salary and complained of his own financial difficulties, particularly
those caused by Alexander Gillon. Because of Laurens' recommendation,
however, he did agree to advance Young £150 (£50 of which Young owed
Laurens) and authorized Grand to pay the amount in French money (3,600
l.t.). Young noted this fact on the bottom of his claim statement. BF told
Young on July 9 that he had been just in time; BF had just received orders
from Robert Morris forbidding salary payments to American ministers and
secretaries: Young to Laurens, July 10 (*Laurens Papers*, XV, 537–40).

2. Young showed BF's recommendation to Benjamin Vaughan, who on
July 19 wrote his own statement immediately below it, affirming that Young's
"frugality has been exemplary, his distress considerable, and his conduct so
meritorious & so perfectly conscientious and discreet, that I [Vaughan] have
intrusted him with the management of a very considerable concern (to the
amount of not a few thousand pounds sterling in money) without any security given on his side."

3. According to Grenville, the courier had arrived the night before. He
carried a letter from Shelburne dated July 5: Giunta, *Emerging Nation*, I, 459.

4. To meet with Vergennes. See BF's response to Lafayette, immediately
below.

5. Lafayette sent a very similar letter to Jay: Morris, *Jay: Peace*, p. 250.

To Lafayette

Reprinted from William Temple Franklin, ed., *Memoirs of the Life and Writings of Benjamin Franklin* . . . (3 vols., 4to, London, 1817–18), II, 386.

In this letter Franklin reports the most important British political development in the course of the peace negotiations, the replacement of Rockingham as prime minister by Shelburne. This permitted Shelburne to take full command of the negotiations.

Rockingham died on July 1. Three days later Shelburne assumed office as first lord of the treasury. On the same day Charles James Fox, frustrated by the cabinet's unwillingness to recognize immediately and unconditionally American independence, resigned as secretary of state for foreign affairs.[6] No one could be certain of the consequences of these developments; it was reported at The Hague that the King insisted that Shelburne oppose "a total unequivocal recognition of the independence of America."[7] Shelburne's first discussion of America after assuming his new office came in the House of Lords on July 10. In answer to the criticism of Fox, he reportedly said that he continued to believe "that the independence of America would be a dreadful blow to the greatness of this country; and that when it should be established, the sun of England might be said to have set." He was willing to give way, but only to necessity, claiming "that though this country should have received a fatal blow by the independence of America, still there was a determination to improve every opportunity, and to make the most vigorous exertions to prevent the court of France from being in a situation to dictate the terms of peace; the sun of England would set with the loss of America," but he was resolved "to improve the twilight, and to prepare for the rising of England's sun again."[8]

6. Fortescue, *Correspondence of George Third*, VI, 70–5; Cobbett, *Parliamentary History*, XXIII, 138–9; Loren Reid, *Charles James Fox: a Man for the People* (Columbia, Mo., London, and Harlow, Eng., 1969), pp. 146–8. On June 30, Fox had proposed to the cabinet that American independence be granted even without a peace treaty, but the supporters of Shelburne prevailed. When a majority voted that independence be accepted only as part of a treaty, Fox announced his intention to resign (but postponed doing so because of Rockingham's illness): Fitzmaurice, *Life of Shelburne*, II, 148; Fortescue, *Correspondence of George Third*, VI, 68–9; Reid, *Fox*, p. 146.

7. This report, dated only "1782", was among BF's papers at one time: Duane, *Works*, V, 326.

8. Cobbett, *Parliamentary History*, XXIII, 193–4. Although his speech left his intentions unclear, Shelburne (like Fox) apparently agreed with Oswald's

Shelburne thus seemed to be hinting at abandoning his idea of using American independence as a bargaining chip to be surrendered
only if Britain's other enemies accepted a return to the peace conditions of 1763, thereby surrendering their own war gains. Franklin,
however, already considered recognition of American independence
as a *sine qua non* and concerned himself instead with other issues; certainly he was not prepared to offer any concessions in exchange for it.
On July 9, Grenville wrote Shelburne that Franklin "the other day, for
the first time, gave me to understand that America must be to have her
share in the N: Foundland Fishery, & that the limits of Canada would
likewise be a subject for arrangement. He seems much dis-inclined to
an idea he expects to be stated, of going into an examination, for the
mutual compensation of the losses of individuals, insisting, perhaps
with reason, upon the endless detail that would be produced by it; nor
does he cease to give the most decided discouragement to any possible plan of arrangement with America, short of compleat and distinct
independance, in it's fullest sense."[9]

Franklin went into greater detail in a two-hour meeting with Oswald on the morning of July 10.[1] Oswald reported that meeting to
Shelburne as follows:[2]

". . . He took out a minute, & from it read a few hints or articles. Some he
said as necessary for them to insist on; others which he could not say he had
any Orders about, or were not absolutely demanded, & yet such as it would

---

assessment that Britain's only way of obtaining an honorable peace was by
separating America from the French alliance: Andrew Stockley, *Britain and
France at the Birth of America: the European Powers and the Peace Negotiations of 1782–1783* (Exeter, 2001), pp. 39, 221n.

9. Quoted in Giunta, *Emerging Nation*, I, 459–60; Lord John Russell, ed.,
Memorials and Correspondence of Charles James Fox (4 vols., London, 1853–
57), IV, 236–8. Some historians have argued that Shelburne did not use recognition as a bargaining chip; see, for example, Bradford Perkins, "The Peace
of Paris: Patterns and Legacies," in Hoffman and Albert, eds., *Peace and the
Peacemakers*, p. 201. Charles Ritcheson believes that before agreeing to recognize independence Shelburne wished only confirmation that BF was prepared to make a separate peace, and that this confirmation was provided by
the Oswald letter quoted immediately below: C. R. Ritcheson, "The Earl of
Shelburne and Peace with America, 1782–1783: Vision and Reality," *International History Rev.*, V (1983), 339–40.

1. BF invited Oswald to the meeting on July 6; see our annotation of BF to
Oswald, June 27.

2. Oswald to Shelburne, July 10: Giunta, *Emerging Nation*, I, 462–4. See
also Oswald to Thomas Townshend, Sept. 11: *ibid.*, 571, 573.

be advisable for England to offer for the sake of Reconciliation, and her future Interest, Viz:

1st. Of the first Class, *necessary* to be granted. Independence full & complete in every sense to the 13 States & all Troops to be withdrawn from thence.

2d. A settlement of the boundaries of *their* Colonies, & the loyal Colonies.

3d. A Confinement of the Boundaries of Canada, at least to what they were, before the last Act of Parliament, I think in 1774, if not to a still more contracted State, on an ancient footing.

4. A freedom of fishing on the Banks of Newfoundland, & elsewhere, as well for Fish as whales. I own I wonder'd he should have thought it necessary to ask for this priviledge. He did not mention the Leave of drying Fish on shore in Newfoundland, & I said nothing of it. I dont remember any more articles which he said they would insist on, or what he calld necessary for them to be granted.

Then as to the *adviseable* Articles, or such as he would as a Friend recommend to be offer'd by England Viz.

1st. To indemnify many People who had been ruind by Towns burnt & destroy'd. The whole might not exceed the Sum of Five or Six hundred thousand pounds. I was struck at this. However the Dr. said though it was a large Sum, it would not be ill bestow'd; as it would conciliate the Resentment of a multitude of poor Sufferers, who could have no other Remedy, & who without some Relief, would keep up a Spirit of secret Revenge & Animosity for a long time to come, against Great Britain: whereas a voluntary Offer of such Reparation, would diffuse an universal Calm & Conciliation over the whole Country.

2d. Some Sort of Acknowledgment in some public Act, of Parliament or otherwise, of our Error in distressing those countries so much as We had done. A few words of that kind the Dr said, would do more good than People could imagine.

3d. Colony Ships & Trade to be receiv'd & have the same priviledges in Britain & Ireland, as British ships & Trade. I did not ask any Explanation on that head for the present. British & Irish Ships in the Colonies to be in like manner on the same footing with their own ships.

4. Giving up every part of Canada."

Oswald had expected to be given the conditions in writing, but "after some Reflection" Franklin said "he did not much like to give such writing out of his Hands" and then arranged for Oswald to meet with Jay. Franklin also said that he wanted to confer with Jay before giving a definite answer and hinted not only at commercial connections but at an eventual federal union with Britain. He discouraged, however, any hope that Britain might maintain any sovereignty as George III had over Ireland. Franklin thought the "American Affair" could be handled apart from the other negotiations by Britain's issuing a separate commission. He agreed to Oswald's suggestion that the power to grant independence should be included in such a commission. (Oswald thereby hoped that the British government could avoid granting independence before beginning discussions.) Franklin did not believe, however, that any compensation to the Loyalists should be included in a peace treaty, and he would not consider using any revenue from territorial concessions to reimburse their losses. In both this and the refusal to give Oswald anything in writing, he was correcting the mistakes he had made in April when he first proposed that Britain offer Canada.[3]

In his letter to Shelburne, Oswald expressed hopes that it would be possible "to put an End to the American quarrel in a short time." To do so, however, would require that Shelburne overcome his reluctance to recognize American independence. Franklin was in a strong position to wait until Shelburne conceded defeat. He had Congress' unequivocal support, at least on this issue, whereas Shelburne had opposition in Parliament from Fox and his followers. Moreover, one of Franklin's greatest strengths as a diplomat was his willingness to bide his time. Five years earlier he and his fellow commissioners had waited many months to begin serious discussions for an agreement with France until they could negotiate from a position of strength. His fellow commissioner Silas Deane had argued for a more active policy, but Franklin's position prevailed,[4] and finally his patience was rewarded. Apparently, Franklin now was prepared to wait as long as necessary in order to negotiate on his own terms; he warned Robert R. Livingston that it would be prudent to suppose "that even another Campaign may pass before all can be agreed."[5]

Dear Sir,   Passy, July 9, 1782.
    Mr. Grenville has been with me in his return from Versailles. He tells me that Lord Rockingham being dead, Lord Shelburne is appointed first Lord of the Treasury; and that Mr. Fox has re-

---

3. See BF's notes for a conversation with Oswald, [on or before April 19], and BF's journal of the peace negotiations.
4. XXV, 207.
5. Above, June 25.

signed; so that both the Secretaryships are vacant.[6] That his communication to M. de Vergennes, was only that no change was thereby made in the dispositions of that Court for peace, &c., and he expects another courier with fuller instructions in a few days.[7] As soon as I hear more I shall acquaint you with it. I am ever with great respect and affection, your most obedient humble servant,

B. FRANKLIN.

Marquis de la Fayette.

From Benjamin Vaughan

ALS: University of Pennsylvania Library

My dearest sir,   London, July 9th:, 1782.

I beg to introduce to your acquaintance My friend Mr Benjn. Savage, a young Gentn., born in South Carolina.[8] By some accident or other, his friends have chosen the wrong side of the question, though he has relations very warmly contending on the right side. Politics however do not much warp his mind, which is as candid a one almost as I ever knew; and his temper to the full as amiable; abounding in attachment & mildness, with a great deal of spirit at the bottom.

This young gentleman's father, an Israelite without guile, married my father in law's sister;[9] and he himself has been four

6. Shelburne's former post of secretary of state for the home department was not filled officially until July 10, and Fox's as secretary of state for foreign affairs until July 17: Sir F. Maurice Powicke and E. B. Fryde, comps., *Handbook of British Chronology* (2nd ed., London, 1961), pp. 115–16.

7. Grenville's account of the meeting with Vergennes is in his July 9 letter to Shelburne, cited above. In the same letter he asked to be recalled. Vergennes' account is in Doniol, *Histoire*, v, 118; an English translation is in Giunta, *Emerging Nation*, I, 460–1.

8. Savage later became a partner in the S.C. banking and merchant firm of Bird, Savage, & Bird, based in London: Harold C. Syrett *et al.*, eds., *The Papers of Alexander Hamilton* (27 vols., New York and London, 1961–87), XIII, 473–4; XVIII, 282–3, 368; XXVI, 142.

9. Merchant and shipowner John Savage (b. 1715) married Ann Scott Allen in 1749; Benjamin was their son. After her death John married a sister of William Manning, who was Vaughan's father-in-law (XXXVI, 59n): Walter B.

years in Mr Manning's counting house, as he intends pursuing business, though heir to a very pretty fortune.— Mr Manning, who is a very able but strict judge, says that his behavior has been in all respects exemplary, and that he never had any thing to correct or suggest in the whole course of time that he was with him.— I have been a daily & hourly witness to his merits for many months past; and can promise you that he will be very able and powerful in his profession as a merchant, and very *much* respected for the general tenor of his life. There is but one thing wanting to him, which is that you should convert him; but good as he is and sure of being citizen, this is the less necessary.

Mr Savage will tell you my situation here, but no one can tell how much I am, my dearest sir, your ever devoted, affectionate, & obliged, BENJN. VAUGHAN

Notation: B. Vaughan, London July 9. 1782.

From Jonathan Williams, Jr.

ALS: American Philosophical Society; copy: Yale University Library

Dear & hond Sir. Nantes July 9. 1782.

I wrote you the 26 June relative to the affair of Mr Springer & his Comrades at Brest. I since hear the prize is condemned to the admiral which tho' I think an unlawfull proceeding may turn out well enough for the admiral in these Cases always gives up the Prize to the Captors. The proceedings of the admiralty at Brest are I believe according to the Laws of France and French subjects; but they have no business to confiscate an american Prize in whatever manner it may be made by american subjects these Men are amenable to the Laws of their own Country if they have done wrong and you not the admiralty should receive the Money if the Prize deserves Confiscation. I beg you will throw in a Memorial on the subject either to the Marquis de Castries or the Duc de Penthievre & I am confident orders will be

---

Edgar *et al.*, eds., *Biographical Directory of the South Carolina House of Representatives* (4 vols. to date, Columbia, S.C., 1974–), II, 594–6.

given to sell the prize & deliver the amount over to the Captors. For the particular Facts I refer you to my last and its inclosure. I am as ever with perfect Respect most dutifully & affecy Yours

JONA WILLIAMS J

Addressed: His Excellency / Doctor Franklin / at / Passy

Excerpts from Chaumont's Revision of His Account with Franklin

Copy:[1] Historical Society of Pennsylvania

Having agreed on July 7 to submit his accounts to arbitration, Chaumont quickly altered his claim. The account he submitted on July 9 was a revised version of what he had initially given to Franklin, published above under the date of [before April 26]. He dropped items 3, 14, and 15, all of which Grand had ruled against in his report of May 7. The three entries we reproduce, below, constitute additions or alterations to preexisting items. In total, Chaumont now claimed that Franklin owed him 179,494 *l.t.* 12*s.* 8*d.*

[July 9, 1782]

Pour change de 25 pour cent
sur les Traites qui devoient
m'être fournies par M. le
Docteur Franklin sur le
Congrès americain en payement
de la derniere partie des
draperies ci dessus, le quel
Benefice étoit à l'avantage de
la France et dont consequement
je dois profiter   107,082.10.

Pour le Fret du Vaisseau le
Marquis de la Fayette Capne.
de Galatheau jaugeant 1684

---

1. In the hand of L'Air de Lamotte. These two sheets are part of Account XXVI (XXXII, 3).

Taux. [Tonneaux] de mer
suivant le Certificat delivré
à Bordeaux le 6. 7bre. 1781.
sur quoi il convient deduire
210. Tonneaux pour autant
d'hommes composant l'équipage
du d. Vaisseau à son depart de
l'Orient, reste 1474 Taux. à
200 *l.t.* suivant le prix fixé
par la Charte partie du 30
Août 1780   294,800.

    Pour le Loyer de l'appartement
occupé par M. Franklin, ensemble
l'indemnité des frais et depenses
pour loger aussi les Commissaires
Americains   20,000.

Franklin's Private Responses to Chaumont's Revised Account: Two Drafts[2]

(I)[3] and (II) AD (draft): American Philosophical Society

[after July 9, 1782]

I.

Remarks upon M. de Chaumont's *second* Account dated July 9. 1782.

Tho' in his *first Acct* he had charg'd a Draft made on me by Mr Williams for 240,000 Livres as being *pour le montant* du fret du Vaisseau le Marquis de la Fayette, and had signed a Receipt in full accordingly, yet in this second Account he charges 294,800

---

2. In these undated memoranda, BF is formulating two different kinds of responses to what he saw as Chaumont's "groundless" charges. It was some-time after writing these that he decided to lay aside the entire matter; see our headnote to the Exchange About Accounts, [before April 26].

3. This two-page draft is included in Account XIX (XXVIII, 3).

livres as the montant of that Freight. Which is an Overcharge of 54,800 Livres.

He gives Credit for 200,000 livres paid by me in Acceptances of his Drafts, but no Notice is taken of the remaining 40,000 livres included in Mr Williams Draft; query, has not that Draft been paid?

He charges 107,082.10.0 livres for an imaginary Advantage he might have had if he had received Paymt. for his Cloth in America; but the Charge is that first Proposition of his, being made at his Request, & for his Accomodation, and if it had not, & if the Charge had not been made no such Advantage could have accru'd to him as he supposes, this whole Charge is groundless.

Suppose the Mere Boby return'd empty.—
 Why did not M C lade her with what
  he had a right to load her
  he might even have put more

II.

Case

A, a Stranger, desirous of sending a Cargo of Provisions to his Island on an Emergency, prevail'd with B to assist him with his Credit in doing it. B procur'd part of the Provisions on Credit, and charter'd a Ship to transport them, on low Freight, but on condition of paying her Value to the Owners in case of Loss. The Ship and Cargo was lost, the Creditors & Owners came upon B for Payment, threatning Suits which would have ruin'd him. He apply'd to A, who delay'd some time, but at last paid the whole, delivering B from his Anxiety by discharging his Engagements.

Question. Whether according to the Custom of Merchants, B has merited some Commission for this Transaction, and what Commission?

To David Hartley

Reprinted from William Temple Franklin, ed., *Memoirs of the Life and Writings of Benjamin Franklin . . .* (3 vols., 4to, London 1817–18), II, 387–88.

Dear Sir,   Passy, July 10, 1782.

I received your favour of the 26th past by Mr. Young, and am indebted to you for some preceding. I do not know why the good work of peace goes on so slowly on your side. Some have imagined that your ministers since Rodney's success are desirous of trying fortune a little farther before they conclude the war: others, that they have not a good understanding with each other. What I have just heard seems to countenance this opinion. It is said Mr. Fox has resigned. We are ready here on the part of America to enter into treaty with you, in concurrence with our allies; and are disposed to be very reasonable; but if your *plenipotentiary*, notwithstanding that character, is upon every proposition obliged to send a courier and wait an answer, we shall not soon see the happy conclusion. It has been suspected too, that you wait to hear the effect of some overtures sent by General Carleton for a separate peace in America. A vessel just arrived from Maryland, brings us the unanimous resolutions of their assembly for continuing the war at all hazards rather than violate their faith with France.[4] This is a sample of the success to be expected from such a measure? if it has really been taken; which I hardly believe.

There is methinks a point that has been too little considered in treaties, the means of making them durable. An honest peasant from the mountains of Provence, brought me the other day a manuscript he had written on the subject, and which he could not procure permission to print. It appeared to me to have much good sense in it; and therefore I got some copies to be struck off for him to distribute where he may think fit. I send you one enclosed. This man aims at no profit from his pamphlet or his project, asks for nothing, expects nothing, and does not even desire

---

4. BF sent a copy of the resolution with his July 6 letter to Vergennes, above. He also read it to Grenville at their July 9 meeting: Giunta, *Emerging Nation,* I, 460.

to be known. He has acquired he tells me a fortune of near 150 crowns a year (about 18 *l.* sterling) with which he is content. This you may imagine would not afford the expence of riding to Paris, so he came on foot; such was his zeal for peace and the hope of forwarding and securing it by communicating his ideas to great men here. His rustic and poor appearance has prevented his access to them; or obtaining their attention; but he does not seem yet to be discouraged. I honour much the character of this *veritable philosophe.*[5]

I thank you much for your letters of May 1, 13, and 25 with your proposed preliminaries. It is a pleasure to me to find our sentiments so concurring on points of importance: it makes discussions as unnecessary as they might, between us, be inconvenient. I am my dear Sir, with great esteem and affection, your's ever, B. FRANKLIN.

To Benjamin Vaughan

Press copy of ALS:[6] Kaller's Historical Documents, Inc., New Jersey (2002)

Dear Sir, Passy, July 10. 1782

I have before me your several Favours of June 7, June 17, & July 9.[7] The Box sent to Mr. Bowens at Ostend is also come to

5. See our headnote to Gargaz's proposed letter, [*c.* July 10].

6. On July 11, seizing the opportunity of a direct conveyance, BF sent this press copy to Vaughan; see BF's letter of that date. Rather than returning the copy, as requested, Vaughan gave it to Shelburne. The ALS has been lost, and for more than two centuries the copy remained at Shelburne's Bowood estate, inaccessible to the public. Only one section was known: the excerpt BF sent to David Hartley on May 8, 1783 (William L. Clements Library). Beginning "By the original law of nations" and ending with "Peace therefore more likely to continue & be lasting", it is an elaboration of BF's earlier thoughts on non-combatants (XXXII, 466–7, 476; XXXV, 134). Hartley circulated the excerpt, calling it "Extract of a Letter from BF to a Friend in England". (Copies are at the Public Record Office, William L. Clements Library, and the Library of Congress; a French translation is at the AAE.) WTF, who only had a copy of the excerpt, published it in *Memoirs*, II, 388, identifying the recipient as Vaughan.

7. The June 7 letter is above. We have found no letter of June 17, and are

hand. It contain'd a Dozen 4to Vols. of my Writings,[8] and a Number of Pamphlets which you have been so good as to chuse for me; but the Remembrancers, & Registers bought for me by Mr Young, and left by him as he tells me with Mr Johnson, to be sent me, were not included, & I hear nothing of them. I beg you would inquire about them.—

I wish you all kinds of good Fortune in your Speculations for America. I think you will be well serv'd by Mr Young, who appears to be [*one line illegible*].[9]

Mr Laurens is gone to the South of France, and has declined acting in the Commission for making Peace. Mr Oswald has not given me the Acct you suppose he may have given, of a certain Person's strange Behaviour.[1] When you have Leisure, acquaint me with it.—

I shall confer with Mr Jay concerning the Bills. There will be no Difficulty in getting them paid if he approves of it. Should his first Opinion continue, I cannot interfere, the Bills being drawn on him. What you tell me, of the first Indorser's going out with a Passport from me, and that these Bills were remitted as part Payment, shows me that I was imposed on by that man; my Passport was obtained on Assurance that the Goods to be carried over were bona fide the Property of the intended Settler; and should not have been used as a Cover for the Goods of English Merchants intrusted to him, to carry on a contraband Commerce.— The Bills of Harley & Drummond[2] which you mention as having been enclosed in the same Letter, afford farther Suspicion of his Situation in that Country, & that the Bills have not been fairly come by.—

Your Sentiments relating to Privateers appear to me very just, & those concerning Arbitrators not less so, tho' perhaps less

---

puzzled by the third reference. While Vaughan did write a letter dated July 9, BF could not have received it by the next day.

8. *Political, Miscellaneous, and Philosophical Pieces* (London, 1779); see XXXI, 210–18. The work was published by Joseph Johnson, mentioned later in this sentence.

9. For Young's plan to join Vaughan in a business venture see our annotation of BF to the Continental Congress, July 9.

1. Laurens; see Vaughan to BF, June 7.

2. A London firm: XVI, 269.

likely to be adopted. I go with you as far as you go, in Proposals for diminishing the Occasions & Mischiefs of War, & perhaps a little farther.— By the Original Law of Nations, War & Extirpation was the Punishment of Injury. Humanizing by degrees, it admitted Slavery instead of Death. A farther Step was, the Exchange of Prisoners instead of Slavery. Another, to respect more the property of private Persons under Conquest, & to be content with acquir'd Dominion. Why should not this Law of Nations go on improving? Ages have interven'd between its several Steps; but as Knowledge of late encreases rapidly, why should not those Steps be quicken'd? Why should it not be agreed to as the future Law of Nations that in any War hereafter the following Descriptions of Men should be undisturbed, have the Protection of both sides, & be permitted to follow their employments in Surety, viz

1. Cultivators of the Earth, because they labor for the Subsistance of Mankind.

2. Fishermen, for the same Reason.

3. Merchants & Traders, in unarm'd Ships; who accommodate different Nations by communicating & exchanging the Necessaries and Conveniencies of Life.

4. Artists & Mechanics, inhabiting & working in open Towns.

It is hardly necessary to add that the Hospitals of Enemies should be unmolested; they ought to be assisted.

In short, I would have nobody fought with but those who are paid for Fighting. If obliged to take Corn from the Farmer, Friend or Enemy, I would pay him for it; the same for the Fish or Goods of the others.

This once established, that Encouragement to war which arises from Spirit of Rapine[3] would be taken away, and Peace therefore more likely to continue & be lasting.—

I send you the Passport you desire for the young Man. His Talents may be useful in a new Country.—

Your Brother John is arriv'd in New York, the Vessel being taken. I have heard nothing more of him since.[4]

---

3. The preceding eight words are obscured by a fold in the press copy; we supply the text from Hartley's extract.

4. John Vaughan went to Philadelphia once he was released on parole; see RB to BF, May 20.

CONCILIATEUR

DE TOUTES

LES NATIONS D'EUROPE,

OU

PROJET

DE PAIX PERPÉTUELLE

Entre tous les souverains de l'Europe & leurs Voisins.

Par P. A. G.

1 7 8 2.

Title Page of a Pamphlet by Pierre-André Gargaz

The Persons you mention to have recommended to me, are not yet arriv'd. I am ever, my dear Friend, Yours most affectionately,   B FRANKLIN

Vaughan

From Pierre-André Gargaz:[5] Proposed Letter from Franklin(?) to Louis XVI

AL: Historical Society of Pennsylvania

When fifty-two-year-old Pierre-André Gargaz arrived at the gate of the hôtel de Valentinois, probably toward the end of May, 1782, he cut an unusual figure. Having served a twenty-year sentence on the galleys at Toulon for a murder he maintained he did not commit and now branded as a convict, Gargaz walked from the south of France to Paris carrying a treatise he had written while incarcerated.[6] Franklin described their encounter in the letter he wrote David Hartley on July 10 (above). A year later, he told the same story to a young British visitor. "In the course of last year," Franklin is quoted as saying, "a man very shabbily dressed—all his dress together was not worth five shillings—came and desired to see me. He was admitted,

5. Gargaz is identified in XXVIII, 540–1n. The information cited there has been to some degree corrected in the recent biography by Ferréol de Ferry, *Pierre-André Gargas (1728–1801), Galérien de Toulon, Réformateur de l'orthographe et de la condition pénitentiaire, inventeur des NATIONS UNIES* (Paris, 2000). The family's name, for example, was spelled with a final "s" by all members except BF's correspondant, whose substitution of the "z" was a result of his personal system of spelling reform. (We will continue to spell his name as he himself signed it.) Gargaz was not a "former teacher" when he wrote BF in 1779; he had followed his father's trade as a merchant before his incarceration and only began teaching after 1782. Gargaz's undated memoir, which we placed under its earliest possible date of *c.* 1781 (XXXVI, 350–1)— in which he refers to himself as a teacher—more likely belongs a year or two later: Ferry, *Pierre-André Gargas*, pp. 21–5, 87–90. Ferry's biography contains a trove of previously unknown documentation from French archives; unfortunately, it does not take into account several previously unpublished letters in American archives, including this one.

6. Gargaz had no family to return to after his release in the spring of 1781. Married at the age of 16, he was widowed by the time he was 24. All three of the couple's children had died in infancy, and his wife died of complications from the third birth: *ibid.*, pp. 21, 24–5.

and, on asking his business, he told me that he had walked from one of the remotest provinces in France, for the purpose of seeing me and showing me a plan which he had formed for a universal and perpetual peace. I took his plan and read it, and found it to contain much good sense. I desired him to print it. He said he had no money: so I printed it for him. He took as many copies as he wished for, and gave several away; but no notice whatever was taken of it."[7]

Gargaz had sent Franklin a preliminary version of this plan in 1779, from Toulon, signing himself as 'galley slave no. 1336.'[8] The version Franklin printed at Passy,[9] entitled *Conciliateur de toutes les nations d'Europe, ou Projet de paix perpétuelle entre tous les souverains de l'Europe & leurs voisins,* was substantially expanded and revised, possibly as a result of discussions at Passy. Forty-six pages in length, the pamphlet began with a definition of peace, a petition to the King, and a circular letter imploring all friends of the human race to do everything in their power to see this plan adopted. The plan itself was divided into eight "infallible means" for establishing and maintaining perpetual peace among all the sovereigns of Europe. Each sovereign was to send a representative to a perpetual Congress in, say, Lyon (instead of Toulon, as Gargaz had earlier proposed), where they would adjudicate international disputes according to a system Gargaz outlined.[1] All nations would agree to be content with their present boundaries, would engage in free commerce on land and sea, and would be allowed to maintain fortresses, warships, and standing armies to protect their territory. In times of peace, the soldiers could be employed in projects for the public good—building roads, bridges, irrigation canals, and so on. The final section of the pamphlet was a series of thirteen common

---

7. At the time he told this story, BF still had copies of the pamphlet "in a closet" and gave one to his visitor: Journal of John Baynes, Sept. 23, 1783, quoted in Sir Samuel Romilly, *The Life of Sir Samuel Romilly, Written by Himself* (2 vols.; 3rd ed., London, 1842), I, 453.

8. XXVIII, 540.

9. Only two copies of the Passy imprint are known; both are at the Hist. Soc. of Pa. For the full text and an English translation, along with facsimile pages of the Passy imprint, see *A Project of Universal and Perpetual Peace, Written by Pierre-André Gargaz . . . reprinted, together with an English Version, Introduction, & Typographical Note by George Simpson Eddy* (New York, 1922).

1. In this as well as previous versions of his text, Gargaz gave credit for the basic plan of a European congress to the proposal attributed to Henri IV and his chief minister Sully, and revised by the abbé de Saint-Pierre in 1712 as *Mémoire pour rendre la paix perpétuelle en Europe.*

arguments in favor of war, with refutations for each. The fourth argument, for example, was the claim that war increases the circulation of money. Gargaz countered with a series of examples of public works projects that could usefully employ the population while ameliorating living conditions, stimulating trade, eliminating famine, establishing funds for victims of natural disasters, and overseeing child welfare. His final suggestion—admittedly difficult and expensive, but not impossible for a united Europe—was to cut through the isthmuses of Panama and Suez.

Franklin printed the pamphlet by July 10.[2] Armed with this privately printed version, Gargaz tried again to approach influential individuals who might help him find a publisher. Although most people ignored him, Vergennes accepted a pamphlet (undoubtedly through Franklin's offices) and deemed it worthy of publication.[3] We suspect that the present letter—in Gargaz's hand, with his characteristic spelling and singular style, and now located in a collection of Franklin's papers—was part of the author's naïve campaign to get Franklin to present a copy to the King. If the American minister did so, he would certainly not have forwarded the pamphlet under cover of this letter.

In addition to their desire to see an end to warfare, Gargaz and Franklin shared another interest. They had both developed systems of phonetic spelling. Gargaz had managed to get a treatise on spelling reform published in Marseille in 1773,[4] an unusual feat for a galley slave. Did they discuss this topic at Passy? Jottings on a random address sheet dating from the second half of June indicate that they did. Franklin began by writing out French word endings that sounded nearly the same: "é, ai, ait, ais, ois, oient." Beneath them, Gargaz copied the endings, indicating that the latter two could also be spelled "es" and "ent." He then demonstrated that his phonetic spelling of "ils mangeroient" would be "iz manjeren." Franklin countered with his own attempt at Gargaz's system: "il fezet."[5] These few snippets of words are our only evidence of what may have been hours of conversation between the American minister plenipotentiary, who at this time was trying to arrange for a durable peace, and the former

2. The day BF sent a copy to Hartley.

3. Gargaz to BF, March 2, 1783 (APS).

4. Pierre-André Gargaz, *Gramère framasone, alfabet consiliateur de l'ortografe* ... (Marseille, 1773).

5. These jottings were made on the address sheet of a letter BF was evidently asked to forward to America, but never did: John Lang's Son & Wienholt to the High and Mighty Lords, the States General of the United Provinces of Nord America. It was dated Bremen, June 19, 1782 (APS).

galley slave who brought him a theory on how a peace might be made permanent.

Sire,   [*c*. July 10, 1782]
    Le 26 Mai dernier, le filosofe Gargaz me presenta un de ses ouvrages ci joint, intitulé, Consiliateur de toutes les Nations d'Europe; ou, Projet de Paix universele e perpetuéle, entre tous les souverains d'Europe e leurs voisins. J'ai lu e examiné plusiers fois cet ouvrage, avec toute l'atention e l'impartialité possibles. Les moïens qe ce filosofe propose, pour etablir e maintenir son sisteme, sont si faciles a metre en usage; si utiles pour le bonheur de toutes les Nations; si interessants pour tous les oficiers, e Aumoniers, emplöiez dans le Militaire; si avantageux a toute la Noblesse; e enfin si conformes aux vüe pacifiqes e bienfaisantes de VOTRE MAJESTÉ, qe je me suis cru obligé en consience, de lui en faire homage. Si Éle les adopte, ainsi qe je l'espere, par sa bonté Paternele envers tous les Peuples, je m'estimerai un des plus heureux mortels, e ce jour sera le plus signalé pour la Gloire, de tous les souverains, de tous leurs principaux Ministres, e de tout le Genre humain.

Au Roi

From Joseph Priestley   ALS: University of Pennsylvania Library

Dear Sir   Birmingham 10 July 1782
    I am far from meaning [to][6] trouble you with letters of recommendation for English Travellers. The bearer of this, Dr Stokes, is a promising young man, who will think himself happy in getting only a *sight* of you, and in this I hope you will have no objection to indulge him. I have given him letters to other persons, who, I hope, will shew him such civilities as may be useful to him.[7]

---

6. The upper right and left margins of the MS are torn. We supply conjectural readings in brackets.

7. Dr. Jonathan Stokes (1755–1831), a botanist, zoologist, and chemist, was embarking on a tour of the continent after completing his medical education at the University of Edinburgh, where he wrote a thesis developing a Lin-

I hope you have received a letter I wrote to you lately, in answer to the [ver]y obliging one with which you favo[red me].[8]
The sun has hardly shone in [*one word missing*] country since, so
that I have not been [a]ble to prosecute my late experiments and
I am afraid that, in the political hemisphere, the gleam of sunshine [we] had some time ago, is almost leaving us. We who have
no influence, must wait the issue, with as much patience as we
can.

With the most perfect esteem I am Dear Sir Yours sincerely

J PRIESTLEY

Addressed: To / Dr Franklin / Paris[9]

Notation: Priestley 10. July 1782.

From Jonathan Williams, Jr.

ALS: American Philosophical Society

Dear & hond sir   Nantes July 10. 1782.

Major Sherburne[1] who will deliver this has already several In-
troductions to you, I cannot however let him go away without
adding my assurances that I think him a Gentleman worthy of

---

naean classification of gases. In June, he delivered a paper attempting a similar classification of "earths" and metals. Stokes began his tour in Paris,
where he had arranged to meet the younger Linnaeus. He continued on to
various northern European cities before returning to London by mid-May,
1783, when he attended a meeting of the Royal Society as Priestley's guest
and joined Priestley as a member of the Lunar Society: Robert E. Schofield,
*The Lunar Society of Birmingham: a Social History of Provincial Science and
Industry in Eighteenth-Century England* (London, Glasgow, and New York,
1963), pp. [3], 223–6, 417–18.

8. These letters, dated respectively June 24 and June 7, are above.

9. Three sketches resembling axes and possibly a hoe appear on the verso
of the address sheet.

1. The future N.H. congressional representative Maj. John Samuel Sherburne (1757–1830), who had been entrusted by John Paul Jones and Richard
Cranch with letters for Europe: Bradford, *Jones Papers*, reel 6, nos. 1354–6;
Adams Correspondence, IV, 282n; *Biographical Dictionary of the American Congress, 1774–1961* (Washington, D.C., 1961), p. 1592.

your Friendship & Civility & I therefore request you will honour him with your particular notice.

I am as ever most dutifully & affecy Your   J WILLIAMS J

Addressed: His Excellency / Doctor Franklin

From Moses Young   ALS: Historical Society of Pennsylvania

Sir   Paris 10th July 1782.

I am exceedingly sorry that Your Excellency gave yourself the trouble to answer my Paper. I did not expect an answer. I was perfectly satisfied with the reasons given for not paying the whole of the Account when I had the honor of waiting on Your Excellency, and only committed to writing what I would have said before I heard those reasons my representation being dated at Paris 8th July.[2]

Your Excellency will observe that I don't say in that Paper that I expect Congress will pay me a salary up to the time I may receive the Money, altho' I believe they have done so in cases nearly similar. If it shall happen that I can prosecute profitable business on my present plan I certainly will not make such a demand. I was not remarked in America for making unreasonable ones on the public, and have been much blamed since the commencement of the war by my friends for being too inattentive to my own interest as I never sollicited any lucrative office in that Country when I believe I might have procured such if I had asked it. I was taken prisoner in the Battle of Long Island in the year 1776 and was four months with the Enemy for which time I neither ask'd nor received any pay.

I most humbly thank Your Excellency for the recommendation to Congress, and have the honor to be, Sir, Your Excellency's much obliged Most humble and obedient Servt.[3]

MOSES YOUNG

His Excellency Benjamin Franklin Esquire

2. His representation was the request for his salary; see the annotation of BF to the Continental Congress, July 9. The matter of Young's salary was still unresolved in 1790: *Laurens Papers*, XV, 538n.

3. BF issued a passport to Young on July 10 for travel to Ostend (Mass.

Franklin's Thoughts on Privateering and the Sugar Islands: Two Essays

(I) Copies: Library of Congress (three), Massachusetts Historical Society, Public Record Office, William L. Clements Library; (II) Copies: Library of Congress (two), Public Record Office, William L. Clements Library

We print these two essays after July 10, 1782, because they elaborate themes addressed in Franklin's letter of that date to Benjamin Vaughan (above). There is no question that Franklin composed them separately, though they have been linked to one another and to Vaughan's letter in various combinations. Franklin himself was responsible for at least some of these groupings. Without access to any of his original versions, we can only suggest the permutations based on surviving copies and early printed versions.

The copies we publish are those that were produced in closest proximity to Franklin: one of three copies of (I) made by L'Air de Lamotte for legation letterbooks *circa* September, 1783,[4] and an independent copy of (II) made by William Temple Franklin. Neither essay was titled. L'Air de Lamotte referred to (I) in one of his tables of contents as "Mr. Franklin's Paper upon the Abolishment of privateering." Franklin endorsed Temple's copy of (II), "A Thought concerning the Sugar Islands."

On May 8, 1783, Franklin sent David Hartley an extract of his July 10 letter to Vaughan along with these two essays. Hartley's secretary made copies of the cover letter and enclosures, labeling (I) "Thoughts on privateering" and (II) "Thoughts concerning the Sugar Colonies."[5] Five months earlier, however, Franklin had sent Richard Oswald a single paper that he said he had already read to him, containing "a Proposition for improving the Law of Nations, by prohibiting the Plundering of unarm'd and usefully employed People." William Temple Franklin, when publishing that letter in 1817, included what he

---

Hist. Soc.; the passport is printed in script type). Young wrote Laurens that day that he planned to return to London on July 11 and then go to Ireland to embark (probably on the *Europa*, a ship chartered by Vaughan): *Laurens Papers*, XV, 539–40.

4. Two of these letterbooks are in the Library of Congress; the other is in the Adams Papers at the Mass. Hist. Soc. The letterbooks do not include (II).

5. Sets of these copies by Hartley's secretary George Hammond are in the Public Record Office and the William L. Clements Library.

claimed was the enclosure: a single essay that seamlessly combined (I) and (II).[6]

Elsewhere in that same edition, however, Temple published the same texts in a different combination that also may have originated with Franklin. In February 1790, Mathew Carey published in the *American Museum* a piece he called "Against privateering: or, reasons in support of new proposed articles, in treaties of commerce, which may be formed by the united states of America. By dr. Franklin."[7] This essay combined the excerpt of Franklin's July 10 letter to Vaughan with the text of (I). Carey most likely received it in that form from the author. Three years later the identical text appeared in a collection of Franklin's writings under the new title, "Observations on War."[8] In 1806, a new collection of Franklin's works reprinted the same text and title, indicating that it was reprinted from the *American Museum*.[9] William Temple Franklin followed suit, placing the "Observations on War" in the final volume of his edition under the section entitled "General Politics and Commerce." Elsewhere in that same section, Temple published as an independent item "A Thought Concerning the Sugar Islands."[1]

[after July 10, 1782]

I.

It is for the Interest of Humanity in general, that the Occasions of War, and the Inducements to it, should be diminished.

If Rapine is abolished, one of the Encouragements to War is taken away, and Peace therefore more likely to continue and be lasting.

The Practice of Robbing Merchants on the high Seas, a Remnant of the Ancient Piracy, tho' it may be accidentally beneficial to particular Persons, is far from being profitable to all engaged in it, or to the Nation that authorizes it. In the Beginning of a War some rich Ships, not upon their Guard, are surprized and

6. BF to Oswald, Jan. 14, 1783 (William L. Clements Library). In WTF, *Memoirs*, II, 420–2, the enclosure (now missing) is called "Proposition relative to privateering, &c. communicated to Mr. Oswald."

7. *American Museum*, VII, 101–2.

8. Benjamin Vaughan, ed., *Works of the late Doctor Benjamin Franklin* . . . (2 vols., London, 1793), II, 151–4.

9. *The Complete Works, in Philosophy, Politics, and Morals, of the late Dr. Benjamin Franklin* . . . (3 vols., London, 1806), II, 435–7.

1. WTF, *Memoirs*, III, 131–2, 168–9.

taken. This encourages the first Adventurers to fit out more arm'd Vessels, and many others to do the same. But the Enemy, at the same time, become more careful, arm their Merchant Ships better, and render them not so easy to be taken; they go also more under the Protection of Convoys, thus while the Privateers to take them are multiplied, the Vessels subject to be taken, and the Chances of Profit are diminished; so that many Cruises are made wherein the Expences overgo the Gains; and as is the Case in other Lotteries, tho' particulars have got Prizes, the mass of Adventurers are Losers, the whole Expence of fitting out all the Privateers during a War, being much greater than the whole Amount of Goods taken. Then there is the National Loss of all the Labour of so many Men during the time they have been employed in Robbing; who, besides, spend what they get in Riot, Drunkenness and Debauchery, lose their Habits of Industry, are rarely fit for any Sober Business after a Peace, and serve only to encrease the Number of Highwaymen & House Breakers. Even the Undertakers, who have been fortunate, are, by sudden Wealth, led into expensive living, the Habit of which continues when the means of supporting it cease, and finally ruins them. A Just Punishment of their having wantonly & unfeelingly ruined many honest innocent Traders and their Families, whose Substance was employed in serving the common Interest of Mankind.

II.

Should it be agreed, & become a Part of the Law of Nations, that the Cultivators of the Earth are not to be molested or interrupted in their Peaceable and useful Employment, the Inhabitants of the Sugar Islands would perhaps come under the Protection of such a Regulation, which would be a great Advantage to the Nations who at present hold those Islands, since the Cost of Sugar to the Consumer in those Nations, consists not only in the Price he pays for it by the Pound, but in the accumulated Charge of all the Taxes he pays in every War to fit out Fleets and maintain Troops for the Defence of the Islands that raise the Sugar and the Ships that bring it home. But the Expence of Treasure is not all. A celebrated Philosophical Writer remarks, that when he consider'd the Wars made in Africa for Prisoners to raise Sugar in America, the Numbers slain in those Wars, the Number that being crowded in Ships perish in the Transportation, & the Numbers that die under the Severities of Slavery, he could scarce look on a Morsel of Sugar without conceiving it spotted with Human Blood.[2] If he had consider'd also the Blood of one another which the white Nations shed in fighting for those Islands, he would have imagined his Sugar not as spotted only, but as thoroughly died red.— On these Accounts I am persuaded that the Subjects of the Emperor of Germany and the Empress of Russia, who have no Sugar Islands, consume Sugar cheaper at Vienna and Moscow, with all the Charge of transporting it after its Arrival in Europe, than the Citizens of London or of Paris. And I sincerely believe that if France & England were to decide by throwing Dice which should have the whole of their Sugar Islands, the Loser in the Throw would be the Gainer. The future Expence of defending them would be saved; the Sugars would be bought cheaper by all Europe if the Inhabitants might make it without Interruption, and whoever imported the Sugar, the same Revenue might be raised by Duties at the Custom Houses of the Nation that consumed it. And on the whole I conceive it would be better for the Nations now possessing Sugar Colonies to give up their Claim to them, let them govern themselves, and put them under the Protection of all the Powers of Europe as neutral Countries open to the Commerce of all, the Profits of the present Monopoly's[3] being by no means equivalent to the Expence of maintaining them.

[*In Franklin's hand:*] A Thought concerning the Sugar Islands

---

2. From a note in Discourse 1, chapter 3, of Claude-Adrien Helvétius, *De l'Esprit*, ed. Jacques Montaux ([Paris], 1988), p. 37n. BF had expressed similar sentiments in 1772: XIX, 188.

3. Exports from the British colonies in the mid-1780s were one-third as large as from Britain itself, while exports from the French colonies were more than two-thirds as large as from France: Michael Duffy, *Soldiers, Sugar, and Seapower: the British Expeditions to the West Indies and the War against Revolutionary France* (Oxford, 1987), p. 7. BF had suggested to Oswald in early May that the sugar islands should be neutral: Gerald Stourzh, *Benjamin Franklin and American Foreign Policy* (2nd ed., Chicago and London, 1969), p. 240.

To Benjamin Vaughan

ALS: partially reproduced in Christie's auction catalogue, "Important Autograph Letters from the Historical Archives at Bowood House" (London, Oct. 12, 1994), p. 34; William Temple Franklin, ed., *Memoirs of the Life and Writings of Benjamin Franklin* . . . (3 vols., 4to, London, 1817–18), II, 388–9.[4]

Dear Sir,   Passy, July 11. 1782.

In mine of yesterday, which went by Mr Young, I made no mention of yours of May 11. it not being before me.[5] I have just now found it. I thank you for the particular Acct. you give me of your own Views, & those your Friends have had for you: Every thing relating to your Welfare concerns me.

You speak of a "proposed dependant State of America, which you thought Mr Oswald would begin with." As yet I have heard nothing of it. I have all along understood (perhaps I have understood more than was intended) that the Point of Dependance was given up, and that we were to be treated with as a free People. I am not sure that Mr Oswald has explicitly said so, but I know that Mr Grenville has,[6] and that he was to make that Declaration previous to the Commencement of the Treaty. It is now intimated to me from several Quarters that Lord Shelburne's Plan is to retain Sovereignty for the King, giving us otherwise an independent Parliament, & a Government similar to that of late intended for Ireland. If this be really his project, our negociation for peace will not go very far; the thing is impracticable and impossible, being inconsistent with the faith we have pledged, to say nothing of the general disposition of our people. Upon the whole I should believe that though Lord S. might for-

---

4. This letter, like the one BF wrote Vaughan on July 10, above, was sold by Christie's as part of Shelburne's Bowood estate. We have been unable to obtain a complete photocopy of the ALS. We print the first part of the letter, and the internal address, from a photograph in the Christie's catalogue of only the first page of the ALS. We reprint the rest of the letter, beginning with the word "similar" (midway through the second paragraph), from WTF's *Memoirs*. The first page of the ALS includes a sentence omitted in WTF's version.

5. Not found.

6. On June 1. See the entry of that date in BF's journal of the peace negotiations.

merly have entertained such an idea, he had probably dropped it before he sent Mr. Oswald here: your words above cited do however throw a little doubt into my mind, and have with the intimations of others, made me less free in communication with his lordship, whom I much esteem and honour, than I should otherwise have been. I wish therefore you would afford me what you can of eclaircissement.

This letter going by a courier will probably get to hand long before the one (preceding in date) which went by Mr. Young, who travels on foot. I therefore inclose the copy of it which was taken in the press. You may return it to me when the other arrives.[7]

By the return of the courier, you may much oblige me, by communicating, what is fairly communicable, of the history of Mr. Fox's and Lord J. Cavendish's resignation,[8] with any other changes made or likely to be made.

With sincere esteem, I am ever, my dear friend your's most affectionately,   B. FRANKLIN.

Mr B. Vaughan

To Richard Oswald

LS:[9] Public Record Office; AL (draft): Library of Congress; copies: Public Record Office (two), Library of Congress, William L. Clements Library

Sir   Passy, July 12. 1782

I inclose a Letter for Lord Shelburne,[1] to go by your Courier, with some others of which I request his Care. They may be put into the Penny Post. I have received a Note informing me, that,

7. Vaughan gave the press copy to Shelburne.
8. Chancellor of the Exchequer Lord John Cavendish (*DNB*) resigned along with Fox and was replaced on July 13 by William Pitt the Younger: Sir F. Maurice Powicke and E. B. Fryde, comps., *Handbook of British Chronology* (2nd ed., London, 1961), p. 105.
9. In WTF's hand, except for the last seven words of the complimentary close, which are in BF's hand.
1. Immediately below.

"some Opposition given by his Lordship to Mr Fox's decided *Plan* of *unequivocally acknowledging American Independency,* was one Cause of that Gentleman's Resignation;" this, from what you have told me, appears improbable. It is farther said "that Mr Grenville thinks Mr. Fox's Resignation will be fatal to the present negociation."[2] This perhaps is as Groundless as the former. Mr Grenville's next Courier, will probably clear up Matters. I did understand from him that such an Acknowlegment was intended previous to the Commencement of the Treaty; and untill it is made, and the Treaty formally begun, Propositions & Discussions seem on Consideration, to be untimely; nor can I enter into Particulars without Mr Jay, who is now ill with the Influenza. My Letter therefore to his Lordship, is merely complimentary on his late Appointment. I wish a Continuance of your Health, in that at present sickly City,[3] being with sincere Esteem, Sir, Your most obedient and most humble Servant

B FRANKLIN

P.S. I send you inclosed the late Resolutions of the State of Maryland; by which the general Disposition of People in America may be guess'd, respecting any Treaty to be proposed by Genl. Carleton, if intended, which I do not believe.[4]

Richd. Oswald Esqre.

Notation: B. Franklin to Mr. Oswald In Mr. Oswald's of the 12th. of July[5]

2. Oswald wrote to Shelburne on July 11 that BF had recently received a communication "from some person in England, who is no friend to the late changes" [in the British government]: Lord John Russell, ed., *Memorials and Correspondence of Charles James Fox* (4 vols., London, 1853–57), IV, 251.

3. The influenza epidemic had by this time reached as far west as Brest: Hector to Castries, July 1, 1782, Archives de la Marine, B³ DCCXX: 18–19.

4. This was the same resolution that BF had sent Vergennes on July 6, above.

5. In a covering letter to Shelburne, dated 3:00 P.M. on July 12, Oswald expressed concern that BF had received a report "of a Reserve intended in the Grant of Independence." Oswald claimed it was the first time he had heard of it and informed Shelburne, "I have in my Letters to your L[ordshi]p, & in Conversation with Dr Franklin, alwise supposed that the Grant was meant to be absolute & unconditional—which last, however, is a Term I never

To the Earl of Shelburne

LS[6] and two copies: Public Record Office; copies: William L. Clements Library, Library of Congress

My Lord   Passy, July 12. 1782
    Mr Oswald informing me that he is about to dispatch a Courier, I embrace the Opportunity of congratulating your Lordship on your Appointment to the Treasury. It is an Extension of your Power to do Good, and in that View, if in no other, it must increase your Happiness, which I heartily wish: being with great and sincere Respect, My Lord, Your Lordship's most obedient and most humble Servant   B FRANKLIN

Honble: the Earl of Shelburne

To Margaret Stevenson   ALS: American Philosophical Society

My dear Friend,   Passy, July 12. 1783. [*i.e.*, 1782][7]
    I had a Line lately from Mr. Theobald,[8] which gave me great Pleasure, as it inform'd me that you and Polly[9] had both got well thro' the Influenza. I had been apprehensive for you particularly, as it is more dangerous to us old People. It is now very rife at Paris. I have had it rather favourably, and, Thanks to God, continue hearty, recollecting but now & then that I am grown old. I still flatter my self that we may meet once more before we die,

---

used, thinking such qualification unnecessary." He enclosed the present letter, saying that BF put "Stoppage upon the preliminaries of Settlement," and asked Shelburne to send him instructions. Public Record Office. Earlier that day Oswald wrote a memoir to Shelburne describing how to restore British rule in America. Unknown to BF, Oswald was a longstanding opponent of American independence: Charles R. Ritcheson, "Britain's Peacemakers, 1782–1783: 'To an Astonishing Degree Unfit for the Task'?" in Hoffman and Albert, eds., *Peace and the Peacemakers*, pp. 79–82.

    6. In WTF's hand, except for the last eight words of the complimentary close, which are in BF's hand.

    7. Dated on the basis of Margaret Stevenson's July 24 reply, below.

    8. James Theobald was RB's brother-in-law and a friend of the Stevensons: xxv, 143n. His note has not been found.

    9. Mary Hewson.

and in that hope I embrace you both most tenderly: being with
sincere Friendship and Affection, Yours ever,　　B Franklin

My Love to Polly; and let me know what is become of Sally
Pearce,[1] &c.

Mrs Stevenson

From William Hodgson　　als: Historical Society of Pennsylvania

Dear sir　　　　　　　　　　　London 13 July 1782
　Since my last in which I acquainted you with my having rec'd
the £200 got by mistake into my namesakes hands in Aldersgate[2]—&c—I have recd your esteemed favor of the 14th Ultimo—[3] I made application immediately for the two Men on
board the Conquistador & was promised that if there, they
shou'd be discharged & sent in the next Cartel Vessell— The
Prisoners are all gone except about 120—who remain for
some sick in the Hospitals & they I expect will go in a very few
days—[4] I shall the first Opportunity of leisure send you my
Acc't of disbursements—[5] Woud you wish me to continue my
attention, in Case the Fortune of War shou'd throw any more
Prisoners into this Country, I shoud be glad to know your plea-
sure on that Head.
　You will have heard what a terrible fracas & blow up the
Death of the Marquiss of Rockingham has occasioned in our
Ministry—it will tend to confirm what I hinted to you in my late
Letters of the Dispositions of Men— I enclose you some News

　1. Sarah Franklin Pearce, bf's first cousin twice removed, lived intermit-
tently with bf and the Stevensons from 1766 to 1773: I, lii; xiii, 446; xx, 145.
For her recent death see Margaret Stevenson's reply, July 24.
　2. See Hodgson's letter of June 7.
　3. Not found.
　4. There were still 157 American prisoners at Forton and Mill on Aug. 28,
however, and, because of new captures of American ships, by Oct. 16 the
number had increased to 284: Sheldon S. Cohen: *Yankee Sailors in British
Gaols: Prisoners of War at Forton and Mill, 1777–1783* (Newark, Del., and
London, 1995), p. 204.
　5. See our annotation of Hodgson to bf, March 22.

papers containing the Speeches of Ministers that were & Ministers that are—as you may wish to see the various reasons each alledge. I wish this does not throw fresh Obstacles in the Way of a General peace— Yesterday a Mail arrived from N. York very first date it seems Genl Carlton wanted to send a Messenger to Congress, who have given positive Orders to Genl Washington to refuse a pass, to such Messenger, indeed I think the attempt to treat separately in America *pending a Negotiation here* was very unwise & very blameable, at least, it so strikes me— If Messr Jones & Paradise are still at Paris I beg you will be pleased to make my respects to them.[6]

The immediate Business of our Correspondence having now in a great measure subsided, I may not be so happy in the frequent reception of your Letters, but I shall presume so far upon your Friendship, as to rest in your Memory on every Occasion that offerrs, assuring you that it will give me the utmost Satisfaction on all Occasions if I can be of the least use to you your Friends & Countrymen, There is one wish My Mind has long entertained which if you wou'd be kind enough to indulge me in I shou'd be very happy, it is this—that you wou'd be pleased to sit for your Picture to one of the best Painters in France for any Acc't. that I may with rapture tell my Children I had the Honor in some degree to enjoy the Friendship of a Man of whom the World thought & think so highly, if you can spare leisure I hope you will not refuse me.—[7] I am with the most sincere regard Dr sr Yours most Respectfully   WILLIAM HODGSON

To His Excellency Benj Franklin Esqr

6. They were. On July 15, BF wrote letters of recommendation for them to Bowdoin, Jefferson, and Livingston (below).

7. BF, who no longer sat for portraits, arranged for Joseph Wright to copy the Duplessis "gray coat" pastel at Passy. The painting was completed by Aug. 29, when Grand paid Wright 192 *l.t.* Although Hodgson fully expected to reimburse the cost (and suggested a means of doing so in October), BF eventually charged the bill to Congress. According to the account entry, a note on the order read, "The same being all the recompense Mr. Hodgson desired for his long Services in takg. care of our Prisoners in England." The painting is inscribed on the back, "This picture of Dr. Franklin was painted at Paris in 1782, & was presented by him to Mr. Wm. Hodgson, of Colman Street, as a token of his Regard and Friendship." It currently belongs to the Corcoran Gallery of Art: Extract of Ferdinand Grand's Account with

P.S. wou'd you wish me to proceed against Digges I think now it may be done without any Risque— The Fellow appears with all possible Effrontery—especially since he was sent or pretended to be sent, by the old Ministry to Mr Adams at the Hague— if he is to be proceeded against you must send me all the Bills & Letters.

Addressed: To / His Excellency / Benj Franklin Esqr

Notation: Hogdson 13. July 1782.

From Sir Edward Newenham

ALS: Historical Society of Pennsylvania

Dear Sir   Dublin 13 July 1782

I most Ardently wish for the hour, that I shall be able to pay my personal respects to your Excellency and thank you for the repeated and unmerited favors you have conferred upon me;[8] Lady Newenham, who accompanies me to Paris & from thence to Neuchatel & Rome, is equaly desirous to pay her respects to that Great & Respectable Character which she has always held in the highest Respect and Estimation; Ancient Rome never produced a more finished Character, than hers, for innate worth & Sincere Patriotism for the Rights & Liberties of all mankind. Two of my Daughters & one of my sons & three Domestics go with us;[9] our wish is to land at Calais or Dunkirk, as a long sea Voyage would injure her health.

Franklin, Account XXVII (XXXII, 4; the extract is also at the National Archives); Hodgson to BF, Oct. 14, 1782 (APS); Sellers, *Franklin in Portraiture*, pp. 418–20, plate 25; Monroe H. Fabian, *Joseph Wright, American Artist, 1756–1793* (Washington, D.C., 1985), pp. 35–6, 86–7, plate 10.

8. The favors known to us were a permit in 1779 (for a sojourn in France) and passports in 1779 and 1781: XXVIII, 331; XXIX, 565; XXXIV, 354–5.

9. Newenham and his wife, Grace Anna, had 18 children. Their son Edward, who wrote BF from Neuchâtel on May 23, was with them in Paris the following October: *DNB* under Sir Edward Newenham; Dixon Wecter, "Benjamin Franklin and an Irish 'Enthusiast,'" *Huntington Library Quarterly*, IV (1941), 216.

May I therefore, Presume to solicit together with your own (which has been lost in the German post office) a Pasport from the Court of France,[1] from the Spanish & Dutch Embassadors, in order to Cross the seas without Interruption, as our family will be too Large to hazard a Capture.

The moment I have the Honor of your Answer I shall leave this Kingdom.

I Sincerely wish you every happiness this Life can afford.

I have the Honor, to be, Dear Sir with Every sentiment of Respect & Esteem your Excellencys most obt: & most obliged Hble Sert   EDWARD NEWENHAM

Addressed: His Excellency Dr: Benj: Franklin / Passy / near / Paris

Notation: Edward Newhenham 13 July 1782.

From Guy(Gui)-Jean-Baptiste Target[2]

ALS: American Philosophical Society

Ce 13. juillet 1782

J'ai l'honneur de présenter mes respectueux hommages a Monsieur Franklin, et de lui adresser un ouvrage anglois que M. de Crevecœur me charge de lui faire parvenir.[3] Je dois des re-

---

1. See Vergennes to BF, [on or after May 24].

2. This friend of Crèvecœur's was one of the most famous lawyers of his day. Like his colleague and close friend Elie de Beaumont, he was concerned with social justice and was associated with the Jansenist opposition to the Maupeou *parlement*. He became a member of the Académie française in 1785, the first lawyer to be elected in more than a century, and helped draft the Declaration of the Rights of Man: David A. Bell, *Lawyers and Citizens: the Making of a Political Elite in Old Regime France* (New York and Oxford, 1994), pp. 131–3; Dena Goodman, *The Republic of Letters: a Cultural History of the French Enlightenment* (Ithaca, N.Y., and London, 1996), p. 262.

3. This was Crèvecœur's *Letters from an American Farmer* (London, 1782), which was already a success in England. Crèvecœur's translation, *Lettres d'un cultivateur américain*, undertaken at the suggestion of Mme d'Houdetot and her friends, was published at Paris in 1784. For an account of the work's publication, reception, and translation see Howard C. Rice, *Le Cultivateur*

mercimens a M. de Crevecœur de m'avoir procuré L'occasion de
me rapeller au Souvenir de Monsieur Franklin et de Lui offrir
Lassurance de mon dévouement et de mon respect   TARGET

Notation: Target 13 Juillet 1782

From William Jones and John Paradise[4]

AL:[5] University of Pennsylvania Library

Paris 15 July 1782.

Mr. Paradise and Mr. Jones present their grateful respects to their
inestimable friend Dr. Franklin, and beg leave to trouble him
with the enclosed letter for Aleppo by the way of Marseilles,[6] requesting him at the same time, if he has not had leisure to write
the letters, with which he kindly intended to favour them,[7] to
send them by the post directed to Mr. Williams at Nantes, as they
propose to set out towards Orleans as soon as the heat of the day
is a little abated. They wish him perfect health and all possible
happiness, hoping again to pay their respects to him on their return from America.

---

américain: étude sur l'œuvre de Saint John de Crèvecœur (Paris, 1933), pp. 59–
106. See also Julia Post Mitchell, *St. Jean de Crèvecoeur* (New York, 1916),
pp. 73–8.

4. The pair left Dover on June 19 for a journey to America, planning to
sail from a French port. Paradise was traveling on family business, while
Jones, frustrated in his pursuit of a judicial appointment in India, considered
practicing law in America. Jay met them when he visited BF on the afternoon
of June 27 and thereafter saw them three or four more times. They so aroused
his suspicion that he warned BF and Lafayette against them and refused to
trust them with letters for America: XXXVI, 655n; Morris, *Jay: Peace*, p. 447;
Wharton, *Diplomatic Correspondence*, VI, 12–14; Garland Cannon, *The Life
and Mind of Oriental Jones: Sir William Jones, the Father of Modern Linguistics* (Cambridge, New York, and Port Chester, N.Y., 1990), pp. 158–65,
174–6; Archibald P. Shepperson, *John Paradise and Lucy Ludwell of London
and Williamsburg* (Richmond, 1942), pp. 155–7.

5. In William Jones's hand.

6. It was from Jones: Cannon, *Oriental Jones*, p. 177. Aleppo (Halab) is in
Syria.

7. We assume these are the three letters of recommendation printed immediately below.

Addressed: A son Excellence / Monsieur / Monsr. Franklin / Ministre Plénipotentiaire / des Etats Unis / &c. &c.

Notation: Paradise 15. July 1782

To James Bowdoin

Facsimile:[8] Reproduced in Charles Hamilton Auction No. 57 (New York; April 20, 1972), p. 28; copy: Massachusetts Historical Society

Dear Sir,   Passy, July 15. 1782.

I take the Liberty of introducing to your Acquaintance, two of my particular Friends, members of the Royal Society of London, Mr. Jones & Mr. Paradise.[9] You will find them men of Learning & Ingenuity, and have great Pleasure in conversing with them. I recomend them warmly to your Civilities; and to your Counsels respecting their intended Journey to the Southward. They are stanch Friends of our Cause & Country. Be pleas'd to make my Respectful Compliments acceptable to Mrs. Bowdoin,[1] and believe me to be, with great & sincere Esteem, dear Sir, Your most obedient & most humble Servant.

B Franklin

Honble. James Bowdoin Esq.

To Thomas Jefferson

LS:[2] Yale University Library

Dear Sir,   Passy, July 15. 1782.

I was in great Hopes when I saw your Name in the Commission for treating of Peace, that I should have had the Happiness of seeing you here, and of enjoying again in this World, your pleasing Society and Conversation. But I begin now to fear that

8. This appears to have been traced from an LS in L'Air de Lamotte's hand.
9. See their letter of this date, immediately above.
1. Elizabeth Erving Bowdoin (XVI, 177n).
2. In L'Air de Lamotte's hand, except for the last seven words of the complimentary close, which are in BF's hand.

I shall be disappointed, as I was in my Expectation of your Company, when I first undertook the Voyage hither.—[3]

Mr. Jones, who possibly may have the honour of delivering this into your hands, is a particular Friend of Mine, and a zealous one of our Cause and Country. I am sure you will be pleas'd with his Conversation, and therefore I make no Apology for recommending him to your Civilities. His Fellow Traveller too, Mr. Paradise an amiable & worthy Character, will merit, your Regards. He has affairs in Virginia, in which possibly your Counsels and Countenance may be of use to him, & which I therefore beg you would afford him.[4] If in any thing I can render you or your Friends any Service here, you will do me a Pleasure in commanding freely, Dear Sir, Your most obedient and most humble Servant   B FRANKLIN

Honble. Thos. Jefferson Esq.

To Robert R. Livingston

LS:[5] New-York Historical Society

Sir,   Passy, July 15. 1782.

I have just received your No 11. dated the 22d. of May. This Line serves chiefly to recommend to your Civilities two of my English Friends, who will probably pass through Philadelphia in their Way to Virginia.[6]

As they are lately from London, they can give you a good Account of the State of Parties there, and the general Disposition of the Nation respecting America; and I am certain you will be otherwise much pleas'd with their Conversation, as they are sound enlighten'd Republicans and warm Friends of Liberty.

---

3. On Sept. 26, 1776, Jefferson had been elected one of the American commissioners to the French court, but two weeks later he declined the honor: XXII, 624–5.

4. Fourteen months earlier BF had requested Jefferson's help for Paradise, who wished to prevent his wife's properties in Virginia from being sequestered: XXXV, 25–6.

5. In L'Air de Lamotte's hand, except for the last seven words of the complimentary close and the address, which are in BF's hand.

6. Jones and Paradise.

With great Esteem, I have the honour to be, Sir, Your most obedient and most humble Servant   B FRANKLIN

Honble. R. Livingston Esq.

Addressed: To / The honble. Robt. R. Livingston, Esquire / Secretary of State for Foreign / Affairs. / Philadelphia

Endorsed: private Docr Franklin 15th. July 1782

From Daniel Mildred[7]   ALS: American Philosophical Society

Esteem'd Friend Benjamin Franklin   London 16. 7mo 1782

My friend Richard Vaux being on his Voyage to America and intending to pass thro' France, I take the liberty of introducing him to thee as a Gentleman and a particular freind of mine.[8] Any Civilities shewn him Shall esteem as confer'd on my Self and Should he have occasion for Cash if thou wilt do me the favour to Supply him to the Amount of One hundred Pounds his draught on Me for that sum shall be duly honoured. And thy Kindness gratefully acknowledged.

7. This is the only extant letter between BF and Mildred, a Quaker merchant and partner in the London firm Mildred & Roberts, which had extensive Philadelphia connections: XVI, 169n; XIX, 292n.

8. On July 24, BF granted a passport for Ostend to Richard Vaux (1751–1790), an English-born merchant who had apprenticed in Philadelphia and engaged during the war in trans-Atlantic trade: XXXVI, 380; *ANB* under his son Roberts Vaux. Two days later BF witnessed and certified Vaux's signed "Affirmation of Allegiance to the United States of America." As a Quaker, Vaux evidently did not swear oaths; the standard oath of allegiance drawn up by L'Air de Lamotte was altered accordingly. The phrase "do swear" was replaced with "Solemnly sincerely and truly Affirm and declare", the closing "So help me God" was crossed out, and the statement of the witness, signed and dated by BF, was changed from "Sworn" to "Affirmed before me" (APS). The certification, written by WTF and signed by BF, was likewise altered to confirm an "Affirmation" of allegiance (Mrs. Daniel Buckley, Broadaxe, Pa. [1955]). Vaux settled in Philadelphia, where in 1784 he married Ann Roberts, the daughter of BF's friend Hugh Roberts. By 1785, he was residing on Front Street: Elaine F. Crane, ed., *The Diary of Elizabeth Drinker* (3 vols., Boston, 1991), III, 2205, 2223; [John] Macpherson, *Macpherson's Directory, for the City and Suburbs of Philadelphia* (Philadelphia, 1785), p. 140.

With unfeigned respect I remain thy Affectionate friend
DANL MILDRED
Addressed: Benjamin Franklin Esq

Contract between Vergennes and Franklin[9]

DS: Archives Nationales;[1] DS,[2] two copies, and transcript: National Archives

[July 16, 1782]

Contrat entre le Roi et les Treize Etats-Unis de l'Amérique Septentrionale, passé entre M. le Cte. de Vergennes et M. Franklin, le 16. Juillet 1782.

À ce Contrat sont annexés les Pleines-Pouvoirs des Plénipotentiaires respectifs.

Contrat entre le Roi et les Treize Etats-Unis de l'Amérique Septentrionale.

Le Roi ayant bien voulu avoir égard aux demandes qui lui ont été faites au nom et de la part des Provinces-Unies de l'Amérique Septentrionale, de les assister dans l'état de guerre et d'invasion où elles gémissent depuis plusieurs années, et Sa Majesté après avoir fait avec les dites Provinces Confédérées un Traité d'amitié et de Commerce en datte du 6 Fevrier 1778.[3] ayant eû la bonté de les soutenir non seulement par ses forces de terre et de mer, Mais encore par des avances de secours pécuniaires aussi abondans qu'efficaces, dans la crise et le besoin où elles étoient réduites, il a été jugé convenable et nécessaire de constater d'une

---

9. Account XII (XXV, 3) is an extract of this contract. BF had asked the French government for clarification of their financial arrangement a year earlier: XXXV, 150–3.

1. Docketing on the cover sheet indicates that on July 24 BF was provided a copy of the contract as well as Vergennes' full powers (not found); see BF's letter to Durival of that date.

2. Printed, with an English translation, in *JCC*, XXIV, 51–63.

3. XXV, 595–626.

maniere positive le montant desdites avances, les conditions sous lesquelles le Roi s'est porté à les faire, les époques auxquelles le Congrès desdits Etats-Unis s'est engagé de les rembourser au Trésor Royal de Sa Majesté, et d'éclaircir enfin cet objet de maniere à prévenir dans l'avenir toutes difficultés capables d'altérer la bonne harmonie que Sa Majesté est résolüe de maintenir et conserver entre Elle et lesdits Etats-Unis; Pour remplir un dessein aussi louable et dans la vüe d'affermir les liens de Commerce et d'amitié qui subsistent entre Sa Majesté et lesdits Etats-Unis; Nous Charles Gravier Comte de Vergennes &ca. Conseiller du Roi en tous ses Conseils, Commandeur de ses Ordres, Ministre et Secretaire d'Etat et de ses Commandemens et finances, muni des pleins pouvoirs de Sa Majesté à Nous donnés à l'effet des présentes.

Et Nous Benjamin Franklin Ministre plénipotentiaire des Etats-Unis de l'Amérique Septentrionale, pareillement muni des pouvoirs du Congrès desdits Etats[4] au même effet des présentes, après nous être düement communiqué nos pouvoirs respectifs, avons arrêté les articles qui suivent.

Article Per.[Premier]

Il a été calculé et vérifié que les Sommes avancés à titre de prêt par Sa Majesté au Congès desdits Etats-Unis pendant les années 1778. 1779. 1780. 1781. et la présente 1782. montent à la somme de Dix huit millions de livres argent de france suivant Vingt-une reconnoissances ci-dessous mentionnées que le Ministre soussigné du Congrès en a fournies en vertu de ses pouvoirs, Savoir:

La 1re. du 28 Fevrier	1778. de 750,000. *l.t.*	
La 2e. du 19 May	id	750,000.	3,000,000. *l.t.*[5]
La 3e. du 3. Août	id	750,000.	
La 4e. du 1er. Novembre id		750,000.	

4. Probably BF's full powers were his Oct. 21, 1778, letter of credence: XXVII, 596–7.

5. For the 3,000,000 *l.t.* loan of 1778 see XXV, 207–8, 675; XXVII, 206; XXVIII, 202n. The contract did not obligate the United States to repay the 2,000,000 *l.t.* loaned by the Royal Treasury in 1777 (for which see Morris to BF, July 1); a Feb. 25, 1783, revised version of the contract (Archives Nationales) specifically lists it as a gift.

La 5me. du 10. Juin   1779. de   250,000.
La 6e. du 16 Septembre id   250,000.
La 7e. du 4. Octobre   id   250,000. } 1,000,000.[6]
La 8e. du 21 Décembre   id   250,000.

4,000,000. *l.t.*

La 9me. du 29 Fevrier   1780. de   750,000.
La 10e. du 23 May   id   750,000.
La 11e. du 21 Juin   id   750,000. } 4,000,000.[7]
La 12e. du 5. Octobre   id   750,000.
La 13e. du 27 Novembre id   1,000,000.

La 14me. du 15 Fevrier   1781. de   750,000.
La 15e. du 15 May   id   750,000.
La 16e. du 15 Août   id   750,000. } 4,000,000.[8]
La 17e. du 1er. Octobre id   1,000,000.
La 18e. du 15 Novembre id   750,000.

La 19me. du 10 Avril   1782. de   1,500,000.
La 20e. du 1er. Juillet id   1,500,000. } 6,000,000.[9]
La 21e. du 5 dudit mois   3,000,000.

Somme égale à celle ci-dessus
de Dix huit millions, Cy   18,000,000. *l.t.*

Par lesquelles reconnoissances le Ministre susdit a promis au nom du Congrès et solidairement pour les Treize Etats-Unis, faire payer et rembourser au Trésor Royale de Sa Majesté le premier Janvier 1788. au domicile du S. Grand Banquier à Paris, ladite somme de Dix huit Millions argent de france avec les intérêts à Cinq pour cent l'an.

Article 2.

Considérant que le remboursement d'un Capital aussi considérable en un seul terme stipulé au premier Janvier 1788. géneroit infiniment les opérations de la finance du Congrès desdits

6. For the 1779 loan see XXIX, 594n; XXX, 345–6.
7. For the 1780 loan see XXXI, 267–8, 563; XXXIII, 309n; XXXIV, 72n.
8. For the 1781 loan see XXXIV, 72n; XXXV, 71–2.
9. For the 1782 loan see XXXVI, 650.

Etats-Unis et seroit même peut-être impracticable sur ce pied, Sa Majesté a bien voulu par ce motif déroger à cet égard à la teneur des reconnoissances que le Ministre du Congrès a fournies des Dix huit Millions de livres Tournois énoncés en l'article cy dessus, et consentir que le remboursement de ce Capital soit fait en argent comptant à son Trésor Royale à Paris, en Douze parties égales de 1,500M. *l.t.*[1] chacune et en douze années seulement, à commencer de la troisieme apres l'époque de la paix.

Article 3.

Quoique les reconnoissances du Ministre du Congrès desdits Etats-Unis portent, que les Dix huit millions de livres dont il s'agit seront payés et remboursés au Trésor Royale avec les intérêts à Cinq pour cent l'an, Sa Majesté voulant donner auxdits Etats-Unis une nouvelle preuve de son affection et de son amitié, Elle a bien voulu leur faire don et remise de la totalité des arrérages des intérêts échus jusqu'à ce jour et de ceux à écheoir jusqu'à l'époque du Traité de Paix; Faveur que le Ministre du Congrès reconnoit émaner de la pure munificence du Roi et la recevoir au nom desdits Etats-Unis, avec une profonde et vive reconnoissance.

Article 4.

Le remboursement des Dix huit millions de livres tournois dont il s'agit, sera fait en argent comptant au Trésor Royale de Sa Majesté à Paris, en Douze parties égales et aux termes stipulés en l'article deux ci-dessus; Les intérêts de ladite somme à Cinq pour cent l'an, commenceront seulement à courir de l'époque du traité de paix, seront acquittés à chaque terme de remboursement partiel du Capital, et diminueront à mesure et en proportion des payemens; Le Congrès et lesdits Etats-Unis restant au surplus libres de devancer le terme de leur libération, par des rembourse-

---

1. *I.e.*, 1,500,000 *l.t.* The repayment schedule proved overly optimistic. For the inability of Congress to meet it see *Morris Papers*, IX, 486n. BF informed Oswald of at least the first two articles of the contract: Oswald to Shelburne, July 11, 1782, in Giunta, *Emerging Nation*, I, 467–8.

mens anticipés, au cas que la situation de leurs finances leur en donnât la facilité.

Article 5.

Quoique l'emprunt de Cinq millions de florins de hollande consenti par les États généraux des Provinces-Unies des Paysbas, aux termes de l'obligation passée le 5 Novembre 1781. entre SA MAJESTÉ et lesdits Etats-généraux, ait été stipulé sous le nom de SA MAJESTÉ et garanti par Elle, Il est néanmoins reconnu par ces présentes que ledit emprunt a été fait réellement pour le comte et le service des Etats-Unis de l'Amérique septentrionale, et que le Capital, montant par évaluation modérée à la somme de Dix millions de livres Tournois, en a été payé auxdits Etats-Unis suivant la reconnoissance du solde de ladite somme que le Ministre soussigné du Congrès en a fournie le sept Juin dernier.[2]

Article 6.

Par la convention dudit jour 5 Novembre 1781. le Roi a bien voulu promettre et s'engager de fournir et restituer au Comptoir Général des Etats Généraux des Pays bas, le Capital dudit emprunt avec les intérêts à quatre pour cent par an, sans aucuns frais ou déduction quelconques pour les prêteurs, de maniere que ledit Capital soit entierement remboursé après l'espace de quinze années, les remboursements devant se faire en dix termes égaux; dont le premier écherra dans la sixieme année à compter de la date dudit emprunt et ainsi de suite d'année en année jusqu'au remboursement final de la susdite somme; Mais il a été pareillement reconnu par le présent Acte, que cet engagement n'a été pris par le Roi à la priere du Ministre soussigné desdits Etats-Unis,[3] que sous la promesse par lui faite au nom du Congrès et solidairement pour les Treize Etats-Unis, de faire rembourser et restituer au Trésor Royale de SA MAJESTÉ à Paris, le Capital, les intérêts et frais dudit emprunt, suivant les conditions et aux époques fixées par la convention susdite du 5 Novembre 1781.

---

2. For the Dutch loan see XXXVI, 16 and *passim*, as well as the statement by BF immediately below. BF's receipt is missing. For the exchange rate between the *l.t.* and the *f.* see XXXVI, 190n.

3. Although the loan was actually solicited by John Laurens, BF assumed responsibility for it: XXXIV, 517n; XXXVI, 231–2, 496.

Article 7.

Il a été arrêté en conséquence et convenu, que la somme de Dix millions des livres Tournois formant par modération le principal de l'emprunt de Cinq millions de florins de hollande ci-dessus mentionné, sera remboursée et restituée en Argent comptant au Trésor Royale de Sa Majesté à Paris, avec les intérêts à quatre pour cent par an, en Dix parties égales d'Un Million chacune et en dix termes dont le premier écherra le 5 Novembre de l'année 1787. Le second au 5. Novembre 1788. et ainsi de suite d'année en année jusqu'au remboursement final de la susdite somme de Dix millions, les intérêts diminuant à mesure et en proportion des remboursements partiels du Capital. Mais par une suite des sentimens d'affection du Roi pour les Etats-Unis de l'Amérique, SA MAJESTÉ a bien voulu prendre à sa charge les frais de Commission et de Banque dudit emprunt, desquels frais SA MAJESTÉ a fait don et remise auxdits Etats, ce que leur Ministre soussigné a accepté avec reconnoissance au nom du Congrès, comme une nouvelle marque de la générosité et de l'amitié de SA MAJESTÉ pour lesdits Etats-Unis.

Article 8.

A l'égard des intérêts dudit emprunt pendant les cinq années qui précéderont celle du premier terme de remboursement du Capital, Comme le Roi s'est engagé à les payer au Comptoir Général des Etats Généraux des Pays Bas, sur le pied de quatre pour cent par an et d'année en année, à compter du 5 Novembre 1781. suivant la convention du même jour, le Ministre du Congrès reconnoit que la restitution en est due à SA MAJESTÉ par les Etats-Unis et s'engage au nom desdits Etats à les faire payer et rembourser aux mêmes époques et sur le même pied au Trésor Royale de SA MAJESTÉ, la premiere année d'arrérages d'intérêts devant être acquitté le 5. Novembre prochain et ainsi de suite pendant chacune des cinq années qui précéderont celle du premier terme de remboursement du capital fixé cy dessus au 5. Novembre 1787.[4]

4. Congress was only able to keep up the interest payments until 1785: Ferguson, *Power of the Purse*, p. 235.

Les hautes parties contractantes se garantissent réciproquement l'observation fidéle du présent Contrat, dont les Ratifications seront échangées dans l'espace de neuf mois à compter de ce jour ou plutôt s'il est possible.[5] En foi de quoi Nous Plénipotentiaires susdits de Sa Majesté Très Chretienne et des Treize Etats-Unis de l'Amérique Septentrionale, en vertu de nos pouvoirs respectifs, avons signé ces présentes et y avons fait apposer le Cachet de nos Armes.

Fait à Versailles le Seizieme jour du mois de Juillet Mil sept cent quatre vingt deux.

GRAVIER DE VERGENNES

[*seal*]

B FRANKLIN

[*seal*]

Franklin: Statement Concerning the Dutch Loan

DS: Musée de Blérancourt

[after July 16, 1782]

Etat des reconnoissances fournies au Trésor Royal par M. franklin, et relatives à l'emprunt d'hollande de dix millions.[6]

Savoir:

		l.t.
18 juillet	1781.	800,000 ″ ″
29 octobre	id	600,000 ″ ″
4 xbre	id	816,000. ″ ″
8 fevrier	1782.	500,000 ″ ″
12 mars	id	500,000 ″ ″
7 juin	id	2,352,899.15. 4
Le dit jour[7]		300,000. ″ ″
		5,868,899.15. 4.

5. Congress ratified it on Jan. 22, 1783: *JCC*, XXIV, 50, 63–4.

6. Neither this statement nor the contract with the French government, immediately above, includes a loan of 416,000 *l.t.* on May 30, 1781, presumably taken from the Dutch loan: XXXV, 71n. We have located loan certificates for the first five payments listed here; see XXXVI, 96–7n, 347n.

7. Perhaps July 16, 1782, the date of the contract with the French govern-

Je soussigné, Ministre des Etats unis de l'Amérique, reconnois que mes sept promesses ci-dessus détaillées, m'ont été rendues, et sont devenues nulles par le traité passé le 16 juillet dernier, lesquelles promesses quoique ne formant que cinq millions huit cent soixante huit mille huit cent quatrevingt dixneuf livres quinze sols quatre deniers nen sont pas moins le Solde des 10 millions de l'emprunt d'hollande n'ayant pas été fourni de reconnoissances pour les 4,131,100.*l.t.* 4.*s.* 8 que j'ai également reçu dans le temps. Paris le   B FRANKLIN

From Antoine-Norbert d'Artus[8]

Two LS:[9] American Philosophical Society

Monsieur   à Belfort le 17 juillet 1782

Je prends la liberté de vous adresser un memoire Relatif au Sr Penet.[1] Linteret que je prends à ce jeune homme depuis sa plus

---

ment. Under the same date, Account XXVII (XXXII, 4) itemizes various sums received from the Royal Treasury, presumably from the Dutch loan: (1) 146,000 *l.t.*, "the Overplus which the Finance has paid on the Subsidy of 1781"; (2) 196,481 *l.t.* 15 *s.* 3 *d.* for 200,000 weight of powder and its transport to Brest; (3) 1,011,248 *l.t.* 5 *s.* 11 *d.* for a provision of cloth made in 1781 at the request of Col. Laurens; (4) 1,800,000 *l.t.* for a second provision, replacing the effects aboard the *Marquis de Lafayette;* (5) 1,052,345 *l.t.* 11 *s.* 6 *d.*, reimbursed to the war department for provisions made in May and June, 1781; (6) a similar payment of 252,275 *l.t.* to the navy department; (7) 293,430 *l.t.* for freight of four vessels from Brest (for which see XXXV, 111n, 518–19); (8) 394,219 *l.t.* 7 *s.* 4 *d.* "for what rests to be furnished with the Freight of Vessels of Transport, valued expecting a final Account".

8. D'Artus (b. 1730) had served with distinction with the French army in Germany during the Seven Years' War: *DBF.* Pierre Penet used d'Artus' residence as a mailing address when he wrote to BF on Oct. 20, 1782 (APS), to explain why he had fled his creditors at Nantes.

9. D'Artus sent duplicates of both this letter and the enclosure on Aug. 7, explaining that he had not yet received a response from BF. APS.

1. The enclosed memoir, signed by d'Artus and dated July 17, claims that Penet had acquitted with "fidelité et intelligence" the mission of acquiring in Europe various supplies for the American army, and blames Congress for exhausting Penet's credit by not providing him with adequate funds. Penet was forced to flee when creditors seized his possessions in Europe and tried to ar-

tendre enfance et mon attachement pour son honnette famille me font ressentir l'amertume de son malheur. Instruit des Causes qui ÿ ont donné lieu, j'ose m'adresser à votre Excellence dans une pleine conviction de sa justice et de sa Bienfaisance, implorant sa bonté pour relever du plus grand des malheurs un Sujet du Roy qui s'est laissé emporté par un desir ardent d'etre de quelq'utilité aux états unis de L'Amerique.

Je suis avec un tres profond respect Monsieur Votre tres humble et tres obeissant Serviteur.

D'ARTUS
chev de st Louis: Lant Colonel D'infanterie

From Thomas Barclay

ALS: American Philosophical Society

Sir   Amsterdam 17 July 1782

I had the honour of receiving your Excellencys of the 5th[2] which I shoud have acknowledged by return of post, but I defer'd doing it for some days, in order to examine my situation and to endeavour to fill in some method of getting away the remainder of the public goods without being further troublesome to your Excellency. I have not hitherto made great progress, nor indeed Can I say what it is possible for Me to do, if you shoud think proper to Continue in the resolution of not accepting any More of My bills, for I am already in that state with respect to the supplies that I shall be very Much Embarrassd indeed— The shirts that I have shipped by the Elizabeth were deliver'd to Me by Mr Peter Buyck of Ghent, and are to be settled for from the British goods, so that I drew for no part of the amount of them.

The other Engagements which I made were for 5200 suits of Cloathing at about 12 shillings sterling per suit which Cost in France 33 livres, 2 Bailes of French Blankets at 5/9 per pair amounting to about £50 Sterling, and 2 Boxes of white Cloth which Cost at Leyden 3766 florins, and which I thought wanting to Compleat the Stores going out, as the Blue Cloths Cou'd be

---

rest him. He hopes that Congress will compensate him by depositing funds with Rochambeau's army, but until then he is seeking an *arrêt de surséance* (XXXV, 541n) from Louis XVI. D'Artus asks BF's assistance in obtaining it.

2. Not found.

of little Use without white facing for the Uniforms. Annex'd is an account of the articles on board the Elizabeth amounting to *f*. 40703. 6. 4.[3] Upon the shirts I am Engaged to pay 12½ per Cent freight on the Value, and on the Blankets 20 per Cent and before I received your Excellencys last letter, I increased the Insurance, which I mention'd to you some time ago, on those goods to 40 thousand florins, It is made at Hambourg under the Guarrantee of a House at Ostend and another here and will Cost altogether 17 per Cent, which is not more than half the premium paid on American Vessells bound to the Continent. For the payment of this freight and premium of Insurance, I stand Bound to Mess. Gerand & Rolland of this place, and to Mess Ingraham & Bromfield for sundry Disbursements on the ship Heer Adams— I beg leave therefore to offer to your Excellencys Consideration the situation I shall be in without farther assistance from You. When I received My Commission from the President of Congress, he informed Me that the Army was in great want of supplys, and that I wou'd immediately on My Arrival in France be furnishd by your Excellency with two Million of livres to supply those wants, at the same time My Instructions Convey'd to me a Credit upon any public loans made in Europe, which Instructions I had the honour to lay before You at Passy.[4] These Considerations, added to the Information that Mr. Morris had written for Cloathing to the amount of two Million of livres[5] induced Me to close for the 5200 suits; especially as there was a saving Made thereby to the public of near one hundred thousand livres. The Goods which I engaged to deliver Mr. Buyck of Ghent in Exchange for the shirts, we Mutualy agreed shou'd be valued by a sworn Broker, they Cost by Mr De Neufville's Invoice *f*. 73248. 17. 8 and were Valued by Mr [Asterlore?] the Broker at No more than *f*. 41575, This great difference is partly

---

3. The enclosure lists goods sent aboard the *Elizabeth, Recovery,* and *Sukey,* as well as those remaining to be sent. About 26,000 *f*. of the *Elizabeth*'s cargo consisted of 65 chests of shirts.

4. *JCC,* XX, 736–7.

5. Morris forwarded BF an invoice from the Board of War requesting nearly 1,800,000 *l.t.* of supplies, mostly clothing: XXXVI, 154–5; *Morris Papers,* III, 289–90.

owing to damage that several of the Bales received by lying in open Boats in the Texel, waiting I am told for Mr. Gillons orders, partly by their being purchased in a hurry and perhaps at too high prices, but principaly I beleive by the Resolve of Congress prohibiting the Importation of British Manufactures into America—be that as it will, I informed Mr Buyck that I wish'd to be excused from delivering him the Goods upon such a Valuation, and that I wou'd Much sooner have them sold by public Auction, to which he readily Acquesced and they stand Advertised for the 23d of this Month. It wou'd have been a Very lucky Circumstance if I had pursued this plan at first, but I did not forsee what happen'd, and on the whole I will not presume to say that I acted properly, but I am sure I did to the best of My Judgement as Circumstances arose. I am Now obliged to Come to the subject of what is to be done with the goods on hand, the particulars of which I also send you. There are some Vessells loading here for America, and to the people who have the Care of them I have Already apply'd— The detention of the ship Congress, and Capture of the navarro, Fox and Heydon, all of whom were intended to load here, have given an opportunity to the other Vessells to put the best freight, and accordingly the people to whom they are Consigned generally reject goods that are Not Valuable— I have endeavour'd to agree for the freight to be paid in America, but I have very little hopes of success with any person but a Mr. Myers who has a Brigantine Bound to America, and who has my proposal under Consideration.[6] I shall be glad to be of any service in my power in Making the settlement with Mess. De neufville & son, but it will be a Very disagreeable office and more than probably payment will be Awarded them for their demand— The Affair having happened prior to My arrival obliges me to ask Your Excellencys instructions as particularly as You think necessary— I have been obliged to trouble You Sir with a longer letter than I Cou'd wish because I Chuse to Acquaint You Minutely with My situation which I beg you will take into Your Consideration. I shall Conclude with the assurance that it was Very far from my intention to add to Your Excellencys

6. See Samuel & Moses Myers to BF, July 22.

Embarrassments by my Engagements here and that I have the honour to be Very respectfully Your Excellencys Most Obedient Humble Servant   Thos Barclay

His Excellency Benjamin Franklin Esqr. Passy near Paris

Since writing the annex'd, Mr Myers has agreed to take the 63 Bales of linen Mention'd in the annexd List on board the Brigantine Grace, George Mitchell Master, paying at Philadelphia 15 per Cent on the Value. The vessell will take them in, and possibly some More of the goods, in two or three days.

From Sally Beckwith   ALS: Historical Society of Pennsylvania

Sir   Convent St George Ghent July 17th 1782

The inclosed Letter[7] which I regret exceedingly not having in my power to deliver in person, I onely had the pleasure of receiving yesterday, its detention has been owing to a long and dangerous illness of the Gentleman to whose care the Paquet was adressed in which it was contained.

The Friendship Mr Strahan has ever testified for our Family & that in particular He has lately shewn towards me in a degree I am ill able to express, makes me apprehensive that a desire of obtaining the Friendship and protection of Dr Franklin may have led him to say in my favor much more than I can possibly hope to merit & makes me almost afraid of what I otherwise should have thought a most singular Happiness the Honor of being known to You.

The very few People I know here & Mr. Bells[8] recent illness at Ostend who proposed to Himself waiting on you previous to his setting off for Philadelphia onely permits me to *hope* how soon I may have it in my power to ask your comands for that part of the world.

7. From William Strahan, May 27, above.

8. William Bell (*c.* 1739–1816), a Philadelphia merchant who had been residing in Amsterdam since 1781. He was quite possibly the Mr. Bell who was a business associate of Benjamin Vaughan's and Moses Young's: *Morris Papers*, VII, 325–6n; Benjamin Vaughan to WTF, Aug. 29, 1782 (APS); *Laurens Papers*, XV, 569.

I must beg pardon for sending these letters by the common Post the retirement in which I live not putting it in my power to find any private Hand on which I can depend. I have Sir the Honor to be your most Obedt & very Hle Servant

S BECKWITH

Notation: S. Beckwith, July 17. 1782.

From the Loge des Commandeurs du Temple[9]

LS: American Philosophical Society

[July 17, 1782]

A La Gloire
du grand Architecte de Lunivers.
d'un lieu éclairé ou regnent le Silence, la paix et La Charité La Loge reguliere des Commandeurs du Temple Seante A Lorient de Carcassonne. Lan de La V∴ L∴ 5782 et Le. 17e. Jour du 5me. mois[1]

Au Trés Digne
Tres Vertueux et Tres Respectable Frere Franklin
Ministre des Etats unis de L'amerique au pres de La Cour de Françe./. Seant à Lorient de Paris
Salut Forçe Union
T∴ C∴ F∴[2]

Chargé des interets dun peuple a qui le dezir de la Liberté a mis les armes a la main, au Sortir de ces conferences Secretes ou lon peze le Destin de lunivers, vous prénes plaisir quelque fois a Sacrifier à L'amitié. La Loge des neuf Sœurs en à été Souvent le temoin. Le Zele que vous y aves témoigné pour nos misteres est parvenu jusques au fonds de nos Provinces.

IL nous donne le droit de nous adresser a vous; notre objet

---

9. The Carcassonne lodge which had last corresponded with BF in September, 1780: XXXIII, 304–6. Their representative in Paris, the baron de La Courtette, visited BF in 1781: XXXIV, 482–3.

1. The masonic year, "de la Vraie Lumière," begins in March.

2. Très Cher Frère.

n'en est point indigne: il sagit de Calmer une Mere éplorée Sur le Sort de son fils.

Celuy cy parti le 1. Janvier du Cap Français (on ne sait Sur quel Vaisseau) était porteur de plusieurs Lettres, dont deux contenant des raports avantageux sur son Compte etaient adressées à sa Mere par des négotians ches lesquels il avait resté.

Les autres étoient pour divers particuliers.

Six mois aprés et il y à environ huit jours ces Lettres arrivent a leur destination. Les deux adressées a la Mere font voir cette Souscription fatale; "le porteur mort à York en Virginie en May dernier."

A Cette nouvelle on laisse à penser le saisissement la douleur qui Semparerent de cette Mere. Il faut Létre pour le Sentir. Des amis genereux Volent à son Secours; ils luy disent que son fils à pû remetre ces Lettres à quelqu'un qui à étté en Virginie et qui y est mort. Elle prete peu loreille a des pareils discours. Cependant comme ils pourroient etre vrais, et qu'il importe de les constater, nous Venons vous prier de vous donner des Soins pour S'avoir quel est le français Mort a York en Virginie en May dernier. Pour que vous ayés plus de facilité, nous vous envoyons cyjoint le signalement du Jeune homme au quel nous nous interessons Son nom, Son Surnom et son âge.[3] Par la comparaison il sera façile de savoir ce que nous desirons.

Si vous nous annoncés que le Jeune homme que nous cherchons n'est pas celui qui est Mort en Virginie vous redonnès la vie à une Mere à la quelle il est cher.

Si vous nous dittes le contraire vous assurés létat dune famille dans la quelle Lincertitude de sa vie ou de sa mort et de linstant ou elle est arrivée peut occasionner des troubles et des disputes pour le partage à faire de son bien. Vous lui rendés encore un autre Service en vous informant de ce que nous vous demandons vous avés la bonté de Savoir si le Jeune homme mort portait des effets avec lui et entre les mains de qui ils Sont tombés. Ainsi dans un seul bienfait vous en reunisses plusieurs.

La Loge des Commandeurs qui s'est toujours fait un devoir de plaindre les malheureux et de les Soulager se flatte que vous

3. The enclosed description has not been found.

offrir loccasion de faire du bien et vous Le voir faire Seront pour vous une meme chose.

Elle Sestime heureuse d'avoir un titre pour sadresser a un S'age L'Espoir de son Pays lobjet de la Veneration du notre.

Elle serait au Comble de Ses dezirs, si pour tranquiliser la Mere éplorée vous luy faisiés la faveur de lui repondre que vous ne perdrés pas du vüe la priere que nous vous adressons.

Nous sommes avec les sentiments de la plus tendre fraternité, par les N∴ M∴ A∴ V∴ C∴[4]

T∴ C∴ F∴

Vos affectionnés et très devoües les officiers de L∴ L∴[5] des Commandeurs   V. VIDAL Venerable[6]

MÊRIC DE RIÊUX,[7] P.S. [premier Surveillant]

ASTOIN avt. [avocat] S.S. [Second Surveillant]

Par Mandement de L. R. L:[8] ROQUES secretaire

L'ABBÉ MERIC DE RIEUX prieur et avt vst(?)

Timbré et sellé par nous garde du timbre et sceaux G DAVID avt

adresse de la Loge à Monsieur David de lafajole avocat au Parlement de Toulouze rüe St. Eulalie à Carcassonne

Notation: David. à Carcassonne

---

4. Nombres Mystérieux A Vous Connus.

5. La Loge.

6. According to a printed *tableau des officiers*, Vidal was an *avocat en Parlement*. The *tableau* was enclosed in a printed letter of Sept. 4 from the Carcasonne lodge to the Neuf Sœurs which alluded to a long delay in the election of new officers that year. The letter was signed by Roques, Astoin, and Mêric de Riêux. APS. The delay was evidently caused by the lodge's recent petition to have its constitutions renewed by the *Chambre des Provinces*, which refused the request: Alain Le Bihan, *Loges et chapitres de la Grande Loge et du Grand Orient de France* . . . (Commission d'histoire économique et sociale de la Révolution française, *Mémoires et documents*, XX, Paris, 1967), 58.

7. For Mêric de Riêux, Astoin, and Roques see XXXIII, 306n.

8. La Respectable Loge.

From William Hodgson

ALS: Historical Society of Pennsylvania

Dear sir   London 18 July 1782

I have recd yours of the 18th, but not that per Mr Young,[9] I immediately set about procuring you the necessary Information Relative to the Marquis de Fayette & inclosed you have an Acc't of the Wine & Salt as per Catalogue for Sale which I hope will be fully Satisfactory—[1] if any thing further I mean Oath & Notarial Certificate shou'd be necessary, please to inform me & it shall be procured— I am going to the Secretarys Office to get this conveyed per Courier—if I shou'd be disappointed in that Conveyance, I shall send you per Some other Conveyance the general Catalogue, & this Letter per post, as the former is too bulky for the post— I am with the greatest Respect Dr sr yours most sincerely   WILLIAM HODGSON

I Wrote you last post via Ostend, under Cover to Mr Grand

His Excellency Benj. Franklin Esqr

From Pierre Colomb, with Franklin's Note for a Reply

LS: American Philosophical Society

Monseigneur   Nimes le 19 Juillet 1782

Voila deux ans et demy d'Ecoulés depuis mon depart de l'amerique Septentrionale, sous le congé qui me fut acordé par le Congrés avec la faculté de venir rejoindre mes drapeaux lorsque Les Circonstances me le permetroient, et que ma Santé Epuisée par les fatigues du service penible que J'y avois fait pend' 3 ans, et de la dure prison que J'y avois soufferte pendant quatre mois de tems par les anglois a Savanah sous le General prevôt[2] ne fut entierement retablie, Je ne dois pas vous laisser ignorer Monseigneur, que pendant ce long Espace de tems, Je ne

---

9. We have no other record of either letter. See BF to Vaughan, July 11, for the sending of letters via Young.

1. For the catalogue see JW to BF, June 18.

2. Augustine Prevost, the British general who repulsed the French and American attack on Savannah in 1779: XXXI, 78n.

648

me suis occupé que du soin de la reparer, mes Medecins et Ceux de la faculté de Montpr [Montpellier] dont je puis vous remetre les certificats ne trouverent d'autre espoir a ma Guerison qui leur parut incertaine que dans le sejour continuel en Suisse dont le Climat plus favorable pût reparer mes forces, en effet J'y ay residé la plus grande partie de Ce tems la, et depuis Quelques mois que J'en suis de retour, Je Jouis de la meilleure santé, et Je ne soupire qu'aprés l'heureux Instant de rejoindre mon Etat et mes drapeaux. C'est dans cette vue que Je prens la Liberté de m'adresser a vous Monseigneur, comme a mon Protecteur, pour m'en faciliter et Indiquer les moyens. L'accueil Gracieux dont vous daignates m'honorer a mon passage a Paris en Janvier 1780. Lors de mon retour de L'amerique Les divers brevets de mon rang de Capne. et ensuitte de Major de dragons, que J'y avois obtenu, et Le Congé du Congrés, que vous avés daigné viser et munir de votre Sceau[3] me permettent desperer votre protection dans ce moment Instant ou Je la reclame Instruit par ces pieces que Je ne puis servir sous les drapeaux Americains pendant la presente Guerre que moyenant mon Echange comme etant jusques la Toujours prisonnier des Anglois Jose vous suplier Monseigneur de me procurer cet Echange, et de hâter par la Le moment de mon depart, et L'employ de mes services que Je brule de Consacrer a l'Illustre Etat que vous representez, Je vous suplie donc d'en hâter le moment et de me fournir les moyens & les secours pour retourner le plutot a mon poste, Puisque mes forces et mes inclinations m'y apellent avec empressement.

Vous voudrés bien me donner pour ce passage une place ou un Employ, Sur Telle fregatte ou tel Batiment destiné pour le Congrés, qui soit a vos ordres, et ou Je Sois apuyé de votre recomandation. J'ose esperer que mon Employ me sera rendu a mon retour, et que Je men aquitteray avec le meme Zele et la meme activitté.

J'ose esperer Monseigneur que vous accederés a la Justice de

3. In December, 1780, BF attested two documents concerning Colomb's service in the American army, one of which listed him as a major even though Congress had refused to promote him to that rank: XXXIV, 76n; *JCC*, XIV, 936–7. For Colomb's meeting with BF eleven months earlier see also XXXI, 39–40n.

ma demande, et que vous ne me refuserés pas dans votre reponse (que Je vous suplie de me faire), le secours et l'apuy que Je reclame de votre bienfaisance et de vos vertus, qui brillent avec tant d'Eclat dans l'auguste place que vous occupés, et qui vous rend le protecteur né de tous ceux qui se sont consacrés au Service de votre Illustre Etat, et qui brulent comme moy de s'y distinguer encore. Dans Cet espoir flatteur Jay Lhoneur detre avec le plus profond respect Monseigneur Votre tres humb et trés obeisst Serviteur COLOMB

major de dragons au service des Etats unis

J'ose vous prier de me dire si depuis mon depart come prisonnier mon Employ a eté remply et si mes apointemens ont courru ou ne courront que du moment de mon retour—[4]

Endorsed:[5] Answer

That I have no Orders to furnish any Officers the Means of going to America, nor any Money put into my Hands for such Purposes. } 2

That I know nothing of his Exchange, and can do nothing in it such Exchanges being made in America } 1

From Mary Hewson

ALS: University of Pennsylvania Library

Dear Sir   Kensington July 19. 1782

Dr Shuttleworth informed me that he intended going to Paris in order to consult you upon some American business of his own, and desired an introduction from me. He attended Mr Hewson's Lectures, and as he has dined several times at our table you probably may have seen him. He was in Maryland with Mr Eden.[6]

---

4. On Aug. 19, Colomb sent another appeal (APS).

5. This endorsement served as a draft of BF's response of Aug. 27 (APS).

6. Dr. John Shuttleworth lived in Maryland in the early 1770s and claimed that during that time he was the physician for Gov. Robert Eden (XVI, 185n): Ronald Hoffman, ed., *Dear Papa, Dear Charley: the Peregrinations of a Revolutionary Aristocrat* . . . (3 vols., Chapel Hill, N.C., and London, 2001), II, 522, 524n, 580, 615; Shuttleworth to George Washington, Dec. 22, 1782 (Li-

I am highly delighted with the importance I am grown into since the change of affairs, but still more so with the frequent opportunities of hearing from you, and writing to you. A letter arrived here two days ago by the penny post, which I knew to be your hand, but I am ignorant of the contents, for as it was addressed to my mother I dispatched it to her unopened.[7] She is upon a visit to Mrs de Ponthieu at Richmond. I do not recollect whether I ever told you the plan Mrs Wilkes was upon at that place. She took a very genteel house for the accommodation of six young ladies at £100 a year each. She had her complement, and by her assiduity in their improvement gave general satisfaction, and gained great applause with a comfortable subsistence.[8] But it is her fate never to be settled. She expected her eldest son from N York to settle in business here, and seeing the impropriety of her house being his home while she had young ladies of 16 & 17 under her care she acquainted their friends, and they were all taken away immediately, except two, one of which was Bolton's daughter,[9] a little girl, and now she is gone; so Mrs W. remains upon an expensive establishment with only £100 a year to support it. The death of Mr Weir[1] obliged Jack to return to N York and by the last accounts I find he, and his brother, who is with him, can do nothing there unless we should have a peace.[2] Mr Wilkes went with Mr Davidson to Algiers, but, as usual, was

---

brary of Congress). For Shuttleworth's present errand see his letter of [Aug. 14].

Dr. William Hewson (XVI, 191n) lectured on anatomy, first with Dr. William Hunter from 1762 to 1771, and then independently from 1772 until his death in 1774: XVIII, 192; XIX, 304; XXI, 209n.

7. BF to Margaret Stevenson, July 12, above.

8. Mrs. de Ponthieu is presumably the mother of Elizabeth de Ponthieu Wilkes, an acquaintance from BF's years in London: XV, 238n. Hewson first informed BF of Mrs. Wilkes's school in 1779: XXIX, 579.

9. Most likely Anne "Nancy" Boulton (c. 1769–1829), daughter of Matthew Boulton, the engineer and manufacturer (X, 39n), and of his second wife, Anne Robinson: H. W. Dickinson, *Matthew Boulton* (Cambridge, 1937), pp. 27, 56.

1. Daniel Wier was British commissary general in New York from May, 1777 until his death on Nov. 12, 1781: Bowler, *Logistics*, pp. 30, 253.

2. Elizabeth Wilkes's sons were John ("Jack") de Ponthieu Wilkes (*DAB* under his son Charles Wilkes) and Charles Wilkes (XXXII, 209).

soon dissatisfied, and returned.[3] The mother[4] is dead, but her jointure you know was made over to creditors long ago, and she left no more than £300 to Israel & his family. What will become of them I cannot tell, nor should I trouble you with this detail had not Mrs W. once hinted that she thought herself qualified to teach English in France, and as we find that is now so much in fashion, perhaps you may be able to recommend her, or at least you can tell us how far such a scheme may be eligible. She is certainly more mistress of the two languages than any woman I know.

I thank you, Sir, for the Books you sent me by Baron Dimsdale; they afforded me much entertainment, and some hints that I hope to profit by. Made de Genlis is quite the mode in England. She has a numerous train of admirers here, and not one censurer that I have heard of. Upon the whole I think she deserves the applause she gains; I honour her for her talents and the use she makes of them, and in general I approve her reasoning; but I detect her sophistry in some points particularly with regard to suckling and stays. You will not wonder, as you know how steadily I persevered in one of my tenets, and I have told you how obstinately I adhere to the other.[5]

You desire my remarks upon the little piece you did me the favour to send of Made de Forbach's.[6] No leisure is required for me to do that, as I cannot make a single objection, and my comment would be only an exact repetition of what she has said.

As you have thus assisted to enlighten my mind you will add

3. Israel Wilkes (XIII, 537n), the husband of Elizabeth Wilkes, had long struggled in business. He went to Algiers in 1779 in search of opportunities: XXIX, 579n.

4. Sarah Heaton Wilkes was the wife of the late Israel Wilkes, Sr., a wealthy distiller: *DNB* under John Wilkes.

5. Thomas Dimsdale conveyed Mme de Genlis' *Adèle et Théodore;* see BF to Hewson, June 13. The work approves of nursing for up to two years (but asserts the propriety of the mother's retreat into the home during this period) and argues that stays, if well-made, can be comfortable and protective of health; see vol. 1, letters XXI and XI, respectively. Hewson suckled her first-born son for at least six months and reported in 1781 her decision to keep her daughter without stays: XVIII, 236; XXXVI, 288–9.

6. See BF to Hewson, June 13.

much to my satisfaction by placing the confidence in me you flatter me with, by sending your grandson to me. I think my daughter and he would soon have both languages at command. To make you some return for what you have sent me, I enclose the rules of the School where my boys are. I should have great pleasure in placing Bache there.[7]

I am with true esteem Dear Sir Your obliged and most obedient hum. Sert   MARY HEWSON

Notation: Hewson, 27. Decr. 1782

From William Hodgson   ALS: Historical Society of Pennsylvania

Dear sir   London 19 July 1782

I wrote you yesterday, in which I acquainted you that I shou'd go to the Secretary's Office, in order to have the pacquet, which I had made up for you, forwarded by a Courier if any was going.

I accordingly went & saw the Earl of Shelburne who entered into a Good deal of Conversation about you & Peace, protested & vowed in the fullest manner & in the most explicit Terms that he was convinced American Independance must be admitted in the most unequivocal Manner, said some one had been *so Wicked*[*8] as to write you, that the present Ministers were averse to the allowing of it—declared it was false & that no Obstacle of that Kind shou'd with him retard a Peace— Seemed to insinuate that he did not see what America coud reasonably ask, that he shou'd not be willing to concede—. I told him that in my poor

---

7. For BF's proposal and the school see BF to Hewson, June 13.

8. Footnote in MS: "Quere have you not said this to B:V—for I conjecture that is the Channell of his Lordships Information; it will put you on your guard in future, was there or was there not any Truth in his Lordships Conjecture." BF did report these rumors to Benjamin Vaughan in his letter of July 11, above. Vaughan was not only a protégé of Shelburne (whom he had met through Benjamin Horne, the brother of John Horne Tooke), but virtually a member of Shelburne's household: C. R. Ritcheson, "The Earl of Shelburne and Peace with America, 1782–1783: Vision and Reality," *International History Rev.,* V (1983), 325; Fitzmaurice, *Life of Shelburne,* II, 165n.

Judgment Improper persons & improper Measures had been pursued in order to obtain what was wished for by all— That I was convinced from what I had the Honor to know of your Disposition that the most open manly & Confidential manner of Treaty was what was most likely to be effectual & that I was confident your Judgment & Penetration wou'd soon see thro' any disguise or Concealment. His Lordship was pleased to say he approved of my frankness—& by his future Conversation seemed to wish much to come to a full & Satisfactory explanation of his own Opinions & that such shou'd be conveyed to you & that he wished me to make the Communication— In consequence of which I returned home to write you this Letter. It will therefore now be in your Judgment if any & what Use can be made of this Overture, for as such I undoubtedly consider it— If you have that Confidence in me which on a former Occasion you were so kind as to express,[9] The Negotiation may be bro't forward here thro' my Intervention in a Tenth part of the Time it will at Paris, or the inadmissibility of the Terms with respect to other Powers be soon brought to a point— If you can confide in me so far as to say *what will do* Matters may be soon bro't to a Crisis with the principals, rather than with the Gentlemen at Paris who wait for explanation on every proposition that Arises— You will please to write me two Letters one private & Confidential the other such a one as I may produce if necessary— I am convinced the Situation of his Lordship is such, that he means to give up entirely the loose Ideas he had adopted from Lord Chatham[1] & that his firm Seat in the Saddle will depend upon his Strait forward Conduct in this Business,

This Letter his Lordship has promised me shall go by the Courier to morrow & I flatter myself that you will upon due Deliberation favor me with such an answer as your maturer Judgment shall direct— For myself I shall only say, that, in whatever way you may judge proper to make use of me I will do my best to merit your approbation & you may rely upon it I will not

9. BF's April 13 invitation to come to Paris, above.
1. Shelburne was a disciple of William Pitt, Earl of Chatham. Both men had advocated ending hostilities and granting America considerable autonomy but not independence: XXV, 213n, 272n; XXVI, 366–71.

abuse your Confidence being with the greatest respect & Esteem
Dr sr Yours Sincerely   WILLIAM HODGSON

P.S. A particular friend wishes to know if the American Privateers belonging to America are restrained by their Instructions
from committing any Acts of Hostility on Land, this I believe is
for a Literary purpose & I shou'd be glad you wou'd inform me
tho' for my own part I cannot conceive any such thing.

His Excellency Benj Franklin Esqr

Notation: Wm. Hodgson 19. July 1782

From Benjamin West   ALS: American Philosophical Society

Sir   London July 19th. 1782
    If I was to permit my friend and nabour Mr. Green to visit
Paris without convaying this to your excellency, I should think
myself defecient in that friendship I have ever wished to shew
him. He is an Artist of distinguished merit in Mezzatinto engraving, and has done most of the esteemed prints in that manner from my paintings.[2] He visits France in the line of his profession, and wishes to have the honor of being known to your
excellency before he leves that country;[3] for that purpose he will
have the satisfaction to present this;—and any favors shewn him
and his son[4] by your excellency will be greatly esteemed by—Sir
Your excellencys greatly Obliged Humble Sert.

                                      BENJN. WEST

His excellency Benjamin Franklin

Notation: B. West July 19 1782.

---

2. For the work of Valentine Green (*DNB*) see George C. Williamson,
ed., *Bryan's Dictionary of Painters and Engravers* (rev. ed., 5 vols., New York
and London, 1903); Alfred Whitman, *Valentine Green* (London, 1902).
    3. Green's visit to Paris in the summer of 1782 resulted in his writing *A
Review of the Polite Arts in France, at the Time of their Establishment under
Louis the XIVth, compared with their Present State in England . . . in a letter
to Sir Joshua Reynolds . . .* (London, 1782).
    4. Rupert Green (*c.* 1768–1804): *DNB* under Valentine Green.

From the Marquis d'Amezaga

AL: American Philosophical Society

Ce Samedy. 20 Jllet. [1782]⁵

Mr. D'amezaga, fait ses Plus Tendres Complimens à Monsieur de franklin, Il luy fait demander Sil dinne demain chés luy, dimanche et Sil veut bien que Mr. Damezaga aille L'embrasser.

From Ferdinand Grand ALS: American Philosophical Society

Monsieur   Passy 20 Juilt 82

Jay lhonneur de joindre icy suivant vos desirs, l'État de Situation du Compte de Mr. Morris, dicy à la fin de l'année;⁶

Vous y verrés monsieur, que les Gros payements faits & à faire absorbent les fonds qu'il à en france, & qu'au lieu de pouvoir contracter de nouveaux Engagements, il faut S'occuper des actuellement des moyens de pourvoir aux anciens qui exigeront comme Vous Le Comprendrés aisement d'apres cet Etat, un secour de deux millions pour etre au Large dans tous les Cas; Jay Lhonneur detre plus que personne Monsieur votre tres humble & tres obeisst Servitr   GRAND

From Richard Penn, Jr.⁷ ALS: Historical Society of Pennsylvania

Dear Sir   Cavendish Square July 20th. 1782

I take the Liberty of recommending to your notice the bearer of this Mr. Philip Livingston⁸ a Gentleman with whom I have had a very great Intimacy for many Years Past both in this Country & on the other side the Atlantic & I will answer for it that you

---

5. The only year during BF's stay in France that July 20 fell on a Saturday.
6. Not found. On March 9, Morris had informed Grand that bills would be drawn on him: *Morris Papers*, IV, 378, 436n, 463.
7. For whom see XXVII, 579–80.
8. Philip Livingston (1740–1810), a first cousin of Sarah Jay's, was touring Europe. He arrived in Paris on Oct. 18 after a visit to Spain: Morris, *Jay: Peace*, pp. 447, 590n.

will find him in every respect worthy of your Acquaintance. My Wife[9] & Family join me in our most sincere Wish's for your Health & happiness. I am My Dear Sir Your very sincere Friend

RICHD. PENN

Addressed: His Excellency / Benjamin Franklin &c &c &c

Notation: Richd. Penn July 20 1782.

From Schweighauser & Dobrée

ALS: Historical Society of Pennsylvania

sir!   Nantes 20 July 1782./.

Altho.' we are without any answer to the Letters we have had the honor of writing to your Excellency the 18 December[1] and the 8 of last Month you will please to permit us to refer thereto.

By Letter received the day before Yesterday from Philadelphia via Cadiz we have inclose a resolve of Congress authorising Joshua Johnson Esqe. to examine our account for the Alliance frigatte and directing your Excellency to pay us the amount, annexed is copy of said resolve.[2]

Mr. Johnson refuses complying with this order for the reason he alledged when you wrote us to apply to him for the same purpose,[3] we most earnestly beg your Excellency would point out to us some method of getting these accounts examined by said Gentleman or would accept the attestation of any regular court of judicature to which we will submit them.

We have waited our due patiently, we have twice prevented our Partners in the house en Comandite at L Orient from arresting this frigatte; the advances we claim were made in a view of serving the public and we have at all times unrelentingly en-

9. Mary Masters Penn: XXVII, 579n.

1. Not found.

2. Congress' resolve of Aug. 24, 1781: *JCC*, XXI, 907. The enclosure is missing.

3. We have not found BF's letter to the firm on this subject. Johnson had previously refused to conduct an audit on the grounds that he could not leave his family: XXXIII, 7–8.

deavored to shew our Zeal & attachement for the good of the United states these Reasons we think ought to induce your Excellency to press the settlement of our accounts wch we earnestly sollicit.

We are with profound Respect Your Excellency's Most humble & most obedient Servants   SCHWEIGHAUSER & DOBRÉE

To his Excellency Benjamin Franklin Esqe Minister plenipotentiary of the United states of America at the Court of Versailles

Notation: Shweighauser & Dobré Nantes 20. July 1782.

From Jean-Baptiste Luton Durival[4]

LS: University of Pennsylvania Library

A Versailles le 21. Juillet 1782.

Si nous devons, Monsieur, avoir l'honneur de vous voir après demain mardy, je vous prie de ne pas oublier d'apporter votre cachet, pour être apposé sur la convention signée le 16. du courant entre vous et M. le Cte. de Vergennes;[5] Si au contraire vous ne deviez pas venir ici, je vous prierois en ce cas de vouloir bien m'adresser par une occasion sure le cachet que je vous renverrois par la même voye.

J'ai l'honneur d'être avec un très parfait et sincere attachement, Monsieur, Votre très humble et très obéissant serviteur

DURIVAL

M. franklin.

Notation: Durival 21. Juillet 1782

---

4. The foreign ministry *premier commis* responsible for financial affairs: XXXIII, 221n.

5. Above.

From Samuel Cooper

AL: American Philosophical Society

My dear Sir   Boston N.E. July 22. 1782.

I wrote you some Weeks ago[6] how pleased I was with the Spirit of my Countrymen in the Manner in which they received the Account that Genl. Carleton was come from the new Ministry to attempt a seperate Peace with these States, and to detach us from our Allies. The Idea was every where treated with Scorn and Indignation. The Legislature of this and the other States have passed solemn Resolutions upon this Occasion to adhere with the utmost Fidelity and Honour to their Engagements with France, and never to listen to any Proposals from the common Enemy but in Concert with the Court of that Kingdom. So that if Britain means to have Peace at all she must seek it upon a fair, open, and general Ground.

We have lately begun to revive the good old Anniversary Solemnity of Commencement. Last Wednesday a vast Concourse of People of all Orders were assembled at Cambridge on that Occasion. The Governor and Council, the Consul and Vice Consul of France,[7] and all the Kings Officers and French Gentlemen in this Town of Distinction, proceeded from hence in Carriages to Cambridge, escorted by a large Body of Continental and Militia Officers in their Uniforms and handsomely mounted, where the Strangers were received with every Mark of Friendship and Respect: They walked in Procession to the Meeting House in the Centre of the Overseers, and had a distinguished Rank thro all the Ceremonies of the Day. They were much pleased with all the Academical Exercises which breathed the Spirit of the Revolution and the Alliance. They returned to His Excellency's House in this Town where they had breakfasted, and supped there with the Council and other Gentlemen of Distinction. The whole Day was particularly pleasing to me, as it afforded a Proof to every Eye of the public Friendship, and tended at the same Time to confirm and cultivate it.[8]

---

6. On June 15, above.

7. Philippe-André-Joseph de Létombe and Jean Toscan, based in Boston: xxxv, 386n; xxxvi, 463.

8. The commencement on July 17 was Harvard's second since 1773. A de-

Mr Temple's Return from Europe has already occasioned Uneasiness and Divisions here, and may produce more. He was at first examined by the Governor and Council who referr'd his Case to the whole Legislature; they returned it to the Governor and Council who laid him under Bonds to say or do Nothing against the public Welfare;[9] and ordered the Attorney Genl. to bring the Matter in to the Course of Law: The Grand Jury found no Bill against him. Mr T. then applies by Way of Memorial to the Legislative, stating his important Services to the Revolution, particularly in procuring and sending to this Country Hutchinson's Letters. Congress writes a Letter to the Governor observing the suspicious Circumstances of Mr. T.'s first Return to America, and of his last Voyage, when he immediately went from Holland to England, conferr'd with L. North &c, desiring the Matter may be sifted.[1] Our Legislature do nothing upon Mr. T.'s Memorial, and say He has not proved the Facts alledged in it. Mr. T. applies again in the following Session, stating that He went to England to oppose the Representations of Mr. Galloway and the Refugees respecting America,[2] and that he was countenanced so to do by Dr Mather, Dr Cooper and others. Those Gentlemen declare they gave no such Encouragement: Mr Bowdoin and Dr Chauncey acknowledge they approved the Design.[3] After some Struggles it obtains in the Senate by a Majority of one, and in the House, of a very few, that Mr T. be released from his Bonds, and considered as an innocent and meritorious Citizen. Mr T. considers himself as qualified for and deserving the most important public Employments. The Resolution of the two

---

tailed account of it appears in the *The Continental Jour., and Weekly Advertiser* of July 25, 1782.

9. For Temple's return and release under bond see XXXV, 669; XXXVI, 274–5.

1. On Feb. 27, Congress had ordered the governor to be so informed. The letter from John Hanson to John Hancock was dated March 1: *JCC,* XXII, 101–2; Smith, *Letters,* XVIII, 364–5.

2. Joseph Galloway and others testified before Parliament that American independence could not be maintained: XXXV, 316.

3. For Congregational minister Samuel Mather see XX, 229n. James Bowdoin was Temple's father-in-law: XIX, 402. Charles Chauncy was the minister of the First Church in Boston: XI, 255n.

Houses was not signed by the Governor, and of Course drops unless renewed again in some future Session. I have ever been disposed to serve Mr Temple as far as Truth and Duty to my Country would allow; but happening to lend to a Member of the Court a Volume of your Works in which was the Advertisement you published in a London Paper respecting Hutchinson's Letters[4] He was much offended, and said to me that I would rob him of his Merit in procuring and sending the Letters; that the Matter was a Secret between him and you, and if he was obliged by this to say any Thing that might be disadvantageous to you, I must answer for it. I replied that I knew you so throughly as to be under no concern for you in this or any other public Matter.

This goes by Mr Rogers a respectable Merchant in this Town who married a Daughter of Col Henry Bromfield. Mrs Rogers accompanies her Husband in his Voyage to Europe in Hopes of re establishing her Health, which has for a long Time been much impaired: I am much interested in their Welfare, and warmly wish them every Thing happy.[5]

I am with every Sentiment of Respect and Affection, Your Excellency's Friend and humble Servt.

Such Subjects as that of Mr. T. I do not love to mention; but thought it incumbent on me to give some brief and fair Account of this Matter

His Excellency Benjn. Franklin Esqr.

---

4. The volume was *Political, Miscellaneous, and Philosophical Pieces . . .* (London, 1779): XXXI, 210–18. It includes BF's Dec. 27, 1773, statement to the *Public Advertiser* claiming responsibility for the Hutchinson letters. For this pronouncement, which appeared in several London newspapers, see XX, 513–16.

5. Daniel Denison Rogers married Abigail Bromfield (1753–1791) in 1781. BF had already met her brother, Henry Bromfield, Jr., now a merchant in Amsterdam. Their father, Henry Sr. (1727–1820), was a Boston merchant. After the war Mr. and Mrs. Rogers lived in England before returning to Boston in 1786. XXXIII, 78; XXXVI, 120n; *Adams Correspondence*, IV, 348n; Daniel D. Slade, "The Bromfield Family," *The New-England Hist. & Geneal. Register*, XXVI (1872), 38, 42.

From Nicolas-Joseph Hüllmandel[6]

ALS: University of Pennsylvania Library

Monsieur   Paris ce 22 Juillet 1782.

Le Pere d'un de mes amis croit avoir fait une découverte en Phisique qui Seroit très importante, il a chargé Son fils de la Soumettre au jugement de la Personne la plus éclairée et Surtout de celle qui l'est assés pour ne pas se laisser aveugler par les prestiges des Sistêmes. C'est vous Monsieur qui avés cet amour de la verité, c'est vous qu'il desire pour juge. Il n'a pas le bonneur de vous connoitre, Son fils Sait que vous avés eu la bonté de me recevoir quelques fois, cet avantage ne suffiroit pas pour m'encourager à une demande indiscrette s'il n'étoit question que de moi; mais l'interest d'un ami m'éxite à vous demander la faveur d'une demi heure ou une heure d'entretien pour lui. J'aurai l'honneur de vous le présenter au jour et à l'heure que vous daignerai nous accorder et nous indiquer.

Si la découverte est réelle, Si elle peut être aussi utile que les experiences ont paru le prouver vous ne me reprocherai pas Monsieur de vous avoir dérobé un tems précieux. Si vous n'en êtes pas complettement Satisfait vous aurai du moins consolé par votre complaisance un vieillard de quatrevingts ans qui a passé Sa vie en recherches intéressantes et qui n'a de confiance qu'en vos Lumieres.

Cette grace particuliere me remplira de reconnoissance et me prouvera que vous avés la bonté d'agréer le respect avec lequel

---

6. An Alsatian composer (1756–1823) who performed on the harpsichord, piano, and glass armonica. He had settled in Paris around 1776 where he frequented Morellet's gatherings and the salon of Mme Vigée-Lebrun. He wrote the article "Clavecin" for the *Encyclopédie méthodique,* but seemed partial to the piano during this period when attitudes toward the two instruments were changing. His recently published sonatas were composed for piano or harpsichord: *Jour. de Paris* of July 16, 1782. See Stanley Sadie, ed., *The New Grove Dictionary of Music and Musicians* (2nd ed., 29 vols., London, 2001); Medlin, *Morellet,* II, 24, 28–9n; Jean-Pierre Guicciardi, ed., *Mémoires de l'abbé Morellet, de l'Académie française, sur le dix-huitième siècle et sur la Révolution* (Paris, 1988), p. 212; Marie-Anne-Elisabeth Vigée Lebrun, *Memoirs of Madame Vigée Lebrun,* trans. Lionel Strachey (London, 1904), p. 36.

j'ai l'honneur d'être Monsieur Votre très humble et très obeissant Serviteur   HÜLLMANDEL

Notation: Hulmandel 22. Juillet 1782.

From Samuel & Moses Myers

ALS:[7] American Philosophical Society

Amsterdam July 22d: 1782

We take the liberty to inform your Excellency that we are fitting out a Brigg for Philadelphia call'd the Grace Bermuda Built 160 Tons Burden Mounts Ten Six pound Cannon, & Forty Men. Commanded by George Mitchell intierly American property for which Vessell we Stand in need of a Commission. Shoud it be convenient to your Excellencey to send One, to Mr. Adams, at the Hague, we will enter into the necessary Security's with that Gentn. for the purpose. The Vessell will Sail in ten or Twelve days at furthest from this time. She has on board a Large quantity of States Goods; which we were induced to take in order to accommodate the public at a More moderate rate than we could have had for Goods of equal quality & Bulk, and for the greater convenience have agreed to receive the frieght in America. Finding that Thomas Barclay Esqr was much Embarras'd to Ship these Goods on reasonable terms we wish'd the more to Convince him, of our Attachment to the Wellfair of our Country which We have truely at Heart and in every instance in our power we shall endeavour to evince that Self interest has not made us unmindfull of the duty we owe as Subjects and patriots.[8]

We shall at all times be happy to Serve your Excellencey to the utmost extent of our abilitys and are with the profoundest respect Your Excellenceys Most devoted & Hble Serts

SAMUEL & MOSES MYERS

7. In the hand of Samuel Myers.
8. See Barclay's July 17 letter. We have found no answer to the present letter, but Mitchell's brig was shipwrecked on Jutland: *Morris Papers,* VII, 314n.

His Excellencey Benjamin Franklin Esqr.

Notation: Myers Mrs. Samuel & Moses July 22. 1782.

From John Adams   Copy: Massachusetts Historical Society

Sir,   The Hague July 23d. 1782.

The two inclosed Accounts have been compared with my List of Acceptations and found right.[9] I am ashamed that they have not been sooner returned: but I have waited for my Clerk who keeps the Account of those Affairs to get well in order to assist me in the business, he having been long confined and disabled with the Fever of this Country,[1] but is now well.

I have the honor to be, Sir, &c

The Honble. Benjamin Franklin Esqr.

From Richard Bache   AL: American Philosophical Society

Dear & Hond. Sir   Philadelphia July 23d. 1782.

Your Favor of 31 March[2] I received some time ago, since which we are without the pleasure of hearing from you— I am unhappy at not having it in my power at present to comply with your request, by remitting you your Interest Money—[3] my accounts as postmr. General are upon the Eve of being settled, on which there is a Balance due me of upwards of five thousand Specie Dollrs.— If I am not paid the *whole* of my account immediately, I shall certainly receive part, when you may rely on my remitting you— Perhaps it would be agreeable to you to have

9. BF had sent JA Fizeaux & Grand's accounts on April 22 (above), asking that he review and return them.

1. John Thaxter, Jr., had been "miserably tormented with the Tertian Ague" since May: *Adams Correspondence*, IV, 359.

2. Not found.

3. In the past RB had regularly forwarded the interest accrued on BF's loan office certificates, but most recently the money was spent on home repairs and ground rents: XXXIV, 188n, 282; XXXVI, 108–9, 187.

this Money vested in a share of the Bank; I recollect you mentioned an intention of becoming a proprietor in one of your last
Letters,[4] and as probably I shall have two or three shares in part
payment of my Salary (for I know it has been the case with
other civil officers that have been paid off) it would be [a] matter of real convenience to me to transfer a share or two; but I
shall not wait your determination on this head with a view of de-
laying the necessary remittances, on the contrary, I shall not feel
satisfied 'till it is made you—

Inclosed is Robert Morris' drt on Monsr. Grand of Paris for
3200 Livres, say 2 Bill, the 1st. I sent you about a fortnight ago
via Boston,[5] and is in full for Moneys received from Christian
Schneider of German Town on account of Ann Catherine
Hocklein of Ebingen in the Dukedom of Wirttemburg, free of
all charges & expences— As it was her request to send the
Money thro' your hands, I take the Liberty of troubling you with
it—[6]

Sally and the Children are in the Country abt. five Miles from
Town, they were all well yesterday; Sally has wrote you,[7] &
there is also a Letter for Benny, whom we wish to hear oftner
from than we do— You have herewith the Newspapers, I send
them by every convenient opportunity, but the Enemy's Cruizers are so vigilent upon our Coast, that few Vessels escape
them—[8] Our Trade this Summer & Spring has been in a most
deplorable situation, and still continues so, I am afraid we shall
not soon see an alteration for the better— I remain with perfect
Duty & Respect Yours &c.

4. XXXVI, 11.
5. See RB's July 3 letter.
6. For BF's role in this transaction see Christian Schneider to BF, April 3.
7. The letter has not been found.
8. RB sent this letter via Baltimore, which was less affected by the blockade than Philadelphia: RB to BF, Aug. 9, below; Richard Buel, Jr., *In Irons:
Britain's Naval Supremacy and the American Revolutionary Economy* (New
Haven and London, 1998), pp. 222–4.

From James Hutton   AL: American Philosophical Society

My old and dear Friend   23 July 82
    I recd last night your kind Note of July 7. with the inclosed.
The principal kind thing is, that you will write in your humane
way to the Pens. Govt. to take effectual Care to protect & save
the Remainder of those unhappy People. These poor Indians
were indeed most unlucky, they had been torn with violence &
Plunder from those Habitations by the Indians Hostile to your
Cause because they would not join in war & Violence against
your People & were in that State of oppression & under Violence for being your Friends, when your Friends, by a sad mistake destroyd them as your Enemies. The article Philadelphia
April 16. is wrong in every circumstance, the Indians, ours had
been removed from the Muskingham. But some came to fetch to
a 100 miles distance some Corn for Bread & were there massa-
cred the next day & not in a night attack according to the circumstances in the printed Paper you have. No body who knows
our Indians can believe that they had any Power to maltreat, or
any will, or any obscene Song to teach the men who says he escaped from them.[9] But where ever Nations are at war, especially
Civil War, the vilest things have happend & will happen the
Consequences of evil Inspirations. In this whole war on all sides
many shocking things have pass'd. & there is no Single man the
cause of it. When I was at Westmr [Westminster] School a Boy
struck me, I returnd the Blow, He was punishd for striking me
and I for returning the Blow for, said the master, the second
Blow, the returnd Blow began the Battle. The first was an Injury,
but the second made the mischief reciporcal. I told you in Jan.
1778 with floods of Tears, there was a Fatal misunderstanding
more than malice in all our war.[1] A small Spark put both people
into a Flame. One for it's Rights, the other to maintain it's Sovereignty whatever it might be. Call all war murther I shall not
contradict it. But do not believe I beseech you, that a farthing is

    9. The April 16 article claimed that two Moravian Indians had once hu-
miliated a captive settler by forcing him to learn an obscene song. See our
annotation to BF's letter to Hutton, July 7.
    1. This must have occurred during his unsuccessful peace mission (xxv,
401–2).

to be paid for Scalps, but rather money to prevent Scalps. That article in the Boston Paper[2] must be Romance. All of it Invention, cruel forgery I hope & believe. Bales of Scalps!!! Neither the K. nor his old ministers nor Haldimand are capable of such atrocities. Nor his new ministers. The Germans are not more murtherers than your French allies, all is murther if you please. I am glad there is to be another Scene by & by when there will be no more wars. Two opportunities were missd—the first, the Petition Penn brought,[3] the second when D Howe was not listend to, as Commissioner.[4] The last day of Decr. 1777 & the first days of Jan. 1778 before the Treaty with France was signed, I thought I saw, ye might have settled with us & we with you. To mutual satisfaction. Time was, is gone. & I have only to sigh bitterly at every missing reconciliation. & to love & thank you, for your Humanity in so many Cases. Your friends in Kens. Square[5] were well last Sunday, but not at home when I went to see them. The Daughter Mrs Hewsons little Girl is a Lively sensible Child like her Mother.[6] The Scalp Bales are so very abominable that I can not prevail upon my self to believe it, as I know the Dispositions here. I am ever my Dear Friend yours most affectionately.

2. "Supplement to the Boston Independent Chronicle," above, [before April 22].

3. Richard Penn carried the Olive Branch Petition: XXII, 280.

4. "Dick," or Richard, Howe had been peace commissioner as well as commander of British naval forces in American waters. At the beginning of 1778, he was unwilling to make use of his peacemaking powers unless the American Army surrendered: Ira D. Gruber, *The Howe Brothers and the American Revolution* (New York, 1972), pp. 290–1 (and for his nickname, "Black Dick," p. 49).

5. Mary Hewson, her children, and her mother recently had moved to Kensington Square.

6. Elizabeth Hewson was about to celebrate her eighth birthday; see XXI, 209n.

From Watson & Cossoul

LS: American Philosophical Society

Sir—   Nantes 23d July 1782.

Being informed by Majr. Shurburn,[7] that your Excellency, had made mention of some Gentleman at Paris,[8] in the Intention of taking their Passage on board the Argo for America—We make free to acquaint your Excellency that the Argo is to our Address; and that she mounts 16—9 lb. & 2—18 lb.[9] & is exceedingly well Calculated for receiving several other Passengers having a double Cabbin, she is a french Frigate built Ship— Should you Occasion to freight the Ship for public Stores for Boston—we shall be able to receive upwards of a hundred Tons—immediately, and intend to dispatch the Ship by the 15th. Augt. We have the Honor to be most respectfully—Yr. Excellency's very Hum. Serts.   WATSON & COSSOUL

The Hon'ble Benjn. Franklin Esqr. Paris.

Addressed: The Hon'ble / Benjn. Franklin Esqr. / Passy

Notation: Watson & Cossoul 23 July 1782—

From Jonathan Williams, Jr.

LS:[1] American Philosophical Society; copy: Yale University Library

Dear & Honoured Sir   Nantes July 23d. 1782

I have Received your Favour of the 15th Inst.[2] by Mr Paradise and Mr Jones who arrived here last evening. I am astonished Mr de Chaumont should persist in such ridiculous as well as unjust Demands, he surely is much altered, for I think I can remember when he would have despised the same conduct in another; Our Defence is so clear and may be so well made in his own Handwriting, that I am more hurt on his Account, in making it, than

7. For whom see JW's letter of July 10.
8. William Jones and John Paradise.
9. *I.e.,* sixteen cannon firing a 9-lb. ball and two cannon firing an 18-lb. ball.
1. In the hand of Gurdon Mumford.
2. Missing.

apprehensive of the Event. You say he claims a vast sum for Freight more than you have paid.[3] I answer if the settlement of the Freight is wrong you have paid too much; I do not pretend however that it is wrong, because I agreed to it & had your Orders to Transact the Business, for it has been, and I hope ever will be the invariable Rule of my Conduct, to perform all my Agreements, let them be what they may. I allowed 1200 Tons because I agreed to pay for her by measurement, and the Admiralty at Bordeaux gave a Certificate of her measuring 1684 Tons. Messrs Jauge & Co at Bordx at first expected payment for the whole 1684 Tons, but after many letters on the Subject it was agreed that the surplus 484 Tons should be allowed for Crew, Artillery Provision &c, In doing this I stuck to the principle of our first agreement & had the Admiralty of Bordeaux for the Authority of just Measurement though it may be thought unreasonable to pay more than for the *hold*, because it is only *there* the Goods can be put; but I repeat I had agreed, & therefore would make no further Contestation.

When I came to Paris Mr de Chaumont desired Mr Jauge to finish the matter because he had been at Bordeaux & knew the whole affair. I went to Mr Jauge, he decided himself, & with his own pen made the Calculation on the blank leaf of the Certificate of Jaugeage; I then came to Mr de Chaumont—paid him, & took his Receipt on the same Paper, therefore, there cannot be on either side the smallest pretence of altering the affair.*[4] I send you this paper inclosed No 1. As to the Period of Paying Freight Mr de Chaumont should have blushed to have said a word about it. I inclose you the agreement with the Decision of two Arbitrations No 2. and I send you his letter No 3 wherein he appoints himself both Arbitrators & Subscribes *d'avance* to their Decision—[5] You will see in this letter he says the Freight of the Ship

3. Chaumont held BF responsible for 1,474 tons of freight: Account XXVI (XXXII, 3).

4. JW added a note in the margin: "*M. de Chaumont was so little inclined to alter Mr Jauge's decision that he of his own accord put in his Receipt 'le Susdit fret est acquit sans retour *depart ni d'autre*' as if he was afraid we should wish to alter it."

5. These three enclosures have not been found. They were probably returned to JW as he requested, below.

made from Bordeaux to L'Orient does not belong to him but us & he should think he *took twice Toll at the Mill* if he received it; Yet he did take it all, & it amounted to something considerable, I do not however make any objection to this for I honestly think it his due, & therefore allow it tho he does not Claim it; but it shows how differently we have conducted with regard to each other.

Mr Tardy is gone down the River to embark for the West Indies, I therefore fear I cannot send you any thing from him, but I will send an express after him & if I catch him you shall by next have the Certificate you desire, in the mean time I send you Copies of my Letters to Congress No 4. 5. 6. which will shew the precautions I thought proper to take relative to surplus freight.[6] If it should be said that we detained the Ship you may make use of a letter Capt Galatheau wrote Mr Moylan & Capt Barry excusing himself for not being ready to take in all his Cargo the 16 March. Yet he was entirely loaded the 18th, and might have been so 18 days sooner. This Letter is inclosed No 7.[7]

These Papers I think must confound all Mr de Chaumont's pretensions, pray return them to me as soon as you have done with them except my Letters No 4. 5 & 6 which you may keep, the others are necessary for my support.

I am with the greatest Respect Your ever dutifull & affectionate Kinsman   JONA WILLIAMS J

you may keep No. 7. if you please as I have another attested Copy.

Endorsed: J Williams July 23. 1782 concerning M. de Chaumont's Demands of additional Freight—Copy of his Receipt

6. The first of these copies, marked "4", is the March 18, 1781, letter summarized in XXXIV, 478–9n. JW also wrote the Committee for Foreign Affairs on May 15, 1781 (National Archives).

7. This copy, marked "No. 7", is summarized in XXXIV, 467–8n.

To Durival[8]

ALS: Fitzwilliam Museum, Cambridge, England

Sir, Passy, July 24. 1782

Being much oppress'd by the Heat of this Weather, I dare not attempt the Journey to Versailles. I therefore send my Grandson, who will affix my Seal to the Instruments, and bring that which appertains to me. I am to request at the same time that you would give Directions to the Tresor Royal, &c, for Returning to me all the Promises I have heretofore given for the Sums now compris'd in the Instrument.[9] With great and sincere Esteem, I have the honour to be Sir, Your most obedient and most humble Servant B Franklin

M. Durivall

Endorsed: Le 24. Juillet 1782/.— repondu verbalement à M. franklin Petit fils, à qui jai remis— l'Expédon. [Expédition] du contrat pour M franklin.

To Lafayette: Extract

Reprinted from William Temple Franklin, ed., *Memoirs of the Life and Writings of Benjamin Franklin* . . . (3 vols., 4to, London, 1817–18), II, 390–1.

Passy, July 24, 1782.

. . . In answer to your questions, Mr. Oswald is doing nothing, having neither powers nor instructions; and being tired of doing nothing, has dispatched a courier requesting leave to return.[1] He has I believe received no letters since I saw you, from Lord Shelburne, Mr. Grenville's return hither is I think doubtful, as he was particularly connected in friendship with Mr. Fox;[2] but if he stays I suppose some other will be sent, for I do not yet see sufficient

8. In answer to Durival's of July 21, above.
9. The "instrument" is the July 16 contract, above, while the "promises" are the loan certificates used by BF for the 21 loan installments recorded in the contract and the seven recorded in the statement concerning the Dutch loan, [after July 16]. For the certificates see XXX, 345n.
1. We have found no confirmation of this.
2. George III recalled Grenville, directing him to tell BF that it was for the

reason to think they would abandon the negociation, though from some appearances I imagine they are more intent upon dividing us, than upon making a general peace. I have heard nothing farther from Mr. Laurens, nor received any paper from him respecting Lord Cornwallis. And since that General's letter written after the battle of Camden, and ordering not only the confiscation of rebels' estates, but the hanging of prisoners,[3] has been made public, I should not wonder if the Congress were to disallow our absolution of his parole, and recall him to America. With everlasting esteem and respect, I am, dear Sir, yours most affectionately, B.F.

To Vergennes   ALS: Archives du Ministère des affaires étrangères

The two extracts inclosed in this letter were brought to Passy as part of a conciliatory mission that backfired. On July 11, Franklin wrote Benjamin Vaughan to express doubts about Shelburne's intentions. Vaughan immediately showed that letter to Shelburne, who denied any grounds for suspicion. Vaughan volunteered to visit Franklin and reassure him in person, rather than answer in writing. Shelburne agreed, instructing him to return in two days and allowing him (for his "private Instruction") to copy in shorthand passages from two important letters that demonstrated Britain's commitment to American independence.[4]

---

purpose of receiving fresh instructions. He left Paris on July 17: Lord John Russell, ed., *Memorials and Correspondence of Charles James Fox* (4 vols., London, 1853–57), IV, 260–1; Fortescue, *Correspondence of George Third*, VI, 82. As BF anticipated, he did not return. His diplomatic mission, paralyzed by the dispute between Fox and Shelburne, had accomplished little, but his lengthy diplomatic and political career was only beginning. It culminated in a six-month tenure (1806–07) as first lord of the admiralty: *DNB*.

3. In mid-September, 1780, a month after the Battle of Camden, Cornwallis ordered the sequestration of estates of "traitors" and threatened to hang two prisoners if the Americans hanged the Loyalist planter John Hutchison (although he also offered an exchange for Hutchison): K. G. Davies, ed., *Documents of the American Revolution, 1770–1783* (Colonial Office Series) (21 vols., Shannon, Ire., 1972–81), XVI, 400; Franklin and Mary Wickwire, *Cornwallis: the American Adventure* (Boston, 1970), p. 174.

4. This account is derived from Shelburne's explanation to Oswald in a letter dated Sept. 3: Giunta, *Emerging Nation*, I, 547–8.

Vaughan violated those instructions once he got to Paris. He transcribed both passages and gave them to Franklin.[5] He volunteered to put "public benefit" above private concerns (his wife was in the final stages of pregnancy) and stay in France for days, months, or even years if the Americans thought he could be useful. Franklin evidently asked him to stay until he composed a response, which he would delay until "a courier should advise the final disposition of the Court of London."[6]

When Shelburne later received Richard Oswald's letter of July 12, also informing him of Franklin's suspicions,[7] he obtained the King's permission to send Oswald full copies of the same two letters he had quietly shown to Vaughan. Oswald, who was not told that Vaughan had already seen them, was encouraged to "communicate to Dr. Franklin such Parts of both, as may be sufficient to satisfy his mind, that there never have been two Opinions since you were sent to Paris, upon *the most unequivocal Acknowledgement of American Independancy*."[8] Far from being satisfied, both Franklin and Vergennes found in the letters confirmation of British duplicity. By the time Oswald received Shelburne's packet, which was dated July 27, not only had Franklin sent the present letter to Vergennes, but Vergennes had also sent copies of the extracts to Spanish Chief Minister Floridablanca.[9]

5. Vaughan's excerpts are in the Franklin Collection at the Library of Congress, mistakenly catalogued as Vaughan to BF, June 5, 1782.

6. Vaughan to WTF, July 26, 1782; Vaughan to Shelburne, July 31, 1782; both at the APS. Vaughan stayed for months, claiming that it was at BF's urging (Vaughan to Shelburne, Aug. 7 and 17, Sept. 11, 1782, APS). BF insisted to Oswald, however, that Vaughan's decision was entirely his own; see our annotation of Hartley to BF, July 26.

7. This letter is discussed in annotation to BF to Shelburne, July 12.

8. Shelburne to Oswald, July 27, 1782, in Giunta, *Emerging Nation*, I, 479.

9. Harlow, *Second British Empire*, I, 271n. See also Vergennes' reply of July 28.

Oswald was alarmed to discover that BF had advance knowledge of the letters he bore. He feared there was a leak in Townshend's office. Shelburne explained the source of BF's information (Sept. 3, cited above), admitting that his own "misjudgment" was to blame for the awkward situation Oswald had found himself in. Shelburne also wondered at BF's "singular Unfairness" in "surprizing and embarassing" Oswald. (This portion of the Sept. 3 letter, not in *Emerging Nation*, is published in Harlow, *Second British Empire*, I, 272.) In addition to presenting these third-party letters, however, Oswald also provided news that unlocked the stalemate in the negotiations: Shelburne had made major concessions concerning peace terms. See the headnote to Shelburne to BF, July 27.

Sir, Passy, July 24. 1782
Inclos'd I have the honour of sending to your Excellency,
Extracts from two Dispatches of the British Ministry, (one of
them to the Commissioners for restoring Peace in America)
which are communicated to me by Order of Lord Shelburne, expressly for the Purpose of restoring Confidence between him
and me. Your Excellency will judge how proper they are for such
a Purpose, when the first is evidently calculated to create Division not only between France & us, but among ourselves;[1] and
the second is contradictory respecting a principal Point, the Independance.[2] I am, with great Respect, Sir, Your Excellency's
most obedient and most humble Servant   B FRANKLIN

M. le Comte de Vergennes

Endorsed: rep

1. The first extract was of a June 5 letter from Shelburne to Lieut. Gen.
Guy Carleton and Rear Adm. Robert Digby, the military and naval commanders in America who served concurrently as peace commissioners. It informed them that the cabinet had directed Grenville "that the Independency
of America should be proposed by him in the first Instance, instead of making it a Condition of a general Treaty." As Harlow points out, the phrase "in
the first instance" meant that Britain was prepared to concede independence
in a preliminary agreement with the Americans before the conclusion of a
general treaty involving all the combatants. It did not mean that Britain
would concede independence in advance of negotiations, as Fox wished:
Harlow, *Second British Empire*, 1, 270. The passage also said that once independence was promised, the French would still be disinclined to terminate
the war. It would then become clear that the war's continuation would benefit not America but France, Spain, and Holland, and would expose the motives of those Americans "devoted to France." French troops in America
would soon become "dangerous enemies" rather than allies. Jay sent a copy
of the excerpt to Livingston on Nov. 17: Wharton, *Diplomatic Correspondence*, VI, 15–16. The full text is published in Giunta, *Emerging Nation*, 1,
421–6.
2. The second extract, in French, was of a June 28 letter from Fox to Russian Minister Ivan M. Simolin acquainting him with Grenville's instructions.

From Castries   L: American Philosophical Society

Vs [Versailles] le 24. Juillet 1782

M de Castries a reçu avec beaucoup de reconnoissance l'ouvrage que Monsieur francklin a eu l'attention de lui envoyer; il a lhonneur de lui en faire ses remerciemens.

From Margaret Stevenson[3]

ALS: University of Pennsylvania Library

My dear Sir   Craven Street July 24th, 82

I have long diclinead(?) the thought of wrightg, but after, your Long Seilece—which has given me the great pleasure, to onse more recive a Line from my dearst friend,[4] you say mr Thabald[5] tells you i am well I wish i was will enuf to injoy that Same hope you mention, but that is to much for me to except not but that Pleasing hope, in soom reeged may be a Suibstet for the Barick, and i will join with your hopes and I will add its the gerats pleasure I can have to see you be fore I goe hence and be nomor seen I cant say: with you: on recolletion that I am old— In dede I am to old for Reefellicton— this I say to you becass in the next Letter you faover me with, pray teach me—for i think of your wisdom as a scund Solmon— So much for that. Pore Sally Peares is dead, She Left forr Children three grils one fine Boy. Which poor Peares writ to her father to take off him but has noe answr his is abot forr years old the olds gril is Egiht and Cliver gril,[6] if I could aford it wo:d take her, Poor Mrs Wilkes,[7] was verey kind to Sally thrue all her Illens & i assited with what I cold

3. This is the last letter of their correspondence.
4. BF's letter to Stevenson, dated July 12, is above.
5. James Theobald.
6. Sarah Franklin Pearce died on Oct. 22, 1781, leaving behind her husband, James; a son, whom we have not been able to identify; and daughters Margaret (b. 1775), Mary (b. 1777), and Frances (b. 1780). Sarah's father was Thomas Franklin, BF's first cousin once removed: I, li–lii; J. Challenor C. Smith, comp., *The Parish Registers of Richmond, Surrey* (2 vols., London, 1903–05), II, 107, 111, 121.
7. Elizabeth de Ponthieu Wilkes.

afford, She was in a Long decline, and the old father & Mothe as Poor ther brothour(?) and have onl thewlf ponds year to live one, thar at Richmond a Frnd to taker of the Children which saves him a searvt, but that cant Last long for i fearr his traed(?) will be son brack ope, but I will not dewll aney Longer one a subject so disstresg to you, God will taker off uss all I trust. Mr & [*illegible*] Send thear Love & best wihs to you & for your Saftiy Pray, you ones my Deer frined, exprest soomthing a wisih forr to have me come to you, but as I had not the Langeueg I could not etempet it, but now hear is a Charing young Lady miss Whitford says she will be my Chaperion if her father will give her Leve,[8] why wee will come in the Later End off September.

Pleas to give my Love to Mr Timple Frankin In I most say Dew my hand Shacke I can say noe more but hurd I am Old(?), as ti is you will receavitt glady from Dear Sir your most obligd &c most Affct Servent   MARGT STEVENSON

Mr. Brown[9] wil pes [*torn*] this Conveaer

Addressed: Dr. Franklin / To the care of Mr. Brown

Endorsed: This good Woman my dear Friend died the first of January following. She was about my Age. BF

Notation: Stevenson 24. 82.

From ——— Faesch   ALS: Historical Society of Pennsylvania

Monsieur!   Paris ce 25. Juillet 1782.

J'ay entendû chez Monsr. Charles, Démonstrateur de Phisique,[1] un harmonica, apartenant au Sr. hulmandel, Professeur

---

8. Julia Whitefoord was the illegitimate daughter of Caleb Whitefoord: XXXII, 208–9; Caleb Whitefoord to WTF, June 30, 1784 (APS).

9. Thomas Brown, Caleb Whitefoord's partner in the wine trade: X, 171n.

1. Jacques-Alexandre-César Charles (1746–1823), once a petty functionary in the finance bureau, was inspired by reading BF's work to learn the elements of experimental physics and in 1781 began offering a public course of lectures. His eloquence and the precision of his experimental demonstrations attracted a wide audience, including members of the Academy of Sci-

de musique,[2] on m'a assuré qu'il était de vôtre Invention, j'en ay été enchanté & je meurs d'Envie d'en posséder un pareil, mais malgré toutes mes recherches, je n'ay encore pû me le procurer, oserais-je vous Suplier de vouloir bien m'indiquer les moyens de parvenir à la possession d'un Semblable Instrument de musique, le plus Délicieux que je Connaisse au Monde, Je vous en aurai une obligation infinie.[3]

J'ay l'honneur d'être avec la plus Respectueuse Considération Monsieur! Vôtre très humble & très obeissant Serviteur.

FAESCH

Rûe & près la Porte St. Denis maison de Mr. sauvage.

From Jonathan Williams, Jr.

ALS: American Philosophical Society; copy: Yale University Library

Dear & hond sir.   Nantes July. 25. 1782.

The inclosed Letter I recvd by this days Post from my House at L'Orient.[4] I am at same Time informed that the Sailors you wrote Williams Moore & Co about are set at Liberty.[5]

I refer you to my last which was on the subject of your affairs with Mr de Chaumont.[6]

I am as ever with the greatest Respect most dutifully & affectionately Yours.   JONA WILLIAMS J

---

ences and BF himself on at least one occasion (XXXVI, lxii). On July 2, Charles began a new course focused solely on fixed air (carbon dioxide), electricity, and light. See *Dictionary of Scientific Biography;* Jean Torlais, "La Physique expérimentale" in *Enseignement et diffusion des sciences en France au XVIIIe siècle,* ed. René Taton *et al.* (Paris, 1964), pp. 633–4; *Jour. de Paris* for June 26, 1782.

2. BF had received Hüllmandel at Passy; see the composer's letter of July 22.

3. For the glass armonica and its manufacture see X, 116–30, 180–2, 235; XI, 426–7; XIII, 253.

4. Missing.

5. Williams, Moore & Co. had written BF about these prisoners on [June 30], above. BF's answer is missing but, according to the notation on the firm's letter, was dated July 9.

6. July 23, above.

Addressed: His Excellence / Benjamin Franklin / at / Passy

Notation: Jona. Williams July 25. 1782.

From Edward Bridgen   ALS: Historical Society of Pennsylvania

Dear Sir   July 26th: 1782

Our Mutual friend the writer of the inclosed[7] wishes me to contrive that it may come safe to your hands. He wishes that he may be instrumental in clearing away any obstructions which may be at present in the path which leades to Peace.

I think it necessary to say that I have not the highest opinion of some of the *present Men*, but that I have not the least apprehension of my Friend being a dupe to any of them; he having all his eyes about him.

God bless you my Dear Sir and preserve you Says Yr. Affectionate & obliged   EDWD: BRIDGEN

When you reply to the inclosed be pleased to Address it under Cover to *Bridgen & Waller a Londres* with a little B just under the Seal and then inclose it a *Monsieur J:B: Hermans au Bureau de Poste a Anvers?*

From David Hartley   Copy:[8] William L. Clements Library

My Dear Friend,   London 26 July 1782

You will have heared before you Receive this that Mr T. Td. is appointed Secretary of State for that department to which the

---

7. Possibly Thomas Pownall, who had asked Bridgen to forward a May 13 letter to BF; see Pownall to BF, July 5.

8. In the hand of Richard Oswald, who forwarded it to Shelburne with a lengthy note of explanation dated "8th Septemr" on the verso. BF had shown Oswald the letter "about three weeks ago" but said he did not understand it. On Sept. 8, when Oswald informed BF that Hartley had "given up his office," BF mentioned having received several letters from Hartley which he had not yet answered. Oswald requested permission to copy the one BF had shown him. BF gave it to him and also allowed him to read Hartley's letters of Aug.

American Corespondence belongs. He is, & has been for many years one of my most intimate Friends.[9] A more honourable & honest Man do's not exist. I have been Requested, in connection with him to undertake one branch of his Office, relating to America. The point which I have been Requested to undertake is the Case, or rather the diversity of Cases of the American Refugees, I understand that in the progress of this business, I shall be referred to a Corespondence with you, as matter may arise. My purpose therfor for the present is only to advertise you of this, in case you Should have any preliminary matter to give or to Receive elucidation upon. I am very Ready to undertake any matter which may be necessary or Instrumental towards peace especially in Connection with my worthy Friend Mr Townshend.

You know all my principles upon American pacification *and Sweet Conciliation.* I Shall always Remain in the Same. But the delegation of a Single point to me, Such as the Case of the Refugees, do's not entitle me to advise upon the great Outlines or principles of Such pacific Negotiation. I shall retain my full Reservation in Such points as Events may justify. My personal

---

16 and 20 (missing), seeming "as if he wished not to be thought to countenance Corespondences of that nature—or that it Should be thought there was any Change in his Sentiments with Regard to Certain Friends he had hitherto esteemed & honored." Oswald "took that opportunity to take nottice of the designed Arts of those, who for Reasons personal to themselves, were apt to misrepresent things . . . Only having mentioned one Gentlemans name—the Doctor seemed to wish that it might not be Supposed that his long Stay here was owing to him. For excepting the first two days he had not Said a word to him on business. I said there could be no harm in his Staying, as I was Certain he meant alwise to do any good in his power—& we had often occasion to be together. The Doctr Said he was getting Acquaintances, & more insight into Naturl philosophy &ca. . . ." The gentleman in question was Benjamin Vaughan; see BF to Vergennes, July 24.

9. Hartley had served in the House of Commons with Thomas Townshend, who represented Whitchurch from 1754 until he resigned in March, 1783, to become Secretary at War: Namier and Brooke, *House of Commons,* III, 554–6. He became part of the new Shelburne government, replacing Shelburne as secretary of state for the home department on July 10: Fortescue, *Correspondence of George Third,* VI, 76–8; Sir F. Maurice Powicke and E. B. Fryde, comps., *Handbook of British Chronology* (2nd ed., London, 1961), p. 115. Shelburne, however, continued to direct the American negotiations.

motive for Saying this to you, is obvious. But in point of justice to those who have at present the direction of publick measures in this Country, I must Request of you, that this Caution of mine may be accepted only as personal to myself, & not as ferential upon the conduct of others, where I am not a party. Having taken a zealous part in the principles & Negotiations of Peace, I wish to Stand clear from any Collateral Constructions which might affect myself, and at the same time not to impose any Collateral or Inferential Constructions upon others. God prosper the Work of Peace & *good Will* as the Means of Peace amongst Men. I am ever your most Affectionat F[riend]   D H

Notations:[1] Memm: 8th Septr Copy of a Letter from Mr H. to Dr Franklin, &ca / Copies of Letters from Mr David Hartley to Dr. Franklin of 26th. July, & 8th. Septr. 1782. / In Mr. Oswald's. of 11th. Septr. 1782

From ———— St. Clair[2]   ALS: American Philosophical Society

Dunkirk july 26th. 1782

Your Excellency will receive this by Mr Joly a Worthy Clergyman who has attended me during part of my confinement and who is gone to Paris on his own affairs as I wrot to your Excellency's Secretary some time ago[3] I shall not enter into a detail regarding the reasons of my Detention but beg humbly leave to

1. The first of which is in Oswald's hand; the last is in Shelburne's.
2. One of the 300 marines from the Volontaires de Luxembourg serving on the *South Carolina:* XXXV, 562n; James A. Lewis, *Neptune's Militia: the Frigate* South Carolina *during the American Revolution* (Kent, Ohio, and London, 1999), pp. 34, 141 (where he is listed as Lt. "Clear").
3. He wrote to WTF on July 5, the "first day of the 7th year of independcy", asking for BF's help. He was being detained at Dunkirk, without benefit of trial, on suspicion of soliciting French sailors to serve in Holland. He had left the *South Carolina* the previous October at La Coruña. His complaint against Gillon had been registered with BF in December while in company with James Searle. He had delayed his return to America until he could be sure of confronting Gillon there; meanwhile, he served on the *Robecq* but also made two trips to Holland, where he had "an advantageous offer". When he heard the rumors about him, he returned to Dunkirk and was taken prisoner. APS.

refer you to Mr Joly who is fully informed on that head both by me and the Grand Bailey every person here seems convinced of my innocency two days ago I received a most gracious letter from the Prince of Robecq[4] wherein he expressed sorrow at not being in power to put an end to my confinement but that he expected daily orders from the Minister[5] on that head the example of others in the same case gives me the greatest uneasiness I find it is not only necessary in such case to be innocent but likewise it is requisite to be reclaim'd there was a Mr De Latre a gentleman of this town who had intered the Dutch service who was taken up for the same reason and with as little foundation he remained a considerable time in Prison and would probably have remained till now had the Dutch Ambassador not reclaim'd him; others that have not been reclaim'd are here four and five months and are as likely to remain as many more. I did not think proper to trouble your Excellency till such time as I was acquainted that my innocency did not avail for the recovery of my liberty and that I would not be brought to trial and that my most sure way of a speedy deliverance would be to sollicit your good offices in my behalf. As I acquainted your Excellency's Secretary's some time ago the manner in which I came to this town and as you probably may recollect me having paid my respects to you the end of last December on my road from Spain to this place I think it unnecessary to repeat any thing on that subject. Upon my arrival here I found the Late St Clair of Roslin was so displeased at my entering the American Service that he left his fortune to my two younger Brothers.

I shall be happy to know if Commodore Gillon is as yet arrived in America[6] as it will then be probably necessary for me to return to America in order to obtain redress for the injury he has done me and continue my Duty. In the firm persuasion of your

4. Anne-Louis-Alexandre de Montmorency, prince de Robecque, the commandant general of French Flanders: XXVI, 693n; *Etat militaire* for 1781, p. 22.

5. Philippe-Henri, marquis de Ségur, the minister responsible for the province of French Flanders: *Almanach royal* for 1782, p. 213.

6. Gillon had arrived in May, but BF did not receive notification of that fact until early August: Livingston to BF, May 30 (above); BF to Livingston, Aug. 12 (below).

Excellency's good offices with the Minister I remain your Excellency's Most humble and most Devoted Servant

ST. CLAIR
Lt of Marines the State of South Carolina

Addressed: A / Son Excellence B Franklin Ministre / Plenipotentiaire des Etats Unies au près / de Sa Majesté tres Chretienne / a / Passy

Notation: St. Clair, Dunkerque, July 26, 1782.

From Benjamin Franklin Bache

ALS: American Philosophical Society

Mon cher Grand Papa   Geneve ce 27 Juillet 1782

Je suis très ètonné de ce que vous ne m'aves pas ecrit il faut que vos affaires vous en empechent car je suis sur que vous ne m'oublies pas:[7] Les affaires de Genêve sont remises en un assez Bon état et par consèquent je suis revenu de Gachet qui est comme je vous ai deja dit la Campagne du Frere de Monsieur de Marignac et nous allons j'espère Bientôt recomencer les etudes en Classe mais quand même nous n'y allons pas nous travaillons tout de meme.[8] Je Languis Beaucoup que vous m'envôyés les exemples pour Bien écrire car je my appliquerai Beaucoup et Je vous prie de me Les envoyer Le plustôt possible et de me dire si vous voulè que J'achète le voyageur François qui a la verité coute Beaucoup plus que ce que vous m'aves donné (il coute 3 Louis et demi) mais cest un Livre qui m'amuseroit et m'instruiroit Beau-

7. BF's last extant letter was written on Jan. 25: XXXVI, 476–7.
8. BFB had written to BF about the retreat outside Geneva the year before: XXXIV, 486–7. Mme Cramer's letters of April 9 and 12, above, describe the recent unrest at Geneva and the precautions taken to ensure BFB's safety. BFB's classes did not resume until Aug. 5, when the troops sent by France, Bern, and Sardinia were quartered throughout the city. Some were at his school, forcing the schoolmasters to hold class in their homes: BFB's journal, Aug. 1, 1782–Sept. 14, 1785. (Two forms of this journal are at the APS: a typescript of the original French, and an English translation made by one of BFB's grandsons.)

coup.[9] Le fils de Monsieur Cramer de Lon,[1] qui etoit dernierement a Paris vous presente Bien ses respect et vous assure qu'il
est bien faché de ce que les affaires de Genêve l'ont fait partir de
Paris sans prendre congé de vous. Je vous prirai Mon cher grand
papa de donner a Johonnot et a moi un augmentation dargent
nous ne vous demandons seulement ce que nous avions a paris
qui fait trente sols d'ici nous avons a present 21 sols. Jai suspendu
pendant le tems que nous etions à Gachet Le compte de mon argent ayant perdu le livre mais je le recomence.[2] Mr et Mdme de
Marignac vous presentent bien leurs respects. Mr Marignac Vous
ayant ècrit si vous vouliez qu'il vous envoya mon compte et celui
de Johonnot et n'ayant point reçu de reponse il m'a chargé de
vous le demander.

Je suis Mon cher grand papa Votre tres Affectioné et très obei-
sant petit fils   B. Franklin Bache

Mes compliments a mon Cousin et a Cockran

Addressed: A Monsieur / Monsieur Franklin / Ministre Plénipotentiaire des / États unis de l'Amerique auprès / de Sa Majesté
très chrétienne / recommandée à Monsieur Grand / Banquier
ruë Montmartre / A Paris

From C. Drogart

ALS: American Philosophical Society

Sir,   Nantes July 27th. 1782
     May I presume to acquaint you that I have directed the Busi-
ness of the House of Penet DaCosta freres & Co. and that of
Penet distinctly whilst I thought their dealings consistent with
the Principles of Honour & Honesty. With the latter I relinquish'd all kind of Intercourse from the time I condescended to
write in Paris Octr. the 30th Ulto.[3] the letter to you touching a

9. See XXXVI, 597n.
1. Jean-François Cramer: XXXVI, 233n.
2. On BF's advice BFB had begun this practice the year before: XXXVI, 80, 85.
3. Both LS of Penet's Oct. 29, 1781, letter to BF (XXXV, 667–8) are in Drogart's hand.

loan he said he could obtain for the State of Virginia amounting to Six hundred thousand livres tournois provided you would be pleas'd to put your visa to his Bills amounting to a 100 pistols each. Your declension on that account was both Prudent & safe for the State of Virginia.[4] Time has Justify'd your measures, as well as my subsequent Conduct my Character. No doubt your Excellency is not ignorant that the Commercial Agent Gl.[5] was oblig'd to disappear & surrender what he could not carry away with him to his Creditors.[6] I am happy to have withdrawn timely & Publicly by that step I saved my Reputation unblemish'd.

My time not being at present engross'd by the little Business I carry on my own account, I would readily embrace some Reputable Connection. Therefore, I beg, when opportunity offers itself that you would be pleas'd to honour me with your recommendation which I would gratefully acknowledge according to my endeavours. I understand tolerably the American Language; the inclosed I have sent as a specimen of my little Knowledge in spelling Political matters. I beseech you would forgive my Temerity; it proceeds from a heart truly attach'd to the Interest of the Americans.

I am with profound Respect. Sir Your most obedient & very humble servant
C∴ DROGART.

His Excellency the Honble. Doctor Franklin.

Notation: Drogart July 27 1782.

From Baron Grantham[7]　　　　LS (draft): Public Record Office

Sir.　　　　　　　　　　　　Whitehall: 27t: July 1782
　　As the first Object of my Wishes, is to contribute to the Establishment of an honourable & lasting Peace, I address myself

---

4. XXXV, 674–5.
5. Penet had been appointed an agent of the Commonwealth of Virginia: *Jefferson Papers,* III, 36.
6. For Penet's difficulties see d'Artus to BF, July 17.
7. Thomas Robinson, 2nd Baron Grantham, was a former ambassador to Spain. He succeeded Fox as secretary of state for foreign affairs on July 17:

without Ceremony to you, upon the Conviction that you agree with me in this Principle. If I was not convinced that it was also the Real System of the Ministers of this Country, I should not now be cooperating with them. The Step they had already taken in sending Mr Grenville to Paris is a Proof of their Intentions; & as that Gentleman does not return to his Station there, I trust that the immediate Appointment of a Person to Succeed him will testify my Agreement with the Principles upon which he was employed. I therefore beg leave to recommend Mr. Fitzherbert to your Acquaintance who has the King's Commands to repair to Paris.[8]

As I have not the Advantage of being known to you, I can claim no Pretense for my Application to you, but my publick Situation, & my Desire to merit your Confidence upon a Subject of so much Importance as a Pacification between the Parties now engaged in a Calamitous War.

I have the Honour to be with great Regard Sir. Your most obedt humble servant   GRANTHAM

B. Franklin Esqr.—

Drat [Draft]

Drat. to Dr. Franklin. July 27t: 1782.

DNB; Namier and Brooke, *House of Commons,* III, 367; Sir F. Maurice Powicke and E. B. Fryde, comps., *Handbook of British Chronology* (2nd ed., London, 1961), p. 116. Contrasting assessments of his abilities are in H. M. Scott, *British Foreign Policy in the Age of the American Revolution* (Oxford, 1990), p. 322, and Andrew Stockley, *Britain and France at the Birth of America: the European Powers and the Peace Negotiations of 1782–1783* (Exeter, 2001), pp. 120, 147–50, and *passim.*

8. Alleyne Fitzherbert (1753–1839) was the former minister plenipotentiary at Brussels. Replacing Grenville, he became minister plenipotentiary and envoy extraordinary at the French court and later participated in the negotiations with the Spaniards and Dutch, a role for which he also received full powers. Charles Ritcheson describes him as "a man of cool and uncommon good sense." *DNB; Repertorium der diplomatischen Vertreter,* III, 162, 167, 177–8; Charles R. Ritcheson, "Britain's Peacemakers, 1782–1783: 'To an Astonishing Degree Unfit for the Task'?" in Hoffman and Albert, eds., *Peace and the Peacemakers,* p. 74. Among BF's papers at the Library of Congress, there is a copy (in Latin) of Fitzherbert's July 24 commission to negotiate with the French court. For his July 27 instructions see Giunta, *Emerging Nation,* I, 475–9.

From the Earl of Shelburne

Reprinted from William Temple Franklin, ed., *Memoirs of the Life and Writings of Benjamin Franklin . . .* (3 vols., 4to, London, 1817–18), II, 392.

On the day Shelburne wrote the following letter, he also accepted as a basis for conducting negotiations the necessary terms that Franklin had communicated to Oswald on July 10.[9] Shelburne informed Oswald on July 27 that "a Commission will be immediately forwarded to you, containing Full Powers to treat and to conclude, with Instructions from the Minister [Townshend] who has succeeded to the Department which I lately held, to make the Independancy of the Colonies the Basis & Preliminary of the Treaty now depending & so far advanc'd, that hoping, as I do with you, that the Articles call'd *adviseable* will be dropp'd, & those call'd *necessary* alone retain'd as the Ground of Discussion, it may be speedily Concluded." He also told Oswald that he had never made a secret of the concern he felt over the separation "of Countries united by Blood, by Principles, Habits, & every Tie short of Territorial Proximity.— But you very well know that I have long since given it up *decidedly* tho' *reluctantly:* and the same motives which made me perhaps the last to give up all Hope of the union, makes me most anxious if it is given up, that it shall be done *decidedly,* so as to avoid all further Risque of Enmity, & lay the Foundation of a new Connection better adapted to the present Temper & Interests of both Countries. In this View, I go further with Dr. Franklin perhaps than he is aware of, & farther perhaps than the profess'd Advocates of Independance are prepar'd to admit." Shelburne confessed that his private opinion would lead him to work for federal union, but questioned whether either country was ripe for it. He also enclosed two documents as proof of his consistency.[1]

Not only did Shelburne concede the necessity of acknowledging American independence as part of a preliminary peace agreement, but he also accepted Franklin's terms demanding the restriction of the borders of Quebec, and American admittance to the fisheries. Franklin had broken off discussions with Oswald on July 12, only two days af-

---

9. Quoted in the headnote of BF to Lafayette, July 9.

1. This letter is published in Giunta, *Emerging Nation,* I, 479–80. For the two enclosures see our annotation of BF to Vergennes, July 24. Shelburne also told Oswald that the powers he would receive had been prepared soon after the passage of the Enabling Act but were delayed because of the view that they instead should be sent to Grenville.

ter presenting his demands.[2] It seems likely that the pressure this put on Shelburne affected at least the timing of the concessions announced here. The winning of those concessions was therefore one of Franklin's greatest accomplishments as a diplomat.

Sir,   Shelburne House, July 27, 1782.
I am much obliged by the honour of your letter of the 12th. instant. You do me most acceptable justice in supposing my happiness intimately connected with that of mankind, and I can with truth assure you, it will give me great satisfaction in every situation to merit the continuance of your good opinion.

I have the honour to be, with very sincere regard, and esteem, dear Sir, your most obedient and most humble servant,

SHELBURNE.

To Richard Oswald

Two copies,[3] press copy of copy, and transcript: National Archives

Sir,   Passy, July 28. 1782.
I have but this Minute had an Opportunity by the Departure of my Company of perusing the Letters you put into my Hands this afternoon; and I return them directly without waiting till our Interview to morrow morning, because I would not give a Moment's Delay to the Delivery of those directed to other Persons. The Situation of Capt. Asgill & his Family aflicts me: but I do not see what can be done by anyone here to relieve them.[4] It cannot be suppos'd that General Washington has the least Desire of taking the Life of that Gentleman. His Aim is to obtain the Punishment of a deliberate murder, committed on a Prisoner in cold Blood by Captain Lippincutt. If the English refuse to deliver up or punish this Murderer, it is saying that they chuse to preserve

2. See BF's letter to Oswald of that date.
3. Both of which are in the hand of L'Air de Lamotte; the press copy is of the copy from which we print.
4. Eventually Vergennes successfully intervened on behalf of Asgill; see our annotation of Livingston to BF, May 30.

him rather than Capt. Asgill. It seems to me therefore that the Application should be made to the English ministers, for positive Orders, directing Gen. Carleton to deliver up Lippincutt which Orders being obtain'd should be dispatched immediately by a swift sailing Vessel. I do not think any other means can produce the Effect desired. The cruel Murders of this kind committed by the English on our People since the Commencement of the War, are innumerable. The Congress and their Generals, to satisfy the People, have often threaten'd Retaliation; but have always hitherto forborne to execute it; & they have been often insultingly told by their Enemies that this Forbearance did not proceed from Humanity but Fear. General Greene, tho' he solemnly & publicly promis'd it in a Proclamation, never made any Retaliation for the Murder of Col: Hayne's,[5] & many others in Carolina; and the People who now think that if he had fulfill'd his Promise, this Crime would not have been committed, clamour so loudly, that I doubt General Washington cannot well refuse what appears to them so just and necessary for their common Security. I am persuaded nothing I could say to him on the Occasion would have the least effect in changing his Determination. Excuse me then, if I presume to advise the Dispatching a Courier immediately to London, proposing to the Consideration of Ministers the sending such orders to General Carleton directly. They would have an excellent Effect in other Views. The Post goes to morrow morning at ten o Clock; but as nine Days have been spent in bringing the Letters here, by that Conveyance, an Express is preferable.

With sincere Esteem, I have the honour to be, Sir, &c. &c &c

(signed) B. FRANKLIN

5. See XXXVI, 162–3n, 268n.

From Vergennes

LS: American Philosophical Society; draft: Archives du Ministère des affaires étrangères

À Versailles le 28. Juillet 1782.

J'ai reçû, Monsieur, la lettre que vous m'avez fait l'honneur de m'écrire le 24. de ce mois, ainsi que les deux piéces qui y étoient jointes. Les contradictions qu'elles renferment sont dignes de remarques; non-seulement elles s'entredétruisent réciproquement, mais elles sont aussi l'une et l'autre dans une opposition manifeste avec[6] les Déclarations Ministérielles faites par M. Grenville.

Il paroit que Le Lord Shelburne a plus en vüe de mettre la division entre le Roi et les Etats-unis que de promouvoir une paix juste et durable: mais il y a lieu de croire que ce Ministre ne tardera pas à être pleinement convaincu que son plan est essentiellement vicieux, et qu'il ne sauroit trop tôt le changer, si la paix fait l'objet de Ses sollicitudes.

Quant au Roi, Monsieur, la bonne foi et la fidélité düe à Ses alliés dirigeront invariablement Sa conduite,[7]—comme la justice et la modération Seront les bazes inébranlables du Système pacifique adopté par Sa Majesté. Si le Ministère Anglois veut rendre hommage à ces principes, il réussira facilement à rétablir la paix à des conditions raisonnables;[8] mais S'il continüe à changer sans-cesse de vües et de marches, s'il ne veut qu'intriguer au lieu de négocier Sérieusement,[9] il S'expose gratuitement à se compromettre, et il prolonge de gaïeté de cœur les calamités de la guerre.

Au reste, Monsieur, c'est au Lord Shelburne lui-même, qui tient actüellement le timon des affaires de l'Angre. [Angleterre], à faire ces réflexions; nous ne pouvons que désirer qu'elles n'échapent pas à Sa Sagacité, et attendre que ce Ministre nous informe des Suites qu'il jugera à propos de donner soit à la négo-

---

6. In Gérard de Rayneval's draft the remainder of this sentence reads, "le systeme pacifique dont M. Grenville a ministeriellement établis la baze"; Vergennes rewrote it.

7. Here either Gérard de Rayneval or Vergennes deleted a phrase in the draft, "la même façon de penser anime certainement le Congrès".

8. The preceding four words were added by Vergennes.

9. The preceding phrase was added by Vergennes.

ciation entamée par M. Grenville, soit à la réponse donnée, en dernier lieu, par le Ministère Anglois aux Cours de Vienne et de St. Petersbourg.[1]

J'ai l'honneur d'être très-parfaitement, Monsieur, votre très-humble et très-obéïssant serviteur. De Vergennes

M. franklin

From James Hunter, Jr.[2]

ALS: University of Pennsylvania Library

Richmond (Virginia) 29th July 1782

Nothing but your promised Favour to Mrs Strange, would induce my so often giving you Trouble;[3] She flatters me of her being in Paris about the Time this reaches, and I can value on no one so proper to apologize with you on this Score, with such Prospect of Pardon as herself.

I am with every Sentiment of Esteem Sir Your most Obedient Servant[4] James Hunter

Addressed: His Excellency / Benjamin Franklin / Paris.

Notation: James Hunter 29. July 1782

1. In mid-June, Catherine II of Russia again had proposed Russian and Austrian mediation of the war. The British government had not yet responded: Madariaga, *Harris's Mission*, pp. 402–3, 417, 419.

2. This letter was forwarded from Philadelphia by Theodorick Bland, who represented Virginia in Congress from 1780 to 1783 (*DAB*). In his Aug. 11 cover letter to BF, Bland indicates that he is also enclosing a letter from Hunter's wife (Marianna Spence) to her cousin (Isabella Strange): University of Pa. Library. See R. Walter Coakley, "The Two James Hunters of Fredericksburg . . . ," *Va. Mag. of History and Biography*, LVI (1948), 9, 15; Isabella Strange to BF, April 23, 1783 (APS).

3. BF served as a conduit for their correspondence; see XXXV, 394.

4. Hunter wrote BF a second letter dated July 29, a one-sentence request that he forward an enclosure to Mr. Strange. APS.

From Patience Wright   ALS: American Philosophical Society

Honor'd Sir   London July 30th 1782

After my most hearty and Sincer love to you and your grand-son—Friends &ce.

I have The pleasure to tell you my hopes is more fixt on you then Ever My Inthuizam encreases Evry day and from good authority Can Say my politicall Creed is well founded: you will be Very Shortly Calld upon by the People—. (Providence Whome I trust) will Call all the wise honest hearted togethr and EXPOSE this Shameful Condoctt of Weckedness: our People are now in good Earnest to be wise and use those powers god and nature has gave them: now is the time for our great and good men to apeare in the behalf of a Ingured and opressd People and do Honor to themselves and to mankind My Confidence in you and high Esteem for Mr Wm Frankling togethr with the Courage Condoct and wisdom of our good men belonging to the diferent Soceatys:[5] will oblige the devil to flye and then the Authors of war will go also with him: and peace and Plenty take Place the Publick Funds is what Keeps all back Pray help our Credit: you Can do it and give the good offic that help to the Bank So Nessecery; a letter in [torn: our(?)] Credet and a line of Friendship to us will bring Thousands your Friends and make Peace on the most Honourable terms to all Nations— Our Manufacterors are going off per way of Ireland to America[6] and the Lyoal town of Manchester feals the *effects* of Sound *Polecy* abroad we now are Eassy things work Round to the grand Reform our old friend Strahn with others is a Patroat it Causes much Chearful Conversation to See Inns and outs— This deferint hops and fears while our great man thinks himself very Safe in his Army with the art and

5. Perhaps the Society for Constitutional Information and its allied organizations: Charles C. Sellers, *Patience Wright: American Artist and Spy in George III's London* (Middletown, Conn., 1976), p. 161.

6. This group of Manchester-based textile manufacturers was led by Henry Wyld. According to British intelligence, most of the party was by this time in Liverpool awaiting Wyld's arrival so that all could proceed together to board a ship in Londonderry, Ireland: John Swindell to Thomas Townshend, Aug. 3, 1782 (Public Record Office), and see our headnote to Wyld's letters of Aug. 12.

deception of his Consort and his first Servants &c Ms Stephenson is well Mrs Hustson sends her love to you and wishs much that I had Calld on her to acompany me to Paris you may See more of your old friends[7] then you Expect if we dont prevent them by Sending for you to DOVER as is Expected by me and others of Strong Faith— I have had the honor to See and hope with good Reasin I beleve my arrivall in London was attended with good: as my opertunitys is great and I find a disposistion to Speak proper truth.

I am very hapy to here by mr whitford and others that My Son is Painting you Portrite[8] We Expect a ordr from the Comon Councill very soon and So by the ordrs of the City or Part of them for your Picture to be Painted by Jos Wright and presented to those or to *whome* or *where* it may do most Honour—the perticulrs are now in Contemplation a few weeks will determen so Pleasing a Vote and So proper act at this time when all Parties Seem to be more in ther Sence, and Joyne with me in wishing to Shew all Possable Testimonies of their love and high Esteem to you by making Publick Declaration and gloring in ther doing Justece to great Men   P. WRIGHT

Addressed: For His Exelency / B. Frankling / Passey

Notation: Wright 30 July—1782.

---

7. Those mentioned here are William Strahan, Margaret Stevenson, and Louise Brandt Hutton, wife of James Hutton: *DNB* under James Hutton (1715–1795).

8. Joseph Wright produced portraits of BF for both Caleb Whitefoord and Richard Oswald (the frontispiece to this volume), in addition to the one BF commissioned for William Hodgson (for which see Hodgson to BF, July 13). All three were copied from the Duplessis "gray coat" portrait. Whitefoord brought his back to London when he returned in 1783. The following year Benjamin West borrowed it for his group portrait of the peace commissioners. Whitefoord had at least two copies of the portrait made, one for himself and another for William Strahan. He considered giving the original to Polly Hewson but ultimately donated it in 1791 to the Royal Society, where it remains. Sellers, *Franklin in Portraiture*, pp. 420–22; Monroe H. Fabian, *Joseph Wright, American Artist, 1756–1793* (Washington, D.C., 1985), pp. 84–5, plate 9.

From Cuming & Macarty   ALS:[9] American Philosophical Society

sir   L'Orient 31st. July 1782
    We take the Liberty again of troubling you with the papers,
relating to a prize taken by the Brig General Galvés Capt.
Silas Jones of Salem—[1]
    We beg leave to request your Execellency will please to Order the necessary paper to be forwarded to us by post, as Soon
as possible.
    We are most Respectfully sir your most obedt Serts.

                                          CUMING & MACARTY

Endorsed:[2] The Anthony, a Brigantine, Captain George Barans,
of London Taken from Africa by the General Galvez Capt. Silas
Jones of Salem in New England the 24th of June. Brought into
L'Orient

Notation: Cuming & Maccarty 31. Juillet 1782.

From Target   ALS: American Philosophical Society

                                              31. juillet 1782
Je presente L'hommage de ma venération a Monsieur Franklin;
plus ignorant quon ne peut dire, dans la Langue Angloise, J'ai
Lu pourtant avec plaisir, l'ouvrage de M. de Crevecœur;[3] par là
je ne sai, si je peux juger quil a du en faire un peu a Monsieur

9. In the hand of William Macarty.
    1. An undated note in Macarty's hand, also at the APS, is evidence of the
firm's previous communication. It states that the ship *Congress,* Capt. Geddes, and the *General Galveʒ,* Capt. Jones, had arrived from Havana. The latter brought in a prize homeward bound from Africa carrying a cargo of elephants' teeth, wax, and dye wood. The ships also brought news of the
capture of New Providence (Bahamas). Macarty promises to "trouble you
soon on the condemnation."
    2. While BF's certificate of condemnation has not been found, these are
evidently his instructions for filling it out. Cuming & Macarty sold the prize
on Aug. 21; a printed announcement of the sale is in Dossiers des prises 9 B
182, Archives départementales de Morbihan.
    3. *Letters from an American Farmer,* which he delivered to BF with his letter of July 13, above.

Franklin; je le souhaite beaucoup et je prens a ses jouissances, Linterêt que Les honnetes gens doivent prendre a toutes celles d'un ami de L'humanité. Il me semble quil y a dans ce livre, bien du naturel et bien de la simplicité. Je desirerois que cela fut aussi decisif en guerre, que respectable au milieu de la paix. Malheureusemt. il faut avoir la guerre pour obtenir la paix, et peutêtre Les qualités dont on a besoin pour se bien batre, sont elles fort différentes de celles qui font le bonheur du monde, quand on s'est bien battu. Je m'en raporte a mon maitre, en morale, en politique, en physique, en tout. Je le salue avec un profond respect, et je le prie de maccorder quelque amitié, pour prix de ma veneration. Je cherche en finissant un autre mot que celui par lequel j'ai commencé et je ne saurois en trouver dautre.

M. de Crevecœur demeure a Caën en normandie, chez M. duperré de Lisle, Lieutenant général, Rue des Croisiés.[4]

TARGET

Addressed: A Monsieur / Monsieur Franklin, ministre / plénipotentiaire des Etats unis / de Lamerique / A Passy

Notation: Target 31 Juillet 1782

From Thomas Cushing[5]   ALS: Massachusetts Historical Society

Sir   Boston July. [*blank*] 1782

Mr William Foster, the Bearer of this Letter, is a Native and a Merchant of this Town, he is a Gentleman of Character and firmly Attached to the Cause of America, Permit me to introduce him to your Acquaintance & to reccommend him to your Friendly Notice.[6] Sir Guy Carlton is at New York, he has not as

4. Nicolas Lebourguignon Duperré-Delisle, *lieutenant-général au bailliage de Caen,* was a relative of Crèvecœur's: Robert de Crèvecœur, *Saint John de Crèvecoeur, sa vie et ses ouvrages (1735–1813)* (Paris, 1883), p. 358n; *Jefferson Papers,* x, 127–8; Julia Post Mitchell, *St. Jean de Crèvecoeur* (New York, 1916), pp. 75, 138.

5. Since 1780, the lieutenant governor of Massachusetts: *ANB.*

6. This is probably the William Foster (1746–1821) who by July 1784, was in partnership with his brother Joseph: Frederick C. Pierce, *Foster Genealogy* (Chicago, 1899), pp. 940–1, 942–3; Butterfield, *John Adams Diary,* III, 164.

yet made any Propositions to Congress, however let him Propose what he will, It appears to be the determination of the United States not to Consent to any Peace but what Includes Independance & Concert with our generous Ally; and the late Extraordinary Change in the British Ministry, I am Confident, will tend to add to the firmness and Vigor of our Councils and Proceedings and The Resolutions of the Several Assemblies, that have been passed since Sr Guy's Arrivall, I am perswaded, will Convince you that they are sensible that their Honor and Interest require a Strict & firm Adherence to the Engagements of their Alliance and a just Veneration for National Faith. I conclude with wishing you Health & All the Happiness you Can desire during the remainder of yr Life & am with great respect yr most obedt humble Sert   THOMAS CUSHING

His Excellency Benja Franklin Esqr LLD

Addressed: His Excellency Benjamin Franklin Esqr / Minister Plenipotentiary of the United States / at the Court of Versailes

Notation: Foster

From Nogaret   ALS: University of Pennsylvania Library

Excellent Docteur et très cher f∴[7]   Juillet 1782

Recevez nos Sinceres remercimens du cadeau sans prix que vous avez eu la bonté de nous faire. Le Peintre ne nous la remis qu'aujourd'hui jeudi.[8] Puissiez vous vivre autant que durera votre portrait. Ce bijou devient un immeuble dont personne de nous ne peut jamais être tenté de se déffaire: il passera dans la famille de pere en fils, et Sera respecté des générations futures

---

7. The masonic symbol for *frère*. In the course of 1782, Nogaret joined two lodges, Saint-Nicolas de la Parfaite Egalité and Le Patriotisme: Le Bihan, *Francs-maçons parisiens,* p. 376.

8. Nogaret requested this miniature on May 24, above; see our annotation there. While the portrait has not been located, Charles Sellers speculates that it might have been the model for miniatures attributed to Jacques Thouron, Jean-Baptiste Weyler, and the miniaturist who signed his enamels "D.C.": Sellers, *Franklin in Portraiture,* pp. 155–6, 162–78, 217–18, 404–7, and plate 34.

qui l'auront, quand la famille de son possesseur sera éteinte. Ma femme devrait vous aller assûrer, chez vous, de toute sa sensibilité; Mais vous avez tant d'affaires, et nous sommes si peu sûrs de vous voir sans vous gêner, que nous croirions commettre une indiscretion, si nous entreprenions ce petit voyage, sans avoir obtenu de vous la faveur d'être avertis du jour où notre présence ne vous Sera pas importune.

Permettez, sage Docteur, Le plus Vénérable de tous les V∴[9] que je vous embrasse trois fois sur les deux joues, cinq si vous voulez; et que je m'engage à avoir la gorge coupée plutot que d'oublier jamais combien m'est precieuse votre amitié paternelle et fraternelle.

Tels Sont les sentimens de votre respectueux et fidele serviteur　　　　　　　　　　　　　　　　　　F∴ FELIX-NOGARET

Notation: F. Nogaret, Juillet 1782

From George Chauncey

ALS: University of Pennsylvania Library

To your Exellency　　　　　　　　　Brest the 1 of august 1782.

Your Exellencÿ will permit me, that on 14th of maÿ Last your petitioner was taken prisonner in the ship Called the nancÿ from boston bound to L'orient and Caried in to plÿmouth were I was in prison till the 18th of june were I found means to Escape into a flemish Vessel were the Captain give me a passage to st malos upon mÿ arival I took a Certificat from the Captain to go to Brest bÿ Land were I traveled without any monÿ or resource to Brest were I thought to find some resource or assistance of a triffle of monÿ to go to Bourdeaux or Nantes but finding no resource in this City have applied to your Exellencÿ for some assistance as my uncle the Hble. Doctor Chauncÿs.[1] at boston will Remit in anÿ Place in America at your Exellencÿs. order or Command I had some Letters of recommandations given me by the Hble. Charles Chaunceÿ Esqr.[2] to your Exellency but Being in Prison

9. The masonic symbol for *vénérable.*
1. For whom see Samuel Cooper to BF, July 22.
2. Charles Chauncy (1729–1809), son of the Rev. Chauncy mentioned

so Long, mÿ Cloaths and Papers have been taken all from me, so that I find mÿ self wholy Destitude and in the Greatest miserÿ in a strange Country without monÿ or Cloaths or anÿ Lodging nor Eating nor Drinking I hop your Exellencÿ will take in to Consideration for the Love of your worthy Country, and the worthy familie were I Decent from, I hope your Exellencÿ will Excuse mÿ freedom, and relive me speedily with a Trifle that I can go to some port or other to find some Vessel to return home with a Passport as I have none and ÿour Exellency will greatly oblige your friends the Hble. Charles Chauncey Esqr. and the Hble. Doctor Chauncéÿ at Boston and much more your Exellencys. Poor Petitioner who is in the utmost Distress, in Expectation of your Exellencÿs speedy relive I Remain with all Submission Possible your most Obedient Hümble Servant

GEORGE CHAUNCEŸ

Be so obliging to Direct for me Chez monsieur Dellour au Lion sur le Reÿ De Brest

Addressed: A / Son Exellence / Doctor Franclin Envoÿ / Extraordinaire Pour Les Etats / De Nouvelle Angleterre A Paris / ou A Versailles

Notation: G. Chainley

From William Vaughan   ALS: American Philosophical Society

Dear Sir   London Aug. 1st. 1782
     I am happy that the inclosed gives me an opportunity of writing a line to one I have ever been taught to revere & respect. There

---

above, was the chair of the Kittery Committee of Safety and in October, 1774, was elected to the first Mass. Provincial Congress. In 1775, the Mass. General Court appointed him Counsellor for the Territory, formerly the Province, of Maine: *Sibley's Harvard Graduates*, XII, 246–51. Another possibility, however, is Charles Chauncy (1747–1823) of Connecticut, who married the daughter of BF's friend Thomas Darling (III, 108n). This Chauncy studied law and was admitted to the bar in 1768. In 1776, he became the state's attorney: *National Cyclopædia of American Biography* (63 vols., New York, 1898–1984), XIX, 221.

are few Events I have so much at heart as once more enjoying your company. I hope from a change of men system & times that day may not be far distant. We have been too long accustomed to misfortunes not to rejoice at the least glymse of hope.

I saw yesterday a lense whose powers you are not perhaps unacquainted with. Platina melts in Seventeen Seconds & other metals yeild to its power. The weather has not been favorable for a variety of experiments. Parker has however many in contemplation with the assistance of our philosophical men here. I beleive it is found superior to the one in France. The lense is solid, & weighs 212 pd.[3]

Our friends Dr. Price & Dr. Preistley are well & would with our family join in sincere wishes for your health & happiness if they knew of this opportunity. I thank you for your generous concern about John who is released on his parole by Sir G. Carleton. He was well at Philadelphia May 10—[4] With great respect & esteem I remain Dear Sir Your sincere & obt Servt

W VAUGHAN

3. What William Parker called his "Large Lens" was in fact an instrument that focused the sun's rays through two lenses mounted in a "Trunkated Cone" of wooden ribs. The larger lens, weighing 212 lb., measured three feet in diameter in the frame. The smaller lens weighed 21 lb. and measured 16 inches in the frame. (For comparison, the lens used by Priestley in his famous 1774 experiments was only 12 inches in diameter.) A wooden bar attached to the cone and extending beneath it held a small adjustable platform on which would be placed the substance to be melted, or "fused." This entire structure was mounted in an iron frame attached to a mahogany pedestal. A set of two engraved plates showing the Large Lens, and a printed key describing its parts, are among BF's papers at the APS. BF also received a handwritten table of 47 "Substances fused" with their weight and their time of fusion; a note on it indicated that some 300 more experiments had been made. This chart (also at the APS) showed that ten grains of platina fused in three seconds.

William Parker and Sons, glass manufacturers of Fleet Street in London, supplied Joseph Priestley with lenses and other glass articles needed for experiments: Robert E. Schofield, *A Scientific Autobiography of Joseph Priestley (1733–1804)* (Cambridge, Mass., and London, 1966), pp. 140–1, 367.

4. See RB to BF, May 20.

From Watson & Cossoul ALS:[5] American Philosophical Society

Nantes. 1st. Augt. 1782
We are extreamly mortify'd that the circumstances of our business obliges us to trouble your Excellency so often: at present we wish to be furnish'd with a commission for the ship to our address mention'd in our last,[6] to qualify her as letter of marque: She is call'd the Argo of 350 Tons burthen own'd in America by Messrs. Saml. R. Trevit & Co. and mounts 20, 9lb. & 18 pounders and is commanded by Saml R. Trevit[7] the ship being nearly ready for sea, we shall be happy to be fav'd with the commission by return of the post.

In case any passengers should offer, it is indispensable that they come on immediately. We are with esteem Your Excellency's Very Hl sts.   WATSON & COSSOUL

His Excellency Doctr. Franklin

Addressed: His Excellency Doct. Franklin / à / Passy

Notation: Watson & Cossoul Nantes 1er. Aout 1782

From the Abbé Jean-Charles Poncelin de La Roche-Tilhac[8]

LS: American Philosophical Society

Monsieur   Paris ce 2. aout 1782.
Votre goût distingué pour la litterature, et la protection que vous accordés à ceux qui cultivent les belles lettres, m'engagent

---

5. In Watson's hand.

6. Above, July 23.

7. Richard Trevett (Trevet) was from York, Massachusetts (later York, Maine). The *Argo* was shipwrecked off that port on Nov. 21, 1782: Kaminkow, *Mariners*, p. 315; Charles E. Banks, *History of York, Maine* (2 vols., Boston, 1931–35), I, 421. On Aug. 31, JW wrote WTF and enclosed an Aug. 7 bond for the ship; both documents are at the APS.

8. Jean-Charles Poncelin de La Roche-Tilhac (1746–1828), lawyer, *conseiller à la table de marbre* for the admiralty, and prolific author, published several works in 1782, including a revised edition of Thévenot's *Art de nager* (XXXVI, 334), a two-volume history of Tahiti, and *Recueil d'évènements curieux et intéressants, ou Tableau politique, historique et philosophique de l'année 1781*

à recourir à vous, pour en obtenir quelques éclaircissements dont j'ai besoin, pour terminer un ouvrage que je me propose de publier. Cet ouvrage, Monsieur, a pour objet l'etat actuel de l'Amerique.[9] Comme j'y fais entrer les noms des principaux Officiers qui composent l'administration de chaque province, oserais-je vous prier d'avoir la bonté de me faire donner la liste de ceux qui sont à la tête des treize provinces unies que vous representés en france. Si je connaissais quelque ouvrage imprimé, ou ce dénombrement se trouvât, je me donnerais bien de garde, de vous importuner sur ce sujet, et de vous derober des moments precieux que vous employés si utilement aux interêts de l'Europe. Je ne prétends pas d'ailleurs exiger de vous que vous vous donniés la peine de faire vous même cette liste. Je me borne à vous prier d'avoir la bonté d'adresser, à ce sujet, vos ordres à l'un de vos secretaires. Permettés, Monsieur, que je vous temoigne d'avance les sentiments de reconnaissance que merite le bienfait que j'ose espérer de vos bontés, et que j'unisse ma voix à celle de toute l'Europe, pour prier le ciel qu'il daigne prolonger le cours d'une vie que vous couvrés chaque jour de nouveaux l'auriers.

J'ay l'honneur d'etre avec un profond Respect Monsieur Votre très humble et très obeissant serviteur[1]

L'ABBÉ DE LA ROCHE-TILHAC,
conseiller à la table de marbre.

(2 vols., Amsterdam [*i.e.*, Paris], 1782): Larousse; Quérard, *France littéraire; Almanach royal* for 1782, p. 350.

9. *Almanach américain, ou Etat physique, politique, ecclésiastique et militaire de l'Amérique* for 1783 was published at Paris. The work included descriptive information on each state as well as lists of military commanders and members of Congress; some of his information, as he stated in his preface (p. x), was taken from Raynal's history. The almanac was announced for sale in the *Jour. de Paris,* Dec. 14, 1782, supplement. On Jan. 25, 1783 (APS), Poncelin thanked WTF for sending his almanac to America and noted that this first edition had sold out in two weeks. He prepared an expanded edition for 1784 and sent the first copy to WTF with a letter of Dec. 16, 1783 (APS). See Durand Echeverria and Everett C. Wilkie, Jr., comps., *The French Image of America* (2 vols., Metuchen, N.J., and London, 1994), I, 532, 570–1.

1. BF must not have replied. On Oct. 21, Antoine-François Quétant wrote WTF on behalf of Poncelin, who wrote WTF the next day renewing his request for information. WTF replied to both on Oct. 22, sending Poncelin copies of the state constitutions and an almanac for the state of Massachusetts, which

Ruë Garanciere Près st. sulpice./.

M. francklin. a Passy

Notation: La Roche Tillac 2 Août 1782.

From —————— Stockar zur Sonnenbourg

ALS: American Philosophical Society

V. Excellence,   Schafhouse en Suisse du 3. d'Aout 1782.
    Un certain M. Pfister, sergent aux gardes Suisses qui remit a
V.E. une lettre de ma part il y a deja plusieurs mois me marqua
dernierement que cette lettre s'etoit perdue parmy d'autres papiers de V.E. et que ne se souvenant plus du Contenu Elle me
permettoit de le Lui rappeller en peu de mots—[2] ma principale
curiosité rouloit sur le sujet de l'Abbé Raynald et de son Histoire
de la revolution en Amerique et ne connoissant parmi touts les
genies superieurs de notre siècle aucun qui par Ses lumieres éten-
dues fut mieux capable d'en juger que Votre Excellence, je desirois tres fort de savoir Son sentiment sur la maniere de penser
de M. l'abbé et sur sa capacité a juger des Ameriquains, ayant eu
quelqu'idée de traduire son petit ouvrage en allemand si V.E.
trouvoit qu'une vraye connoissance de Son Sujet en faisoit le
fond; Je ne crains pas d'etre prévenu par un autre par ce que je
n'en Souffrirois pas beaucoup, étant deja condamné par ma situation a ne rien faire et par mon inactivité naturelle a ne faire
que des riens. La renommée de V.E. qui s'ètend sur l'un et l'autre
Hemisphere tant en qualitè de Ministre public que dans celle de

---

listed officers in the state militia and in the American army. On Oct. 29, Poncelin pointed out to WTF that the list of congressional delegates did not include those of North Carolina. He also asked WTF to supply for the next edition the list of members of the Philadelphia academy "qui doit Sa naissance
à L'illustre M. franklin." In a later, undated letter Poncelin thanked WTF for
the "Service essentiel que vous m'avez rendu" and enclosed for BF and for
WTF copies of two of his works. All these letters are at the APS.
    2. The lost letter was dated Dec. 6, 1781: XXXVI, 204–6. Stockar must also
have enclosed with the present letter the duplicate copy on which BF drafted
notes for a reply. We have dated those notes [before Dec. 14, 1782]. Hist. Soc.
of Pa.

genie transcendant dans les Sciences m'engagea naturellement, comme voyageur, de rechercher Sa connoissance pendant mon petit Sejour a Paris et de Lui rendre l'été passè mes honneurs a Sa Maison de Plaisance a Passy en compagnie d'un autre compagnon et l'accueil gracieux que nous fit Votre Excellence m'enhardit ensuite de Lui ecrire tant pour cultiver cette connoissance infiniment interessante que pour m'informer du sus-dit Sujet. Je fais des voeux pour le Bien general en faisant de tres sinceres pour Sa Conservation en particulier et je suis avec le plus profond respet De Votre Excellence Le tres humble et tres obbeissant serviteur   STOCKAR ZUR SONNENBOURG

Notation: Stockar 3. Août 1782

From Jonathan Williams, Jr. Copy: Yale University Library

Dr & hond sir   Nantes 4th Augt 1782

This will be delivered to you by Mr W Burgess late a london Merchant but now bound to America.[3] In his passage through Paris to come hither he wishes to pay his personal Respects to you. I therefore beg leave to introduce him & shall esteem every Civility shewn him as a Favour confered on me.

I am as ever most Dutifully & affectionately

His Excellency Doctor Franklin— Passy

---

3. In March, William Burgess had asked JW's opinion on immigrating to America. JW suggested that he might be successful in either Philadelphia or Boston. Burgess was now in Amsterdam awaiting passage. JW sent him this letter, in case he should need to come to Paris. He may not have presented it, however, as he was said to have sailed to Massachusetts via the Netherlands: JW to Burgess, March 26 and Aug. 4 (Yale University Library); Smith, *Letters*, XIX, 640n.

To Alexander Martin[4]

ALS: John Carter Brown Library; copy: North Carolina Office of Archives and History

Sir   Passy, Augt. 5. 1782

Mr Edward Bridgen, Merchant of London, a particular Friend of mine and a zealous one of the American Cause, acquaints me that his Lands on the Sound in Cape Fear River, with his Negroes & Debts owing to Bridgen & Waller have by virtue of some late Laws of your Province been all Confiscated.[5] I have not seen those Laws, but I would hope there may be some Exception in them favouring the Property of our Friends, as it would grieve me to see those suffer as Enemies, who have from the Beginning of our Difference with England, uniformly, openly & firmly espoused the Interests of our Country, which to my certain Knowledge is the Case of Mr Bridgen.— I therefore beg leave to request your Excellency's Protection & Interposition in favour of that Gentleman, that so, if by no Construction of the Laws as they stand his Estates may be exempted, he may however obtain a subsequent Law to set aside the Confiscation & restore his Property, an Indulgence which it appears to me his Conduct has justly merited.— I give with Pleasure this voluntary Testimony in favour of a very worthy Man, but it will afford me infinitely more if it may be of some Utility to him. With great Respect I have the honour to be, Sir, Your Excellency's most obedient and most humble Servant   B FRANKLIN

His Excellency the Governor of N. Carolina

Notation: No. 10. Dr. Franklin for Bridgon. Registered got over

4. This is the only extant correspondence between BF and Gov. Martin (*c.* 1740–1807), who began serving as North Carolina's chief executive when the sitting governor, Thomas Burke, was captured by the British. Martin was subsequently elected to six terms (1782–84, 1790–92). *ANB.*

5. See Bridgen's letter of June 25.

From William Jones   ALS: American Philosophical Society

My dear Sir,   Nantes 5 Aug. 1782.
    We have been here above a fortnight, but I am sorry to find
that there will not be a good opportunity of embarking for
America till the beginning of next month, if so soon. I have been
on board all the ships here, that are bound for *the land of virtue
and liberty*, and have given the preference in my own mind to the
Annette, which will sail in about 5 weeks for Philadelphia or Virginia.[6] Had a ship been ready, we should have embarked immediately; but, on my return yesterday from Painbeuf, I found
letters from England requiring my immediate presense on domestick business. I have therefore promised Mr. Paradise to return to him here in three weeks, which will be long enough, I
fear, before the ships will sail, and I am informed that they will
leave the port together.[7] Should my family affairs or my profes-
sional views prevent my going this year, I shall write to my
friend, whom I have importuned with fruitless intreaties to go
without me, and, if he should refuse to go alone, he will have no
man to blame but himself, if his strange pertinacity should prove
ruinous to his children.[8] As my shortest way of returning
(though it would give me infinite pleasure to see you once more
at Passy) will be through Rennes and Alançon to Calais, I shall
be extremely obliged to you, if you will send me a passport *for
myself and one servant* to *embark for* England at *Ostend*, though

    6. Possibly the Virginia ship *Annett*, carrying 12 cannon and a crew of 45,
and commanded by John Audobon: Charles H. Lincoln, comp., *Naval
Records of the American Revolution, 1775–1788* (Washington, D.C., 1906),
p. 227.
    7. Jones is being somewhat less than candid. He had been in correspon-
dence with Shelburne about a judicial post in India. Encouraged by Shelburne, he decided to investigate the situation. After arriving in England on
Sept. 9, he canceled his trip to America: Garland Cannon, *The Life and Mind
of Oriental Jones: Sir William Jones, the Father of Modern Linguistics* (Cam-
bridge, New York, and Port Chester, N.Y., 1990), pp. 177–9.
    8. Paradise made plans to accompany Henry Laurens to America. When
Laurens delayed his departure, Paradise returned to Paris and went back in
September to London: Archibald B. Shepperson, *John Paradise and Lucy
Ludwell of London and Williamsburg* (Richmond, 1942), pp. 176, 179–80;
Laurens Papers, xv, 557n.

I should prefer Calais, if there should be an opportunity: be so kind as to order the passport to be sent to me at Calais at the *poste restante.* We have received great civilities from Mr. Williams, to whom I shall ever think myself highly obliged. Mr. Laurens came hither a few days ago, but was not determined, when I saw him, in what vessel he should embark.[9] How weak must my poor friend Paradise be, if he declines the opportunity of going with Mr. Laurens, in case of my necessary continuance in England! As to myself, if the English are too indolent or too dastardly to preserve their popular rights, I neither will nor can live among them; and must earnestly request you, my ever-respected friend, to give me information concerning the profession of a *lawyer* in the state of Pensylvania, and to let me know whether you think that I should be acceptable among your countrymen in that character. My long study of the laws of ancient and modern nations might make me a *useful assistant* in the necessary work of framing their *private codes.* My best compliments to Mr. Franklin, and our common friends; and assure yourself that I can never cease to be with the highest veneration, my dear Sir, Your much obliged and ever faithful friend   W. JONES.

From Williams, Moore & Co.

ALS:[1] American Philosophical Society

L'Orient 5th. Augt. 1782

We beg leave to trouble your excellency for information respecting the disposal of some Powder, taken in a Prize Consigned us. Believing a liberty is allowed to every American to sell any Article to the highest Bidder, (if for exportation) We yesterday made an Offer of a quantity of Powder at 20 *s.* a lib to the Comissary at Port Louis. He declined giving more than 10 *s.*, at sametime desired Us not to sell, 'till he heard from Paris respecting Our right of disposal. If We have liberty, We mean to take this Powder Ourselves, or Sell to any American Merchant,

9. See Laurens to BF, Aug. 7.
1. In James Moore's hand.

that will give more than Us.— In Brest We have a Prize nearly in similar Circumstances loaded with Spars,[2] detained by the Commandant of that Port.— Being at a loss how to Act, hope your excellency will be kind enough to inform Us. With great Respect We remain Your Excellencys Most devoted & humble Servants   WILLIAMS MOORE & CO

Addressed: Monsieur / Monsieur B. Franklin / Ministre Plenipotentiaire des Etas-unis / de l'Amerique, à la Cour de france / Passy./.

Notation: Williams Moore & Co.—L'orient 5 Août 1782.

Franklin: Certificate for Gustavus Conyngham[3]

DS:[4] Joseph Kleiner, Trenton, New Jersey (1968)

[August 7, 1782]

I do hereby certify whom it may concern, that the Commissioners of the United States of America at the Court of France, did issue on the first Day of March One thousand seven hundred & seventy seven, to Captain Gustavus Conyngham a Commission of Congress appointing him a Captain in the Navy of the said States and to command a Vessel then fitting out at Dunkerque on their Account to cruise against their Enemies, in which Vessel he took the English Packet Boat going from Harwich to Holland.[5]

2. For which see their letter of June 31 [*i.e.,* on or after June 30].

3. In response to Conyngham's June 8 letter to WTF, written from Nantes. It asked WTF to remind BF of his promise to either retrieve Conyngham's commission from Vergennes or grant him a certificate of its existence. Hist. Soc. of Pa.

4. In WTF's hand. Upon returning to America after the war, Conyngham entrusted this certificate to Col. Walter Stewart and presented a copy to Congress, along with a memorial requesting a new commission as a captain in the American Navy: Neeser, *Conyngham*, pp. 206–7. The matter was referred to a congressional committee headed by Arthur Lee, which refused the request on the grounds that commissions issued by the commissioners were only for temporary expeditions: *JCC*, XXVI, 7. Congress had not specified such limits: *JCC*, VI, 1036; illustration of Conyngham's commission in Neeser, *Conyngham*, facing p. 16.

5. In May, 1777: XXIII, 585n; XXIV, 5–6, 48–9.

But their being no War at that Time between France & England, and the Clandestine Equipment of an armed Vessel in a French Port to cruise against the English being therefore an unjustifiable Proceeding, he was apprehended by Order of the French Government[6] and his Papers seized, among which was the said Commission, which was never restored, and cannot now be found.[7] It is therefore that at the Request of the said Capt. Conyngham, and to ascertain the Fact that such a Commission was issued to him, I give this Certificate, at Passy, this 7th. Day of August, 1782.	B FRANKLIN
Minister Plenipotentiary from the United States
of America at the Court of France.

Vergennes to Ministers of Foreign Courts[8]

AL (draft): Archives du Ministère des affaires étrangères

[August 7, 1782]

Circulaire.

J'ai lhr [l'honneur] de vous envoyer M une ordonnance que le Roi a jugé a propos de rendre, pour rappeller les dispositions des anciens Réglemens qui défendent aux domestiques, gens de livré et à toutes personnes Sans état, de porter aucuns armes, épés, Couteaux de chasse &.[9] Sa majesté m'a ordonné, M, de vous donner connoissce. de cette ordonnance et de vous prier de Vouloir bien tenir la main à son execution en ce qui vous con-

---

6. XXIV, 64n, 73–4, 243; Stevens, *Facsimiles*, XV, no. 1530.

7. The commission (XXIV, 243n; XXX, 246, 386, 414–15; *Deane Papers*, II, 52) disappeared for almost 125 years before being offered for sale: Neeser, *Conyngham*, pp. xxii–xxiii. Conyngham was issued a replacement, but it was captured by the British: XXIV, 243n; Stevens, *Facsimiles*, XVI, no. 1589.

8. Filed with this draft is a list of the 27 recipients, including BF; asterisks indicate that all the ministers responded. It is similar to the list of "Ministres des cours étrangères résidens près le roi" in the *Almanach royal* for 1782, pp. 147–9, except that the representatives of Trier and the Hanseatic League are not listed, and the chargé d'affaires of the Neapolitan delegation, Luigi Pio, is listed in place of the ambassador. We have not located BF's response.

9. An *ordonnance* of July 6: François Isambert *et al.*, comps., *Recueil général des anciennes lois françaises . . .* (29 vols., Paris, 1821–27), XXVIII, 203.

cerne, Soit dans les gens qui composent létat de votre Maison, Soit par raport aux personnes de votre nation qui sont actuellement à Paris ou qui pourroient y venir. Votre Zéle pour le maintien du bon ordre ne me permet pas de douter M, que vous ne Concouriez avec plaisir en ce qui vous regarde à l'execution de la volonté de Sa maté. [majesté] à cet égard. Je vous serai très obligé de vouloir bien m'accuser la réception de cette Lettre, pour que je puisse en rendre compte à sa mté.

J'ai lhr d'etre tres parfaitement.

Minutte d'une Lettre écrite par ordre du Roi, aux Ambassadeurs et Ministres des Pais étrangers près sa maté.

In another hand: M. [?] Vls le 7. Aout 1782.

From Henry Laurens

Draft:[1] University of South Carolina Library; incomplete copy:[2] Library of Congress

Sir,   Nantes 7th Augt. 1782

Very late in the evening of the 12th of July I had the honor of recieving at Vigan your favor of the 2d. By the dawn of day the next morning I had mounted the chaise in order to prosecute my journey to this place & here I arrived in a very shattered state of health on the 30th. & have been ever since confined to my bed & to my chamber & my condition is still so weak & feeble as renders me incapable of writing. I dictate in the best manner I can, & my son Harry who will have the honor of delivering this, is my amanuensis. He is going to the South of France in order to conduct his sisters to this place where if I can find a proper embarkation, I mean to make use of it for our return to America sometime in September or as early as possible in October, I could

---

1. In the hand of Henry Laurens, Jr., with revisions by his father, who changed the date from Aug. 6 to Aug. 7. We print the revised text; for the original wording see *Laurens Papers*, xv, 549–52.
2. Consisting only of a fragment of the final sheet, containing most of the postscript.

not allow him to pass thro' Paris without paying mine & his own respects at Passy.

Mr. Adams had no doubt sufficient reasons for his silence respecting my name in the commission, I have recently heard from him, that he was ready to relinquish the mission for Money-borrowing into my hands, but the intelligence comes indirect, & much too late.[3] I am fairly acquitted & as I think happily delivered from that business, which at a great expence to myself, I once offered, as my duty prompted, to take upon me. & there's an end of that affair.

Some men would have found the late shuffling conduct of the British Ministry very troublesome, you have viewed it with tranquility & you know how to manage them, they will find it necessary by & by to be sincere & decided, I hope nevertheless you are drawing them to a point & that you have made some progress in the work of peace. Lord S. [Shelburne] may be satisfied now that all crooked & indirect tamperings with different parties end in exposing the Duplicity of those who practice such measures.[4] The repeated rebuff lately recieved from Congress may perhaps impress this lesson upon His Lordship's mind.— He might as well have sent Messengers to the man in the moon, & with less hazard of degrading himself & his Court. His Lordship had been told, that if he was in earnest about the work of peace, it might it must be transacted at his own door. But he thought it necessary once more to feel pulses at a thousand leagues distance, he surely flatters himself in a belief that he has an influence over the Americans which they know nothing of, & he never once reflected upon the futility & the danger of projects to wheedle, after having failed in every exertion to beat.

The completion of the exchange of Lord Cornwallis, even in the cautious manner in which you have performed it[5] affords me great pleasure, I have not the least doubt of its having proved

3. The intermediary was Edmund Jenings: *Laurens Papers*, XV, 550n. For Laurens' dispute with JA see Laurens' June 24 letter to BF.
4. Laurens altered this sentence, which had ended with "exposing his own duplicity." This was a direct criticism of Shelburne for his attempts to use Gen. Carleton and Adm. Digby as peace intermediaries.
5. See BF's discharge of Cornwallis from his parole, June 9.

satisfactory to His Lordship, nor do I think you will be further troubled on that affair, by any different arrangement or alteration on the part of Congress.[6] My Daughter expressed her sensibility of the notice you were pleased to take of her in your letter 'tis not improbable she will have an opportunity of paying her respects to you in person in her way hither.

I have the honor to be with very sincere Esteem & Regard Sir, your most obedient & most humble Servt

P.S. My worthy friend Jas. Bourdieu Esqr. of London, is exceedingly anxious lest the Count Vergennes & yourself should have been imprest with an Opinion, that he had been improperly officious, in the commencement of the late or present, what shall I call them, sham-treatings; & has earnestly desired me to explain his conduct; this would require a great deal of time, & might be unecessarily taking up yours, as I am rather of opinion that neither Count Vergennes nor yourself have heard or said any thing to his detriment—but should it be otherwise I can explain, & send you a narrative of his whole conduct at the time when he offered his service to go to the Court of France, a little before Mr Oswald had been applied to.[7] Mr. Bourdieu is a great stickler for American Independence, & I believe a faithful friend to his own Country, but Lord S is pleased to think him much too much in the French Interest & has treated him in my Opinion as a bystander, in a very unwarrantable manner. I beg Sir you will do me the honor to present my compliments to Mr & Mrs Jay.

Doctor Franklin.

Notation: Copies to Mr. Oswald Doctr. Franklin. J Laurens & M. Laurens. 7th. August.

6. Members of Congress were outraged at both Laurens and BF for discharging Cornwallis, and Congress refused to ratify the exchange: *Laurens Papers*, XV, 503n; *JCC*, XXIII, 753.

7. James Bourdieu (1715–1804), a business associate of Laurens', wished to promote a negotiated settlement between Britain and America: *Laurens Papers*, XV, 406–7, 527n.

From Hugh Williamson[8]

ALS: American Philosophical Society

Sir   Philada 7th Augt 1782.

When you have a few minutes to spare from the more weighty concerns of State I wish to interest you in favour of two young men belonging to NorthCarolina who are now Prisoners in England. They saild from Edenton about the month of Augt. 1780 in the Brig Fair-American, Captn Smith bound for France and were captured on their outward Passage.[9] They are Twins, and were, if I recollect well, about 14 Years old when they left Home. They are neither Soldiers nor Sailors, for they never had been at Sea before; and on that occasion they went through meer whim. The father of those Lads, Coll. Saml: Lockhart[1] is a worthy and respectable Citizen of NorthCarolina. Having served with him in the southern Army, in the most perilous Times, it is not only my duty, but among the first of my wishes that I might render him a Service. The Coll. apprehends that, considering the Age of his Boys and other circumstances, the Enemy will not make a Point of detaining them. They are supposed to be in Fortin Prison.[2] At the first time you may have occasion to enquire concerning any of our People who are Prisoners in England, will you be so good as cause Enquiry to be made concerning these Boys. If you should effect their Release you will be so good as

8. One of BF's former political enemies, Williamson moved to North Carolina early in the war and served as surgeon general of N.C. troops, 1779–82. He had recently been elected to Congress: X, 266–7n; *Biographical Directory of the American Congress 1774–1961* . . . (Washington, D.C., 1961), p. 1826. This is his only extant letter to BF, and we have no evidence that BF responded. Williamson's name is on a list BF drafted earlier in the year of people he distrusted: XXXVI, 375–6.

9. See XXXIV, 23n. The letter cited there establishes the date of capture as Oct. 6, 1780: *Laurens Papers*, XV, 440.

1. Samuel Lockhart, of Northampton County, held the rank of lieutenant colonel when he resigned his commission in October, 1777: Heitman, *Register of Officers*, p. 268; William L. Saunders, Walter Clark, *et al.*, eds., *The Colonial and State Records of North Carolina* (30 vols., Raleigh, 1886–1914), X, 165, 501.

2. John and Thomas Lockhart were committed to Forton Prison on Nov. 30, 1780, and escaped in mid-March, 1782: Kaminkow, *Mariners*, p. 118; Sheldon Cohen, *Yankee Sailors in British Gaols: Prisoners of War at Forton and Mill, 1777–1783* (Newark, Del., and London, 1995), p. 184.

give them such Instructions and Assistance as may enable them to return to any Port in the united States. Any Expence you are at, on this Accot: shall be immediately repaid to your order in Philada: where my duty in Congress may detain me for the present Year. I have the Honor to be With the utmost Esteem Sir Your most obedt and very Hble Servt   Hu WILLIAMSON

Benjamin Franklin Esqr

Addressed: The Honourable / Benjamin Franklin Esqr / Minister Plenip / Passy

To Vergennes   LS:[3] Archives du Ministère des affaires étrangères

Sir,   Passy, Augt. 8. 1782

Yesterday Mr Oswald communicated to Mr. Jay and me a Paper he had just received from his Court being a Copy of the King's Order to the Attorney or Sollicitor General to prepare a Commission to pass the great Seal, appointing him to treat with us &ca.[4] and he shew'd me a Letter from Mr Secretary Townshend, which expresses his Concern that the Commission itself could not be sent by this Courier, the Officers who were to expedite it being in the Country, which would occasion a Delay of eight or ten Days; but that its being then sent might be depended on, and it was hoped the Treaty might in the meantime be pro-

3. In the hand of WTF, except for the last six words of the complimentary close, which are in BF's hand.

4. Following a cabinet recommendation of July 25 (Fortescue, *Correspondence of George Third*, VI, 91), the King had Townshend write the order that same day. It asked that a bill be prepared for the King's signature empowering Oswald to negotiate with any commissioner or commissioners named by the thirteen "Colonies or plantations or with any Body or Bodies, Corporate or Politick or any Assembly or Assemblies or Description of Men or any Person or Persons whatsoever a Peace or a Truce with the said Colonies or plantations or any of Them, or any part or parts thereof": Giunta, *Emerging Nation*, I, 471–3; BF's copy, in L'Air de Lamotte's hand, is at the Library of Congress and another copy is at the AAE. Oswald's instructions of July 31 (Giunta, *Emerging Nation*, I, 481–4) authorized him to allow any persons with whom he treated "to describe themselves by any Title or Appellation whatever."

ceeded on. Mr Oswald left with me a Copy of the Paper, which I enclose for your Excellency's Consideration,[5] and am with great Respect, Sir, Your Excellency's most obedient and most humble Sert   B FRANKLIN

His Exy Count de Vergennes

From Vergennes

Copies: Library of Congress (two), Massachusetts Historical Society, National Archives

Versailles le 8 août 1782.

Je recois, Monsieur, la lettre de ce jour dont vous m'avez honoré et la Copie du Pouvoir que M. Oswald vous a communiqué. La forme dans laquelle il est conçû n'etant pas celle qui est usitée,[6] Je ne puis pas arreter mon Opinion a une premiere vue, Je vais l'examiner avec la plus grande attention et si vous voulez bien

5. Oswald received the King's order (serving as a draft commission) and his instructions on the evening of Aug. 6. The following morning he showed the draft commission to BF. According to Oswald, BF was relieved to see it, since Vergennes' own negotiations with Fitzherbert were stalled until it arrived; Vergennes had told BF that "both treaties must go on together hand in hand." BF "seemed to be satisfied, and said, as on a former occasion, He hoped we should agree; and not be long about it": Morris, *Jay: Peace*, pp. 286, 292, 295.

Oswald then took his draft commission to Jay, who remarked that independence should be expressly granted by Parliament in advance of negotiations for a treaty: Morris, *Jay: Peace*, p. 287. On Aug. 8, BF and Jay called on Oswald, after having seen Fitzherbert, and informed him of BF's present communication with Vergennes.

The conversation between Jay and Oswald marked the beginning of a crisis which paralyzed negotiations until Oswald received a revised commission, issued on Sept. 21, specifically empowering him to treat "with any Commissioners or Persons vested with equal powers, by and on the part of the Thirteen United States of America": Morris, *Jay: Peace*, pp. 292–3, 298–308, 310–11, 360–2.

6. Vergennes described Oswald's draft commission to La Luzerne on Aug. 9: "la commission de M. Oswald était en forme de lettres patentes et conçue comme un acte domestique du gouvernement anglais, mais que les Colonies n'y étaient présentees ni comme rebelles, ni comme sujettes de la couronne britannique": Doniol, *Histoire*, V, 110.

vous rendre ici samedi matin[7] Je pourrai en conferer avec vous et avec M Jay s'il lui etoit commode de vous accompagner—

J'ai l'honneur d'etre très parfaitement, Monsieur, Votre tres humble et très obeissant serviteur DE VERGENNES.

A Mr Franklin

To Vergennes LS:[8] Archives du Ministère des affaires étrangeres

Sir,   Passy, August 9. 1782.

The American Commerce in general, and that between France and America in particular having suffered greatly of late, from the Number of Frigates employed by the Enemy to cruise on our Coasts, I am directed to communicate to your Excellency the Paper on that Subject which I have the honour now to enclose,[9] wherein the Means of protecting that Commerce, and the Advantage such Protection would be to both Nations and to the Common Cause are briefly and clearly stated. I beg leave to request that your Excellency would take the same into Consideration, and thereupon advise such Measures as to your Wisdom may appear proper and convenient. With Respect, I am, Sir, Your Excellency's.—most obedient and most humble Servant

B FRANKLIN

Mr. Le Comte de Vergennes.

Notation: rep le 23.

7. Aug. 10. BF and Jay met with Vergennes on that date and discussed the form and essence of Oswald's commission. Vergennes argued that the language of the commission should be accepted. BF agreed, but Jay did not. The Americans did agree that they should deliver a copy of their full powers to Oswald, but should defer negotiations until Oswald's official commission arrived: Wharton, *Diplomatic Correspondence*, VI, 14–15; Giunta, *Emerging Nation*, I, 527. After this meeting BF, Jay, Aranda, and Fitzherbert dined with Vergennes: *Courier de L'Europe*, XII (1782), 139.

8. In L'Air de Lamotte's hand, except for the last six words of the complimentary close, which are in BF's hand.

9. The enclosure, also at the AAE, was a copy of Robert Morris' "State of American Commerce . . . " (although its author was not identified): *Morris Papers*, V, 145–57. Another copy, with supporting documents, is with BF's papers at the Library of Congress. Livingston had sent BF at least one copy with his letter of May 22, above.

From Richard Bache

ALS: American Philosophical Society

Dear & Hond. sir   Philadelphia August 9—1782.

The foregoing is Copy of my last to you via Baltimore,[1] since which a number of French Ships of the Line having arrived from Cape Francois on our Coast,[2] the British Cruizers have retired into Newyork, & our port is once more open—this affords me an opportunity of sending you the third Bill[3] of the sett within mentioned, and of letting you know that we are all well;— None of the Claret that you were so kind as to order me, has yet reached me; I have received a Letter from Mr. Bonfield of Bordeaux dated in March, which informs me that he had sent ten Boxes to LOrient, to be forwarded me from thence, but the Letter is all I have received.[4]

You will herewith I hope receive the Newspapers as there are two Vessels now bound for France, I shall transmit some in both— Sally and the Children are still in the Country, they return to Town next Week— We present our joint Love & Duty— I am ever Dear & Hond. Sir Yours affectionately

RICH BACHE

Dr. Franklin.

Addressed: Dr. Franklin

---

1. RB TO BF, July 23, above.
2. The marquis de Vaudreuil, who commanded the French fleet in the West Indies after de Grasse's capture, sent 13 ships of the line to Boston for repairs; see our annotation of Livingston's May 22 letter. One of them, the *Magnifique*, 74, ran aground off Lovells Island (about six miles east of Boston) on Aug. 9 and had to be abandoned. A portion of Vaudreuil's fleet was detached to Portsmouth, N.H.: Dull, *French Navy,* pp. 284, 299–301, 333; Rice and Brown, eds., *Rochambeau's Army,* 1, 74n, 257; Morison, *Jones,* p. 326.
3. A duplicate of a Robert Morris draft on Ferdinand Grand; see RB TO BF, July 3.
4. The previous October BF had asked John Bondfield to ship RB three casks of claret. Bondfield planned to ship one on the *St. James,* which sailed in January, 1782, and arrived safely in March: xxxv, 645; xxxvi, 110. Bondfield charged 1488 *l.t.* 10 *s.* for the three casks and their transport: Account VI (xxiii, 21).

From Joseph Banks ALS: University of Pennsylvania Library

Dear Sir   Soho Square Augst. 9 1782
Tho the difference of our pursuits has for so long a time en-
strangd us from Each other[5] I trust if ever peace should return
that philosophy & your old Friends would resume that share of
your time which when in their possession they so much valued.
Not doubting but that if I was within your reach I still should
enjoy a part of your time & some share of your Friendship I take
the liberty to request that the Bearer Dr. Broussonet[6] may as my
Proxy be allowd sometimes to visit you he will write me word
what you think of me & what you think of the Calm pursuits
which I have ever been steady to he will tell you that I have
never Enterd the doors of the house of Commons & I will tell
you that I have escapd a Million of unpleasant hours & preservd
no small proportion of Friends of both Parties by that fortunate
conduct thank god times are not yet so bad as to Oblige all men
to enlist in one or the other party at least I hope not.
With the sincere wishes of a moderate man that such measures may be taken by both parties as may tend to the Elevation
of both rather than the destruction of either beleive me Your
Hearty Friend & Faithfull Servant   JOS: BANKS

Broussonet has studied Fish with no small success he has been
near two years in england & spent much time with me beleive
me when I tell you that you will find him much above par in
Common sence as well as in Learning

Addressed: Dr. Franklin / &c. &c. &c.

---

5. Banks's last letter, in 1780, thanked BF for supplying a passport to Capt.
James Cook: XXXII, 176–7.
6. Pierre-Marie-Auguste Broussonet (1761–1807) received his doctorate
in medicine in 1779 and soon moved to London to pursue his interest in
ichthyology. He became friends with Banks and classified for him the extensive collection of exotic fish gathered during Cook's first expedition. The
catalogue was published as *Ichthyologia sistens piscium descriptiones et icones*
(London, 1782), and Broussonet was made an honorary member of the
Royal Society. After returning to Paris, Broussonet presented several memoirs to the Academy of Sciences and was elected a member in 1785: *DBF;
Dictionary of Scientific Biography.*

Endorsed: From Sir Joseph Banks, Bart. President of the Royal Society

Notation: Jos. Banks

From Robert R. Livingston

Three LS:[7] University of Pennsylvania Library; AL (draft): New-York Historical Society; transcript: National Archives

Dear sir   Philadelphia 9th. August 1782.

Having written to Mr Jay, who I presume is with you, I do not think it necessary to repeat what I have mentioned to him.[8] We have not heard from you since March,[9] a very long period, considering the interesting events that have taken place between that time and this—many vessels have arrived without bringing us a line from you— I am apprehensive that Mr Barclay does not communicate to you the frequent opportunities that offer of writing— I shall write to him upon the subject— Sir Guy Carleton and Admiral Digby have informed the General, that a negotiation for a general peace is now on foot, and that the King his master has agreed to yeild the independence of America, without making it conditional— I shall enclose a copy of his letter at large, which refers to an other object,—the exchange of Prisoners, this great point once yielded.[1] I see nothing that will obstruct your negotiations, except the three points of disenssion,

7. According to a notation on the transcript, the original was sent by the ship *Washington*, the duplicate by the ship *Queen of France*, and the triplicate by the ship *St. James*. We print from the triplicate because it alone bears BF's endorsement and his decipher of the passages in code.

8. Livingston wrote Jay on Aug. 8, enclosing a congressional resolution giving Jay permission to leave Spain: Morris, *Jay: Peace*, pp. 312–15.

9. On May 30, above, Livingston told BF he had received his letter of March 30. BF's March 4 letter to Robert Morris (XXXVI, 649–52) was delivered to Congress by Morris on May 24: *JCC*, XXII, 290.

1. Guy Carleton and Robert Digby to George Washington, Aug. 2, 1782: Jared Sparks, ed., *The Writings of George Washington . . .* (12 vols., Boston, 1834–37), VIII, 540–1. Carleton and Digby had just received Shelburne's June 5 letter (for which see BF to Vergennes, July 24).

which I have before written to you about,[2] I wish it had been possible to obtain the estimates I mention, as they might have been rendered useful to you upon one of them— But the negligence of the Governors or Legislatures of the several states have rendered all my endeavours hitherto unsuccessful, Notwithstanding repeated promises to give this subject their earliest attention—[3] the restoration of confiscated property has become utterly impossible, and the attempt would throw the Country into the utmost confusion—the fisheries are too important an object for you to lose sight of, and as to the back lands, I do not concieve that England can seriously expect to derive any benefit from them that will be equivalent to the Jealousy that the possession of them would awaken and keep alive between her and this Country. The claims of Spain[4] are the dreams of one who sighs for what he has no title to, and which if attained, would only add to the misery he has already hoarded. The Degree of estimation in which she stand with us you will judge from the Resolution transmited to Mr Jay—[5] I write to him in your cypher being No. 4. of the Cypher which Mr Morris sent you,—this is also written in the same cypher—[6] I would wish you to use that as I have no great reliance upon the one you have written in formerly, it has passed thro' too many hands— I transmit you a bill for 71.380. Livres, being the amount of one quarters Salary to yourself Messrs. Jay, Adams, Carmichael, Dana & Dumas— No provision is made for the private secretaries or contingencies, not having been furnished with an account of them— I also send bills for the first quarter commencing in January, so that you will on the receipt of this be enabled to pay one half years salary to our foreign Ministers—and their Secretaries.

2. The three points of dissension that Livingston expected were the territorial boundaries of the United States, American access to the Newfoundland fishery, and the fate of the Loyalists: XXXVI, 390–400.

3. Apparently estimates of the damages caused by the British, about which Livingston had long hoped to gather information: XXXVI, 128–9.

4. To land east of the Mississippi, a subject of some concern to Livingston: Morris, *Jay: Peace*, p. 313. This phrase, through "dreams," was encoded.

5. This sentence was encoded, except for "estimation" and "Mr. Jay."

6. Livingston had been using this code for the previous eight months: XXXVI, 262.

I just now learn that Carlton has published his, and Digby's letter to the General,[7] the design of this must either be to see whether the People of this Country will catch so eagerly at the proposition for a peace which yields them their Independence, as to be careless about the Alliance, or to impress them with an Idea that we are indebted for our freedom to the generosity of Great Britain, rather than to the attention of France to our interests in the general Treaty—it is not to be doubted that the good sense, and the gratitude of this Country will defeat both these objects.

I have the honor to be sir with the highest respect & esteem your Excellency's most obedient humble Servant

ROBT R LIVINGSTON

NB If Mr. Jay should not be at Paris, I must beg you to open and decypher for him, the letter of this month, and the resolution contained therein, marked on the back below the seal *Augt.* and send it to him by the earliest opportunity.

No. 15. 3plicate

His Excellency Benjamin Franklin

Endorsed: Mr Secry. Livingston No. 15 Aug. 9. 1782 Sundry Points of Negociation Bills transmitted

From Benjamin Vaughan[8]

Copy:[9] Massachusetts Historical Society

My Dearest Sir   Paris August 9th: 1782

To avoid pressing you with conversation, & to shew how little I expect you to enter into any answer or dispute, I leave with

---

7. It was published in the Aug. 7 issue of James Rivington's *Royal Gazette*.

8. The subject of this letter, the confiscation of property from Loyalists, was of interest to Vaughan's fellow Briton Richard Oswald, who may have discussed the matter with Vaughan. Oswald's instructions included an article calling his attention to such confiscations: Giunta, *Emerging Nation*, 1, 483, 505.

9. In a hand we do not recognize, with later editing marks (which we do our best to ignore) in another unknown hand.

you upon paper, my thoughts concerning your American confiscations; that you may take as much or as little of them as you please.

I know of two principles, which your American friends will say influenced them in this matter; Retaliation & the just rights of society— Let us begin with Retaliation; from which, however I may exclude maritime captures; because you have seemed of opinion, that America has something like revenge in that article, by making similar captures.

I am sensible the Injuries done you, have very feelingly provoked Retaliation. It is, however a fact in criminal Law, that tho' there are no bounds to crimes, yet every wise society determines that there are bounds to Punishments. If a Villain tortures my Brother, there is no civil law that determines reciprocal torture for that Villain; & still less for that Villain's Brother, who perhaps was wholly averse to the crime. Where the Practice was otherwise, Brutus (according to Voltaire) would say, "C'est agir en tyrans, nous, qui les punissons"—[1] It is not the practice of our modern Europians, I am sure, to confiscate in this manner; for in the hottest wars that we have known among us, we have seen Enemies respecting the private property of each others Subjects, wether in Lands or in Funds, when left in their power; & this, even where the Individual has taken a personal part in the war & it's success. And notwithstanding the brutality which a part of our people have exercised beyond the Atlantic; & notwithstanding our Ministry (as you say) by declaring you traitors, virtually determined your whole property to be confiscated, & meant to have confiscated that of particular persons; yet I know of no one public Confiscation of such American Property existing in England itself notwithstanding the many debts still due from America to England, nor Do I believe your example will yet be pleaded with us, in order to induce our legislature to confiscate such American property.— And indeed there was no time of the war, in which an act would not have been in danger of being highly unpopular in England. The Case which I put were it to happen would be highly distressing to many; as I know some who are in the predicament of having property & friends on both

1. Voltaire, *Brutus* (Paris, 1731), Act IV, Scene vii.

sides of the quarrel; & who would in consequence be greatly divided which of the two places to chuse for their residence & Party.

As to the detention of the money in the funds, belonging to the province of Mary land;[2] I think the case admits of a very natural explanation, without considering it as an act of public confiscation; a measure, which the English for the sake of their public credit & policy, would as much avoid I believe in the case of America, as they do in the case of Holland. The money in question was I think was deposited in our funds by the hands of private commissioners; & as it depended upon an Event (vizt: the fate of the war) whether the new Government of Mary land was to be held legitimate or not, the commissioners wished to avoid the risque of paying the money twice over; for having been intrusted with it by the proprietary Government, they were afraid that a receipt given on the part of the new popular Government only, might not be deemed as a sufficient Acquittal for them, should the old proprietary Government be restored by the force of the British Arms.— In this affair, therefore, the commissioners acted as private men; & tho' the opinions that led them, were obtained from Crown Lawyers, yet their advice was given as private advice; &, coming from lawyers, was framed according to statutes, & not according to Policy or justice.— Besides, considered as a public sum, it was very small; only £30,000; & for this £30,000, a general confiscation took place, of refugee & absentee property;[3] without, considering whether it was not more than a proportionate Reimbursement; even supposing the money should be finally sequestered, contrary to probability.— But I may be told, that the principles of society admit & require these measures towards offending subjects, independant of Retaliation.— When I think, however, of any punishment for guilt, I am always apt to reflect by what means the unhappy Parties became guilty.— In England, the Sin of the bad politics that pre-

2. The British government prevented the trustees of Maryland from selling Bank of England stock: XXXI, 336n; XXXIII, 254–5.

3. Maryland required absentees in the British dominions to return to the state by March 1, 1782, under penalty of forfeiture of their property: XXXV, 179.

vailed, arose very much from distance, bad education, & industrious deceptions; & often times when it appeared the act of the many, it was really the act of the few. Such Sins therefore of the few, are to be punished on the many with some measure of relenting; and so far as the punishment is meant for prevention, something should be considered as to the frequency of the occasion which is said to require the prevention, & the real efficacy of the example itself for preventing— Among the refugees, I am convinced that some (for want of a better reason) took side in order to follow their relations; others took side from some accidental injury; others from fear of the issue, in a struggle where they thought more was to be lost, than could be gained (a Maxim, which ought to have fair influence in all situations, & which cannot be held worthy of the Bitterest punishments); not to mention, that it is but candid to allow, that as Mankind differ on all other subjects, so it is possible for some [few?] honest men to have differed on this, & that some persons also may have been influenced by the oaths they were made to take, or by the personal danger that was supposed at times to threaten them. Refugees of this discription, one should think, deserved at least a degree of lenity.

But what are we to say to the confiscation of the Estates of distant innocent absentees, among whom were many Women & Youths; Absentees, who never took a hostile part, or who perhaps were usefully employed in Europe in combating prejudices or distributing information, or who were otherwise attached to some particular connection or Profession, or some place of Residence or education. They left their Estates answerable for paying their full proportion of taxes, & have themselves rarely received one farthing of Revenue in the interim.— It is true, these absentees yielded no personal service in the field; nor were all of them calculated for yielding it; but neither have many of your own subjects yielded personal services; & in what are such subjects better than absentees; & why are the one allowed to provide Substitutes for themselves in the Militia, & not the other? The Estates of the absentee was ready to contribute towards the substitute, & I presume was taxed, with a view to it; & as the proprietor of it was not upon the spot to mitigate his share of the tax, it is probable he was not spared so much as the resident.—

The only point of essential difference that I see between them, is, that the Resident has probably taken oaths which the absentee has not taken; but as Experience shews, the facility with which such oaths are taken and broken, this difference becomes of less importance. The resident in defiance of his oath may have secretly spread causes of terror and distress, thro' his country, which seldom can be imputed to the other; so that he may be found no otherwise to have taken a side, than by contributing his effects; in which shape probably the Absentee has taken his side still more seriously. Risques attending the passive residents from the events of war are put a good deal out of the question when it is candidly considered how easy it is for the resident to avoid giving offense & even to gratify the Loyalists; so as to secure their protection, in spite of his oaths, his contribution to taxes, & his backward service in the Militia, & perhaps, all things considered, to make his situation more useful to himself, than that of the absentee. In short, tho' I think I have heard all that is usually said about the right of Society to command the persons, Effects, & landed property of it's members; yet the present case I believe exceeds the usual theory, as well as practice of Europe, on these occasions; especially when it is remembered, that the military service is so easily, & has in fact in America so often been, compounded for, either in money or taxes.

If these Estates are said to be confiscated, to furnish a fund out of which to indemnify your own sufferers, I cannot but reply, that if those sufferers are provided for inconsistently with justice, they will create other Sufferers. They will occasion Violence to those private rights, which are not less the pillars of Society, than those sterner Virtues that produce civil Revolutions. They will eject others from honest acquisitions, made in peaceable times by private citizens, either by purchase, economy(?) or labor; & this too, when most of the States have other natural ways of assisting the sufferer, by considerations of vacant Lands, or immunity from taxes, & the like. Besides whenever the English evacuate any of their Posts, much of this private property will be restored again to your people; not to mention, that it is in some little degree to be considered, that English subjects have suffered in Florida & Canada by a simular course of war; & may still again suffer, either there, or in the West Indies.—

There are suspicions, however, that these late confiscations, are made chiefly as a substitute for taxes, which have only lately begun to be imposed in America; & those suspicions are confirmed, from finding you have been so little disposed to retaliate for personal injuries. And there are reports here, on this side the Atlantic, (which I pray may not be authentic), that a language is uttered & principles are espoused on some of these occasions, not very favorable to the encouragement of public humanity or private charity; & in some cases, to the breach of personal gratitude, & the improper indulgence of private interest & private pique.— There is no doubt, that the several parties whose property is in question, must expect more or less to suffer considerable levies upon it; but (excepting a few,) I think not to the lenth of complete Sequestration.— Besides, it is worth considering, that the gain of the public has in no degree been in proportion to the injury of the individual; the Estates having in many Cases produced less than their value, & especially formerly, when they were paid for with a falling currency.— A General Confiscation likewise, with a design of Restitution in favor of deserving individuals, I conceive must end in injustice, either to the sufferers or yourselves; first, because all retributions is difficult; & next, because it will be particularly hard for yourselves to restore a value, where you did not receive a Price; & if you mean to do precise justice, by returning the specific property sequestered, you may do injustice to the purchasers; who may have ventured upon considerable improvements, as well as withstood other bargains in the interim, for the sake of it. Instead therefore of confiscating the whole number of these Estates indiscriminately, & afterwards reinstating the innocent; it seems a truer method, to begin only with what are known to belong to the guilty, & add the rest in proportion as they come to light.— But as a friend to the prosperity of America, I beg to ask, whether the principle of imposing Residence upon purchasers or traders in that country, may not in some views be impolitic; as Many Europians or West Indians might employ their capitals in cultivating Trade or Lands in America, so as to make the remaining Lands more valuable; & more abounding in useful labours, for by their situation they might easely Send over provided they were allowed to preserve to themselves the Choice of Residence out of the Country; for at present, it appears as a Rule, that no Europian can vest a Capital in trade or lands, nor any American depart from his trade or Lands, without (what is every where else unheard of) a formal leave of Absence.

But as it is time to conclude, I shall only add, that the farther these things are proceeded in, the more obstacles are thrown in the way of affectionate Reconciliation. The present English Ministry & government, are not your wrong doers, & will perhaps feel themselves, with the rest of the English Nation, somewhat hurt, at not discovering things returning into an immediate train of happy Settlement.— The business however of deciding concerning the more obnoxious refugees, is an affair left in the hands of Persons fully authorized on the subject; & what I write on this occasion, you know to be the more Spontaneous Measure of an individual, (who feels warmly for America,) in favor of Refugees or absentees, who have proved either innocent or neutral in the public Contest.

I am well aware you have no present powers to act in this Subject, nor has even the Congress itself, which has commissioned you. But you can communicate Opinions on this head, to your different Countrymen; & perhaps procure the Revision or suspension of what is going forwards that relates to it, in the different States.— At all events, as peace & the mode of it is a general Import, I conceive not wholly impracticable for the different States to receive the advice of Congress, & for Congress in return to receive the instructions of the different States, for concluding this matter in a general national way, with Great Britain. And the Instructions to their Commissioners here, may either arrive in time for the general treaty; or else serve in bringing on a special Settlement of the affair; supposing the States unwilling to take the redress of the grievance upon themselves.

I am, my dearest Sir, with the utmost respect, Your ever devoted, affectionate & grateful,   BENJN. VAUGHAN

From Edmund Burke[4]   ALS: American Philosophical Society

Dear Sir,   Beconsfield Augst. 10. 1782.

I flatterd myself that by this time we might have shaken hands as publick friends as I hope we always should have done as private. In the Latter Case States have no power, though in other respects they may & do put us in odd & awkard Situations. Two friends of mine are going to Paris one of whom I know for a long time & have valued just in proportion as I have known him, He is one of the first men in Bristol with regard to commercial consideration, & in every other light one of the first men that can be found in any place. His constitutional principles, his private honour, his sound & comprehensive understanding, & his general knowlege will recommend him to a Mind like yours. He is ambitious of being known to you, & will cultivate you during his short stay in Paris with his Son a most promising young Gentleman. I think you will be pleased both with the father & the Son. Mr. Harford's is merely a tour of pleasure.[5] The other Gentleman Mr. Hill, I only know by Character; but I know him by that Channel, in the most advantageous manner. He is a Spanish Merchant, & as his Business to Spain, to which he proposes to go through France, is purely mercantile no difficulty I think is to be apprehended; but as in a time of War which is a time of Jealousy, especially with a Jealous Nation, he may possibly meet some obstruction, I shall be much obliged to you to obtain proper passports for him from the Spanish Minister at Paris, assuring You that I have reason to be persuaded that his call to Spain is altogether commercial & unmixt with any political purpose whatever.[6] Anxiously longing for the happy moment of peace, when

4. The final extant piece of correspondence between Burke and BF.

5. Joseph Harford (1741–1802) was a political supporter of Burke's when the latter represented Bristol in the House of Commons. His son was Charles Joseph Harford (1764–1830): Thomas W. Copeland *et al.*, eds., *The Correspondence of Edmund Burke* (10 vols., Cambridge and Chicago, 1958–78), v, 27n; Dixon Wecter, "Burke, Franklin, and Samuel Petrie," *Huntington Library Quarterly*, III (1939–40), 337n.

6. A J. Hill, Jr., wrote BF from the Hôtel du Bain-Royal, rue Richelieu, on Aug. 31 to inquire about the success of his application to the Spanish ambassador for a passport (APS). On Sept. 6, *Lieutenant-Général de Police*

all Languages will speak the Language of amity, at least that those will at last speak it whose original [Tongue?] has been for several Years so confounded, I remain in all Seasons with the greatest Esteem & Regard My dear Sir Your most faithful & obdt. humble Servt.   EDM BURKE

Endorsed:[7] 1782 apeid boike 1776 Ind:apois

From ——— Destouches[8]

LS: University of Pennsylvania Library

Monsieur   Dunkerque Le 10. aoust 1782./.

Le zêle dont le Capitaine Bennet Negus[9] a donné des preuves dans le Commandement des Corsaires La Civilité, et Le franklin, les Combats honorables qu'il a soutenu, les prises quil a faites ont merité l'attention de Votre Excellence, et elle a dit dans le tems à M. Le Roÿ quelle cherchoit à temoigner sa bienveillance à ce Capitaine son compatriote. Le Sr. Bennet Negus en est d'autant plus digne quil se trouve la Victime de son activité et de son Empressement à nûire à l'Ennemi et servir L'Etat. Il n'a pu rester dans L'inaction Tandis qu'au retour de sa Croisiere, l'été dernier, on s'est occupé à reparer son Batiment, et à le matter en Brigantin, et il a pendant cet Intervalle pris le Commandement d'un petit Corsaire avec lequel il a eté pris. Il traine depuis ce tems des jours malheureux dans Mill prison,[1] près Plÿmouth, n'en aÿant pu obtenir son échange que pour l'amerique, ou il ne pouvoit se resoudre à aller pour ne pas perdre de Vüe sa nouvelle Croisière au rearmément du franklin. Il a meme tenté de s'echapper des prisons, mais malheureusement il a eté atteint en fuÿant

---

Lenoir wrote BF that passports had been delivered to Harford and his son to return to London, and to Hill to go to Spain (University of Pa. Library).

7. Written on the verso; its meaning eludes us.

8. A *conseiller* of the Admiralty of Dunkirk, he was a cousin of Jean-Baptiste Le Roy: XXXV, 267n.

9. Negus, a former officer aboard the *Black Prince,* had become a privateer captain: XXXV, 126–7, 267.

1. Where he was committed on Oct. 2, 1781: Kaminkow, *Mariners,* p. 140.

d'une balle de fusil à la Cûisse,[2] et il est depuis plusieurs mois de
Soins et de remèdes encore fort mal de sa Blessûre dont il sera
Estropie toute sa vie. Sa Santé ne lui permet pas même le passage
à L'amérique de sorte qu'il desire pouvoir revenir en france pour
se remettre plus facilement, et promptement qu'il ne le fait en angleterre, et en prison, et commander ensûite Le franklin; mais
sans la protection la réclamation de Votre Excellence c'est en
vain quil espéreroit cet acte d'hûmanité. On a Tenté en vain
Toutes les autres Voÿes, le Capne. Bennet Negus aÿant un Bre-
vet de Lieutenant de fregate[3] de S.M. [Sa Majesté] a eté demandé
en Echange par le ministre, mais etant américain il est regardé en
angleterre Comme sûjét du Congrés, il ne peut donc que se reclamer de Votre Excellence et il espère qu'attendu les efforts qu'il
a fait pour en bien mériter, et surtout la Circonstance de sa
Blessure Votre Excellence voudra bien s'intéresser à lui, et demander pour lui son Echange pour la france; il ÿ a près d'un an
qûil souffre la Captivité. Sa bravoure et ses Taléns connus prés
de trois millions de prises qu'il a faites, les plus Baux combats
dont il est sorti victorieux, donnent de lui des Espériance fon-
dées, et le plus beau le plus fort Corsaire quil ÿ ait eu dans le port
de Dunkerque, et le méilleur voilliér, le franklin, est dans L'inaction en l'attendant, par ce qu'on espère qûil ne faudroit que le
Changement d'air, la Liberté, la satisfaction et l'espoir de se
venger pour retablir bientot la santé du Sr. Negus. Je vous aurai, Monsieur, ainsi que lui les plus grandes obligations de ce
que vous voudréz bien faire en sa faveur, et j'ose dire en faveur
de Justice par ce que son Echange peut entrer en Ballance avec
celle de quelque officier anglois de rang et d'Importance. Les
Sieurs Charles et Edouard Hagues sont les Correspondans à
Londres du Sr. Negus et du Sr. Pre. Salomez l'ainé[4] son armateur, negociant en cette ville, vous pourrez, Monsieur, faire cor-

2. This happened on Feb. 14, 1782: Charles F. Jenkins, ed., "John Claypoole's Memorandum-Book," *PMHB*, XVI (1892), 179, 188.

3. Negus was one of six Americans or supposed Americans to receive that
rank. Although he claimed to be from New Bedford, he actually was Irish:
Clark, *Ben Franklin's Privateers*, p. 50; Henri Malo, *Les Derniers Corsaires:
Dunkerque (1715–1815)* (Paris, 1925), pp. 129–30.

4. Pierre Salomez l'aîné was the principal owner of Negus' former command, the *Franklin:* XXXIV, 102n.

respondre les personnes que vous Emploirez à la Cour d'angleterre, avec ces Correspondans. Je dois avoir aussi l'honneur d'obsérver à Votre Excellence que le Sr. Bennet negus, cache en angleterre son desir, et son dessein de retournér en france pour ÿ Commander, et quil ne parle que de raisons de santé, qui malheureusement pour lui n'existent que trop réellement. Je serai aussi fort obligé à Votre Excellence de vouloir bien m'honorér de sa reponse le plustot quil sera possible, et de me marquér le degré d'espoir qu'il ÿ a du prochain retour du Sr. Bennet negus, par ce que le Sr. Salomez ne peut differer bien longtems à prendre un parti et faire choix d'un Capitaine pour le franklin.

Je suis avec un tres profond Respect Monsieur Votre tres humble & tres obéissant Serviteur   DESTOUCHES
conseiller de l'amirauté

P.S. Le Capitaine Bennet Negus a eté pris a bord du Corsaire Le marquis de Morbecq[5] le 18. septembre 1781. armé a Dunkerque par Le Sr. Salomez l'ainé.

Notation: Destouches le 10. aout 1782

From Nogaret   ALS: University of Pennsylvania Library

Monsieur   Paris ce Samedi 10 [August, 1782][6]
Je reçois une Lettre de me femme, par laquelle J'apprends que vous nous avez fait l'amitié de nous venir voir.[7] Elle a du vous dire que j'étais à Paris pour une bonne oeuvre. Un ami agé de 85 ans me charge de recevoir Ses fonds: je m'acquitte à cette heure de cette commission. Je Serai *sûrement Libre Jeudi jour de la Vierge:* J'aurai l'honneur de repondre à votre invitation, et celui de vous renouveller les assûrances de mon respect et de ma gratitude. Ce sont Les Sentiments avec les quels je fais profession

5. Or possibly *Marquise-de-Morbecq:* Malo, *Les Derniers Corsaires*, p. 279.
6. This date is based on Nogaret's reference to the feast of the assumption of the Virgin, which fell on Thursday, Aug. 15, 1782.
7. BF was at Versailles meeting with Vergennes on Aug. 10; see our annotation of Vergennes' letter of Aug. 8.

d'être pour la vie Monsieur Votre très humble et très obeissant Serviteur[8]   FELIX-NOGARET

Addressed: A Son Excellence / Monsieur Franklin / Ministre Plenipotentiaire / des Provinces unies de / L'amerique / a Passy / Près Paris / pressée

To Robert R. Livingston

Copy, incomplete press copy of copy,[9] and transcript: National Archives

Sir,   Passy, Augt. 12. 1782.

I have lately been honour'd with your several Letters No. 10. March 9. No 11. May 22. and No. 12. May 30.[1]

The Paper containing a State of the Commerce in North America, and explaining the Necessity and utility of Convoys for its Protection, I have laid before the Minister, accompany'd by a Letter pressing that it be taken into immediate Consideration;[2] & I hope it may be attended with Success.

The Order of Congress for liquidating the Accounts between this Court and the United States, was executed before it arrived.[3] All the Accounts against us for money lent, and Stores, Arms, Ammunition, Clothing &ca furnished by Government were brought in and examined, and a Ballance received which made the Debt amount to the even Sum of Eighteen Millions, exclusive of the Holland Loan for which the King is Guarantee. I send

---

8. On another unspecified Saturday, Nogaret wrote from Versailles to explain his absence when BF called. He asked BF to send word by his servant when he would be free to accept their "petit diner bourgeois", and they would set a date then for dinner at BF's. APS.

9. Both the copy we print, and the one from which the press copy was made, are in L'Air de Lamotte's hand.

1. The first of these is in XXXVI, 675–6; the rest are above.

2. Livingston sent the paper with his May 22 letter, and BF forwarded it to Vergennes with a covering letter of Aug. 9, above.

3. The congressional resolution was enclosed with Livingston's letter of May 30. BF's having already executed it refers to his July 16 contract with Vergennes, above.

a Copy of the Instrument to Mr. Morris. In reading it you will discover several fresh marks of the King's Goodness towards us, amounting to the Value of near two millions. These added to the Free Gifts before made to us at diferent times, form an object of at least twelve Millions for which no Return but that of Gratitude & Friendship are expected. These I hope may be everlasting. The constant good Understanding between France and the Swiss Cantons, and the steady Benevolence of this Crown towards them, afford a well-grounded Hope that our Alliance may be as durable and as happy for both Nations; there being strong Reasons for our Union, & no crossing Interests between us. I write fully to Mr. Morris on Money affairs,[4] who will doubtless communicate to you my Letter, so that I need say the less to you on that Subject.

The Letter to the King was well received.[5] The Accounts of your Rejoicings on the News of the Dauphin's Birth give pleasure here; as do the firm Conduct of Congress in refusing to treat with General Carleton, and the unanimous Resolutions of the assemblies of different States on the same Subject. All Ranks of this Nation appear to be in good humour with us, and our Reputation rises thro' out Europe. I understand from the Swedish Ambassador that their Treaty with us will go on as soon as ours with Holland is finished;[6] our Treaty with France, with such Improvements as that with Holland may suggest, being intended as the Basis.

There have been various misunderstanding and mismanagements among the Parties concern'd in the Expedition of the Bonhomme Richard which have occasion'd Delay in dividing the Prize Money. Mr. de Chaumont who was chosen by the Captains of all the Vessels in the Expedition as their Agent, has long been in a State little Short of Bankruptcy,[7] and some of the Delays have possibly been occasioned by the Distress of his Affairs.

4. Immediately below.

5. It was enclosed with Livingston's May 22 letter.

6. See BF to Creutz, April 24.

7. Chaumont had been in financial difficulty for more than two years; for its beginnings see XXXIII, 445–6. For the agreement or concordat among the squadron's captains see XXX, 223n, 459.

He now informs me, that the Money is in the Hands of the Minister of the Marine.[8] I shall in a few Days present the memorial you propose with one relating to the Prisoners,[9] and will acquaint you with the answer. Mr. Barclay is still in Holland. When he returns he may take into his Hands what Money can be obtained on that Account.[1]

I think your Observations, respecting the Danish Complaints thro' the Minister of France, perfectly just. I will receive no more of them by that Canal; & will give your Reasons to justify my Refusal.[2]

Your Approbation of my Idea of a Medal to perpetuate the Memory of York & Saratoga Victories gives me great Pleasure, and encourages me to have it struck. I wish you would acquaint me what kind of a Monument at York the Emblems required are to be fix'd on; whether an Obelisk or a Column; its Dimentions; whether any Part of it is to be Marble, and the Emblems carved on it; and whether the Work is to be executed by the excellent artists in that Way which Paris afford; and if so to what Expence they are to be limited?[3] This puts me in mind of a Monument I got made here and sent to America by order of Congress 5 Years since.[4] I have heard of its Arrival and nothing more. It was admired here for its elegant antique Simplicity of Design, and the various beautiful Marbles used in its Composition. It was intended to be fix'd against a Wall in the State house at Philadelphia. I know not why it has been so long neglected. It would me thinks, be well to enquire after it, and get it put up some where. Directions for fixing it were sent with it. I enclose a Print of it. The Inscription in the Engraving is not on the monument: It was merely the Fancy of the Engraver.[5] There is a white Plate of

---

8. BF had known this since February: XXXVI, 529–30.

9. The proposed memorials are the ones on prize money mentioned in Livingston's letter of May 30 and on prisoners mentioned in his letter of May 22.

1. *I.e.*, whatever prize money could be obtained.

2. Livingston objected in his May 30 letter to France's transmitting protests against American ships.

3. See XXXVI, 262–3, 644, as well as Livingston to BF, May 30.

4. Caffiéri's monument to Gen. Richard Montgomery: XXX, 472n.

5. Augustin de Saint-Aubin made the engraving in 1779 with the inscrip-

Marble left smooth to receive such Inscription as the Congress should think proper.

Our Countrymen who have been Prisoners in England are sent home, a few excepted who were sick, & who will be forwarded as soon as recovered. This eases us of a very considerable Charge.

I communicated to the Marquis de la Fayette the Paragraph of your Letter which related to him.[6] He is still here: And as there seems not much likelihood of an active Campaign in America, he is probably more useful where he is. His Departure however, tho' delay'd, is not absolutely laid aside.

The second Changes in the Ministry of England have occasioned or have afforded Pretences for various Delays in the Negociation for Peace. Mr. Grenville had two successive imperfect Commissions. He was at length recall'd, and Mr Fitz-herbert is now arriv'd to replace him, with a Commission in due form to treat with France, Spain & Holland. Mr. Oswald, who is here, is inform'd by a Letter from the new Secretary of State, that a Commission impowering him to treat with the Commissioners of Congress will pass the Seals & be sent him in a few Days. Till it arrives this Court will not proceed in its own Negociation. I send the Enabling Act as it is called. Mr. Jay will acquaint you with what passes between him & the Spanish Ambassador respecting the proposed Treaty with Spain. I will only mention[7] that my Conjecture of that Court's Design to coop us up within the Allegheny Mountains is now manifested. I hope Congress will insist on the Mississippi as the Boundary and the free Navigation of the River from which they would entirely exclude us.[8]

---

tion "A la gloire de Richard de Montgommery Major Général des Armées des Etats unis Américains tué au siege de Quebec le 31 Decembre 1775 agé de 38 ans": Charles H. Hart and Edward Biddle, *Memoir of the Life and Works of Jean Antoine Houdon* . . . (Philadelphia, 1911), illustration facing p. 62. BF had it sent to Jay shortly after it was issued: XXX, 472–3.

6. In Livingston's May 30 letter.

7. From here to the end of the paragraph BF wrote in cipher. The English is interlined on this copy and is also given in the transcript.

8. Jay began discussions with Aranda on Aug. 3: Morris, *Jay: Peace,* pp. 268–73. He and BF had dined with Aranda on July 6: *Gaz. de Leyde,* July 16, 1782.

An Account of a terrible Massacre of the Morravian Indians has been put into my Hands.[9] I send you the Papers that you may see how the Fact is represented in Europe. I hope Measures will be taken to secure what is left of those unfortunate People.

Mr. Laurens is at Nantes, waiting for a Passage with his Family to America. His State of Health is unfortunately very bad. Perhaps the Sea Air may recover him, & restore him well to his Country. I heartily wish it. He has suffered much by his Confinement.[1]

Be pleased to present my Duty to the Congress, and assure them of my most faithful Services.

With great Esteem, I have the honour to be, Sir, &ca signed
B. FRANKLIN

Honble. Robt. R. Livingston Esqe.

Notation: Letter 12 Aug 1782 Doct Franklin Read Decr. 13. 1782 Secret— Decr. 27 At the request of Mr Howell the injunction of Secresy taken off so far as respects the latter part of the paragraph on the second page marked between Brackets () and of the first paragraph of the letter of Sept 3. 1782[2]

To Robert Morris

Copy and transcript: National Archives

Sir   Passy August 12th 1782.

I have received, many of them at the same time, your sundry letters of March 23. April 8 & 17 May 17 18, two 23 two and 29. It would be a Satisfaction to me if you would likewise mention from time to time the Dates of those you receive from me.

Most of your Letters pressing my obtaining more money for

---

9. See BF to Hutton, July 7.

1. See William Jones's letter of Aug. 5 and Laurens' of Aug. 7.

2. The paragraph beginning "The Letter to the King" is marked with brackets. R.I. congressional delegate David Howell requested that the sentence within it beginning "All Ranks of this Nation" and part of a sentence from BF's Sept. 3 letter to Livingston (beginning "It affords me much satisfaction") be sent to the executive of his state: *JCC,* XXIII, 832–3; XXIV, 32–6; *Morris Papers,* VI, 172–3n; Wharton, *Diplomatic Correspondence,* V, 682.

the Present year. The late Losses suffer'd in the W. Indies, and the unforseen necessary Expenses the Reparation there and here must occasion render it more difficult, and I am told impossible. Tho' the good Disposition of the Court towards us continues perfect. All I can say on the Head of money more than I have said in preceding Letters, is, that I confide you will be careful not to Bankrupt your Banker by your Drafts, and I will do my Utmost that those you draw shall be duly honored.

The Plan you intimate for discharging the Bills in favor of Beaumarchais, tho' well imagined was impracticable.[3] I had accepted them,[4] and he had discounted them, or paid them away, or divided them among his Creditors. They were therefore in different Hands with whom I could not manage the Transactions proposed. Besides, I had paid them punctually when they became due, which was before the Receipt of your Letter on that Subject. That he was furnish'd with his Funds by the Government here is a Supposition of which no foundation appears. He says it was by a Company he had formed: and when he sollicited me to give up a Cargo in Part of Payment he urg'd with Tears in his Eyes the Distress himself and associates were reduc'd to by our Delay of Remittances.[5] I am glad to see that it is intended to appoint a Commissioner to settle all our public Accounts in Europe.[6] I hope he will have better Success with M. Beaumarchais than I have had. He has often promised solemnly to render me an Account in two or three Days. Years have since elaps'd and he has not yet done it. Indeed I doubt whether his Books have been so well kept as to make it possible.

You direct me in yours of May 17th. "to pay over into the

3. See Morris to BF, May 29.

4. On June 25, BF had paid Beaumarchais 2,544,000 *l.t.:* Account XXVII (XXXII, 4).

5. In 1776, the French government had sought to minimize the risks of providing arms to the Americans by having it handled by a private company, Beaumarchais' Roderigue Hortalez & Cie. The government loaned the company 1,000,000 *l.t.* with which to purchase supplies to sell to America: XXII, 453–4. For the final disposition of Beaumarchais' financial claims see *Morris Papers*, v, 321–8n.

6. It was not until Nov. 18, however, that the plan was given final approval and Barclay elected to carry it out: *Morris Papers*, v, 128–9n.

Hands of Mr Grand on your account such monies belonging to the United States as may be in Europe distinct from those to be advanced for the current Year." I would do it with Pleasure if there were any such. There may be indeed some in Holland rais'd by the new Loan,[7] but that is not in my Disposition, tho' I have no Doubt that Mr Adams will on occasion apply it, in support of your Credit. All the Aids given by the Crown, all the Sums borrow'd of it, and all the Dutch Loans of ten Millions: tho' the Orders to receive have been given to me, the Payments from the *Tresor Royal* have all been made on my orders in Favor of Mr. Grand, and the Money again paid away by him on my Drafts for Public Services and Expences, as you will see by his Accounts, so that I never saw or touched a Livre of it, except what I received from him in Discharge of my Salary and some Disbursments. He has even received the whole Six Millions of the Current Year,[8] so that I have nothing in any Shape to pay over to him. On occasion of my lately desiring to know the State of our Funds that I might judge whether I could undertake to Pay what you were directed to Pay Mr William Lee by Note of Congress "as soon as the State of Public Finances would admit"[9] Mr Grand wrote me a Note with a Short Sketch of their then supposed situation which I enclose.[1] You will Probably have from him as soon as possible a more perfect Account but this will serve to show that I could not prudently comply with your wish in making that Payment to Mr Lee, and I have accordingly declin'd it; the Less unwillingly as he is intitled by the Vote to Interest.[2]

I send herewith the Accounts of the supplies we have received in Goods which I promised in my last.[3] The sum of their Value

---

7. A new loan undertaken by JA raised more than $650,000 by November: Ferguson, *Power of the Purse*, p. 128.

8. For which see BF's July 16 contract with Vergennes.

9. The quotation is from a Sept. 12, 1781, resolution of Congress (*JCC*, XXI, 955) sent with Morris' first letter of Nov. 27: XXXVI, 155.

1. Probably the now-missing enclosure to Grand's July 20 letter to BF, above.

2. Lee wrote on July 8, above, asking for the money.

3. BF's last letter to Morris was that of June 25, above. The enclosed accounts are missing, but see our annotation of Franklin's Statement Concerning the Dutch Loan, [after July 16].

is included in the Settlement made with this Court mentioned in a former Letter.[4] Herewith I also send a Copy of the Contract, which has been long in hand, and but lately compleated. The Term of the first yearly payment we are to make, was readily changed at my request from the first to the third year after the Peace;[5] the other marks of the Kings bounty towards us will be seen in the Instrument. The Interest already due, and forgiven, amount to more than a Million & half; what might become due before the Peace is uncertain. The Charges of Exchange, Commissions, Brokerage &ca. &ca. of the Dutch Loan, amount to more than 500,000 Livres, which is also given, so that we have the whole sum net; and are to Pay for it but 4 per cent. This Liquidation of our Accounts with the Court was compleated before the Vote of Congress directing it came to Hand.[6] Mr Grand examined all the Particulars, and I have no doubt of its being approved.

Mr Grand to whom I have communicated your letter of April 17th. will soon write to you fully. We shall observe the general Rule you give respecting 5th, 6th 7th & 8th Bills.[7] The attention, care and pains necessary to prevent by exact Accounts of those accepted, and Examination of those offered, Impositions which are often attempted, by presenting at a distant time the 2nd. 3rd. &ca is much greater than I could have imagined. Much has been saved by that attention, of which of late we keep an Account; But the Hazard of Loss by such attempts might be diminished together with the Trouble of examination, by making fewer small Bills.

Your Conduct, Activity and address as Financier and Provider for the Exigencies of the State is much admired and praised here, its good Consequences being so evident, particularly with regard to the rising Credit of our Country, and the Value of Bills. No one but yourself can enjoy your growing Reputation more than I do.

Mr Grand has undertaken to Pay any Ballance that may be

4. Perhaps that of March 4: XXXVI, 650.
5. See the second article of the July 16 contract.
6. As BF also told Livingston, immediately above.
7. See Morris to BF, March 23.

found due to Messrs. le Couteulx, out of the Money in his hands. Applying for so small a Sum as 5000 Livres would be giving Trouble for a Trifle as all application for money must be considered in Council.[8]

Mr Grand having already received the whole six Millions either in money or accepted Bills payable at different Periods, I expect he will deliver up to me the Bills for that Sum which you have drawn upon me; the rather as they express Value received by you. I never heard any mention here of intended Monthly Payments, or that the money could not be obtained but by your drafts. I enclose a Letter by which the Payment was ordered of the last three Millions.[9]

I observe what you mention of the Order that Ministers Salaries are to be hereafter paid in America.[1] I hereby impower and desire you to receive and remit mine. I do not doubt your doing it regularly and timely; for a Minister without Money I perceive makes a ridiculous Figure here, tho' secure from arrests. I have taken a quarters advance of Salary from the 4th of last Month, supposing it not intended to *muzzle* immediately *the mouth of the ox that treadeth out the Corn.*[2]

With great Esteem, I am, Sir, Yours &ca. &ca.

(signed) B. Franklin

Your Boys are well Mr Ridley & Mr Barclay still in Holland.[3]

Honble R Morris Esqr.

---

8. See Morris' second letter of May 18.

9. The enclosure is missing, but according to the July 16 contract the last 3,000,000 *l.t.* from the French government's 1782 loan were paid on July 5. Morris had mentioned the supposed monthly payments in his letter of May 17, above.

1. On May 29, Congress passed a resolution that the salaries of the American ministers in Europe should be paid by Morris: *JCC*, XXII, 308. It probably was enclosed with Livingston's May 30 letter to BF (above).

2. Deuteronomy 25:4.

3. Ridley returned from Rouen on Aug. 27. The following day he saw Robert Morris, Jr., and Thomas Morris at John and Sarah Jay's, and on Aug. 31 he and Barclay went to the theater: Klingelhofer, "Matthew Ridley's Diary," pp. 101, 103.

Notation:[4] Copy of letters of 8 April and 12 August 1782 from Doct Franklin to the Superintend of finance, which were recd and read in Congress 27 Decr. 1782 Jany 2d. 1783[5] Pursuant to the order of Congress of this day[6] I deliverd this copy into the hands of M Howell, but to my surprise after Congress adjourned found it left on the table CHA THOMSON

From Richard Bache   ALS: Historical Society of Pennsylvania

Dear & Hond. Sir   Philadelphia Augt. 12th. 1782.

I have wrote you by two different Conveyances,—[7] Another now pressents which I embrace to let you know we are well, & to send you the Dutch News papers— Wishing them safe to your hands— I remain with unfeigned Love & Duty. Yours affectionately   RICH. BACHE

Dr. Franklin—

Addressed: Doctor Franklin

Notation: R. Bache Augt. 12. 1782.

From Thomas Barclay   LS:[8] American Philosophical Society

Sir   Amsterdam 12th. Augt. 1782

I have been for Some time past in hopes of having the pleasure of hearing from your Excellency in answer to what I had the honour of writing to you the 17th. of last month. Since that time Mess De Neufville have totally rejected any Arbitration relative to the Settlement of their demand and have applied to Congress— Consequently my Stay here on their account will be intirely unnecessary and with respect to the Continental goods I

---

4. In Charles Thomson's hand.
5. *JCC*, XXIV, 3.
6. *JCC*, XXIV, 32–6.
7. His last two extant letters are above, July 23 and Aug 9.
8. The last six words of the complimentary close are in Barclay's hand.

have got Clear of them tollerably well. I have put on board the Brigantine Grace 64 Packs of linen the freight to be paid in America, and by the Brigantine four Friends a Neutral Vessell 82 Bales, the freight of which is also payable in America, except that of 23 Bales of Soldiers Socks and mittens which is of no great Consequence, and which must be paid here as the Value Cannot be ascertained in America.[9] I hope to have the honour of Seeing you before this Vessell Sails and of being able to prevail on you to order Insurance on the Value as it may be done at a low premium, and I think it is better not to run the risk. By the Brigantine Temmink I have Shipped 22 Bales and have been obliged to value on your Excellency of the 9th. for amount of the freight and Primage Viz in favour of Sampson Marcus & Co. at Six Months No. 25 for 3143 Ecus which I must rely on your Excellencys Goodness to honour.[1] Next post will Convey you my account Current, and I must depend on your assistance a little farther, It shall be as little as posible, but in truth there was no other way of getting away the goods, I Know they are much wanted in America, and Ruin of them would be the Consequence of their remaining here. This has been experienced on Supplies purchased by Mr. Beaumarchais which lay in the West Indies untill they were render'd intirely unfit for use by the Moth and became not worth twenty Shillings the Bale,[2] There lyes at Mess. De Neufville 9 Bales of French Cloth left there by Mr. Gillon I Know not the value, but I Suppose about £500.—and at Mr. Van Arps 4 Bales of the Same Kind of goods—the value is So very inconsiderable in Comparison of the Sale which he made to Col. Lawrence [Laurens] that I think I had better not medle with them— But Should your Excellency think other ways, both Mr. De Neufville and Mr. Van Arp Say they are ready to deliver them. The letter which I Shall write you next post will be the last I Shall have the honour to address you from Holland,[3] I am Sir

9. For the *Grace* see Samuel & Moses Myers to BF, July 22. The *Four Friends* eventually reached Philadelphia: *Morris Papers*, VII, 314n.

1. An *écu* was equal to three *livres tournois*. Grand honored the bill on Feb. 17, 1783: Account XXVII (XXXII, 4).

2. See XXX, 472.

3. We have no trace of that letter. Barclay arrived in Paris by Aug. 31: Klingelhofer, "Matthew Ridley's Diary," p. 103.

very respectfully your Excellency Most Obedient & Most Hum
Sert.   THOS BARCLAY

His Excellency Benjn. Franklin Esqe.

From Caffiéri   ALS: American Philosophical Society

Monsieur   De Paris ce 12 Aoust 1782
    Jay lhonneur de vous faire remettre plusieurs Epreuve de Tom-
beau que vous mave demender,[4] je profite de cette occasions pour
vous offrier La Statue de Pierre Corneille qui est une fidelé copie
de celle que jay executer en marbre pour Le Roy de qui a merité
les applaudissement du Public,[5] jose vous Supliér de vouloire bien
L'accepter Comme un hommage que je Rens a votre Rare Merite
qui vous ont acquis Ladmirations de tout Les Nations.
    Je Sui avec un tres profon Respec Monsieur Votre tres hum-
ble et tres obeïssant Serviteur   CAFFIERI

Notation: Caffiery 12. Aout 1782.

From Jonathan Williams, Jr.   Copy: Yale University Library

Dr & hond sir   Nantes Augt 12 1782
    The present serves only to inform you that agreable to the
permission contained in Billy's letter of the 23 June I have this
day drawn on you for my advances to Prisoners in favour of Mr
Grand as per accot on the other side amounting to £1697..10..0
which please to honour I inclose the original Vouchers to each
charge.—[6] I am as ever &c &c

His Excellency Doctor Franklin Passy

    4. Caffiéri offered on April 1, above, to sculpt funerary monuments or stat-
ues.
    5. The marble statue of the playwright, exhibited at the Salon of 1779, was
universally admired: Bachaumont, *Mémoires secrets,* XIII, 226; *Jour. de Paris*
for Sept. 27, 1779. The copy Caffiéri sent BF was most likely one of the terra-
cottas manufactured at Sèvres: Jules Guiffrey, *Les Caffiéri, sculpteurs et fondeurs-
ciseleurs* (Paris, 1877), pp. 299–300.
    6. JW had first requested reimbursement for these expenditures in his let-

From Henry Wyld: Two Letters

(I) and (II) ALS: American Philosophical Society

Franklin had last heard from Wyld and his group of English textile manufacturers, who wanted to emigrate to America, through their representative Edmund Clegg in mid-June. Buoyed by having received Franklin's passport and letters of recommendation, and ignoring his admonitions against sailing before a peace was declared, the core group had consolidated their assets and sent one of their number to Ireland to scout out ships and make arrangements for the passage. Clegg decided to stay behind, at least for the time being.[7] Wyld, eager to enlist experts in all aspects of the trade, approached several additional highly regarded engineers. One of them, the subject of letter (I), below, was John Swindell of Stockport, inventor of a cotton carding and roving machine. His involvement, as it turned out, was the group's undoing.

On August 3, Swindell turned informer. Assuring Secretary of State Thomas Townshend that he had won the trust of these defectors "far beyond my most sanguine expectations," he spelled out their plans in enough detail to ensure credibility. Henry Wyld, he wrote, had visited Franklin in Paris and had received both a passport and the promise of congressional backing. The group had retained a ship in Londonderry with a payment of twenty guineas. Franklin had also written Wyld a letter—which Swindell alone had been shown—that mentioned a "certain latitude" where their ship could meet with a huge convoy bound to a destination that Swindell was prepared to divulge. Since the emigrants were due to leave for Ireland in six days, "no time is to be lost."[8]

Townshend immediately notified the lord lieutenant in Dublin, who in turn notified customs officials in Londonderry. Townshend also instructed the head of the Secret Service to investigate.[9] An agent was dispatched to Stockport to interview Swindell, who provided

---

ter of March 26, above; see also his letter of May 22. A copy of the enclosed invoice follows the present letter in JW's letterbook (Yale University Library) and includes expenses for various Americans' board through June 9.

7. Edmund Clegg to BF, June 16, above.

8. John Swindell to Thomas Townshend, Aug. 3, 1782, Public Record Office.

9. Robert Glen, "Industrial Wayfarers: Benjamin Franklin and a Case of Machine Smuggling in the 1780s," *Business History*, XXIII (1981), pp. 316, 324.

more details. The agent's report, submitted to Whitehall on August 8, gave names and descriptions of many of the emigrants and specified that Wyld, who was leaving the following day to join the group in Liverpool, was lame, walked with a crutch, and was said to conceal his passport in the sole of his shoe. Their ship was to meet the Rhode Island–bound convoy thirty leagues off the Azores. When the group arrived in Londonderry, they were to apply to a Mr. Wood.[1]

I.

Most Excellent Sir   Hatherlow 12th. August 1782

I Am sorry to inform you, that M. Jno. Swindles Engine Maker of Stockport[2] can not attend the Co. 'though he originally designed so to do; Yet as circumstances occur I am perswaded he will for the next six years be of more use to us in Stockport than he could be with us, and knowing from the professed principles he possesseth, that he will hazard much for the sake of us and the Cause of the United States, I humbly recommend him to your notice, and beg you would give him an Answer by the return of post, to what he proposeth by the inclosed,[3] knowing that his abilities in Machinery equal, if not surpass any Mans in this Country, if we have any occation to make use of him I hope you

1. The emigrants named in the report, besides Wyld, were Joseph Schofield, "a tall genteel man 25 years of age," who had gone to Londonderry and paid 20 guineas to detain a ship until the group arrived from Liverpool; Henry Royle, a calico printer between 20 and 30 years old; John Rowbottom, a weaver; William Schofield, "a weaver and cotton spinner upon a machine"; Arnfield, "a common Engine maker"; Tolkington, "a weaver and Farmer"; and Edmund Clegg, formerly a Manchester tradesman but now a Baptist teacher, and his two sons. Many more were evidently in the company, but the agent could not get their names. William Clark to Thomas Townshend, Aug. 8, 1782, Public Record Office. The convoy, as described by Swindell, does not coincide with any group of transports sailing in the summer of 1782, but does sound like the convoy carrying Rochambeau's troops that sailed to Rhode Island in 1780.

2. Certain of Swindell's inventions were described in the *Manchester Mercury*, April 30, 1782: Glen, "Industrial Wayfarers," pp. 315, 324.

3. Wyld must have anticipated giving the present letter to Swindell, advising him to write a letter of his own. We assume that the enclosure was Swindell's letter to BF, Aug. 18, 1782 (APS). It, too, was sent care of Grand, and the notations on both letters indicate that they were received the same day.

will forward our Orders to him during the continuance of the present unhappy disputes betwixt the persons in power in this Kingdom, and the Citizens of the United states of America (whose preveledges we wish to in part injoy and whose oppressions we will participate) and forward his returns to us, and by you so doing and complying with my other request you will am perswaded be of great use to us as Manufacturing Subjects of those states and use to our common Friend am Honour'd Sir Your very humble and most obedient servant   HENRY WYLD

Addressed: M. Ferdinand Grand Mercht.[4] / Paris / Haste

Notations in different hands:[5] hatherlon le 12 aoust 1782: henry Wyld / Recue le 30 aoust Reple

II.

Most excellent Sir   Hatherlow 12th. August 1782

The person who writes the Postscrip,[6] being originally one of our Company, and one who designed to accompany the Expedition, but is put by, through an uncommon disappointment yet he wishes to be in Pensilvania, and I am fully persuaded he means to follow, if his business would be worth carrying over, of which you only can inform him of, and whereas sundry honest and industrious Artisans wish to acompany him which perhaps may be of use to us I humbly desire you will return him Answer to the questions he may propound to you respecting their Business; as they may be of use to the persons already gone, and perhaps be instrumental in introducing some useful mechanical Inventions, I hope they are people of confidence, and though not companions; yet well wishers to the undertaking, and the Inditer of the post script a person in whom I place the greatest Confidence, I

---

4. Wyld here reverts to the cover address he had used earlier: xxxvi, 567–8.

5. The notations here and on (II) were made in Grand's office, the first by an unknown clerk, and the second by Grand himself.

6. William Cheetham. Though written on the verso and labeled a postscript, Cheetham's communication is in all other respects a separate letter, written from a different location and dated Aug. 20. We will publish it under that date.

am for him and self, Sir Your excellencies most obedient Humble Servant   HENRY WYLD

Addressed: Mr. Ferdinand Grand Mercht. / Paris / Haste

Notations in different hands: Hatherlon le 12 aoust 1782 Henry Wyld / Recue le 5 7bre Réple

From John Shuttleworth[7]   ALS: American Philosophical Society

                    Hotel d'Hambourg Ruè Jacob.
Sir   Wednesday Afternoon [August 14, 1782][8]
    Since I had the honor of conversing with you,[9] it has occurred to me, that much of the expence, danger of capture, and inconvenience attending my intended voyage would be prevented by going to New York: the difficulty of getting from thence to Maryland seems, to me, to be that of being received into General Washington's lines; I have been a little acquainted with him from having met him at Sir Robert Eden's table, when he was Governor of Maryland,[1] but so many years have elapsed since that time, and his mind has been so continually employed in affairs of importance that he most probably may have forgotten me, entirely; I imagine a few lines from you, such as I might send by a flag of truce, expressive of my intention of settling in America would entirely remove all difficulties of that sort perhaps too, my profession would be no bar to my reception, especially if it be considered that there are very few Gentleman who have had those opportunities of acquiring professional Knowledge which I have happily experienced: If, therefore, you should

7. Introduced by Mary Hewson in her letter of July 19, above.
8. Dated on the basis of Shuttleworth's next letter, of Aug. 17 (University of Pa. Library).
9. We do not know precisely when Shuttleworth arrived at Passy, but he later reminded BF that he had discussed his desire to serve as a physician in the American army and his and Henry Harford's "affairs," presumably land claims: Shuttleworth to BF, Nov. 24, 1784 (APS). Harford (*ANB*) was the last proprietor of Maryland, and Shuttleworth owned vast acreage there: Shuttleworth to BF, Oct. 13, 1785 (APS).
1. Eden served from 1769 to 1776: *DAB.*

see nothing improper in favoring me with an introduction of that kind to the General I should esteem myself extremely obliged to you for it.

As an interested person I may see this affair in a different point of view to that in which your experience may lead you to consider it; but I beg leave to assure you that I wd not presume to sollicit a favor which I foresaw might be attended with any inconvenience to yourself, and I must beg that you will attribute any impropriety in my request to my want of Reflection.

It is my intention to leave paris on Saturday morning on my return to England, (for a few days), by way of Lisle and ostend; and I will do myself the honor of calling upon you on Friday morning, when you may depend [*torn:* on?] my care of any letter or message with which you may please to favor me. I am with very great respect Sir yr obliged and very obedt Servt

JOHN SHUTTLEWORTH

Addressed: Doctor Franklin / Passÿ

Notation: Shuttleworth

Index

Compiled by Jonathan R. Dull.

(Semicolons separate subentries; colons separate divisions within subentries. A volume and page reference in parentheses following a main entry refers to an individual's first identification in this edition.)

Commons, British House of (*continued*)
Laurens presents petition to, 441n; mentioned, 10, 716. *See also* Burke, Edmund; Parliament

Compiègne, Collège royal de, 412–13

Complete Collection of the ... Works of John Fothergill, A (Elliot), 423n

Conciliateur de toutes les nations d'Europe, ou Projet de paix perpétuelle entre tous les souverains de l'Europe ... (Gargaz), xxviii, lviii, 607–8, 611–14

Condorcet, Marie-Jean-Antoine-Nicolas Caritat, marquis de, 101n

Conductivity. *See* Metals

Confederacy (frigate, U.S.N.), 45

Congress (merchant ship?), 643

Congress (ship), 693n

Conseil d'état. *See* Council of State, French

Considerations on the sovereignty ... of New Ireland (McNutt), 129n

Considérations sur l'état présent de la colonie française de Saint-Domingue ... (Hilliard d'Auberteuil), 132n

Constantinople: Vergennes, H. Grenville members of diplomatic corps in, 302

Constitution and Frame of Government of ... New Ireland, The (McNutt), 129n

Constitutions of the Several Independent States of America ..., The (translation of La Rochefoucauld edition), 20n, 332

Consuls: neutral, in Bordeaux, request information, 13; Martin requests post as, 40; Livingston sends draft convention concerning, 535

Continental Congress: approves new instructions for privateers, 13n: Bank of North America, 265; appoints peace commissioners, 18–19, 55–6, 78–9, 136–7, 156, 165, 243, 245, 524, 528, 530–1, 630, 709: JA as minister to make peace, 55, 56n: Laurens to raise loan, 378, 417, 477n, 523, 709; authorizes commissioners to borrow money, 23: seizure of British ships by their crews, 578; orders respect for neutral shipping, 23: payment of d'Arendt, 33n: BF to repay Beaumarchais, 74, 182, 405–6, 426–7: to pay salaries of JA and his secretary,

146–7n: to consult with Lafayette, 305: to intercede on behalf of Jones's men, 429–30, 731–2: liquidation of accounts with France, accounts of American ministers abroad, 431n, 569, 730, 735, 737: Morris to pay ministers' salaries, 431n, 738: Barclay to desist from further purchases, 540n: BF to pay W. Lee, 580–1, 595: to furnish funds to Barclay, 642: Barclay to purchase military supplies, 642–3: copies of BF letters given to Howell, 739; prohibits trade in British goods, 42, 183, 227, 359; and auditing of Deane's accounts, 43–4, 74, 76–7, 365: Laurens-Cornwallis exchange, 109n, 243–4, 334, 336, 417, 451–2, 464, 528–30, 565, 672, 710: prisoner exchange, 153, 357, 401, 422, 447, 537, 732: Loyalist grievances, 171n, 725: parole for Macleod, 322, 433–4: proposed Laurens-Burgoyne exchange, 336, 451–2, 464, 529–30, 565: exchange of Cornwallis' staff officers, 341, 465–6: Tousard's pension, 518: *Den Eersten* claims, 519: Swedish treaty proposal, 538, 567n: Colomb, 648–9; uses bills of exchange, 44n, 261; pays Lomagne-Tarride, grants him leave, 64; suspends granting of passports, 82; La Luzerne communicates with, 113; requisitions money from states, 120–1, 571; BF inquires about reaction of, to Spanish claims, 138: sends copy of his journal of peace negotiations, 291–2n: urges to maintain French alliance, 566; accused of issuing letters of marque against Portuguese ships, 139; instructs commissioners to undertake nothing without French concurrence, 171n: JA to propose military alliance with Netherlands, Spain, 263; is part-owner of *Heer Adams*, 199; grants commissioners power to make commercial treaties, 204; Danish protest forwarded to, 204n, 538; Holker refused payment by, 221, 224–5; Carleton makes overtures to, 344–5, 399, 566, 574, 586, 626, 695, 709, 731; congratulates Louis XVI on birth of dauphin, 398n, 481; refuses BF's resig-

France (*continued*)

George III wishes vigorous exertions against, 112; Morris wishes to prevent further solicitations from government of, 121; occupies Dutch colonies, 137n; passports not needed by Englishmen to enter, 146; difficulties of American trade in ports of, 168–9, 484–90; production of salt in, 169n; commissioners instructed to undertake nothing without concurrence of, 171n; U.S. remains economically dependent on, 171n, 177n: faithful to alliance with, claims Livingston, 399–400, 429, 431, 518, 719: claims BF, 584, 607, 623: claims Cooper, 659; Fizeaux, Grand & Cie. appointed banker to government of, 182; Hartley discusses relations between Britain and, 252–8; Shelburne wishes to break alliance between U.S. and, 282n, 598–9n; ships of, seized in 1755 before declaration of war, 294; and Spain continuing war for own aggrandizement, argue British, 314n, 320; and threat to Ottoman Empire, 333; possessions of, guaranteed by U.S., 335n; public in, censures de Grasse, prefers d'Estaing, 340: favors America, 731; opposition to American war in, 385, 386n; Britain foments rebellion in, 385–8; press censorship in, 386n; British, Austrian intrigues in, 387; peace much discussed in, 393; various states affirm loyalty to American alliance with, 399–400, 480n, 584, 586, 607, 623, 659, 695, 731; contract for repayment of American debt to, 542–3, 633–9, 639–40n, 658, 671, 730–1, 737; foreigners need permission of court to remain in, 555n; would benefit from giving up sugar islands, argues BF, 620; interest rates charged by, on loans to U.S., 636–8; Congress unable to maintain interest payments to, 638n; continuation of war will benefit, claims Shelburne, 674n; alliance of, with Swiss canton, 731. *See also* Army, French; Convoys; Duties; Navy, French; Peace negotiations, British-American; Peace negotiations, British-French; Regiments, French; Treaty of

Alliance, American-French; Treaty of Amity and Commerce, American-French; Vergennes; West Indies, French

Franklin, Benjamin

—books and reading: assists Hilliard d'Auberteuil with book, lix, 132–3, 148, 356, 360, 375, 392–3, 420, 453–4, 495, 546–7; sent *Letters of an American Farmer*, lix, 628–9n: Gastellier's works, 30: Cowper poems, 105, 284: copy of *Senator's Remembrancer*, 229; subscribes to various journals, 3; purchases works by Bonnet, Rousseau, 3n; asked for, sends various books to Livingston, Morris, 4n, 71, 74, 214–15, 543; quotes Bible, 116, 416, 738; Helvétius on colonialism, slavery, 619–20; requests permission for books to bypass *Chambre syndicale*, 128, 214–15; McNutt sends pamphlets to, 129; inventory of library of, 129n; Hillegas sends Clarkson book inquiries to, 240; asked to order *Encyclopédie* for Library Company, 240n; Hopkinson asks for subscription to *Encyclopédie méthodique*, 240–1; Richard sends poetry to, 247–8, 262; has lost relish for reading poetry, 284; orders Greek and Roman classics, 347–8; Percival sends books to, 361; Pownall sends books to, 371, 448n, 582–3; encourages Soulavie to publish in *Journal de Paris*, 384n, 385–6, 390; Lacepède wishes to give copy of new book to, 403–4; paraphrases Montaigne, 444; sends Hewson works of Genlis, Deux-Ponts, 471; Vaughan sends books to, 608–9

—business and financial affairs: disputes accounts with Chaumont, lix–lx, 215–25, 473–5, 497–500, 588–9, 604–5, 605–6, 668–70; purchases shares in Caisse d'escompte, 3–4; salary of, 4, 381; estate of, 4n; asked for, provides financial assistance to Jay, 5–6, 8, 67, 72–4, 106, 107, 114, 118–19, 198, 261, 573n; bills of exchange drawn on, presented to, cashed by, 5–6, 8, 31, 44–5, 67, 72, 114, 119–21, 261, 278, 437–9; sends money to Hodgson, 31, 79, 357–8, 422, 446, 625: copy of accounts to

Franklin, Benjamin (*continued*)
obligations, and gratitude, 308: dangers faced by peacemakers, 415–16: importance of press, 472–3: slavery, unprofitability of West Indian colonies, 617–20; interested in phonetic spelling, lviii, 613–14; recommends liquidating debt to Spain, 6, 68; believes military supplies in America are adequate, 41–2: British weary of war, 97: Dutch should not accept separate peace, 138: frontiersmen the most disorderly of people, 170: U.S. should not solicit alliances, 310; calls Netherlands, Spain slow, 71, 78: himself a friend to honest, industrious people, 82: Louis XVI "our good Friend & Ally," 414: frugality an enriching virtue, 520; urges continued vigilance against British, 71, 73, 88–9; predicts British evacuation of New York, Charleston, 77–8: Britain will have a large share of American commerce, 158; wishes to finish "this devilish contest" as soon as possible, 80: for wise and honest men as British negotiators, 95: for permanence of friendship, alliance with France, 731; advises would-be emigrants to wait, 82, 226; compares U.S. to Hercules, 88, 432: the English to pirates, 191–5: Battle of the Saintes to Battle of Lepanto, 315; argues that idea of natural enemies should be abolished, 95: American liberty will weaken despotism elsewhere, 97: Mississippi should be boundary of U.S., 733; suggests release, good treatment of prisoners will further reconciliation, 96, 229, 269, 302n, 352, 363: U.S. should have consideration for Netherlands, 321; discusses with Shelburne promoting happiness of mankind, 103; tells Cooper conversing with nobility will increase his love of the French, 111; warns against trusting British, 116; fears Spain wishes to shut U.S. within Appalachians, 138, 733; claims peace only ingredient wanting to his felicity, 145: they who threaten are afraid, 295: there has never been a good war or bad peace, 457; blames Loyalists

for war, 326; supposedly regards Louis XVI as leading founder of U.S., 390; does not make dedications, does not wish to receive any, 519–20; expresses belief in divine providence, an afterlife, 587–8

—writings: keeps journal of peace negotiations, xxvii, liii, 291–346; "Supplement to the Boston Independent Chronicle," xxvii, lvii–lviii, 96n, 184–96, 197, 206–7, 268, 373, 667; "Thoughts on privateering," lviii, 617–19; "Thought concerning the Sugar Islands, A," lviii, 617–20; "Question Discussed . . . , The", 20n; "Dialogue entre La Goute et M.F.," 54; *Political, Miscellaneous, and Philosophical Pieces . . .* , 133, 609n, 661; *Interest of Great Britain Considered, The*, 170n; "Plan of Conduct," 175n; publishes satire in *Affaires de l'Angleterre et de l'Amérique*, 185n; "Apology for Printers," 191n; 1775 journal of negotiations in London, 291n; "The Ephemera," 360; "Observations on War," 618

Franklin, Deborah (BF's late wife), 520
Franklin, James (BF's late brother), 271
Franklin, John (BF's late brother), 17n
Franklin, Thomas (BF's cousin), 675–6
Franklin, William, 148n, 482n, 691
Franklin, William Temple: and JW, 11–12, 12, 42, 168, 376n, 402n, 699n, 741: Elie de Beaumont, 47–8n: Hazlehurst, 48n: Ingenhousz, 212, 468–9: Barbançon and his seeds, 230n: RB, 230n, 231n, 392: R. West, 236n: Foulke, 360n: La Roche, 396n: B. Alexander, 453, 560: Ridley, 463: Mumford, Tardy, 517n: BFB, 550n, 683: Cheminot, 568: Moylan, 582: Carmichael, 593: formalizing of BF's contract with Vergennes, 671: M. Stevenson, 676: St. Clair, 680n: W. Jones, 705: Conyngham, 706n; greetings to, 12, 174, 237, 392, 453, 463, 545, 560, 568, 593, 676, 683, 705; claims he does not ask favors of BF, 40n; will send paper, ink to Nantes, 42; visits Bertin, 51n; present when toad found at Chaumont's quarry, 100n; helps decipher Morris letters,

Jones, Sir William (*continued*)
629; Jay warns against, 629n; judicial
appointment in India for, 629n, 704n;
corresponds with Shelburne, 704n; re-
quests passport to England, 704–5;
sends greetings to WTF, 705; letter from
Paradise and, 629–30; letter from,
704–5
Joseph II, Holy Roman Emperor, 469
Journal de Paris, 133n, 274n, 384n, 385–90,
410n, 436n, 454n, 700n
Journal de physique (Rozier), 151, 533
"Journal of the Peace Negotiations". *See*
Franklin, Benjamin, writings
Juigné de Neuchelles, Antoine-Eléonor-
Léon Le Clerc de (archbishop of Paris),
412
Julien, ——— (*commissaire*), 4

Karl August, Duke of Saxe-Weimar, 231
Karl Theodor, Elector Palatine, 63
Keay, (Philip?): and Cheminot, 568; sends
report of accident in Philadelphia, 568;
letter from, 568
Kemp, John (escaped prisoner), 202
Keppel, Augustus (first lord of Admi-
ralty), 28n
Kingston, Elizabeth Chudleigh, Duchess
of, 20n, 21
Kingston, Evelyn Pierrepont, Duke of, 21n
Kingston-upon-Hull (constituency in
House of Commons): Hartley elected
to represent, 553n
Kinsale, Ire.: American prisoners at, 49,
59, 79, 125, 153, 229, 285, 447, 556n
Klinglin, ———, abbé de: asks recom-
mendation for La Coste, 40
Knox, Maj. Gen. Henry: appointed by
Washington to negotiate prisoner ex-
change, 462
Kuiebel, Hermanus (captain of *Le Plus
Ultra*), 497
Kurowski, Capt. ———, 62

La Bassée, Charles-Marie-Hubert de: recommends son for commission, 61–2
La Bassée, Mathieu (Charles-Marie-Hubert's son): recommended for commission, 61–2

Labat de Mourlens, ———, abbé: sends
copy of speech, 58; letter from, 58
La Blancherie, Claude-Mammès Pahin de
Champlain de (XXXVI, 357n), 274n
Lacepède, Bernard-Germain-Etienne de
La Ville-sur-Illon, comte de: and Le
Roy, 403; wishes to give BF copy of his
new book, 403–4; letter from, 403–4
La Coruña: arrival of convoy at, 72n
La Coste, ——— (would-be emigrant),
40
La Courtette, ———, baron de, 645n
Lady Greene (brigantine), 456–7
Lady's Adventure (cartel ship), 447n
Lafayette, Marie-Adrienne-Françoise de
Noailles, marquise de, 208n
Lafayette, Marie-Joseph-Paul-Yves-
Roch-Gilbert du Motier, marquis de:
plans return to America, 4n, 71, 74–5,
88, 113, 115, 322, 333, 431–2, 568; and
Jay, 6, 534, 534–5, 597n, 629n: Oswald,
Grenville, 305–6, 333, 351, 355–6: Ver-
gennes, 315, 341–2, 502: exchange of
Cornwallis, other officers captured at
Yorktown, 330, 332–4, 336, 341, 465–6,
484, 672: A. Ross, 333–4, 336n, 465,
484: Livingston, 431–2, 534n, 537, 733:
Washington, 465–6, 484, 534: Morris,
539, 568; proposes plan for Americans
to escape Forton Prison, 60; had recommended Lomagne-Tarride, 64; will discuss "petite affaire" with BF, 149; helps
compile list of British cruelties, 185;
Congress orders BF to consult with, 305;
postpones return to America, 305, 534,
537, 539n, 733; role of, in peace negotiations, 305–6, 315, 333, 341–2, 502, 515,
534, 537, 597, 601–2, 671–2; dines with
BF, expresses uneasiness about progress
of negotiations, 322; attends review
with Grand Duke Paul, 332; inquires
about Enabling Act, 484; works for religious rights of Protestants, 514n; uses
Castries' courier to carry letters to U.S.,
534; to carry journal of peace negotiations to America, 537; warned against
Jones, Paradise, 629n; letters from, 149,
465–6, 484, 502, 515, 534, 597; letters to,
60, 534–5, 598–602, 671–2

Netherlands (*continued*)

355, 374n; Dumas reports political, diplomatic developments in, 66, 113, 159–60, 564; pro-British party in, 66, 264n, 268, 289–90; should change policy toward U.S., argues Jay, 67; government of, called slow by BF, 71, 78; George III wishes vigorous exertions against, 112; American affairs go well in, reports BF, 113, 115; Barclay detained in, 115, 215, 540, 732, 738; Jay bills held in, 118–19; commercial relations between Britain and, 137, 266; France occupies colonies of, 137n; Russia as mediator between Britain and, 137n, 316–17, 329, 332, 333, 337, 355, 477; military, naval operations of, 138, 593; possible alliance between U.S. and, 197; G. Grand official French banker in, 198; shortage of cash in, 264; BF fears his correpondence with JA may be opened by postal authorities in, 282: supposedly is ready to make peace without concurrence of, 313n; Vergennes will inform of Grenville mission, 304, 352, 434; diplomatic corps in, refuses to return JA's visits, 310; Grenville's powers to negotiate with, 314n, 339; American obligations to, as issue in peace negotiations, 320–1, 435, 674n; U.S. should have consideration for, suggests BF, 321; Britain declares war against, 321n; Dumas wishes official post in American legation in, 373n; Howe cruises off coast of, 463; JA believes U.S. can obtain lasting friendship of, 476; criticisms in England of war with, 527; selects P. J. Van Berckel as minister to U.S., 564n; continuation of war will benefit, claims Shelburne, 674n. *See also* Loans; Navy, Dutch; States General of the Netherlands; Treaty of Alliance, proposed American-Dutch; Treaty of Amity and Commerce, proposed American-Dutch

Neuf Sœurs, Masonic Lodge of, 47n, 133n, 360n, 436–7, 645, 647n

Neufville, Jean de (Amsterdam banker, XXVII, 344n), 321n, 572–3

Neufville, Jean de, & fils (merchant firm): and Mumford, 85: Dana, 354: Barclay, 493–4, 541, 560, 572, 642–3, 739–40; forwards letters, 572; reports retirement of J. de Neufville, 572–3; letter from, 572–3

Neufville, Leendert de (Jean's son), 573n

Newburyport, Mass.: arrival of ship from, 93

Newcastle, Eng.: textile workers in, wish to emigrate, 130–1

Newcomb, Bryant (exchanged prisoner), 167–8n

Newell, Capt. Thomas, 582

Newenham, Sir Edward (XXVIII, 330n): directs son to forward newspapers, 406; and wife, request passport to visit Paris, 413–4n, 627–8; letter from, 627–8

Newenham, Edward (son of Sir Edward and Grace): sends newspapers, predicts Irish independence, 406; meets parents in Paris, 627n; letter from, 406

Newenham, Grace Anna (wife of Sir Edward), 413, 627

New London, Conn.: arrival of *Alliance* at, 381n, 404

Newman, Joseph (British prisoner), 168n

Newport, R.I.: residents of, praise French army, 286

New Providence (island in Bahamas): Spaniards capture, with American help, 346, 433, 693n

Newspapers: English, BF sends to Livingston, 69–70, 112, 428: report British political news, 80: print false news about U.S.-Portuguese relations, 138–9: received by BF, 331–2: Pownall advertises map in, 371: brought by Dawes, 557; American, print Treaty of Alliance, 332: sent by Livingston, 399: requested by Ingenhousz, 468: carry accounts of murder of Moravian Indians, 586–7n, 588, 666: sent by RB, 665, 715; Irish, sent by Newenham, 406; help mold public opinion, argues BF, 472–3; European, sent to Livingston, 734; German-language, sent by RB, 739

New York (city): JA argues for attack on, 57; British evacuation of, 73n, 77–8, 249n, 319n; garrison of, forced to re-

Peace negotiations, British-American (*continued*)

300, 306: returns for second time to London, 306–7, 313n, 314, 364–5, 417, 418n: and Grenville believe BF ready to make separate peace, 307n, 309n, 313n, 319n: comes to Paris again, 317–18, 319n, 396, 417, 421: holds formal discussions with BF, 318n, 323–30, 335–9, 341–4, 558n, 599–601, 623–4n: says Britain's enemies have the ball at their foot, 323: wishes to make quick peace with America, 601: supposedly requests leave to return to England, 671; compensation for Loyalists as issue in, liv–lv, 171, 282n, 325–6, 601, 718; Shelburne keeps secret the notes given by BF to Oswald, liv–lv, 171–2n: appointed prime minister but continues to direct, lv, 218, 598, 601–2, 623, 624, 679n: hints to House of Lords about recognizing American independence, lv, 601: concedes BF's necessary articles, informs Oswald, lvi, 673n, 686–7: sends BF letter of recommendation for Oswald, 102–4: and cabinet, King, approve Oswald's return to Paris, 224–5, 234–5, 249n, 270, 281–2, 298–9, 352: rejects BF's proposal for cession of Canada, 282n, 299n: informs Carleton, Digby about peace negotiations, attempts to use them as intermediaries, 302n, 672–4, 686, 689, 709n, 717n, 719, 731: leaves BF choice of Oswald's status, 325, 327–8, 341–2, 551: gives memorandum to Oswald, 325–7, 344, 551: tells Laurens he is reluctant to part with America, 525–6: wishes confirmation BF prepared to make separate peace, 599n: attempts to reassure BF about his intentions, 672–4: claims continuation of war will benefit France, Spain, Netherlands rather than U.S., 674n; American boundaries as issue in, liv–lvi, 321n, 416, 527, 599–600, 686, 718, 733: obligations to France as issue in, lv, 157–8, 282n, 301, 302n, 307–8, 309n, 317n, 320–1, 331–2, 674n: trade with Britain as issue in, lvi, 600–1: debts to British merchants as issue in,

282n: obligations to Spain, Netherlands as issue in, 320–1, 435, 566, 674n; Fox, Grenville offer immediate acknowledgement of American independence, lv, 319, 320–1n, 338, 621; Grenville's role in, lv–lvi, 249n, 270, 285, 287, 299, 301–9, 313n, 314n, 317–22, 327–8, 332, 335, 337–9, 341–2, 346, 350–1, 355–6, 434–5, 516, 522, 551, 558–9, 574, 575n, 599, 607, 621, 686n; recognition of American independence as issue in, lv–lvii, 102, 157, 162–3, 235n, 249n, 263–4, 271n, 282, 293, 299, 309n, 313n, 319, 320–1n, 435, 594–5, 598–601, 621–2, 623, 653–4, 672–4, 686, 713n, 717; relationship with British-French negotiations, lv–lvii, 102–3, 157–9, 179, 263, 282, 301, 302n, 303, 305n, 307–8, 309n, 313n, 314n, 316, 318n, 320–1, 325, 329n, 370, 429, 434–5, 566, 598–9, 672–4, 689–90, 713n, 733; Newfoundland fishery as issue in, lvi, 158n, 321n, 416, 527, 599–600, 686, 718; British reparations, acknowledgement of war guilt as issues in, lvi, 296, 600; compared to 1777–78 American-French negotiations, lvi, 601; King's order used as temporary commission by Oswald, lvi, 712–13, 713–14; Jay's role in, lvi–lvii, 67–8, 206, 600–1, 623, 712–13, 714n; Oswald's credentials, instructions for, lvi–lvii, 245, 282n, 298–9, 317n, 574, 601, 671, 686, 712–13, 713–14, 719n, 733; culminate in Nov. 30 preliminary peace agreement, lvii; and British negotiations with Netherlands, Spain, 6, 102–3, 300, 328n; Hartley volunteers services in, gives suggestions about, 18–19, 257–8, 313, 369–70, 418–19, 553; documents relating to, sent to Gérard de Rayneval, Vergennes, 22–3, 102n, 140, 235n, 270, 271, 294, 335, 345; Hodgson volunteers services in, is promised advance notice of progress of, 32–3, 80, 104n, 126–7, 146, 358, 422, 447–8, 654–5; authorized by Enabling Act, 69–70, 424–5n; Shelburne's, Fox's objectives in, 102; are independent of France, Digges tells Shelburne that JA said, 109n; Laurens

Pownall, Thomas (*continued*)
582: inquiries about settling in America, 583; unable to serve in peace negotiations, 371–2, 582; letters from, 370–2, 582–4

Précorbin, ——— Moisson de (Alexandre-Félix's father), 65

Précorbin, ——— Moisson de (Alexandre-Félix's mother): asks commission for son, 60, 64–5; letter from, 60, 64–5

Précorbin, Alexandre-Félix Moisson de: commission sought for, 60, 64–5

Prevost, Maj. Gen. Augustine, 648

Price, James (merchant): recommends Lynch to assist prisoners, 40

Price, Richard (clergyman, XI, 100n): discusses controversy about lightning rods, 150–1n; dines with Hodgson, Priestley, Jones, Paradise, 357; Laurens carries letter from, 377; expresses desire for peace, 394; introduces Brown, Milford, 394, 472; Hodgson asked to convey BF's love to, 422; Shipley family seldom sees, 455; and fellow members of Club of Honest Whigs, 472–3; BF sends his thoughts about importance of press, 472–3; W. Vaughan sends greetings from, 698; letter from, 394; letter to, 472–3

Price, Thomas (Amiens manufacturer): testifies to Allcock's honesty, 272n, 276, 277; letter from, 277

Priestley, Joseph (scientist, XIII, 185n): and Ingenhousz, 212: fellow members of Club of Honest Whigs, loved by BF, 445: La Rochefoucauld, 445, 532: Parker & Sons, 698n; dines with Hodgson, Price, Jones, Paradise, 357; Hodgson asked to convey BF's love to, 422; BF writes views to, on war, procreation, the nature of mankind, 444–5; conducts scientific experiments, 444–5, 532–3, 615, 698n; sent report of Lavoisier experiment, 445–6; Shipleys plan to dine with, in Birmingham, 455; asks assistance for Russell, 532; submits results to Royal Society, *Journal de physique*, 532–3; political views of, 533, 615; introduces Stokes, 614; as member of Royal Society, Lunar Society, 615n; W. Vaughan sends greetings from, 698; letters from, 532–3, 614–15; letter to, 444–6

Pringle, John (physician, VI, 178n), 100n

Prisoners, American: exchange of, lvii, 32, 70, 79–80, 124–6, 130, 152–4, 156–7, 167, 181–2, 184n, 206, 228–9, 236, 237, 269, 297, 309–10, 340–1, 352, 356–7, 362–3, 395–6, 401, 418, 422, 446–7, 527–8, 537, 625, 732–3; assisted by BF, 5, 7n, 31, 79, 183, 202n, 357–8, 374n, 402n, 537, 577n, 677: Coffyn, 5n, 7, 59n, 183, 202, 374–5: Bondfield, 12–13: Saurey, 31n: Wren, 31n: Hodgson, 31–3, 79, 357–8, 537, 625, 626n: JW, 58–9, 246, 376, 402, 480, 741: Schweighauser & Dobrée, 450–1; BF asked to assist, 12–13, 16–17, 49, 58–9, 116–18, 130, 148–9, 232–3, 241–2, 270–1, 285, 696–7; escaped, sufferings of, 12–13: at Bordeaux, 40, 59: Nantes, 49, 59, 117, 402, 450–1, 480, 741: Brest, 53, 118, 450–1, 696–7: Lorient, 116–18, 241–2, 567, 677: St. Malo, 117, 450–1: Le Havre, 118, 232–3: Morlaix, 450–1; Digges misappropriates funds for relief of, 25–6n, 29, 95, 537; number of, 31, 96, 125, 153, 206, 340–1, 447, 625n; in Ireland, 49, 59, 79, 96, 124n, 125, 153, 167, 206, 229, 285, 341, 447, 556n: North America, 401n, 462, 650, 672, 717; Lafayette proposes plan for mass escape of, 60; Beaumarchais not involved in assistance to, 80, 81; release, kind treatment of, will further reconciliation, suggests BF, 96, 184n, 229, 269, 302n, 352, 363; exchanged, at Cherbourg, 167; mistreatment of, 167, 193–4, 228; release of, is tacit recognition of American independence, claims BF, 181–2, 206; escape prison at Bristol, 183: Forton Prison, 242; slops furnished to, 341, 357, 422, 446–7; Cooper hopes for general release of, 483. *See also* Cartel ships; Forton Prison; Mill Prison